Reading and Learning to Read

Reading and Learning to Read

THIRD EDITION

Jo Anne L. Vacca
Kent State University

Richard T. Vacca
Kent State University

Mary K. Gove
East Cleveland Schools

HarperCollins*CollegePublishers*

Executive Editor: Christopher Jennison
Developmental Editor: Joe Budd
Project Editor: Andrew Roney
Design Manager: Wendy Ann Fredericks
Cover and Chapter Opener Illustrations: Christine Orlando
Art Studio: Vantage Art, Inc.
Photo Researcher: Carol Parden
Electronic Production Manager: Valerie A. Sawyer
Manufacturing Manager: Helene G. Landers
Electronic Page Makeup: Ruttle, Shaw & Wetherill, Inc.
Printer and Binder: RR Donnelley & Sons Company
Cover Printer: The Lehigh Press, Inc.

Reading and Learning to Read, Third Edition

Library of Congress Cataloging-in-Publication Data
Vacca, Jo Anne L.
Reading and learning to read / Jo Anne L. Vacca, Richard T. Vacca, Mary K. Gove.—3rd ed.
p. cm.
Includes bibliographical references (p.) and index.
ISBN 0-673-99089-3
1. Reading (Elementary) 2. Language arts (Elementary) I. Vacca, Richard T. II. Gove, Mary K. III. Title.
LB1573.V32 1995
372.4—dc20 94-26317
CIP

97 98 9 8 7 6 5 4 3

To our professional partners:

Colleagues and friends from Albany, Syracuse, DeKalb,

Boston, Troy, Storrs, East Cleveland, and Kent;

Knowing you has sustained us over the years.

Brief Contents

Detailed Contents

Preface

The conversation today in education circles is about partnerships. Concerns about our collective practice in the 1990s bring us together as literacy educators committed to providing quality instruction for *all* children. It's simply not acceptable for any child to fail. Our purposes in this, the third edition of *Reading and Learning to Read,* revolve around three major themes: *including* new and experienced teachers, specialists, aides, parents, and authors in creating the best practices for the delivery of reading instruction; *valuing* individual beliefs, multiple perspectives, cultural and language differences through learning and communicating; and *seeking* the most current and meaningful information available to update our knowledge base about all aspects of reading and learning to read.

You will be exploring and sharing ideas about what works and why as you read *Reading and Learning to Read.* You will, we hope, be challenged to think about each major topic while also anticipating the connections across topics and chapters. Perhaps the color insert, *Literature Across Cultures,* is the best illustration of how an important contemporary topic adds depth to our teaching portfolio and connects us to literature-based instruction and materials, diverse learners, response to literature, and communities of readers.

At the request of colleagues who have used *Reading and Learning to Read,* we continue to offer a range of instructional approaches for teachers to consider after reflecting on their beliefs. Special features such as the insert on multicultural literature in Chapter 10, interviews with reading program authors in Chapter 11, authentic assessment and portfolio development in Chapters 13 and 14, and differentiating instruction for diverse learners in Chapter 15 speak to the most current trends in the field of literacy. While there is something new in virtually every chapter, we've retained the essence of *Reading and Learning to Read* from beginning to end:

- Lenses on the reading process
- Family literacy and literate environments
- Shared reading and writing
- Writing workshops
- Story structure and comprehension
- Vocabulary in literature and content material
- Modeling word identification strategies
- Fluency in young readers
- Choosing and responding to literature

- Literature-based instruction
- Content-area texts and literature across the curriculum
- Using portfolios in authentic assessments
- Cooperative learning and classroom communities
- Literacy and diversity

Each chapter opens with a preview called *Between the Lines* and a list of *key terms* appears at the end of each chapter and in the *glossary.* Supplements, in addition to a printed *Instructor's Manual,* include *Overhead Transparencies* and an *Electronic Portfolio* featuring both a student and faculty version. The student version classifies and stores student responses to text questions and activities, from very specific prompts to responses to boxes, teacher-action researcher activities, and journal entries. Materials can be combined into a course portfolio. The disk can also be applied to E-mail submission of assignments, Listserv discussions, on-line discussions in real time, and distance learning. The faculty disk includes all material from the student disk, plus a test bank that can be modified and custom-printed.

The beautiful cover and chapter-opening illustrations by the New York artist Christine Orlando keep us all centered on children who are reading and learning to read. Our partners in this project are dedicated professionals who share our commitment to children's success in literacy. Lee Williams and Harry Noden conducted research through their lenses as experienced teachers. Our reviewers, James W. Wiley of Baylor University, Judith Cohen of Adelphi University, Patricia DeMay of Livingston University, Peggy Ransom of Ball State University, and Peter J. Quinn of St. John's University, were insightful, knowledgeable, and direct, yet gentle in their commentaries.

Our editors, Chris Jennison and Joe Budd of HarperCollins, know about partnerships, care about quality, and understand the delicate balance between process and product. Their persistence moved us toward a higher level—and an unlisted telephone number. Andrew Roney and Wendy Ann Fredericks of HarperCollins guided the book through the production stages and ensured that our vision became the book you now hold.

Jo Anne L. Vacca
Richard T. Vacca
Mary K. Gove

About the Authors

Jo Anne L. Vacca is Professor and Chair of the Department of Teaching, Leadership, and Curriculum Studies at Kent State University in Kent, Ohio.

Richard T. Vacca is Professor of Teaching, Leadership, and Curriculum Studies at Kent State University. He was recently elected Vice President of the International Reading Association and will become president in 1997. JoAnne and Rich have a daughter, Courtney, and a grandson, Simon. They live in Aurora, Ohio.

Mary K. Gove is a Reading Consultant in the East Cleveland Schools. She has a daughter, Jessica, and lives in Cleveland Heights, Ohio.

Reading and Learning to Read

CHAPTER

1

Lenses on the Reading Process

BETWEEN THE LINES

In this chapter you will discover:

- **How beliefs about reading influence instructional decisions and practices.**
- **What the metaphor *lenses on the reading process* means.**
- **How teachers construct personal, professional, and practical knowledge.**
- **The images associated with classroom teachers of reading.**
- **Why reading must be viewed from multiple human perspectives.**
- **How different reading models describe what readers do to construct meaning.**

On an unusually warm and humid day in May, the furnace at Lincoln Elementary School is blasting hot air into one of the first-grade classrooms. Two building custodians are trying to turn off the heat while the teacher and the students are trying to work despite the physical discomfort. The windows are wide open; a fan moves the hot air around the room, but to little avail.

Lincoln Elementary, an old red brick building, is an inner city school. Although the physical plant shows its age (the heating system breaks down now and again and needs repair), minor inconveniences don't get in the way of teaching and learning. For example, in the midst of all the commotion in the first-grade classroom, one of the students is at her desk, busy with paper and pencil, as she writes a note. She folds it in half, writes the teacher's name on the front, and delivers it post-haste. The teacher opens the note and, much to her delight, reads:

Plese turn of
the fan Them
guys smell like
my brother when
he mos the
grass.
Toni P.

This vignette has much to say about literacy-in-the-making. As lighthearted as it may appear on the surface, it's what Harste, Woodward, and Burke (1984) call a *language story*. Language stories illustrate how children use language to construct meaning and to interact with others in environments that foster literacy learning and development. A good language story provides insights that help us to think about reading and learning to read, the role that writing plays in children's literacy development, and the connections between human interaction and literate activity.

Just ask yourself, for example, "Does Toni know what writing and reading are for? Does she get her message across effectively? Does she have a sense of the teacher as a reader?" And as a language user, "Is Toni empowered? Is she willing to take risks?" Questions such as these are far more revealing about Toni's literate development than noting the grammatical and spelling errors that she made.

But there's more to the story. When the teacher reads Toni's note, she acts upon the plea—quickly we might add—by turning off the fan. And at the same time, she can't help but appreciate Toni's use of language to communicate. The teacher recognizes that a powerful and authentic **literacy event** has just taken place between a writer and a reader. She decides, on the spot, to extend the transaction that has just occurred between a writer and a reader. So she, too, writes a note, folds it in half, and gives it to Toni.

Dear Toni,

Thank you for the note. It made me smile on a very crazy day. ☺ Let's hope the workers fix the radiator soon!

This day reminds me of the story we shared about Alexander who had the TERRIBLE, HORRIBLE, NO GOOD VERY BAD DAY!

I'll read it again to the class so we can all feel better about this morning!

Love,
Mrs H ☺

The teacher's decision to continue and extend the communication reflects not only what she knows about reading and learning to read, but also what she values and believes about teaching, learning, and the process of becoming literate. Consider what she does: Connecting the events of the morning to *Alexander's Terrible, Horrible, No Good, Very Bad Day* (Viorst, 1982) is an opportune, authentic way to demonstrate one of the *language functions* that reading serves. As we discuss later in the chapter, reading can be put to use in different ways for different purposes, one of which is to entertain—or in the classroom situation that the first graders find themselves—to provide some pleasure and relief from the heat in the room.

In addition, sharing the book with the class results in a "commercial" for another book, Patricia Reilly Giff's *Today Was A Terrible Day* (1980) which is part of the classroom library collection. This is a story about a boy named Ronald who has a terrible day in school until he discovers that he can read (without any help) a personal note written to him by the teacher. Toni's teacher previews the story with the class and makes a connection between the notes that she and Toni have exchanged and the note that the teacher in the story writes to Ronald. She then builds anticipation for the story by inviting the students to think about the "terrible days" experienced by Alexander and Ronald, what contributes to making a day terrible, and what people can do to turn a bad day into a good one.

Throughout the remainder of the day, as you might anticipate, children asked if they could leaf through or read *Today Was A Terrible Day* between class activities. Some of them even wrote about terrible days in their journals, which are an integral part of the literacy curriculum in this first-grade classroom.

All of the reading and writing activities that evolved from the unanticipated events of the morning provided children with a demonstration of the *intertextuality* of stories. Stories are products of the imagination, but the problems and themes that they portray reflect the human experience. Intertextuality is a ten-dollar word used by literary theorists to describe the connections that exist within and between texts. Think about the personal connections made by Toni and her classmates. They were able to build on the morning's heating crisis to make connections between the two stories shared by the teacher, as well as the texts that some of them created by writing in their journals. The children in Toni's class are exploring what it means to be *meaning-seekers* and *meaning-makers*. Their use of texts to construct meaning is the nexus by which they link the stories and explore a theme that will recur throughout their lives.

Not a bad day's work on a hot, muggy day in May. The work of teachers sometimes takes unexpected twists and turns, "teachable moments" if you will, which usually beget reasons for reading and writing. Yet taking advantage of a teachable moment, as Toni's teacher did, requires a vision of reading and learning to read. Some educators call this vision a *world view* or *perspective;* others, a *philosophy;* still others, a **belief system.**

For one reason or another, some teachers probably would have reacted differently to Toni's note. Some may have been too busy or preoccupied with the heating crisis or other matters to respond to the note in a manner that connects literacy learning to life in the classroom. Other teachers may have missed the teachable moment because they did not understand or appreciate the literacy event that occurred.

In the pressured world of teaching, it is sometimes easy to lose sight of what we know and believe about children, reading, and how children learn to read. In the case of Toni's teacher, however, her response to the note suggests that she views the reading process through *lenses* that create images of her role as a classroom teacher.

Through what lenses do you view the reading process? How should reading and writing be taught? Or what roles do reading and writing play in learning? Throughout your teaching career, from the time you begin studying to become an elementary teacher and all the while you practice the profession, you continually will be focusing and refining the lenses through which you view the reading process and how it is played out in the classroom.

Different Belief Systems, Different Instructional Decisions

Just about every teacher we've ever talked to agrees on the main goal of reading instruction: to teach children to become independent readers and learners. Differences among teachers, however, often reflect varying beliefs and instructional perspectives on how to help children achieve independence. Because they view the reading process through different lenses, teachers will have different instructional concerns and emphases. The decisions they make will vary. Compare the way Arch and Linda handle the complexities of reading and learning to read in their classrooms.

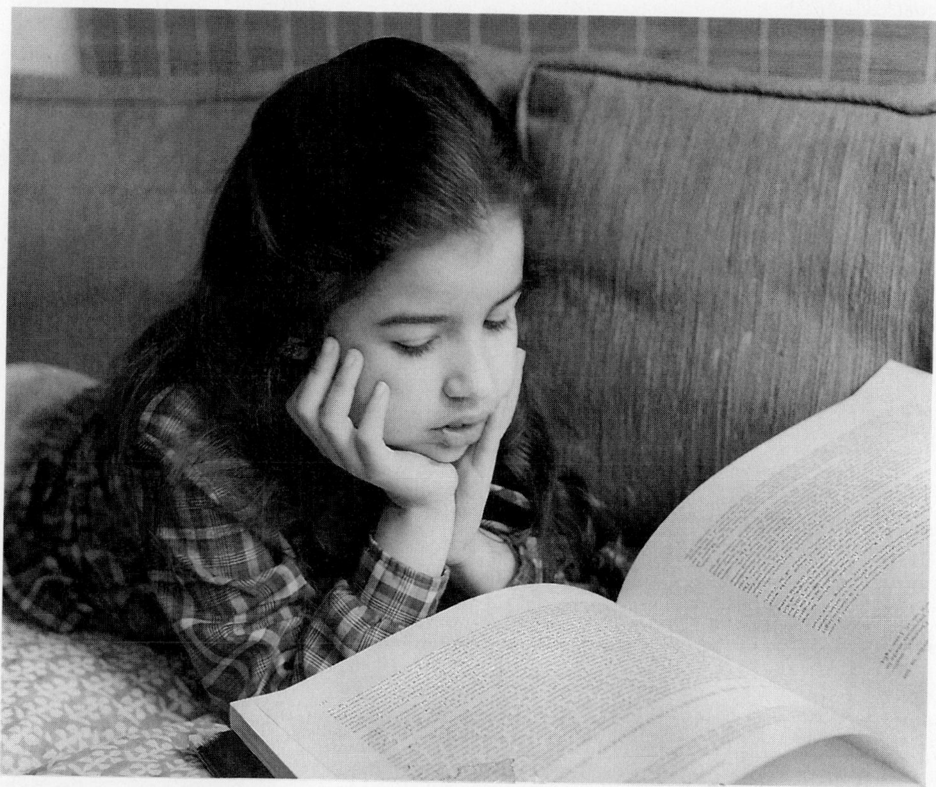

The main goal of reading instruction is teaching children to become independent readers and learners.

Arch is an oddity at Clark Lane Elementary School. Not only is he the only male first-grade teacher, but he is also the self-acknowledged "renegade" of the instructional staff at his school. By his own admission, Arch doesn't do anything by the book.

The "book" in Arch's case is the teacher's manual of the basal reading program that is used extensively by the other teachers at Clark Lane. Arch eschews basal reading instruction in favor of what he calls "invitations" to learn. He invites his first graders to explore and experience the uses of oral and written language in a variety of instructional situations. Early in the year, for example, Arch's class will read "anything that's real and important to the kids": signs, boxtop labels, and most importantly, their own writing. His pupils write (and dictate) a lot. They also listen to Arch read, as well as engage in discussions about stories before "ever getting into any kind of formal reading instruction. You know . . . identifying letters and words . . . learning the skills of reading."

Arch places little importance on his students' recognizing every word as they read. He says, "I tell my students not to let one or two words prevent them from reading; that they might be able to understand what the story is about and to enjoy it without identifying all of the words."

Linda also teaches reading to 6-year-olds. But her approach is decidedly different from Arch's. She believes quite strongly that beginning readers must start with sound-letter correspondences, translating print into speech. Other than occasional "experience charts" in the first weeks of the school year, Linda doesn't even attempt to introduce writing until most of her children make the monumental "click" between the black squiggly marks on a page and the sounds they represent.

Of the "click," Linda says, "You can't miss it." When she sees children making the connection between print and speech, Linda begins to aim for mastery. She teaches sound-letter correspondences thoroughly. She believes in having beginning readers overlearn decoding skills to the point where they can use them automatically in translating print to speech.

Linda says, "My students learn to read by blending sounds into words and putting words together into sentences." She explains why: "I think it is important for students to overlearn their consonant and vowel sounds so that they can recognize each word." Comprehension is important to Linda as it is to Arch, but the two differ in perspective. Although both Linda and Arch believe that the most important instructional goal is for children "to read by themselves, to read for enjoyment, and to learn new information," Linda assumes her students "must first have word attack skills to read."

The lenses from which Linda and Arch view the reading process reflect different beliefs about reading and learning to read and result in different instructional decisions. Each works hard to develop able readers. Yet they are worlds apart. What Linda does instructionally reflects beliefs that embody a *skills* perspective; what Arch does underlies a belief system that reflects a *whole language* perspective. Much of the recent debate in the field of literacy has centered around these two opposing perspectives, both of which will be examined in various parts of this book.

So you ask, "Why the debate? Why isn't there more consensus on how to teach children to read?" These questions are not unlike those asked by novice and veteran teachers alike. It's not unnatural to want to know "the right way" to do something. Fagan (1989), however, argues that rather than being empowered, some teachers are dependent on others to tell them how to help children develop as readers. Disempowered teachers rely heavily on curriculum materials rather than professional expertise and judgment to get the job done.

Empowered teachers, on the other hand, use their beliefs about reading and learning to read to make instructional decisions. The ability to decide what is best practice for readers brings to mind the French proverb, "Between two stools one sits on the ground." Although teachers like Linda and Arch may have different belief systems, they exercise professional judgment in making choices and decisions. Arch and Linda are decisive, even though their practices differ. Wanting to know the right way to teach reading, nonetheless, can leave some teachers sitting on the ground waiting for "someone else" to decide how best to work with their students in classroom situations.

Next you ask, "Are some belief systems better than others?" The answer to the question lies not with authors telling you the best way to teach, but in the process of coming to know. The more you know about what readers and writers do, and the roles that reading and writing play in the lives of children, the more empowered you are to respond to a question of such personal and professional importance.

Ways of Knowing

Teachers come to know in different ways. For example, in a lifetime of interaction with the world about us, we acquire knowledge about reading and learning to read by *building it from the inside,* as we interact with people, processes, ideas, and things. Jean Piaget's theory of **constructivism** provides a compelling explanatory framework for understanding the acquisition of knowledge. Piaget, one of the preeminent child psychologists of the twentieth century, theorized that children do not internalize knowledge directly from the outside but construct it from inside their heads, in interaction with the environment (Kamii, 1991). When constructivist thinking is applied to the acquisition of knowledge about teaching and learning, it holds that teachers engage in a process of seeking and making meaning from personal, practical, and professional experiences.

Constructing Personal Knowledge

Personal knowledge of reading and learning to read grows out of a teacher's history as a reader and a writer. Consider, for example, the influences in your life that have shaped the literate person that you are. From birth, you have interacted with *people* (parents, teachers, siblings, friends, significant others) and *things* (all kinds of literacy artifacts and texts, including books, signs, letters, labels, pencil and paper, word processors) to construct

● BOX 1.1

Developing a Reading Autobiographical Sketch

Reflect on how you learned to read, the reading habits you have formed, home and school influences on your reading development, and the kinds of reading you do. Prepare an autobiographical sketch that captures these personal memories. How did you learn to read? What home reading experiences do you recall? What kinds of instructional activities and practices were you involved in as an elementary school child? Which ones do you recall fondly? Which, if any, do you recall with regret? In retrospect, what belief systems and views of reading and learning to read did your elementary school teachers seem to hold? Were you effectively taught how to handle the variety of reading tasks you are faced with in the real world?

knowledge about the *processes* of reading and writing. By engaging in reading and writing, you come to know in a very personal way what readers and writers do, and the contributions that reading and writing make to a life. You belong to what Frank Smith (1992) calls the *literacy club* by virtue of the fact that you read and write.

The development of an autobiographical narrative is a powerful tool that helps you link your personal history as a reader to instructional beliefs and practices. Not all teachers like to read, even though they know how to. Some may read well and be well read. But others may have struggled as readers and bear the emotional scars to prove it. How do these realities affect what teachers do in classroom situations?

An *autobiographical narrative* helps you to inquire into the past so as to better understand what you do in the present and what you would like to do in future classroom situations. Teachers who engage in narrative inquiry explore mental pictures of memories, incidents, or situations in their lives. The inquiry allows you to reflect, make connections, and project. As Connelly and Clandinin (1988) put it, "Where we have been and where we are going interact to make meaning of the situations in which we find ourselves" (p. 6).

To develop a reading autobiography, consider the questions in Box 1.1. You may wish to share your narratives with others. What beliefs, values, and attitudes are an integral part of your stories? How do your personal histories of reading and learning to read influence where you are in your thinking about reading and where you would like to be?

Constructing Practical Knowledge

Teachers also construct practical knowledge, which is closely related to personal knowledge in that it grows out of experience both in and out of classrooms. The more that you work with and observe children in literacy situations in classroom and community contexts, and reflect on their behavior *and* your own, the more you develop theories about what is the best practice for the readers and writers with whom you work. Practical knowledge is characterized by the beliefs, values, and attitudes that you construct about readers and writers, texts, reading and writing processes, learning to read and write, and the role of the teacher in the development of children's literate behavior.

In teacher education programs, field experiences and student teaching are vehicles for acquiring practical knowledge. In addition, interactions with and observations of practicing teachers influence the way you might think about reading and learning to read in classroom situations. Often, preservice teachers find incongruities between what is taught in education courses and what they observe in the field. These incongruities create conceptual conflict, which is healthy, because it helps reflective students of literacy to think more deeply about their own understandings, beliefs, and practices.

The construction of practical knowledge extends beyond classroom situations and includes interactions within the cultural context of school and community. For example, a teacher's beliefs about reading and learning to read may be affected by peer pressure, the beliefs of colleagues and administrators, school board policies, curriculum guidelines, the publishing and testing industry, public opinion, and state (and eventually national) standards for teaching reading.

Constructing Professional Knowledge and Expertise

As an integral part of their professional development, teachers interact with the world of ideas. Professional education organizations, such as the International Reading Association (IRA), refer to what teachers ought to know to teach reading well as *standards* or the *knowledge base.* In Figure 1.1, study the framework established by IRA for the development of the knowledge base for reading professionals.

The categories graphically displayed in Figure 1.1 represent broad areas of professional knowledge that require the attention of classroom teachers. **Professional knowledge** is knowledge acquired from an ongoing study of the practice of teaching. What teacher education programs do best is help preservice and inservice teachers build a knowledge base that is grounded in current theory, research, and practice. Throughout their professional development, the books and journals teachers read, the courses and workshops they take, and the conferences they attend contribute to the vision they have of reading and learning to read.

The instructional differences among teachers reflect the knowledge they put to use in classroom situations. While few would argue that nothing is as practical as a good theory, we embrace the notion, "There's nothing so theoretical as a good practice." Teachers construct theories of reading and learning to read, based on their ways of knowing, which influence the way they teach, including the way they plan, use and select texts, interact with learners, and assess literate activity. In turn, the decisions teachers make about instruction influence students' reading behavior and their perceptions of and attitudes toward reading, as illustrated in Figure 1.2.

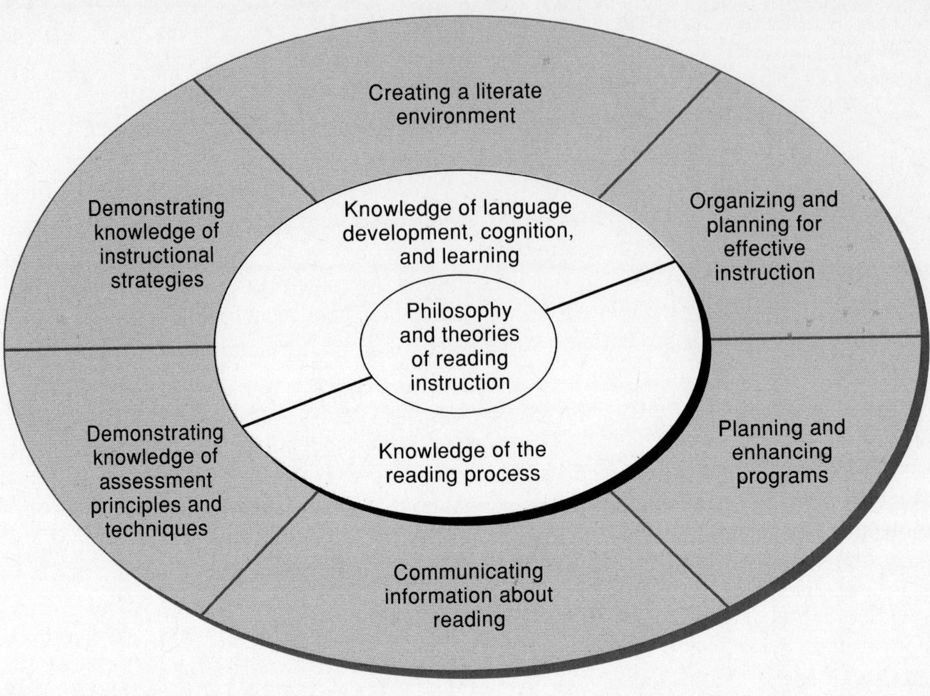

● **FIGURE 1.1** IRA's framework of the knowledge base for reading professionals

Source: Standards for Reading Professionals (Newark, DE: International Reading Association, 1992). Reprinted with permission.

Images of Teachers

What are our **images of teachers?** Our use of the metaphor *lens* implies that as teachers construct knowledge, they form images in their heads about teaching and learning in general and reading and learning to read in particular. These mental pictures represent concepts or *schemata,* a term that we explain more fully in the next section. When images are evoked and reflected on, they will give teachers insights into what they know, believe, and value about reading, readers, the reading process, and reading instruction.

Knowledge is constructed from the inside and images of what it means to be a teacher of reading will differ, because they are created from personal experience, professional study, work in classrooms, and, to some extent, the way teachers have been depicted in the popular media. Recall a time, for example, when you have watched a movie or television

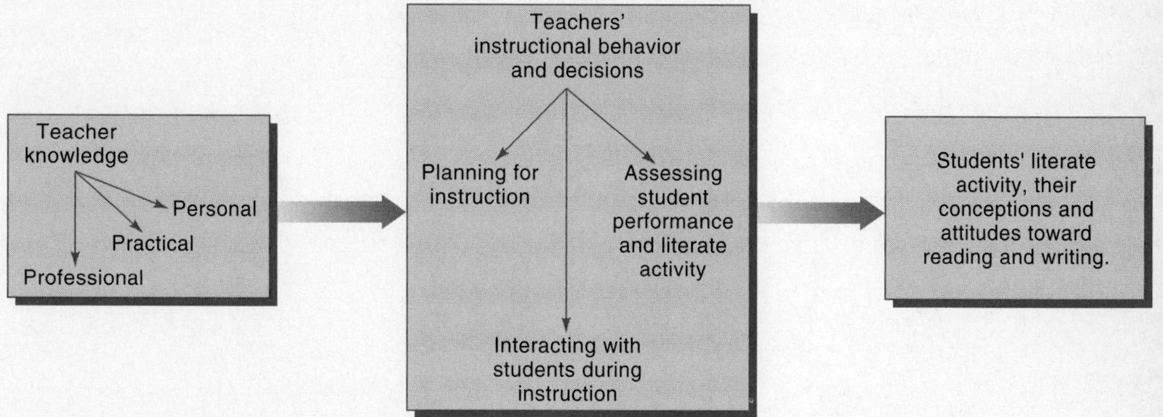

● **FIGURE 1.2** Relationships among teacher knowledge, decisions and actions, and students' literate activity and attitudes toward reading and writing

program in which someone is being taught to read. The popular concept in our culture, as portrayed on the screen, is of someone in the role of a teacher who works with a reader (or group of readers) to unlock the mysteries of print. What we often see on film are images of unsure, word-by-word readers who labor painfully at sounding out words that they don't know, and sympathetic teachers who interrupt at points of error to provide correction. As stereotypical as these images may appear, they work their way into the public psyche and affect popular conceptions of what it means to teach reading.

Yet no single image is likely to capture the complexity of what it means to be a teacher of reading or to engage in good teaching. Figure 1.3 identifies some of the images that have been associated with teachers of reading and shows how multifaceted and interrelated these images can be. What are some of the images that flash in your mind when you use the phrase *teacher* to describe the work you do (or plan to do) in literacy situations? Compare the images you form with the mental pictures and concepts that are stimulated by in Figure 1.3.

Teachers as Experts

After four or more years of college preparation, on-the-job experience, and continuing education, a teacher undoubtedly has the kind of professional expertise in the education of children that a lay person does not. It should thus come as little surprise that school boards and communities alike expect elementary teachers to have expertise in the teaching of basic processes such as reading and writing.

Yet the specialized knowledge that comes from education courses is not the same as the expert knowledge that grows out of classroom practice and our own literate activity in the world outside of classrooms. A crucial juncture in our development as teachers is the

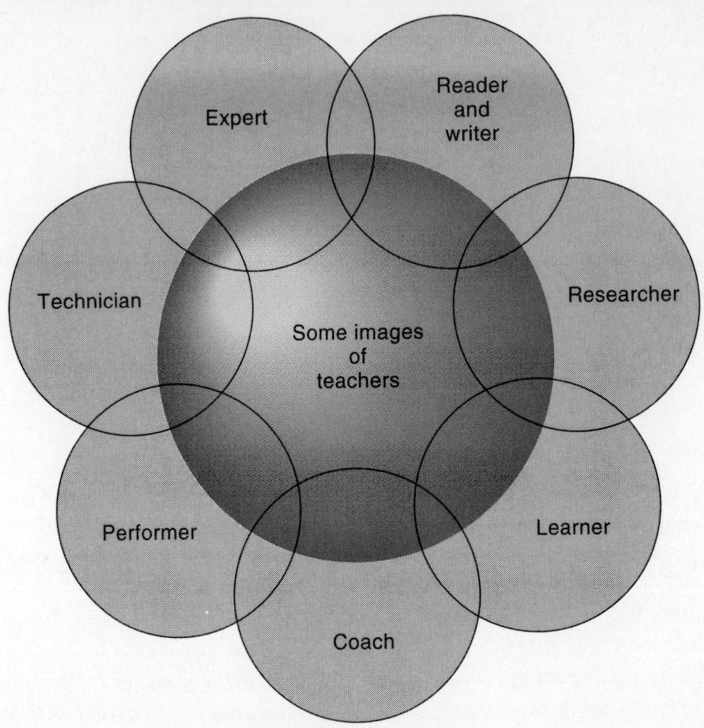

● **FIGURE 1.3** Images associated with teachers of reading

image that we develop of ourselves, not only as professionals with expertise in the education of children, but also as skilled readers and writers in the real world. Students expect their teachers to know what readers and writers do and to share those strategies with them. No wonder Linda Crafton (1991) reminds teachers to demystify literacy by making our thinking as skilled readers and writers an integral part of classroom life: ". . . part of what we have to do as teachers is to demonstrate the ins and outs, the ups and downs of our proficiencies" (p. 14). Students want their teachers to let them in on the secrets of literate behavior. To what extent and under what conditions, then, do teachers project an image of themselves as readers and writers in classrooms?

Teachers as Readers and Writers

Autobiographical narratives often reveal whether you like to read or not, the types of texts you read, and the occasions in which you use reading as a tool for enjoyment, learning, or solving problems. Some of you may be avid readers, while others may rarely read for pleasure, but know how to use reading effectively when the functional need to read arises. If reading, however, does not play an important and functional role in a teacher's life outside of the classroom, what messages about reading will wittingly or unwittingly be telegraphed to students inside the classroom? The same question can be asked about writing.

Studies of teachers' reading habits and attitudes paint a disappointing picture about their personal reading practices (Cardarelli, 1992). In most of the research that has been conducted, fewer than half of the teachers surveyed claim to engage in reading for personal fulfillment or enjoyment on a regular basis. Personal reading is more the exception than the rule in their lives.

We suspect that an even greater percentage of teachers do not engage in writing on a regular basis for personal purposes. In college-level courses that we teach, informal surveys uniformly reveal that most preservice and inservice teachers alike do not view themselves as writers nor do they like to write. Yet the role of the teacher as a *model* for reading and writing is at the very core of literacy instruction.

If the adage, "People find time for the things they value" holds true, then prospects seem slim for extended reading and writing activity in classes with teachers who themselves read and write only rarely. Indeed, as we explain in Chapter 10, some teachers attest to the importance of reading, but devote relatively little time in a school day to engaging students in personal reading situations. This is why the Teachers as Readers project is one of the most exciting literacy initiatives in education today.

The Association of American Publishers (AAP) has joined forces with the IRA, the National Council of Teachers of English (NCTE), and the American Library Association (ALA), to promote a nationwide program for encouraging teachers to read new children's and young-adult trade books and to integrate them into the school curriculum. The premise behind Teachers As Readers is straightforward enough: In school districts throughout the country, teachers, principals, librarians, district administrators, and parents meet regularly in book groups to read and discuss new children's books. The results of these book groups are dramatic: "Teachers As Readers groups rekindle the love of literature and the sharing process that can result, first among teachers and administrators; later among teachers and their students" (*Reading Initiative News,* Fall 1992). As a result of book groups, teachers who may not perceive themselves as readers gain experience and confidence with natural book talk and become models of enthusiasm for their students.

Teachers as Technicians

Many teachers engage in the techniques or technical aspects of teaching reading—matters related to the scope and sequence of skills, planning lessons, and managing activities, for example. Technicians usually are good at what they do, but what they do is often limited to specific methods or prescriptive programs of instruction. Teachers who are technicians often reduce the complexity of teaching and learning to a set of instructional routines which may include a variety of drill-and-practice techniques, a heavy reliance on seatwork, and question-and-answer recitations. Nanci Atwell (1993) reflects on her beginnings as a "teacher-technician:"

● BOX 1.2

Teachers as Readers Book Groups

What Is a Book Group?

The *Teachers as Readers Project* is designed to gather teachers together in "book groups" to talk about children's books, adolescent literature, professional books, and adult books. Teachers can then use the knowledge and ideas they've shared to create richly literate classrooms where students read with confidence and pleasure.

Teachers as Readers Book Groups consist of teachers who agree to meet at least six times each year to discuss books.

Why Form a Book Group?

- To share quality literature with colleagues.
- To gain experience and confidence in talking about books.
- To learn from the ideas and experiences of others.
- To become familiar with a wider range of children's and adolescent literature.
- To learn strategies for guiding students to become lifelong readers.

Guidelines for Organizing a Book Group

- Organize a group of approximately ten members, one of whom ideally should be a school administrator.
- Consider inviting parents, community members, and school board members to participate.
- Select a group leader or discussion facilitator.
- Determine six or more meeting dates.
- Establish a regular meeting place and time.

Determine Reading Material

- Consult your local librarian for suggestions.
- Study book reviews.

(continued)

- Check recommended reading lists (such as Teachers' Choices, Young Adults' Choices, or Children's Choices).
- Consult the Teachers as Readers article in each issue of *Reading Today.*

Variations

- Select books by theme.
- Read several books by the same author.
- Focus on literature about or from a particular culture.
- Meet in special places or at unique times (Monday afternoon tea, breakfast, brunch).
- Extend format (STAR: Student Teachers as Readers; PAR: Parents as Readers; PAR: Professors as Readers).
- Encourage participants to maintain reading response journals.

Adapted with permission from the International Reading Association. *Teachers As Readers Book Groups: Explore Your Own Literacy. Form a Book Group!* (Newark, DE: International Reading Association.)

> In 1974, when I became a teacher, the work was not real. I was the classic teacher-technician, and my work was classroom management. I managed the kids, the programs, and the paperwork. I viewed academics as the experts who were going to manage me, and I looked to them to be the "someone elses" who would tell me what to do with my students in my classroom. When the methods didn't work or didn't work with everyone, I blamed the experts. Or worse—I blamed the kids. Then I looked around for new gurus and recipes. (pp. vii–viii)

Not until Atwell began to change her image of what it means to be a teacher did she begin to view teaching as "real work." Instead of orchestrating assignments and managing programs, she began to observe learners, ask them questions, and reflect on their—and her own—behavior, ". . . so I could teach them what they needed to know." Her image of herself as a technician gradually changed to one as a learner.

As she reflects on her transformation as a teacher-learner, Atwell (1993) acknowledges, "I was a teacher of writing and reading who did not know what writers and readers actually do when they use language to make meaning; nor did I know the individual writers and readers who passed in and out of my classroom all day long" (p. vii). Her transformation as a teacher began as she began to make inquiries into literacy learning in the context of real classroom situations. Gradually she came out "from behind my big desk," gave up the technical security of teacher-controlled pedagogy, and began to observe and learn from her students as they engaged in the work of reading and writing.

Teachers as Learners and Researchers

In schools throughout the country, teachers are taking their roles as learners seriously and are engaging in problem-solving and reflective inquiry related to classroom practice. Teacher-researchers, like Nanci Atwell and those who are described in the book *Teachers Are Researchers* (Patterson, et al., 1993) are tackling tough questions as they inquire into the nature of problems and uncertainties that they face in the classroom. According to the coeditors of *Teachers Are Researchers,* teachers who engage in "action research" form new visions of themselves as teachers—and of their students as learners—by asking questions and discovering answers.

Teachers are researchers in the sense that they are careful observers of what children do in literacy situations. They often use the tools of action research—observation, interview, anecdotal note taking, survey, and analysis of students' writing samples—to understand reading and writing from the student's perspective. Such is the case of Marné Isakson who describes how she got started on a research project in her classroom (Isakson and Boody, 1993).

> "My son has read more in the last six weeks than he has in the last six years. I don't know what you are doing in that classroom of yours, but whatever it is, it's working."
>
> This comment, made by a father at a parent-teacher conference . . . started me thinking. . . . Why? What was occurring (in my classroom) that supported them (my students) as readers? (p. 26)

Isakson's curiosity led to other questions. She recognized that she could have listed the techniques, materials, strategy lessons, activities, and other student activities that she had initiated in her class, but these planned activities would tell her little "about what was really going on, especially from the perspective of individual students" (p. 27). Her inquiry into why students "turned on" to reading in her classroom included the use of field notes, interviews, and analyses of students' writings in response to what they were reading.

What effect did the inquiry have on Isakson's teaching? Here is what she says:

> I think I have grown more as a teacher since I started looking closely at what was happening in my classroom than ever before in my professional life. I started looking at people instead of at lesson plans. I became involved in the class-

In the school context, the concept of the teacher as a coach creates images of child-centered practices.

> room—reading with the students, writing with them, puzzling over difficult questions with them—instead of just directing activities. I started to take risks with my learning. (p. 33)

The axiom, "to teach is to learn" takes on new meaning for teacher-researchers who eschew tightly controlled, product-oriented methods to read, write, and learn along with their students. As they change, their images change. Often teachers will use words like *partner* or *coach* to describe what they do in the classroom.

Teachers as Coaches

Coach is a concept that more than likely evokes images of playing fields and athletic contests rather than classrooms and learning events. Applied to school contexts, however, the word *coach* creates images of child-centered practices.

Consider what it means to coach another person's work. Coaches know that the burden of responsibility to do well always rests with the people with whom they work.

Coaches try to get the most out of the natural talent of their players and performers. The teacher who coaches prepares, models, guides, supports, and stretches students to the limits of their potential as readers and writers.

Coaches will tell you that the key to successful coaching lies in the attitude they bring to their work. Kirby, Latta, and Vinz (1988), for example, describe an interview with Quincy Jones, the Grammy Award-winning musician and record producer. Quincy Jones captured "the secret to coaching anyone's work" when he was asked how he was able to draw out the best work from the world-class singers, songwriters, and musicians with whom he has worked. His response: "You have to love what they do, and you have to try to understand what they do and not be promiscuous with what they do." Rather than focus indiscriminately on what they can't do, a great coach leads students to what they can become.

Teachers as Performers

A concluding image. Consider the mental picture that flashes through your mind when you think of a teacher as a performer. Some teachers burn out believing that they must create "dog and pony" shows to motivate students to read and to hold their interest in learning. Mel, for example, is a first-grade teacher who says quite emphatically, "I want my classroom to be lively, entertaining, and still have kids get something out of it. You want to make reading as interesting as possible. The kids have TV in front of them at home at all hours. If you're not as interesting as TV, they turn you off. So you have to be a super entertainer."

Lively, relevant experiences with texts are part of good teaching, but this involves much more than just putting on a good show for your students. Grant Wiggins' (1993) study of "the secrets of great teachers" is an ambitious inquiry into what teachers do to make learning meaningful and engaging. He distinguishes "great" teachers from those "egocentric" teachers who maintain a powerful presence but "are often very poor at making themselves obsolete" in classroom learning situations.

Consider the strain and energy it must take for Mel to be on center stage all the time. How is the performer different from the coach, the partner in learning, or the teacher-researcher?

Coming to know what readers do is no easy matter. Part of the challenge that teachers encounter comes from the elusive nature of the reading process. Who can ever really *know* a process that takes place in the head? The best we can do is develop images, concepts, and theories that organize knowledge about reading into a system of beliefs, assumptions, principles, and procedures. Theories allow us to predict and explain phenomena which otherwise are unexplainable. In recent times, new knowledge related to how reading works has resulted in multiple human perspectives on the reading process.

Reading, for example, has been viewed from a *psychological* perspective. People "think with print." Reading is a cognitive process and should be taught and thought of as such. Yet viewing reading and learning to read strictly from a psychological perspective is not sufficient. One of the important ways people think and learn is by using language. Reading, therefore, can also be viewed from a *language perspective.* Goodman (1986b) put the matter of language learning this way: "Language enables us to share our experiences, learn from each other, plan together, and greatly enhances our intellect by linking our minds with others of our kind. . . . Written language greatly expands human memory by making it possible to store far more knowledge than the brain is capable of storing. . . . Written language links us with people in faraway places and distant times, with dead authors" (pp. 11–12).

Learning to read needs to be understood in terms of learning to use written language effectively. Children are language users; for them, learning to read is inherently social. If children perceive little use for written language, then they will have a difficult time learning to read and write. However, if written language is meaningful, the *social and cultural situations* in which it is used allow children to discern what reading and writing are all about.

Reading from a Psychological Perspective

A university colleague of ours, a cognitive psychologist by training, says he's been researching and studying the reading process for more than 15 years because he's interested in "how the mind works." How the mind works is another way of saying that he's interested in understanding *cognitive and metacognitive processes* in reading. His inquiries into the reading process embrace a psychological perspective.

How children think and reason with print is an important concern in this book. A cognitive view of reading suggests that the reader's ability to construct meaning is at the core of the process. The constructive processes characteristic of reading comprehension have been of intense interest to cognitive psychologists and reading researchers for more than a decade. In particular, they have studied the role that *schemata* play in comprehending texts.

Schema and Meaning-Making

Schemata reflect the prior knowledge, experiences, conceptual understandings, attitudes, values, skills, and procedures a reader brings to a reading situation.

BOX 1.3

What Is the Passage About?

The procedure is quite simple. First you arrange things into different groups. Of course, one pile may be sufficient depending on how much there is to do. If you have to go somewhere else due to lack of facilities that is the next step, otherwise you are pretty well set. It is important not to overdo things. That is, it is better to do few things at once than too many. In the short run this may not seem important but complications can easily arise. A mistake can be expensive as well. At first the whole procedure will seem complicated. Soon, however, it will become just another facet of life. It is difficult to foresee any end to the necessity for this task in the immediate future, but then one can never tell. After the procedure is completed one arranges the materials into different groups again. They can be put into their appropriate places. Eventually they will be used once more, and the whole cycle will then have to be repeated. However, this is part of life. (Bransford and Johnson, 1973, p. 400)

Children use what they know already to give meaning to new events and experiences. **Schema** is a technical term used by cognitive psychologists to describe how humans organize and construct meaning in their heads. Schemata (the plural of schema) have been called "the building blocks of cognition" (Rumelhart, 1982) and "a cognitive map to the world" (Neisser, 1976) because they represent elaborate networks of concepts, skills, and procedures that we use to make sense of new stimuli, events, and situations.

For example, do you possess the schema needed to interpret the passage in Box 1.3?

Upon first reading, Bransford and Johnson's passage may seem difficult to understand unless you were able to activate an appropriate schema. How many of you recognized that the passage had to do with washing clothes? Once a schema for washing clothes is activated, the words and phrases in the passage take on new meaning. Now try rereading the passage. Upon rereading, you will probably react by saying, "Aha! Now that I know the passage is about washing clothes, it makes sense!" Ambiguous words such as "procedure" and word streams such as "A mistake can be expensive" are now interpreted within the framework of what you know about washing clothes. The more you know about washing clothes, the more comprehensible the passage becomes. When readers activate appropriate schema, *expectations* are raised for the meaning of the text. Your expectations for the passage above help you to anticipate meaning and to relate information from the passage to existing knowledge.

The more we hear, see, read, or experience new information, the more we refine and expand existing schemata within our semantic language system.

Schemata, as you can see, influence reading comprehension and learning. For comprehension to happen, readers must activate or build a schema that fits with information from a text. When a good fit occurs, a schema functions in at least three ways to facilitate comprehension. First, a schema provides a framework that allows readers to *organize* text information more efficiently and effectively. The ability to integrate and organize new information into old facilitates retention. Second, a schema allows readers *to make inferences* about what happens or is likely to happen in a text. Inferences, for example, help children to predict upcoming information or to fill in gaps in the material. And third, a schema helps readers to *elaborate* upon the material. Elaboration is a powerful aspect of reasoning with print. When children elaborate on what they have read, they engage in cognitive activity that involves speculation, judgment, and evaluation.

Metacognition

Metacognition, defined generally by Ann Brown (1985), refers to knowledge about and regulation of some form of cognitive activity. In the case of reading, metacognition refers to (1) *self-knowledge:* the knowledge students have about themselves as readers and learners; (2) *task knowledge:* the knowledge of reading tasks and the strategies that are appropriate given a task at hand; and (3) *self-monitoring:* the ability of students to monitor reading by keeping track of how well they are comprehending.

Consider the following scenario, one that is quite common when working with reading beginners: A first-grader, reading orally, comes to a word in the text that he doesn't recognize. Stymied, he looks to the teacher for help. The teacher has at least four options to consider in deciding how to respond to the reader: (1) tell him the word; (2) ask him to "sound it out"; (3) ask him to take an "educated guess"; or (4) tell him to say "blank" and keep on reading.

What would you do? A rationale, based on what you know and believe about teaching reading, can be developed for each of the options or, for that matter, a combination. For example, "First, I'd ask him to sound out the word, and if that didn't work, I'd tell him the word." Or, "First, I'd ask him to take a good guess based on what word might make sense, and if that didn't work, I'd ask him to say 'blank' and keep on reading."

Options 2 through 4 represent strategies to solve a particular problem that occurs during reading—identifying an unfamiliar word. Sounding out an unfamiliar word is one strategy frequently taught to beginners. When using a sounding-out strategy, a reader essentially tries to associate sounds with letters or letter combinations. An emphasis on sounding out in and of itself is a limited strategy because it doesn't teach or make children aware of the importance of monitoring what is read for comprehension. A teacher builds a child's metacognition when sounding out is taught in conjunction with making sense. For example, a teacher follows up a suggestion to sound out an unfamiliar word by asking, "Does the word make sense? Does what you read sound like language?"

Option 3, taking an educated guess, asks the reader to identify a word that makes sense in the context of the sentence in which the word is located and/or the text itself. The **implicit** message to the reader is that reading is supposed to make sense. If a child provides a word other than the unfamiliar word, but preserves the meaning of the text, the teacher would be instructionally and theoretically consistent in his or her actions by praising the child and encouraging him to continue reading.

The fourth option, say blank and keep on reading, is also a metacognitive strategy for word identification because it shows the reader that reading is not as much a word-perfect process as it is a meaning-making process. No one word should stop a reader cold. If the reader is monitoring the text for meaning, she may be able to return to the word and identify it or decide that the word wasn't that important to begin with.

The teacher can make the implicit messages about reading strategies **explicit.** Throughout this book we will use terms associated with explicit instruction: *modeling, demonstrating, explaining, rationale-building, thinking aloud,* and *reflecting.* From an instructional point of view, these terms reflect practices which allow the teacher to help students develop *metacognitive awareness and strategic knowledge.* For example, Arch, the first-grade teacher discussed earlier in this chapter chooses to engage the reader, after she takes a good guess at the unfamiliar word and completes reading, in a brief discussion of the importance of identifying words that "make sense" and "sound like language" in the context of what's being read. Such metacognitive discussions have the potential to build self-knowledge and task knowledge, and also to strengthen the reader's self-monitoring abilities.

Self-Knowledge. Do children know what reading is for? Do they know what the reader's role is? Do they know their options? Are they aware of their strengths as readers and learners? Do they recognize that some texts are harder than others and that all texts should not be read alike? Questions such as these reflect the self-knowledge component of metacognition. When readers are aware of *self* in relation to *texts* and *tasks,* they are in a better position to use reading strategies effectively (Armbruster, Echols, and Brown, 1982).

Task Knowledge. Experienced readers are strategic readers. They use their task knowledge to meet the demands inherent in difficult texts. For example, they know how to analyze a reading task, reflect on what they know or don't know about the text to be read, establish purposes and plans for reading, and evaluate their progress in light of purposes for reading. Experienced readers often are aware of whether they understood what they have read. And, if they haven't, they know what to do when comprehension fails.

Self-Monitoring. Reading becomes second nature to most of us, as we develop experience and maturity with the process. Experienced readers operate on "automatic pilot" as they read, until they run into a problem which disrupts smooth, fluent reading. Read, for example, the short passage below:

> The boys' arrows were nearly gone so they sat down on the grass and stopped hunting. Over at the edge of the woods they saw Henry making a bow to a little girl who was coming down the road. She had tears in her dress and also tears in her eyes. She gave Henry a note which he brought over to the group of young hunters. Read to the boys it caused great excitement. After a minute but rapid examination of their weapons, they ran down the valley. Does were standing at the edge of the lake making an excellent target.

Now reflect on the experience. At what point during reading did a "built-in sensor" in your head begin to signal to you that something was wrong? At what point in the passage did you become aware that some of the words you were misreading were homonyms and that you were choosing the inappropriate pronunciations of one or more of the homonyms? What did you do to rectify your misreadings? Why do you suppose the "sensor" signaled disruptions in your reading?

As experienced readers, we expect reading to make sense. And as we interact with a text, the metacognitive "sensor" in each of us monitors whether what we're reading is making sense.

What reader hasn't bumped into a homonym or two on occasion only to choose the inappropriate pronunciation, or come across a concept too difficult to grasp, or become "lost" in the author's line of reasoning or organizational scheme? What experienced reader hasn't sensed when a text is just too difficult to understand the first time around? The difference, of course, between the experienced and inexperienced reader is that the former knows when something's wrong and often utilizes correction strategies to "get back on track." This is what monitoring comprehension is all about.

Metacognitive ability is related to both age and reading experience (Stewart and Tei, 1983). Older students are more strategic in their reading than younger students, and good readers demonstrate more ability to use metacognition to deal with problems that arise during reading than readers with limited proficiency. Nevertheless, the instructional implications of metacognition are evident throughout this book. Becoming literate is a process of becoming aware, not only of oneself as a reader, but of strategies that help to solve problems that arise during reading. A classroom environment that nurtures metacognitive functioning is crucial to children's literacy development.

Reading from a Language Perspective

Cognition and language are critical components in human development. Although the acquisition of language is a complex process, many children understand and use all of the basic language patterns by the time they are 6 years old. The child's apparent facility with language is best understood by recognizing the active relationship between cognition and language.

Jean Piaget (1973) spent most of his life observing children and their interactions with their environment. His theory of cognitive development helps to explain that language acquisition is influenced by more general cognitive attainments. As children explore their environment they interpret and give meaning to the events that they experience. The child's need to interact with immediate surroundings and to manipulate objects is critical to language development. From a Piagetian view, language reflects thought and does not necessarily shape it.

Lev Vygotsky (1962, 1978), the acclaimed Russian psychologist, also viewed children as active participants in their own learning. However, at some point in their early development, children begin to acquire language competence; as they do so, language stimulates cognitive development. Gradually they begin to regulate their own problem-solving activities through the mediation of egocentric speech. In other words, children carry on external dialogues with themselves. Eventually external dialogue gives way to inner speech.

According to both Piaget and Vygotsky's views, children must be actively involved to grow and learn. Merely reacting to the environment isn't enough. An important milestone in a child's development, for example, is the ability to analyze means-end relationships. When this occurs children begin to acquire the ability to use language to achieve goals.

The linguistic sophistication of young children cannot be underestimated or taken for granted. Yet the outdated notion that children develop speech by imitation still persists among those who have little appreciation or knowledge of oral language development. The key to learning oral language lies in the opportunities children have to explore and experiment with language toward purposeful ends. As infants grow into toddlers, they learn to use language as an instrument for their intentions: "I want. . . " becomes a favorite phrase. No wonder M. A. K. Halliday (1975) described learning oral language as a "saga in learning to mean."

When teachers embrace reading as a language process, they understand the importance of learning oral language, but are also acutely aware that written language develops in humans along parallel lines. Children learn to use written language in much the same manner that they learn to use oral language—naturally and purposefully. As Goodman (1986b) put it: "Why do people create and learn written language? They need it! How do they learn it? The same way they learn oral language, but using it in authentic literary events that meet their needs" (p. 24).

Ultimately, there's only one way to become proficient as a writer and reader—and that's by writing and reading. When opportunities abound for children to engage in real literacy events (writing and reading), they grow as users of written language.

When language is splintered into its parts, and the parts are isolated from one another for instructional purposes, learning to read becomes more difficult than it needs to be. Hence, the term **whole language,** coined by Kenneth and Yetta Goodman, reflects the way some teachers think about language and literacy. They plan teaching activities which support students in their use of all aspects of language in learning to read. Keeping language "whole" drives home the point that splintering written language into bits and pieces, to be taught and learned separately from one another, makes learning to read harder, not easier. According to Goodman (1986b):

> Many school traditions seem to have actually hindered language development. In our zeal to make it easy, we've made it hard. How? Primarily by breaking whole (natural) language up into bite-size, but abstract little pieces. It seemed so logical to think that little children could best learn simple little things. We took apart

> the language and turned it into words, syllables, and isolated sounds. Unfortunately, we also postponed its natural purpose—the communication of meaning—and turned it into a set of abstractions, unrelated to the needs and experiences of the children we sought to help. (p. 7)

Support for whole language teaching comes from two areas of language inquiry: **psycholinguistics** and **sociolinguistics.**

Psycholinguistics and Reading

A psycholinguistic view of reading combines a psychological understanding of the reading process with an understanding of how language works. Psycholinguistic inquires into the reading process suggest that readers act upon and interact with written language in an effort to make sense of an author's text. Reading is not a passive activity, but an active thinking process that takes place behind the eyes. Nor is reading an exact process. All readers make mistakes—"miscues," according to Kenneth Goodman (1973b). Why? Miscues are bound to occur because readers are continually *anticipating* meaning and *sampling* a text for information cues based on their expectations. As a result, a reader searches for and coordinates *information cues* from three distinct systems in written language.

Graphophonemic System. The print itself provides readers with a major source of information: the graphic symbols or black squiggly marks on the page represent the relationship between speech sounds and letters. The more experiences readers have with written language, the more they learn about regular and irregular sound-letter relationships. Experienced readers acquire enough knowledge of sounds associated with letter symbols that they do not have to use all the available graphic information in a word in order to decode or recognize it.

Syntactic System. Besides having semantic knowledge, readers possess knowledge about how language works. *Syntactic information* is provided by the grammatical relationships within sentence patterns. In other words, readers use their knowledge of the meaningful arrangement of words in sentences to help construct meaning from text material.

The arrangement or order of words provides important information cues during reading. For example, although children may be able to read the words, "*ran race the quickly children the,*" they would make little sense out of what they read. The meaning is not clear until the words are arranged like so, "*The children quickly ran the race.*" In addition, a reader uses syntactic information to anticipate a word or phrase which "must come next" in a sentence because of its grammatical relationship to other words in the sentence: "I saw a red ______." Most children reading this sentence would probably fill in the blank with a noun, because they intuitively know how language works.

Semantic System. The semantic system of language stores the schemata that readers bring to a text in terms of background knowledge, experiences, conceptual understandings, attitudes, beliefs, and values.

Sociolinguistics and Reading

In the child's first several years, skill in spoken language develops naturally and easily. Children discover what language does for them. They learn that language is a tool that they can use and understand in interactions with others in their environment. They also learn that language is intentional; it has many purposes. Among the most obvious is communication. The more children use language to communicate, the more they learn the many special functions it serves.

Halliday (1975) viewed language as a reflection of what makes us uniquely human. His monumental work explored how language functions in our day-to-day interactions and serves the personal, social, and academic facets of our lives. Frank Smith (1977) expanded Halliday's functions of language by describing ten of its uses. He proposed that "the uses to which language is put lie at the heart of language comprehension and learning." The implications of this proposition for learning to read will become apparent throughout this book.

The ten uses of language are described below (Smith, 1977, p. 640):

1. *Instrumental:* "I want." (Language as a means of getting things, satisfying material needs.)
2. *Regulatory:* "Do as I tell you." (Controlling the behavior, feelings, or attitudes of others.)
3. *Interactional:* "Me and you." (Getting along with others, establishing relative status). Also, "Me against you." (Establishing separateness.)
4. *Personal:* "Here I come." (Expressing individuality, awareness of self, pride.)
5. *Heuristic:* "Tell me why." (Seeking and testing knowledge.)
6. *Imaginative:* "Let's pretend." (Creating new worlds, making up stories, poems.)
7. *Representational:* "I've got something to tell you." (Communicating information, descriptions, expressing propositions.)
8. *Divertive:* "Enjoy this." (Puns, jokes, riddles.)
9. *Authoritative/contractual:* "How it must be." (Statutes, laws, regulations, agreements, contracts.)
10. *Perpetuating:* "How it was." (Records, histories, diaries, notes, scores.)

Children recognize the meaningfulness of written language once they become aware of its uses. As Halliday (1975) noted, if children have difficulty learning to read, it is probably because beginning instruction often has had little to do with what they have learned about the uses of oral language.

The work of Harste, Woodward, and Burke (1984), which explores the literacy development of preschool children, reveals that even 2-year-olds use language strategies, often in concert, to make sense of written language. Four strategies, in particular, characterize the literacy expectations of beginners:

Text Intent. Children expect written language to be meaningful. Their encounters with text support the expectation that they will be able to recreate and construct an author's message.

Negotiability. Because children expect print to make sense, they use whatever knowledge and resources they possess to negotiate meaning—to create a meaningful message. Negotiation suggests that reading is a give-and-take process between reader and author.

Risk-Taking. Children experiment with how written language works. They take risks. They make hypotheses and then test them out. Risk-taking situations permit children to grow as language users.

Fine-Tuning Language with Language. An encounter with a written language becomes a resource for subsequent literacy events and situations. The more children interact with authentic authors and texts, the better they get at constructing meaning.

Because reading is uniquely human, learning to read requires sharing, interaction, and collaboration. Parent/child, teacher/child, and child/child relations and participation patterns are essential in learning to read. To what extent do children entering school have experience operating and communicating in a group as large as that found in the typical classroom? Children must learn the ropes. In many cases, kindergarten may be the first place where children must follow and respect the rules that govern how to operate and cooperate in groups. They must know not only how and when to work independently versus share and participate with one another; they must also learn the rules that govern communicative behavior.

Communicative competence, as defined by Hymes (1974), develops differently in children because they have not all had the same set of experiences or opportunities to engage in communication in the home or in the community. Some preschoolers have acquired more competence than others as to *when to* and *when not to speak,* and as to *what to talk about, with whom, where,* and in *what manner.* As hard as it may appear from an adult perspective, the sociolinguistic demands on a 5- or 6-year-old are staggering.

Since a large part of learning to read will depend on the social and cultural context of the classroom, opportunities must abound for discussions and conversations among teacher and child and children and other children. Within this context, children must show: (1) an eagerness to be independent; (2) an unquenchable zest to explore the new and

● BOX 1.4

Class Works

Social Learning in an Inner City Classroom

In an inner city elementary school, where about 80 percent of the students are from minority backgrounds, a first-grade class was nearing completion of a thematic literature unit on bears. Most of the students in the class were black, except for several white children and Pha, who at the beginning of the school year was a non-English-speaking child from Laos.

As a culminating activity in the unit, one group of the first graders chose to make masks of the characters from *Goldilocks and the Three Bears* and then to perform the story as a play. Pha played the part of Baby Bear.

Pha performed wonderfully as Baby Bear. When he discovered that somebody had eaten his porridge, he noted with much surprise, "Somebody ate my soup!" And when he found that his chair was broken, he shouted indignantly, "Somebody broke my chair!" And in the final episode of the play, when the bears find Goldilocks in bed, Pha was the first to make the discovery and exclaimed, "Somebody's in my bed, AND THERE SHE BE!"

Pha's teacher marveled at his use of *black dialect* and made an "on-the-spot" decision not to correct Pha's use of English, but to celebrate his full participation in a literacy activity.

Reflective Inquiry

- How does this classroom vignette illustrate how children use language as they interact with one another in environments that foster literacy learning and development?
- What roles do culture, social learning, and collaboration play in literacy events?
- What does Pha's teacher value and believe about the process of becoming literate?

unknown; (3) the courage to take risks, try things out, experience success as well as some defeat; and (4) the enjoyment of being with others and learning from them (Gans, 1963).

Kay, a kindergarten teacher with over 25 years of professional experience, confided in us her "secret" for teaching reading: "A hug for every child and lap-time whenever it's needed." Every child has a need for acceptance, love and affection, and individual attention. Certainly children differ in their emotional make-up and feelings of worth. But no child needs ever to experience overwhelming failure or rejection in learning to read.

Models of Reading

Models of the reading process often depict the act of reading as a communication event between a sender (the writer) and a receiver of information (the reader). Generally speaking, language information flows from the writer to the reader in the sense that the writer has a message to send and transmits it through print to the reader who then must interpret its meaning. Reading models have been developed to describe the way readers use language information to construct meaning from print. *How* a reader translates print to meaning is the key issue in the building of models of the reading process. This issue has led to the development of three classes of models: **bottom-up, top-down,** and **interactive.** A brief definition of each type of reading model follows.

Bottom-Up Models of Reading. These are models of reading that assume that the process of translating print to meaning begins with the print. The process is initiated by decoding graphic symbols into sounds. Therefore, the reader first identifies features of letters; links these features together to recognize letters; combines letters to recognize spelling patterns; links spelling patterns to recognize words; and then proceeds to sentence, paragraph, and text level processing.

Top-Down Models of Reading. These models of reading assume that the process of translating print to meaning begins with the reader's prior knowledge. The process is initiated by making predictions or "educated guesses" about the meaning of some unit of print. Readers decode graphic symbols into sounds to "check out" hypotheses about meaning.

Interactive Models of Reading. These are models of reading that assume that the process of translating print to meaning involves making use of both prior knowledge and print. The process is initiated by making predictions about meaning and/or decoding graphic symbols. The reader formulates hypotheses based upon the interaction of information from semantic, syntactic, and graphophonemic sources of information.

The terms *top-down, bottom-up,* and *interactive* are used extensively in the fields of communication and information processing. When these terms are used to describe reading, they also explain how language systems operate in reading.

Models of reading attempt to describe how readers use semantic, syntactical, and graphophomenic information in translating print to meaning. It is precisely in these descriptions that bottom-up, top-down, and interactive models of reading differ Figures 1.4 and 1.5 generally show the flow of information in each kind of reading model. Note that the illustrations are general depictions of information processing during reading and do not refer specifically to models such as those in Singer and Ruddell's *Theoretical Models and Processes of Reading* (1985).

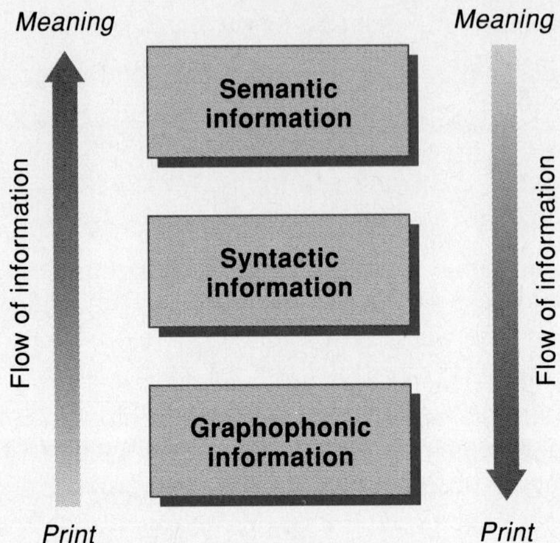
TOP-DOWN PROCESSING:
The act of reading is triggered by the reader's prior knowledge and experience in order to construct meaning.
Meaning
Meaning
Semantic information
Syntactic information
Graphophonic information
Flow of information
Flow of information
Print
Print
BOTTOM-UP PROCESSING:
The act of reading is triggered by graphophonic information such as letters, syllables, and words in order to derive meaning from print.

● **FIGURE 1.4** Bottom-up and top-down models

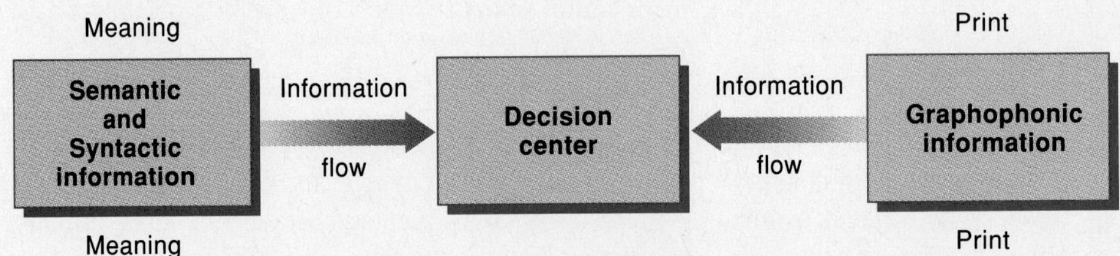
Meaning
Semantic and Syntactic information
Meaning
Information
flow
Decision center
Information
flow
Print
Graphophonic information
Print
INTERACTIVE PROCESSING: The act of reading is triggered by the reader's prior knowledge and experience as well as graphophonic information in order to construct meaning.

● **FIGURE 1.5** Information processing in interactive models of reading

Bottom-Up Models

As illustrated in Figure 1.4, the process of deriving meaning from print in bottom-up models is triggered by graphic information embedded in print. This is why bottom-up models are described as being "data driven." Data in this case are the letters and words on the page. A prototype model for bottom-up processing was constructed by Gough (1985), who attempted to show what happens in "one second of reading." In Gough's model, reading involves a series of steps that occur within milliseconds in the mind of the reader. The reader takes one "linguistic step" after another, beginning with the recognition of key features in letters and continuing letter-by-letter, word-by-word, sentence-by-sentence until reaching the top—the meaning of the text being read.

The reading model by Laberge and Samuels (1976) is also essentially bottom-up. However, the Laberge-Samuels model incorporates the idea of *automaticity.* The concept of automaticity suggests that humans can attend to only one thing at a time but may be able to process many things at once so long as no more than one requires attention. Automaticity is similar to putting an airplane on automatic pilot and freeing the pilot to direct his or her attention to other things.

In reading, **decoding** and **comprehending** vie for the reader's attention. Readers must learn to process graphophonic information so rapidly that they are free to direct attention to comprehending the text material for meaning.

The young reader is similar to the novice automobile driver. When learning to drive a car, the beginner finds the mechanics of operating the automobile so demanding that he or she must focus exclusively on driving. However, with practice, the skilled driver pays little conscious attention to the mechanics of driving and is able to converse with a passenger or listen to the radio. Likewise, the beginning reader must practice decoding print to speech so rapidly that decoding becomes automatic. As beginners become more fluent in decoding, they can devote their attention to comprehending the writer's message.

Top-Down Models

Top-down models emphasize that information processing during reading is triggered by the reader's prior knowledge and experience in relation to the writer's message. Obviously there are no pure top-down models because readers must begin by focusing on print. As opposed to being data driven, top-down models are said to be conceptually driven. That is to say, ideas or concepts in the mind of a reader trigger information processing during reading. As Frank Smith (1979) put it, "The more you already know, the less you need to find out" (p. 15). In other words, the more readers know in advance about the topic to be read, the less they need to use graphic information on the page.

To get a better idea of how reading is conceptually driven, read the following story:

FLAN AND GLOCK

Flan was a flim.
Glock was a plopper.
It was unusual for a film and a plopper to be crods, but
Flan and Glock were crods. They medged together.
Flan was keaded to moak at a mox. Glock wanted to kead
there too. But the lear said he could not kead there.
Glock anged that the lear said he could not kead there
because he was a plopper.

Although you've never heard of Flan and Glock nor know what a flim or a plopper is, it is not difficult to interpret from this short story that Glock was discriminated against. How did you figure this out? Your knowledge of capitalization may have led you to hypothesize that Flan and Glock are proper names. Knowledge of grammar, whether intuitive or overt, undoubtedly helped you to realize that flim, plopper, crods, and mox are nouns and that medged and keaded are verbs. Finally, your knowledge of the world led you to predict that since the lear said, "Glock could not kead there because he was a plopper" Glock probably is a victim of discrimination.

Note that these interpretations of the story are "educated guesses." However, both prior knowledge and graphophonic information were required to make these guesses. From our perspective, reading is rarely totally top-down or bottom-up. A third class of models helps to explain the interactive nature of the reading process.

Interactive Models

Neither prior knowledge nor graphophonic information is used exclusively by readers. Interactive models suggest that the process of reading is initiated by formulating hypotheses about meaning *and* by decoding letters and words. According to Kamil and Pearson (1979), readers assume either an active or passive role, depending upon the strength of their hypotheses about the meaning of the reading material. If readers bring a great deal of knowledge to the material, the chances are that their hypotheses will be strong and that they will process the material actively, making minimal use of graphophonic information. Passive reading, on the other hand, often results when readers have little experience with and knowledge of the topic to be read. They rely much more on the print itself for information cues.

Effective readers know how to interact with print in an effort to understand a writer's message. Effective readers adapt to the material based on their purposes for reading. Purpose dictates the strategies that readers use to translate print to meaning. Two of the most appropriate questions that readers can ask about a selection are, "What do I need to know?" and "How well do I already know it?" These two questions help readers to establish purposes for reading and formulate hypotheses during reading. The questions also help decide how to *coordinate* prior knowledge and graphophonic information.

Note that the models of reading just described don't take into consideration the social nature of reading and learning to read. In this sense, they're incomplete. However, models are useful in some respects; they help you to reflect on your beliefs, assumptions, and practices related to reading instruction—the topic of Chapter 2.

SUMMARY

We organized this chapter around the metaphor *lens* to suggest that teachers view what they do in the classroom through lenses that focus and clarify their instructional decisions and practices. They form images in their heads about reading and learning to read. These images (mental pictures) bring into focus what teachers know, believe, and value not only about their roles as classroom teachers of reading, but also about reading, readers, curriculum, and instruction. We explored the role that the teacher's belief system plays in instructional decisions and practices. Teachers develop belief systems about reading and learning to read through personal, practical, and professional study and experience.

Because we believe that all teachers are theorists in that they have reasons for their instructional decisions, we examined the reading process from cognitive, linguistic, and social perspectives and described three models that involve the processing of language information.

The next step in thinking about reading and learning to read is to study how belief systems influence instructional practices and strategies. Chapter 2 explores the teaching of reading from two major instructional perspectives: skills and whole language.

TEACHER-ACTION RESEARCHER

Teachers who engage in reflection and inquiry find themselves asking questions and observing closely what goes on in their classrooms. As one teacher put it, "My concerns produced a need to examine everything that was happening in the classroom. What was I doing? What were the children's responses? What did they say? What did they do? What and how did they read and write?" (Avery, 1990, p. 34). Action research is a way for teachers who want to use reflection and inquiry to better understand within the context of their own teaching more about themselves as teachers and their students as learners. At the end of each chapter, several ideas for action research projects are presented.

1. Observe a teacher in an elementary school. Record what you see and hear during reading instruction time. Based on the interactions recorded between teacher and students, what image(s) of teaching do you associate with the teacher?
2. Using the idea of the reading autobiography, prepare an autobiographical narrative following the directions in Box 1.1. Share your autobiographical sketch with other members of the class or with colleagues in your school, or with a family member or roommate. What differences in reading development and attitude are evident? What similarities exist?
3. Join a book group in your school or methods class. What affect does participation in book discussions have on you? What teaching insights do you gain as a result of participation?

KEY TERMS

literacy event
professional knowledge
metacognition
whole language
bottom-up
decoding
belief system
images of teachers
implicit
psycholinguistics
top-down
comprehending
constructivism
schema
explicit
sociolinguistics
interactive

CHAPTER 2

Lenses on the Reading Curriculum

Connecting Beliefs to Practices

BETWEEN THE LINES

In this chapter you will discover:

- **How different reading models are connected to beliefs about reading.**
- **The differences between a skills-based and a whole language curriculum.**
- **The major approaches to the teaching of reading.**
- **How teachers enact the reading curriculum in their classrooms.**

Gay's gift wasn't what she had expected. Her mother's Christmas present in years past had always been unusual, but this year she had outdone herself. Wrapped in shiny foil, much to Gay's surprise, was a worn out, overstuffed, red-covered notebook. There it was—Gay's old red notebook which she hadn't seen for more than 20 years—reunited once again with its owner (Fawcett, 1990).

Between the covers of the red notebook were those wonderful, creative, misspelled stories that Gay had written as a child. She was about 8 years old when she penned her first story, "Hankie and the Hawk." Story after story filled hundreds of pages now yellowed with time. And then the idea struck her. Gay could hardly wait to get back to the students that she taught and share her childhood stories with them.

Since then, Gay introduces "the old red notebook" to her students on the opening day of each school year. In her own words, "the book" has become the centerpiece of a strategy she uses to introduce her third-grade class to reading and writing: "Here I am, starting the morning of the first day of the school year by reading stories to my class that sound like something the children would have written. The book is falling apart, the pages are yellow, and the crazy teacher is grinning like a fool! Soon, however, an 'ah ha' or two can be heard as I read the author's name with each story: 'Hankie and the Hawk' by Miss Gay Wilson, April 3, 1957; 'How the Pig Got a Curly Tail' by Miss Gay Wilson, December 10, 1959; 'Sue's Birthday' by Miss Gay Wilson, February 21, 1958.

"The dates and the name Wilson carry little meaning, but a few of my students recognize the name Gay as mine and soon catch on to what's happening. 'These are stories *you* wrote when you was a little girl,' blurts a precocious listener. The looks on the children's faces are worth their weight in gold. Sheer delight!

"They beg for more, and I promise more another day. There are enough stories to read every day for most of the school year. So I make a promise to them that I will not break: 'Every day this year you'll get to read, and every day this year you'll get to write.' I want them to feel the specialness of this promise. Then we discuss the author in each of them.

"What do we do next? Write, of course. Do any of the children say, 'I don't know what to write about?' Not at all. Of course, not all of them do write; some, on the first day, draw. But all the children approach writing with confidence. What do they do next? Read, of course. Since I read to them what I had written as a child, they now read to one another."

First days are important. Why did Gay make the decision to use her childhood writings on the first day of school as an instructional tool? "It was a natural decision to make," says Gay, "because I believe strongly in my role as a model. What better way to model what it means to be an author and a reader than to use my own childhood stories." So the old red notebook became part of a strategy—a plan of action—designed to build community, set expectations, and contribute to a classroom environment that supports literacy development.

Gay's story opens this chapter because it illustrates how a teacher's beliefs about learning to read and write influence what she does in the classroom. Making the connection between belief systems and models of reading is an important step in understanding what classroom teachers of reading do and why. In this chapter, we invite you to take a step further in making the link between theory and practice. How do belief systems relate to approaches and strategies used in the teaching of reading?

Gay's classroom reading program doesn't come prepackaged. It isn't synonymous with the published "reading program" she's required by school district policy to use. Nor is it defined narrowly as objectives and activities compiled in the school district's curriculum guide. A curriculum guide is just that—a guide, a set of guidelines. Instead, Gay's reading program reflects the way she *enacts* the curriculum in the classroom.

Gay views the literacy curriculum in her classroom through lenses that focus and clarify how she plans instruction, makes decisions, uses instructional strategies and materials, and interacts with children.

What Gay does to teach reading mirrors her **beliefs about reading** and learning to read. She is often *theoretically consistent* in her instructional practices and the decisions she makes. When teachers are theoretically consistent, there is a congruency between what they do and why they do it.

Alan Watts, a contemporary philosopher dealing with existential questions such as "Who Am I?" and "Where am I going?" once said, "Trying to define yourself is like trying to bite your own teeth." Throughout this book, we invite you to engage in a process of defining and refining your beliefs about reading and learning to read. The task is not easy, but unlike trying to bite your own teeth, it *is* in the realm of the possible.

Connecting Models to Beliefs About Reading

Throughout this book we urge you to recognize that instructional decisions and practices are theoretically related. We encourage you to make the connections between your beliefs and practices and to expand your repertoire of instructional strategies. Moreover, we contend that teachers of reading should reflect a strong interactive view of the reading process. This view recognizes the definite interplay between the reader and the text and the situation in which learning occurs.

One important way to define who we are as teachers of reading is by talking about *what* we do and *why* we do it or by observing one another in a teaching situation and asking *why* we did what we did. Another way is through self-examination and reflection. The tools which follow help you to inquire into your beliefs about reading in relation to instructional practices.

The Beliefs About Reading Interview

Your beliefs about how students learn to read in all likelihood lie on a continuum between concepts that reflect bottom-up models of reading and concepts that reflect top-down models of reading. By participating in the Beliefs About Reading Interview (see Appendix A), you will get a *general indication* of where your beliefs about learning to read lie on the continuum.

Your responses in the interview will often mirror **units of language** emphasized for instructional purposes. For example, the smallest units of written language are letters; the largest unit is the text selection itself. In Figure 2.1, concentric boxes help to illustrate units of written language. The largest box represents the text as a whole. It may be a story, a poem, or an article on the Civil War. This unit of language is made up of *paragraphs,* which are made up of *sentences,* which are made up of *words,* which are made up of *letters.*

Teachers who possess a bottom-up belief system believe that students must decode letters and words before they are able to construct meaning from sentences, paragraphs, and larger text selections. Consequently, they view reading acquisition as mastering and integrating a series of word identification skills. Letter/sound relationships and word identification are emphasized instructionally. Because recognizing each word is believed to be an essential prerequisite to being able to comprehend the passage, accuracy in recognizing words is seen as important. If you hold a bottom-up set of beliefs, you may consider the practice of correcting oral reading errors as important in helping children learn to read. Or you may believe that helping students to read a passage over and over or to read orally into a tape recorder are important instructional activities because they develop accurate word recognition. Teachers who hold bottom-up conceptual frameworks of reading often emphasize the teaching of skills in a sequential and orderly manner.

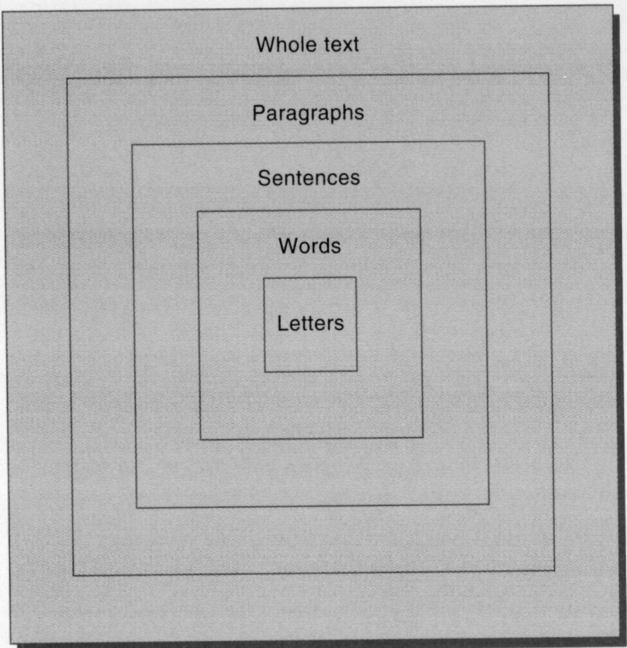

● **FIGURE 2.1** Units of written language

Teachers who have a top-down belief system consider reading for meaning an essential component of all reading instructional situations. Therefore, they feel that the majority of reading/language arts instructional time should involve students in meaningful activities in which they read, write, speak, and listen. They may also emphasize the importance of students choosing their own reading material and enjoying the material they read. Sentences, paragraphs, and text selections are the units of language emphasized instructionally. Since recognizing each word is not considered an essential prerequisite to comprehending the passage, word errors during oral reading may not be corrected. Instead, they may advocate noninterference during oral reading or encourage a student to use the context or meaning of the passage to determine unrecognized words.

Table 2.1 summarizes the beliefs defining the bottom-up and top-down belief systems.

Theoretical Orientation to Reading Profile (TORP)

The **Theoretical Orientation to Reading Profile (TORP),** designed by Diane DeFord (1985), is a survey instrument that uses a Likert Scale to determine teacher beliefs about practices in reading instruction. DeFord identifies three belief systems or theoretical orientations which are associated with instructional practices: *phonics, skills,* and *whole language.* These belief systems fall on a continuum of instruction as illustrated in Figure 2.2.

● TABLE 2.1

Defining Bottom-Up and Top-Down Beliefs About Reading

	Bottom-Up Beliefs About Reading	Top-Down Beliefs About Reading
Relationship of Word Recognition to Comprehension	Believe students must recognize each word in a selection to be able to comprehend the selection.	Believe students can comprehend a selection even when they are not able to recognize each word.
Use of Information Cues	Believe students should use word and sound-letter cues exclusively to determine unrecognized words.	Believe students should use meaning and grammatical cues in addition to graphic cues to determine unrecognized words.
View of Reading	Believe reading requires mastering and integrating a series of word recognition skills.	Believe students learn to read through meaningful activities in which they read, write, speak, and listen.
Units of Language Emphasized Instructionally	Letters, letter/sound relationships, and words.	Sentences, paragraphs, and text selections.
Where Importance Is Placed Instructionally	View accuracy in recognizing words as important.	View reading for meaning as important.
Evaluation	Think students need to be tested on discrete skills.	Think students need to be tested on the kind of knowledge constructed through reading.

The Beliefs About Reading Interview and the TORP help teachers examine the relationships between their beliefs about reading and instructional practices. Bottom-up practices, for example, are essentially equivalent to phonics and skills instruction. Top-down instruction embodies a whole language perspective.

Appendix B contains the TORP survey and guidelines for scoring.

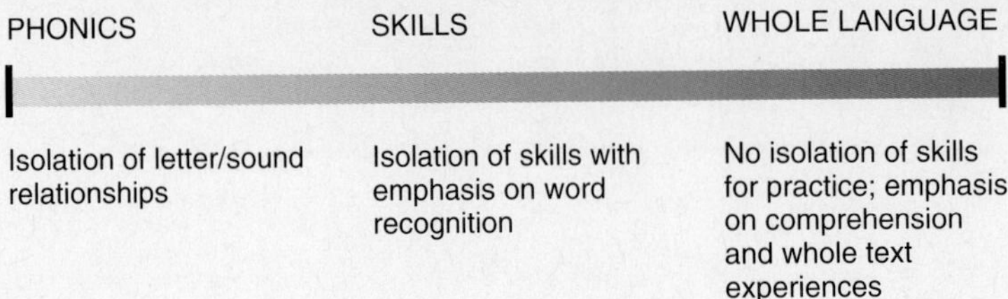

● **FIGURE 2.2** Continuum of instruction

Two Images of the Reading Curriculum

Teachers form images in their head about the reading curriculum. These images are mental pictures of what the curriculum should look like when it is enacted in the classroom. Images of the reading curriculum are brought into focus by belief systems. Belief systems influence the teaching of reading and contribute to decisions involving, among other things: (1) the instructional goals the teacher emphasizes for the classroom reading program; (2) the materials the teacher selects and uses for instruction; (3) the environment the teacher perceives as most conducive to reading growth; (4) the behaviors the teacher perceives as reflecting good reading behavior; and (5) the practices, approaches, and strategies the teacher uses to teach reading.

Questions every elementary teacher has struggled with (or is struggling with) concern the teaching of reading skills: Which reading skills are important? How do I teach reading skills? Should I be teaching reading skills? Two images of the reading curriculum, each supported by differing belief systems, result in dramatically different practices and decisions related to the teaching of skills.

The dominant approaches to the teaching of reading in the twentieth century have been from a **skills view.** Only in the past decade has a skills perspective been seriously challenged by educators. Today, a **whole language view** has been transforming the way teachers think about and teach reading.

A Skills-Based Curriculum

If you believe in a skills view, then you probably think that learning to read successfully presumes the acquisition of a finite but sizable number of skills and specific abilities. We liken this skills perspective to the image of a railroad track shown in Figure 2.3.

Imagine that the sequence of skills in the teaching of reading is analogous to the railroad track, on which one tie (a skill) is followed by another and another as far as one travels. The railroad track captures the *linear progression* associated with skills development. In schools, children are often required to learn certain skills before they are taught other skills. The scope and sequence of skills reflects the linear progression underlying skills development.

● **FIGURE 2.3** An image of the skills-based curriculum as a railroad track

From a skills perspective, children are expected to walk one tie at a time, whether they need to or not, as they progress on the "skills track." If you have ever walked a railroad track, you have experienced how difficult it is to maintain a steady pace, without stumbling, when you walk a tie at a time. What happens when a child stumbles on the skills track? Often, teachers prescribe additional skills instruction before a child can step to the next tie. The skill in question is singled out for additional practice and reinforcement, usually in the form of workbook exercises, until the child's performance reflects a satisfactory progress.

Is reading a skill or a set of separate skills? John Downing (1982), a noted reading researcher, wondered if reading could be defined as a skill or a set of skills. He reasoned that if reading could be classified as either a skill or as a set of skills, then all that is known in psychology about the nature of a skill and a set of skills could be applied to reading. As Downing surveyed the psychological literature, he found a comprehensive definition of a skill provided by McDonald (1965): "From a psychological point of view, playing football or chess or using a typewriter or the English language correctly demands complex sets of responses—some of them cognitive, some attitudinal, and some manipulative." McDonald stresses that it is not merely a matter of motor behavior. The player must also understand the game, enjoy playing it, and have appropriate attitudes about playing the game. McDonald went on to state: "The total performance . . . is a complex set of processes—cognitive, attitudinal, and manipulative. This complex integration of processes is what we usually mean when we refer to 'skill'" (p. 387).

Downing points out that psychologists have technical terms for parts of a skill, that is, *subskills* or *subroutines.* Maybe that is what reading skills are. What do psychologists mean by subskills or subroutines of a skill?

Does the skill of reading have subskills or prerequisite skills that students need to be able to perform in order to read? Downing (1982) makes a very strong statement about the alleged "reading skills" described in many reading method texts: "These bits of alleged behavior . . . mostly have no basis in objective data from studies of actual reading behavior. In other words, these so-called 'reading skills' are largely mythical" (p. 535).

Taking a more moderate stance than Downing, Samuels (1976) believes that it may be possible to determine a true hierarchy of subskills in reading. However, he admits, "Despite the fact that . . . commercial reading series, with their scope and sequence charts, order the reading tasks as if we did know the nature of the learning hierarchy in reading, *the sad truth is that the task is so complex that a validated reading hierarchy does not exist*" (p. 174, emphasis added).

Yet all basal reading programs—in fact, just about all published reading programs—have scope and sequence charts, which are lists of skills to be taught. When these scope and sequence charts or management systems are compared, there is little agreement as to sequence. Some first-grade and kindergarten programs begin with the alphabet, proceed through consonant sound/letter association, and then begin introducing vowel sound/letter association. Others begin with rhyming elements and graphic shapes and then present some words and sound/letter associations. Likewise, there is little agreement to be found when comparing lists of skills from different commercial publishers of middle- and upper-grade reading programs. Stennett, Smythe, and Hardy (1975) reviewed a number of published reading programs and concluded that "*none provide a sound rationale or adequate documentation for either the relevance of their skill content or the sequence of instruction*" (pp. 223–224, emphasis added).

Two major national reports published in the mid-1980s affirm that reading and learning to read are more involved processes than some educators believe. Reading is "a complex skill . . . a holistic act" according to the Commission on Reading's *Becoming a Nation of Readers* (1985, p. 7). Instructionally speaking, this report later advises that ". . . no matter how children are introduced to words, very early in the program they should have experience with reading these words in meaningful texts" (p. 43). The second report, *What Works: Research About Teaching and Learning,* recommends "direct experience with written language as requisite for reading" (1986, p. 9).

Images of the reading curriculum as mastering sets of skills or as involving students in a holistic process can be traced to our beliefs about reading. The view of learning to read by mastering word recognition and comprehension subskills is based on a bottom-up belief. On the other hand, a whole language view is based on the top-down and strong interactive beliefs that students learn to read through meaningful experiences. These experiences include students reading, writing, speaking, and listening about things important to them.

A Whole Language Curriculum

Whole language means different things to different people. In practice, however, teachers often associate whole language with what they do in their classrooms. They believe that a whole language curriculum creates child-responsive environments for learning that are supported by literature-based instruction and curriculum integration. Not only are the language arts integrated, but so is curriculum across content areas. Language is for learning. Teachers develop curriculum *with* students (Watson, 1989). Together, teacher and students enact and negotiate a whole language curriculum day by day throughout the school year.

Whole language teachers believe in weaving into their teaching the use of authentic texts for children to read, discuss, listen to, or write about. In Figure 2.4, we liken a whole language curriculum to a spider's web. The spider's web image underscores how children in a whole language classroom weave a web of meaning around authentic texts for authentic reasons. The various strands of language—reading, writing, speaking, and listening—serve as threads in the construction of the web.

One of the main goals of a whole language curriculum is to support children in the skillful use of language. They develop skills and strategies, but they do so in the context of meaningful learning. The development of skills and strategies is not assumed to occur in linear progression as in a skills-based curriculum. Instead, as the spider's web image suggests, children grow as readers and writers, both vertically and horizontally. Some children will experience periods of accelerated learning followed by plateaus in their development. Some may need more time than others to "roam in the known" before they make noticeable progress in their use of language. Teachers provide the type of supportive environment that enables learners to develop confidence and competence with language and its many uses.

Although classroom descriptions of whole language practices may vary from teacher to teacher, some basic principles guide every teacher's actions. For example, teachers believe that language serves the personal, social, and academic facets of children's lives. Language, therefore, cannot be severed from a child's quest to make sense; language and meaning-making are intertwined. In addition, whole language teachers recognize that oral and written language are parallel processes; one is not secondary to the other. Language, whether oral or written, involves a complex system of symbols, rules, and subsystems that govern the content and form of language in the context of its use. For the whole language teacher, keeping language "whole" means not breaking it into bits and pieces or isolating the subsystems of language for instructional emphasis.

The predominant image of the child in a whole language curriculum is that of a language user. Through language use, children learn to reflect upon their own experience, to express themselves symbolically, to make meaning and create knowledge, and to share their meanings with others. Gordon Wells (1986) depicts children as "meaning-makers" who, in the process of learning language, use language to describe, explain, and inquire

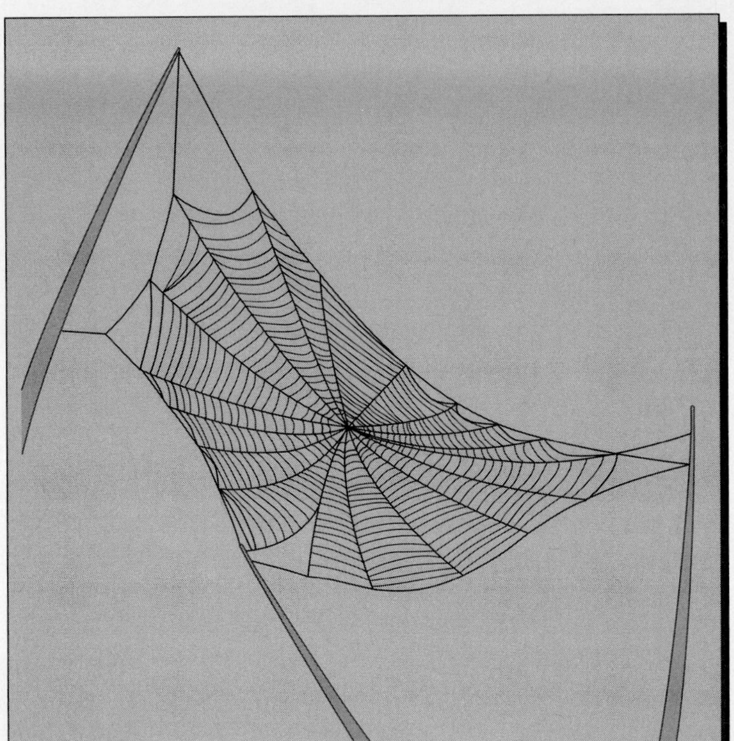

● **FIGURE 2.4** An image of the whole language curriculum as a spider's web

about the world around them and to share their knowledge with others. Wells' 15-year study of language users describes patterns of oral and written language development and explains children's individual differences in learning language and literacy. He concludes from his longitudinal study that parents and teachers best serve children's language and literacy development as collaborators in learning. If parents and teachers are to help children to achieve their full potentials as meaning-makers then their role is to guide, encourage, and facilitate.

Another strong image of children in a whole language curriculum is that of learner. Respect for the child as a learner is paramount to a successful classroom environment. Whole language teachers believe that children are natural learners who best learn how to read and write under natural conditions. Because learning to read and write involves trial and error, whole language teachers hold firm to their convictions that children must learn to take risks in classroom contexts. Child development experts often characterize young children from birth through age 5 as "examiners," "experimenters," "explorers," "exhibitors," and "experts" (Owens, 1988). Teachers extend these images of children into their classrooms.

In the whole language curriculum, classrooms are communities of learners, with children coming together to engage in reading, writing, and other collaborative activities.

Classrooms are "communities" in a whole language curriculum. Teacher and students come together as a community of learners to engage in reading, writing, and other collaborative acts of meaning-making. Language learners help one another. They talk to each other about what they are writing and what they are reading. They engage in partnerships around projects and thematic studies. They share their understandings of how to solve problems encountered while reading and writing.

Certain conditions for learning permeate classroom learning communities. These conditions have been described by various whole language theorists and educators such as Goodman (1986), Atwell (1987), Cambourne (1987), and Smith (1989). For example, *immersion* and *authenticity* are two necessary conditions for a whole language curriculum. Children must be immersed in written language. As learners, they need to engage in explorations of a wide range of texts which include those they produce by writing and those they use for reading. They need to be surrounded with all kinds of literature. When they are immersed in literature, children are given numerous occasions to explore real texts to satisfy real needs. In a whole language curriculum, authentic texts may include children's actual writings as well as books representing different literary genres. Books may be big or little in size, wordless, predictable, informational, imaginary, biographical, historical, or realistic. Books may be anthologies of poetry or collections of short tales. In addition, genuine texts may also serve the functional, everyday needs of children and may include "environmental print" (e.g., street signs, posters, and boxtop labels), reference materials, textbooks, newspapers, and magazines.

In addition, *demonstration* and *engagement* are essential conditions for whole language learning. Teachers and students alike demonstrate the role literacy plays in their lives. Demonstrations show how reading and writing can be used to satisfy the user's purposes and functional needs. As Frank Smith (1989) observes, a teacher who is bored by what she or he is teaching demonstrates to children that what is being taught is boring. Likewise, a reading skills workbook containing meaningless exercises demonstrates to children that reading can be meaningless. In a whole language curriculum, children encounter numerous demonstrations of reading and writing in use. Sometimes demonstrations are strategic in nature. The teacher, for example, models a learning strategy which shows students how to solve a problem encountered during a reading or writing.

Engagement suggests the learner's commitment, mental involvement, and willingness to participate in a demonstration. In a whole language curriculum, there is a strong expectation that children who are engaged in learning will succeed. Teachers create environments which reinforce the expectation that children will be successful and then provide the means by which they will succeed.

Ownership, time, and *response* are also conducive to learning in a whole language curriculum. Children take ownership for their own learning, but teachers play an important role in helping children assume responsibility for their learning. For example, teachers may plan and gather resources for a thematic unit, but they include their students in setting goals and making decisions about texts, activities, and patterns of participation. Learning is invitational. Harste, Short, and Burke (1988) define "invitations" to learn within the framework of choice and hypothesis testing: "Choice is central in curriculum because students test different hypotheses according to their different needs, interests, and experiences. Children should be invited rather than forced to engage in specific literacy activities" (p. 15). Invitations to participate in literacy events allow children to retain ownership of the processes in which they are engaged during a learning activity.

Time to read and write also is essential. Children need time to engage in literacy events. In whole language classrooms, opportunities for reading, writing, speaking, and listening occur throughout the day and are not pigeonholed or compartmentalized into periods or time blocks.

If children are to realize their potential as language users, they not only need time to read and write, they also need response. Whole language teachers recognize this and build systems for response into their classroom procedures. In whole language classrooms, it is not uncommon to see children "conferencing" with one another or with the teacher as they share what they are reading or writing. It is also not uncommon to observe them talking about books or using journals to write their personal responses to what they are reading.

Another condition involves *approximation.* Cambourne (1987) suggests that children approximate written language as they learn to read and write. They experiment with written language as they put literacy to use in purposeful situations. With trial comes error. Conditions that favor *trial and error* learning help children to become risk-takers. Nonconventional spellings, the child's "inventions," are interpreted as signs of growth as children develop toward conventional spelling competency. Oral reading errors, also known as *miscues,* may represent a child's attempt to construct meaning during reading and should not be discounted as mistakes that must be remedied. Errors are welcomed, not frowned upon, in a whole language curriculum. Knowing *when* and *why* to correct are important functions of whole language teaching.

Skill-based and whole language perspectives are on opposite ends of an instructional continuum. Various approaches to the teaching of reading can be explained within the context of this continuum. Let's take a closer look.

Approaches to Reading

What **approaches to reading** are available? The reading curriculum may include several approaches on the skills to whole language instructional continuum. Reasonably speaking, however, a major approach should meet these two basic criteria: First, it must be observable in actual classroom instruction around the country; second, it must be derived from a theoretical base that is top-down, bottom-up, or interactive. The major approaches to reading instruction include adhering to these criteria, prescriptive, basal reading, language-experience, writing process, and literature-based programs. Figure 2.5 illustrates their relative positions on the skill-holistic continuum.

The term *individualizing reading instruction* has different meanings to teachers. One kind of individualization is associated with bottom-up theory: Heavy emphasis is placed on *prescribing linguistic and other sequential skills.* Another kind of individualization is associated with top-down theory: Heavy emphasis is placed on personalizing instruction through literature. Consequently, the term *individualizing* refers to two distinct approaches.

Basal reading programs come the closest to an eclectic approach. That is, within the basal reading program itself some elements of the other approaches are incorporated. Yet basal reading programs, built on scope and sequence foundations, traditionally have been

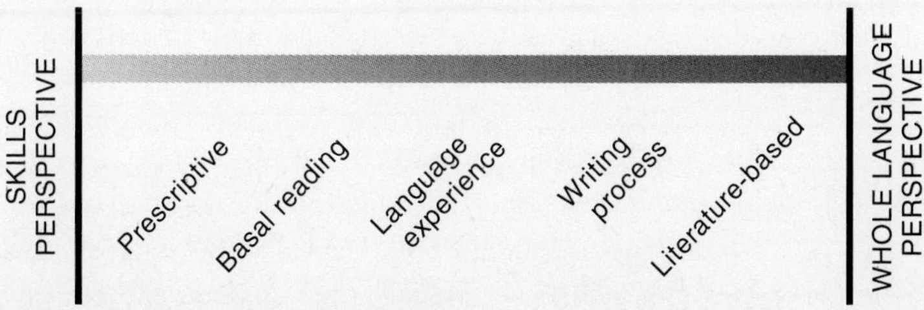

FIGURE 2.5 Range of approaches on an instructional continuum

associated with bottom-up theory. This association has been modified over the years with the addition of language experience and literature activities.

Language experience, located on the holistic side of the continuum, is tied closely to an interactive or top-down theory of reading and writing. This approach is often considered a kind of beginning reading approach, although strategies connected to the writing process, in which links to reading and writing are made, are becoming more and more prevalent in today's elementary classrooms.

Prescriptive Approaches

The **prescriptive** type of individualized instruction is often favored by teachers who devote large chunks of the reading period to work on phonics or linguistics. They focus on sound-letter relationship instruction advocated by linguists such as Bloomfield and Barnhart in *Let's Read: A Linguistic Approach* (1961). While there are some variations in the teaching procedures offered by the programs labeled *linguistic,* the stress by and large is on small language units such as letters, syllables, spelling patterns, and words.

The Bloomfield-Barnhart method emphasized that reading instruction should begin with teaching the letters of the alphabet. Then students should be taught phonics through a method similar to *analytic phonics.* In analytic phonics, students learn sound-letter relationships by seeing how parts of words sound alike and are written similarly. For example, teachers may teach the digraph *sh* by having students compare "*sh*ell" and "da*sh.*" The students would see the graphic and auditory similarities in "di*sh,*" "fi*sh,*" and "wi*sh.*" Bloomfield and Barnhart thought letter-sounds should be taught in sentence contexts, while comprehension was of secondary importance in the early stages of reading. Bloomfield and Barnhart believed that the major emphasis in beginning reading instruction should be on decoding, that is, associating the phonemes or sounds of our language with their most regular grapheme representations, or letters or groups of letters.

Fries is another linguist who endorsed this approach and coauthored a basal reader series, the *Merrill Linguistic Readers,* in 1966. Other linguistic programs published at about the same time include *SRA Basic Reading Series* (1964) published by Science Research Associates, the *Linguistic Readers* (1965) published by Harper & Row, and *Programmed Reading* (1963), a programmed linguistic series published by McGraw-Hill.

These programs include stories written so that there is a gradual introduction and numerous repetition of specific sound-letter relationships. The readers were comprised of sentences such as "The fat cat sat on the mat" and "The car was parked at the market." Patterns that were considered simpler such as the "cat, hat, mat" pattern were introduced before more difficult ones such as the "car, park, market" pattern.

Other linguistic programs advocate *synthetic phonics* rather then the analytic phonic approach. Whereas in the analytic phonic method students break words down into grapheme-phoneme (letter-sound) units, in synthetic phonics students build words up letter-by-letter. In using the synthetic phonic method, teachers show beginning readers that "c" goes with a /k/ sound, "a" goes with an /a/ sound, and "t" goes with a /t/ sound. When these phonemes or minimal sound units are blended together, the child would read "c-a-t—

cat." This is where the term *sound it out* comes from. In using synthetic phonics, the students "sound out" words in a letter-by-letter fashion.

The *Lippincott Basal Program* (1968) emphasized the teaching of synthetic phonics. *The Distar Program,* in use since the late seventies, also gives teachers explicit directions for teaching students by the synthetic phonics method.

Another characteristic associated with an individualized-prescriptive approach is *skills management.* Often, this involves the purchase and use of commercially boxed skill cards organized into prescription modules.

Let's take a minute and look at a fourth-grade teacher. It is September and Mrs. Winkley is eager to meet her students and begin teaching her favorite subject, reading. The week before school started, she and her colleagues attended an in-service class on a recently adopted skills management system to be used with their basal reader. During the in-service Mrs. Winkley heard that the school system is working toward adopting some "basic minimal standard" in the teaching of both mathematics and reading. In doing this, the school system will become more accountable for the students' education.

After a coffee break, the in-service program leader got around to what Mrs. Winkley wanted to know—how to actually use this skills-management system in her classroom. A list of behavioral objectives was given to her as well as mastery tests that were to be used to periodically test the students' performance on the set of objectives or subskills. She was told students had "mastered" a reading skill if they were able to correctly answer 80 percent of the items testing that skill. For each reading skill, she was given a list of workbook pages, ditto sheets, games, and other activities to drill the students who had not mastered the reading skill, that is, had not passed the mastery test for that skill. Mrs. Winkley even was given a set of cards for each skill that could be sent home to get parents involved in drilling a child on needed skills.

After some consideration, Mrs. Winkley decided the skills management system made a lot of sense. She remembered last year when she taught her middle reading group the skill of determining how many syllables were in words. She had drilled the whole group of students on this reading skill. Some of the students already seemed to know how to do this; others in the group struggled. "With this management system," she thought, "I will be able to know which students need to be taught particular skills and which students won't need further instruction in them."

Skills management systems usually include a sequentially ordered set of skills written as objectives, sets of tests to measure these objectives, directions for determining what level of achievement constitutes mastery, and resource files of specific workbook pages, dittos, games, and other activities that can provide instruction and practice for each of the skills. These systems also have a method of organizing and reporting which skills students have or have not mastered.

In addition to *phonics instruction* and *skills management,* a third characteristic is becoming associated with an individualized-prescription approach: *computer assisted instruction.*

Since the early 1980s, computer assisted instruction (CAI) has become a "hot topic" in the education business. With increasing advances in computer technology, schools are now being supplied with computers. Individual classrooms will soon have several terminals networked to a larger computer that serves the entire school. This school computer will be connected to a CPU serving the school district.

Students will have school access to computers similar to those presently under development at the Xerox Research Center in Palo Alto. These computers are being designed to store and allow students to here access to the equivalent of an encyclopedia of information and to create artistic creations or musical compositions (Mason, Blanchard, and Daniel, 1983).

Books will *not* become obsolete and neither will teachers. Rather, computers provide another tool for teachers to use in teaching. Books and the computer terminals will simply be recognized as two sources of information for both students and teachers alike.

Specialized devices such as Speak-N-Spell, Speak-N-Read, the Talking Picture Book, and Alphamaster are in many classrooms. Such battery-powered reading devices may become more widely accepted than their predecessors, plug-in devices that were hampered by inadequate wiring in many of our school buildings. Videodisc systems are becoming available in schools in the 1990s, as predicted by Mason, Blanchard, and Daniel (1983). Television monitors and videodiscs, similar to movie projectors of the 1970s, are used by numerous teachers.

As a major approach to reading instruction, individualized instruction is observable in elementary classrooms in phonic lessons, skills practice, and some forms of computer assisted instruction. Individually prescribed instruction, akin to programmed learning, emanates from bottom-up models of the reading process.

Basal Reading Approaches

Basal reading programs, the dominant approach to classroom reading instruction, are examined at length in Chapter 11. Teachers who traditionally use the reading lesson or story with a small group of students during a specified time in a regular location are most likely to use the basal reading approach. They constitute the majority in terms of numbers of classroom teachers around the country using a particular approach.

Most of today's basal programs are advertised as literature-based. They now feature anthologies and journals, while providing a scope and sequence of skills and strategies to be taught at various levels and grades, along with control for some of the vocabulary words in the stories. Depending on your beliefs, basal instruction could be considered an example of the bottom-up (presenting skills to be taught in a sequence) or the top-down (featuring unedited children's literature selections and writing opportunities) approach. We asked three authors of major basal programs to comment on their instructional versatility in interviews which are featured in Chapter 11.

In addition to having scope and sequence charts and controlled vocabulary, basal reading series outline a standard lesson framework with slight variations in differing basal programs. The Directed Reading Activity (DRA) is the common label for the lesson framework in basal series. The DRA has four major instructional components: (1) motivation and background building; (2) guided reading; (3) skill development and practice; and (4) follow-up enrichment. These components are discussed in Chapter 11 and are important because they are based on interactive assumptions that students learn to read by reading, writing, and talking about meaningful topics. As a major approach to reading instruction, basal reading is easily observable in elementary classrooms in small reading groups. It spans a large segment of the skills-whole language continuum due to its relationship to both bottom-up and interactive theories of reading. Basal reading, frequently described as eclectic, runs the gamut from word attack skills practice to extended and meaningful reading, discussing, and writing.

Language Experience and Writing Process Approaches

Teachers often use language experience in combination with other approaches to reading instruction. Language experience is also, however, a major approach to teaching reading to children from kindergarten through second grade and on into the intermediate grades. This approach is examined in several chapters throughout this textbook.

There is more to the language experience approach (LEA) than just recording the ideas of first graders after they have taken a trip to the school nurse or the zoo. LEA includes planned and continuous activities such as individual- and group-dictated stories, the building of word banks of known words, creative writing activities, oral reading of prose and poetry by teacher and students, directed reading-thinking lessons, the investigation of interests using multiple materials, and record keeping of student progress.

Russell Stauffer (1970) and R. Van Allen (1976) have been strong proponents of LEA. Allen has summed up the theory behind the language experiences from the young reader's point of view: What I think about, I can talk about; what I can say, I can write or someone can write for me; what I can write, I can read; and I can read what other people write for me to read.

Teachers who subscribe to LEA have common viewpoints about children and their language. For example, they probably would agree that children's oral and written expression are based on their sensitivity to classroom and home environments. Further, they would support children working with their *own* language.

Thus the language experience approach is based on the idea that language should be used to communicate thoughts, ideas, meaning. It is very much an interactive approach to teaching reading. As such it is placed on the right side of the skills-whole language continuum. Teaching strategies that are part of LEA are interspersed throughout this book. How to use dictated stories and word banks, the directed reading thinking procedure with comprehension strategies, and ways to extend children's writing and reading into more writing and reading are all examples of related instruction.

In Chapter 5, we explore the connections between reading and writing. When teachers introduce a **writing process** program in their classes, they are teaching reading in a subtle-but-powerful manner.

Literature-Based Approaches

Literature-based reading programs are used by teachers who want to provide for individual student differences in reading abilities and at the same time focus on meaning, interest, and enjoyment. Veatch and Acinapuro (1966) designed a program for individualizing reading and articulated the how-tos of this approach. In this approach teachers encourage their students to personally select their own trade books (another name for popular books).

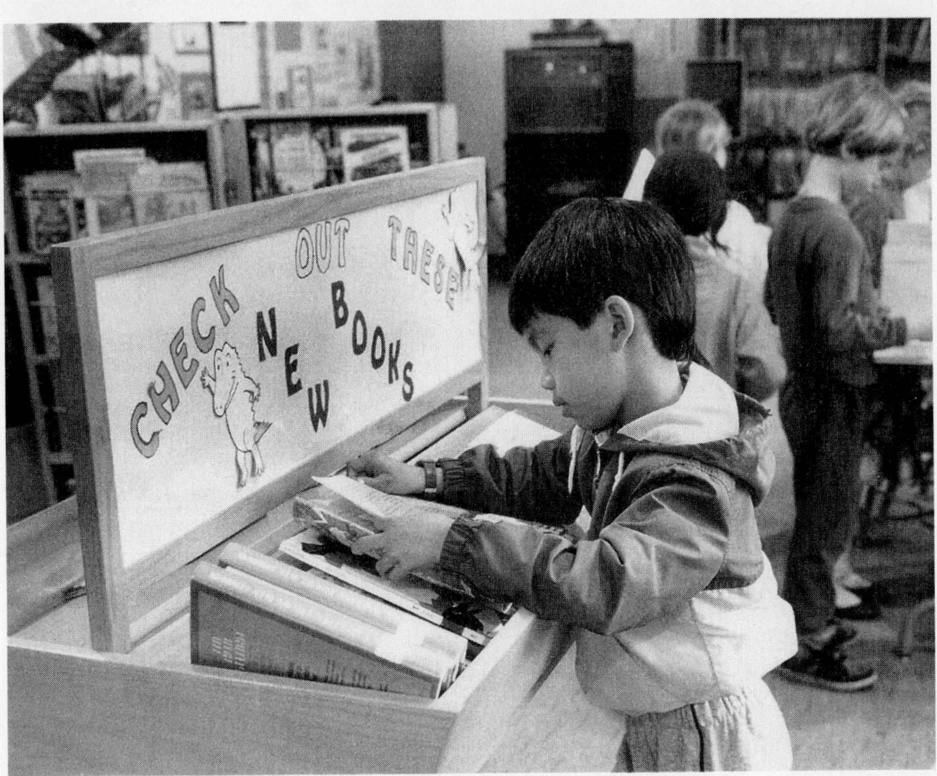

In literature-based reading programs, students are encouraged to personally select their own trade books to read.

The teacher has conferences once or twice a week with each student. During these conferences students might be asked to read aloud parts of the book they have read which they especially enjoyed. Teachers take notes on the type of miscues students make as they read. Also, students discuss with teachers words with which they had difficulty. The overall emphasis of the individualized program as described by Veatch and Acinapuro is on meaning and on having students apply and extend the ideas in their reading.

Some proponents of the individualized reading program contend that reading skills should *not* be taught; they argue that these skills will be learned as the child reads (Farr and Roser 1979, p. 146). The main thrust of the individualized approach, even as explained in the 1960s, is that importance is placed on reading for meaning and for enjoyment. Children in classes in which the individualized approach to reading is used read more and read a greater variety of materials than children in other classes. Further, they read more for their own enjoyment and interest.

In the late 1970s and early 1980s articles suggesting a literature base reappeared in reading instruction journals. The development of a literature base is the core of the personalized individual approach. Students are surrounded with books, and time is set aside for reading and talking about books. The teacher reads books to students and helps them to read some of those same books as well as other books. Students act out and make things they read about.

In classrooms using literature in this way children delight in the exploits of Curious George, Madeline, Encyclopedia Brown, and Pippi Longstocking. The rationale is that an important part of classroom life should be *reading:* reading literature that makes children wonder, weep, laugh, shiver, and gasp.

Pieces of literature are used as springboards for writing. Children can write differing endings for stories or incidents in their own lives that reflect conflicts similar to ones about which they have read. Students also look at story structures such as the repetitive structure in "The Three Little Pigs" and devise stories using the same kind of structure. Further, the conflicts between characters in literature can be used to help students gain insights into their own life situations. Students are encouraged to write about these also.

Self-selection of trade books or literature books is part of personalizing reading through the individualized approach. Teachers hold conferences with individual students about the books they are reading. Other forms of organization are also used. For example, a group of students read and respond to the same piece of literature. Or students read different books with similar themes and then share and compare insights gained. Reading instruction delivered in this way emanates from assumptions about the reading process that are interactive and top-down. Thus, the other side of the individualized-prescriptive approach is an individualized-personalized one which falls on the holistic side of our approach continuum. It depends on teachers who know children's literature and classroom organization. These topics are discussed in Chapters 10, 11, and 14.

How the Reading Curriculum Plays Out in Actual Practice

We have connected theory to practice in this chapter by moving from belief systems to images of the reading curriculum to approaches for instruction. The final step is to connect approaches to **instructional strategies** and the decisions that teachers make.

Strategies are the key to reading instruction; they are the hour-by-hour, day-to-day evidence of what is really happening in the classroom. Often, teachers don't have a voice in choosing the major approach to instruction in their school. For instance, a district as a whole or a particular school may have recently adopted a new basal series and committed the entire staff to staff development on how to manage these materials. In fact, it would be more unusual today to find a school in which each teacher has the option of independently deciding which approach to use. It's only when teachers put into play specific strategies—that is, tactics or plans or practices—that they are enacting the reading curriculum.

In the Class Works descriptions that follow, you will meet three teachers at different stages of their development. First, there's Kara, a student teacher grappling with the problem of planning and teaching reading over an extended period of time for the very first time. (See Box 2.1.) Even though she has an excellent model in her cooperating teacher,

Kara relies heavily on a teacher's manual from the basal reader to plan and guide reading instruction.

Katie, the second Class Works case, is a first-year teacher who finds herself struggling with reading as she tries to survive the day-to-day pressures of the first year. (See Box 2.2.) Even though she brings a whole language perspective to the teaching of reading, she feels the pressure to teach skills from administrative mandates, a highly structured curriculum, and a schoolwide testing program.

The third Class Works case is Gay's story. (See Box 2.3). You met Gay at the beginning of this chapter. She's a veteran teacher with more than 18 years of professional experience. Gay views herself as continually in transition as a teacher. Through her practice, which is rooted firmly in a theoretical perspective, she models for her students what it means to be literate, the kinds of decisions a reader and writer must make, and the personal satisfaction that comes from being a reader and writer. As a result, she makes literacy come alive in her third-grade classroom.

● **BOX 2.1**

Class Works

Kara, a Student Teacher

Kara, 21 years old, attends a public university in a midwestern city once known for its steel industry. Most of the mills have since closed, and, as a result, the entire region served by the university is economically depressed. Kara's father is a laborer; he works for a cement company. He doesn't have a high school diploma, but staunchly values the college education that Kara is receiving. She'll be the first in the family to earn a college degree.

Kara's preparation for teaching reading includes three reading courses. Since the university is on a trisemester, the courses are each ten weeks long. The first course relates learning theories to reading and introduces students to methods and materials used in teaching reading. The goal of the course is to provide a balanced perspective on how to teach children to read. Kara has spent a considerable period of time learning about phonics, the basal reader and how to use it, and whole language techniques. The second course is taught on a school site. Kara has prepared and taught lessons designed around the different skill areas to individual children. The third course is an overview of reading diagnostic techniques. In this course, Kara has learned "how to use different kinds of tests" to find out what difficulties a child has with reading. "We give a child different types of tests and then try to figure out what his problem is and how to best help him with the problem," she says.

Kara student-taught for a period of ten weeks in a K-6 suburban elementary school with an enrollment of 600 students. Her cooperating teacher, Mrs. Taylor,

(continued)

has taught in the school for 13 years, the past 7 at the second-grade level. She's competent and confident, "a masterful teacher," according to the school's principal. She teaches reading from a basal reader, but augments basic reading instruction with children's literature: "I'm required by the administration to use the basal, but young children also need to be exposed to lots of good reading." Even though Mrs. Taylor uses a basal reader, she says that she exercises a great deal of judgment and flexibility in making decisions about what to emphasize during reading instruction. She spends a goodly portion of instructional time on story discussion and on activities involving "writing and reading together." She explains the writing-reading connection this way: "It's important for children to write about what they read and to share what they write with each other."

Kara did not begin teaching reading on a regular basis until the fourth week of student teaching. It was the final subject for which she assumed responsibility. Why? She and the cooperating teacher believed that Kara would benefit from extensive observation of reading instruction. According to Kara, "Mrs. Taylor knows a lot about reading and I learn from her, especially how to get the kids interested in reading." Mrs. Taylor also confided that teaching reading is "one of the toughest and most important things an elementary teacher can do. I'm always reluctant to give it up when I have a student teacher."

For planning, Kara relies heavily on the teacher's manual of the basal reader used in the school. Here's what she said about using the teacher's manual to plan instruction: "The manual knows what it is doing or it wouldn't be published, and it goes through reading like I remember from when I learned to read."

Two weeks into the teaching of reading, Kara has significantly altered some of the activities that Mrs. Taylor emphasized during reading instruction: "The kids talk too much, especially during reading. I'm going to cut back on the discussion time. The kids just talk about themselves anyway. There really isn't too much to these stories and we don't need to discuss them so much. The book [the teacher's manual] doesn't suggest all the things we [a reference to Mrs. Taylor's instruction] have been doing."

Another week into planning and instruction, Kara comments, "Although I learned a lot from my cooperating teacher, especially how important it is for children to write, I'll probably include writing with reading when I have a class of my own." In her final two weeks of student teaching, Kara eliminated all time for writing during the reading class.

Instead, Kara emphasized skills. She reflects on her decision to teach skills: "I use more drill work than Mrs. Taylor. The worksheets help. The kids hate them, but that's how they learn the skills."

(continued)

● BOX 2.1 *(continued)*

Toward the end of student teaching, a typical lesson taught by Kara looks like this: A story from the basal reader usually takes three days to teach. On the first day, Kara introduces the story by presenting vocabulary words. She writes the words on the board and then asks various children to read each word aloud. When children can not pronounce words successfully, Kara asks them to sound out the words using "phonics clues." After all the words are pronounced correctly, she then asks children to tell what each word means. When the vocabulary list is completed, the class reads the story silently and then completes a comprehension worksheet. Each child works individually to complete the comprehension sheet.

On the second day, the class reads the story orally, taking turns, and then discusses what they read through question and answer exchanges. These exchanges prompt the students to retell different parts of the story. The third day is usually spent on skills development. Kara assigns the students skills-related worksheets to complete. These sheets are from the "practice book" that accompanies the basal reader or from other commercially published materials that deal with reading skills introduced and taught in conjunction with the story.

Kara summarizes her student teaching experience this way: "I believed that the kids already liked to read, so I didn't need to motivate them. Sometimes, they didn't know words so we worked on words. I would add a list of sight words to every story if it were my class. A teacher should help kids that have trouble reading. They need more drill. I remember lots of drill when I was in school. I hated it, but it worked."

REFLECTIVE INQUIRY

- Do you (or are you planning to) teach reading the way you were taught to read? What would you keep the same? What would you change?
- How are your beliefs, understandings, and values about teaching reading similar to or different from Kara's?
- How does Kara differ from Mrs. Taylor as a teacher of reading?
- Mrs. Taylor seemed to have had limited influence on Kara's teaching of reading. If you were Mrs. Taylor, how would you have handled the differences between the way you plan and teach reading and the way Kara does?
- Speculate on Kara's future as a teacher of reading. Will her beliefs and values change with more experience? Are they likely to cause her difficulties? What will she need to do to continue to grow as a teacher of reading?

● **BOX 2.2**

Class Works

Katie, a First-Year Teacher

Katie began her first teaching position at the age of 23—a first-grade assignment in an urban, racially mixed elementary school. The challenge of teaching beginners was buoyed by the elation of her first job: "I know it's not going to be easy, but I can't wait to get started!"

Katie attended a private college located in a suburb of the city. The college offered a small teacher education program. Katie's reading and reading-related courses included elementary reading, children's literature, and language arts. The reading and language arts courses were taught by the same instructor. Katie participated in numerous hours of field experience throughout the junior and senior years of the program. She especially enjoyed her reading courses because the instructor "challenged us to think about reading as language, not just skills to be taught in itsy-bitsy pieces." During many of her visits "in the field," the instruction that Katie observed wasn't congruent with what she was learning in her reading classes. The incongruity was the subject of much inquiry and debate: Should future teachers maintain the status quo or should they be innovators who bring new ideas into the teaching profession, especially about the teaching of literacy?

Katie's school is situated in the inner city. About 70 percent of the children are from minority backgrounds. The principal is considered a "strong instructional leader." She believes that an "effective school must maintain high expectations for student achievement, an orderly climate, and a rigorous assessment program to monitor children's educational progress." As a result, the principal is a proponent of a "teach-test-teach" model for instruction. She indicates to Katie that it is okay to try out new teaching strategies, "as long as you are teaching the skills the children need." How well children scored on achievement tests is one of the main indicators of how successful a teacher is in her building.

Katie feels the pressure of "having to teach skills in isolation." This approach, she admits, is not "what I believe in," but she feels obligated to follow the curriculum "like all of the other teachers."

Prior to the opening of school Katie had spent two weeks planning what she was going to do. One of her first tasks was to fix up the room so that it would "invite kids to learn." The room has a reading corner and a "writer's nook." Both areas are stocked with children's books, paper, pencils, markers, scissors, and posters. The reading corner has a throw rug, a book rack, and an old couch that Katie borrowed from her parents. The writer's nook has a round table and an electric typewriter.

(continued)

BOX 2.2 *(continued)*

On the first day, Katie plans to have "print cover the room" so that the children will get used to written language in their environment. The children have blank name tags ready so that they can write their first name on it "any way they want to." Katie also plans to create "experience stories" with different groups of children to get them off to a good start with reading, and to read "at least two good books every day."

The reality of teaching reading skills is omnipresent, despite Katie's attempts to provide meaningful experiences for her first graders. Periodically, she is required to test children to determine mastery of the skills in the basal program. The principal also requires weekly lesson plans to be in her office in advance on Friday afternoons. Katie's plans are returned on Monday morning, before the start of school, with comments and notations.

In practice, Katie tries valiantly to teach a dual reading curriculum. She teaches the skills using the basal reading program and supplementary workbooks in the morning, and she "smuggles in the good stuff" whenever she can find the time. Needless to say, Katie goes home each day exhausted and frustrated. She complains that she spends more time giving tests than she spends on instruction. "But that's what's expected of me," she adds. The reading corner and the writer's nook often are underused. "At least," she says, "I still read the class a story every day."

REFLECTIVE INQUIRY

- If you have yet to teach, are your beliefs, understandings, and personal values likely to result in the frustration that Katie experienced during her first year of teaching reading? If you currently teach, do you experience conflicts between what you believe you should be teaching and what you actually teach?
- Was Katie's school situation unusual or typical, especially in terms of administrative and curricular influences on the teaching of reading? Explain.
- If you were in Katie's situation, what would you have done differently?
- How appropriate was it for Katie to try to teach a dual reading curriculum? What would you have done?
- If you were to visit Katie's classroom three years later, predict the kinds of changes you might see in the way she teaches reading.

● **BOX 2.3**

Class Works

Gay, a Veteran Teacher

Gay has been teaching for 18 years. For many of those years, she taught first graders, but recently switched to the third grade "for the change and the challenge of working with children at a different stage in their development."

Gay is highly respected as a teacher by all who come in contact with her work: children, parents, principals, professors, student teachers, and colleagues. In the past several years, she has been recognized for her excellence in teaching with several awards, including "Teacher of the Year" in her own school district.

Gay is active professionally. She belongs to several local, state, and national professional organizations, where she has participated in leadership roles. In addition, she has continued to pursue her study of teaching.

Gay approaches reading from a whole language perspective. But as she says, her philosophy of reading and teaching reading is rather simple, "so simple, in fact, that by the end of September most of my students can articulate it."

Gay believes that reading is a thinking process. Her role in the process is to "model strategies that will allow my students to read and write on their own." She attempts to make students consciously aware of strategies and to know when and why they use them. Discussions, therefore, are frequent in Gay's class. Often they're initiated by the students themselves: "Do you know what I did when I was reading. . . ?" or "I know Matthew's a good reader because he. . . " As part of Gay's belief system, she views learning to read as an integration of language processes: talking, listening, writing, and reading.

Gay is required by Board of Education policy to use a basal reading program in her class. Within the spirit of the Board's mandate, she integrates language activities through flexible planning and use of a two-hour block of time for reading and language arts instruction. She divides the time by focusing on three components: (1) group reading lessons using basal stories; (2) a period of sustained silent reading in which the students self-select books, read at their own pace, and then follow up by book sharing; and (3) writing process instruction.

Gay plans whole class, individual, and group instruction for children, but she does not make grouping decisions based on ability. As she explains, "I group children by need, not ability." She elaborates by suggesting:

"It's difficult to explain exactly how I plan because it is all done very informally, as I observe children. Rather than choose a group of children all with the same

(continued)

BOX 2.3 *(continued)*

observed problem, I try to group one or two students who are having trouble in a specific area with several stronger ones. The point is never made—'Bill, you need to work on making inferences today with this group.' I just say, 'Bill, for a few days I'd like for you to come with this group.' At the beginning of the year a child will sometimes ask why, and I simply say, 'We all work together at some point in the year. You'll be in lots of groups.' The children get used to it really fast and it becomes a natural part of reading groups."

If a visitor observed a typical morning of instruction, here is what might be happening in Gay's class: Children arrive on staggered bus schedules during the half hour before school starts. They are permitted to socialize (speaking and listening) with peers and the teacher, write in journals or other writings of choice, read books of choice, or work on late or overdue assignments. At 9 A.M., morning announcements are made. A student then takes attendance while another passes out assignment sheets. At 9:05 A.M., the first small group meets for 30–40 minutes. Two other small groups meet following this period. While Gay is teaching the small groups, the children at their desks complete activities that usually include a math assignment and a reading selection (sometimes self-selected, sometimes assigned) to which they respond in "literature response logs." When they are finished, they may work in small groups at the computer, listening center, story center, or reading center or choose from teacher-made learning games.

There is a lot of movement and quiet conversation. Gay's classroom is not a still, quiet classroom, but the students demonstrate a high degree of on-task behavior. She firmly believes in the importance of shaping ideas through talk, so students are not discouraged from conversing. She also believes in a cooperative learning climate, so they are encouraged to go to one another for assistance before coming to her.

Recently, Gay received district permission to use a literature-based reading program as an alternative to the basal program. Instruction is built upon the following principles: (1) self-selection; (2) multilevel grouping; (3) critical thinking; (4) cooperative learning; and (5) quality children's literature with natural text. Students read their selections and then meet in small groups to discuss and complete related activities. Gay serves as facilitator, moving from group to group and assisting as necessary. She notes, "I have been impressed with the independence and self-directedness the children have as learners when provided the opportunity."

REFLECTIVE INQUIRY

- How are your beliefs, understandings, and personal values related to reading and teaching reading the same as or different from Gay's?

(continued)

- If you were in Gay's situation, what would you find difficult to implement as you plan and teach reading?
- How easy or difficult would it be for you to "model" reading strategies? What does modeling require of a teacher?

SUMMARY

An underlying assumption in this book is that when teachers are in touch with their beliefs about reading and learning to read, they are in a better position to enact curricula in the classroom. When you analyze your beliefs, connecting what you practice with what you know and believe, you are better able to understand what you do and why. The reading autobiography suggested in Chapter 1 lends itself to a narrative inquiry that helps teachers discover some of the events and experiences that contribute to the development of beliefs and attitudes related to reading and learning to read. In this chapter, the Beliefs About Reading Interview and the TORP survey were suggested as tools that also permit teachers to inquire into their beliefs.

We explored two predominant images of the reading curriculum, one based on a skills perspective and the other based on a whole language perspective. Is reading a skill or a set of separate skills? What principles underlie a whole language curriculum? These questions allowed us to make distinctions between two very different curricular views associated with the teaching of reading. We showed how different instructional approaches to reading lie on a continuum between skills-based and whole language perspectives. These approaches include prescriptive reading programs, basal reading programs, language experience/writing process programs, and literature-based programs.

Teachers enact curriculum in varied and complex ways based on their images of the reading curriculum and the particular contexts in which they teach. We introduced several cases in the Class Works activities to illustrate how the reading curriculum plays out in varying classroom contexts.

TEACHER-ACTION RESEARCHER

1. If you haven't already done so, go back into Chapter 2 and answer the reflective inquiry questions for each of the Class Works cases that were presented. If at all possible, do this with a colleague so that you may compare your reflections on the student teaching experience or your projections about student teaching. If you are yourself a veteran teacher, what experiences have most contributed to your growth and change as a professional over the years?

2. Is there someone you now work with or a teacher who stands out in the school in which you are either interning or working, whom you believe would be interesting to profile? Organize your description of this teacher with the following: (a) background information including some personal history, (b) beliefs about reading, (c) the school context, and (d) how he or she plans and teaches reading.

3. Interview and observe a teacher who uses a whole language curriculum or is in the process of making a transition from a skills-based curriculum to a whole language curriculum. How does the teacher encourage children who don't want to read? Describe how the teacher keeps track of what each child is reading and how he or she is progressing in reading. How does the teacher encourage children to respond to what they read?

4. Interview and observe a skills-based teacher. How does the teacher differ in practice from the teacher described in Question 3?

5. Interview an elementary school teacher, using the Beliefs About Reading Interview (Appendix A). Analyze the teacher's implicit theories of reading as suggested in this chapter. If there is time, ask a colleague to interview another colleague and form a small group to compare the various responses.

KEY TERMS

beliefs about reading
units of language
Theoretical Orientation to Reading Profile (TORP)
skills view
whole language view
approaches to reading
basal reading
language experience
prescriptive
writing process
literature-based
instructional strategies

CHAPTER

3

Literacy Learning in Early Childhood

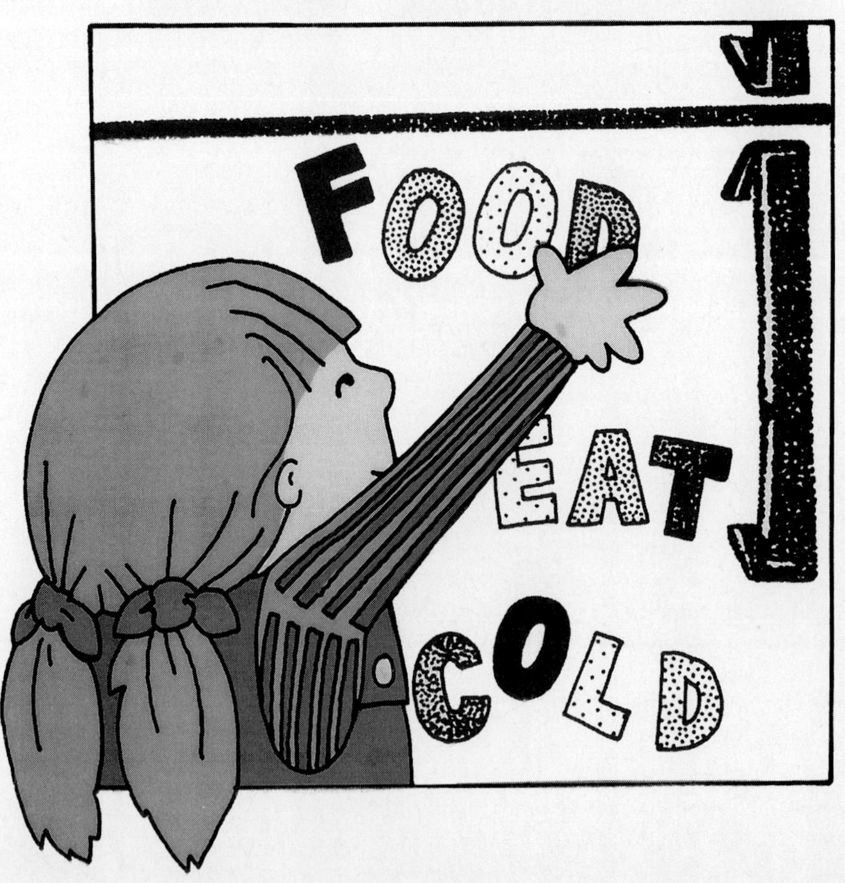

BETWEEN THE LINES

In this chapter you will discover:

- **What family literacy means.**
- **How young children learn to use written language.**
- **Why intergenerational literacy programs can break the cycle of illiteracy.**
- **Why developmentally appropriate practice supports literacy learning.**
- **How to create literate environments in kindergarten and first grade.**
- **How to plan and use literacy strategies, play centers, and language experiences.**

Beginnings are important. Literacy beginnings, as crucial as they are to children's development as readers and writers, often take diverse paths. For example, when Leslie Ann was born, her grandmother, a reading specialist by trade, gave her granddaughter the book *Goodnight Moon.* And she gave Leslie Anne's dad (her son) some motherly, if not professional, advice, telling him that it was time to begin reading aloud to his daughter. According to the grandmother, Margaret Moorehead (1990), her son "looked at me like I was crazy. 'Mom, Leslie Anne is only 2 days old. This is silly. She wouldn't understand' " (p. 332). Moorehead countered her son's incredulity, saying that Leslie Ann already was being talked to, even though she didn't understand everything that was being said. Then why not read to her?

On that auspicious occasion Leslie Anne began her journey to literacy. Her parents developed the habit of reading to her daily. At 6 months, Leslie Anne was sitting on her grandmother's lap, helping to hold a book, when she began "reading" in a voice distinctively different from her usual cooing and babbling. According to Moorehead (1990), Leslie Anne read aloud, "'A baa baa, a baa baa,' and turned the page. Six months old, and already she knew that you hold a book up, that there are just a few sounds on each page, that those sounds are different from ordinary talking, and that you turn a page and say something else" (p. 332). The love of books, quite naturally, blossomed for Leslie Anne in a family environment that supported and nurtured literacy learning. Going to the library and listening to stories became as routine a family activity as grocery shopping.

Leslie Ann, as you probably have surmised, is in the process of becoming literate in a family context that values reading and communicates strong feelings and attitudes about literacy to her. The family's own interest in reading, manifested by a willingness to spend time talking and reading with Leslie Anne, provides the supportive, natural learning environment that she needs in order to grow as a reader.

Irma, by way of contrast, is a third-generation housing project child who lives in East Los Angeles with her mother and four younger siblings. Her mother can't read. Neither she nor her brothers and sisters have ever heard a nursery rhyme or story. According to LaVergne Rosow (1992), Irma is trapped in a cycle of illiteracy that is passed from one generation to another: "Irma had never had a chance even to hold books before entering school" (p. 525).

Now during the first week of the first grade, Irma checked out two library books. But what was she expected to do with the books? Where were the models of literate activity in her life? For one reason or another the books disappeared once she brought them home. The school sent a note to the home, pinned to Irma's shirt, requesting the return of the books, lest Irma's family pay a fine and she lose her library privileges: "But the note to the nonreading mom, who herself had never had library privileges, failed to recover the books or collect the fines, so Irma spent her first year in school without books. She had no one to read to her, and she had no hope of reading to herself" (Rosow, 1992, p. 525). As bleak as the prospects for Irma's **literacy development** may seem, Rosow reminds us that Irma's story could be different. To realize the promise of literacy in Irma's life, appropriate school experiences could very well bring the intergenerational cycle of illiteracy to an end.

The stories of Irma and Leslie Anne—two young children from culturally diverse family backgrounds—underscore the importance of understanding the needs of all children and the conditions underlying their literate development. If we are going to make a difference in children's literacy development, we must be aware of the learning environment of the home, respect the diverse cultural milieus from which children learn to use language, and develop strategies to build on family strengths. Irma and Leslie Anne will not bring the same kinds of knowledge, values, attitudes, and strategies for literacy learning to school. Yet their school experiences will play a pivotal role in realizing their full potential as literacy learners.

This chapter is about literacy beginnings. It is forged on the dynamic and powerful interplay between a child's oral language and written language development. Keep in mind several main ideas about literacy learning as you prepare to study this chapter. First, many children come to school with some, if not considerable, knowledge of and experiences with written language. Second, preschool and school-aged children develop literacy knowledge as they interact with others. Third, literacy learning occurs as young children participate in purposeful and meaningful activities. And, fourth, speaking, writing, and reading are interrelated, mutually supporting activities. Oral language competence is the common denominator in learning to read and write.

In this chapter we tackle important issues related to the early literacy learning of children before they enter school, and the implications of such learning for beginning instruction. What do teachers of young children need to know about young children's knowledge of and experiences with literacy? How can teachers make the child's first encounter with formal reading and writing instruction smooth and developmentally sound?

Family Literacy: How Young Children Learn to Use Written Language

The roots of reading and writing begin at home. Families serve to support and nurture children's literacy development. The term **family literacy** is a relatively new concept that describes how family interactions influence the language development of young children and provide the context in which they learn to read and write (Taylor, 1983).

How Reading Develops

Most children enter school with expectations that they're "gonna learn how to read." It doesn't matter to Michael, a-year-old, that he already can read many signs—for example, "Stop" and "Zoo"—which have a great deal of meaning to him. It also doesn't matter that Michael "knows" most of the alphabet by name and often "reads along" by reciting favorite passages from bedtime stories that his mother and father read to him. Nor does it matter that Michael's mother still chuckles over his behavior at around age 2 when he first recognized a McDonald's billboard from the backseat of the family car. Michael "oohed" and "aahed" and chanted, "Stop! Stop! Hungry, Mommie."

Michael doesn't grasp the significance of these events because he is on the threshold of starting school. Nor does his mother recognize the importance of these abilities. Despite Michael's observable reading and reading-like behaviors at home, there remains a trace of uncertainty on his mother's part. Although the groundwork has been laid for Michael to continue to grow as a reader, his mother expresses some concern as to whether he will achieve success in learning to read. She is sure that he will but adds, "We'll wait and see."

Does Michael's mother need to assume a "wait and see" attitude? A child such as hers grows up immersed in a print-oriented world. Children see written language all around them—in books, supermarkets, department stores, fast-food restaurants, and on television, signs, and a variety of printed materials from *TV Guide* to labels on household products. Print is everywhere. When aren't children confronted with written language in some form in their immediate environment? The child may also see parents, brothers, sisters, and others using written language to some degree—whether to read recipes, follow directions, do homework, solve problems, acquire information, or enjoy a story. The plethora of print that confronts young children on a daily basis plays a subtle but important role in their desire to understand written language and use it for personal and social means.

Today's preschooler acquires much more intuitive and conscious knowledge about print and its uses than most adults would imagine. As early as 1958, James Hymes observed that reading "sells itself" to the young child because written language is in the "limelight" constantly. Everyday living "beats the drums" for reading with a bombardment of print that no formal program of instruction could ever match.

Although this may be the case, informal "teachable moments" await children in a print-rich world. Parents (and teachers) should make a *conscious* effort, whenever appropriate, to create awareness of print in meaningful and functional ways. By way of illustration, four-year-old Sandy's parents seize whatever opportunity is available to demonstrate the purposeful nature of print. Whenever they go to a restaurant, for example, they encourage Sandy to "read" the menu and to select the foods she prefers. Although Sandy may not be able to read most of the words on the menu, she "pretend reads." Her parents support her use of print by showing her the menu, by engaging in dialogue with her over possible food choices, and by pointing to the printed words as they read the menu with her.

This example, simple and straightforward as it may appear, illustrates the subtle but powerful role that parents play in literacy learning. *The parent's role (and the teacher's) is to lead, model, and facilitate literacy learning by being supportive, by socializing children in the uses of written language, by engaging them in conversation about written language, and by encouraging and accepting children's constructions of meaning through written language.*

Michael and Sandy already know a lot about written language, and have had some valuable early literacy experiences. They are learning to read informally through family interactions. More than likely, they will continue their growth as literacy learners and should experience success in school. As teachers, we have much to gain from the study of family literacy. Box 3.1 illustrates this point. Read it and reflect on the family interactions that occur between a mother and her children as they are grocery shopping.

Some children learn to read naturally. They develop the ability to read through a process that can best be described as trial-and-error learning. These early readers make discoveries about written language in a *low-risk* family environment that is relatively free from anxiety and criticism.

In school, however, the stakes are usually high and the risks involved in learning to read are greater than at home. The margin for error isn't what it was at home, especially if the emphasis in school is on learning through memorization, analysis, and recitation. As a result, children are often introduced to reading instruction with emphasis on the smallest possible print units, for example, letters. For those children who have little background experience with print, confusion mounts quickly in what often becomes a high-risk learning situation. In such contexts, little, if any, time is spent on functional, meaningful literacy activity. Children are denied the opportunities to experience and learn from their participation in the uses of written language.

The amount of written language confronting a child can come as a surprise to an adult who normally pays only passing attention to it. But adult readers have

● **BOX 3.1**

Class Works

Kid Watching at the Supermarket

One of our students, Meg, plans on teaching in the primary grades. As part of a field experience, she decided to "shadow" unobtrusively a mother and her two children as they shopped in a local supermarket. Here are Meg's observations as recorded in her field notes.

> The mother pushed the shopping cart with the younger of the two children sitting in the child seat. I learned that the two children were named Brian and Kate when overhearing the mother talking in line. Brian was around 14 months old and Kate about 3 or 4 years old. Kate sat on the bottom shelf of the cart. When the mother stopped in the produce area, she said to the children, "Look at the bananas. Don't they look good?" Brian looked at the bananas and said, "Bananas." The mother continued in an easy, slow voice to comment on the color of the bananas and what she planned to use them for. At this time, I decided to observe Kate more closely.
>
> As her mother went up the dairy aisle, Kate walked between the cart and her mother. As Kate walked around the store, she asked questions like "What's this?" pointing to specific items on the shelves. Her mother would always answer and explain about the item if more questions were asked. At one point, a can was thrown out of the cart by Brian while the mother was looking over the cereals. She walked over to the cart, picked up the thrown can, and asked Kate what had happened. Kate pointed to Brian saying, "He throwed it." The mother then asked Kate to find the cereal that she was looking for. (I couldn't hear what kind.) Kate roamed the aisle looking for the cereal and eventually found it. Throughout shopping, Kate was quite active and inquisitive. She would look at items in the store and always wanted to know more about them. For some products she would finger the letters on the box or can and ask, "What does this say, Mommy?"

REFLECTIVE INQUIRY

- What does this case tell you about the uses of language?
- In what ways does the older child demonstrate knowledge of written language?
- How does the mother's interaction with the children support and encourage language learning?

> learned to ignore this plethora of print, while to an inquiring, learning child it must be a stimulating situation. (Smith, 1976. p. 298)

Perhaps this is why most adults form the expectation that learning to read is a function of formal instruction in school. Does a similar expectation exist for a child's growth and development in spoken language? Of course not. Most parents play an important role in the oral language development of their children. Yet few, until recently, had begun to believe that learning to read begins through interaction with parents and other significant members of a family. The foundations of literacy are built on children's social and linguistic interaction with their world and the persons in it. Home is where literacy learning begins.

Studies of early readers indicate that learning to read is strongly associated with positive home environments (Teale, 1978). Early readers have access to a variety of easy reading materials in the home. Not only do young readers have easy availability to books at home, but they can also use the local library. Moreover, early readers are attracted to reading *anything* that interests them in their immediate everyday print environment, from labels on cans and cereal boxes to television supplements in local newspapers to cookbooks, telephone directories, and bus timetables.

While books, billboards, and cereal box labels are all potential sources for reading in a young child's home environment, children must learn how print functions in their lives. In this respect, reading aloud to children is one of the most important contributing factors in the learning environment of early readers. Early readers' homes are frequently characterized by one or more parents and older siblings who read regularly.

As a result, children learn about reading by observing the significant people in their lives modeling reading behaviors naturally—for real purposes—in a variety of ways. They might see, for example, a parent reading a recipe while cooking or baking, studying a map on the family's vacation, singing from a hymnal at church, or reading the assembly instructions for a new bike. Some children will rivet their attention on the television screen as words flash before them during a commercial. Others quickly become aware that newspapers and magazines impart information about events occurring locally and in the world. Others realize that books may be read to learn and to entertain. Indeed, reading is part of their environment. Children need to become aware of the many purposes for reading, and become involved in different kinds of reading activity frequently.

The quality of interaction that the child has with family members—whether they are parents, older siblings, grandparents, aunts, or uncles—plays heavily in reading development. Often, however, assistance in learning to read is not consciously given. Instead, significant others, such as parents, read to children repeatedly (by reading certain stories over and over) and *answer questions that children ask about reading.* What better way to help the child make the connection that print is meaningful than to respond to the question, "What does this say?" as the child points to a printed page.

As you might surmise, a **literate environment** for young children is one that fosters interest in and curiosity about written language and supports children's efforts to become readers and writers. Learning, not instruction, is the dominant force in a child's literacy development. Early readers thrive in environments where parents and other significant persons hold a high regard for reading. Reading to children is a highly valued and recur-

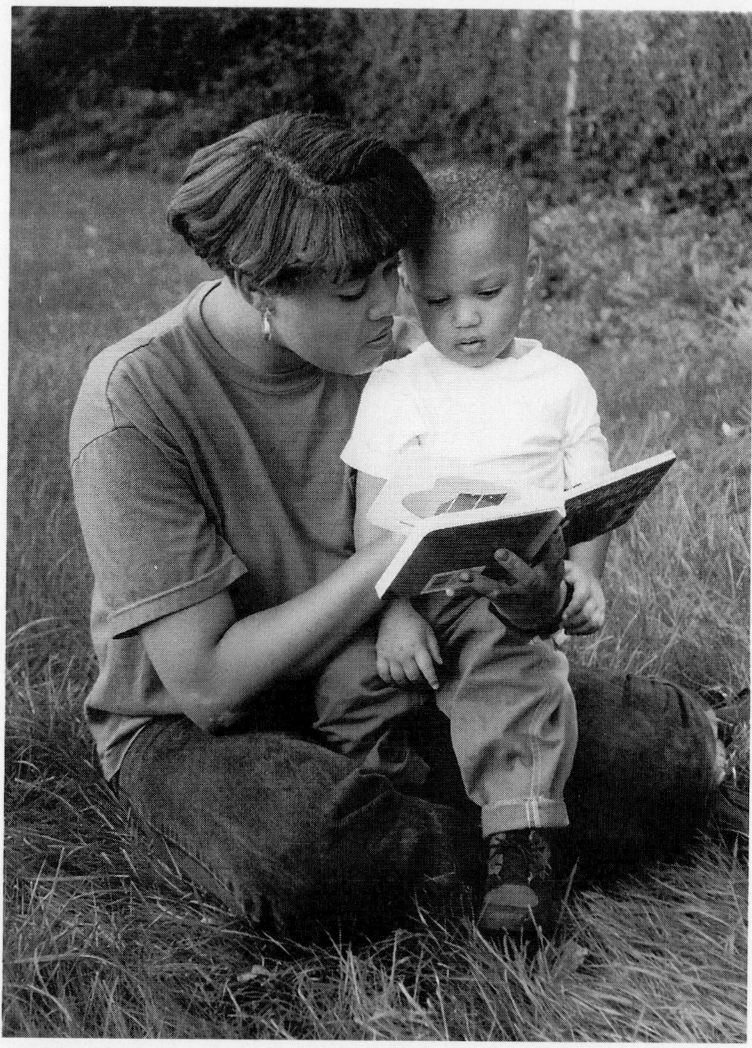

Reading aloud to children is one of the most important contributing factors in the learning environment of early readers.

ring event. The environment is punctuated by a genuine willingness to respond to children's questions about print. Within a literate environment, there is also a preoccupation with scribbling, drawing, and writing—so much so that Durkin (1966) characterizes children who learn to read naturally as "paper-and-pencil kids."

Early readers spend significant amounts of time expressing themselves through scribble writing, drawing, copying words, and inventing spellings for words. Writing is an important, often underestimated, factor in learning to read. Materials that encourage and facilitate writing should be readily accessible to young children. Crayons, markers, pencils, pens, paper, postcards, stationery, and chalkboards invite self-expression and should be kept in reach of children. Parent-child activities, such as the ones listed below, extend children's interest in and knowledge about written language by providing opportunities to observe, as well as participate in, meaningful, functional writing activities.

- Parents should encourage their children to help write the family shopping list.
- Parents and children may communicate with one another through written messages, such as writing notes. A bulletin board or a chalkboard provides a designated location for writing and receiving notes.
- Parents should create occasions to write, such as writing a Christmas list or a letter to Santa. In the same vein, they should encourage children to correspond with a responsive pen pal, perhaps a "best friend" or a relative living in another area who's about the same age. Writing invitations for a birthday party or a sleep over, or writing the instructions to give to the person who will temporarily care for a pet, provide meaningful writing occasions.

How Writing Develops

Some young children are prolific with pencil and paper. Others are just as handy with crayon, ink marker, or paintbrush. Sometimes a convenient wall or refrigerator door substitutes nicely for paper. The common denominator for "paper-and-pencil kids" is a strong desire and a need for self-expression and communication.

The noted Russian psychologist Lev Vygotsky (1962) suggests that an infant's gestures are the first visible signs of writing: "Gestures are writing in air, and written signs frequently are simply gestures that have been fixed." As Calkins (1986) explains: "The urge to write begins when a baby, lying in her crib, moves her arms and we draw close to the crib, our faces lighting into smiles. 'She's waving at us,' we say. Because we attach meaning to what could be called meaningless gestures, the gestures assume meaning. Babies learn the power of their gestures by our response to them" (p. 35). As infants learn about the power of signs and symbols, there is, in Vygotsky's words, "a fundamental assist to cognitive growth."

Klein (1985) distinguishes between the terms *writing* and *written expression.* Written expression comes earlier than writing. Scribbles and drawings are examples of written expressions *if* they have symbolic meaning to the child. The difference, then, is in the child's ability to produce units of written language; that is, letters, words, and sentences. For Klein, a working definition of writing should include written expression: writing is the "*ability to employ pen or pencil and paper to express ideas symbolically so that the representations on the paper reflect meaning and content capable of being communicated to another by the producer*" (pp. 3–4). How youngsters move from various representations of written expression to units of written language is a natural and an important evolution.

Young children learn writing through exploration. As Clay (1988) observes, most 5-year-olds "have definite ideas about the forms and uses of writing gained from their preschool experience—exploring with a pencil, pretending to write, inventing messages, copying an important word like one's name, and writing labels, messages, or special words in favorite story books" (p. 20). The key to early writing development is not found in a child's motor development or intelligence, but in the *opportunities* he or she has to explore print. According to Clay, new discoveries about writing emerge at every encounter a child has with paper and pencil: young children write "all over the paper in peculiar ways, turning letters around and upside down and letting the print drift over into drawing and coloring from time to time. We should be relaxed about this exploration of spaces and how print can be fitted into them" (p. 20). What can be learned from observing how young writers progress in their development?

Progressing from Scribbling to Writing

Scribbling is one of the primary forms of written expression. In many respects, scribbling is the fountainhead for writing and occurs from the moment a child grasps and manipulates a writing tool. Children take their scribbles seriously, if Linda Lamme's (1984) quotation from a scribbler is any indication: "Dat's not a scrwibble. It says, 'What's for dinner, Mom?'" Lamme has described the progression of scribbling in children's writing development in her excellent handbook for parents.

Early Scribbling. Early or uncontrolled scribbling is characterized by children making random marks on paper. Evidence of early scribbling can be gathered for most youngsters before their first birthday. Very young children who scribble soon learn that whatever it is that is in their hands, it can make marks. Early scribblings, according to Lamme, compare with babbling in oral language development. In Figure 3.1, Taylor, at 21 months, is constantly preoccupied with her scribbles and often talks spontaneously as she expresses herself with paper and pencil. She tells her mother as she scribbles that she likes to make lots of "tapes" and points to a "face" in the upper-right-hand corner of the scribble in Figure 3.1.

Since early scribbles are not usually representational (i.e., they do not convey meaning), parents and teachers should suppress the urge to ask a child, "What is this?" Instead, encourage a child to make markings on paper without pressure to finish a piece of work or tell what it's about, unless they are eager to talk about it.

Controlled Scribbling. Movement away from early scrawls becomes evident in children's scribbles as they begin to make systematic, repeated marks such as circles, vertical lines, dots, and squares.

Controlled scribbling occurs in children's written work between the ages of 3 to 6. The marks are often characterized as *scribble writing* in the sense that the scribbles are linear in form and shape and bear a strong resemblance to the handwriting of the child's culture. Notice for example, Dawn, Najeeba, and Dalia's scribble writing in Figure 3.2.

In Figure 3.2, Harste, Woodward, and Burke (1984) demonstrate how much knowledge children between the ages of 3 and 6 actually have about the purpose and form of written language. For example, when asked "to write everything you can write," three 4-year-olds from different countries produced, organized, and identified print that reflected

● **FIGURE 3.1** Taylor's scribbling.
She points to a "face" in the upper-right-hand corner.

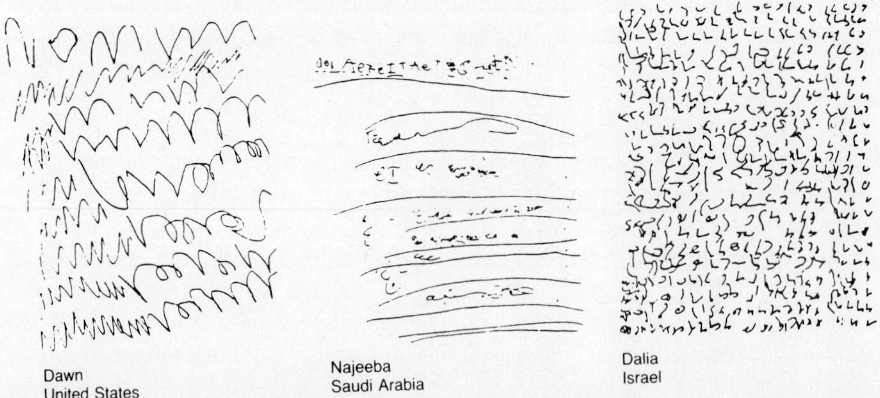

● **FIGURE 3.2** Dawn, Najeeba, and Dalia's writing samples show they have more knowledge about print than adults would expect.

their native languages (English, Arabic, and Hebrew). The writing samples of Dawn, Najeeba, and Dalia show that these young children have more knowledge about print than some adults might have anticipated.

According to Harste and his collaborators, Dawn's controlled scribbles look undeniably English. When Najeeba finished her writing she said, "Here, but you can't read it because it is in Arabic." Najeeba went on to point out that in Arabic one uses "a lot more dots" than in English. Dalia is an Israeli child whose whole writing bears the predictable look of Hebrew. Kindergarten and first-grade children build on their knowledge of written language by participating in planned and spontaneous writing activity. In doing so they acquire knowledge about reading *by* writing.

In the remainder of this chapter and in Chapters 4 and 5 we show how beginners can explore the natural relationship between writing and reading through language experiences and independent writing.

Scribble writing stands in contrast to *scribble drawing,* which is more pictographic in expression. Children use drawing as a means of written expression. According to Klein (1985), "*Drawing is possibly the most important single activity that assists both writing development and handwriting. It is critical to the child's evolving sense of symbol, and it directly assists muscle and eye-hand coordination development*" (p. 40). Children between the ages of 4 to 6 use drawings or pictographs as a form of written expression in their work.

Name Scribbling. Name scribbling is an extension of scribble writing. Scribbles become representational to the child-writer: The scribbles mean something. At this point, parents or teachers should begin to model writing and write with children. This is where the language experience activities described in the previous chapter play an important role in the writer's development. Make cards, lists, or signs with child-writers; label things. Have children dictate stories as you write them as well as encourage independent writing.

When children differentiate between drawing and scribbling as means of written expression, they begin to make great strides in their knowledge of print. Name scribbling underscores this differentiation and results in the formation of valuable concepts about written language; namely, that markings or symbols represent units of language such as letters and words, which in turn represent things and objects that can be communicated by messages.

Four-year-old Matthew engaged in name scribbling in Figure 3.3. His writing represents a thank-you note. What do you notice in Matthew's writing?

When Matthew's mother asked him to read the thank-you message aloud, he approximated a speech-to-print match. That is, he matched *his spoken words to the letters and marks on each line of print.* Here's what he read line by line.

> *This is Matthew Padak*
> *speaking, Rich Vacca*
> *and Jo Anne Vacca. Thank you*
> *for coming to our house.*

What does Matthew's written expression tell us about his development? Matthew is acutely aware of the message-sending function of writing. He has developed a "message

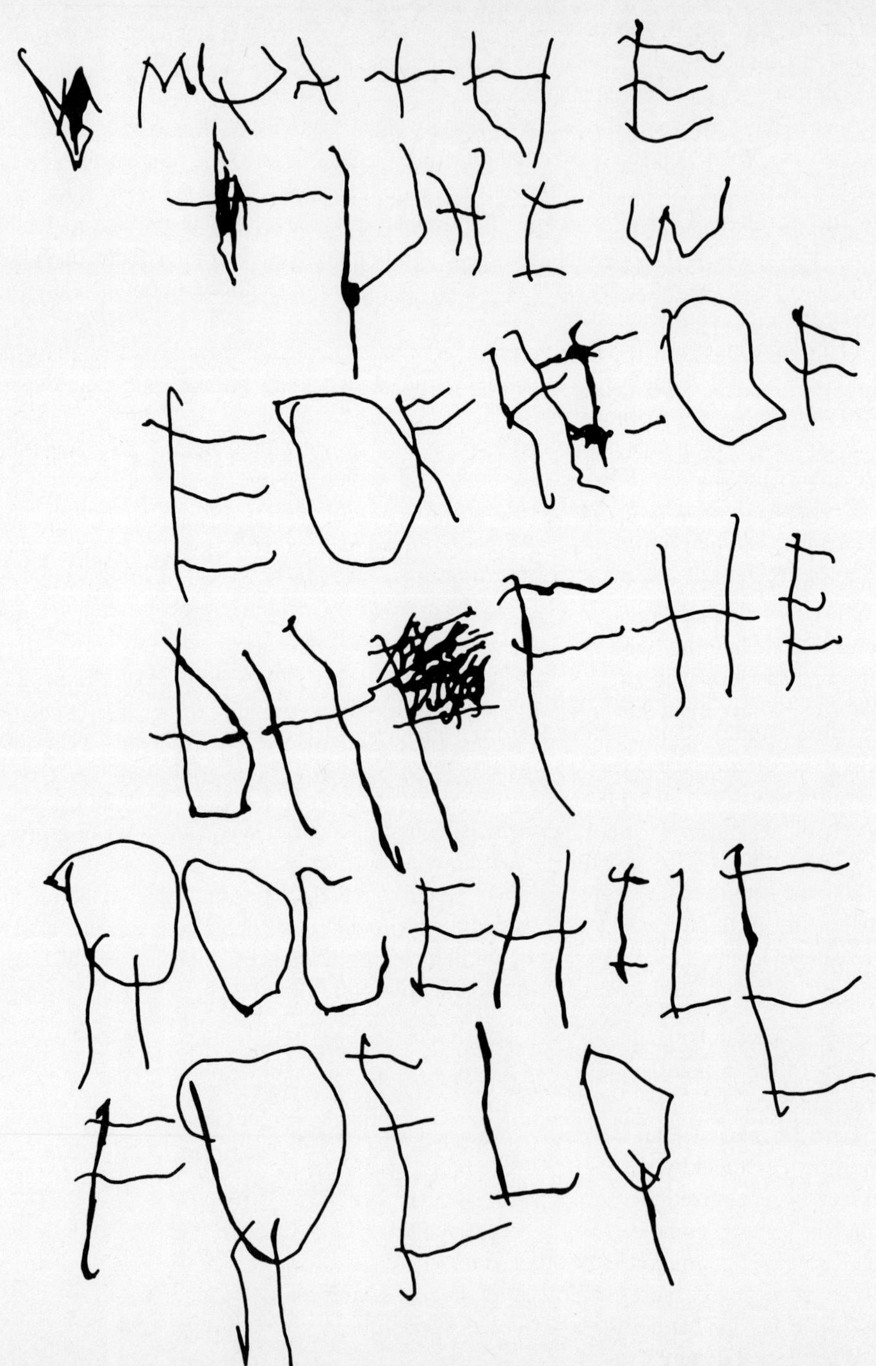

● **FIGURE 3.3** Matthew's thank-you note

concept." Through his many encounters with print in his environment, Matthew has also developed alphabet-letter awareness. He knows, too, some of the conventions of writing peculiar to the English language. Writing, for example, moves from left to right, then back to the left at the end of a line, and from top to bottom on a page. Also, Matthew has developed an awareness of audience—in this case, the Vaccas. His thank-you message is direct and to the point. In case you're wondering what the two solid markings are that appear at the beginning and end of the first line, Matthew's explanation is both sensible and pragmatic: "That's where they [the Vaccas] can put the nails through." In other words, when the Vaccas display Matthew's thank-you note on their bulletin board, they'll know where to place the thumbtacks!

Matthew's note is also revealing by what it doesn't reflect. At age 4, Matthew's writing doesn't indicate word awareness (i.e., that words are composed of letters and are separated from one another by "boundaries" or white spaces). Matthew might be called a one-letter speller. A letter or several letters on each line of text may represent a word, phrase, or an entire sentence.

As Matthew continues to grow as a writer, his writing will become increasingly more sophisticated. He will develop a concept of word and a knowledge of sound-letter correspondence. We are confident that Matthew will soon be writing words and sentences with the aid of invented spellings. Spelling invention will give way to convention as he gains greater knowledge and control of sound-letter relationships. Other writing conventions, such as punctuation and capitalization, will also evolve with continued writing experiences in an environment that encourages growth and supports Matthew's literacy development. How parents and teachers view the conventions of writing, particularly invented spellings, in beginning situations is crucial to writing development.

How Spelling Develops

Invented spelling is a name given to children's misspellings before they have learned the rules of spelling. Most children don't begin school having mastered sound-letter correspondence. Yet children come to school having varying degrees of knowledge about the structure of written language because of their early explorations with reading and writing. Children, through their use of invented spellings, expect their writing to make sense and have meaning.

Take the case of Paul Bissex, an early reader/writer, whose mother documented his literacy development by keeping a detailed diary of his progress (Bissex, 1980). At age 4, Paul clearly recognized the connection between writing and reading. For example, when he read his writing, complete with invented spellings, he explained: "Once you know how to spell something, you know how to read it" (p. 1). As Bissex observes, Paul developed multiple strategies because of his use of invented spellings: "Paul seemed to be asking himself not only 'What does this word *sound* like?' and 'What does this word *look* like?' but 'What does it mean?'" (p. 102).

Invented spellings signal to parents and teachers that children are beginning to analyze speech sounds in print. By first grade, for example, most children know something about letters. They may know the names and shapes of some letters. Others may be making associations between sounds and letters. The more that children explore letter-sound associations in their writing, the more progress they make toward conventional spelling. Bobo, a second grader, is a case in point.

Bobo was an "average" second grader in Sharon Piper's class. A regular classroom event in Mrs. Piper's room is journal writing. Early in the school year, Bobo's journal entries indicated that he was using several systematic strategies in his writing. His entries on October 27 and 28, for example, indicated that he was employing both a letter-name strategy (*cam* for *came*) and what Henderson and Beers (1980) describe as a transitional strategy showing awareness of lax vowels and the *e* marker (*scerry* for *scary; gucy* for *guy*).

Mrs. Piper decided to follow Bobo's development as a speller by examining words that recurred through different entries over time. Here's what she discovered.

	today		**snow**
a. Nov. 3	to daey	Nov. 20	sarrow
b. Nov. 20	taooday	Dec. 9	sniwing
c. Dec. 3	teay	Jan. 18	snowing
d. Jan. 5	today		

	yesterday		**tomorrow**
e. Nov. 19	ewastdoaday	Nov. 7	tamarro
f. Dec. 11	yesdday	Apr. 28	tomorrowe
g. Feb. 5	yesterday	Apr. 29	tomrrow

	opening my presents		**vacation**
h. Dec. 14	opting my poisis	Dec. 7	waicing
i. Dec. 18	opning my pisins	Dec. 16	facishin

	coming		**outside**
j. Dec. 17	ciming	Nov. 5	altt
k. Feb. 4	caming	Nov. 20	aitsadd
l. Feb. 11	comming	Dec. 9	awtside
m. Apr. 16	comeing	Jan. 21	owtshd
n.		Feb. 24	outsid
o.		May 3	outside

All of the examples show progress toward a correct form. The important point, however, is that Bobo's progress reveals how children *invent* and *reinvent* spellings as they experiment with written language. Chomsky (1970) points out that the child doesn't *memorize* spellings, but instead reinvents them each time in order to more closely approximate correct spelling. Invention, then, reflects that spelling is a process that is refined over time, and that children have little trouble making the transition to conventional spelling when they have many opportunities to write freely.

Advantages of Invented Spelling. The gradual sophistication in children's invented spellings should be celebrated by teachers and parents as a display of intelligence and emerging competence with written language. When "correct spelling" isn't an obstacle in the path of young writers, they are free to get their ideas down on paper. Invented spellings help children place ideas before notions of correctness. Every primary teacher knows the interruptions that can occur in class when youngsters constantly ask for the correct spelling of practically every word they don't know. What we sometimes fail to recognize, however, is that children probably seek correct spellings because they perceive that the teacher values accuracy in their writing. When children are bound by notions of correctness, writing becomes a laborious undertaking rather than a meaning-making act. A supportive learning environment, however, encourages children to try to spell words as best they can during writing and to experiment with written language without the restrictions imposed by demands for accuracy and correction.

Sowers (1982) lists the advantages of not placing a premium on accuracy:

1. Children build independence because they don't have to ask for every word they don't know.
2. By emphasizing ideas rather than correctness, children become fluent in their writing. They can elaborate and play on paper without interruptions.
3. Children move efficiently through the stages of spelling development when they have opportunities to apply strategies about sound-symbol correspondences at their own pace and level of sophistication.
4. Children develop control and responsibility for their writing by taking risks and trying out the "rules" that they are forming about spelling. As Sowers noted, "The worst outcome of an unsuccessful invention is that communication stops temporarily." But if the invention succeeds, so does the child: "Real rewards await the child who writes fearlessly about a FROSHUS DOBRMAN PENSR instead of a BAD DOG" (p. 48).

The whole idea behind encouraging spelling invention is to build on the emerging competence of the beginner. As children put their ideas ahead of concerns for correct spelling, they will develop confidence in their ability to write; they will recognize the value of taking risks.

Developmental Stages of Spelling. During the past decade, spelling researchers have explored the developmental relationship between spelling ability and reading and writing (Read, 1971, 1975; Clay, 1979c; Bissex, 1980; Henderson and Beers, 1980). From their work it is clear that young children apply systematic strategies to relate speech sounds to print. These strategies are applied through definable **developmental stages of spelling.** These stages, are broadly defined below.

Prephonemic Spelling. Once children know some letters, they begin to experiment with the relationship between the letters and their sounds. One early concept that develops is that there is a one-to-one correspondence between the initial consonant or final consonant of a word and the words. The word *back* is spelled with a *B* or *sink* with a *K.* This concept is gradually expanded to include the consonant boundaries of words. For example, ML = *mail* and DR = *dear.* Matthew, whose thank-you note is illustrated in Figure 3.3, is an early prephonemic speller.

Phonemic Spelling. At this stage, vowels begin to appear in children's invented spellings. Six- and seven-year-olds learn to sound their way through a word making sound-letter matches as they write. There is still a tendency to use a one-to-one match although it is now much more refined than in the previous stage. For example, MAL = *mail;* ESTR = *Easter;* COT = *coat;* SRPRIS = *surprise.* Note that long vowels are represented with the corresponding letter name. Often, logical substitutions are made for short vowels, such as SEK = *stick* or JRAS = *dress.*

Transitional Spelling. As a result of extended opportunities to read and write in and out of school, children begin to abandon the notion that there has to be a one-to-one match between a spoken sound and a graphic symbol. They now actively search for chunks or patterns of letters that represent spoken sounds. They begin to develop greater spelling awareness by observing the consonant-vowel-consonant (CVC) pattern, that is, GET; the CVVC pattern, that is, MALLE = *mail;* DAER = *dear;* CEAP = *keep;* the CVCe patterns, that is, TAKE = *take;* LIKE = *like;* CAER = *care.*

Conventional Spelling. By the third grade children have developed many accurate notions of how to spell words that conform to the standard rules of the language. They use correct spellings more and more often in their attempts to communicate.

Realizing the Literacy Potential of All Children

Although children of poverty are often identified as at risk of academic failure upon entering school, young children from middle class or affluent home situations may also be at risk for a variety of reasons. If television is used as a continual babysitter, regardless of children's socioeconomic status, literacy development may suffer from a lack of parental role model, socialization to print, or potentially rich parent-child interactions around print. Also, a parent who wants to "hurry" a child into reading may increase, quite unwittingly, the pressure on the child to learn to read. Such pressure on young children may lead to stressful situations and negative associations with print. It may also create a high-risk learning environment by engaging the child in inappropriate (from a language perspective) activities that lack meaning and a functional purpose—for example, drilling children to recognize isolated sound-letter relationships before they are linguistically and cognitively able to do so.

Children from single parent homes, or homes where both parents work, may also be at risk as literacy learners if they are placed in less than optimal child-care situations. If the provider of child care is uneducated or untrained, perhaps illiterate or marginally literate, chances are that the child will miss important literacy experiences. It is imperative that parents choose child-care providers judiciously.

Poverty has a devastating influence on the social, emotional, and intellectual development of young children. Intellectual deprivation during a child's preschool years is likely to have profound and long-lasting effects. In family contexts where parents are either illiterate or semiliterate, it is not likely that children will be read to or have reading models, nor will they have easy access to books or writing materials. Poverty and illiteracy become *intergenerational.* That is to say, when children are unsuccessful in school, it is not likely that they will become economically successful adults. Thus, a cycle of poverty and illiteracy tends to be perpetuated from one generation to another.

Intergenerational Literacy Programs. **Intergenerational literacy** is another term for family literacy, although it is often used in connection with family intervention programs designed to break the cycle of illiteracy from one generation to the next. Illiteracy need not breed illiteracy. Family intervention programs underscore the close relationship between adult and child and treat literacy as a social activity that influences both young and older learners. They range in scope from federally funded interventions such as **Head Start** and Even Start to local school and community efforts that enlist low-literate parents' aid in the development of their children's reading. Such family literacy programs are sensitive to the literacy needs of parents and attempt to build their competence and confidence with literacy activities. In addition, parents learn strategies such as *readalouds* and *readalongs* to enrich on family interactions with books and also engage in literacy events such as group book discussions or story hours on the weekend.

In 1965, the United States government initiated an effort to break the "cycle of poverty" by focusing attention on education for underprivileged preschool children and their families. Project Head Start programs were developed in communities throughout the United States to provide a nursery school environment to compensate for developmental differences that are apt to exist between poor children and their more advantaged counterparts. These programs were designed to prepare children intellectually and socially to begin kindergarten and first grade on a more equal basis with advantaged children.

Head Start provides a comprehensive program to serve the needs of the "whole child." In addition to provisions for cognitive and social development, the program includes social and mental-health services, a nutritional component, and a parent participation requirement. Early intervention programs such as Head Start have positive, long-lasting effects. Simply put, children of poverty who participate in early intervention programs are more likely to be successful in school (Maeroff, 1989).

Patricia Edwards (1989) decribes how she volunteered to serve as a parent consultant for a local Head Start center in a rural community in northern Louisiana. In this role, she created a book reading project in which she met with low socioeconomic black families periodically for nine months to build on family strengths. She showed them how to better support their children's reading both at the Head Start center and in the public school setting. The main focus was on how parents could interact with their children during the reading of storybooks. Throughout the project the parents learned how to use strategies to maintain children's attention, respond to their comments and questions, relate the storybooks to life experiences, initiate discussions, share personal reactions, and encourage children to respond in a like manner.

In 1990, another federally legislated program, Even Start, was designed to assist parents of children from birth to age 7 who live in the area of an elementary school with Chapter 1 services. One of the stipulations of Even Start is that parents must qualify for participation in an adult basic education (ABE) program. As part of the Even Start program, added to the literacy instruction that they get through ABE, parents receive education and become directly involved in their children's literacy learning through early childhood intervention programs.

Success for Head Start and Even Start interventions as well as for the multitude of school and community-based family literacy programs hinges on the provisions they make for developmentally appropriate literacy and language practices.

Developmentally Appropriate Literacy Experiences. All children benefit from **developmentally appropriate practice** regardless of the learning situation. The idea of developmentally appropriate practice suggests that the curriculum match or be geared to children's developing abilities (Bredekamp, 1987). From a literacy development perspective, a child's first contact with a language arts curriculum in school should match his or her level of emergent literacy.

David Elkind (1989) argues that developmentally appropriate practice takes into account one's beliefs and conceptions of the learner, or the learning process, of knowledge, and of the goals of education. From a developmental perspective, the child, as a learner, is viewed as having *developing* abilities. All children, perhaps with the exception of those who are mentally, emotionally, or linguistically impaired, are capable of attaining these abilities. However, not all children will attain these abilities at the same age. In terms of literacy learning, not all children entering school will have developed abilities to read and write at the same level of proficiency or rate of growth. Thus, the differences in children should weigh heavily in planning initial literacy experiences.

Elkind also contends that a teacher's conception of the learning process and of knowledge affects developmentally appropriate practices. From a developmental viewpoint, learning always involves *creative* activity. Nowhere is this proposition more evident than in literacy learning. As we have already observed, young children must "try out" literacy on their own terms by exploring and experimenting with written language. Not only is the learning process creative, but the learner is always involved in the *construction* of knowledge. Within a literate environment, young children act upon objects (e.g., paper, pencil, books, etc.) and events (e.g., a bedtime story) to make sense of written language.

Teachers' conceptions of the aims and goals of education are interlaced with their conceptions of the learner, the learning process, and knowledge. Elkind put it this way: "If the learner is seen as a growing individual with developing abilities, if learning is regarded as a creative activity, and if knowledge is seen as a construction, then the aim of education must surely be to facilitate this development, this creative activity, and this construction of knowledge" (p. 115).

Effective teachers of literacy know how to plan developmentally appropriate experiences and how to rally instruction around children's diversity. Individual differences, however, need not suggest a unique program of instruction for each child. Individualizing a literacy program is as much a state of mind as it is a fixed or prescriptive approach to instruction. How teachers go about individualizing says more of their beliefs about reading and learning to read than it does about any specific method.

Individualized instruction sometimes is narrowly translated to mean "learning small things in small steps," where each child completes an individualized program "except for some differences in pacing" (Moffett, 1975). A teacher's responsibility, first and foremost, is to establish a classroom environment in which individual learning takes place during literacy instruction. Holdaway (1979) argues that it is impossible to determine the right level, content, pace, and style of learning for each child, each day. But teachers can set the conditions for learning by giving enough instructional support to each child to learn to read and write successfully.

Since ideal conditions for literacy growth may not exist for all children, what, then, do some of the insights from literacy learning in early childhood hold for initial school experiences?

Instructional Implications for Kindergarten and First Grade

Reading instruction in kindergarten today is more the rule than the exception. In 1977, a statement of concerns about present practices in pre-first-grade reading instruction was issued by a joint committee made up of members from seven national and international professional educational associations.[1] The concerns expressed by the committee focus on the highly formalized, structured instructional practices that run counter to natural language

[1]Sponsors of the joint statement of concerns and recommendations for the improvement of reading in pre-first grade included the American Association of Elementary/Kindergarten/Nursery Educators, the Association for Childhood Education International, the Association for Supervision and Curriculum Development, the International Reading Association, the National Association for the Education of Young Children, the National Association of Elementary School Principals, and the National Council of Teachers of English.

learning and the development of the "whole child." The recommendations of the committee listed in Box 3.2 highlight provisions for a *language-centered* curriculum for beginners. Not only does the committee support a language-centered curriculum, but they also underscore the need for an instructional environment for learning to read that is *home centered.*

Creating a Literate Environment in the Classroom

Insights from the early reading experiences of preschool children have yet to fully influence beginning reading in schools. Instruction for 5-year-olds should not be a carbon copy of practices that are appropriate for older children or that emphasize drill, repetition, and memorization. Instead, the beginner in kindergarten needs supportive, meaningful situations in learning to read. In this respect, there is much to be learned from the behavior of parents of preschool readers.

A teacher of beginners should consider focusing reading instruction around the natural methods of parents whose children learned to read before school entry. A literate classroom environment for reading places less attention on instructional methods and more emphasis on individual attention and a warm, accepting relationship between child and teacher. A literacy learning environment in school establishes ideal conditions for learning to read in much the same way that the home environment of the child establishes ideal conditions for learning to speak.

In a classroom environment that promotes literacy development, children feel free to take risks because errors are expected and accepted. Risk taking is an important factor in literacy learning. Beginners should feel free to ask questions with the expectation that interested adults will listen and respond constructively. As Routman (1988) noted, respect for each child is a critical factor: "If they [children] feel respected, they will feel secure and be able to take risks. So it is with us as adults too. Respect is necessary for optimal learning" (p. 32).

Holdaway (1982) describes some of the characteristics of a natural, or home-centered, language learning environment that operates efficiently in a preschooler's mastery of oral language.

1. *Young children are allowed to develop in their own way and at their own rate using language functionally to meet their needs.*

2. *Parents are positive and rewarding in their reception of most responses that children attempt.* In learning oral language, children have a built-in support system provided by their parents that does not stress criticism or correction but allows for trial and approximations.

3. *Parents demonstrate tremendous faith and patience.*

4. *Parents do not create competitive situations in which children learn language.* Parents may compare a child's performance with what he or she did yesterday or a week ago, but rarely do they make close comparisons of their child's performance with another child.

● BOX 3.2

Recommendations from the Joint Committee on Reading in Pre-First Grade

1. Provide reading experiences as an integrated part of the broader communication process that includes listening, speaking, and writing. A language experience approach is an example of such integration.
2. Provide for a range of activities that is broad both in scope and in content. Include direct experiences that offer opportunities to communicate in different settings with different persons.
3. Foster children's affective and cognitive development by providing materials, experiences, and opportunities to communicate what they know and how they feel.
4. Continually appraise how various aspects of each child's total development affects his or her reading development.
5. Use evaluative procedures that are developmentally appropriate for the children being assessed and that reflect the goals and objectives of the instructional program.
6. Ensure feelings of success for all children in order to help them see themselves as persons who can enjoy exploring language and learning to read.
7. Plan flexibility in order to accommodate a variety of learning styles and ways of thinking.
8. Respect the language the child brings to school, and use it as a base for language activities.
9. Plan activities that will cause children to become active participants in the learning process rather than passive recipients of knowledge.
10. Provide opportunities for children to experiment with language and simply to have fun with it.
11. Require that preservice and in-service teachers of young children be prepared in the teaching of reading in a way that emphasizes reading as an integral part of the language arts as well as the total curriculum.
12. Encourage developmentally appropriate language learning opportunities in the home.

5. *Children learn in meaningful situations that support the language being learned.*
6. *Children have models to emulate.* Because the language learning process is innately rewarding, they spend much of their time voluntarily practicing.

It is evident from the studies reported in the previous sections that many of the conditions necessary for language learning were operating in the lives of early readers. Teachers of reading beginners must approximate these ideal conditions in their classrooms. Consider, then, establishing some of the hallmarks of a home-centered environment for learning to read.

Reading to Children

There is no better way to create a love for books than by reading to children. Reading to children sparks their imagination and gives them a sense of wonder. According to Cramer (1975), reading to children will help them appreciate the gift of literature, develop and enrich their own language, and build implicit concepts about reading and writing.

Reading to children helps them learn to read in subtle but important ways. It is through reading that children develop a schema or a sense for stories. In Chapter 6, we discuss the role of *story structure* in learning to read and how children can use their schema for stories to comprehend material. A story schema is developed early in the lives of children who have been read to frequently. Moreover, reading to children provides models for writing as they develop a sense of plot, characterization, mood, and theme.

Cramer (1975, pp. 461–62) provides valuable guidelines for reading to children.

1. *Plan each day's reading selection in advance.* Normally one should have certain days reserved for the reading of a continuing story. It is also useful to reserve at least one day a week for special selections—poetry, surprise readings, or readings designed to mesh with other daily or weekly classroom activities.
2. *Select reading material best suited for the children being read to.* Keep in mind age and interest levels. Many teachers choose to consult various sources in selecting appropriate books.
3. *Interpret the mood, tone, and action of the passage being read.* Don't be afraid to be dramatic. Inhibition, shyness, or fear of making a fool of oneself often prevents teachers from entering into the drama of a story.
4. *Differentiate the reading-to-children time for the directed reading-and-listening-activity time.* It is neither necessary nor desirable to make the reading-listening time into a structured lesson. The primary objective is enjoyment.
5. *When reading a narrative that will be continued the next day, stop at a point that is likely to invite anticipation for the next episode.* Judicious use of this device can have

a positive effect on attendance and sustained high interest level in the selection being read.

Reading activities may be planned to focus on children's authors and illustrators. Children may learn about the authors and illustrators by reading or listening to their stories, by corresponding with them, by creating stories in their style, or by comparing and contrasting the stories.

Jim Trelease's *The New Read-Aloud Handbook* (1989) is an invaluable resource for parents and teachers who want to make reading to children a regular routine. Not only does Trelease provide the dos and don'ts of reading aloud, but he also includes annotated references of readaloud books that can be used to make reading come alive for children.

Shared Book Experiences

Reading to children is an important way of sharing books. The act of sharing books with children provides invaluable stimulation for relating speech to print. Almost all of the early readers in various studies came from book-oriented homes. Reading to and with children captures their fascination with print. They progress from sheer delight in the human experience of story sharing to recognition that the pictures in books "tell a story" to the awareness that the black squiggly marks (not the pictures on a page) have a direct association with spoken language.

Books may be shared in a variety of contexts. Young children will hear good children's literature during a library story hour or on television programs such as "Reading Rainbow." Excellent literature is also available to children through book and cassette combinations that are sold in bookstores or may be borrowed from a public library.

The Shared Book Experience. Holdaway (1979) popularizes a teaching strategy called the **shared book experience** to incorporate the facilitating features of the bedtime story. The idea behind the strategy is to use a "big book" (usually constructed by the teacher in a 24- by 15-inch format). The big book allows all the children in the class or in a small group to actively participate in the reading of the story. Because the print and illustrations are large enough for all the children to see, the teacher captures their attention immediately and focuses instruction around key goals. For example, the teacher should read the story aloud often enough so that children learn it by heart. The story then becomes the basis for discussion and language-related activities (i.e., story dramatization) as well as teaching children about directionality and other print-related concepts.

Steps in the Shared Book Experience. The shared book experience involves the teacher and a class of beginners partaking in the reading and rereading of favorite stories, songs, poems, and rhymes. Andrea Butler (1988) likens the shared book experience to a ritual that should occur daily in the classroom lives of teachers and children. She recommended the use of shared book experience as a way of creating opportunities for children to learn what a book is, what an "expert" reader does with a book as it is read, and what makes a story a story (p. 3). Butler suggested a three-step process in conducting a shared book experience: (1) introduce a new story; (2) reread familiar stories; and (3) encourage independent reading.

Introduce a New Story. As part of the story's introduction, show the children the cover of the book and invite discussion of the illustration: "What does the illustration on the cover remind you of?" "What do you think this story will be about?" Then tell the children the title of the story and invite further predictions as to the story's content. Next, read the story dramatically.

Once the students have experienced the joy of hearing the story, invite conversation: For example, "What did you enjoy about the story?" "Were the characters like you?" It is better not to overdo the discussion with lots of questions. Accept the children's personal reactions and responses, and support their efforts to express their enjoyment of the story and to talk about the meaning that it had for them.

You might have the children retell the story in their own words. Allow them to use picture clues to help them if they do not remember certain parts of the story. Then, reread the story, inviting the children to participate in some way, perhaps by focusing on repetitive elements, or chants, in the story and by having them join in with you. To avoid a high-risk situation, it isn't necessary to require total participation in the rereading; keep the emphasis on meaning and enjoyment.

Reread Familiar Stories. Once several stories have been introduced and are familiar to the children, ask them to choose a favorite to be reread. Strive for increased participation by the children by creating a readalong situation. Also, consider developing students' book knowledge. As you read, point to the words in the text, and demonstrate skills such as page turning and directionality (e.g., left to right, top to bottom). Teach children about book conventions (e.g., front and back cover, title and author/illustrator page, pictures support the story), or make them aware of the conventions of written language (e.g., words, pages, spaces between words, the use of capital letters in proper names or in the beginning of a sentence, punctuation marks, quotation marks to indicate dialogue between the characters).

As children progress in the sharing and rereading of favorite stories, teach them reading strategies such as comprehending and discovering meaning, developing oral reading expression and fluency, skipping over an unknown word, using context to identify words, building a sight-word vocabulary, and showing sound-letter relationships in words. These strategies and others will be explained in subsequent chapters.

Encourage Independent Reading. Develop a classroom library of books that have been shared and reread many times. Encourage students to read favorite books on their own. Motivation to do so will be high.

Whether a teacher uses a big book format or not, sharing books is an invaluable experience for beginners. In Chapter 10, we explore ways to share books.

Repeated Readings of Favorite Stories

Repetition of favorite stories and eventually "memory reading" play a crucial role in the child's understanding that print is supposed to sound like language. The phenomenon of memory reading involves the child recalling and rehearsing favorite segments of stories by heart. Young children learn to use a variety of strategies to achieve some sense of independence over their favorite stories. As part of sharing books and reading aloud, the teacher should be ready and willing to read and reread favorite books and to invite children to participate as much as possible. The language patterns of the books should be predictable, melodic, and rhythmic. In Chapter 9 we will have more to say on predictable materials and book choices for young children.

Two additional suggestions to consider are: First, create a listening library for the classroom by recording stories on audiotapes for children to listen to as they follow the story in the book. Second, children will enjoy repeating and retelling favorite stories by using a flannel board or puppets, or through creative play and dramatics.

Some adults are quick to point out that children who memorize stories are just pretending to read, just "going through the motions." Pretending, however, shouldn't be discouraged. In fact, imitation establishes good models. The readinglike behaviors associated with an imitative stage in reading provide children with important early book experiences. Just consider some of the print concepts they learn: Books have pages, the pages can be turned, books have a right and wrong way up, the pictures help to tell a story, and books are a source of enjoyment and pleasure.

In Chapter 9, we elaborate on the uses of repeated readings to develop a child's oral reading fluency.

Assisted Reading

Parents of early readers answer questions when their children ask for assistance. The parent usually follows the child's lead, not vice versa. Children choose their own activities and materials, and when questions arise a parent or a significant other is there to help.

One of our preservice students who is studying to be an elementary school teacher observed her two children, Ben and Matt, interact with each other just before bedtime. The brothers share the same bedroom and often read bedtime stories together. Ben is 8 and Matt is 5.

Ben: Matt, pick out a story. (*Matt proceeds to do so while Ben plays with the dog.*)
Matt: Ben, can I read the big words?
Ben: (*points to the book*): Are these the big words?
Matt: Yeah, those words.
Ben: Why don't I read the black words and you read the red ones? OK?
Matt: (*points to book*): You mean these?

Ben: Yeah.
Matt: But I don't know all the words.
Ben: Well, I'll just help ya—OK?
Matt: OK, I'll try. (Matt sighs and the story begins.) Will you help me with that? (*Matt points to a word on the page.*)
Ben: Scissors.
Matt: Scissors.
Ben: Yeah, good. That's right. (*The story continues until Matt reads the word "fish" for "goldfish."*)
Ben: No. What kind of fish?
Matt: Goldfish?
Ben: Yeah, good. (*Ben points to a picture of the goldfish. After a while Ben gets tired of giving Matt hints about the words.*)
Ben: Can I read the rest?
Matt: Yeah, but I want to read the last page.
Ben: OK. (*Ben reads the book until the last page.*) Are you goin' to read this?
Matt: Yeah. (*Matt attempts the last page and does fairly well with Ben's occasional assistance.*)
Ben: Good. Matt! You're learnin' to read real well.

Matt has acquired knowledge of written language and has developed concepts of reading by being immersed in stories from a very early age. He is learning how to read *by* reading with help from Ben and his parents, and on his own. Matt seeks assistance when he needs it and doesn't recognize such help as corrective or critical.

Hoskisson (1975) recommends a strategy that he devised called **assisted reading** that combines all of the features of home-centered learning: reading with children, sharing books, repeating favorite stories, memorizing text, and providing assistance as needed. Parents or teachers can easily adapt the three stages associated with the strategy.

STAGE 1. Read to children and have them repeat the phrases or sentences after the person doing the reading. This encourages memorizing. It is sometimes referred to as *echo reading,* because children are to repeat the phrases and sentences exactly as they were read. It is during echo reading that children are working out the connection between print and speech and developing a concept of *word.*

STAGE 2. Children begin this stage when they recognize that some of the words occur repeatedly in stories they are reading. At this point, the teacher can leave out some of the words that they think children know. The children fill in the blanks left as they read.

STAGE 3. Children enter this stage of assisted reading when they do most of the reading and the teacher fills in the words the children may not know or may have trouble recognizing. The goal is to maintain as smooth a flow of the reading as possible. When children hesitate or seem unsure of a word, a teacher should supply the word rather than ask them to "sound it out" or require them to practice word identification strategies.

Not only is a literate classroom environment home centered, it is also playful. A play-centered environment allows young children in day care or kindergarten classrooms to develop a "feel" for literacy as they experiment with written language.

Literacy Play Centers

In 1908, M. C. Bettinger, an assistant superintendent of the Los Angeles City Schools, is attributed with having said, "If parents and teachers are to hold their own in their efforts at language teaching, in competition with the playground, they must take their cue from the playground" (King, 1908, p. ii). To this astute comment, Kathleen Roskos (1988), a literacy researcher, adds another timely observation: As researchers continue to explore the ways in which children learn literacy, they are just beginning to see how play serves children's literacy development and may, in turn, inform literacy teaching. The literacy play center is a powerful context in which to observe, as Roskos noted, "literacy at work in play."

What Happens During Play?

Literacy play centers in preschool and kindergarten provide an environment where children may play with print on their own terms. Play provides a natural context for beginners to experiment with literacy. Play centers promote literacy by giving children opportunities to observe one another using literacy for real reasons (Schickendanz, 1986).

Roskos (1986, 1988) closely observes eight children, ages 4 and 5, for six months during free-play situations to analyze the kinds of reading and writing activities they engaged in naturally during play. As a result of the study, she was amazed to discover the quantity and quality of early literate activity in pretend-play situations.

In free-play situations, the children Roskos observed were involved in literacy in two fundamental ways. First, during **pretend play,** they commonly engaged in "story making." The stories that were spontaneously created during play frequently included a setting, characters, a goal or central concern, specific events that constituted a plot, and a resolution. Some of the stories that children created included taking trips to Sea World and domestic problems like "the naughty daughters."

Second, literacy socialization—what children know about reading and writing from living in a literate society—was also observed during spontaneous free-play activities. The young children in Roskos's study were highly aware of the reading and writing activities that occur naturally on a daily basis, and they exhibited their knowledge of literacy when they used it during pretend play.

As a result of the study, Roskos makes three recommendations for teachers in day-care, preschool, and kindergarten settings.[2]

1. Create and frequently use play centers that facilitate sustained pretend play and prompt experimentation with reading and writing. In addition to the traditional house-keeping and block areas, teachers should consider developing play centers like the office, the travel agency, the store, the bank, or the play school that stimulate young children to explore the routines, functions, and features of literacy.
2. Ask young children to share their pretend-play stories, which can then be recorded on chart paper and used for extended language experience activities. From play accounts like these, teaching points about story sense, print forms, directionality, and sight vocabulary can easily be inserted.
3. Begin to observe more closely the literacy at work in the pretend play of youngsters. These observations tell us much about the young child's literacy stance and may guide us in our instructional efforts to connect what is known about written language to the unknown. Scribbled recipes from the housekeeping area, stories created at the sand table, and book handling in the play school are literacy signals that should not be ignored.

How Do Literacy Play Centers Work?

Usually **literacy play centers** are designed around familiar contexts or places (e.g., the kitchen, a bank, a doctor's or dentist's office, the post office), but are kept general enough for children to create their own stories and themes as they engage in play talk and action. Play centers are located within a designated area of the classroom, labeled accordingly at children's eye level, and are furnished with real props found in the environment. The props may be used for dramatic effect (dramatic props) or for literacy-related activity (literacy props). McGee and Richgels (1990), for example, outlines the dramatic and literacy props in a "doctor play center." Dramatic props included a play doctor's kit (with stethoscope, light, etc.), a nurse's hat, a blanket for an examining table, dolls as the patients, and a white shirt for the doctor. Literacy or "print" props included patient charts, prescription pads, sign-in sheets, bill forms, checkbooks, and magazines for the waiting room. In Table 3.1 Neuman and Roskos (1990) list the types of literacy props that may be used in several different literacy play centers. The appropriateness of props in a play center depends on

[2] Adapted from Kathleen Roskos, "Literacy at Work in Play." *The Reading Teacher* 41(6): 562–66.

● TABLE 3.1

Types of Props Found in Literacy Play Centers

Kitchen center	Office center	Post office center	Library center
Books to read to dolls or stuffed animals	Calendars of various types	Envelopes of various sizes	Library book return cards
Telephone books	Appointment book	Assorted forms	Stamps for marking books
A telephone (preferably a real one)	Message pads	Stationery	A wide variety of childrens books
Emergency number decals on or near telephone	Signs, e.g., open/closed	Pens, pencils, children's	Book marks
Cookbooks	Books, pamphlets, markers magazines	Stickers, stars, stamps, stamp pads	Pens, pencils, markers
Blank recipe cards	File folders	Post office mailbox	Paper of assorted sizes
Small plaques or decorative magnets	Racks for filing papers	A tote bag for mail	A sign-in/sign-out sheet
Personal stationery	In/out trays	Computer address labels	Stickers
Food coupons	Index cards	Large and small plastic cups	ABC index cards
Grocery store ads/fliers	Business cards	Calendars of various types	A telephone
Play money containers	Assorted forms	Small drawer trays	Telephone books
Empty grocery containers	Play money and checklike pieces of paper	Posters and signs about mailing procedures	Calendars of various types
Small message board or blackboards	Ledger sheets		Posters of children's books
Calendars of various types	Typewriter or computer keyboard		File folders
Notepads of assorted sizes pens, pencils, markers	Clipboards		
Large plastic clips	Post-its™ and address labels		
	Notecards		
	Large and small plastic clips		
	Pens, pencils, markers		
	Trays for holding items		

their authenticity, use, and safety. Any literacy-related item found in the "real world" might be included in a center.

Teachers often assume the role of a participant in a play episode, but their main responsibility is to facilitate literacy-development, which may involve appropriately intervening to create opportunities to include children in literacy-related activities during play. This may entail suggesting the need for making a list, recording an appointment, requesting a telephone number, checking food labels, or reading a bedtime story.

Notice how a kindergarten teacher, Ms. Green, participates in and facilitates two timely literacy routines:

Four children are busily working in the housekeeping area when the teacher walks by.

Ms. Green: Mmmm! It smells wonderful in here. What are you cooking?

Lonnie: I'm making applesauce.

Tim: Well, I'm making some pizza.

Ms. Green: Applesauce and pizza will make a terrific lunch!

Karen: Yeah! Let's have pizza and applesauce for lunch. Pizza is my favorite.

Ms. Green: Even the baby can eat applesauce. He can't chew pizza yet because he doesn't have teeth, but he can eat applesauce.

Karen: Oh, no! The baby is crying again. That baby is crying too much!

Ms. Green: I will help you take care of the baby while you fix lunch. Let's see. I think that he would like to hear a story. (The teacher selects a small board book from the bookshelf in the housekeeping center and sits down to read to the "baby.") Yes, the baby should enjoy this book. This is a story that my children liked to hear when they were babies. (The teacher holds the doll and reads the book. Several children come over to watch as she reads to the baby.)

Emily: OK, lunch is ready. Do you want some lunch, Ms. Green?

Ms. Green: I would love to have lunch with you. I like pizza and applesauce.

(Everyone pretends to eat.)

Tim: Well, how do you like my pizza, Ms. Green?

Lonnie: How's my applesauce?

Ms. Green: Everything is delicious. Will you both share your recipes for pizza and applesauce with me?

Tim and Lonnie: Sure!

The teacher then provides paper for Tim, Lonnie, and the other children to write their recipes. The children's writings used a combination of scribbles, letters, and invented spellings.

Teachers may also wish to extend and elaborate on a play episode by inviting children to think about and discuss what they did during play. Pictures, three-dimensional materials, and written work (involving children's scribbles or invented spellings) may provide a basis for children to recall what they did and what they liked about the play episode.

In a post office center, a kindergarten teacher, Mrs. Chones, provided additional experiences and activities designed to extend children's prior knowledge of the responsibilities of postal workers and the process of transporting mail. She began by guiding a discussion to determine what the children already knew about the post office, what they needed or wanted to know, and any misconceptions they may have had. The children's responses were recorded on chart paper and were posted on the wall near the post office center. As a follow-up to the discussion, the teacher showed the children an interesting, current, age-appropriate video about the post office. A brief discussion followed to determine if the video provided answers to any of the questions or clarified any misconceptions.

In addition, the children were taken on a field trip to the local post office. The remaining unanswered questions from the wall charts were transferred to smaller strips of paper for the children to carry with them to the post office. The children drew pictures to accompany their questions and to serve as visual aids to help them remember what questions they wanted to ask. A postal worker served as a tour guide and patiently answered the children's questions, impromptu and planned. When the children returned to their classroom, they helped the teacher to revise the wall charts based on the knowledge gained from the field trip.

As a result, the play episodes that occur in the post office center are likely to be more involved and sophisticated, because the teacher provided relevant experiences designed to extend the children's knowledge and to stimulate their interest. At times, the teacher guided the children's play in the post office center by acting as a participant. For example, she mailed a package, she bought stamps and requested a receipt, and she asked for help in locating an address for a letter that she was sending.

A home-centered, play-centered environment extends children's literacy learning in developmentally appropriate, creative ways. A language-centered environment provides language experiences that are crucial to a beginner's growth as a literacy learner.

Language Experiences

Young children need to have the time and space to explore language in order to clarify its uses and gain facility in its production and reception. Children who experience language and its intricacies take giant steps on the road to becoming literate.

It is no coincidence that many preschool readers are also early writers. They have a strong desire to express themselves in symbolic terms through drawing, scribbling, copying, and, ultimately, producing their own written language. Exploring written language through paper and pencil helps children form expectations that print is meaningful.

Talking, Creating, Singing, and Dancing

The main feature of a language experience approach is that it embraces the natural language of children and uses their background experiences as the basis for learning to read.

Language experience activities in beginning reading instruction permit young children to share and discuss experiences; listen to and tell stories; dictate words, sentences, and stories; and write independently. The teacher can revolve language experiences around speaking, listening, visual expression, singing, movement, and rhythmic activities.

Use conversation to encourage individual or group language experience stories or independent writing. A language experience story is one, as we explain in the next chapter, that is told by the child and written down by the teacher for instructional purposes.

1. *Talk about everyday sights and occurrences.*
2. *Provide problem-solving tasks* (e.g., making a milk shake) or *highly motivating situations* (e.g., making peanut butter and jelly sandwiches) *to elicit oral language.*
3. *Tell stories through pictures.* Wordless picture books are particularly useful for stimulating language development through storytelling and creative writing.
4. *Discuss enjoyable occasions* (e.g., birthdays, holidays, special events such as the World Series, the class picnic).
5. *Use visual experiences to stimulate conversation* (e.g., television, book illustrations, art work). Visual expression through art activity, in particular, provides exciting opportunities for language experiences.

Use art as a vehicle for personal expression. Artistic expression represents a powerful force in children's lives. Through various forms of aesthetic and manipulative activity, children learn that there are many ways to express what they are thinking or feeling. What children draw, paint, or sculpt today can be the basis for what they talk or write about tomorrow and, then what they eventually read.

Every classroom for young children should provide enough space to work on and display art projects. Art materials should include crayons, colored chalk, clay, paints, felt-tip pens, scissors, paste and glue, paper, newsprint (unprinted newspaper), and an assortment of junk (e.g., straws, wire, boxes, soap bars, toothpicks, Styrofoam, pipe cleaners, and anything else that might lend itself to manipulative activity).

Singing, dancing, and other rhythmic activities are valuable means of expression in their own right. Such activities can also be linked easily and naturally to reading and writing instruction. For example, you can:

1. *Encourage readalongs as children sing familiar and favorite songs.* Create large cue cards that contain the lyrics to the songs. As children sing, the teacher directs their at-

tention to the lyrics, moving her hand across the card, left to right, top to bottom, pointing under each word, and synchronizing the movement with the music.

2. *Create new lyrics for familiar songs that have a highly repetitive pattern.* In one kindergarten class, the children changed "Old MacDonald Had a Farm" to "Old MacDonald Had an Amusement Park." Imagine the new lyrics that were contributed by the children!

3. *Create dances that tell a story.* Songs such as "The Eensy Weensy Spider" can be used to encourage movement and interpretation through dance.

4. *Improvise movement stories inspired by poems and familiar stories.* Chenfeld (1978) suggests that as you read with the students, include movement as a way to further express and interpret the reading material. Children make fine choreographers creating spontaneous movement sequences for "The Gingerbread Man," "Peter Cottontail," or other action stories.

Role Playing and Drama

Young children delight in pretending. Role playing and dramatic activities in a beginning reading program not only stimulate the imagination, but also provide many opportunities to use language inventively and spontaneously.

Role playing affords children the chance to approach ordinary or unusual events and situations from different perspectives and points of view. Children begin to recognize that there are different levels and uses of language appropriate for different situations. Role playing can be easily adapted to stimulate writing and to enhance reading comprehension throughout the elementary grades.

The objective of drama in the classroom is self-expression. Children "play along" in structured and unstructured situations. **Dramatic play** activities require very little planning and involve unstructured, spontaneous expression such as pretending to be a leaf falling from a tree or an astronaut going to Mars. *Creative drama,* on the other hand, is more structured in the sense that children often have definite parts to play as they act out a favorite story or event. Props, costumes, and scenery may be called for. A third kind of dramatic activity, *pantomime,* involves wordless communication in which children use their bodies to translate reality and convey meaning.

The teacher should have a dress-up area for dramatic activities. Because drama is so unlike traditional classroom activities, the teacher's approach, much like a parent's, is one of continuous encouragement and facilitation. Consider some of these language experiences.

1. Use children's literature for drama. Folk tales such as *Little Red Riding Hood* or *Henny Penny* provide simple plot structures and clearly defined characters. Action-filled poems can be valuable for pantomime and movement activities.

2. Engage children in problem situations as a start for spontaneous dramatic activity. Rose (1982) suggested the following problems:

Improvisation and creativity expand and enhance classroom self-expression.

- You have been called at school to go home immediately.
- You are waiting in line at McDonald's or Burger King and are very hungry. On two occasions people get ahead of you. What do you do the third time it happens?
- You have just broken your mother's pearl necklace and the pearls are scattered on the floor. You are picking them up when your mother enters the room.
- You run into the police station to report that your bicycle has been stolen. The police seem to doubt your story.

So far, we have scratched the surface in presenting some of the implications of early reading for beginning instruction. However, in the next chapter we will continue the discussion.

SUMMARY

In this chapter we dealt with the developmental aspects of literacy learning in relation to some children's early literate activity. We inquired into the nature of beginning reading instruction by looking at preschoolers' knowledge of and experiences with print. Children bring much to reading. Topics pertaining to a child's cultural, cognitive, and language background were presented.

Young children use what they have learned and experienced daily to make sense out of new events and experiences. As they build positive associations with books through such natural activities as the bedtime story and other types of storybook interaction, children are developing a "set for literacy." Preschoolers are immersed in a world of meaningful print; they exhibit early reading behaviors well before they enter a classroom. What kinds of experiences, then, are needed to get the kindergarten child off to a good start?

Beginning readers benefit from a curriculum that is home-centered, play-centered, and language-centered. Home centered refers to those supportive, individual situations in which a warm, accepting, and patient relationship develops between the teacher and child. Reading to children, sharing books, and assisting with reading are among the activities that can be easily transferred from the parent to the teacher. Play-centered refers to activities that allow children to explore literacy in spontaneous play contexts. Literacy play centers are powerful contexts for helping children experiment with literacy. Language-centered refers to those experiences in which children explore spontaneous activities. Speaking, visual expression, singing, movement and rhythmic activities, role playing, and drama are all instructional devices for teachers who want to approximate ideal conditions for learning to read in their classrooms.

TEACHER-ACTION RESEARCHER

1. Locate a kindergarten or preschool classroom that has a play-centered environment in which children can develop a "feel" for literacy as they experiment with written language. Collect data describing how children experiment with literacy in a natural context. How do play centers promote literacy? What do children do as they pretend play that will assist in their literacy development? Collect information as Avery (1990) did by tape-recording conferences that occur, interviewing children, collecting anecdotes of interactions among the children, and compiling all the information into a study of one or more children in literacy learning.

2. Refer to the Class Works case titled "Kid Watching at the Supermarket," in Box 3.1. Observe a preschool child or several children learning about reading and writing in a natural setting. Unobtrusively record what you see and hear as the child interacts with written language. What do your notes tell you about the child's use of language? In what ways does the child demonstrate knowledge of written language? If an adult is observed interacting with the child, how does the adult's behavior support and encourage language learning? (If possible, observe in a multicultural preschool setting.)

3. Observe a kindergarten or first-grade class during language arts time. Note what the teacher does, the amount of time spent on instructional activities, and the kinds of learning activities initiated during instruction. Keep the following questions in mind to guide your inquiry:

a. Were children read to or were stories told to them?
b. How much time was spent in listening to stories?
c. Describe the instructional situation and how children responded.
d. Describe situations in which a child was given encouragement and support, perhaps with a hug or an accepting word, within the learning situation.
e. Do children spend time completing worksheets?
f. How much time was spent on worksheets?
g. Describe the nature of the exercises in the worksheets and the children's participation in the instructional situation.
h. Did children spend time scribbling, drawing, or writing? If so, how much time was spent in activities such as these? What did the children draw or write? Describe the instructional situation and the children's participation.
i. Describe the classroom discourse and language interactions that occurred during each instruction. How did bilingual children or children with limited English proficiency interact with others? What were the topics of conversation between the teacher and the children and the children with each other? Compare the data you gathered and analyzed with those of other members of the class. What conclusions can be drawn?

4. Analyze the invented spellings of first, second, third, and fourth graders from writing samples that you have collected or from those provided by your instructor. What are the developmental stages of spelling of the children whose writing you have analyzed? What does the analysis of spelling tell you about each child's knowledge of words and of sound-letter relationships? How would you design instruction to help each of the children continue to grow and develop as spellers?

KEY TERMS

literacy development
family literacy
literate environment
scribbling
invented spelling
developmental stages of spelling
intergenerational literacy
Head Start
developmentally appropriate practice
shared book experience
assisted reading
pretend play
literacy play center
language experience activities
dramatic play

CHAPTER 4

Inviting Beginners Into the Literacy Club

BETWEEN THE LINES

In this chapter you will discover:

- **What it means to be a member of the literacy club.**
- **The differences between reading readiness and emergent literacy.**
- **How to immerse beginners in storybook experiences.**
- **How to use language experience stories to build children's confidence and competence with print.**
- **Why beginners must understand the language of instruction.**
- **How to develop phonemic awareness.**
- **How to assess emergent literacy behaviors.**

The first day of school is always full of anticipation and excitement for children and teachers alike. Thoughts of children from previous years flash through Sandra's mind a half hour before she meets a new group of first graders. The room's ready. She's ready. And she's sure that the children will be ready to continue their growth as literacy learners.

This is Sandra's fourth year as a teacher. She's just as eager to get started as she was on her very first day and as full of expectation as her children. She's confident about her ability to work with 6- and 7-year-olds. She knows that she must anchor the teaching of reading and writing in knowledge of what children bring to her classroom, how they learn, and how language works.

Sandra understands that children come to school expecting to learn to read. Sandra begins the first day of the first grade by introducing the children to a poem, which she has printed and illustrated on a large piece of poster board. She reads the poem to the children several times as she points to each word.

SOMETHING ABOUT ME[1]

There's something about me
That I'm knowing.
There's something about me
That isn't showing.

I'm Growing!

When Sandra feels that the children are sufficiently familiar with the poem, she invites individuals to read the poem and to tell the class something about themselves. As each child responds, she creates an "About Me" story by recording on chart paper exactly what each child has said, and then reading the poem aloud.

Joey said, "My best TV show is 'Muppet Babies.' "

Sally said, "I like to eat pizza."

Jeff said, "I have a new baby brother. His name is Tyler."

Jenny said, "My cat wakes me up every morning."

Sandra then makes copies of the poem and the "About Me" story to send home with the first graders at the end of the school day to share with their families.

Through the social interactions that occur in the classroom, Sandra invites all of her students into the **literacy club** on the first day of school. In this club, there are no dues; nobody's excluded from joining. Sandra recognizes that when young children identify themselves as part of a community of readers and writers, and are accepted as readers and writers, they will build upon the literacy behaviors they bring to school. Confidence with print breeds competence.

Frank Smith (1985) coined the term *literacy club* to describe the group of written language users with whom a child interacts. In many ways, the term dramatizes much of the theoretical developments and research findings related to literacy learning in early childhood. If children are to understand reading and what reading is for, they must become members of the literacy club. According to Smith, the only requirement for membership is a mutual acknowledgment of acceptance into a group of people who use written language. That is to say, children must perceive themselves as readers and writers and, in turn, be perceived by others as readers and writers.

Nowhere does knowledge of reading and learning to read play a more significant part in the development of literacy learners than in children's initial encounters with reading instruction in kindergarten and first grade. How teachers view and assess literacy development, plan beginning reading and writing experiences, and interact with learners builds a sturdy bridge between young children's varied interests, backgrounds, and skills, on the

[1] *Read-Aloud Rhymes for the Very Young.* Selected by Jack Prelutsky. New York: Alfred Knopf, 1986.

other hand and the initial confusion they often experience during beginning instruction on the other.

Emergent Literacy or Reading Readiness—What's the Difference?

Reading readiness evolved from the belief that readiness is largely the result of maturation to the present-day conception that children benefit from instructional experiences before engaging in reading. Although early proponents of reading readiness contended that children must reach a certain level of physical, mental, and emotional maturity to profit from teaching, there has been a dramatic shift from a maturational perspective to an instructional emphasis.

From the 1930s, readiness has implied that there is a best time to benefit from reading instruction. The idea of a best time often translated into one-dimensional indicators of reading readiness such as a child's mental maturity as reflected by a score on an intelligence test. The importance of mental age, for example, was supported by the views of Morphett and Washburne (1931). For many years, a 6.5 mental age became the benchmark upon which to decide matters of reading instruction. Even today, there are remnants of the best-time-for-teaching-reading theory; we still award children performance scores on a reading readiness test. But reliance on a single readiness test score, or for that matter mental age, tends to minimize the differences that children bring to reading instruction and negates a developmental view of learning to read.

During the past three decades, there has been a momentous social and cultural push in America toward formal reading instruction for 5- and 6-year-olds. As a result, beginning instruction has focused on the **prereading skills** young children need to learn in order to read. The prevailing thought behind formal instruction is that young children need not wait for a best time to benefit from instruction, *if* the instructional program is carefully designed. Young children *can* be taught the prerequisite skills necessary to learn to read—the earlier the better—through carefully sequenced instruction. Today, every major publisher of basal reading programs provides a readiness strand for its beginning program in kindergarten and first grade.

Reading readiness programs, for the most part, have changed very little in the past 30 years. Readiness programs are based on a logical analysis of reading skills grounded in a bottom-up view of the reading process. As a result, most programs generally include activities to develop prerequisite skills such as auditory memory and discrimination and visual memory and discrimination. In addition, children are expected to master the smallest units of written language (e.g., recognizing letter names and sounds) before progressing to larger units (e.g., letter combinations, words, simple sentences). To facilitate mastery, readiness programs are organized around a "scope and sequence," a hierarchy of skills through which children progress. Monitoring a child's skills acquisition through periodic assessment is a major feature of today's readiness programs.

A predominant view of reading readiness has been to treat it as a period of transition extending over several weeks or months. According to Clay (1979b), a transitional view of readiness upholds the notion that children gradually change from nonreaders to beginning readers. At best, such a view pays lip service to a developmental concept of reading. It leads to the unwarranted assumption that children bring little, if anything, to school in the way of knowledge about and experience with print. Most children are bound to have some knowledge of print and book experiences before entering school, as limited as they may seem in some cases.

Teale and Sulzby (1986) contend that reading readiness, as institutionalized by schools, curricula, and publishers of tests and instructional programs, is no longer an appropriate way to conceptualize instruction for beginners. In its place, they suggest **emergent literacy** as a developmentally appropriate view upon which to build literacy curricula, instructional practice, and assessment for beginners.

Emergent literacy, as we began to develop it in Chapter 3, is a concept that supports learning to read in a positive home environment where children are in the process of becoming literate from birth. Literacy development begins from the time children hear their first nursery rhymes and stories. The acquisition of reading should be as natural as oral language development, given ideal learning conditions. What happens in the classroom impacts on children's emerging literacy skills and concepts of reading, as well as their motivation to read. Children need good role models, invitations to learn, and support in their development toward skilled reading and writing, much of which they can get from effective teachers. Beginning instruction, then, should serve to extend literacy development in early childhood.

Three questions underlie instruction and assessment in an emergent literacy program: (1) What does a child already know about print? (2) What reading behaviors and interests does a child already exhibit? and (3) What does a child need to learn? Answers to these questions will demonstrate that beginning instruction for 5- and 6-year-olds is not a period of time in which children progress from nonreading to reading behavior. When planning beginning instructional experiences for 5- and 6-year-olds, a basic principle of emergent literacy should guide your actions: Rather than thinking about getting children ready for reading, consider what must be done to get literacy instruction ready for children.

Table 4.1 compares readiness and emergent literacy along several dimensions.

If beginners are going to make a smooth transition from emergent to fluent literacy, they must feel from the onset that they belong to a classroom community of readers and writers. The challenge of working with beginners lies in scaffolding learning and weaving together experiences that build on children's knowledge of language and their previous interactions with texts. Working with beginners requires knowing about the book experiences they have had, their desire to read, and their awareness of concepts related to print. Because young children come to school with diverse family literacy backgrounds, their

● TABLE 4.1

Comparison of Emergent Literacy and Reading Readiness

	Emergent literacy	Reading readiness
Theoretical Perspective	Children are in the process of becoming literate from birth and are capable of learning what if means to be a user of written language before entering school.	Children must master a set of basic skills before they can learn to read. Learning to read is an outcome of school-based instruction.
Acquisition of Literacy Skills and Strategies	Children learn to use written language and develop as readers and writers through active engagement with their world. Literacy develops in real-life settings in purposeful ways.	Children learn to read by mastering skills arranged and sequenced in a hierarchy according to their level of difficulty.
Relationship of Reading to Writing	Children progress as readers and writers. Reading and writing (as well as speaking and listening) are interrelated and develop concurrently.	Children learn to read first. The skills of reading must be developed before introducing written composition.
Functional-Formal Learning	Children learn informally through interactions with and modeling from literate significant others and explorations with written language.	Children learn through formal teaching and monitoring (i.e., periodic assessment) of skills
Individual Development	Children learn to be literate in different ways and at different rates of development.	Children progress as readers by moving through a scope and sequence of skills.

acquaintance with texts will vary dramatically. Some will have little or no prior knowledge or experience with books and little interest in learning to read. Others will have rich experiences and considerable desire to extend what they already know about print. Many will fall somewhere between the two extremes. Invitations into the literacy club build on the instructional implications of literacy learning in early childhood. Bethany's story in the Box 4.1 illustrates this point. Storybooks and their many uses beckon young children to membership.

● **BOX 4.1**

Class Works

Bethany's Membership in the Literacy Club: In, Out, and In Again!

Bethany's encounters with reading instruction in kindergarten capture the *disempowerment* that occurs when a young child feels excluded from participation in a literate community (Searcy, 1988). Before entering school, Bethany was an active member of the literacy club. She engaged in much of the literate activity of early readers and writers described in the previous chapter. For example, at 13 months she pointed to a logo in the corner of a place mat at a local fast-food restaurant and read, "Pepsi." By age 2, she was enjoying books and joining in on the reading by supplying words for predictable text. Throughout her early literacy development, Bethany had learned that she did not have to be perfect to belong to the literacy club, and that taking risks was part of what it meant to be a user of written language. But when she entered kindergarten, Bethany soon found that she was "into school and out of the literacy club."

Kindergarten was not what Bethany had expected. Although her teacher was warm, caring, and enthusiastic, the *reading readiness program* was contrary to everything she had learned about literacy and what it meant to be a user of written language. For most of the year, Bethany's "reading" consisted of doing worksheets designed to teach letter names and to associate sounds with letters. For example, early in the school year one worksheet task consisted of drawing lines from "Mr. B with Beautiful Buttons" to pictures whose labels started with the sound of the letter *b.!* Whenever she erred on tasks such as these, her mistakes were corrected in red pencil by the teacher. Eventually, the red marks convinced Bethany that she could not read. It wasn't until April of her kindergarten year that Bethany began to regain her confidence and restore her self-concept as a reader. Her class had finally progressed through the readiness worksheets to exercises that involved reading simple sentences, but the key to her return to the literacy club occurred outside of school at the public library. The children's librarian had encouraged Bethany to read a book by reassuring her that she "could do it." Literacy was beginning to make sense again.

REFLECTIVE INQUIRY

- What is the significance of Bethany's story?
- How do the actions of teachers help or hinder children's literacy development?

Immersing Beginners in Storybook Literacy Experiences

Storybook experiences unlock the mysteries of reading, rivet children's attention to print, and provide models of writing which build upon and extend the young child's concepts of texts and how they work. In the previous chapter we explored the value of reading storybooks aloud, repeated readings of familiar stories, and shared reading experiences around the use of **big books**—enlarged versions of children's storybooks. As Figure 4.1 illustrates, a literature-rich curriculum for young children will offer numerous opportunities to interact with storybooks. Literacy lessons immerse children in storybook experiences. These experiences aren't mutually exclusive, but as the illustration in Figure 4.1 suggests, they are interlocking and connected. All are designed to further children's explorations with texts and to develop concepts related to print as well as strategies to construct meaning.

Immersing beginners in storybook literacy experiences, which include readalouds and readalongs, **shared reading** and **shared writing,** rereadings of favorite texts, and independent reading and writing, helps to accomplish a variety of instructional goals, all of which are designed to:

- Motivate beginners to want to read and write.
- Interest beginners in listening to, reading, and writing stories with emphasis on predicting, sharing, and extending personal meanings.
- Help beginners understand what reading and writing are all about.
- Encourage beginners to respond to stories by drawing, writing, and dramatizing their explorations of texts.
- Invite beginners to construct meaning through the use of picture cues and storybook illustrations.
- Help beginners to gain familiarity with "book language" and the meaning of terms that figure in literacy instruction.
- Teach beginners about directionality, the left-to-right, top-to-bottom orientation of written language.
- Teach beginners the meaning of *word* and the function of space in establishing boundaries between words.
- Teach beginners to predict words that "must come next" in a sentence.

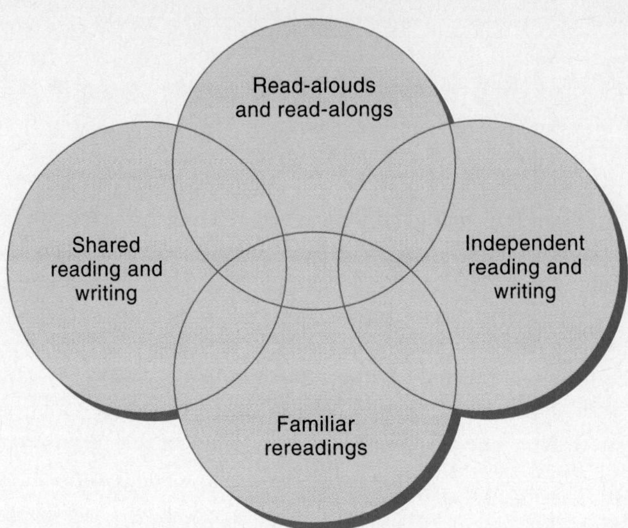

● **FIGURE 4.1** Storybook literacy experiences for beginners

- Teach beginners to recognize words that they are interested in learning or that occur frequently in meaningful contexts.
- Teach beginners alphabetic/symbolic principles of written language.

These goals are not sequential in the sense that one must be accomplished before another is attempted. In classrooms where storybook experiences are an integral part of the school day, several or more may be accomplished over time in combination or simultaneously. The translation of these goals into classroom activities and experiences lies in having a developmental perspective of beginning reading. Big books, as hinted in the previous chapter, are a recent phenomenon in American classrooms and provide a developmentally appropriate context for shared reading and writing experiences.

The Big Book Phenomenon in American Classrooms

Big books are one of the easiest and most effective ways to get beginners involved in the exploration of texts. The use of big books as an instructional resource began in the late 1960s in New Zealand, when teachers began to make their own big books from heavy brown butcher paper. Teacher-made big books retold nursery rhymes, poems, and popular stories such as "The Gingerbread Man." The critical feature common to these big books was that the stories and poems provided beginners with strong rhythms and predictable patterns of language.

The predictability of the plot and language of big books makes them easy to understand and remember. For example, after two or three readings, most 5- and 6-year-olds easily memorize Joy Cowley and June Melser's *Hairy Bear* (Wright Group), Mem Fox's *Hattie and the Fox* (Macmillan, 1987), or Bill Martin Jr.'s *Brown Bear, Brown Bear, What Do You See?* (Holt, Rinehart, and Winston). Big books such as these with their simple, repetitive refrains, colorful animal illustrations, and cumulative plot endings allow children to make predictions and participate immediately in shared reading experiences.

New Zealand researchers, spearheaded by the pioneering work of Don Holdaway, observed and documented the influence of big book teaching on children's literacy development and their social interactions in the classroom (Holdaway, 1979). Children were learning to read naturally in the company of other children and the teacher. In the 1970s, authors such as Joy Cowley and June Melser began publishing the first big books in New Zealand for use in classrooms. Cowley's amazingly popular *Mrs. Wishy Washy* is used today in classrooms for beginners throughout the world. According to Cowley (1991), the popularity of her big books is in the inherent appeal they have for children: "It is important to me . . . that the big books I write relate directly to the child's world and not to an adult view of what the world is or should be" (p. 19). (See Box 4.2.) Today's big books not only capture the child's view of the world, but they range in content from traditional tales, to books of poems, to informational books in different content areas.

The popularity of big books in New Zealand coincided with whole language movements throughout English-speaking countries. Big books soon began to appear in classrooms throughout the United States and became associated with whole language teaching. In addition to the pleasure and enjoyment that children get when they participate in shared readings and rereadings of big books, big book formats are versatile in helping to achieve all of the above-listed instructional goals for beginners. The chart in Figure 4.2 suggests some of the activities that teachers and children engage in when they use big books.

Shared Reading and Shared Writing

When the teacher and children engage in shared reading and writing experiences, they demonstrate that literacy learning is social and collaborative. In shared reading, they collaborate to construct meaning and enjoy a story. And in the process, children develop strategies and concepts related to print. In shared writing, the teacher and students collaborate to create a text together. The texts that are created—lists, letters, labels, story retellings, alternative texts (of stories that have been shared), experience charts, and the like—demonstrate some of the important uses of written language and show children what reading is all about.

Shared reading and shared writing, as you might surmise, are reciprocal processes. What children read together is the basis for what they will write together; and in turn, what they write together is the basis for what they will read together. And what they read and write together often is the springboard for independent reading and writing.

During shared writing, there are many opportunities for explicit instruction in which teachers demonstrate early writing strategies (Clay, 1985). Following steps associated with the language experience approach, the teacher becomes a scribe for a text dictated by the

● BOX 4.2

Joy Cowley on Big Books

Big book reading is a big plus for all children. It puts children in a no-risk situation where they can read with a group at their own skill level. Children who lack confidence in reading will especially benefit from big book reading. Their reading is reinforced by their peers, and they can enjoy the pleasure of stories within a group until they are ready to attempt the stories on their own.

Enthusiasm is the key emotion associated with big book reading. A confident, enthusiastic teacher will readily communicate those feelings to his or her students. Usually I introduce a big book by reading the story a couple of times to the class and inviting discussion. Then the students and I can read the book together. Big books invite student participation, not just in reading but in using a pointer for following along, turning pages, and so on. Children may extend the large group experience by reading to each other in smaller groups, reading individually, dramatizing the text, making recordings complete with sound effects, and writing their own books using a similar theme or pattern.

Whatever the follow-up or innovation, it is important to remember that reading and writing are activities we do to share ourselves with others. Big books are especially good tools for sharing. It's for that reason, I think, that teachers around the world are having such success in using big books to bring literature to the lives of children.

Source: Joy Cowley, "Joy of Big Books," *Instructor* (October, 1991), p. 19.

What the teacher does	What the child does	Objective
Before reading		
(1) Stimulates discussion about relevant content and concepts in text.	(1) Talks and listens to others talk about relevant content and concepts.	(1) To focus listening and speaking on vocabulary and ideas about to be met in print. To activate background knowledge related to text.
(2) Reads aloud title and author; uses words *title* and *author* and briefly explains what they mean.	(2) Notes what the words on the book cover represent.	(2) To build vocabulary and concepts: title, author, authorship.
(3) Asks children what they think story might be about, based on title, cover. Or, thinks aloud about what s/he thinks this story might be about.	(3) Uses clues from title and cover together with background knowledge to formulate predictions about the story. Or, observes teacher model the above.	(3) To use clues from text and background knowledge to make inferences and formulate predictions.
(4) Shows pleasure and interest in anticipation of the reading.	(4) Observes as teacher models personal interest and eagerness toward the reading.	(4) To build positive attitudes toward books and reading.
During reading (teacher reads aloud)		
(5) Gives lively reading. Displays interest and delight in language and story line.	(5) Observes teacher evoke meaningful language from print.	(5) To understand that print carries meaning.
(6) Tracks print with hand or pointer.	(6) Follows movement of hand or pointer.	(6) To match speech to print. Directionality: left to right.
(7) Thinks aloud about her/his understanding of certain aspects of the story (self query, making predictions, drawing conclusions, etc.).	(7) Observes as teacher monitors her/his own understandings.	(7) To develop an understanding of the reading process as thinking with text.
(8) Hesitates at predictable parts in the text. Allows children to fill in possible words or phrases.	(8) Fills in likely words for a given slot.	(8) To use semantic and syntactic clues to determine what makes sense.
(9) At appropriate parts in a story, queries children about what might happen next.	(9) Makes predictions about what might happen next in the story.	(9) To use story line to predict possible events and outcomes.

● **FIGURE 4.2** Big book activities before, during, and after reading

Source: L. Galda, B. Cullinan, and D. Strickland, *Language, Literacy, and the Child* (Fort Worth, TX: Harcourt Brace Jovanovich, 1993), pp. 102–103. Reprinted by permission.

What the teacher does	What the child does	Objective
After reading		
(10) Guides discussion about key ideas in the text. Helps children relate key concepts.	(10) Participates in discussion of important ideas in the text.	(10) To reflect on the reading: to apply and personalize key ideas in text.
(11) Asks children to recall important or favorite parts. Finds corresponding part of the text (perhaps with help of children) and rereads.	(11) Recalls and describes specific events; parts of text.	(11) To use print to support and confirm discussion.
(12) Guides group rereading of all or specific parts of text for errorless repetition and reinforcement.	(12) Joins in the reading in parts s/he feels confident about.	(12) To develop fluency and confidence through group reading.
(13) Uses cloze activities (flaps to cover words) to involve children in meaningful prediction of words. Gives praise for all meaningful (contextually plausible) offerings. Discusses response with children.	(13) Fills in possible words for a given slot.	(13) To use semantic and syntactic clues to determine what words fit in a slot and why.
After reading, for repeated readings only		
(14) Focuses children's attention on distinctive features and patterns in the text: repeated words, repeated word beginnings (letters, consonant clusters), punctuation marks, etc. Uses letter names and correct terminology to discuss these features. Extends discussion to developmentally appropriate level.	(14) Notes distinctive features and patterns pointed out by teacher and attempts to find others on her/his own.	(14) To analyze a known text for distinctive features and patterns. To develop an understanding of the elements of decoding within a meaningful context.
(15) Makes books and charts available for independent reading.	(15) Select books and charts for independent reading and reads them at own pace.	(15) To increase confidence and understanding of the reading process by practicing it independently.

● **FIGURE 4.2** (Continued)

children. The focus, first and foremost, is always on the composing of the text. The teacher, as well as the children who volunteer, will often read, then reread, the text for emphasis and make additions and changes to clarify meaning. Within this meaningful, collaborative context, opportunities abound to demonstrate early writing strategies such as word-by-word matching, left-to-right directionality, use of space to create boundaries between words, and other print conventions. As children gain experience with the conventions of print, the teacher uses shared writing activities to focus on spelling patterns and word analysis.

Let's take a look at how shared reading and shared writing are played out in Stephanie Hawking's first-grade class (Hawking, 1989). Stephanie and the children have been sharing Jack Kent's *The Fat Cat* (Scholastic). After the third rereading, she and the children decide to write an alternative text to the story, which they titled, "The Fat Cat at Big Boy." The inspiration for the alternative story is the Big Boy restaurant which is located near the school.

The children wondered what would happen if The Fat Cat ever prowled for food at the Big Boy. So their first shared writing experience involved brainstorming a list of what The Fat Cat would eat at Big Boy. One student, Miranda, suggested that The Fat Cat could eat men. Stephanie invited her to write the word "men" on a list, saying, "You know how to write 'ten.' Can you use ten to help you write men?" (p. 7). Miranda first practiced on the blackboard and then wrote *men* on a chart titled "Big Boy." The class worked on the chart for several days, and when it was finished, the children taped it to the wall to use as a resource.

Stephanie and the children then began writing the alternative text together. Talk, as you might predict, was crucial to the success of the story. As Stephanie explains, "The talk surrounding shared writing is a rich source of information. . . . As the children discuss what to write and how it should be written, the teacher finds out more about their developing concepts of story and their understanding of the writing process" (p.7). The class began by talking about how to begin the story. Everyone agreed that it should begin with the words "once upon a time" because it was going to be a "fake" story. Stephanie used this "teachable moment" to briefly underscore the connection the children made between their story and the fairy tale genre. She told them that another name for a particular kind of fake story is a folk tale.

As the text began to develop, Stephanie wrote on the chart as children dictated, but she also invited the children to add to the story by volunteering to write parts. This strategy is sometimes called **interactive writing.** Stephanie observed what the children who volunteered knew about the mechanics and conventions of writing and listened to their comments and suggestions as other children added to the text. When she served as a scribe for the children, she was able to focus their attention on the use of quotation marks for portions of the text that contained dialogue. As the class finished each page of the chart, the children would tape it to the wall so that they could refer to it whenever necessary to check on continuity of story line. At other times, they would search for the spelling of a word they knew had already been written on a previous page.

The shared interactive writing of "The Fat Cat at Big Boy" eventually was made into a class big book by the children. The children illustrated the story with drawings, decided on the sequencing of pages, and assembled the entire big book text, rereading each page several times. Stephanie served as proofreader for the final copy—the public copy—of the big book by changing children's invented spellings to conventional forms. The big book's construction followed guidelines similar to those given in Box 4.3.

Stephanie's class was so proud of the big book they had created that they decided to dedicate it "To All the Cats in the Neighborhood."

Alternative texts such as *The Fat Cat at Big Boy* are popular forms of shared writing in Stephanie's class. Some of the children were so excited about the project that they wanted to write Fat Cat stories on their own. And they did. What began as a shared reading of a popular storybook for young children turned into independent reading and writing:

> As children finished writing and illustrating their own books, they read their stories to the rest of the group. We began with a shared reading of Jack Kent's *The Fat Cat* and ended with independent reading of their own stories. Nestled in between was our shared writing of an alternative text. That shared writing evolved from the shared reading and in turn gave birth to their own independent reading and writing.
>
> (Hawking, 1989, p. 9)

A child doesn't learn to read and write overnight. Nor, as we have shown, is it just in school that children learn all that they need to know to be able to read and write. Concepts of literacy develop gradually. As children progress, certain kinds of learning are necessary. These types of learning precede and accompany literacy behavior.

Learning What Reading and Writing Are All About

First of all, the child must be able to figure out what spoken language and written language have in common. Without learning the relationship between speech and print, the beginner will never make sense of reading or achieve independence in it. Earlier we suggested that reading often to children, repeating favorite bedtime stories, and providing opportunities to draw, scribble, and interact with print in their immediate environment are

● BOX 4.3

Publishing Big Books in the Classroom

Big book publishing is an excellent collaborative group writing activity. Because children love big books, they will enjoy their own published stories. The models and directions below will involve children in creating their own big books for classroom use.

MODELS

Use commercially published big books as models for the types that children will make. Consider these possibilities:

- Poem books
- Alternative books (based on stories read in class)
- Alphabet and number books
- Reaction books (the scariest thing I ever saw)
- Riddle and rhyme books
- Informational books (based on theme studies)
- Innovations on a text (imitative stories based on the predictable language patterns of books read in class)

DIRECTIONS FOR MAKING BIG BOOKS*

Mural Style

- Fold even-size pages of butcher paper in a back-and-forth manner (each page should be 12 inches wide). Fold one page per child, plus one each for the cover and the title page. If you plan to display sculpturally (see *display options*, below), make sure to back each page with oaktag or cardboard.

Source: Ethel Huttar, "Do-It-Yourself Big Books." *Instructor,* October 1991, p. 21.

(continued)

● **BOX 4.3** *(continued)*

- Children can draw and color directly onto their assigned pages, or glue on illustrations and text. This kind of big book does not easily lend itself to lamination.

Construction-Paper Style

- Have students draw and write directly onto 12-by-18-inch white construction paper.
- After each page is decorated, laminate or cover with contact paper.
- Put pages in sequence. Turn the first two pages face-down, lay on a flat surface and bind with masking or colored craft tape. Continue taping pages to the already-bound ones, in right-to-left fashion. Be sure to fold the hinged pages back and forth as you finish each one to keep the book flexible.

Variations

- Create a book that never stops by continuing the story line and illustrations right around the back of the last page, ending up on the reverse of the title page.
- Make an upside-down topsy-turvy book by turning the book over and using the reverse side in regular left-to-right fashion. This can be done with two separate stories or with two madeup versions of a favorite fairy tale.
- Use real objects as illustrations if they complement the story. Some you might try include photos, stickers, wrappers, and yarn. Staple, glue, or stitch in place before laminating. There will be a tiny bulge on any page you decorate this way.
- Use colorful sentence-strips to fit the pages above or below the illustrations. Have the children write text onto the strips.

Display Options

- Hang with clothespins from an overhead wire; use a clamp to hold the book's pages while you read aloud (if the clamp has holes, hang the book from a hook); display sculpturally on the floor or around a table; hang across a bulletin board.

some of the ways that children naturally learn to make sense out of reading and its uses. Nevertheless, many 5-year-olds enter school with only vague notions of the purpose and nature of reading. They are not yet aware that what is said can be written, that written language is made up of words and sentences, or that reading involves directionality, attending to the spacing between words, punctuation cues, and other conventions of print. There are several ways of going about this important instructional task.

Making Beginners Aware of the Uses of Written Language

From the beginning of their school experience children must learn that the value of reading or writing lies in its uses as a tool for communicating, understanding, and enjoying. A 5-year-old or a 75-year-old should engage in reading and writing for real reasons and in real situations. Effective teachers make their own opportunities, and should consider teaching about the uses of written language when any interesting or natural occasion arises in the classroom.

> *ITEM:* The teacher and children are gathered around the guinea pig cage discussing their new pet. The teacher is explaining the food guinea pigs eat and is showing the children the food they will be feeding the pet. One of the children remembers that the class goldfish died because too much food was put in the bowl. The teacher suggests that the class make a sign to put on the package telling the right amount of food and a chart to put near the cage to be checked on the day he is fed. She discusses the reasons these written records will help. (Taylor and Vawter, 1978, p. 942)

Situations such as the guinea pig scenario evolve naturally in the classroom. Nevertheless, seizing the opportunity to help children recognize the value of reading and writing requires a certain amount of awareness and commitment. For example, Taylor and Vawter (1978) illustrates how two teachers approach an everyday event differently. As children prepare for a field trip to a farm, one kindergarten teacher passes out name tags routinely and without explanation. Another teacher, however, poses a problem to be solved by the children: "If the farmer wants to ask one of us a question, how can we help him know our names?" Through give-and-take discussion, the children offer solutions that range from "tell him," to "I don't know," to "wear our names." As the discussion progresses, the teacher passes out the name tags and suggests that names are written so that someone can read them and that writing a name helps to identify someone.

In Chapter 1 we outlined the **uses of oral language.** These language functions can and should be adapted to print at the beginning of instruction. Not only will children become aware of the purposes of written language, but many of the activities outlined below build word awareness. Therefore, beginners should be introduced to some of the more obvious uses of print.

In general, the classroom should reflect a living example of written language put to purposeful ends. The classroom environment should be filled with print to suit specific instructional goals. Print should be evident everywhere in the form of labels for classroom

Monday	Tuesday	Wednesday	Thursday	Friday
awful	foggy	sunny	________	________
rainy	cloudy	clear	________	________
sticky	dark	dry	________	________

objects, simple messages, rules, directions, and locations where a specific activity takes place such as a story-reading area or an art center. Specifically, consider these uses of written language.

Perpetuating Uses. Show children how to bridge the gap between time and space through print, or *perpetuate.* To do this, *keep records and charts of a daily activity.* For example, Durkin (1980) recommends developing a weekly weather chart with the days of the week at the top and slots for inserting descriptive cards under each day. The children can then use words to describe the day's weather.

Post the names of room helpers for each week. Each morning, make a point of going to the chart and having the children identify who will help the teacher for the day.

Vote or poll children on various classroom events or activities and tally the results. For example, ask children to suggest names for the new pet rabbit. List the names, limiting the number to three or four possible choices, and tally the results for the children to see.

- Thumper
- Whitey
- Long Ears

Use children as messengers to deliver notes to other teachers or to parents. Explain the purpose of the note and why it was written. Or *display notes from the principal congratulating children for work well done.* Also post thank-you notes, letters, the school lunch menu for each day, as well as a host of other forms of communication.

Finally, *keep a classroom scrapbook, beginning from the first day of school and including important events throughout the year.* For example, use Polaroid photographs or magazine pictures, and record the importance of each event.

Regulatory, Authoritative-Contractual Uses. Show children how print can be used to control and direct behavior, and to establish rules and agreements. For example, *list classroom rules and use print to give directions such as lining up for the bus or going to the library. Establish official written contracts with children for various classroom activities (e.g., clean-up after art activities, taking milk count for the week).*

> OFFICIAL CONTRACT
>
> ____________________ *hereby agrees to* ____________________
> (*name*) (*activity*)
>
> for ______________
> (*date*)

To use print to give directions a teacher can *make recipe charts for cooking projects* that may include pictures and words explaining what to do. Pictures can depict *ingredients* such as flour, sugar, or eggs (cut from a magazine advertisement) or *processes* (e.g., a sketch of eggs being broken). In addition, children can *follow directions with clue cards that use pictures and simple words or they can play scavenger hunt using simple messages to direct the hunt.*

Instrumental Uses. Children should learn that print can be used to express personal needs. Teachers and children can *list materials needed to participate in various activities:*

Art	**Music**	**Building**
a. clay	bells	wood
b. scissors	shakers	glue
c. paint	piano	cardboard
d. brushes	record player	blocks

Planting	**Field Trip**	**Sleepover**
e. seeds	lunch	toothbrush
f. water	boots	P.J.'s
g. pots	warm clothes	pillow
h. tools	25¢	teddy bear

The teacher can write (dictated by the children) Christmas lists or birthday wishes. Signs can be used to invite children to participate in various activities:

It's storytime!

Line up for the playground.

Diversion Uses. Demonstrate the value of print as a tool for enjoyment, or *diversion. Read aloud to children on a daily basis.* Also consider storytelling. (In Chapter 9 we will explain a variety of reading aloud and storytelling procedures and activities.) In particular, introduce children to humorous and nonsensical literature. Consider such classics as Dr. Seuss's *Cat in the Hat* (1957), Mayer's *The Billygoofang* (1968), Pincus's *Tell Me a Mitzi* (1970), and Krauss's *The Backward Day* (1950). Read to children those that you especially enjoy.

Tell puns, jokes, riddles, brain teasers, and the like. For example, ask children, "What's white and can be poured in a glass?" and record the responses. Or consider posting a riddle and joke on a section of the bulletin board, with the answer or punch line written on the inside flap.

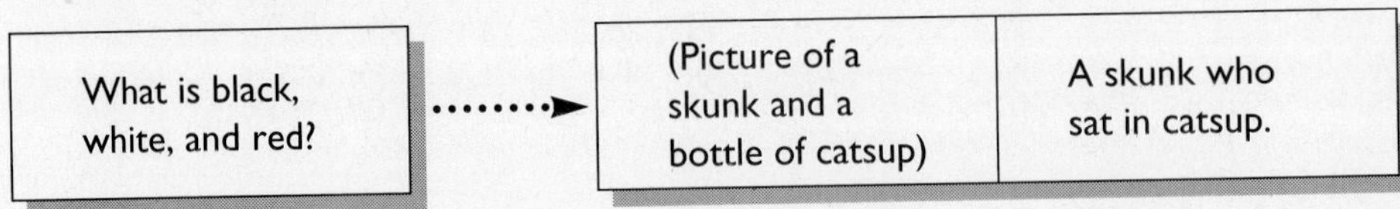

Use simple language patterns to introduce children to the rhythms of language. Later in the year use **patterned stories** and poems to model language patterns in writing. These patterned stories are highly predictable, enjoyable, and repetitious enough that children are naturally attracted to them. Bill Martin's *Instant Readers* or Dr. Seuss's materials develop children's sensitivity to hearing language. The following lines by Dr. Seuss (1960) provide an example:

One fish, two fish.
Red fish, blue fish.

This one has a little star.
This one has a little car.

As the year progressed in one kindergarten class, children were creating their own writing by dictating familiar patterns to the teacher.

One bear, two bear.
White bear, brown bear.

This one has a big red nose.
This one has big fat toes.

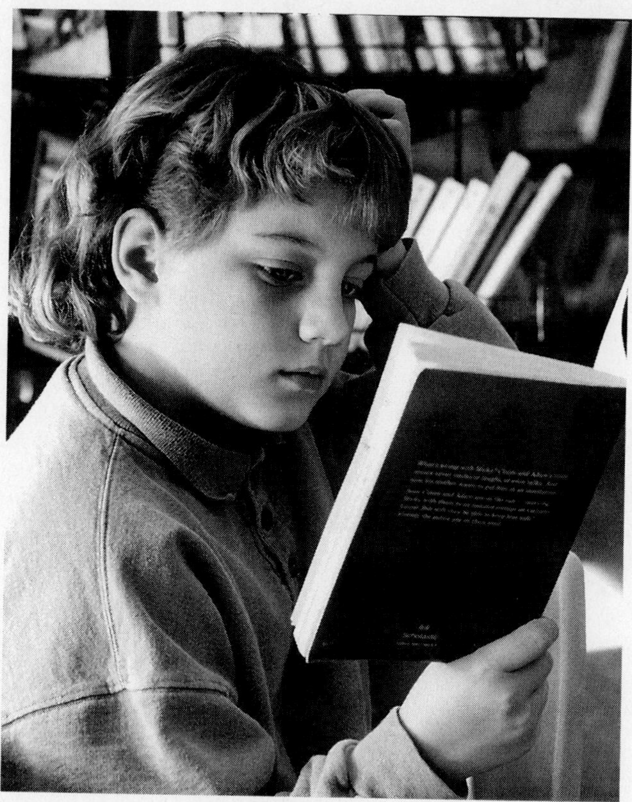

Some children show consistent interest in reading books on their own.

Personal Uses. Children need to learn that written language can be used to express individuality, pride, and awareness of self—a *personal* use of language. *Develop a "this is me" book for each child.* The book might be bound and contain the child's drawings and descriptions of self and family. The first page might begin, "This is me," and include a self-portrait drawn by the child. Other pages may include: This is my family, this is my pet. My favorite game is ______________. My favorite book is ______________. I like ______________. I want to be ______________. My best friend is ______________.

In a similar vein, have the students make *"me" cards that tell the names of pets, favorite toys, books, colors, television programs, or movies. Names of places of interest, places recently visited, or exciting places to explore in the community can also be included.*

As children develop letter and sound awareness, have them suggest self-descriptive words for each letter in their names: jolly, open, happy, nice. *Ask children for "best" words and write them on the blackboard.* Then read them to other members of the class. *Write words that name special people, such as family members or friends.* Then attach a photograph of the person to accompany the name.

Creating Awareness Through Language Experience Stories

What more appropriate way to help children understand what reading is all about than to show them how language is transcribed into print. A **language experience** story is just what it implies—an account that is told aloud by a child and printed by another person. In the beginning of instruction there are numerous ways to involve children in producing experience stories. For example, many of the suggestions for teaching about the uses of written language in the previous section can serve to stimulate the child's dictation or, for that matter, a group-dictated story. Not only does an experience story vividly show the relationship between speech and print, but it also introduces children to the thrill of personal authorship.

This doesn't mean that children should not engage in independent writing experiences. However, when language experience stories are coupled with regular writing time, children make great strides in learning about written language. Some argue that language experience activities are superfluous in light of the recent emphasis on writing process. (Read Chapter 5 for an extended discussion.) We disagree. From a learning-to-read perspective, young people will benefit greatly from *both* language experience and writing.

The value of language experience lies in the physical ease by which text is produced *to achieve reading instructional goals.* When a child dictates, the physical burden of writing is removed. This often results in more of a child's ideas being put in print than would otherwise be possible in beginning situations. In Chapter 5, we advocate regular, ongoing writing activity from the first day that children enter school. Dictated language experience stories should be phased out as children's independent writing fluency increases.

When children have opportunities to converse naturally and spontaneously, their language is likely to be colorful and expressive, to have an almost poetic quality. For example, the following language experience story was based on a conversation among a group of 5-year-olds as they experienced the visit of a pet mouse. It was recorded verbatim by Mrs. Ruttan, their kindergarten teacher.

This mouse is soft.
Soft as a baby sister?
Soft as a little tiny ball?
She's so small somebody could step on her.

I'm afraid to hold her.
I'll touch her and pet her,
But I'm afraid to hold her.
Does her tail tickle?
Does it really?
Are you scared of a mouse?
No. But they tickle, you know.

Feels like a pillow in my hand.
Feels like I could sleep on her.
Feels like a feather.

I just love mouses.
I wish we had our very own mouse.
I held her for just a minute.
Her claws tickled me.
She was soft though.
I told you I liked mouses.

Study another language experience story based on a conversation a group of children had about a new baby guinea pig in Mrs. Ruttan's class.

We have a baby guinea pig.
Her name is Nothing.
She's not much of anything at all.
She doesn't even weigh a pound.

She wants to hide from us.
Maybe she's scared.
Why should she be scared?
This is the first time she saw us.
I think she's scared of us.

Maybe she's just not used to us.
Maybe she's just playing hide-and-go-seek.
Maybe she's got to take lessons about knowing about people.

Much can be learned about what young children think and know and how they feel through language experience-based instruction. An emergent literacy curriculum becomes more relevant, meaningful, and appropriate when it is based on children's own language, existing knowledge, and interests.

Steps to Follow in Producing Language Experience Stories. A child can dictate a complete story, or several children can collaborate on an account by contributing individual sentences. In either case, the first step is to provide a stimulus (e.g., a classroom guinea pig, pictures, concrete objects, an actual experience a child has had) that will lead to dictation. Whatever the stimulus, it should be unusual and interesting enough for children to want to talk about it and to remember it two or three days later when the dictation is reread.

As children dictate, it's important to keep their spoken language intact. Therefore, write down exactly what is said regardless of whether grammatical differences exist in the dictated account or sentences are less than complete. By capturing language just as it is spoken, the teacher preserves its integrity and ensures the child's total familiarity with the print to be read.

Once the story is written down, the teacher should read it aloud several times, carefully but steadily moving left to right, top to bottom, and pointing to each word or line as it is read and then sweeping to the next line. Next, the account should be read in unison with the teacher continuing to model left-to-right, top-to-bottom orientation to print.

A dictated story need not be long. It can represent free-flowing language or controlled responses elicited by guiding questions. Suppose students are conversing about their summer activities. The teacher might say, "Let's tell each other what we did on our summer vacations." Jim begins, "I went fishing for the first time." As he says this, Mrs. Phillips, the kindergarten teacher, writes this verbatim on an "experience chart" (a large sheet of newsprint). The other children contribute to the story with Mrs. Phillips writing each contribution beginning with the child's first name. The account was dictated as follows:

Jim said, "I went fishing for the first time."

Dory said, "We went to my grandma and grandpa's in Florida."

Tony said, "I didn't do nothing but swim."

Sheila said, "My family and me fished too."

Michele said, "I went to Sea World."

The Value of Language Experience. Examine what can be accomplished when young children engage in the writing of language experience stories (Durkin, 1980). You can:

- Motivate children to want to read.
- Personalize instruction.
- Demonstrate the connection between spoken and written language.
- Demonstrate left-to-right, top-to-bottom orientation of written English.
- Demonstrate that the end of the line does not always mean the end of a thought.
- Demonstrate the value of written language for preserving information, ideas, and feelings.
- Teach the meaning of "word" and the function of space in establishing word boundaries.
- Teach the function of capitalization and punctuation.

In Mrs. Phillips's case, the story was read three times as the children watched her move left to right, top to bottom. Next, they read the story aloud two more times as she continued to model left-to-right orientation. She then had each child read his or her contribution, directing the children to "read it the way you said it." As a child read, she moved her hand along the bottom of each line coordinating pointing with the child's voice, and reading in unison with each child.

Mrs. Phillips wanted to build confidence among her readers as she unobtrusively provided them with valuable learning opportunities. In addition to a "reading experience," she also spent time engaging the children in building the concept of "word." First, she read the entire story in a natural speaking manner, pointing to each word as it was being read. By suggesting to the children that they read their individualized contributions, she reinforced word understanding. Mrs. Phillips also asked the children questions such as, "Which word appears the most?" and discussed how space separates one word from another. Finally, Mrs. Phillips asked the children to draw an illustration for the sentence or part that each contributed to the account. These illustrations were pasted around the chart as they were completed and the chart was posted on a bulletin board for other class members to read.

Learning About the Language of Instruction

Children's understanding of the relationship between speech and print is a vital first step in learning to read. They become aware of what reading is all about by recognizing the functionality of reading—that the purpose of reading, in its broadest sense, is to communicate ideas. A second step, or stage, is to become aware of the technical features of reading (Downing, 1979). These technical features (e.g., printed letters, words, sentences, syllables, sounds, punctuation marks, etc.) make up children's "technical vocabulary" for reading, or according to J. F. Reid (1966), the language available to children "to talk and think about the activity of reading itself" (p. 57). To understand the technical features of reading, children must develop **linguistic awareness.**

Five- and six-year-olds may not be aware that words are language units. Spoken language, after all, is a steady stream of sounds that flow one into the other. Words and other print conventions (e.g., punctuation marks) were created to better represent spoken language in print, and thus, facilitate the reading of written language. For the 5-year-old, the six-word written message—*Did you visit the fire station?*—sounds like one big word—*Didjavisitthefirestation?* Even more difficult concepts for young children to learn are that spoken words are made up of smaller sounds, phonemes, that written words are made up of letters, and that in a written word there is a close approximation between letters and sounds.

If children are to succeed in reading, they must acquire linguistic awareness and understand the language of reading instruction. They must learn the technical terms and labels that are needed to talk and think about reading and to carry out instructional tasks. What, for example, is the child's concept of "reading"? Of a "word"? Of a "sound"? Does the child confuse "writing" with "drawing" and "letter" with "number" when given a set of directions? Without an awareness of these terms, cognitive confusion in the classroom mounts quickly for the child (Downing, 1979). The teacher's job is to make explicit what each child knows implicitly about written language.

The technical features of written language are learned gradually by children and are best taught through real reading and readinglike activities, and through discussions designed to build concepts and to untangle the confusion that children may have. Within the context of shared-book experiences, language experience stories, and writing activities, children will develop linguistic sophistication with the technical features of print. These vehicles for instruction provide teachers not only with diagnostic information about children's print awareness, but also form the basis for explicit instruction and discussion.

Agnew (1982) shows how to use language experience stories to assess young children's emerging print awareness. She proposed several procedures and tasks, some of which are outlined below:

PROCEDURES[2]

1. Obtain a short dictated story by the child.
2. Print three or four nouns or verbs from the story on index cards.
3. Print two sentences from the story on separate pieces of paper.
4. Have available a supply of separate letters made from wood, felt, cardboard, etc.
5. Ask the child to complete any or all of the tasks outlined below. Record responses and impressions on the evaluation form.
6. Results should be viewed as tentative hypotheses about the child's print awareness. You'll want to validate results through classroom observation.

TASKS

1. Ask the child to point to any word on the chart story, then to "cup" his or her hands around or circle the word. (The child does not have to say the word, but only show that he or she knows where a word begins and ends.) Ask the child to repeat the task with three or four other words.
2. Ask the child to match an individual word card with the same word in the story. (The child does not have to say the word; he or she simply needs to make a visual match.) If the word occurs more than once in the story, ask the child to locate the word in another place in the story. Repeat the task with several other word cards.
3. Ask the child to match a sentence with its counterpart from the story. (The child does not have to read the sentence.) Repeat the task with the other sentence.
4. Show the child an individual word card and provide him or her with the individual letters necessary to spell the word. Ask the child to build the word he or she sees on the card, using the separate letters. Ask the child for the names of the letters he or she is using. Probe the child about his or her understanding of the difference between letters and words. Repeat the exercise with two or three other word cards.
5. Ask the child to point to any letters he or she can name in the story. (Note whether the child points to letters rather than words.)

As part of a research study to investigate young children's acquisition of concepts about print, Marie Clay (1979a) developed the Concepts About Print Test. She examined not only what knowledge of print children possessed, but also how their understanding of

---

[2] Adapted from "Using Children's Dictated Stories to Assess Code Consciousness" by Ann T. Agnew, *The Reading Teacher,* January 1982, pp. 451–52. Reprinted by permission of Ann T. Agnew and the International Reading Association.

print changed. The underlying question that guided the study asked, "To what degree do young children possess reading-related concepts and linguistic abilities considered to be essential in learning to read?"

The Concepts About Print Test is individually administered to a child within the context of an interview. The examiner asks the child if he or she will help in the reading of a story. For example, if the test were being used by a teacher to acquire diagnostic information, particularly for children experiencing difficulty in a beginning program, the teacher might tell the child, "I'm going to read you a story, but I want you to help me." A child's book, *Sand,* is then introduced to the child to begin the assessment interview. During the interview, which usually takes 15 to 25 minutes to complete, up to 24 questions may be asked to evaluate concepts about print such as directionality and the differences between word and letters.

In addition to *Sand,* Clay (1979d) developed a second child's book, *Stones,* to also be used to assess concepts of print. Full instructions for the administration of the *Concepts About Print Test* may be found in Clay's book, *The Early Detection of Reading Difficulties: A Diagnostic Survey with Recovery Procedures* (1985). In Box 4.4 the types of reading-related and linguistic concepts tapped by Clay's assessment tool are examined.

In subsequent sections of this chapter, additional strategies for instruction and assessment are suggested.

● **BOX 4.4**

Reading-Related and Linguistic Concepts Assessed in the Concepts About Print Test

by Marie Clay

Print Concept	Child's Task
a. Front of book	Identifies the front of the book.
b. Difference between a picture and a page of print	Identifies a page of text (and not the picture on opposite page) as the place to begin reading.
c. Left-to-right directionality	Identifies the direction of reading as a left-to-right process.
d. Return sweep	Identifies the return sweep as the appropriate reading behavior at the end of a line.
e. Word pointing	Points out words as a teacher reads a line of print slowly.
f. Beginning and end	Identifies the first and last parts of a story, page, line, or word.

(continued)

● **BOX 4.4** *(Continued)*

Print Concept	Child's Task
g. Bottom of a picture	Identifies the bottom of a picture that is inverted (upside down) on a page.
h. Inverted page of print	Identifies the appropriate place to begin, left-to-right direction, and return sweep.
i. Line order	Identifies line sequence as the correct answer, when asked, "What's wrong with this?" (The teacher reads a printed sentence in which the line sequence is jumbled.) *Example:* and began to swim. I jumped into the water
j. Left page begins a text	Identifies the left page as place to begin reading when two pages of text are side by side.
k. Word order	Identifies word order as the correct answer when asked, "What's wrong with this?" (The teacher reads a printed sentence in which the word order is distorted.) *Example:* I looked and looked I but could not find the cat.
l. Letter order	Identifies that the letters in simple words are not sequenced properly when the teacher reads, as if correct, a text in which the letters of words are out of order. *Example:* The dgo chased teh cat thsi way and thta way. The cta ran pu a tree.

Learning About the Alphabetic Principle in Written Language

Language experience stories help children to discover that the string of sounds in spoken language can be broken down into units of print made up of words and sentences. But children must also learn that a word can be separated into sounds and that the segmented or separated sounds can be represented by letters. Such learning involves the beginnings of *phonic analysis.* In Chapter 8, we examine more closely issues related to phonics. For now, however, note that a *phone* is defined as the smallest sound unit that is identifiable in spoken language. While phones describe all the possible separate speech sounds in language, they are not necessarily represented by the letters of the alphabet. *Phonemes,* however, are minimal sound units that can be represented in written language. The **alphabetic principle** suggests that letters in the alphabet map to phonemes. Hence, the term *phonic analysis* is used here generally to refer to the child's identification of words by their sounds. This process involves the association of speech sounds with letters. In the beginning of reading instruction, key questions that need to be asked are, "Is the child able to hear sounds in a word?" "Is the child able to recognize letters as representing units of sound?"

One of the first indications that children can analyze speech sounds and use knowledge about letters is when they invent their own spellings during writing (Read, 1975; Henderson and Beers, 1980). Invented spellings are a sure sign that children are beginning to be conscious of sounds in words.

In Table 4.2, study the invented spellings from several samples of writing from three kindergartners. In the case of Monica, Tesscha, and James, their spellings reflect varying levels of sophistication in hearing sounds in words and in corresponding letters to those sounds. Gentry and Henderson (1980) contend that Monica demonstrates the most phonological awareness and James the least. A perusal of Monica's list of words indicates that she has learned to distinguish sounds in sequence and can correspond letters directly to the surface sounds that she hears. Tesscha has also developed an awareness of sounds and letters, although this awareness is not as evident or developed as Monica's. James is the least ready of the three to benefit from sound-letter instruction. The fact that he uses numbers

● **TABLE 4.2**

Spellings by Three Kindergartners

Word	Monica's spelling	Tesscha's spelling	James's spelling
monster	monstr	mtr	aml
united	unintid	nnt	em3321
dressing	dresing	jrasm	8emaaps
bottom	bodm	bodm	19nhm
hiked	hikt	hot	sanh
human	humin	hmn	menena

for letters is indicative of his confusion and lack of letter and word awareness. For James (and other 5- and 6-year-old children at a similar level of performance) analyzing sounds in words and attaching letters to those sounds is beyond present conceptual reach. Making initial reading tasks too abstract or removed from what James already knows about print will not help him progress in reading.

Children can easily become confused when taught to identify sounds in words or correspond letters to sounds if they have not yet developed a concept of what a word is. Likewise, the level of abstraction in recognizing a word is too difficult for children if they have yet to make any global connection that speech is related to print. From an instructional point of view, a beginning reading program that starts with a strong "bottom-up" premise, introducing letter recognition and speech-to-print rules to all children, puts the proverbial cart before the horse, especially for 5- and 6-year-olds who have yet to acquire basic understandings about written language. Certainly this doesn't mean that program goals for studying words, analyzing sounds in words, or recognizing correspondences between sounds and letters are not worthwhile. However, they must be put into perspective and taught to beginners in meaningful contexts and as the need or opportunity arises.

Recognizing Letters

Letter recognition has been a well-established predictor of first grade success in reading (Durrell, 1958). However, studies by Ohnmacht (1969) and Samuels (1972) show that teaching children to master the recognition of letters does not necessarily help them to become better readers at the end of the first grade. Therefore, teachers of beginning reading should not assume that the relationship between letter naming and reading success is *causal.* The ability to recognize letters and to succeed in reading probably results from a more common underlying ability. Venezky (1978) contends that letter recognition scores on a reading readiness test can be interpreted as a sign of general intelligence or positive home experiences and a child's early exposure to print.

No doubt, today's 5-year-old brings more letter knowledge to beginning reading instruction than the 5-year-old of a decade ago. Television plays a big part in this phenomenon. Children's programs such as "Sesame Street" are largely responsible for increasing children's letter awareness.

The kindergarten teacher should capitalize on children's knowledge of letters in a variety of ways. Plan instruction in letter recognition around daily classroom routines and activities. Also help children discriminate small but significant differences among letters, not necessarily in isolated activity, but in meaningful written language contexts. Traditionally, visual perception tasks have involved letter identification and discrimination. While these tasks are more justifiable than discrimination activities involving geometric shapes, the teacher should move quickly to letter recognition and discrimination within words and sentences. Consider the following instructional tasks:

Discuss letters in the context of a language experience story, or key words that children recognize instantly because they are personal and meaningful. (See Chapter 8 for a discussion of key-word instruction.) For example, ask children to find at least one other child in the room whose first name begins with the same letter. If a child can't find a match, ask the class to brainstorm some names that begin with the same letter as the child's name. Write the names on the board for discussion and analysis.

Use alphabet books. Every kindergarten class should have a collection of alphabet books. Ask children to find the page that a certain letter is on. Compare and contrast the illustrations of the letter in the different books. The children can illustrate their own rendition of the letter, and over time the class can develop its own alphabet book.

Target a letter for discussion. Have children search for the letter on labels of cans and other commercial products (e.g., "Special K"), in magazines, newspapers, and other sources of print. Children can make a letter collage by cutting the letters they find and arranging and pasting them onto a big letter poster that the teacher has made from construction paper.

Tie letter recognition to writing. Begin with each child's name. Encourage children to write their names by tracing copies of the letters or writing independently. Ask children to count the number of letters in their names, to examine their names for repeating letters, and so on.

Create letters through art activities. Art plays a very important part in the child's school experience, by giving children the opportunity to learn that there are many ways to express their thoughts, feelings, and points of view. Art also heightens children's awareness of their physical environment, involving them through the manipulation of different materials and the development of visual and sensory capacities. For this reason, one small but significant form of expression might be to create letters through drawing, finger painting, sculpting, and making collages such as the letter poster previously described.

Helping Beginners to Become Aware of Phonemes in Words

One of the most difficult concepts related to print that beginners must become aware of is that a word is made up of a series of sounds. Yopp (1992) explains that young children typically lack **phonemic awareness,** an understanding that speech is composed of a series of individual sounds: "Cat . . . is simply a cat, a furry animal that purrs. Young children are unaware that the spoken utterance *cat* is a word that is made up of a series of sounds, or phonemes, /k/, /a/, and /t/.. . . " (p. 696). Phonemic awareness is a powerful predictor of children's later reading achievement (Juel, 1988). The lack of phonemic awareness contributes to children's inability to identify unknown words. If beginners are to benefit from word identification strategies (which we explain more fully in Chapter 8), they must develop a certain degree of phonemic awareness.

The Russian psychologist Elkonin (1973) argued that one of the critical features in learning to read is for the child to hear sounds in sequence in a word. In American schools, teachers of beginners gear instruction so that children go from *letter recognition* to *sound association.* However, Elkonin's work shows that making the correspondence between sounds and letters is easier if children are first aware of the number of sound segments in a word.

Separating sounds in words has been referred to as *phonemic segmentation.* The following procedures can be incorporated into individual or small-group instruction once the children are identified as ready to benefit from training in phonemic segmentation. In order to benefit from such instruction, children must have developed strong concepts of print as "talk written down" as well as a concept of "word." Because the initial stages of training in segmenting a word into sounds is totally aural, children need not be aware of letters to profit from this type of instruction. Eventually, children learn to attach letters to sounds that are separated.

Procedures for Segmenting Sounds in Words

1. *Give the child a picture of a familiar object.* A rectangle is divided into squares according to the number of sounds in the name of the object. Remember that a square is required for every sound in a word, not necessarily every letter. For example, if the picture were of a boat, there would be three squares for three sounds:

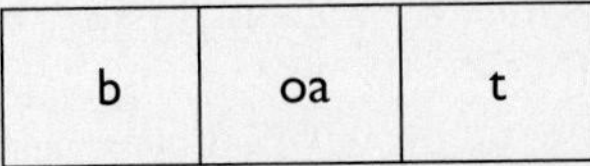

2. *Next, articulate the word slowly and deliberately, allowing the child to hear those sounds that can be naturally segmented.* Note that research has shown that it is easier to hear syllables than individual phonemes in a word (Liberman et al., 1974).
3. *Now, ask the child to repeat the word, modeling the way you have said it.*
4. *Continue to model.* As a word is articulated, show the child how to place counters in each square according to the sounds heard sequentially in the word. For example, with the word *boat,* as the teacher articulates each sound, a counter is placed in a square:

0	0	0

5. *Walk the child through the procedure by attempting it together several times.*
6. *Show another picture, then the word.* Ask the child to pronounce the word and separate the sounds by placing the counters in the squares. The teacher may have to continue modeling until the child catches on to the task.

7. *Phase out the picture stimulus and the use of counters and squares.* Eventually the child is asked to aurally analyze words independently.

In time, the teacher should combine phonemic segmentation with letter association. As the child pronounces a word, letters and letter clusters can be used instead of counters in the squares. The child can be asked, "What letters do you think go in each of the squares?" At first, the letters can be written in for the child. Clay (1979c) suggested that the teacher accept any correct sound-letter correspondence the child gives and write it in the correct position as the child watches. She also recommends that the teacher prompt the child with questions such as: "What do you hear in the beginning?" "In the middle?" "At the end?" "What else do you hear?"

Hearing sounds in words is no easy reading task for 5- and 6-year-olds. The research of Liberman and her associates (1977) pointed out that preschool and kindergarten children have a more difficult time with segmentation tasks than do first graders. As we suggested earlier, helping children to sound out words and learn sound-letter correspondences may be premature if they have not made the connection between speech and print or developed a good sense of what a word is.

For those beginners who can profit from sound separation and show an interest in instruction, we strongly recommend that the teacher move quickly from the training task described above to applying it in real situations. The writing by children is a natural occasion to apply phonic analysis principles to purposeful activity. To illustrate, Cramer (1978) provided an account of how one teacher helped a first-grade child to approximate the spelling of a word she needed for writing. The teacher-child interaction went like this:

Jenny: Mrs. Nicholas, how do you spell *hospital?*
Mrs. Nicholas: Spell it as best you can, Jenny.
Jenny: I don't know how to spell it.
Mrs. Nicholas: I know you don't know how to spell it, honey. I just want you to write as much of the word as you can.
Jenny: I don't know any of it.
Mrs. Nicholas: Yes, you do, Jenny. How do you think *hospital* starts? (Mrs. Nicholas pronounced hospital distinctly with a slight emphasis on the first sound, but she deliberately avoided grossly distorting the pronunciation.)
Jenny: (very tentatively): h-s.
Mrs. Nicholas: Good! Write the *hs.* What do you hear next in *hospital?* (Again Mrs. Nicholas pronounced hospital distinctly, this time with a slight emphasis on the second part.)
Jenny: (still tentatively): p-t.
Mrs. Nicholas: Yes! Write the *pt.* Now, what's the last sound you hear in *hospital?* (While pronouncing hospital for the last time, Mrs. Nicholas emphasized the last part without exaggerating it unduly.)
Jenny: (with some assurance): l.

Mrs. Nicholas: Excellent, Jenny, *h-s-p-t-l* is a fine way to spell *hospital.* There is another way to spell hospital, but for now I want you to spell words you don't know just as we did this one.

Because Mrs. Nicholas was willing to tolerate misspellings in a beginning situation, Jenny benefited. Not only did she have an opportunity to apply her knowledge of sound-letter correspondences, but Jenny also had the opportunity to test the rules that govern English spelling in an accepting environment.

Assessing the Beginner's Emerging Literacy

An important instructional principle for beginning reading is to assess a child's literacy development by providing abundant, varied opportunities to read. In short, a teacher must *assess through teaching* and then adjust instruction appropriately for individual children.

Reading readiness assessment is often treated ritualistically at the beginning of the school year. Children are usually given a standardized reading readiness test to determine if they are ready for the school's reading program. The limitations in using a readiness test score have already been mentioned. While most standardized tests attempt to evaluate pre-reading skills, they are limited by the test author's views concerning which variables are essential for success in reading. Compare the subtests of six popular standardized readiness tests in Table 4.3.

Although it may be difficult in some cases to determine the nature of some of the subtests by their title, it is easy to recognize that almost all of the subtests are predicated on a bottom-up view of the reading process. If the instructional experiences that you plan for beginners reflect an emergent literacy view, it is *imperative* that informal assessment through teaching and **observation** reflect the instructional conditions in your classroom.

Observing Reading and Readinglike Behavior

Beginning teachers can evaluate children's readiness for reading through a wealth of information garnered from daily classroom interactions. The teacher, however, has to tune in to children's reading behavior. You must be a good listener and observer. Through many of the instructional activities that have been suggested in this and the previous chapter, important information will emerge to help make instructional decisions. For example, as you interact with children, ask yourself these questions as suggested by McDonnell and Osburn (1978).

TABLE 4.3

Comparison of Subtests from Standardized Readiness Tests

Test	Subtests
Clymer-Barrett Prereading Battery	Recognition of letters, matching words, discrimination of beginning sounds in words, discrimination of ending sounds in words, shape completion, copying a sentence.
Gates-MacGinitie Reading Tests—Readiness Skills	Listening comprehension, auditory discrimination, visual discrimination, following directions, letter recognition, visual-motor coordination, auditory blending.
Harrison-Stroud Reading Readiness Profile	Using symbols, making visual discriminations, using the context, making auditory discriminations, using context and auditory clues, giving names of letters.
Lee-Clark Reading Readiness Test	Matching, cross-out, vocabulary, following directions, identification of letters and words.
Metropolitan Readiness Tests	Word meaning, listening, matching, alphabet, numbers, copying, draw-a-man.
Murphy-Durrell Reading Readiness Analysis	Phonemes, letter names, learning rate.

Do children attend to the visual aspects of print? If I am reading a story, can the child tell me where to start and where to go next? Is the child able to point to words as I read them, thereby demonstrating knowledge of directional patterns of print? Does the child understand the concepts of words and letters? Can he or she circle a word and letter in the book? To eliminate the good guesser, this ability should be demonstrated several times.

Do children use their intuitive knowledge of language? Can the child look at a picture book and invent a story to go with the pictures? Does the invented story, when the teacher begins to write it down, indicate the child is using a more formalized language that approximates the language used in books (i.e., book talk) rather than an informal conversational style? Does the child recognize that the print and the pictures are related? Can the child "read the words" of a memorized text such as a nursery rhyme, even though the spoken words are not completely accurate matches for the print? Is this recall stimulated or changed by the pictures?

● **BOX 4.5**

Checklist for Beginning Reading Behaviors

Name: ____________________ Date: ____________________

Skill Area	Seldom or Never	Usually	Always
A. Basic Literacy Concepts			
1. Recognizes the uses of written language			
2 Demonstrates left-right progression			
3. Recognizes sentences			
4. Recognizes words			
5. Recognizes letters			
6. Recognizes sounds			
B. Uses of Language			
7. Interested in communicating ideas			
8. Uses variety of words			
9. Invents story to go with pictures			
C. Integrates Skills			
10. Begins to read sentences word by word			
11. Begins to use information cues			
12. Self-corrects without prompting			

Are children beginning to show signs of integrating visual and language cues? Are they beginning to read single sentences word by word, pointing to each word with a finger while reading? Can the child use all the cues available to a reader: the predictability of language, word order, a beginning sound, and an appropriateness to context while reading? Does he or she stop and correct, without prompting, when a visual-vocal mismatch occurs?

Does the child expect meaning from print? Does he or she demonstrate that a message is expected by relating a sensible story?

These questions easily lead to the development of checklists that can help the teacher make systematic evaluations. The checklist in Box 4.5 provides a representative example of a checklist that can be used for this purpose.

Another integral part of informal assessment is consideration of a child's background. The checklist in Box 4.5 lends good insight into what to observe related to a child's cognitive, language, social, emotional, and physical development.

SUMMARY

In this chapter we explored the difference between reading readiness and emergent literacy as views upon which to begin instruction. If reading is viewed developmentally, then teachers will make use of children's preschool experiences with and knowledge of print to get beginners started in reading and writing. The principle behind instruction is to teach for literate behavior. In other words, beginning reading and writing should center around readinglike situations rather than on activities that are unrelated to having children interact with printed language.

Three strands of instruction characterize beginning reading. First, children should participate in storybook literacy experiences as well as learn what reading is all about. To this extent, we showed how to use stories and incorporate language functions into instructional practices. Through these activities children will learn that the string of sounds in spoken language can be broken down into units of print made up of words and sentences. Moreover, they should be getting instruction in which they learn that a word can be separated into sounds and that these separated sounds can be represented by letters. Finally, a third phase should center around children learning about the language of instruction. They must learn the terms and labels that are needed to talk about reading and carry out reading tasks.

We emphasized informal assessment over a standardized reading readiness testing, because informal assessment provides teachers with daily judgments of children's preparedness and progress in beginning reading situations. Assessment through teaching and observation yields valuable information about a child's abilities, as well as about the teaching methods that seem to be easiest and of greatest interest to individual children.

TEACHER-ACTION RESEARCHER

1. Follow the procedures in the chapter to use language experience stories to assess print awareness. Select several children that you are interested in obtaining more data

about and follow the procedures beginning with a short dictated story for the child. What conclusions could you draw about the child's emerging print awareness?

2. Informally interview several kindergarten and first-grade teachers on their views of emergent literacy. Develop your interview questions using Table 4.1 in this chapter that compares emergent literacy and reading readiness. In constructing your questions, use "newer" terminology from emergent literacy. What are the teachers' concepts of emergent literacy? Do they subscribe to a separate program more in line with construct of readiness instruction? What do they value as children's first school experiences with reading?

3. Plan and teach a lesson to a small group of children in which the children dictate an experience story. Plan the language experience activity by deciding how best to stimulate this story and how to involve children further in literacy learning once the story is written. Do the same type of lesson with the same children in several weeks. How do the children interact? Are there any observable differences in growth in the children's literacy development over the three or four week period? Is there one child in particular who seems to have blossomed? Describe and develop some recommendations for the next instructional steps with this group.

4. Plan and teach a lesson using a storybook. In what ways do children become involved in the story? How do the children interact with the text?

KEY TERMS

literacy club
emergent literacy
shared reading
uses of oral language
linguistic awareness
observation
reading readiness
storybook experiences
shared writing
patterned stories
alphabetic principle
prereading skills
big books
interactive writing
language experience
phonemic awareness

CHAPTER 5

Connecting Reading and Writing

BETWEEN THE LINES

In this chapter you will discover:

- **What the connections are between reading and writing.**
- **What conditions contribute to a classroom environment that supports reading and writing together.**
- **How to use journals to integrate reading and writing.**
- **Why it is important to have a predictable classroom structure for writing.**
- **How to organize writing workshops and guide the writing process.**

In Megan Woodrum's elementary school, the fifth grade students participate in a family living class where they explore a variety of social, emotional, and psychological issues that, in Megan's words, "teaches us growing up." A textbook and supplementary materials, including imaginative and informational trade books, pamphlets, magazines, and newspaper articles, provide numerous reading opportunities for the students. An integral part of the class is to examine adolescent behavior and its effect on the family.

"Teenagers," Megan hears her teacher say in class discussion, "worry about a lot of things." "What things?" Megan wonders to herself, but the question is left unexplored as the discussion shifts gears to another subject.

When she gets home from school that day, the question of what teenagers worry about is still on Megan's mind: "I didn't have much to do and I was kinda bored, so I began to draw about what teenagers think." In her notebook, she sketches the drawing shown Figure in 5.1 and titles it, "What Most Adolescents Think." In the process, she captures the angst of adolescence in a series of questions.

● **FIGURE 5.1** "What Most Adolescents Think," by Megan Woodrum

The next day Megan brings her drawing to class and shows it to the teacher. Delighted, the teacher invites Megan to share the drawing with other class members. Later that morning, as the students write in *dialogue journals* (where they engage in written conversation with one another), a classmate asks Megan about her drawing and why she thinks teenagers worry about such things as being normal, looking good, and fitting in. Megan responds to her writing partner with the journal entry below,

As this vignette illustrates, Megan explores and clarifies ideas encountered in class and in her own life experiences through the use of paper and pencil activities. She has a strong desire for self-expression; yet she knows, perhaps intuitively, that meaning-making, whether it manifests itself through art, music, drama, movement, or literacy is a process that allows her to explore the things she already knows and to transform that knowledge into new meanings and insights. Megan constructs meaning to gain perspective on her world.

In this chapter, we show how writing helps children to understand as well as to be understood. Writing is thinking with paper and pencil, and therein lies one of its important links to reading. Our emphasis throughout the chapter is on the strong bonds that exist between learning to write and learning to read. These connections are powerful enough to suggest that children probably learn as much about reading by writing as they learn about writing by reading.

Why do I think that's what adolecents think? Well, for starters, I have a sister who is 17. Exsperence, I guess. Also, we have a teacher who teaches us about growing up. And she's defently had experence! So, I guess that's that.

From
Megan
Woodrum
The Artist of "What most Adolecents think."

How Reading and Writing Are Connected

Common sense tells us that writing is intended to be read. When children are writing, they can't help but be involved in reading. Before writing, they may be collecting and connecting information from books, and during and after writing, they are revising, proofreading, and sharing their work with others. Children should be invited to write about what they are reading and to read about what they are writing. Therein lies the real value of the **reading-writing connection.**

Writing and reading have been described as two sides of the same process (Squire, 1984). Yet in many elementary schools, writing and reading are strangers to one another, isolated and taught as separate curriculum entities. In many schools, teachers follow a much-traveled road to literacy instruction. Along the way, reading and writing are taught separately and sequentially. The premise underlying this instructional path is that reading ability develops first, and writing ability follows. Nevertheless, with new knowledge about literacy development emerging daily, teachers are recognizing that when young children are engaged in writing, they are using and manipulating written language. In doing so, children develop valuable concepts about print and how messages are created.

There is compelling evidence to suggest that writing and reading abilities develop concurrently and should be nurtured together. Carol Chomsky (1970, 1979) was one of the first language researchers to advocate that children write first and read later. She contends that writing is a beneficial introduction to reading, because children acquire letter and word knowledge through invented spellings. Marie Clay (1979c) also supports the powerful bonds between writing and reading. She views reading and writing as complementary processes. Literacy development demands that children engage in reading and writing concurrently.

The connections between reading and writing have been examined formally through research studies and theoretical explorations (Shanahan 1990; Tierney and Shanahan, 1991. How are reading and writing connected? The following are some of the conclusions about the relationships between reading and writing that can be drawn.

1. Reading and writing processes are correlated; that is to say, in general, good readers are good writers and vice versa.
2. Students who write well tend to read more books than those who are less capable as writers.
3. Wide reading may be as effective in improving writing as actual practice in writing.
4. Good readers and writers are likely to engage in reading and writing independently, because they have healthy concepts of themselves as readers and writers.

These conclusions suggest that reading and writing are related. The two processes share many of the same characteristics: Both are language and experience based, both require active involvement from language learners, and both must be viewed as acts of making meaning for communication. This is why children's writing should be shared with an audience composed of readers, in *and* out of the classroom. As Tierney and LaZansky (1980) suggest, readers must think about writers and writers must think about readers.

As much as reading and writing are similar, Shanahan (1988) warns that the body of research suggests that the two processes may be different as well. Some good readers, for example, aren't good writers and some good writers may indeed be poor readers. Nevertheless, if writing is to have an impact on reading, and vice versa, then instruction in writing and reading must be integrated throughout the instructional program.

Integrating writing and reading is no easy task. An occasional foray into creative writing will not appreciably affect children's writing or reading development. Where does a teacher begin? How do you get started? How do you guide children's writing day in and day out throughout the school year?

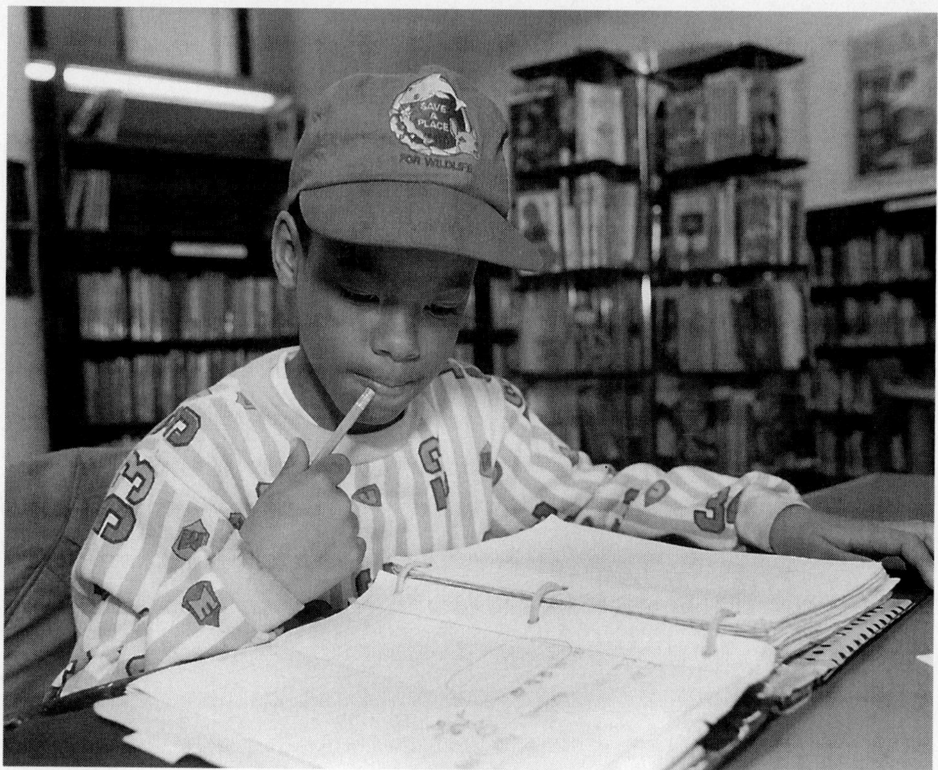

Reading and writing are related, and both are acts of making meaning for communicating.

Creating Environments to Support Reading-Writing Connections

Since the mid-1970s, Donald Graves (1983) and Jane Hansen (1987) have conducted research on the writing and reading development of elementary children. Extensive field work in primary and intermediate classrooms has yielded valuable insights into the influence of the learning environment on children's writing and reading. Graves and Hansen have shown that *informal* learning environments increase the volume of writing and reading produced by elementary children. Not only do they write and read more, but they also take greater control over and responsibility for their writing and reading. Children need much less external motivation to write and read from their teachers when they have time to read and write and have the chance to select their own writing topics or reading material.

In school, children develop fluency and power in their reading and writing when they have *time* and *choice* on their side. In Chapter 10, we explore in greater depth the importance of student choice and the uses of instructional time in a literature-based reading program.

Children must have numerous occasions to write freely about things that are important to them. This is why a teacher's positive attitude toward invented spellings contributes greatly to children's writing development. Concerns for the form and mechanics of writing matter greatly, but must be viewed from a developmental perspective. The first order of business in establishing an environment that supports writers should be on the exploration of topics that matter to young writers.

A classroom environment that supports reading and writing has much in common with the characteristics of a natural learning environment outlined in Chapter 3. In an informal classroom context, where reading and writing are connected, children are encouraged to develop in their own way and at their own rate. Teachers are positive and rewarding in their reception of children's written work and their interactions with print. A "built-in support system" supports the learner. There is tremendous faith and patience that children will develop as readers and writers. A willingness to wait permeates the environment, especially at times when some children seem to be at a plateau or even regressing in their development as readers and writers.

In addition, miscues or errors are viewed as natural in reading and writing and provide the teacher with valuable insights into a child's development as a language user. In an environment that supports the reading and writing development of children, there should *never* arise a situation such as the one that happened to Sean, a 5-year-old, whose story we convey in Box 5.1.

What's the moral of Sean's story? Simply this: There's the old adage about "sticks and stones may break your bones. . . ." Well, sticks and stones may break your bones, but words are capable of breaking your heart. Criticism and inappropriate correction by teachers must give way to children's trial-and-error forays into writing and reading. Teachers and children must celebrate the experience of writing, reading, and sharing their efforts with one another.

Examine Ron Cramer's (1978) suggestions for encouraging classroom writing, and note our italics, which underscore the connections he suggests between writing and reading.

1. Use children's experiences and encourage them to write about things that are relevant to their interests and needs. Children must choose topics that they care about. Yet a fear that teachers often harbor is that students will have nothing to say or write about if left to select their own topics. Rarely is this the case. Children want to write. But before they begin, they should have good reason to believe that they have something to say. How can you help? Guide students to choose topics that they have strong feelings about; *provide opportunities for reading* **literature,** discussion, and brainstorming before writing; and show students how to plan and explore topics by using lists, jotting notes, and clustering ideas.

   Not only must children recognize that they have something worthwhile to say, but they should have good reason to believe that they will succeed. As Cramer noted,

● **BOX 5.1**

Class Works

Sean's Story

Sean, a 5-year-old, asked his kindergarten teacher if he could read a story by Dr. Seuss, *Hop on Pop,* to his classmates during share time. "No," said his teacher. "We already had our story reading time."

Sean is a child who has developed literate behavior before entering school. Not only does he like to read his favorite books to others, but he likes to write. A favorite game he likes to play with his mother is "let's write messages."

Sean came home from kindergarten one day looking quite troubled and with tears in his eyes. He wouldn't talk about what was bothering him. The next day he came home and crumpled up a worksheet from school, saying, "I'm not going to write anymore."

Apparently, Sean, who writes his name completely in upper-case letters, was told by his teacher that on his worksheets he incorrectly spelled his name. The teacher said, "You're supposed to use small letters." Well, on his next worksheet, Sean wrote his name, shrinking it to about half the size that he normally writes it. What was the teacher's response? "Sean, it's still wrong." That day Sean announced to his parents that he was never going to write again.

it's fruitless to force children to write on assigned topics for which they can generate little enthusiasm or background knowledge.

2. Develop sensitivity to good writing by reading poetry and literature to children. Young writers need to listen to written language. In Chapter 10, we explain ways to *bring children and literature together. Although literature is a mirror that reflects good writing to children, Cramer is quick to point out that the writings by other children also serve as a powerful model.* Sharing good literature and children's writing helps young writers feel that they are capable of producing similar work.

3. Invent ways to value what children have written. Children need praise and feedback, the two mainstays of a built-in support system for classroom writing. *Sharing writing in progress is an important way* to ensure response, or feedback, in the classroom. *Displaying and publishing writing is another.*

   Children's writing reflects the functions of written language. Children, like adults, don't engage in writing for the sake of writing. Because their efforts are purposeful, their writing must result in products. Later in this chapter, *we explain ways to value children's products through publication. Certainly one of the best ways to value writing and reading is through bookmaking. Nowhere do children build a sense of authorship better than by writing and illustrating their own books.*

4. Guide the writing personally. As children are writing, you should circulate around the room to help and encourage. As Cramer put it, writing time is no time to perform other tasks. Conferencing, then, becomes the primary means to respond and to give feedback in the writer's environment. Teacher-student and peer conferences help to create a collaborative, noncompetitive environment in which to write, *try out work in progress, and share what has been written with others.*

5. Write stories and poetry of your own and share them with your students. *Sharing your writing with students* or discussing problems that you are having as a writer signals to children that writing is as much a problem-solving activity for you as it is for them. What better way to model writing than to let students in on the processes you use as a writer. Children need to know that writing is as exciting for you as it is for them.

6. Tie writing in with the entire curriculum. Content area activities may provide the experiences and topics that can give direction and meaning to writing. *Writing to learn will help children discover and synthesize relationships among the concepts they are studying in social studies, science, mathematics, art, music, and health. The connection between reading and writing are especially meaningful when children explore concepts through written language.*

7. Start a writing center in your classroom. A writing center represents a place where young writers can go to find ideas, contemplate, or *read other children's writing.* The center should be well equipped with lined paper of various sizes and colors; lined paper with a space for a picture; drawing paper of all sizes; stationery and envelopes; tag board; index cards; a picture file; pencils, colored pencils, crayons, and magic markers; paper clips; white glue and paste; paper punches; *book display stands;* **informational texts** *such as magazines, dictionaries, and encyclopedias; a classroom library for students' writing; and an address file of book authors, sports figures, celebrities, and magazines that print students' work.* A writing center isn't a substitute for having a classroom program where children work every day at developing the craft of writing. Instead, the center is a visible support that enhances the writing environment in your classroom.

When teachers begin a writing process program, children engage in reading activities in varied and unexpected ways. An environment that connects writing and reading provides students with numerous occasions to write and read for personal and academic reasons.

Environments that connect reading and writing encourage students to write with an **audience** in mind. Wolf and Vacca (1985) argue that the following opportunities to write give students a real sense of purpose and audience.

Pen pal arrangements with other classes within the building

Pen pal arrangements with a class from another school within the city

Pen pals in other cities or countries

Secret pen pals who leave messages for each other in the classroom

Writing for a school or class newspaper

Writing for a school or class literary magazine

"Author of the Week" bulletin board that features a different student writer each week

Entering writing contests within the community

Opportunities for students to read pieces of writing over the school's public-address system

Weekly "radio broadcast" on the school's public address system

Opportunities for students to read selected pieces of writing to a younger class

Outings where students can read selected pieces of writing to children in a day-care center

Displays of student writing within the classroom and in the corridors of the school

Videotapes of students reading their pieces of writing

Slide presentations with student-authored scripts

Play festivals featuring student-authored scripts

Student-written communication for requests for change within the school

Student-written correspondence used in search of information for a research topic

Student-made publicity for school events

Student-written speeches for school assemblies and programs

Young author festival to highlight student-authored books

Student-prepared speech in the voice of a character from a story or from social studies

Daily journals and diaries (real and imaginary)

Biographical sketches based on interviews or research

Letters requesting free material (many items are listed in *Free Stuff for Kids,* Meadowbrook Publishing Co., Deephaven, MN 55391)

Songwriting

Reviews of movies or television programs

Student-written directions on how to do something

Writing cartoon scripts

Integrating Reading and Writing Through Journals

When journals are part of the writing environment, children use them to write about things that are important to them and that they have strong feelings about. Journals can be used to help children to examine their personal lives and to explore literary and informational texts. A journal is a gold mine for generating ideas and a place to record thoughts and feelings, and is a way to bring children in touch with themselves. All forms of written expression and types of writing are welcomed in journals—doodles, comments, poems, letters, and, for the purpose of the next section, written conversations between child and teacher and child and child.

Using Journals to Engage in Written Conversation

If journals are to be used to generate ideas, time must be set aside by the teacher to read and respond to children's entries on a regular basis. Because child and teacher enter into a personal relationship through the vehicle of journal writing, there are, as we have seen, many occasions for a dialogue in writing. According to Gambrell (1985), the **dialogue journal** emphasizes meaning while providing natural, functional experiences both in writing and reading. Child and teacher use dialogue journals to converse in writing. A teacher's response to children's entries may include comments, questions, and invitations to children to express themselves.

In Figure 5.2, study how second-grade teacher Sharon Piper responded to Tammy Lynn's September 20 journal entry. Mrs. Piper's dialogue with Tammy Lynn encourages a response and a continuation of the conversation through subsequent journal writing.

Gambrell suggested the following guidelines for using dialogue journals in the classroom:

1. Use bound composition books. (Staple appropriate writing paper inside a construction paper cover. The paper should be large enough for several journal entries so children can see the developing dialogue.)

2. To motivate students, tell them journals are like letters. They will write to you and you will write back. Encourage writing about any topic of interest or concern to them.

3. For best results, write daily. Set aside a special time for writing and reading. For children in grades one and two, 10 minutes might be appropriate, whereas older children may need 20 minutes.

4. Focus on communication. Do not correct entries; instead, model correct forms in your response.

5. Respond in a way that encourages written expression such as, "Tell me more about . . . ," "I'd like to know more about. . . ," "Describe. . . ."

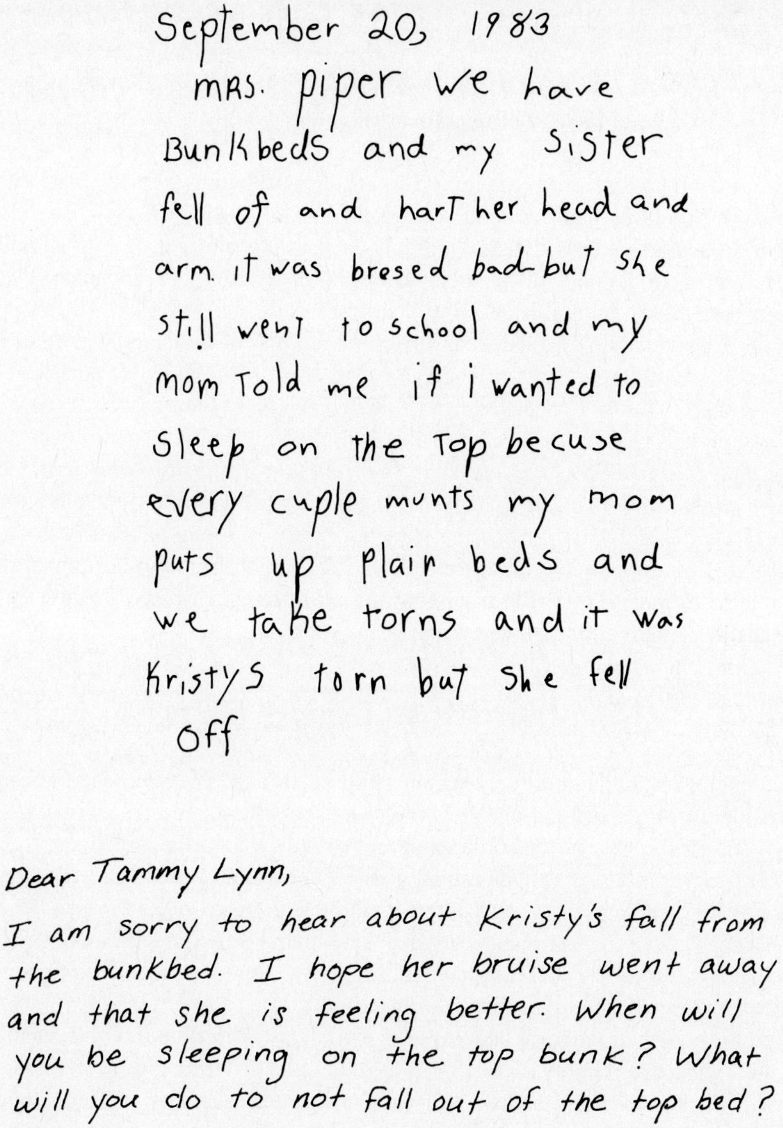

September 20, 1983
mRS. piper we have Bunkbeds and my Sister fell of and harT her head and arm. it was bresed bad but She still wenT to School and my mom Told me if i wanted to Sleep on the Top becuse every cuple munts my mom puts up plair beds and we take torns and it was Kristys torn but She fell off

Dear Tammy Lynn,
I am sorry to hear about Kristy's fall from the bunkbed. I hope her bruise went away and that she is feeling better. When will you be sleeping on the top bunk? What will you do to not fall out of the top bed?

● **FIGURE 5.2** Tammy Lynn and Ms. Piper's dialogue entries

6. Dialogue journals are private. Convey to students that they belong to the two of you, but they may share their journals if they wish. Sharing should always be voluntary.

A **buddy (or partner) journal,** as the name implies, encourages written conversation between children using a journal format (Bromley, 1989). Before beginning buddy journals, children should be familiar with the use of journals as a tool for writing, and also be comfortable with the process of dialoguing with a teacher through the use of dialogue journals. To get buddy journals off and running, divide the students into pairs. Each child may choose a buddy (a friend) or buddies may be selected randomly by drawing names from a hat. To maintain a high level of interest and novelty children may change buddies periodically.

Buddies may converse about anything that matters to them—from sharing with one another books they have been reading to sharing insights and problems. As Bromley (1989) advised, teachers who use buddy journals for natural writing occasions should promote student interaction, cooperation, and collaboration: "Buddy journals enhance socialization since they allow students a forum for learning about each other" (p. 128).

Figure 5.3 depicts a dialogue between two third graders, Michele and Krista, in which Michele provides Krista with support and sympathy in their buddy journal entries of December 2 and December 6.

When using buddy journals as part of a writing-reading program, guard against their overuse. Rotate their use every two weeks or so with other forms of journal writing, such as a solitary journal in which students are writing for themselves or a dialogue journal in which the teacher is conversing with the students. Also, as mentioned earlier, consider switching buddy pairs regularly. In any event, buddy journals are highly motivating, and serve a functional, meaningful role in connecting writing and reading, because children love to read what other children have written.

Using Journals to Explore Texts

Journals create a nonthreatening context for children to explore their reactions and responses to literary and informational texts. Readers who use journals regularly are involved actively in the process of comprehending as they record their feelings, thoughts, and reactions to various types of literature. Journals create a permanent record of what readers are feeling and learning as they interact with texts. As a result, they also have been called *logs* because they permit readers to keep a visible record of their responses to texts. Such responses often reflect thinking beyond a literal comprehension of the text and engage students in inferential and evaluative thinking.

Several types of journals may be used to explore texts: **double-entry journals, reading logs,** and **literature response journals.** What do these different types of journals have in common? Each integrates reading and writing through personal response, allowing readers to feel and think more deeply about the texts they are reading.

Double-Entry Journals. A double-entry journal provides students with an opportunity to identify text passages that are interesting or meaningful to them and to explore—in writing—why. As the name of the journal implies, students fold sheets of paper in half lengthwise, creating two columns for journal entries. In the left-hand column, readers select quotes from the text—perhaps a word, a phrase, a sentence or two—that they find interesting or evocative. They then copy the text verbatim and identify the page from which each text quote is taken. In instances where the quoted passage is several sentences

12-2-88
My new sister is a pain
she wakes me up at night
all the time. motly at
3:30 in the morning Then
she gos back to sleep
and wakes me up at
7:00.

Krista

She shire
is a piane. you
stile love her don't
you? do you have eney
older sisters or
brothers?

Michele

12-6-88
my mom dos't pay
any atenchen to me
she pays most atenchen
to Jennifer.

Krista

that's not far is it?
if she pase moreatenchen
to Jennnifer.

Michele

● **FIGURE 5.3** Krista and Michele's buddy-journal

or a paragraph long the student may choose to summarize rather than copy the passage verbatim.

Across from each quote, in the right-hand column, readers enter their personal responses and reactions to the text quotes. As Yopp and Yopp (1992) explain, students' responses to a text will vary widely: "Some passages may be selected because they are funny or use interesting language. Others may be selected because they touch the student's heart or remind the student of experiences in his or her own life" (p. 54).

Children as early as first grade have used double-entry journals with success, once they have developed some confidence and fluency reading simple stories (Barone, 1990). Teachers, however, must model and demonstrate how to respond to text using the two-column format. With reading beginners, teachers sometimes follow these steps:

1. Help children interact with a text through a shared reading experience.
2. After sharing a story several times, have young readers gather around an experience chart.
3. Divide the chart paper into two columns; label the left column, "What I Liked the Best" and the right column, "Why I Liked It."
4. Illustrate how to use the double-entry format for response by sharing with the class a text quote or two that you like. You might say, "One of my favorite parts of the story is on page 5. . . ." Then you turn to page 5 and read it to the class. Next, copy the text quote in the left-hand column. Tell why you like the text quote; how it makes you feel or what it reminds you of. Write your personal reaction in the right-hand column.
5. Then invite children to volunteer some of their favorite words, lines, or parts from the text. Encourage them to share their reactions. Serve as a scribe by writing their quotes and reactions on the chart paper.
6. Vary the demonstrations with subsequent interactive writing experiences; for example, ask children to volunteer to write on the chart paper.
7. Introduce the class to double-entry journals. Begin by showing them how to make their own journals using 8 1/2 by 11-inch lined paper. Encourage children to use the double-entry journal as a follow-up to a shared reading. Share the journal entries as a group. Phase children into the use of double-entry journals for texts read independently.

Older children will not need as many demonstrations before they develop the knack of using double-entry journals, yet the payoffs will be readily evident in class discussions. One of the big benefits of a double-entry journal is that it encourages interactions between reader and text. Another benefit is that it makes children sensitive to the text and the effect the author's language has on them as readers. A third payoff is that as students explore texts for personally relevant ideas, the teacher can begin to develop an awareness that some parts of a text are more meaningful than other parts. Such awareness is the foundation for sophisticated reading and study strategies that involve identifying main ideas and organizing text information.

Reading Logs. Another type of journal has been called a reading log (if used with literary texts) or a learning log (if used in conjunction with informational texts in content areas). In contrast to double-entry journals, logs provide students with more structure and less choice in deciding what they will write about. The teacher often provides a prompt—a question, for example—to guide students' writing after a period of sustained reading. Logs are usually used with a common or *core* text that everyone in a class is reading.

Prompts may include generic-type "process" questions such as the following: What did you like? What, if anything, didn't you like? What did you think or wonder about as you were reading? What will happen next? What did you think about the story's beginning? Its ending? What did you think about the author's style? Did anything confuse you? At times reading logs use prompts that are more content-specific, asking readers to focus on their understanding of an important concept or some relevant aspect of plot, setting, character, or theme.

As second graders finished a class study of Donald Hall's *Ox-Cart Man,* a story set in the distant past about a farmer and his family, the teacher, Laura Scott, prompted the students to write in their reading logs: "Would you like to be one of the ox-cart man's children?"

The children were eager to answer the question. One reader responded to the prompt in the affirmative:

I wolwd like to be the
ox cart mans son bcose
he wolwd by me a
knife. also becose
he grow food.

Another child responded from an alternate perspective:

I wod not like to be in his family becuse
I wod have to wlak to
the markit And I wod
not like it if I wod have
to eat the food
I Do not like.
And I wod have to
live on a farm and
I'am not talking
abut the farming today
but abut long go.

Many of today's basal reading programs are cognizant of the importance of reading-writing connections and often include a journal or log as part of the overall program. In fact, some basal programs have replaced the traditional workbook with a journal. Workbooks are designed, first and foremost, for readers to practice and apply skills rather than to explore meaning. While journals represent a significant step forward in the evolution of basal programs, some basal reading journals remain workbooks in disguise. Teachers need to pay close attention to the prompts and activities that are contained within basalized journal formats. Do the prompts engage students in personal response and the exploration of meaning or are they designed to reinforce specific skills?

Literature Response Journals. Response journals are treated in Chapter 10 in more detail than space permits here. The main difference between a reading log and a response journal is the amount of prompting that teachers use to elicit students' reactions to a text. Response journals invite readers to respond to literary texts freely, without being prompted. Hancock (1993) suggests an extended set of guidelines (see Box 5.2) for students who use response journals. These guidelines are perhaps best suited for intermediate and middle-grade students but can easily be adapted to the primary level.

Gloria Reichert, a sixth-grade teacher, introduces students to response journals with a letter at the beginning of the school year. In one section of the letter, she explains response journals this way:

> I'm sure you are wondering about what a response journal is. It is a place where you will be able to write about books and stories that you will be reading throughout the year in our class. The response journal will be a great way to help us explore what we are feeling and thinking about what we are reading.
>
> What will you be writing in your response journals? You can write anything you want about the book or story you are reading. You can express your thoughts, your feelings, or your reactions. How do you feel about the book? What does the book make you think about? What do you like or dislike about it? Who are the characters? Do you like them? Can you relate to their problems? What does the story mean to you?

Gloria then shows the class some different types of responses that she has collected from past students who read Wilson Rawl's *Where the Red Fern Grows.* One entry that she shows mixes literary commentary with personal involvement in the story:

> I thought chap. 5 was very good. I'm glad Billy got the dogs. I thought it was really, really mean that all the people were laughing at him because he was carrying the pups in the gunny sack. I mean, come on. He had nothing to carry them in, and they needed air to breathe. I can't believe a fight would actually start because it got so bad. The part where the mountain lion came, and the two pups saved Billy by howling was amazing. I thought the chapter had good action.

Another entry critiques a chapter from the perspective of someone who has had dogs as pets:

> I didn't like chapter two. How can a kid get so sick from just not having a dog. Dogs are not always perfect anyways. They wake so early in the morning by barking there head off and sometimes they run around the house making a ruckus.

In Chapter 10, we will more closely examine some of the different types of responses that children write. Recognize, however, that by showing different examples of entries to her class, Gloria is making students aware that they should try to avoid just telling what the text is about.

● BOX 5.2

Guidelines for Literature Response Journals

- *Feel free to write* your innermost feelings, opinions, thoughts, likes, and dislikes. This is your journal. Feel the freedom to express yourself and your personal responses to reading through it.
- *Take the time to write* down anything that you are thinking while you read. The journal is a way of recording those fleeting thoughts that pass through your mind as you interact with the book. Keep your journal close by and stop to write often, whenever a thought strikes you.
- *Don't worry* about the accuracy of spelling and mechanics in the journal. The content and expression of your personal thoughts should be your primary concern. The journal will not be evaluated for a grade. Relax and share.
- *Record the page number* on which you were reading when you wrote your response. Although it may seem unimportant, you might want to look back to verify your thoughts.
- *One side only* of your spiral notebook paper, please. Expect to read occasional, interested comments from your teacher. These comments will not be intended to judge or criticize your reactions, but will create an opportunity for us to "converse" about your thoughts.
- *Relate the book* to your own experiences and share similar moments from your life or from books you have read in the past.
- *Ask questions* while reading to help you make sense of the characters and the unraveling plot. Don't hesitate to wonder why, indicate surprise, or admit confusion. These responses often lead to an emerging understanding of the book.
- *Make predictions* about what you think will happen as the plot unfolds. Validate, invalidate, or change those predictions as you proceed in the text. Don't worry about being wrong.
- *Talk to the characters* as you begin to know them. Give them advice to help them. Put yourself in their place and share how you would act in a similar situation. Approve or disapprove of their values, actions, or behavior. Try to figure out what makes them react the way they do.

(continued)

● **BOX 5.2** *(continued)*

- *Praise or criticize* the book, the author, or the literary style. Your personal tastes in literature are important and need to be shared.
- *There is no limit* to the types of responses you may write. Your honesty in capturing your thoughts throughout the book is your most valuable contribution to the journal. These guidelines are meant to trigger, not limit, the kinds of things you write. Be yourself and share your personal responses to literature through your journal.

Reprinted with permission of the International Reading Association and M.R. Hancock, 1993. *The Reading Teacher, 46,* 6, p. 472.

When using response journals, some students, especially beginners, will be inclined to write about the plot of a story. Vacca and Newton (1995) illustrate how Eli, a third grader, responds in his journal to two of Cynthia Rylant's books for young readers.

ELI'S RESPONSE TO *GREEN TIME:*

I liked it. In the beginning, Henry and Mudge went on a picnic. There was a bee on Henry's pear. When Henry picked it up he got stung. He was yelling Ow! Ow! After awhile the pain went away and Henry was fine.

ELI'S RESPONSE TO *SMALL PIG:*

I didn't like it. It was about a pig that liked to sit in the mud and sink. One day the farmer's wife was cleaning the house. Then she cleaned the farm and sucked up the mud in the vacuum. So he went to the city and sat in wet concrete and it dried. The farmer had to get him out.

In both entries, Eli's expression of like or dislike is followed by a plot summary. For young readers, such responses are typical, as Vacca and Newton explain, particularly in cases where classroom time is spent on *story structure* or different elements of a story that comprise its plot. Retellings, however, often give way to personal response when teachers provide regular opportunities for students to use response journals and when they encourage children, as Gloria Rieckart does in her class, to respond beyond retelling.

In addition to minilessons where teachers demonstrate different kinds of responses, one-on-one reading conferences or group book discussions may also be used to discuss the reader's role in responding to texts. In Chapter 10, we explain how response journals, conferences, and book talks play an integral role in *reading workshops.*

Response journals can be used flexibly to incorporate the features of dialogue and buddy journals. Several options are possible. The students engage in a dialogue with the teacher or with one another. In Rieckart's sixth-grade class, she will often respond to students' entries directly or invite them to correspond with one another by writing **literary letters,** a response technique popularized by Nanci Atwell (1987).

When a literary letter becomes the discourse form for a response, it is written in the journal and delivered to the teacher or a classmate. The rule of thumb for returning a literary letter is this: If someone in the class receives a letter, he or she should write a response, in the form of a letter, in the sender's journal within twenty-four hours. Students in Riechart's class can write as many literary letters as they wish, but they are expected to write at least two letters per week, one to her and one to another student. She uses the opportunity to respond to students' letters as a means of validating their thinking and helping them to further explore their reactions.

Here's an example of an exchange of letters by Nick and Brian, two of Rieckart's students, in response to *Where the Red Fern Grows:*

> Dear Brian,
>
> I think Billy is veary strange. I would take his older sister's idea about him being crazy.
>
> It was cool how his dogs chased that coon all over God's creation.
>
> Personally I don't think the coon's up in that big old tree. Do you?
>
> Dear Nick,
>
> I think he is crazy too. But I think Ann would be smart enough to catch that coon. I do think that coon is up that tree.

Journals, in no matter which format, reflect writing in which children use language loosely as if they are engaged in talk. Such writing does not place a premium on perfection or mechanics—spelling, punctuation, or grammar, for example. Indeed, teachers encourage children to write freely, placing their reactions and responses ahead of concerns for correctness.

Journal writing is a vehicle for developing writing fluency among students. Students who write regularly in journals find that the more they write the easier it becomes to express their feelings and thoughts about what they are reading. Not only does the volume of writing increase over time, the facility to explore and clarify ideas is also sharpened.

Encouraging the Use of Computers for Word Processing

Take advantage of what the **word processor** can offer. The screen lends a public quality to writing that can encourage sharing and communication. It can encourage children to perceive text as flexible and malleable and it can increase teacher involvement in writing and, paradoxically, student independence.

Avoid some of the pitfalls of word processing. For some children and some writing tasks, the screen can become too public. Rearranging the setting can ameliorate this problem. Do not allow yourself to get carried away by overediting children's writing. Avoid

Word processors can encourage children to see text as flexible and malleable.

viewing any printout (as nice as it may look) as a final draft. Finally, think about your students' ability to type. If they have insufficient typing skills, they may (at first) write less, be less spontaneous, or be loath to delete.

Some additional suggestions for teaching word processing follow.

Become familiar with the program yourself first. Use it for your own writing. While learning, you may wish to make a poster and/or a duplicated sheet of major editing commands for your students.

Start simple. Teach only a few basic commands, then add more to students' repertoires as necessary.

Consider introducing word processing in a whole-class language experience story setting. As each command or key is pressed, discuss why it is needed and how to do it.

Work intensely with a small group to develop your first "experts." Post children's names with the instructions for using the program so that others can ask them for help.

Continue presenting short, direct lessons to the class followed by work on the computer in pairs.

If few computers are available, rotate groups using the word processor for compositions. Or, have students write their first draft in pencil. When they are done, they can sign up for a 20- to 30-minute session at the computer. Working in pairs, one student types in his or her own composition as the other student reads it, suggesting changes along the way. (If possible, try to work for just a minute with students during this time; it is exciting to be a coach during the writing rather than a critic afterward.) The children then switch places. One teacher who had only one computer every third week had a parent-volunteer type in students' work after school during the two weeks in which the class did not have access to the computer. In the third week, students would read and revise their programs. Although these methods are compromises to an extent, students can still benefit from using the computer, especially in reviewing and revising, the final, crucial step in writing.

Model and follow the writing process as described in this chapter.

Because students find themselves writing more, and more easily, on word processors, their work may be less organized and need more revision than paper-and-pencil writing. Fortunately, this free, continuous writing followed by reflection and revision is one of the best ways to compose. The computer can also help with revisions.

Compositions can be reviewed either as paper printouts or on the computer screen. "Reviewing" should mean that both the teacher and other students read and react to a child's writing. The real advantage for students is the ease of making corrections. Rather than messy erasures, confusing lines and arrows, and unwelcome rewriting, editing on the computer is like a game. Press a key—poof!—a paragraph disappears. Move to an earlier spot in the composition and press another key—the paragraph reappears in its new location. Or press a few keys and, in less than a second every "din't" becomes "didn't."

In sum, word processors, used correctly, can help children write. Words are not carved in stone; they are painted in light, a medium that encourages effortless manipulation. The more students intelligently manipulate text—the more they read their work and revise—the better writers they will become.

Establishing a Predictable Structure for Writing

No two writing classrooms are the same; nor should they be. Instructional routines and procedures vary from classroom to classroom. However, effective classrooms often have certain characteristics in common.

One classroom characteristic is that children have freedom of movement. Allowing them to choose where they want to write contributes to the writing environment. Many will choose to write at their desks or a nearby writer's table. Some may opt for the writing center or a private area of the room designated "The Writer's Nook" or "The Writer's Hideaway." Arrange the room so that movement and easy access to classmates are possible. Access to classmates, in particular, will become an important part of trying out work in progress, reading drafts, and holding peer conferences.

A second characteristic involves continuity from day to day. It's crucial to establish a regular writing time that children will come to expect and anticipate. Set aside 45 to 60 minutes every day, if possible, for writing. This is not to suggest that children shouldn't be encouraged to write at other times of the day. However, it does suggest a set time for writing that will provide students with a sense of continuity and regularity.

When there's a special time for writing every day, children learn to anticipate writing *when they are not writing* (during lunchtime, on the playground, or at home). Writing, in Nancy Atwell's (1985) words, becomes habitual: "In situations where students can't write every day, three days each week are enough for developing the habit of gathering and considering ideas for writing. And I think the three days should be regular and consecutive—e.g., every Monday, Tuesday, and Wednesday—this provides the sense of continuity and routine writers need" (p. 37).

In addition to journals, another integral part of the routine of classroom writing involves the use of folders or writing portfolios. In process-centered classrooms there is often a box of writing folders that contain the collected pieces of the children. The written pieces are chosen by the children or the teacher. They may be selections that represent the children's best work or pieces that demonstrate growth in writing. The folders often are stored in a brightly decorated cardboard box or in a filing cabinet within easy reach of the children.

Some teachers recommend using two writing folders: a *daily folder* that contains a child's immediate work in progress, and a *permanent portfolio* for completed pieces of writing. The permanent portfolio has at least two important purposes. First, it documents students' writing development during the school year. Children (as well as parents or the principal) can study their progress and the changes that have occurred in their own writing. They enjoy reading and reviewing the topics they've written about and the types of writing they've completed. Teachers find that folders are invaluable for helping students better understand the writing process. Second, when students accumulate their writings, they can see the investment that they have made. The folder, then, helps to build a sense of pride, accomplishment, and ownership. It is a visible record of a child's growth as a writer.

A process-centered classroom should be guided by rules and procedures that set clear expectations for behavior and interaction and give children a sense of structure and stability. Rules or guidelines will emphasize different things in different classrooms. Yet you may want to consider some of the following:

> When engaged in drafting, writers shouldn't be disturbed. There will be plenty of time to talk about their writing and to share work in progress.
>
> Talk is an important part of writing, but there are limits set on the number of persons who share with one another at any one time.
>
> The class writes and shares every day (Graves, 1983).

Organizing the Writing Workshop

Many teachers think about writing time each day as a workshop. The classroom is the student-writer's studio. Begin each day's **writing workshop** by providing students with the structure they need to understand, develop, or use specific writing strategies, or by giving them direction in planning their writing or in revising their drafts. The **minilesson,** as the name implies, is a brief, direct instructional exchange (usually no longer than ten minutes) between the teacher and the writing group (which may include the whole class). The exchange isn't a substitute for individual guidance; instead, it is meant to get students started on a writing project or to address their specific problems or needs. For example, a minilesson can help to stimulate topic selection; brainstorm ideas and rehearse for writing; illustrate interesting versus dull writing; model literary style by reading passages from literature; illustrate good sentence and paragraph structure; teach and/or model strategies for revision; and teach a mechanical skill.

Calkins (1986) provides several in-depth examples of different types of minilessons that she has seen used by elementary teachers.

Following the minilesson is the actual time that the students spend "in process," whether they're collecting information, drafting, revising, or editing their work. For part of this time, you may find yourself working on your own writing. In addition, your role is primarily to facilitate the workshop by responding to the needs of writers as specific situations demand.

Two plans that teachers have followed in facilitating the writing workshop are outlined below:

PLAN 1

I. Minilesson (3–10 minutes)

II. Writing workshop
   A. Circulate to help individuals (10 minutes).
   B. Work with children in a group conference (15 minutes).
   C. Hold scheduled individual conferences (15 minutes).

III. Group share session (10 minutes)

PLAN 2

I. Minilesson (3–10 minutes)

II. Writing workshop
   A. Write with class (5–10 minutes).
   B. Circulate to help individuals (10–20 minutes).
   C. Hold scheduled individual conferences (10–15 minutes).

III. Group share session (10 minutes)

The main purpose of a **group share session** is to have writers reflect on the day's work. "Process discussions" focus on concerns implicit in the following questions:

How did your writing go today? Did you get a lot done?

Did you write better today than yesterday?

Was it hard for you to keep your mind on what you were writing?

What do you think you'll work on tomorrow?

What problems did you have today?

Calkins (1983) provided these guidelines to facilitate reading and discussion of children's drafts.

RAISING CONCERNS: A writer begins by explaining where he or she is in the writing process, and what help he or she needs. For example, a child might say, "I'm on my third draft and I want to know if it's clear and makes sense," or, "I have two beginnings and I can't decide which is best."

READING ALOUD: Usually, the writer then reads the writing (or the pertinent section) out loud.

MIRRORING THE CONTENT AND FOCUSING PRAISE: The writer then calls on listeners. A classmate begins by retelling what he has heard: "I learned that. . . " or "Your story began. . . " Sometimes a listener may begin by responding with praise or showing appreciation for the writing.

MAKING: SUGGESTIONS Questions or suggestions are then offered about the concern raised by the writer. Sometimes other things will come up as well.

Besides reflecting on the day's writing, reserve the share session for celebrating finished work. Ask volunteers to share their writing with an audience. The author's chair, a strategy we discuss in the next section, is an integral part of the sharing experience. The celebration that children take part in reflects their payoff for the hard work that writers go through to craft a piece of writing to their satisfaction. In Box 5.3 notice how Liz Crider, a second grade teacher, makes the writing workshop an integral part of the school day.

Guiding Writing (and Observing Reading)

When teachers guide the writing process, they will have many opportunities to observe children in real, functional reading situations. Hornsby, Sukarna, and Parry (1986), in fact, show the kinds of reading opportunities that children have when they are involved in the writing process. Table 5.1 depicts these opportunities.

In a process-centered classroom, children quickly become aware that writing evolves through steps and stages. The **stages in the writing process** have been defined by different authorities in different ways. In this book, the stages include *rehearsing, drafting, revising and editing,* and *publishing.* These stages aren't neat or orderly. No wonder they have been described as *recursive.* Writing, as Lindemann (1982) noted, is "a messy business, rarely in real life as tidy as textbook descriptions portray it. We don't begin at step one, 'find a topic,' and follow an orderly sequence of events to 'proofreading the paper.'

● **BOX 5.3**

Class Works

A Typical Day in a Writing Workshop

Liz Crider is a second-grade teacher who makes the writing workshops an integral part of the school day. Here's how she describes a typical day for her students in a writing workshop:

> I teach writing through demonstrations that show my students "what good writers do." To begin my writing program at the beginning of the school year, I invite a published writer to come into the class to let the children know that adult writers have some of the same problems in writing that children do. This year and last year, I invited Mrs. Regie Routman to come and speak to my class. She brought her manuscripts and a variety of interesting personal stories about her experiences as a writer. One of my students was so inspired that he made a statement that I will always remember. He said, "I'm writing a book too, but it's still in my head. I haven't even started writing it yet." This is a profound statement for a second grader to make and the other students in the class responded by telling how writing also begins in their heads.
>
> Not only do my students write in their literature response journals, but they also engage in the writing workshop. Before the workshop begins, I may conduct a focused minilesson to teach whatever skills the students might show a need for at the time. I frequently use the writing of other second graders and my own writing as a means of teaching these lessons.
>
> The children write abut 30 minutes a day. While they are writing I conduct one-on-one conferences with as many students as I can during that half-hour period. I usually can see no more than two or three during that block of time. While I am conferencing with a student, partners conduct peer conferences. I model throughout the year, so that the children will know what a good conference looks and sounds like. They work at being gentle, yet honest with their responses.
>
> At the close of the workshop, two or three children read their writing. The piece that they read might be completed or in progress. They sit in the special "author's chair." They tell the group what their needs are: 1) if they would like the group to just listen; 2) if they would like suggestions; or 3) if they would like comments. This is used as a whole class conference. I constantly model, even during this activity. I record the students' comments on a large Post-it and give it to the author to attach to the story that she/he shared. I frequently remind the children that authors own their writing. They may choose to accept or ignore our input.

(continued)

● **BOX 5.3** *(continued)*

All topics are generated by the children themselves. They write on whatever topic they desire. The children frequently choose to involve themselves in research during writing workshop. They write a report of their findings, complete with a simple bibliography. They then stand as the expert on whatever subject they investigated.

During the workshop, students' desks are arranged in groups of four for collaboration. Children freely share ideas and information. They support one another. The writing center is an important area in my room. There they gather to revise, edit, peer conference, and share ideas about their writing. Though there is movement and noise in my classroom, children are engaged and active learning is taking place.

Certainly, we plan what we want to say before we begin drafting, but the act of writing generates new ideas and shapes new plans" (p. 23).

Rehearsing. *Rehearsing* is everything that writers do before the physical act of putting ideas on paper for a first draft. "Getting it out" is a useful mnemonic, because it helps us to remember that rehearsal means activating background knowledge and experiences, getting ideas out in the open, and making plans for approaching the task of writing.

The rehearsing stage has also been called *prewriting,* a somewhat misleading term because "getting it out" often involves writing of some kind (e.g., making lists, outlining information, jotting notes, or free writing in a journal). Regardless of terminology, rehearsing is a time to generate ideas, stimulate thinking, make plans, and create a desire to write. In other words, rehearsing is what writers do to get "energized," to explore what to say and how to say it: "What will I include?" "What is a good way to start?" "What is my audience?" "What form should my writing take?"

The teacher's job is to make students aware that the writing process must *slow down* at the beginning. By slowing down the process, the students can then discover that they have something worthwhile to say and that they want to say it.

There are many ways to rehearse for writing: *talking, reading to gather information, brainstorming* and *outlining ideas, role playing, doodling, drawing, cartooning, jotting down ideas, taking notes, interviewing,* and even *forming mental images* through visualization and meditation.

Drafting. "Getting it down" is an apt way to describe *drafting.* Once writers have rehearsed, explored, discovered, planned, and talked (and done whatever else it takes to get ideas out in the open), they are ready to draft a text with a purpose and an audience in mind. A child is reading when he or she is drafting a piece. The writing workshop

● TABLE 5.1

Opportunities to Read During Writing

Writing	Reading opportunities
Before Writing	Poetry reading
(Rehearsing)	Oral reading of stories in draft and published form Short story reading Play reading "Read-along" taped stories
During Writing (Drafting and Revising)	Children's oral reading of their drafts to selves and in conferences Silent reading during composition of drafts (to check meaning; to remind oneself of where the writing has been and where it should go; to regain momentum; to provide a breathing space or even to avoid writing) Researching books for material for stories Functional reading and the development of reference, library, and study skills Reading aloud to check sense; to hear the sound of the language
After Writing (Publishing)	Oral reading for audience response Silent reading of own and other children's published stories Borrowing books from class and school libraries Choosing to read again a favorite book/story Reading and performance of plays written by children

Source: Adapted from David Hornsby, Deborah Sukarna, and Jo-Ann Parry. *Read-On: A Conference Approach to Reading. (Portsmouth, NH: Heinemann,* 1986) p. 117.

provides the in-class time for first draft writing. As children draft, the teacher regulates and monitors the process. For example, while students are writing, teachers should not be grading papers or attending to other nonrelated chores. Instead, they should either be writing themselves or keeping writers on task.

Drafting is a good time to confer individually with students who may need help using what they know to tackle the writing task. The teacher can serve as a sounding board, ask probing questions if students appear to be stuck, and create opportunities for a child to read what he or she is writing. A teacher may want to ask the following questions:

How is it going?

What have you written so far?

Tell me the part that is giving you a problem. How are you thinking about handling it?

I am not clear on __________. How can you make that part clearer?

Are you leaving anything out that may be important?

What do you intend to do next?

How does the draft sound when you read it out loud?

What is the most important thing that you're trying to get across?

Once completed, a first draft is just that—a writer's first crack at discovering what he or she wants to say and how he or she wants to say it.

Revising. Each interaction that occurs when a writer seeks a *response,* either from the teacher or another writer in the class, constitutes a *conference.* Children have many opportunities to read their work critically during conferences. Simply stated, a conference may be held when a writer needs feedback for work in progress. The conference may last five seconds or five minutes depending on the writer's needs. However, once a student decides to rework a first draft, conferencing becomes a prominent aspect of *revising* and *editing.*

Conferencing. When writers work on a second or third draft, they have made a commitment to rewrite. Rewriting helps students to take another look. This is why good writing often reflects good rewriting and rereading of a piece.

To conduct a teacher-child conference, a teacher must learn to define his or her role as listener. Graves (1983) noted that when conducting a conference, the child leads and the teacher intelligently reacts.

To elicit clarification of a piece of writing, a teacher might focus the conference with a specific question or two appropriate to the writer's needs.

The following general steps will help in conducting a conference.

1. The writer *reads* the draft out loud.
2. The teacher *listens* carefully for the meaning of the draft.
3. The teacher then *mirrors the content* ("Your draft is about. . . "); *focuses praise* ("The part I liked the best about your draft is. . . "); *elicits clarification* ("Which parts are giving you the most trouble?"); *makes suggestions* ("I think you should work on. . . "); and *seeks the writer's commitment* ("Now that we have talked, what will you do with the draft now?").

To illustrate how effective a conference can be in helping children to revise their work, Wolf (1985) described her work with Jessica, a second grader. Jessica's first draft, displayed in Figure 5.4, is a fluent but rambling piece on a topic that evolved from a social studies lesson on the problem of pollution in big cities.

In this draft, Jessica's content is remarkable; her voice is strong. In conference with the teacher, Jessica realized that her ideas "jumped around." Jessica brings a "writer-as-reader" perspective to her draft, and would need to help the reader to keep the ideas straight. Here is the strategy that she and the teacher worked out: Jessica used a green marker to underline all those ideas about factories and how they pollute the air, and a red marker to underline all those things about how pollution made people and animals sick. Jessica mentioned to the teacher that she also wanted to include her mother's problems with pollution. As a result, she underlined all of those ideas with a yellow marker. She then rewrote a second draft, putting all the ideas underlined in green together, all the ideas underlined in red together, and all the ideas underlined in yellow together. The conference was a perfect opportunity to discuss paragraphing and the idea of indentation. Jessica's second draft is displayed in Figure 5.5.

Teachers who have regular conferences with students quickly realize two things: (1) it's an overwhelming, if not impossible, task to conference with every student who needs feedback during a day's writing, and (2) the class must assume responsibility for providing response to fellow writers.

Peer conferencing provides an audience of readers for a writer to try out work in progress. A child may arrange during the writer's workshop to hold a conference with another child, if it doesn't interfere with the other child's writing. In addition, time might be set aside for peer-conference teams to meet.

A peer-conference team consists of two, three, or four members. At first, a team responds to a writer's draft from questions that the teacher has prepared and modeled through class discussion, demonstration, and individual student conferences.

> What did you like best about this paper? What worked very well?
>
> Was there anything about this piece of writing that was unclear to you?
>
> What feeling did this piece of writing convey to you?
>
> Where in the paper would you like to see more detail? Where could the writer show you something instead of telling you about it? In other words, where could the writer use more description?

Editing. During revision, students will be messy in their writing. In fact, they should be encouraged to be messy. They should be shown how to use carets to make insertions, and be allowed to make cross-outs or to cut and paste sections of text, if necessary. The use of arrows will help students show changes in the position of words, phrases, or sentences within the text.

Once the content and organization of a draft are set, children can work individually or together to edit and proofread their texts for spelling, punctuation, capitalization, word choice, and syntax. Accuracy counts. "Polishing" or "cleaning up" a revised draft

Pollushein! By Jessica
I hate pollushun! It
comes from fackters. They pollut
the air. Pollushun can make you
sick! I su jest you stay away
from pollushun! Every day fater
ys pollut the air even more.
When I go to teleto
I go in a car. We see
Lots of fackters polluting
The air. We see all sorst
of fackterys. facktery chimnis
are what pallut the
air If thay wod tink
about other pepill.

● **FIGURE 5.4** Jessica's first draft on pollution

Maybeifthay wodspend ther
money on geting their chimneys
clean the peopill won't
have to Wach the air.
for the dascusting things in
it. Like my mom
she works down town
All so cars and
turuks polluth the air
When my mom parcks
her car she walks
To her offices. Whill
She is walking to her
ofies she smels the discust
ing smells in the air
When facktters dump ther junck

(continued)

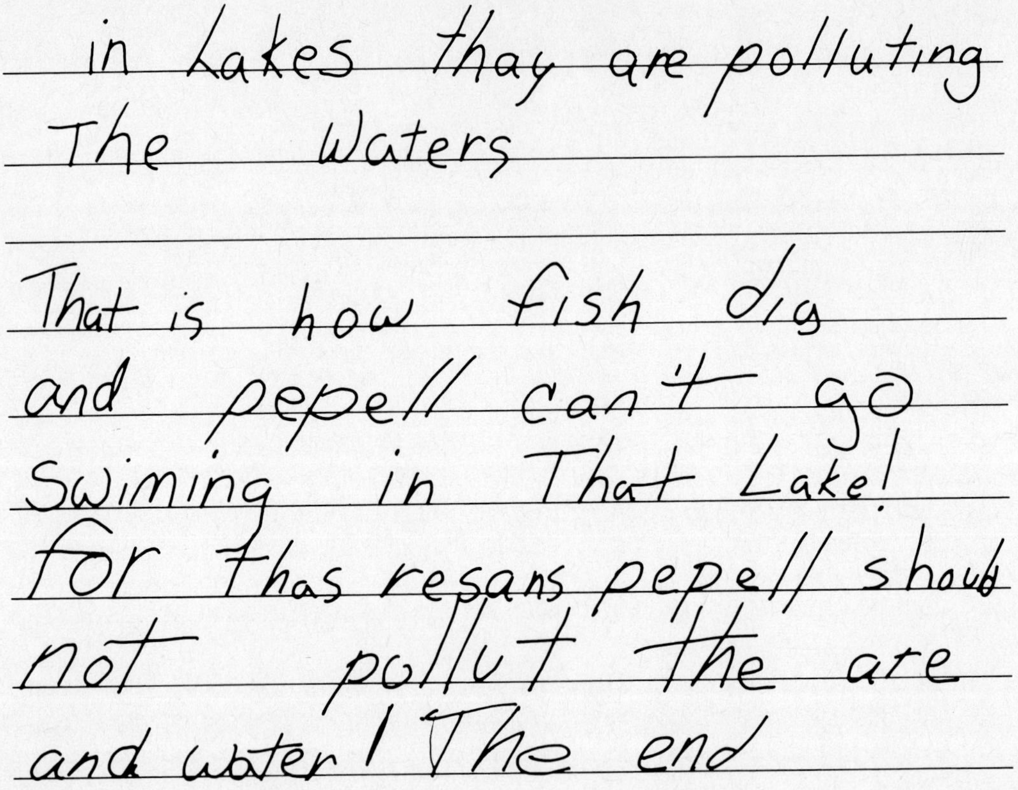

in Lakes thay are polluting
The Waters

That is how fish dig
and pepell can't go
Swiming in That Lake!
for thas resans pepell shoud
not pollut the are
and water! The end

● **FIGURE 5.4** *(continued)*

shouldn't be neglected, *but students must recognize that concern for proofreading and editing comes toward the end of the writing process.*

Children should edit for those skills that are appropriate to their ability and stage of development as writers. An editing conference should provide a *focused evaluation* in which one or two skill areas are addressed. If children have edited their writing to the best of their ability, the teacher may then edit the remainder of the piece for spelling and other conventions.

Publishing. If writing is indeed a public act, then it is meant to be shared with others. Writing is for reading, and children learn quickly to write for many different audiences. When young writers have a sense of their audience, the task of writing becomes a real effort at communication.

The pride and sense of accomplishment that come with *authorship* contribute powerfully to the development of writers. As Kirby and Liner (1981) noted, publishing involves the ego; it provides a strong incentive for children to keep writing and rewriting. But more

By Jessica Second Draft

Pollashn By Jessica

I Hate pollashn! It came from fackters thay pallut the air Every day faterys pallut the air even more We see lots of fackters pullating the air. We see all sorst of fackterys facktery chimns are What pallut the air. When fackterys dump ther junck into lakes thay are polluting the water That is how fich days and pepell can't go swiming in that Lake

Pollushn can make you sick! I sujest you stay away from pollushn! When I go to taketo I go in a car I see lots of fack. faktery chimny s are What pollut the eir. May be if they Whod spend ther monny on chimnys clean pepell whod not have to Whach out for the air for the dasgusting things in it. when fackterys

dump ther junk in the Lakes they are polluting the water that is how fish diys pepell can't go swiming in that lake!

If thay wod thingk about other pepell. may be if thay wod spend ther mony on getting ther chimnys eleand then pepell wod not have to woch the air for the dascusting thing in it. Like my Mom she works downtown allso cars & tracks pollut the air. when my mom parks her car she wocks to her offes. She smells the disgusting tings in the air!

● **FIGURE 5.5** Jessica's second draft on pollution

than anything else, publishing in the classroom is fun. Consider the following vehicles for reading, displaying, sharing, and publishing student work.

We recommend the frequent use of readaloud sessions as a way of sharing and celebrating writing. In this way, all children will at one time or another have an opportunity to read their work to the group. The group-share session described earlier creates the opportunity for a child to present his or her work. Establish a tone of acceptance during oral readings of finished work. Having a child read a completed piece of writing from the author's chair is one way to celebrate authorship, because it dignifies the hard work and effort that has been put into the writing.

Young people take great pride in writing and illustrating their own books. Often, book writing provides the impetus for the writing and justifies all the hard work that goes into the final product. Writing a book creates a meaningful context and a natural motivation for youngsters to revise and edit stories for content, organization, complete sentences, interesting words, and correct spelling. Young writers are especially inspired to write books when they are exposed to children's literature on a regular basis—a topic we explain thoroughly in Chapter 9. They are also eager to make books when they can choose the type of book they want to write. Some possibilities for bookmaking are given in Figure 5.6.

Class-produced newspapers, magazines, anthologies, and books are excellent ways to publish student writing. The students should be involved in all phases of the publication's production. We suggest that children participate not only as writers, but that they also work in groups to assume responsibility for editing, proofreading, design, and production. Production of a class publication need not be elaborate or expensive. Dittoed publications have the same effect on student writers when they see their work in print.

Display student writing. As Kirby and Liner (1981) found, "a display of finished products attracts attention and stimulates talk and thinking about writing" (p. 217). Establish an author's day or a reading fair in which students circulate around the room reading or listening to as many pieces as they can. In their book, *Gifts of Writing* (1980), the Judys outline numerous formats for one-of-a-kind publications. These publications "preserve" students' writing in a variety of forms.

Letters, community publications, commercial magazines, and national and state contests are all vehicles for real-world publishing outside of the classroom and school. Letters, in particular, are valuable because there are so many audience possibilities.

In addition to letters, the local newspaper, PTA bulletin, or school district newsletter sometimes provide outlets for class-related writing activity. Commercial magazines and national, state, local, or school writing contests also offer opportunities for publication. Commercial magazines and writing contests, of course, are highly competitive. However, the real value of writing for commercial publication lies in the authenticity of the task and the real-world audience that it provides. Several magazines that publish the work of young writers are listed below.

Chart Your Course. P.O. Box 6448, Mobile, AL 36660. Material by gifted, creative, and talented children. Ages 6–18.

Ideas for Making Books

Type of Book	Sample	Construction
Shape books Stories about animals, objects, machines, people, etc.; poems; nursery rhymes; innovations	 I Like girls Bubbles TALL TALES	Make pages in the shape of your book. Bind together with staples or masking tape or lace with yarn.
Ring books Group stories; word fun; poems; collection of poems	 BOOKS	Punch holes in pages and use notebook rings or shower curtain rings to bind together.
Stapled books Individual stories; group contributions; alphabet books; word books; poems	 the Silly KiD!	Pages and cover are stapled together, then bound with masking tape for added durability.
Fold-out books Poems; patterns; sequence; stories	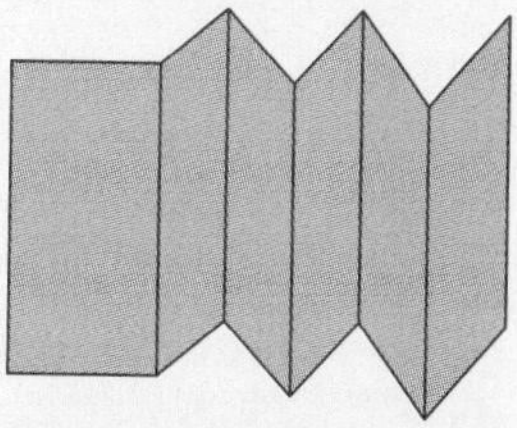	Pages folded accordion-style and then stapled or glued to covers.
Bound cloth books Poems; collections of poems; stories that have been edited and prepared for printing	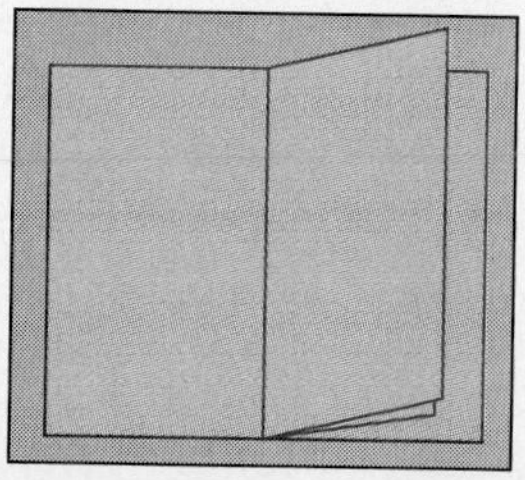	(See extended directions on next page.)

● **FIGURE 5.6** Ideas for making books

Extended Directions for Bound Cloth Books

Supplies: 1 piece of lightweight fabric (approximately 1/2 yard), several needles, white paper, dry mount tissue, cardboard, masking tape, an iron, and an ironing area.

1. Each child should have 6 or 7 sheets of paper. This will give him a finished book with 10 to 12 pages, but will not be too difficult to sew. Fold each sheet of paper in half (one-by-one). (Fig. 1).

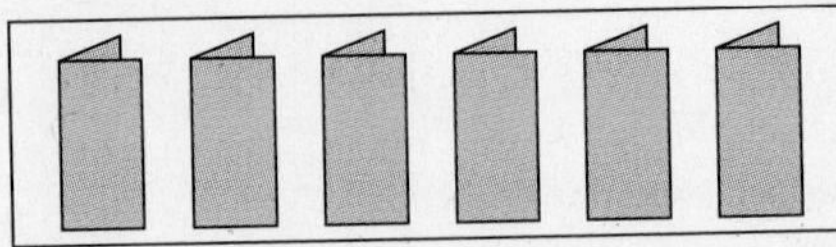

Figure 1

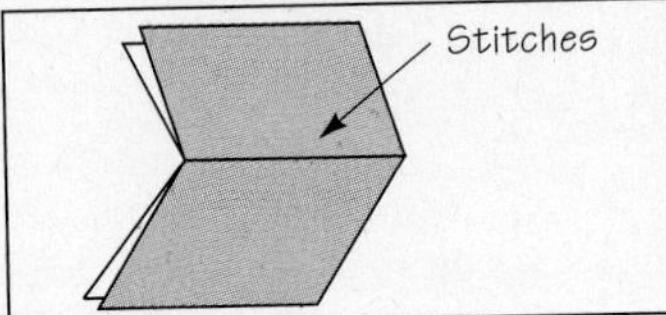

Figure 2

2. Bring the sheets together and sew along the fold. *Hint:* Start on the outside of the fold so the knot is not seen when finished. (Fig. 2).

3. Cut out the fabric to measure 12" x 15". Prepare some templates from cardboard for students to use as guides. (Fig. 3).
4. Spread out the materials as pictured. (Fig. 3).

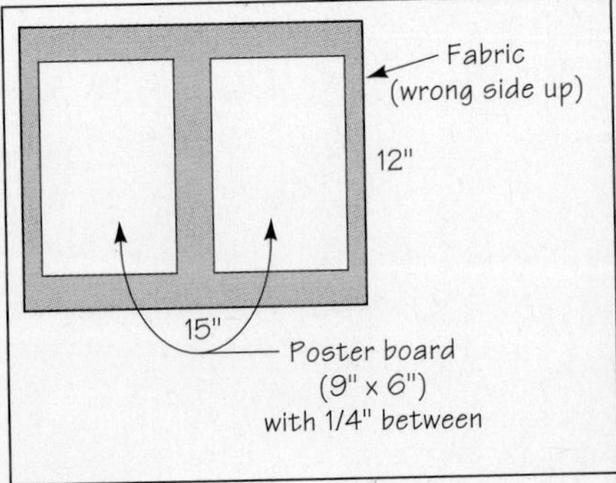

Figure 3

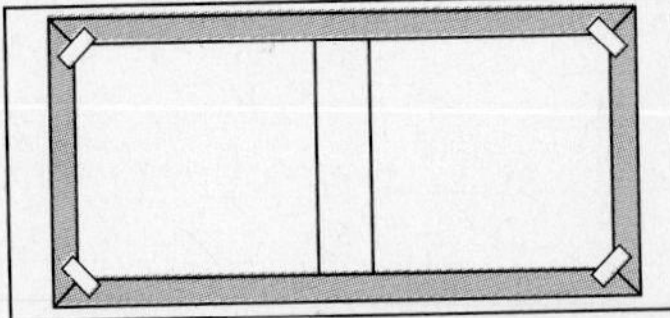

Figure 4

5. Fold the edges of the fabric over the two boards and tape in place at the corners. (Fig. 4).

6. Now, make a sandwich using the cover, then a piece of dry mount tissue (8 1/2" x 11"), then the sewn pages, and iron in place as pictured. Iron only on the endpapers since the pages can be scorched. (Fig. 5).

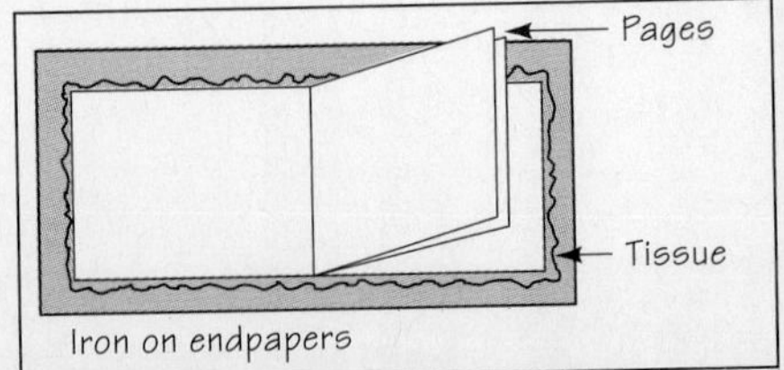

● **FIGURE 5.6** *(continued)*

Child Life. The Children's Better Health Institute, 1100 Waterway Blvd., Indianapolis, IN 46206. Ages 8–10.

City Kids. 1545 Wilcox, Los Angeles, CA 90028. Ages 11–14.

Cobblestone: The History Magazine for Young People. 20 Grove Street, Peterborough, NH 03458. Each issue devoted to a particular theme. Ages 8–14.

Cricket. Box 100, LaSalle, IL 61301. Note: Considers *only* material that complies with current contest rules and descriptions (see each issue for current contest rules). Ages 5–13.

District: Young Writers Journal. 2500 Wisconsin Ave., N.W., #549, Washington, DC 20007. For District of Columbia students and residents only. Ages 9–14. Currently in planning stages. Write for information.

Ebony Jr.! 820 S. Michigan Ave., Chicago, IL 60605. Specializes in material about blacks. Ages 6–12.

Paw Prints. National Zoo, Washington, DC 20008. Specializes in wild exotic animal conservation and other animal-related material. Ages 6–14.

Sprint. Scholastic, Inc., 730 Broadway, New York, NY 10003. Publishes student writing based on assignments in its previous issues. Ages 9–11.

Stone Soup. P.O. Box 83, Santa Cruz, CA 95063. Ages 6–12.

Wee Wisdom. Unity Village, MO 64065. Ages 6–13.

SUMMARY

Learning to write is as natural to children as learning to read. Recent research has resulted in compelling evidence that suggests that reading and writing develop concurrently. Rather than teaching reading and writing as separate curricular entities, they should be taught in tandem.

One of the keys to writing and reading connections in classrooms rests with the environment that teachers create. Natural environments for learning provide encouragement and a built-in support system, and there is tremendous, patient faith that children will develop as writers. Time for writing, response to writing, and ownership of one's own writing are the hallmarks of a natural learning environment.

Writing leads to reading. Getting started with writing instruction is challenging. Teachers must establish a routine for writing. For example, there should be time to write every day, freedom of movement in the classroom, and occasions to write.

Reading is a natural springboard into children's writing. Making the connection between children's literature and writing and informational texts in content areas and writing is important because writing is a way of comprehending. Through journals, children can respond personally to text to explore, clarify, and extend meaning. Writing, we believe, can help children grow in every facet of reading. Journals and writing folders should be the focal point of the classroom-writing program.

Process-centered classrooms allow for great flexibility, not anarchy, and have a predictable structure. Guidelines need to be established to set clear expectations for behavior and interactions within the classroom. In process-centered classrooms, students are encouraged to choose topics that matter to them and to rehearse for writing through talking, reading, brainstorming, and other prewriting strategies. Talking and journal writing, in particular, will help children discover and select topics for writing.

Drafting, revising, and editing are commonplace occurrences in process-centered classrooms. Throughout the stages of writing, children need a response from the teacher and other children. Conferences are the vehicles by which teacher and writers respond to one another in order to try out work and to get ideas on how to improve their drafts. Revising means that the writer will resee or rethink a piece. Once the content of writing is set, then editing becomes a major responsibility of the writer. Editing means preparing the writing for an audience, and involves polishing the writing by attending to such matters as spelling, punctuation, and usage.

Publishing provides the payoff for the hard work that goes into the writing process. Encouraging Students to value writing is crucial. Some suggestions include providing an author's chair; sponsoring class publications, bookmaking, oral presentations, and contests; and advising students about submission to magazines that publish student work.

TEACHER-ACTION RESEARCHER

1. Observe an elementary school teacher during writing instruction time, taking notes on what the teacher says and does. What provisions does the teacher make for writing instruction? Is the teacher's approach to writing process-or product-centered? Analyze the lesson and your notes in order to answer the questions.

2. Locate a classroom in which process writing, including conferences, is used. Observe the interactions that occur when writers seek a response to their writing, either from the teacher or other writers in the class. Do the children seem to have sufficient opportunities to read their work critically during conferences? How long do the conferences tend to last? In a week or two, collect the same type of data based on observations in another classroom either at the same or another grade level. Or revisit the same classroom each week for the same amount of time during the course of a month. Do you notice any changes in the conduct of the conferences? The interactions among the children?

3. Conduct a writing-process conference with an elementary-grade student who has just completed a draft (use some of the suggestions in this chapter for conducting the conference). Describe what happened during the conference. What did you learn from the experience? (Tape-record, if permissible.)

4. Collect several journal entries of children at different grade levels. What do children write about? What kinds of responses do they make to literary texts? How would you plan instruction to help each child continue to grow and develop as a journal writer.

KEY TERMS

reading-writing connection
audience
double-entry journal
literary letters
minilesson
literature
dialogue journal
reading log
word processor
group-share session
informational text
buddy journal
literature response journal
writing workshop
stages in the writing process

CHAPTER 6

Reading Comprehension

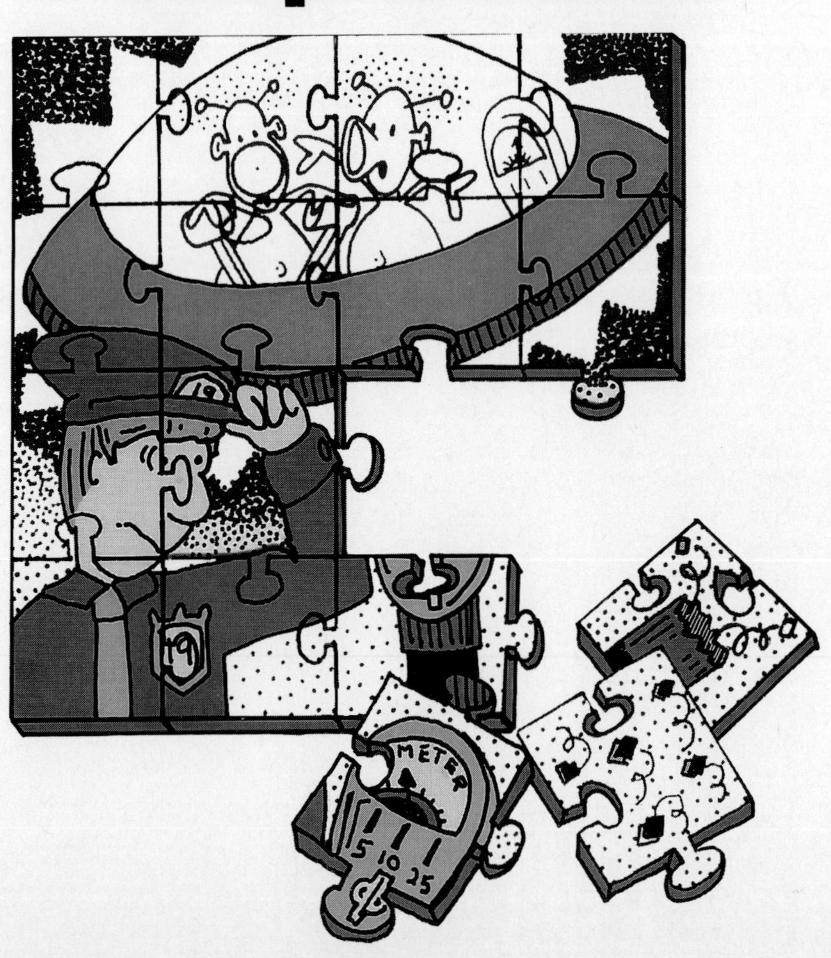

BETWEEN THE LINES

In this chapter you will discover:

- **Why an awareness of story structure aids comprehension.**
- **Strategies to make readers aware of story structure.**
- **Strategies to activate and build schema for comprehension.**
- **Strategies to guide reader-text interactions.**
- **Strategies to promote text discussions.**

It's reading-workshop time in Gay Fawcett's third-grade class. After finishing silent reading, the children are sharing their stories with one another.

Hannah is eager to start and jumps at the opportunity to tell her classmates, "I read this story about a girl who's spoiled and she's going to have a baby sister."

Gay, modeling a listener's response for her students, asks, "Does the author tell you she's spoiled? Does the author come right out and say, 'That girl's spoiled'?"

Hannah doesn't waste a second in replying, "Well, no. But I just knew."

"How did you know? Were there some clues?"

"Yeah," Hannah answers. "She was always yelling at everyone and she had to have her own way all the time."

In response, Gay moves from modeling to an explanation to reinforce one of the concepts she and her students have been working on during the year—an awareness of *sources of information* in text. "That's really good, Hannah! Authors give us information in different ways, don't they?" She then waits for Hannah's reply.

"Sure," Hannah says. And she proceeds to recite the names she has learned for the sources one can turn to in seeking answers after a reading. "Right There, Think and Search, Author and You, and On Your Own."

And to Hannah's classmates Gay ask, "Which one of those do you think Hannah used to figure out that the girl in her story was spoiled?"

"Think and Search," several of the children respond in unison.

The exchange between Gay and her students takes about thirty seconds. The children then return to sharing the content of their stories, which takes most of the time allotted for the reading workshop.

A thirty-second opportunity to indirectly teach children about one of the ways a reader interacts with text is no small feat. Gay likes to take advantage of what are often called teachable moments. To recognize a teachable moment when it arises requires that you know why you're doing what you're doing. Gay's instruction is theoretically sound; she knows what reading is for. Reading is for comprehending.

Who claims to read without comprehension? Our position throughout this book has been that reading involves meaning in the transaction between reader and author. Without comprehension, the act of reading is an empty, vacuous event. Children's earliest home experiences with print are often purposeful, meaningful, and enjoyable. Should school experiences be anything less?

In the past three decades, reading researchers have taken dead aim on understanding the reading process, with comprehension the bullseye. Fueled with federal funding, major research projects have undertaken to better understand how readers comprehend written discourse. As a result, more is known theoretically and practically about comprehension today than ever before. With this knowledge has come a renewed commitment to teaching comprehension as a meaning-making process.

In this chapter, our focus will be on how teachers can apply comprehension strategies to narrative and informational texts, with emphasis on narrative texts. In Chapter 12, we will continue to examine how comprehension strategies may be adapted to various types of texts, with emphasis on informational texts. This division is arbitrary, if not awkward, and is not meant to suggest that the process of comprehending stories and other imaginative works is vastly different from that of comprehending texts of an informational nature.

Meaning, as we suggested in Chapter 1, doesn't lie hidden in text like buried treasure, waiting for readers to dig it out. On the contrary, texts, whether narrative or informational, provide cues that help readers to construct meaning. This is why children must learn to interact with texts to make meaning. From an interactive point of view, comprehension is triggered by the knowledge that the reader brings to print. Not only must children use prior knowledge to comprehend, they must also bring into play knowledge about the text itself. As readers mature, they become more sophisticated in recognizing how texts are organized in narrative and informational writing. To engage in reading as a meaning-making activity, readers must search for and find structure in everything they read.

Building a Schema for Stories

Most authors aren't in the habit of writing carelessly or aimlessly. They impose structure on their writing. Perceiving structure in text material improves learning and retention. When students follow relationships in a reading selection, they're in a better position to construct meaning and to distinguish important from less important ideas and events. In this section, attention is paid to the underlying elements that make up the structure of simple, well-told stories.

Stories are basic to any school's reading curriculum. Because stories are central to children's reading development, much time and effort have been spent attempting to understand how stories are comprehended. A child's knowledge of stories begins to develop at an early age. In Chapters 3 and 4, we explained how children hear and tell simple stories, and then read and view them in both home and school experiences. Children learn implicitly that well-told stories are predictable. There is an underlying structure that all simple stories appear to have in common. As children develop a **story schema,** they begin to sense what comes next.

A simple story actually isn't as simple as it might appear on the surface. During the past decade it has been shown how complex the underlying structure of a story can be. Attempts have been made to identify the basic elements that make up a well-developed story (Mandler and Johnson, 1977; Thorndyke, 1977; Stein and Glenn, 1979). These efforts have led to the development of several variations of **story grammar.** Just as sentence grammar provides a way of describing how a sentence is put together, story grammar helps to specify the basic parts of a story and how those parts tie together to form a well-constructed story. What do most well-developed stories have in common? While individual story grammars may differ somewhat, most would agree that a story's structure centers around *setting* and *plot.*

Elements in a Story Grammar

The setting of a story introduces the main character (sometimes called the *protagonist*) and situates the character(s) in a time and place. The plot of a story is made up of one or more *episodes.* A simple story has a single episode. More complex stories may have two or several episodes, as well as different settings. Each episode is made up of a chain of events. Although the labeling of these events differs from story grammar to story grammar, the following elements are generally included:

A beginning or initiating event: either an idea or an action that sets further events into motion.

Internal response (followed by a goal or problem): the character's inner reaction to the initiating event, in which the character sets a goal or attempts to solve a problem.

Attempt(s): the character's efforts to achieve the goal or alleviate the problem. Several attempts may be evident in an episode.

An outcome(s): the success or failure of the character's attempt(s).

Resolution: the long-range consequence that evolves from the character's success or failure to achieve the goal or resolve the problem.

A reaction: an idea, emotion, or a further event that expresses a character's feelings about success or failure to reach a goal or resolve a problem, or that relates the events in the story to some broader set of concerns.

The events in the story form a causal chain. Each event leads to the next one as the main character moves toward reaching a goal or resolving a problem.

Keeping the elements of story grammar in mind, read the story, "People of the Third Planet," in Box 6.1, and then analyze its structure. To help you map the story's structure, use the chart in Figure 6.1. In the spaces provided on the chart, write what you believe to be the major story parts, including the setting and chain of events.

After you have completed the chart, compare your mapping of the story elements with those of other members of your class. Although there will undoubtedly be some differences in the way the story elements are interpreted, there will probably be a fair amount of similarity among ideas of in what constitutes the elements of story grammar in "People of the Third Planet."

Knowing the underlying elements of a story benefits both teacher and students. You can use story organization to plan instruction more effectively and to anticipate the problems students might have in following a specific story's action, especially if it lacks one or more story elements. Students, on the other hand, can build and use story schema to better understand what they read. The closer the match between the reader's story schema and the organization of a particular story, the greater the comprehension is likely to be. This is why a *story map* is an important planning tool in the hands of teachers.

Mapping a Story for Instructional Purposes. An analysis of a story's organizational elements strengthens instructional decisions. Beck and her associates (1979) recommend creating a *story map* as a way of identifying major structural elements—both explicit and implicit—underlying a story to be taught in class. A chart such as the one in Figure 6.1 helps you to map the relationships that exist among the major events in a story. Once these relationships are established, they form the basis for developing a line of questions that will help students grasp the story parts under discussion. According to Beck, students should thoroughly understand the general framework of the story before broader, evaluative questions can be considered.

The following generic questions are easily applied to specific stories. As you examine these questions, consider how you would adapt them to "People of the Third Planet."

SETTING: Where did the story take place? When did the story take place? Who is the main character? What is ____________ like? What is ____________'s problem? What did ____________ need? Why is ____________ in trouble?

INTERNAL RESPONSE AND GOAL/PROBLEM: What does ____________ decide to do? What does ____________ have to attempt to do?

● BOX 6.1

People of the Third Planet

by Dale Crail

The silver flying saucer came down silently and landed in a parking lot in a small town on earth. It was one o'clock in the morning, and the streets were dark.

Slowly a section of the saucer slid open. Two creatures from another world stepped out. For a moment they thought no one was near. Then they noticed a line of figures standing before them.

One creature whispered to the other, "Over there I see some people of the Third Planet. But they do not come forward to greet us. Perhaps this is not the time to tell the people of the Third Planet about our world."

The other creature shook his head. "No, our orders are clear. Now is the time. We must approach these earth people and arrange a meeting with their leader."

He stepped forward and began to speak. "People of the Third Planet—or Earth, as you call it. We greet you in peace. We are messengers from a world that is millions of years older than your own. We wish to establish a peaceful link between our two worlds and exchange ideas with you. We would like to speak to someone of importance on your planet. Please direct us to such a person." No one in the line of figures moved. They did not even seem interested in the space creature's words.

After several seconds the creature stepped back and whispered to his friend, "These earth people act as if they do not understand what I am saying. How can that be? We monitored their radio signals and listened to them speak. I am sure we are using their language correctly."

"Stay calm," said the other creature. "I will speak to them."

He raised his voice and said, "Earth friends! Perhaps you are frightened by our sudden appearance. Or perhaps you do not fully understand our message. I assure you that it is of the greatest importance. It is necessary that we speak to the leader of the Third Planet. Please tell us where we may find this person."

The figures remained absolutely still.

"We will not harm any of you," the space creature went on. "We only wish to talk with your leader. But—if you do not cooperate—we will be forced to take one of you with us for questioning."

Not one figure moved or said a word.

The creature from the saucer began to get angry. He clenched his fists and whispered to his friend, "Apparently these Earth people will not tell us anything. Let us take one aboard. We will force the Earth person to speak."

He shouted at the figures standing before him, "You have left us no choice! We will have to use force."

He was amazed that even these words had no effect. The figures did not turn and run. They did not move at all.

(continued)

● **BOX 6.1** *(continued)*

In a fury he raced up to the first figure in line and said, "You are my prisoner. March forward to the saucer!"

Nothing happened.

Then he hit the figure hard, but still the figure did not move.

"It is no use," he said. "I cannot force this Earth person to walk. It is as if the Earth person has roots that go deep into the ground."

"Use your ray gun!" his friend yelled. "Cut the Earth person away from the Earth that these people love so much."

There was a single flash of fire from the space creature's gun. The Earth person fell noisily to the ground.

Even then none of the other figures moved.

This was more than the space creatures could believe.

"People of the Third Planet!" the first creature said. "We greeted you in peace, and you did not answer us. We captured one of your people, and you did not stop us. You are strange people with no feelings for anyone. Farewell, people of the Third Planet. Farewell."

The two creatures put the captured figure into their saucer and then climbed in themselves. With a sudden flash of light the flying saucer took off from Earth.

A police car was coming down the street just as the saucer flashed up into the sky.

"What was that?" one of the police officers asked.

"Looked like an explosion in the parking lot," his partner said. "Better see what happened."

The car raced toward the lot and screeched to a stop. The driver jumped out and flashed his light and found the officer down on one knee, pointing to a metal base that was still hot to the touch.

"Something sliced off this thing," the police officer said. "Did a neat job of cutting too. But what for? They could only get away with a few pennies. Why would anyone want to steal a parking meter?"

ATTEMPTS AND OUTCOMES	What did ____________ do about ____________? What happened to ____________? What will ____________ do now? How did (*the attempt*) turn out?
RESOLUTION:	How did ____________ solve the problem? How did ____________ achieve the goal? What would you do to solve ____________'s problem?
REACTION:	How did ____________ feel about the problem? Why did ____________ do ____________? How did ____________ feel at the end?

<table>
<tr><td colspan="2">Setting</td></tr>
<tr><td>Time and place:</td><td>Character(s):</td></tr>
<tr><td colspan="2">Chain of Events</td></tr>
<tr><td>The beginning event that initiates the action</td><td></td></tr>
<tr><td>Internal response and goal/problem</td><td></td></tr>
<tr><td>Attempt(s) and outcome(s)</td><td></td></tr>
<tr><td>Resolution</td><td></td></tr>
<tr><td>Reaction</td><td></td></tr>
</table>

● **FIGURE 6.1** A chart for mapping story structure

When students have responded to questions related to the story line, engage them in discussion centered around other important aspects of the story such as its theme, character development, or the reader's personal response to the story.

THEME:	What is the moral of the story? What did you learn from the story? What is the major point of the story? What does this story say about (*unusual truth*)? Why do you think the author wanted to write this story?
CHARACTERS:	Why do you think (*character*) did that? What do you like about (*character*)? Dislike? Does (*character*) remind you of anyone else that you know?
PERSONAL RESPONSE:	Is there anything you would have changed in the story? How did the story make you feel? Happy? Sad? Angry? Bewildered? Was there anything about the story that didn't make sense?

Not only is story mapping useful for planning questions, but it also provides you with information about "break points" during reading. A break point occurs whenever students are asked to stop an in-class reading to discuss story content. When and where to stop reading, as we will explain later in this chapter, is one of the most important decisions you can make when guiding a *Directed Reading-Thinking Activity.*

Is It Necessary to Teach Story Structure?

We don't advocate teaching story elements for the sake of teaching story elements. Such practice can turn out to be as mindless as teaching reading skills for the sake of reading skills. However, making children aware of the predictability of a well-developed story is appropriate, especially if the children don't appear to use story schema during reading. You can put story structure to good use in the classroom when there is access to reading materials that are written around recognizable story structures. Moreover, avoid using narrative selections that masquerade as stories. These so-called stories go nowhere; they're incomplete and severely lacking in one or more story parts.

The following activities and suggestions will help students build a sense of story and reinforce their awareness of story structure.

Read, Tell, and Perform Stories in Class. There is no better substitute for building experience with stories or extending students' knowledge of how stories are put together than to read, tell, and perform stories in class on a regular basis. These types of experiences with stories are as paramount in the upper grades as they are in the beginning grades. In Chapter 10, we will emphasize the nuts and bolts of storytelling. In earlier chapters, we have explained the importance of reading stories aloud, writing stories, and performing stories through dramatic play. Language experiences such as these are integral to the development of concepts related to literacy.

Don't Teach the Language of Story Grammar as an End in Itself. Although children need to be aware of the language of instruction, avoid teaching jargon for the sake of learning technical terms. Children develop story schema gradually and implicitly, mainly through direct experience and interaction with stories. However, when teaching story parts explicitly to children, use language that is simple and familiar. For example, instead of asking a child to identify the initiating event in the story, you may want to phrase the question in more familiar language such as, "What happened in the beginning of the story to get things started?"

Build on children's concepts of *problem* and *trouble.* You might ask "What does trouble mean? Have you ever been in trouble with a parent or a friend? What kind of trouble happens in stories you have read? How did (the main character) get into trouble? How did (the main character) get out of trouble?"

The concept of trouble is closely related to the central problem in a story. Most fiction in the elementary and middle grades revolves around a problem. Because a problem gives coherence to a story, it is probably one of the most important story parts for readers to recognize. For this reason, build on students' sense of problems in their own lives. Categorize the types of problems that they have experienced (e.g., problems related to needing, wanting, feeling, etc.). Then relate these problems to stories children have read and will read.

Show Relationships Among Story Parts. Diagrams and flowcharts depicting the relationships that exist among events in the story give children a visual image of how stories are organized. Gordon and Braun (1983) suggest giving students copies of a diagram without the story information. As information is discussed relating to the story parts depicted on the diagram, students can write what is being said on their own copies.

Pearson (1982) claims that children as young as 8 years old are successful, with much teacher modeling, at representing a story on a flowchart. Flowcharting can take many different forms such as the one illustrated in Figure 6.2. Study the generic format and how a second-grade teacher adapted that format to develop a story map based on students' suggestions during discussion.

The value of diagramming or flowcharting lies in the discussions that take place before, during, and after the activity. Discussions should revolve around the relationships of one event to another. The goal behind a discussion is to make students consciously aware that events in a story form a causal chain. With much teacher-led discussion, modeling, and guided practice, many students beginning in the second or third grade will grasp how to diagram story parts and make flowcharts on their own. Once this is the case, have students share their products with one another. Rather than emphasize accuracy during sharing sessions, ask for reasons and rationales. Encourage speculation and risk taking. Also, allow students the opportunity to revise or alter their individual efforts based on the discussion.

Reinforce Story Knowledge Through Instructional Activities

Children's understanding of story structure can be extended through varied instructional tasks. Whaley (1981) suggests two activities: **macrocloze stories** and **scrambled stories.** A third activity involves the use of **story frames.**

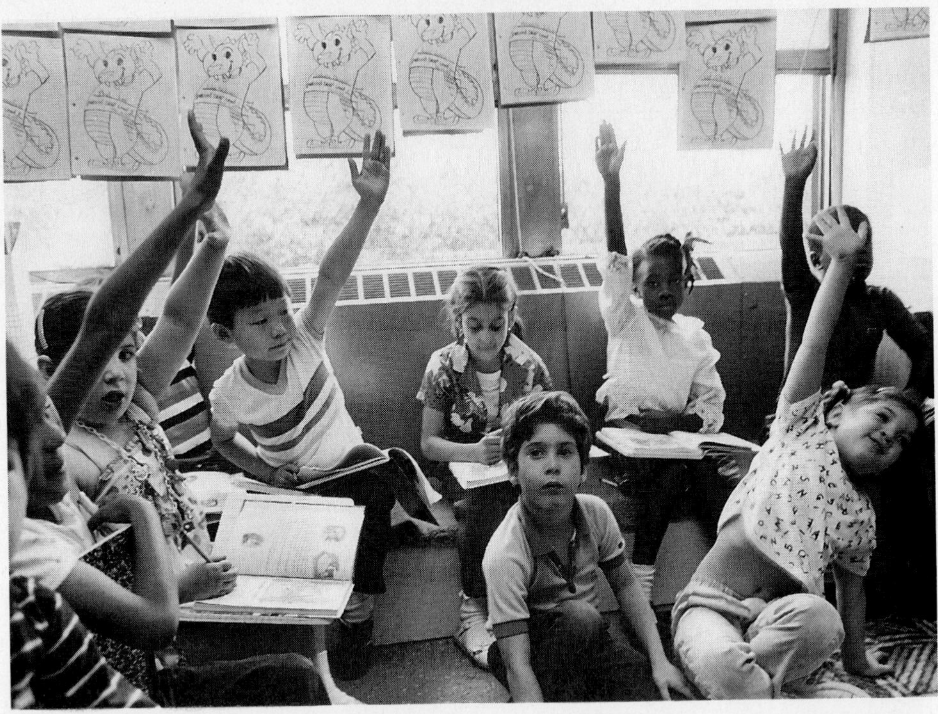

How did the story make you feel? Is there anything you would have changed? Did any of the characters remind you of someone you know?

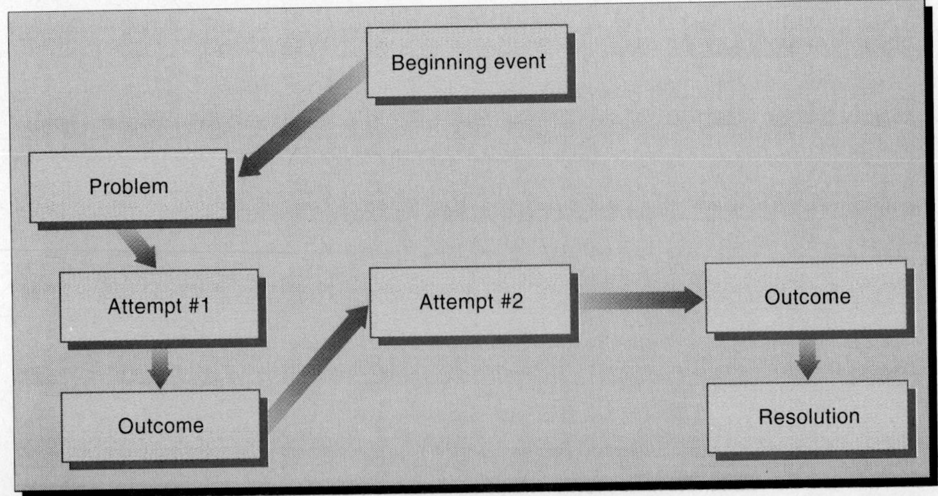

● **FIGURE 6.2a** Generic flowchart for mapping a story and a classroom example of the format

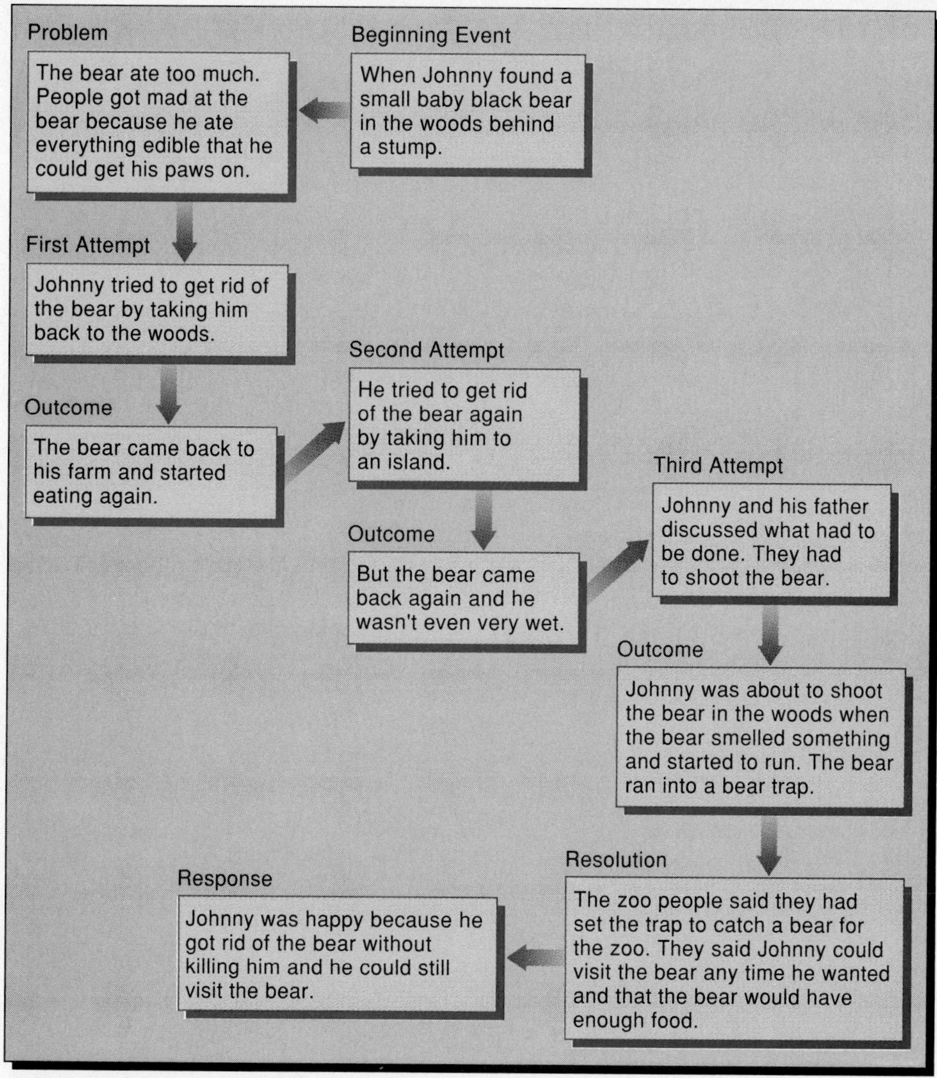

Problem
The bear ate too much. People got mad at the bear because he ate everything edible that he could get his paws on.
Beginning Event
When Johnny found a small baby black bear in the woods behind a stump.
First Attempt
Johnny tried to get rid of the bear by taking him back to the woods.
Outcome
The bear came back to his farm and started eating again.
Second Attempt
He tried to get rid of the bear again by taking him to an island.
Outcome
But the bear came back again and he wasn't even very wet.
Third Attempt
Johnny and his father discussed what had to be done. They had to shoot the bear.
Outcome
Johnny was about to shoot the bear in the woods when the bear smelled something and started to run. The bear ran into a bear trap.
Resolution
The zoo people said they had set the trap to catch a bear for the zoo. They said Johnny could visit the bear any time he wanted and that the bear would have enough food.
Response
Johnny was happy because he got rid of the bear without killing him and he could still visit the bear.

● **FIGURE 6.2b** Classroom example: a second-grade group-constructed story map

Macrocloze Stories. A macrocloze story is based on the same principle that operates for a cloze passage (see Chapter 13 for a fuller explanation). A teacher constructs cloze material by deleting single words from a passage. Children are then given copies of the cloze passage and are required to supply the missing words. When constructing a macrocloze story, instead of omitting single words, delete one or more parts from the story; for example, a sentence, several sentences, or an entire paragraph. Reproduce copies of the story with rules indicating where the text deletions have been made. Students should then read the story and discuss the missing information orally or in writing.

Scrambled Stories. A second instructional task involves scrambled stories. As the name implies, a story is separated into its parts and jumbled. Students must then read the scrambled story and reorder it. Try your hand at reordering the story events in Figure 6.3 from Aesop's fable, "The Crow and the Pitcher." Decide which story event comes first, second, third, and so on. Compare your reordering with others in your class.

Story Frames. Story frames present a third way of heightening an awareness of stories. Fowler (1982) showed how story frames may be particularly appropriate in the primary grades or in situations where students are at risk in their development as readers. A story frame provides the student with a skeletal paragraph: A sequence of spaces tied together with transition words and connectors that signal a line of thought. Fowler identified five story frames, each with a different emphasis: *plot summary, setting, character analysis, character comparison,* and the story's *problem.*

In Figure 6.4, examine how two third graders completed a frame for the story, "Owl at Home." The frame centers on the story's problem. The children bring differing abilities to the task, yet both capture the central focus of the story.

Example of story-frame formats suggested by Fowler are illustrated in Figure 6.5.

As students become familiar with using story frames, you may want to involve them simply in writing summary paragraphs that focus on different elements of the story.

Building a schema for stories is an important aspect of comprehension instruction. No less important is how children activate and use schemata in general to predict and anticipate meaning during reading. Prediction and anticipation are valuable tools for helping students read for meaning. In the next section, we explore how strategies related to prediction and anticipation help remove potential roadblocks to comprehension.

Activating and Building Schema

A common sense imperative emerges from a schema theory of reading comprehension: help students act upon and interact with the main ideas of a reading selection *before* they encounter them in print. The value of *prereading preparation* lies in helping comprehenders recognize what they know and what they need to find out more about. Two pivotal questions that readers must ask as they approach a reading selection are, "What do I already know about the reading selection?" and, "What do I need to know?"

"What do I already know?" agitates thinking. Readers must learn how to take inventory of their own store of knowledge and experiences. Helping children reflect in this manner is crucial from an instructional point of view. For one thing, it's a great confidence

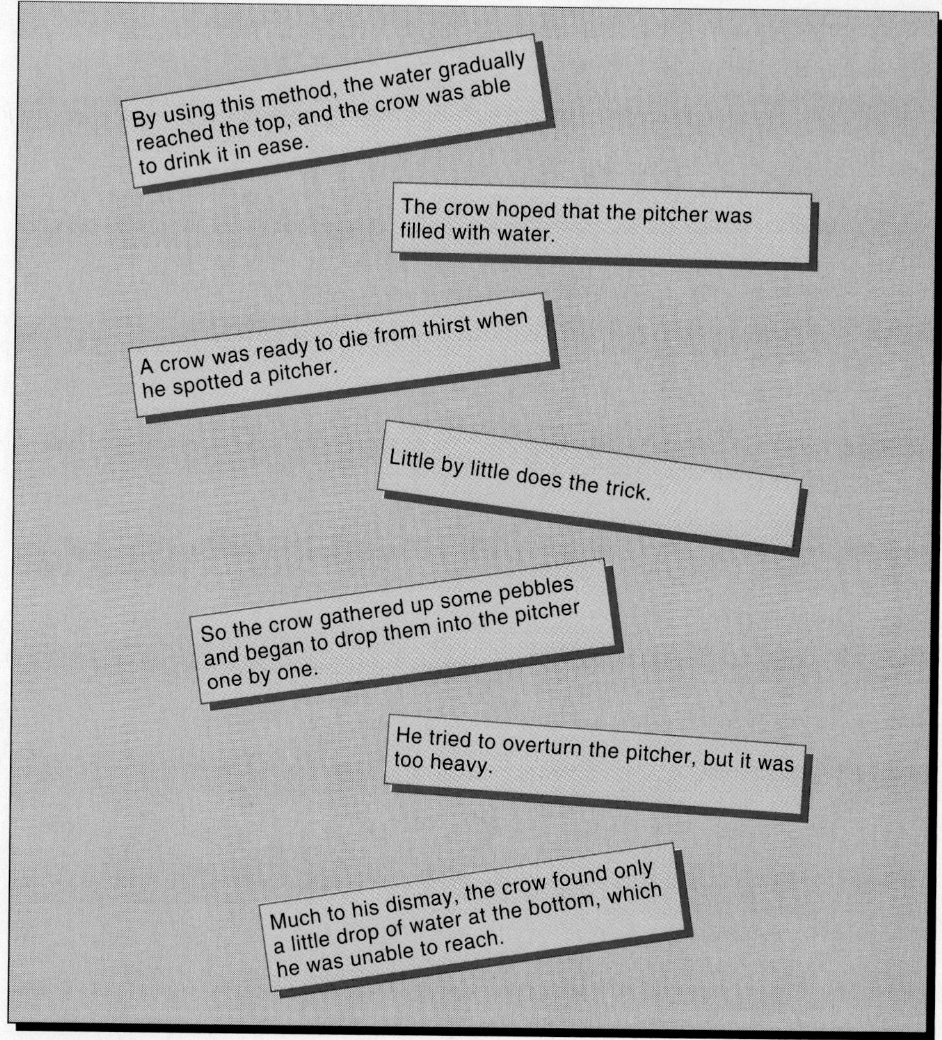

By using this method, the water gradually reached the top, and the crow was able to drink it in ease.
The crow hoped that the pitcher was filled with water.
A crow was ready to die from thirst when he spotted a pitcher.
Little by little does the trick.
So the crow gathered up some pebbles and began to drop them into the pitcher one by one.
He tried to overturn the pitcher, but it was too heavy.
Much to his dismay, the crow found only a little drop of water at the bottom, which he was unable to reach.

● **FIGURE 6.3** An example of a scrambled story

booster to know that you know something about a subject to be encountered in print. One of the challenges of teaching is convincing children that they know more about a text than they often give themselves credit for.

On the other hand, "What do I already know?" helps children recognize what they don't know, *but* will learn more about from reading. When faced with a text selection, they may lack an *available* schema for comprehending the material. Here's where background building activities will help develop a frame of reference for children to handle incoming information in text. In the next chapter, the "Cone of Experience" is explained

Tanner's Frame

In this story the problem starts when Owl thought the moon was following home.

After that, He started walking and he said that the moon was ~~[illegible]~~ following him.

Next, He was almost home and he still thougt the moon was still following him.

Then, he went inside his house and he got his p.J's on.

The problem is finally solved when Owl looks out the window and says night to the moon and went to bed. The story ends with owl sleeping.

Renee's Frame

In this story the problem starts when everything was dark.

After that, a tip of the moon appeard over the seashore.

Next, Owl watched the moon go higher, higher.

Then, They became good friends.

The problem is finally solved when Owl went to bed

The story ends good

● **FIGURE 6.4** Comparison of story frames for "Owl At Home"

STORY SUMMARY WITH ONE CHARACTER INCLUDED:

Our story is about ____

______________________________. ______________________________ is an important character in our story. ______________________________ tried to ____.

The story ends when ____

____.

IMPORTANT IDEA OR PLOT

In this story the problem starts when ______________________________

____. After that,

____.

Next, ____

______________________________. Then, ______________________________

____. The problem is finally solved when ____

____. The story ends ____________

____.

SETTING

This story takes place ____

____. I know this because the author uses the words " ____

____." Other clues that show when the story takes place are ______________________________

____.

CHARACTER ANALYSIS

____ is an important character in our story. ______________________________ is important because

____. Once, he/she

____. Another time,

____. I think that

____________________ is ____
(character's name) *(character trait)*

because ____.

● **FIGURE 6.5** Story frame examples

CHARACTER COMPARISON

_______________ and _______________ are two characters in our story. _______________ (character's name) is _______________ (trait) while _______________ (other character's name) is _______________ (trait). For instance, _______________ tries to _______________ and _______________ tries to _______________. _______________ learns a lesson when _______________.

● **FIGURE 6.5** *continued*

within the context of concept development. Edgar Dale (1969), the cone's originator, provides valuable insights into building real and vicarious experiences for reading and learning tasks. When children lack a schema for reading, concrete, extended discussions focusing on the key ideas *before* reading takes place should be the rule and not the exception. The use of film, video, pictures, and filmstrips are excellent experience builders.

Although children may have a schema for reading they may fail to bring it to bear as they read. Maturing readers are often unaware that prior knowledge is of any consequence in the reading process. However, when strategically engaged in exploring what they know and what they need to know, young readers soon recognize the importance of establishing goals and plans for reading. Searching for answers to questions such as, "What do I need to know?" leads to prediction making and goal-directed behavior.

Story Impressions

Story Impressions is the name of a strategy that helps children anticipate what stories *could* be about. As a prereading activity, this strategy uses clue words associated with the setting, characters, and events in the story (the story impressions) to help readers write their own versions of the story prior to reading. McGinley and Denner (1987), originators of the strategy, describe it this way: "Story impressions get readers to predict the events of the story that will be read, by providing them with fragments of the actual content. After reading the set of clues, the students are asked to render them comprehensible by using them to compose a story of their own in advance of reading the actual tale" (p. 249).

Fragments from the story, in the form of clue words, enable readers to form an overall impression of how the characters and events interact in the story. The clue words are selected directly from the story and are sequenced with arrows or lines to form a descriptive chain. The chain of clue words triggers children's impressions of what the story may be about. Children then write a "story guess" which predicts the events in the story.

As McGinley and Denner explain, "The object, of course, is not for the student to guess the details or the exact relations among the events and characters of the story, but to simply compare his or her own story guess to the author's actual account" (p. 250). They suggest the following steps to introduce Story Impressions to the class for the first time:

1. Introduce the strategy by saying to the students, "Today we're going to make up what we think this story *could* be about."
2. Use large newsprint, a transparency, or a chalkboard to show students the story impressions (See Figure 6.6 for an example), saying, "Here are some clues about the story we're going to read." Explain that the students will use the clues to write their own version of the story and that, after reading, they will compare what they wrote with the actual story.
3. Read the clues together and explain how the arrows link one clue to another in a logical order. Then brainstorm story ideas that connect all of the clues in the order that they are presented, saying, "What do we think this story could be about?"
4. Demonstrate how to write a story guess by using the ideas generated to write a class-composed story that links all of the clues. Use newsprint, the chalkboard, or a transparency for this purpose. Read the story prediction aloud with the students.
5. Invite the students to read the actual story silently, or initiate a shared reading experience. Afterwards, discuss how the class-composed version is like and different from the author's story.
6. For subsequent stories, use story impressions to have students write individual story predictions or have them work in cooperative teams to write a group-composed story guess.

Story Impressions works well in primary and intermediate classrooms. Younger readers may need more than one introductory lesson to model the strategy. With older readers, Story Impressions can easily be adapted for longer literary texts which may involve several chapters or more. In Gloria Riechert's sixth-grade class, for example, readers use story impressions to predict events from the novel, *Where the Red Fern Grows* by Wilson Rawls. Figure 6.6 shows the story impressions for Chapter 9 and compares the story guesses of two students. A class discussion of the strategy revealed that students felt that the clue words aided in making predictions about the story easy. According to some of the students, Story Impressions helped them to key in on important events and aroused their curiosity about the chapter.

Student-Generated Questions

When students learn to ask questions before, during, and after reading, they put themselves in the strategic position of generating their own organizers for learning. Showing children how to ask questions is no easy task, because it cuts against the grain of typical

Story Guess

Billy uses his ax to chop down the big sycamore tree. He doesn't chop it down, and he goes to his Grandpa for help. His grandpa teaches him a trick. He shouldn't give up, and chop all day, and then, if it is not down, put a scarecrow by it. Then, go home and eat dinner. Billy did that, and he got some sleep. He had a lot of blisters in his hands. He went next day, and he tried to chop down the tree, but he didn't chop it down, and he had a lot of discouragement. He said a prayer that night, and at night, a gust of wind blew down the tree.

● **FIGURE 6.6** Story impressions for Chapter 9 of *Where the Red Fern Grows* classroom discourse. As early as first grade, children learn two of the main rules that usually govern classroom talk: (1) the teacher talks in questions and, (2) the students talk in answers. The following strategies alter the rules of classroom interaction by promoting students' self-questioning behavior.

Active Comprehension. Whenever children are engaged in a process of generating questions throughout reading, they are involved in **active comprehension.** According to Singer (1978), teachers encourage active comprehension when they *ask questions that elicit questions in return.* A first-grade teacher, for example, might focus attention on a picture or an illustration from a story or a book. Instead of asking, "What is the picture about?" the teacher poses a question that gets questions in response: "What would you like to know about the picture?" In return, students might generate questions that focus on the details, main idea, or inference from the illustration.

Ms. Mayer, a sixth-grade teacher, read the opening paragraph of *The Best Christmas Pageant Ever* to her class.

> The Herdmans were absolutely the worst kids in the history of the world. They lied and stole and smoked cigars (even the girls) and talked dirty and hit little kids and cussed their teachers and took the name of the Lord in vain and set fire to Fred Shoemaker's old broken-down toolhouse.
>
> The toolhouse burned right down to the ground, and I think that surprised the Herdmans. They set fire to things all the time, but that was the first time they managed to burn down a whole building.
>
> I guess it was an accident. I don't suppose they woke up that morning and said to one another, "Let's go burn down Fred Shoemaker's toolhouse" . . . but maybe they did. After all, it was a Saturday, and not much was going on.

She then asked, "What more would you like to know about the Herdmans?" As her sixth graders responded, Ms. Mayer wrote their questions on the board.

> Why were the Herdmans so bad?
>
> Did they enjoy setting fire to the toolhouse?
>
> Did they feel guilty after the toolhouse burned down?

Not only do these questions stimulate interest and arouse curiosity, but they also draw students into the story. In the process, students' reading behavior will be more goal directed. That is, they will read to satisfy purposes that *they* have established, not the teacher.

Nolte and Singer (1985) explain that teachers can show students how to generate their own questions for a story by adhering to a "phase-in, phase-out" strategy. Phase-in, phase-out simply means that you gradually shift the burden of responsibility for question-asking from your shoulders to those of your students. A good deal of this strategy involves modeling question-asking behavior and making students aware of the value of questions before, during, and after reading. The following plan will ensure a smooth transition from teacher-directed questions to student-generated questions. Although the steps in the plan were recommended for 9- and 10-year-old students, they can easily be adapted for younger or older readers.

1. Discuss the importance of asking questions as you direct students' comprehension of a story.
2. Model the types of questions that can be asked about central story content, including setting, main character, problem or goal, and obstacles encountered while attempting to resolve the problem or achieve the goal.
3. As you work through a story, ask questions that require questions in response; for example, "What would you like to know about the setting of the story?" "The main character?" "What would you like to know about what happened next?" Spend several class periods guiding question generation in this manner.
4. Divide the class into small groups of four to six children. One student in each group is designated to serve in the role of teacher by eliciting questions from the other members. Circulate around the room to facilitate the group process. Spend several class periods in small group question-generation. Allow several minutes toward the end of each class period for debriefing with students; for example, "How did the questioning go?" "Were there any problems?" "Why does question-asking make a story easier to read?"
5. Have students work in pairs, asking each other questions as they read.
6. Have students work on their own to generate questions. Discuss the questions they raise as a whole group.

In following these steps, Nolte and Singer found that training students to ask questions resulted in superior comprehension on the part of 9- and 10-year-olds as compared to 9- and 10-year-olds who did not receive such training.

ReQuest. **ReQuest,** or reciprocal questioning, can easily be used to help students think as they read in any situation that requires reading. ReQuest encourages students to ask their own questions about the material being read (Manzo, 1969; Vacca and Vacca, 1993).

Should you use ReQuest, consider the following steps.

1. Introduce ReQuest to students in their reading groups.
2. Both the students and the teacher silently read a common segment of the reading selection. Manzo recommended one sentence at a time for poor comprehenders. This may also be appropriate for beginning readers. Consider varying the length of reading for older students. For example, both teacher and students begin by reading a paragraph.
3. The teacher closes the book and is questioned about the passage by the students.
4. Exchange roles. The teacher now asks students questions about the material.
5. Upon completion of the student-teacher exchange, the next segment of text is read. Steps 3 and 4 are repeated.
6. At a suitable point in the text, when students have processed enough information to make predictions about the remainder of the assignment, the exchange of questions

stops. The teacher then asks broad questions such as, "What do you think the rest of the assignment is about?" "Why do you think so?"

7. Students are then assigned the remaining portion of the selection to read silently.
8. The teacher facilitates follow-up discussion of the material.

The ReQuest procedure also works well in groups when you alternate the role of student-questioner after each question. By doing so, you will probably involve more students in the activity. Also, once students understand the steps and are aware of how to play ReQuest, you may also try forming ReQuest teams. A ReQuest team made up of three or four students challenges another ReQuest team.

Whenever students are asked to generate questions, some will not know how to do so. Others will ask only literal questions, because they don't know how to ask any others; they don't know how to ask questions that will stimulate inferential or evaluative levels of thinking. One way to deal with these situations is to provide a model that students will learn from. Your role as a questioner should not be underestimated. Over time you will notice the difference in the ability of students to pose questions and in the quality of questions asked.

Notice how in one third-grade class, the teacher used her children's penchant for asking detailed questions to an advantage. ReQuest was being played from a social studies textbook, and the text under consideration consisted of two pages: one explaining map symbols and the other a map of the city of Burlington to practice reading the symbols or key. The children sensed that it would be difficult for the teacher to recall every detail relating to the map of Burlington. So they zeroed in, hoping to stump the teacher with precise questions. Notice how the teacher (T) uses the occasion to make students (S) aware of how to interact with the text.

S: Where is the lake in Burlington?
T: Oh-oh. I'm not sure I studied the map well enough. Let me think (closes eyes). I'm making a picture in my head of that map. I can almost picture that lake. I think it's in the northeast corner of Burlington.
S: You're right.
T: I'm glad I made that mental picture as I was reading.
S: Where are the railroad tracks in Burlington?
T: I'm not sure. My mental picture is pretty good, but I don't have every single detail.
S: Close to City Hall.
S: Where is the hospital?
T: (closes eyes) Near the center of town.

Questioning continued in this manner with the teacher knowing some of the answers and the students informing her of others. At the conclusion of the lesson, the teacher summarized this way: "Who would have ever thought you'd get so many questions from two short pages of social studies? I'm glad you asked all those. I sure learned a lot about reading maps! When we do ReQuest, I do two things that might help you, too. First, if there's a chart, picture, or map, I try to make a picture of that in my head. Then if you ask me questions about it, I can bring it up in my memory. Also, as I'm reading, I ask myself questions that I think you might ask me. Then I'm ready for them! This is a good thing to do anytime you're reading. Stop, ask yourself questions, and answer them. That helps you understand and remember what you have read."

Your Own Questions. Another schema-based strategy involving self-questioning is called **Your Own Questions.** As the name implies, this strategy helps students set purposes for reading and directs their reading behavior. They are encouraged to generate questions and then search the reading situation for answers. Here's how Your Own Questions works.

1. Have students preview a title and pictures and/or listen to or read a portion of text from the beginning of a selection.
2. Encourage students to write or ask as many questions as they can that they think will be answered by reading the remainder of the selection.
3. Discuss some of the questions asked by the students before reading. Write the questions on the board.
4. Students then read to see if questions are answered.
5. After reading, which questions are answered? Which weren't? Why not?

Your Own Questions teachers children to approach reading material inquisitively. Discussing student-generated questions before reading raises expectations and helps to determine what content readers judge to be important. The strategy, then, is similar to the ReQuest and active comprehension strategies in that it allows readers to achieve self-defined goals.

Guiding Interactions Between Reader and Text

On the road to reading maturity, young readers need to become aware of and skilled at recognizing when shifts in thinking occur during reading. The shift may involve an author's transition to a new topic, changes in setting, twists in the plot, and so on. Or the author may put demands on the reader's ability to make inferences. For whatever reason, many youngsters run into trouble while reading because they don't know *how* or *when* to adjust their thinking as a particular reading selection demands.

Suppose you were teaching a class in which most of the students had appropriate background knowledge for the reading selection. Discussion before reading activates schema, and students approach the selection with anticipation of what lies ahead in the material. But somewhere during reading, you sense that the readers are having trouble understanding the story. Some look confused as they read; a couple raise their hands to ask for clarification. Others just plow ahead; whether they are comprehending is anyone's guess.

Readers sometimes get lost in a welter of details or bogged down in the conceptual complexity in the selection. The prereading activity that was initiated at the beginning of the lesson, while necessary, wasn't sufficient to maintain readers' interactions with the text. As a result, they're able to process only bits and pieces of information, but fail to grasp in any coherent way the author's intent and message. How can you help?

Assigning questions *after* reading may help to clarify some of the confusion, but does little to show readers how to interact with the author's ideas *during* reading. This is why guiding reader-text interactions is an important part of comprehension instruction. In this section, we explain three strategies that teachers have found useful for this purpose.

Directed Reading-Thinking Activity

The **Directed Reading-Thinking Activity (DR-TA)** builds critical awareness of the reader's role and responsibility in interacting with the text. The DR-TA strategy involves readers in the process of predicting, verifying, judging, and extending thinking about the text material. Throughout this process, the teacher agitates thinking by posing open-ended questions. The learning environment for DR-TA lessons must be supportive and encouraging so as not to stifle or inhibit students' participation. For example, never refute the predictions that children offer. To do so is comparable to pulling the rug out from under them.

"Think time" is important in a DR-TA lesson. We suggest that you pause several seconds or more for responses after posing an open-ended question. If there is silence during this time, it may very well be an indication that children are thinking. So wait and see what happens.

To prepare a DR-TA for a story, analyze its structure first. Map the story as we suggested earlier. Once you have identified the important story parts, decide on logical stopping points within the story. In Figure 6.7, we indicate a general plan that may be adapted for specific stories.

Linda Fleckner, a sixth-grade teacher, used the DR-TA to guide reader text interactions for the short story, "People of the Third Planet." Earlier you were invited to map the elements of this story. Study the dialogue that occurred between Ms. Fleckner and two students at the beginning of the lesson.

Ms. F.: *(Writes title on the board before assigning the story.)* What do you think this story's about?
Student: It's about outer space.
Ms. F.: Why do you say that?
Student: Because it's about a planet.
Ms. F.: *(Writes the prediction on the board.)* Let's have some more predictions.
Student: This is about space, I think. But something happens on Earth.
Ms. F.: Why do you think it's about Earth?
Student: Earth is the third planet from the sun, right? *(Ms. F. writes the prediction on the board.)*

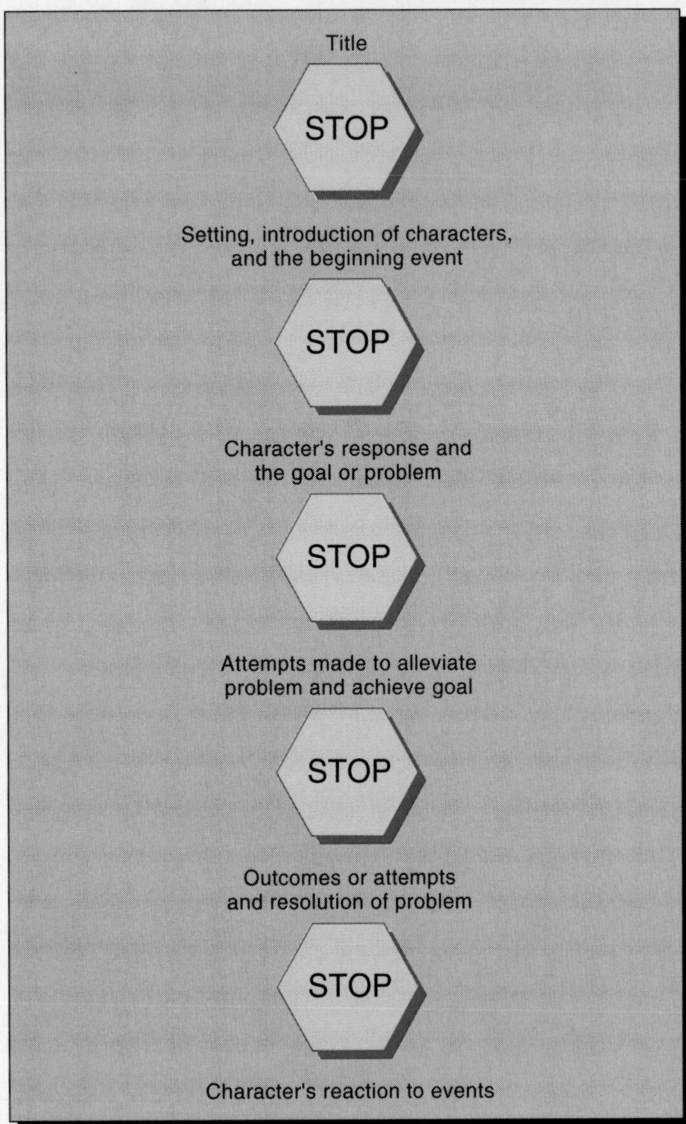

● **FIGURE 6.7** Potential stopping points in a DR-TA

Comments: First note that Ms. Fleckner used two open-ended questions and resisted posing additional questions to clarify students' predictions. In doing so, she set a tone of acceptance and didn't turn the question-response exchange into an interrogation session. In addition, she wrote the predictions on the board. Later, she returned to the predictions and asked students to verify their accuracy, reject them outright, or modify them in light of information gained from reading.

After five or six predictions about the title were written on the board, Ms. Fleckner assigned the first segment of text. Students read through the story's initiating event, the first eight lines from the story. Study the exchange that followed with the student who predicted that the Third Planet was Earth.

Ms. F.: *(pointing to the board):* Well, how did some of your predictions turn out?
Student: I was right. It's about Earth.
Ms. F.: You certainly were! So what do you think is going to happen now that the space ship has landed on Earth?
Student: War will break out. Someone's going to report the space ship. The creatures are going to come out and capture the people.
Ms. F.: Why do you say that?
Student: Because that's what happens in the movies.
Ms. F.: That's a possibility! *(She turns her attention to the class and asks for other predictions.)*

Comments: Initial predictions are often off the mark. This is to be expected since students' predictions are fueled by background knowledge and experience.

The DR-TA begins with very open-ended or divergent responses and moves toward more accurate predictions and text-based inferences as students acquire information from the reading. Compare the DR-TA to *Inferential Strategy,* which also makes substantial use of students' ability to use background knowledge and make predictions.

Inferential Strategy

Inferential Strategy was designed for elementary children, especially those in the primary grades (Hansen, 1981). Unlike the DR-TA, Inferential Strategy does not require stopping points throughout the reading selection. Instead, it relies on several questions *before* reading and discussion afterward.

Consider the following steps in Inferential Strategy:

1. Analyze the content selection for important ideas central to the material. Before assigning the class to read the material, select three ideas that are important or might be difficult to understand.

2. Plan prereading questions. Develop *two* questions for *each idea* identified in the content analysis. One question is posed to tap background knowledge relative to the idea; the other, prediction. For example:

   (Background) How do you react when you feel uncomfortable in a social situation? *(Prediction)* In the selection you are about to read, Tim feels unsure of himself on his first blind date. How do you think Tim will react when he meets his date?

   Ask students to write predictions before discussion takes place.

3. Discuss responses to background and prediction questions *before* reading. Discuss both students' previous experience with the topic and their predictions for the selection.

4. Upon finishing the prereading discussion, assign a selection to read.

5. After reading, relate predictions to what actually happened in the selection. Evaluate the three or four ideas that motivated background and prediction questions.

For example, in Mrs. Conti's second-grade class, the children read "The Lion and the Mouse" from their basal reader. It contained the following story line:

SETTING: A happy little mouse is running and jumping in the grass in the morning.
BEGINNING EVENT: The mouse gets lost in the grass and is picked up by a lion who says he wants to eat him.
INTERNAL RESPONSE: The mouse is frightened; he wants to be set free.
ATTEMPT: The mouse promises to help the lion if the lion will set him free.
OUTCOME: The lion laughs in disbelief, but decides to let the mouse go free.
RESOLUTION: The lion gets caught in a net and the mouse chews him free.
REACTION: The lion is grateful—a little mouse helped him after all.

Mrs. Conti chose three ideas around which to ask background questions and prediction questions: (1) a kindness is never wasted; (2) everybody needs someone; and (3) you can use your head to get out of trouble.

Study the background and prediction questions that Mrs. Conti asked for the third idea. *Background question:* All of us have probably been in trouble at some time, maybe with a friend, a brother or sister, or a parent. Sometimes we have to use our heads to get out of trouble. What are some of the things that you have done to get out of trouble? *Prediction question:* In this story, a mouse got caught by a lion who wants to eat him. What do you think he'll do to get out of trouble?

During the prereading activity, the children shared their answers to the questions. They had much to contribute. They then read the story in its entirety. After reading, the predictions that were made were compared with inferences derived from the story.

K-W-L (What Do You *Know*? What Do You *Want* to Find Out? What Did You *Learn*?)

K-W-L, as described by Ogle (1986), is a three-step teaching plan designed to guide and to motivate children as they read to acquire information from expository texts. The strategy helps students to think about what they know or believe they know about a topic; what they need to find out by reading the text; and finally what they learned by reading and what they still need and want to learn about the topic from other information sources. The

TABLE 6.1

K-W-L Chart

K—What do you know?	W—What do you want to find out?	L—What did you learn?
Categories of information you expect to use:		
A.	E.	
B.	F.	
C.	G.	
D.	H.	

K-W-L model is outlined on a chart that children use as they proceed through the steps of the strategy (see Table 6.1).

The first two steps in the model are prereading activities. The beginning step, K—What do you know, involves brainstorming with a group of students to help them focus on their current knowledge of a topic. The teacher's questions should lead children to think about and to respond *specifically* to the topic being discussed. The purpose of this process is to activate children's prior knowledge to help them understand what they will read in the text. The children's responses will be recorded on the board or on an overhead projector. The teacher, however, will not merely accept children's ideas or statements. As the discussion progresses the teacher will encourage children to extend their thinking by asking questions that require them to consider the source, as well as the substance of their information. Children will be asked to reflect on where they learned their information and on how they might prove that what they said is accurate.

Organizing children's statements into general categories of information that they may come across as they read, and discussing the kinds of information that they are likely to find in the article will provide additional structure, guidelines, and direction for children as they read. The teacher will demonstrate how key categories are determined and will invite children to offer additional categories. Students who are not ready for or accustomed to this level of thinking may need additional support and practice.

The next step, W—What do you want to learn, evolves naturally from assessing the results of the brainstorming and categorizing activities. As children identify areas of controversy and/or key categories that contain little or no information, a purpose for reading is developed. Although this step is done mainly as a group activity, each student will write the questions that he or she is most interested in learning about on their worksheet. Students' personal interests will guide and motivate their reading. The length and the complexity of the material will determine whether children can effectively read and derive information by reading the entire text or if the piece should be read in steps that provide opportunities for children to think, at logical intervals, about what they are reading.

During the final step of the K-W-L process, L—What did you learn, the students will record their findings on their worksheets. They have the option of writing down information either as they read or immediately after they finish reading. With teacher guidance and assistance the students will assess whether their questions and concerns were satisfactorily answered by reading the text. When students need or want additional information about a topic, they should be guided to other sources of information.

In Box 6.2 examine the K-W-L chart that was developed by a third-grade class. Also, study the interactions that occurred between the teacher (T) and students (S) as they developed the chart.

T: Fold your paper into three columns. In the first column write a *K*. That stands for things you know. The next column will be titled *W*. That stands for what you want to know. The last column should be labeled *L*. That is for what you learned when the story is all finished. Now what is the title of the story?

S: "Eastern Chipmunks."

T: What kinds of things do you already know about chipmunks that you could put in the first column?
(The children's responses are listed in the first column of the worksheet. They were not certain, however, whether or not chipmunks were nocturnal. They decided to move that question to the next column—What you want to find out.)

T: Now take a look at what you have here. We are going to put what you believe you know about chipmunks into groups. We'll make concept groups like we do when we do concept circles. Does anyone have a group or concept?

S: Where they live.

T: Which things would go into that group?

S: They live in the ground.

S: They live in forests.

T: What other groups do you see?

S: Things like run fast.

T: What else could go with that?

S: Climb trees.

T: These seem to be things that they do. Could we call this group behaviors?

S: Yes.

S: Food.

T: Good. Find all the statements on your page that refer to their food and read them to yourself.

● BOX 6.2

K-W-L Chart

K—What you know	W—What you want to find out	L—What you learned and still want to learn
1. They run fast. 2. They eat nuts. 3. They dig holes. 4. They climb trees. 5. They are afraid of pe-ople. 6. Some are brown.	1. Do they come out in the the daytime or at night? 2. How old are they when they live on their own? 3. How long do they live? 4. What colors are they? 5. How fast can they dig? 6. How fast can they run? 7. How deep can they dig.	1. I learned that they live under rocks. 2. Their holes are 20 to 30 feet long. 3. Cats eat them. 4. Baby chipmunks grow up in one month. 5. Chipmunk is an Indian word. 6. They have two pouches for storing food. 7. They work, play and rest at different times during the day and night. 8. They have eyes on the side of their heads. 9. They have sharp claws and teeth. 10. They are good at hid-ing. 11. They nibble on leaves.

CATEGORIES OF INFORMATION YOU EXPECT TO USE:

A. Where Chipmunks live (homes)

B. How they look (appearance)

C. How they act (behaviors)

D. What they eat

S: I know another one. How they look.
T: Which ones would go there?
S: They are brown with striped tails.
S: They are small.

The same type of questions were asked to help the children think about what more they wanted or needed to know about chipmunks.

As the class completed the prereading phase of the K-W-L strategy, they were assigned the text to read. After reading, the discussion that followed went something like this.

T: Now write in the last column on your chart the things that you learned when you read the story. Was there anything that we wanted to know that was not in the story?
S: How deep their tunnels are.
T: How could we find out?
S: I have an encyclopedia at home. I could bring it in tomorrow.
T: Great! Bring in the encyclopedia volume with chipmunks in it and we'll look it up. We might find some other things that we didn't know about chipmunks also.

The kinds of questions asked in the DR-TA, and Inferential Strategy, and K-W-L help to guide reader-text interactions and promote comprehension. In the next section, we explain in more detail how you can use questions to help children to discuss their understanding of texts.

Using Questions to Promote Discussion

Questions are only as good as the context in which they're posed. If questions fail to create an active, problem-solving environment for readers, then much will be lost in the transactions that occur among you, the students, and the text. If questioning is to promote reading comprehension, it must first and foremost serve as a springboard to conversation and discussion.

Questions as a Springboard to Discussion

Whereas recitation is concerned chiefly with recall and regurgitation of what has been read, discussion initiates thinking by going beyond right answers to inference making, reaction, and evaluation. Dillon (1983) maintains that the ultimate goal of discussion is to

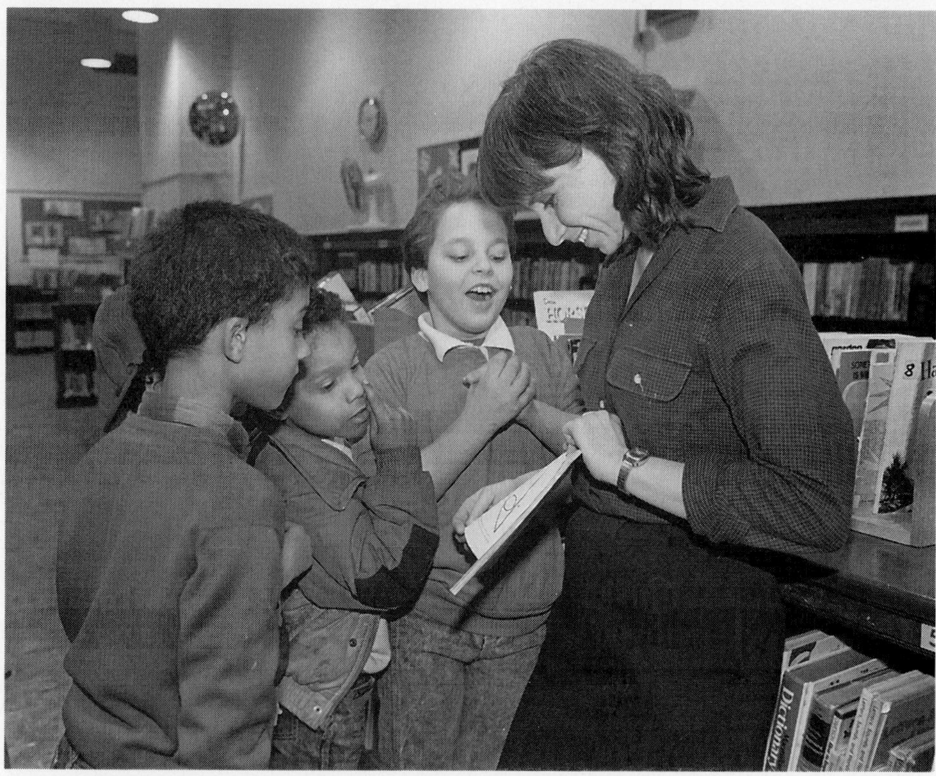

Discussion initiates thinking by going beyond right answers to inference, reaction, and evaluation

have students add to their knowledge or judgment on the matter being discussed. Therefore, questions should be based in perplexity. There should be a gnawing inside each student to explore, clarify, and find out more. If this is the case, certain principles must be inherent in classroom behavior, including orderliness, mutual trust and respect for one another, and the right to maintain or hold differing opinions and points of view.

A good discussion has no hidden agenda: There are no predetermined conclusions to reach. As a result, the discussion hinges on teacher modeling and class reflection. A few questions—carefully planned to provide direction—are the rule, not the exception. Plan key questions in advance by writing them in clear, understandable language. Avoid rapid-fire question-answer exchanges or asking questions off the top of your head. Otherwise, discussion will soon wither. Three types of questions at key points in a discussion will keep students on task: (1) a preliminary question to identify a problem or issue; (2) a question or two to clarify or redirect the discussion; and (3) a final question or two that can tie together loose ends or establish a premise for further discussion.

One way to get a discussion off to a good start is by asking a question about a perplexing situation or establishing a problem to be solved. If you are working with a story, raise an issue related to the central problem or theme. From time to time, it may be necessary to refocus attention to the topic by piggy-backing on comments made by particular students: "Tim's point is an excellent one. Does anyone else want to talk about this?" During small group discussions, a tactic that keeps groups on task is to remind students of time remaining in the discussion. In order to keep the focus or redirect a discussion you may want to ask a question to clarify a student's question. You may want to ensure that everybody understands a particular student's comment. Often, keeping the discussion focused will prevent the class from straying from the task.

Alternatives to Questions

Dillon (1983) explains several alternatives to questions to stimulate student thought and response and to encourage participation.

Declarative Statement. Instead of using a question, express a thought that has occurred to you in relation to what a student has just said. The effect of a straightforward statement in response to a student's comment is to have the student and others examine your thinking instead of trying to guess what's in your head. As Dillon puts it, a question says, "Supply this bit of information and then stop." In contrast, statements invite further response and enhance student thought.

Example: Mrs. Cross, a kindergarten teacher, overheard a child's conversation as the child pretended to drive a "car" that she had built with hollow blocks:

Mandy: I drive day and night so I never go to sleep. Sometimes I go to sleep steering, but then I take my foot off the gas peddle.

Mrs. Cross: It could be very dangerous to fall asleep while you are driving.

Reflective Restatement. Sometimes it is valuable to "mirror" the content of a student's response. A reflective restatement, then, lets the students know that you are listening and informs them of the extent of your understanding of what is being said. Restate by saying, "I get from what you say that. . . " or "So you think that. . . " (Dillon, 1983, p. 31). What you'll find, more often than not, is that a student will agree with your reflection and then elaborate. For example:

Example: After reading *Alexander and the Terrible, Horrible, No Good, Very Bad Day* by Judith Viorst, Mark was working on a story frame.

Mark: Mrs. Ralph, I can't write anything about the resolution because there wasn't one in the story.

Mrs. Ralph: You finished reading the story and you don't think that Alexander's problems were solved?

Mark: They weren't. Alexander had a really bad day and then he went to bed. Nothing good happened to him all day.

State of Mind. At certain points in a discussion share with students your state of mind. For example, if you are confused by a student's point, say, "I'm sorry, I'm not getting it" or "I'm confused about what you're saying." At other points in the discussion, you might wish to express your state of mind by pondering what has been said: "I was just thinking about what you said. Could it be that. . . " Here is another example:

> *Example:* As part of a second-grade social-studies unit on interdependence, Mrs. Green read *Old Henry* by Joan Blos to her students and encouraged them to talk about the problems between Henry and his neighbors.
>
> *Tom:* I think the neighbors were really mean to old Henry. They didn't have to be mad at him all the time. They could have helped him fix his house and clean up his big mess.
>
> *Mrs. Green:* I am a little surprised by what you just said. Could it be that you think the neighbors caused all of the trouble in the neighborhood and that Henry didn't have any part in the problem?

Deliberate Silence. According to Dillon (1983), "Deliberate silence is the most intriguing alternative to questions and one of the most effective" (p. 38). He suggested that when a student finishes a response, or falters, you might consider maintaining a deliberate silence for three to five seconds. Often, the silence results in the student extending his or her comments or another student will enter into the discussion. To be effective at the use of silence, you must practice timing. One second can seem like an hour in a teacher-student exchange; three seconds, an eternity. However, a minimum of three seconds is necessary for silence to be noticeable.

Discussion Webs

Discussion Webs require students to explore both sides of an issue during discussion before drawing conclusions. When classroom discussions occur, they can quickly become dominated by the teacher or a few vocal students. In an effort to move the discussion forward, the teacher may ask too many questions too quickly. Usually children are more reticent to participate or become involved when discussions are monopolized by teacher talk or the talk of one or two students.

Donna Alvermann (1991) recommends the use of Discussion Webs as an alternative to discussions that are teacher-dominated. The Discussion Web strategy makes use of cooperative learning principles that follow a "think-pair-share" discussion cycle (McTighe and Lyman, 1988). According to Alvermann, ". . . students *think* individually about the ideas they want to contribute to the discussion and then discuss these ideas with a partner. Next, the partners *pair* up with a different set of partners to work toward consensus. . . . Finally, the two sets of partners, working as a group of four, decide which ideas a spokesperson from the group will *share* with the entire class in the whole-group discussion that follows" (p. 93).

The Discussion Web strategy utilizes a graphic aid to guide children's thinking about the ideas they want to contribute to the discussion. The graphic aid takes the shape of a web and is illustrated in Figure 6.8. In the center of the web is a question. The question reflects more than one point of view. Students explore the pros and cons of the question in the NO and YES columns of the web—in pairs, and then in groups of four. The main goal of the four-member group is to draw a conclusion based on the discussion of the web.

Alvermann suggests the following steps in the use of Discussion Webs for classroom discussions:

1. Prepare students for reading by activating prior knowledge, raising questions, and making predictions about the text.
2. Read the selection and then introduce the Discussion Web by having students work in pairs to generate pro and con responses to the question. The partners work on the same Discussion Web and take turns jotting down their reasons in the YES and NO columns. Students can use key words and phrases to express their ideas and need not fill in all of the lines. They should try to have an equal number of pro and con reasons represented on the web.
3. Combine partners into groups of four to compare responses, work toward consensus, and reach conclusion as a group. Explain to students that it is okay to disagree with another member of the group, but they should try to keep an open mind as they listen to others during the discussion. Dissenting views can be aired during the whole-class discussion.
4. Give each group three minutes to decide which of all the reasons given best support the group's conclusion. Each group selects a spokesperson to report to the whole class.
5. Have students follow up the whole class discussion by individually writing their responses to the Discussion Web question. Display students' responses to the question in a prominent place in the room so that they can be read by others.

When students use Discussion Webs there is usually a high degree of participation; they are eager to hear how other groups reach consensus and draw conclusions. In Gloria Rieckert's class, sixth graders use Discussion Webs to think about several dilemmas that Billy, the main character, faces in the book, *Where the Red Fern Grows.* The Discussion Web shown in Figure 6.8 asks the question, "Should Billy have cut down the big, old sycamore tree in order to get the coon?" Reyna, Pam, Jessica, and Kim reach a yes consensus on the question, but Reyna still has her doubts and Jessica clearly voices a dissenting view. Each member follows up the discussion by writing his or her response to the question.

Reyna: I felt that Billy shouldn't have cut the sycamore tree down because he could have really hurt himself. Plus the tree was part of nature, and that coon didn't deserve to die. The tree is a living thing. But I sort of changed my mind about Billy cutting the tree down after listening to Pam and Kim. Keeping your word is important.

Pam: I think Billy should of cut down the big tree because a promise is worth more than a tree and he was proud.

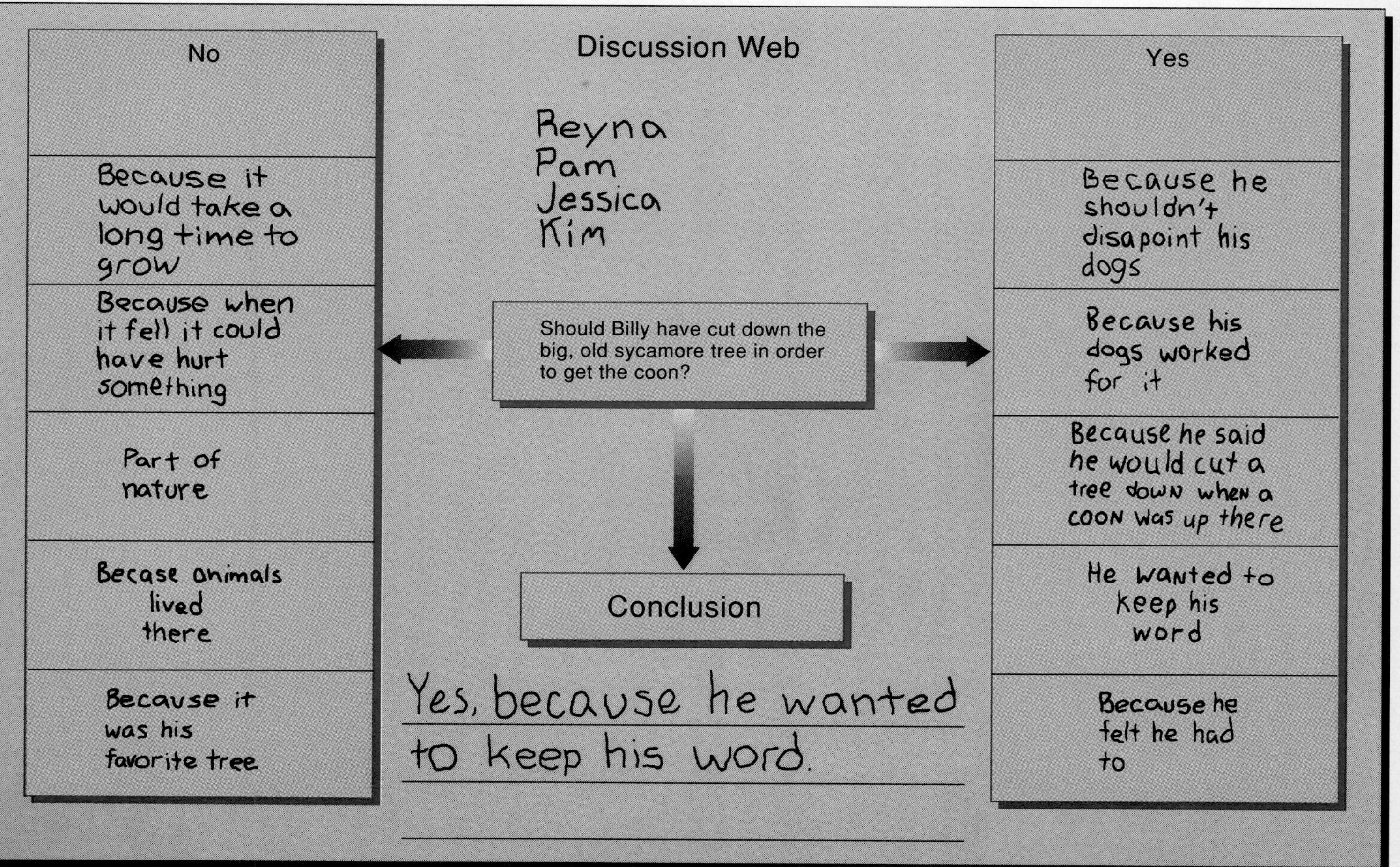

● **FIGURE 6.8** Discussion web for *Where the Red Fern Grows*

Kim: I think he should've cut down the tree because he promised that coon to his dogs. It was also his first coon. If he wouldn't of cut down that tree he would've never of gotten his coon skin hat. If he didn't cut down that tree he wouldn't have been a hunter.

Jessica: I don't think he should have cut down the tree because it takes a long time to grow back. It hurt the environment and Billy didn't even think about that. I don't think he should have done it because it is a bad thing to do.

It is evident from these responses that discussion plays a role in guiding students' interpretation of what they are reading. Readers have an opportunity through Discussion Webs to view and refine their own interpretations of a text in light of the points of view shared by others.

Question-Answer Relationships

When asking questions, special attention should be given to the most likely source of information the reader needs to answer the question. Certain questions can be thought of as *textually explicit* because they promote recall or recognition of *information actually stated in the text.* Other questions are *textually implicit* because they provoke thinking. Readers must search for text relationships and think about the information presented. If students are to integrate ideas within a text, then textually implicit questions are likely to be the most useful. Finally, some questions usually place the reader's knowledge of the world at the center of the questioning activity. Such questions are *schema-based.* Students must rely on their own resources as well as the text to solve problems, discover new insights, or evaluate the significance of what was read.

Question-Answer Relationships (QARs), as proposed by Raphael (1986), help learners know what information sources are available for seeking answers to different types of text questions. Through this strategy, readers become more sensitive to the different mental operations and text demands required by different questions. As a result, teachers and students become cognizant of the three-way relationships that exist among the question, the text to which it refers, and the background knowledge and information at the reader's disposal. QARs enhance children's ability to answer comprehension questions by teaching them how to find information they need to answer questions. Explicit instruction will make students sensitive to two information sources where answers can be found.

The first information source is the *text.* Some answers to questions can be found *right there* in the text. Other answers found in the text, however, demand a *think-and-search* strategy in which students *search* the text for information and *think* about the relationships that exist among the bits of information found.

The second information source is the *reader.* Some questions signal to the reader: I am on my own. Other questions may signal: It's up to the author and me. On either case, the text may help, but answers must come from inside readers' heads. The use of *Right There, Think and Search, Author and You,* and *On My Own* are mnemonics to help readers recognize question-answer relationships. A chart such as the one in Figure 6.9 can be used to make readers aware of QARs.

Where are Answers to Questions Found?

In the Text:

Right There!

The answers in the text. The words used in the question and words used for the answer can usually be found in the same sentence.

Think and Search!

The answer is in the text but the words used in the question and those used for an answer would not be in the same sentence. You need to think about different parts of the text and how ideas can be put together before you can answer the question.

Or

In My Head:

On My Own

The text got you thinking, but the answer is inside your head. The author can't help you much. So think about it and use what you know already to answer the question.

Author and You

The answer is not in the text. You need to think about what you know, what the author says, and how they fit together.

FIGURE 6.9 Introducing Question-Answer Relationships

As students become sensitive to question-answer relationships, you will find it easier to guide reader-text interactions. Not only will readers develop strategies for responding to questions, but they will also realize that they have an active role to play in comprehending text selections.

SUMMARY

In this chapter, we approached the heart of contemporary reading instruction—comprehension—from an active, meaning-making stance. After examining the elements of story grammar, strategies were discussed for building and reinforcing children's awareness of a story's underlying structure. There is, however, no substitute for building children's experiences with stories (and developing concepts) by reading, telling, listening, and performing them on a regular basis.

Instructional activities and strategies were described for building and activating readers' schema. Prereading preparation, if anything, involves engaging children in exploring what they already know and what they need to know in order to comprehend text effectively. Advance organizers and student-generated questions activate background knowledge and create a set for comprehending reading material.

Three strategies, the Directed Reading-Thinking Activity (DR-TA), the Inferential Strategy and K-W-L, are useful in helping to guide reader-text interactions. Each involves the use of prediction and background knowledge, and engages children actively in constructing meaning and making inferences during reading.

Without doubt, questions promote comprehension. They should serve as springboards to discussion and reflection. Modeling question-asking behavior is crucial to reading comprehension instruction.

TEACHER-ACTION RESEARCHER

1. Working with several class members or colleagues, plan to teach a reading selection. First, decide on the selection to use and develop a story map. Then brainstorm comprehension instructional activities appropriate for the selection and think of ways to guide comprehension before, during, and after reading. Each person should try out the lesson independently with his or her students at the appropriate level and write notes immediately following the lesson. Then reconvene as a group to discuss the results. How were experiences similar? How were they different? What adjustments would need to be made in order to improve the lesson?

2. Discuss with a group of children a story they have just read, and tape-record the conversation. Analyze the discussion to see if you followed these guidelines to keep students on task: (a) ask a preliminary question to identify a problem or issue; (b) insert a question or two as needed to clarify or redirect the discussion; and (c) pose a final question or two to tie together loose ends or establish a premise for further discussion. Also check to see if you used declarative or reflective statements, state-of-mind queries, or deliberate silence as alternatives to questions.

3. Choosing different grade levels, observe three elementary school classrooms during reading instruction time. Take notes on what the teacher does to facilitate comprehension. Also watch what students are doing when they are not working directly with the teacher: Are they completing worksheets, reading selections longer than one or two sentences or a paragraph in length, or writing about what they have read? Are they involved in other instructional activities? Categorize what you see in terms of types of activities and instruction according to ideas presented in this and previous chapters

KEY TERMS

story schema
story grammar
story maps
macrocloze stories
scrambled stories
story frames
Story Impressions
active comprehension
ReQuest
Your Own Questions
Directed Reading-Thinking Activity (DR-TA)
Inferential Strategy
K-W-L
Discussion Webs
Question-Answer Relationships (QARs)

CHAPTER 7

Vocabulary Knowledge and Concept Development

BETWEEN THE LINES

In this chapter you will discover:

- **The relationship among children's experiences, concepts, and words.**
- **Principles that guide the teaching of vocabulary in elementary classrooms.**
- **Instructional strategies for teaching vocabulary using a variety of activities.**
- **Why vocabulary functions differently in literature and in content material.**

It's like day and night: the difference between classrooms where children experiment and play with words and classrooms in which words are maintained in lists. Teachers in the former take advantage of the natural spontaneity of children, knowing that part of the joy of teaching is the uncertainty of what children will say or do. They create classroom environments in which opportunities to experiment with words abound. Every time a decision is made by a student-writer as to which word is best in a piece of writing, vocabulary learning takes place. Mark Twain said that the difference between the right word and the almost-right word is the difference between lightning and the lightning bug. Children experiment with words whenever they hear unfamiliar words read aloud in literature or whenever they encounter new words while reading. They develop an ear for language and an eye for the images created by language.

Nevertheless, the problems teachers face daily in developing vocabulary knowledge and concepts in their classrooms are real. In a nutshell, the practical problem and challenge is one of teaching vocabulary words *well enough* to enhance children's comprehension of written language (Beck and McKeown, 1983). If children are not readily familiar with most words they meet in print, they will most certainly have trouble understanding what they read.

Too often, we assume that children will develop an understanding of words from such staple activities as discussing, defining, and writing the words in sentences. We do little else instructionally. Yet, students must not only be able to define words, they must also experience unfamiliar words in frequent, meaningful, and varied contexts. A major premise of this chapter is that *definitional knowledge* is necessary, but students must also develop *contextual* and *conceptual knowledge* of words in order to comprehend fully what they read.

Defining and using words in sentences are insufficient to ensure vocabulary learning. Students need to be involved in *constructing* meaning rather than memorizing definitions. In addition, they need to experiment with the relationship between the meanings of terms (Beck, Perfetti, and McKeown, 1982). The more that children encounter vocabulary in as many language contexts as possible, the more they will come to know and use words.

Have you ever heard a student who encounters a difficult word say with confidence, "I know what that word means!"? We share a concern that there are not enough children developing the I-know-that-word attitude. This chapter will emphasize ways to increase children's sensitivity to new words and their enjoyment in word learning. What instructional opportunities can be provided to influence the depth and breadth of children's vocabulary knowledge? What are the instructional implications of vocabulary for reading comprehension? How do students develop the interest and motivation to *want* to learn new words? How can students grow in independence in vocabulary learning? To answer these questions, we must first recognize that vocabulary development is not accidental. It must be orchestrated carefully not only during reading time, but also throughout the entire day.

The Relationship Between Vocabulary and Comprehension

The relationship between knowledge of word meanings and comprehension has been well documented by researchers and acknowledged by children. There are many students, like Joe, a fifth grader who said, "Sometimes I don't understand what I'm reading because the words are too hard. You know, I don't know what they mean." The seminal work of F.B. Davis (1944) and other researchers such as Thurstone (1946) and Spearitt (1972) have consistently identified vocabulary knowledge as an important factor in reading comprehension.

Various explanations are used to account for the strong relationship between vocabulary and comprehension. Anderson and Freebody (1981) proposed three hypotheses: **aptitude, knowledge,** and **instrumental.** These three hypotheses are capsulized in Box 7.1.

We believe that all three hypotheses have merit in helping to understand the relationship between word knowledge and comprehension. Surely the implications of the aptitude and knowledge hypotheses signal the importance of reading aloud to children and immersing them in written language. Wide reading experiences develop a facility with written language. Further, the instrumental hypothesis is important to us as teachers: Teach word meanings well enough and students will find reading material easier to comprehend. Unfortunately, vocabulary instruction research has provided contradictory evidence on this effect. Nagy (1988/1989) summarizes some of the research this way:

Children experiment with words whenever they encounter new words while reading.

> Imagine an experiment with two groups of students who are about to read a selection from a textbook. One group is given typical instruction on the meaning of some difficult words from the selection; the other group receives no instruction. Both groups are given passages to read and are tested for comprehension. Do the students who received the vocabulary instruction do any better on the comprehension test? Very often they do not. (p. 1)

According to several studies, many widely used methods generally fail to increase comprehension (Mezynski, 1983; Pearson and Gallagher, 1983; Stahl and Fairbanks, 1986). Why might this be the case? One explanation may involve the very nature of practices associated with vocabulary instruction. This instruction usually involves some combination of looking up definitions, writing them down or memorizing them, and inferring the meaning of a new word from the context. These activities do not create enough *in-depth* knowledge to increase comprehension of difficult concepts. Good definitions and illustrations of how words are used in natural sounding contexts seem to be minimal requirements for good instruction in vocabulary. Other studies indicate that comprehension is facilitated when vocabulary is taught *in depth* before reading begins (Beck, Perfetti, and McKeown, 1982; Stahl, 1983; Beck, McKeown, and Omanson, 1987). Blachowicz and

● BOX 7.1

Three Hypotheses for the Strong Relationship Between Vocabulary and Comprehension

The Aptitude Hypothesis:	Both vocabulary and comprehension reflect general intellectual ability. A large vocabulary as measured by test performance is a solid indicator of verbal and mental ability. The relationship is explained this way: The more intellectually able the student the more she or he will know the meanings of words and, therefore, comprehend better while reading. It is best to guard against the pessimistic attitude that only the most intelligent child profits from instruction in vocabulary. A child's environment and experiences, including those in the classroom are crucial in learning concepts and words.
The Knowledge Hypothesis:	The Knowledge Hypothesis suggests that vocabulary and comprehension reflect general knowledge rather than intellectual ability. In other words, students with large vocabularies related to a given topic also have more knowledge about the topic, which in turn produces better comprehension. Closely tied to the schema view of reading, the knowledge hypothesis proposes that vocabulary words must be taught within a larger framework of concept development.
The Instrumental Hypothesis:	The Instrumental Hypothesis establishes a causal chain between vocabulary knowledge and comprehension. The Instrumental hypothesis can be defended thus: If comprehension depends in part on the knowledge of word meanings, then vocabulary instruction ought to influence comprehension.

Lee (1991) conclude that: ". . . judicious attention to vocabulary can build knowledge of specific vocabulary and can have a positive, though modest, impact on comprehension" (p. 191).

In our observations we've noticed that many teachers spend instructional time introducing vocabulary words *before* students read, but do not spend much time on vocabulary *after* students have read. For example, few teachers encourage children to use significant vocabulary words *after* reading texts in such activities as retelling, and written, oral, artistic, and dramatic response to what has been read. Researchers are also looking into the connection between intensive vocabulary instruction and writing. They are finding that students write better after intensive, in-depth work on vocabulary related to the writing topic (Duin and Graves, 1987; Beyersdorfer and Schauer, 1989).

Though wide reading provides students with rich and meaningful contexts for word learning, vocabulary instruction is also important. This seems to be particularly true for the less able reader who begins school knowing fewer school-type words (Becker, 1977) and those who have limited networks or meanings for the words that are familiar to them (Graves and Slater, 1987). Contextual reading does not automatically result in word learning (Jenkins, Stein, and Wysocki, 1984). Instructional interventions such as encouraging students to notice new words can increase the likelihood that students will learn from context (Elley, 1989; Jenkins et al., 1984). Poorer readers are at a double disadvantage in increasing their vocabulary if they are unmotivated or unable to do the amount of contextual reading required to extend their vocabularies. Further, McKeown (1985) found that less able readers do not use strategies to gain new word meanings from context as their more skilled classmates do.

Moreover, the instrumental and knowledge hypotheses have many instructional implications, which we address in the remainder of this chapter. Words need to be taught directly and well enough to enhance comprehension. Students must have quick access to word meanings when they are reading. Quick access can be achieved through a variety of strategies that make use of children's definitional, contextual, and conceptual knowledge of words.

Before examining instructional strategies, the relationship among children's experiences, concepts, and words needs to be explored. What are concepts? What does it mean to know words?

Experiences, Concepts, and Words

One way to define **vocabulary** is to suggest that it represents the breadth and depth of all the words we know—the words we use, recognize, and respond to in meaningful acts of communication. *Breadth* involves the size and scope of our vocabulary; *depth* concerns the level of understanding that we have of words.

As children progress through their school years, they learn to identify and use as many written as spoken words.

Vocabulary has usually been classified as having four components: *listening, speaking, reading,* and *writing.* These components are often said to develop in breadth and depth in the sequence listed. Five- and six-year-olds, for example, come to school already able to recognize and respond to thousands of spoken words. Children's first vocabulary without much question is listening vocabulary. However, as a child progresses through the school years, he or she eventually learns to identify and use as many written as spoken words. By adulthood, a person's reading vocabulary often outmatches any of the other vocabulary components.

For this reason, it is more or less assumed that listening and speaking vocabularies are learned in the home, whereas reading and writing vocabularies fall within the domain of school. Although this assumption may generally hold, it creates an unnecessary dichotomy between inside and outside school influences. It is much safer to assume that both home and school are profoundly influential in the development of all components of vocabulary.

Words Are Labels for Concepts

Although words are labels for **concepts,** a single concept represents much more than the meaning of a single word. It might take thousands of words to explain a concept. However, answers to the question, "What does it mean to know a word?" depend on how well we understand the relationship among words, concepts, and experiences. Understanding this relationship provides a sound rationale for teaching vocabulary within the larger framework of concept development.

Concepts are learned through our acting upon and interaction with the environment. Edgar Dale (1969) reminded us how children learn concepts best: through direct, purposeful experiences. Dale's Cone of Experience in Figure 7.1 depicts the levels of abstraction from the most concrete, nonverbal experiences beginning at the base of the cone to the most abstract and removed experiences at the tip of the cone—verbal symbols. For a child who has never eaten a banana split, the most intense and meaningful learning would occur

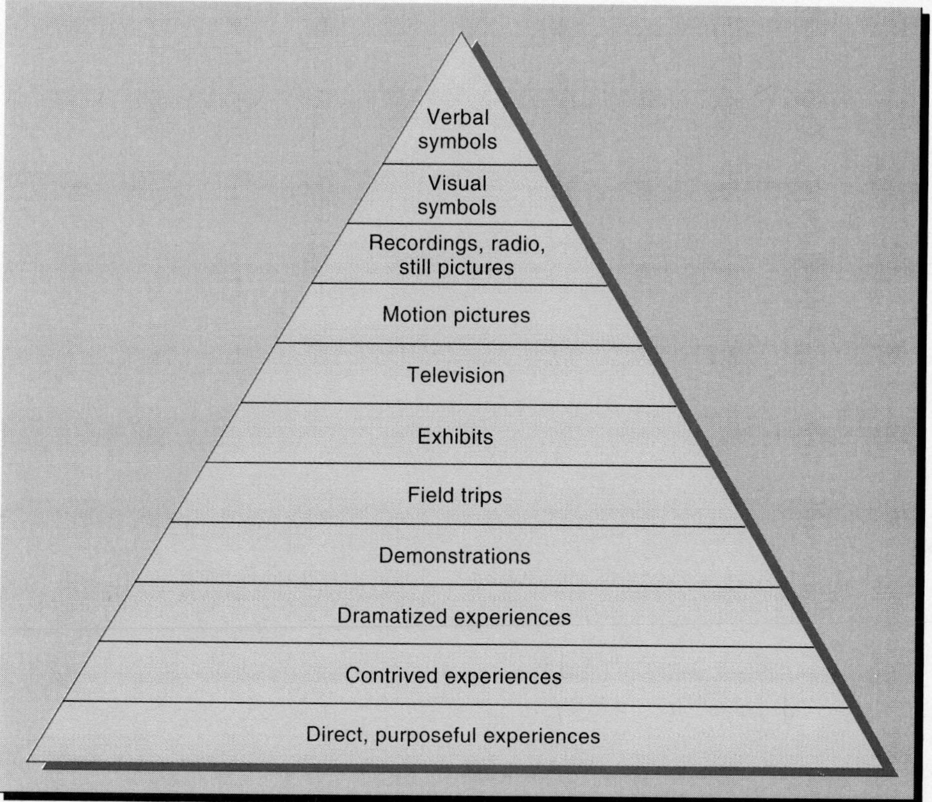

● **FIGURE 7.1** Dale's Cone of Experience

during a trip to an ice-cream parlor! The relationship of experiences to concepts and words sets the stage for an important principle of vocabulary instruction: In order to learn new or unfamiliar words it is necessary to have experiences from which concepts can be derived.

Words and Concepts: A Closer Look

One way of thinking about a concept is that it is a mental image of something. By something, we mean anything that can be grouped together by common features or similar criteria—objects, symbols, ideas, processes, or events. In this respect, concepts are similar in nature to schemata.

Concepts are synonymous with the formation of categories. We would be overwhelmed by the complexity of our environment if we were to respond to each object or event that we encountered as unique. So we invent categories (or form concepts) to reduce the complexity of our environment and the necessity for constant learning. Every canine need not have a different name to be known as a dog. Although dogs vary greatly, the common characteristics that they share cause them to be referred to by the same general term. Thus in order to facilitate communication, we invent words to name concepts.

Scan a page from any dictionary and you will encounter word after word—most of which represent the names of concepts. The only place that these words stand alone is on a dictionary page. In your head, concepts are organized into a network of complex relationships. Suppose, for example, you were to fix your eyes on the word *baboon* as you scanned the entries in the dictionary. What mental picture comes to mind? Your image of *baboon* probably differs from that of another person. Your background knowledge of *baboon,* or the larger class to which it belongs known as *primates,* will very likely be different from someone else's. So will your experiences with and interests in baboons, especially if you are fond of frequenting the zoo or reading books about primate behavior. The point is that we organize background knowledge and experiences into conceptual hierarchies according to class, example, and attribute relations. Let's take a closer look at these relationships.

Class, Example, and Attribute Relations

What do we mean by *complex relations?* We stated earlier that the concept *baboon* is part of a more inclusive class called *primates,* which in turn is a member of a larger class known as *mammals,* which in turn is a member of an even larger class of animals known as *vertebrates.* These *class relations* are depicted in Figure 7.2.

Class relationships in any conceptual network are organized in a hierarchy according to the **superordinate** and **subordinate** nature of the concepts. For example, in Figure 7.2 the superordinate concept is *animals.* There are two classes of animals known as *vertebrates* and *nonvertebrates,* which are in a subordinate position in the hierarchy. However, *vertebrates* is superordinate in relation to *amphibians, mammals, birds,* and *fish,* which, of

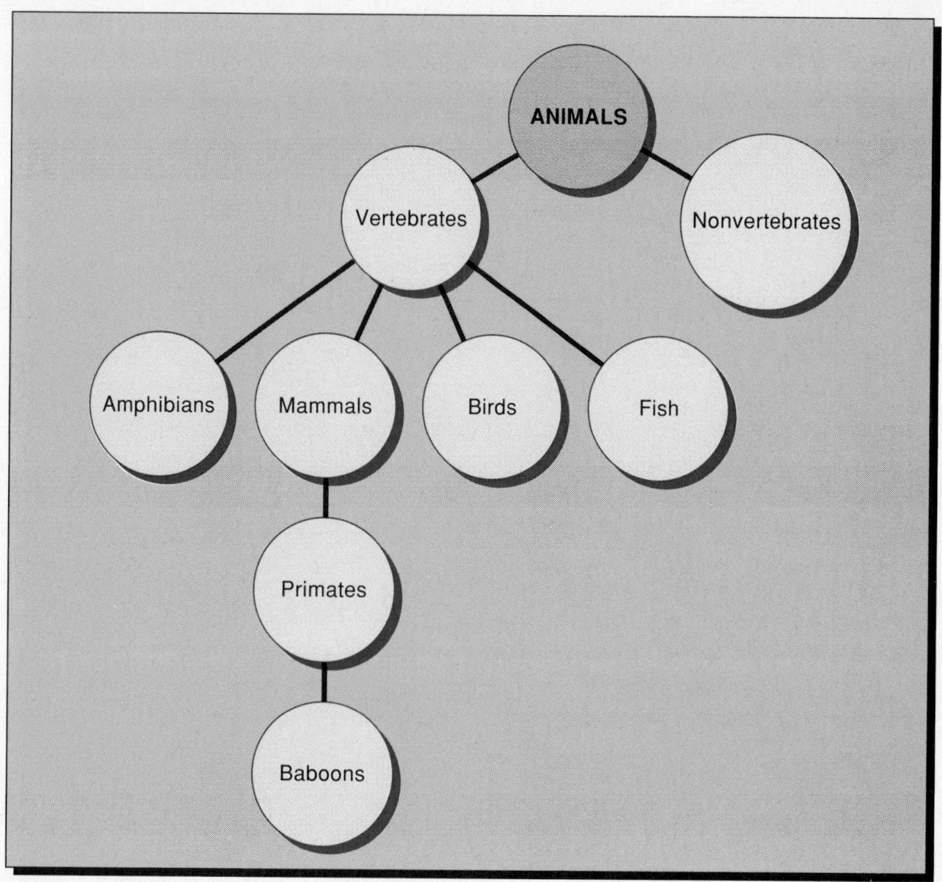

● **FIGURE 7.2** An example of a concept hierarchy

course, are types or subclasses of vertebrates. To complete the hierarchy, the concept *primates* is subordinate to *mammals,* but is superordinate in relation to *baboons.*

By now you have probably recognized that for every concept there are examples of that concept. In other words, an *example* is a member of any concept under consideration. A *nonexample* is any instance that is not a member of the concept under consideration. Class-example relations are reciprocal. *Vertebrates* and *nonvertebrates* are examples of *animals. Mammals, birds, fish,* and *amphibians* are examples of *vertebrates.* A *primate* is an example of a *mammal,* and so on.

To extend this discussion, suppose we were to make *primates* our target concept. In addition to baboons, what are other examples of primates? No doubt, *apes, monkeys,* and *Homo sapiens* come quickly to mind. These examples can be shown in relation to each other.

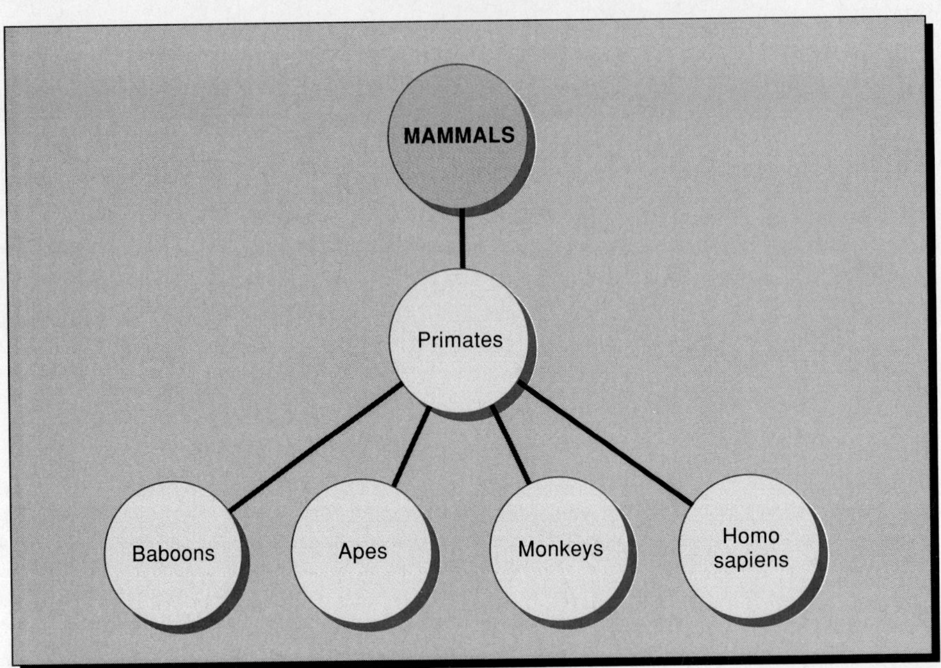

● **FIGURE 7.3** Class-example relations for the target concept *primates*

Note that the examples of primates given in Figure 7.3 are not exhaustive of all possible primates that we could have listed. Nevertheless, we might ask, "What do baboons, apes, monkeys, and *Homo sapiens* have in common?" Answers to this question would force us to focus on relevant *attributes,* those traits, features, properties, or characteristics that are common to every example of a particular concept. In other words, the relevant attributes of primates refer to the characteristics that determine whether baboons, monkeys, apes, and *Homo sapiens* belong to the particular class of mammals called *primates.*

All primates, from baboons to human beings, have certain physical and social characteristics, but not every primate shares each of these features. Nearly every example of a primate can grasp objects with its hands and/or feet. A primate has nails rather than claws. Vision is a primate's most important sense. Most species of primates live in groups, but some live alone. A social group is often considerable in size and highly organized. Primates have the capacity to communicate with one another by means of signals based on scent, touch, vision, and sound. And, of course, primate infants depend to a large extent on their mothers.

This discussion began when we asked you to form a mental image of *baboon.* The clarity with which you were able to picture a baboon in your mind depended, as you may have surmised, on how familiar you were with the characteristics of primates in general and baboons specifically. Baboons, apes, monkeys, and *Homo sapiens* share common characteristics, but they are also different.

In what ways are baboons similar to other primates? How are baboons different? These are important questions in clarifying your concept of baboon and sorting out the relations that exist among the various examples. Concept learning involves to a large extent the search for and listing of attributes that can be used to distinguish examples from one another and to distinguish examples from nonexamples.

To promote students' conceptual understanding of key vocabulary, Simpson (1987) culls an instructionally useful answer to the question "What does it mean to know a word?"

Suppose, for example, that a concept to be developed in a third grade social studies unit was the *wigwam.* Students would need to be able to generate that it was a shelter or home for Indians, and that it was not as sturdy as the house they live in. They could relate the wigwam to a tent they may have used on a camping trip or a Scout outing, although wigwams were made of light wooden poles covered by layers of bark or reed mats. But suppose the concept in a science unit was a more abstract one like *energy.* In this case, students would need to be able to generate that they needed energy to play and work, but that they did not need much energy to sleep or to watch television. As the concept energy was explored further, students would realize that our bodies need fuel or food to produce energy, just as cars and airplanes need gasoline fuel to keep running. Students could even come up with the notion that nuclear reactors split atoms to produce electrical energy, which lights their houses and runs their television sets and video games.

Through such understandings, children will gain depth in their word learning. Next, before we examine teaching strategies, let's look at some guidelines for establishing vocabulary programs throughout the elementary grades.

Principles to Guide Vocabulary Instruction

In this section, we consider six principles to guide the teaching of vocabulary in elementary classrooms. They evolve from common sense, authoritative opinion, and research and theory on the relationship between vocabulary knowledge and reading comprehension.

Principle 1: Select Words That Children Will Encounter While Reading Literature and Content Material

Readers can tolerate not knowing some words while reading; they can still comprehend the text selection. So when introduced to and taught relatively *few* new words prior to a reading selection, chances are that vocabulary instruction will not lead readers to better

Map to *The Paperbag Princess*

Characters:
1. Elizabeth: a princess with expensive clothes.
2. Ronald: a prince
3. dragon: dragon smashed castle, burned Elizabeth's clothes, and carried off Ronald

Problem:
Elizabeth wanted Ronald back.

Resolution:
Elizabeth outwitted dragon by telling him he was the "fiercest" dragon and got Ronald back. Ronald told her to "Come back when dressed like a real princess." Elizabeth told Ronald he looked like a prince but he was a bum.

"Big" Ideas:
* Sometimes using you brains wins out over physical strength.
* At times what you do is more important than what you wear.

● **FIGURE 7.4** Map to *The Paperbag Princess*

comprehension. However, when vocabulary learning is centered around acquiring a large percentage of words from actual selections that will be read in class, comprehension is likely to be enhanced (Stahl, 1982; Beck and McKeown, 1983). Which words are the best choices for vocabulary instruction? Which aren't?

Words shouldn't be chosen for instructional emphasis just because they are big or obscure. Teaching archaic, or difficult, words just because they are unusual is not a legitimate reason for instruction. A reader learns to use monitoring strategies, such as those we will discuss in the next chapter, to overcome such obstacles. Nor should difficult words be chosen if they do not relate to the central meaning or important concepts associated with passage content. Maps or organizers of the reading material can be used to help identify the words for study. This is true of literature as well as for content area vocabulary instruction. For example, for the book, *The Paperbag Princess,* by Robert N. Munsch (1980) Ms. Belle chose the vocabulary from a map she constructed (see Figure 7.4).

Further, consider the following ways to choose words for instructional emphasis:

Key Words. Key words come directly from basal, literature, or content text selections. These words convey major ideas and concepts related to the passage content and are essential for understanding to take place. Key words need to be taught, *and taught well,* because they present definite obstacles to comprehension that cannot be overlooked by the reader.

Useful Words. Useful words are relevant. Children encounter useful words repeatedly in a variety of contexts. In some cases, a child may be familiar with useful words, having been taught or introduced to them in earlier stories or units, or in previous years. However, it cannot be assumed that these words are old friends; they may be mere acquaintances.

Interesting Words. Interesting words tickle the imagination and create enthusiasm, excitement, and interest in the study of words. Words that have unique origins, tell intriguing stories, or have intense personal meaning for students make good candidates for instruction. Children can get hooked on words through the study of interesting words.

Vocabulary-Building Words. Classroom instruction should include words that lend themselves readily to vocabulary-building skills: **Vocabulary-building skills** allow children to seek clues to word meanings on their own. Words should be selected for instruction that will show students how to inquire into the meaning of unknown words—through structural analysis (i.e., drawing attention to word parts) or context analysis (Vacca and Vacca, 1993).

Principle 2: Teach Words in Relation to Other Words

Vocabulary words are often crucially tied to basic concepts. Children, as we have contended earlier, develop definitional knowledge when they are able to relate new words to known words. When words are taught in relation to other words, students are actively drawn into the learning process. They must use background knowledge and experiences to detect likenesses and differences. When words are taught within the context of concept development, children develop a greater sensitivity to shades of meaning in communication. Rather than learning words randomly, children should deal with words that are related semantically and belong to categories.

Henry (1974) outlined four basic cognitive operations associated with learning concepts and words. The first involves the act of *joining,* or "bringing together." Comparing, classifying, and generalizing are possible through the act of joining. Asking children to explain how words are related or having them sort through word cards to group words together involves the act of joining.

The act of *excluding* is another conceptual operation worth considering when teaching words in relation to other words. Children must discriminate, negate, or reject items because they do not belong within a conceptual category. When a child must decide which word does not belong in a set of words, the process involves exclusion. In this case, a child would search through his or her background knowledge to distinguish examples from nonexamples or relevant attributes from irrelevant attributes.

So when a child is asked to decide which word does not belong in the list—flower, music, perfume, skunk—upon what set of criteria is a decision made? One immediate response may have been that music doesn't belong since it has little to do with the concept of smell.

A third conceptual activity or operation involves the act of *selecting.* Children learn to make choices and to explain why they made their choices based on what they have experienced, know, or understand. Synonyms, antonyms, and multiple-meaning words lend themselves well to the act of selecting. For example, select the *best* word from those given in the sentence.

Tyrone's quiet behavior was mistaken for ______________________
SHYNESS/MODESTY/TERROR

Any of the choices might be acceptable. Yet the value of the activity is in providing a rationale for your choice by judging the worth of several potentially correct answers.

A fourth aspect of thinking conceptually involves the act of *implying*. Is a child able to make decisions based on if-then, cause-effect relations among concepts and words? Dupuis and Snyder (1983) contended that the most common form of vocabulary exercise using implication is the analogy. They believe that the act of completing an analogy is such a complex activity that it actually requires the use of joining, excluding, and selecting processes.

Principle 3: Teach Students to Relate Words to Their Background Knowledge

Judith Thelen (1986) likened children's schema of differing subjects to having file folders inside the brain. Let's suppose a math text reads "a negative number is on the left of a number line." If Joe has a well-developed file folder for some schema for number line, this explanation of a negative number will be useful to Joe. But suppose Helen has heard of number line, but has an underdeveloped file folder for number line. In that case, the sentence defining negative numbers will have little meaning for Helen.

Pearson (1984) admonished educators by saying that we have asked the wrong question in teaching vocabulary. Instead of asking, "How can I get this word into the students' heads?" we should be asking, "What is it that students already know about that they can use as an anchor point, as a way of accessing this new concept?" If we ask the latter question, then we will always be directing our vocabulary instructions to the file-folder issue—where does this word fit? Following Pearson's line of thinking, Joe and Helen's teacher could help each of them think about "How can I use what I know about a number line to learn what a negative number is?" In Helen's case, the teacher needs to show her a number line and have her work with it to develop her notions of number line.

Principle 4: Teach Words in Prereading Activities to Activate Knowledge and Use Them in Postreading Discussion, Response, and Retelling

Through **prereading activities,** vocabulary words can be focused on *before* students read to help activate background knowledge in activities involving predicting. For example, Ms. Belle, a second-grade teacher, used vocabulary words she had chosen from *The Paperbag Princess* in a technique called *Connect Two* (Blachowicz, 1986). Her students predicted ways the terms would be connected in the story. (See Figure 7.5) Then, since the words she chose reflected the story line, her students used them quite naturally when responding *after* reading. Here is a retelling given by Albert, a second-grader:

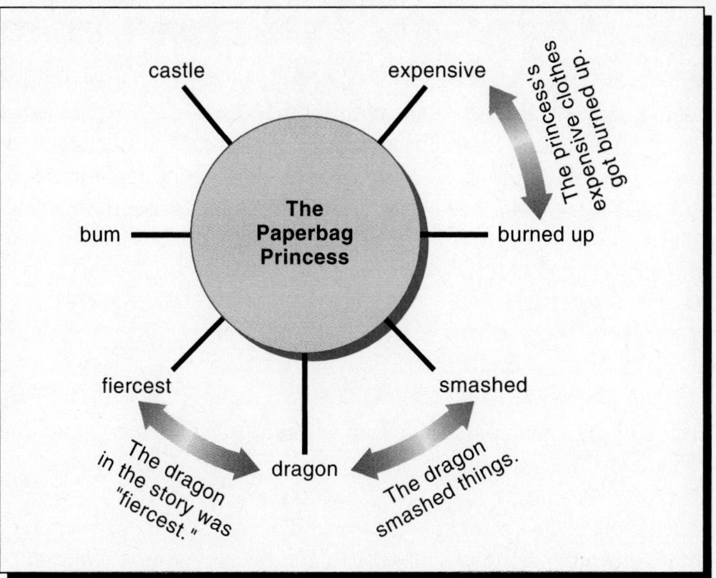

● **FIGURE 7.5** Example of Connect Two strategy for *The Paperbag Princess*

> Elizabeth was a princess who wore *expensive* clothes and was going to marry a prince named Ronald. A dragon *smashed* her castle and took Ronald. Elizabeth told the dragon, "Aren't you the *fiercest* dragon in the world?" and "Can't you burn up ten forests?" and stuff like that. The dragon did this stuff and got so tired he went to sleep so Elizabeth got Ronald. Then Ronald told her, "Come back when you look like a real princess." Elizabeth told him he looked like a prince but he was a *bum*.

In this way, Albert was able to integrate the words *expensive, smash, fiercest, and bum* as he retold the story.

Principle 5: Teach Words Systematically and in Depth

Teaching a word in depth means going beyond having students give back a definition. It even means more than having students do something with a definition like finding an antonym, fitting the word into a sentence blank, and classifying the word with other words. All these are excellent activities, and do need to be a part of a systematic vocabulary program. However, researchers are finding that for students to process vocabulary *in depth,* they must *generate a novel product using the term:* They could restate the definition in their own words, compare the definition to their own experiences with the concept, or make up a sentence that clearly demonstrates the word's meaning. These novel products can be written. But, in fact, class discussion leads students to process words deeply by drawing connections between new and known information (Stahl, 1986).

By teaching systematically, we mean following a vocabulary program similar to the ones proposed by Beck, McKeown, and Omanson (1987) and Duin and Graves (1987). In these programs ten to twelve conceptually related words were taught and reinforced over a seven- to ten-day period. Networks of meanings of these words were established as well as links to students' experiences. The activities included timed word matchings to facilitate students' automatic retrieving of new meanings. Finally, in the Duin and Graves study, students were engaged in group writing activities on a topic, using the vocabulary words in their writing.

Principle 6: Awaken Interest in and Enthusiasm for Words

The case too often in elementary classrooms is that vocabulary learning is one of the dullest activities of the school day. Children tend to associate vocabulary instruction with dictionary drill: looking up words, writing out definitions, and putting words in sentences. While these activities have some merit, they quickly become a meaningless routine. Children need to know *why, when,* and *how* to use dictionaries.

Nothing can replace the excitement about words that a good teacher can generate. The teacher's attitude toward vocabulary instruction can be contagious. What you do to illustrate the power of words is vital in improving children's vocabulary. Ask yourself whether you get excited by learning new words. Share words of interest to you with your students, and tell stories about the origin and derivation of words.

Help students play with words, as Cindy's third-grade teacher did. In one activity, her teacher, through discussion and demonstration, developed for the children the concept of facial expression, or "mugging." With a Polaroid camera she took "mug shots" of her students, and placed them prominently on the bulletin board. The children learned to "mug" for the camera by acting out "mug" words (e.g., happy mugs, sad mugs, angry mugs, etc.). The very last mug the children learned was the smug smile of satisfaction, or the "smug mug." Cindy's teacher explained that when a child knew something that no other person knew or took great pride in an accomplishment, he or she was to flash the "smug mug."

Strategies for Vocabulary and Concept Development

Vocabulary instruction should not be neglected in the elementary classroom. Teachers in most grades worry that they "don't have the time to spend on vocabulary instruction." Direct vocabulary instruction need not take more than 20 minutes a day. Moreover, opportunities for incidental instruction and reinforcement arise in content-area instruction throughout the school day.

Effective vocabulary instruction begins with the teacher's commitment to teach words well. So start slowly, and gradually build an instructional program over several

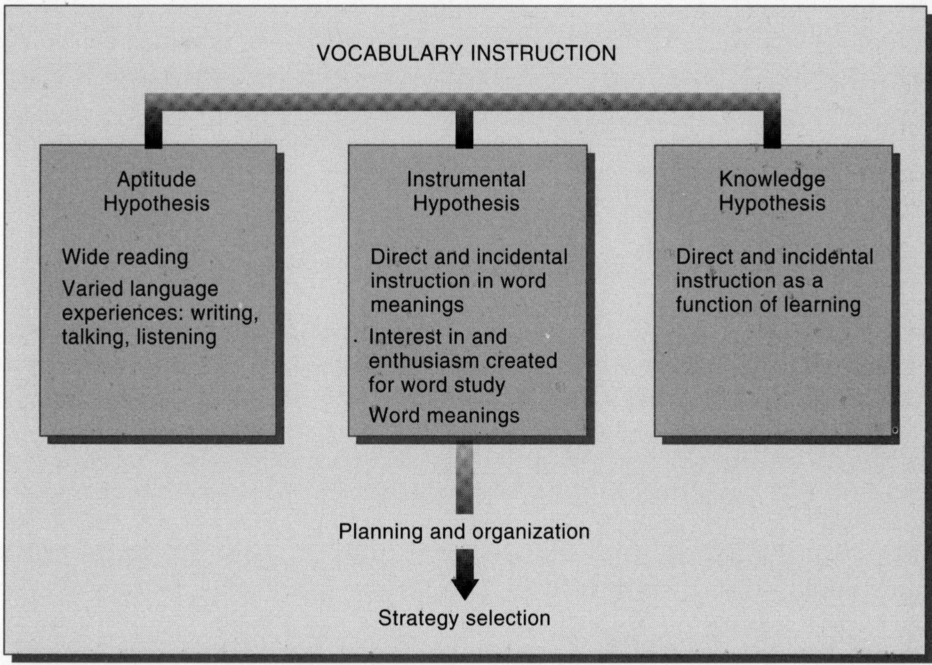

● **FIGURE 7.6** A three-component approach to classroom vocabulary instruction

years. We have already recommended that words be selected for emphasis that come from the actual materials that children read during the year, basal and literature selections as well as content-area text selections. We further suggest that the program evolve from the instructional implications of the knowledge, instrumental, and aptitude hypotheses discussed earlier. Therefore, consider a three-component approach to classroom vocabulary instruction as illustrated in Figure 7.6.

Instructional strategies are not unique to any one component illustrated in Figure 7.6. In fact, strategies for teaching vocabulary should cut across components. Therefore, select strategies based on planning decisions that include provisions for a variety of activities, the types of information you wish to convey about words, and ways to link concepts to the children's experiences.

Relating Experiences to Vocabulary Learning

Dale's Cone of Experience (Figure 7.1 on page 233) is a good place to begin in planning and selecting vocabulary strategies that are experienced based. The more direct, first-hand experiences that students have, the better.

However, in place of first-hand experience, different levels of vicarious experience can establish the bases for vocabulary learning. Vicarious experiences are second-hand experiences, yet they are valuable in their own right. Dale's Cone of Experience indicates the possibilities that are available in planning experiences that are vicarious: demonstrations, simulations, dramatization, visual and audio media, reading to children, and reading on one's own.

Next, we will consider how wide reading is useful for growth in vocabulary learning, and how to help students use context to extend this growth.

Using Context for Vocabulary Growth

Teachers and experts know that in addition to defining new terms, children also need some examples of the concept; that is, children need to hear the new words used in differing contexts. Hearing a dictionary definition is not enough to learn a new word.

Defining a word and using the word in a sentence or *a context* is a common and useful practice. In studying sound, a third-grade class learned that the definition of *vibrate* was "to move rapidly back and forth." They also discussed different contexts for vibrate—like how a violin string vibrates, and how blowing into a bottle or a flute makes the air vibrate. Even though we know that using context while reading is an important avenue for vocabulary growth, we agree with Nagy (1988/1989) that when *teaching new meanings,* context used alone is not effective. We know that the context provided in most texts tells us something about the word's meaning, but seldom does any single context give complete information (Deighton, 1970; Shatz and Baldwin, 1986). Nevertheless *we suggest that the instructional goal should be to teach students to use context to gain information about the meanings of new terms.* Buikema and Graves (1993) suggest that students can be shown that using context is like solving a riddle. For example, Judy led a group of first graders in reading a big book entitled *Skylab* (Ribgy, 1986). First, when she asked the children what they thought a Skylab was, Jan said, "A lab in the sky, of course," Judy wrote this on the board. As Jan and the first graders read the book together, they made a list of what a skylab is:

It is a space station.

A rocket takes a skylab into space.

A skylab goes around the earth.

Astronauts stay on a skylab.

A Skylab has big solar collectors. Solar collectors change sunlight into electricity.

Helping students learn to use context to gain information about words new to them is particularly important for less fluent readers of any age. In addition, children need to know that they must accept partial word knowledge, some degree of uncertainty, and occasionally misleading contexts as they meet new words in their independent reading (Beck, McKeown, and McCaslin, 1983).

In the last section of this chapter, we examine ways to help children grow in independence by using differing contexts to extend their vocabulary knowledge. But first, we look at more direct instructional strategies to develop word meanings.

Developing Word Meanings

Definitional knowledge or the ability to relate new words to known words can be built through synonyms, antonyms, and multiple-meaning words.

Synonyms are words that are similar in meaning to other words. **Antonyms** are words that are opposite in meaning to other words. Synonyms and antonyms are useful ways of having children define and understand word meanings. Antonyms, in particular, can demonstrate whether children really comprehend the meanings of new words. Moreover, words that have multiple meanings tend to confuse students, especially when they are reading and encounter the uncommon meaning of a word used in a passage.

Synonyms. Synonym instruction has value when a child has knowledge of a concept but is unfamiliar with its label—the new word to be learned. In such cases, the focus of instruction is to help the student associate new words with more familiar ones. This particular strategy is a good example of the cognitive principle of bridging the gap between the new and the known.

For example, a fifth-grade teacher provided a synonym match for words that children were studying in a unit on ecology. Several of the matching items were:

Column A: New Words	Column B: Words That You Already Know
cultivate	change
erode	surroundings
environment	wearing away
modify	work

The children were directed to match the words from Column B with the words from Column A. A discussion followed with students giving reasons for their matchups. The discussion led to further clarification of each new term and the realization, as one child put it, that "some words just look hard but really aren't."

In another synonym-related activity, students were given overworked or unimaginative words in sentences or paragraphs, and asked to supply alternative words that would make each sentence or the paragraph more descriptive and interesting. Words such as nice, swell, and neat are good candidates for this type of activity.

> Our trip to the zoo was *neat.* The entire family had a *swell* time. Dad thought that seeing the monkeys on Monkey Island was *fun.* So did I. But Mom *said,* "The monkeys were *okay,* but I liked the reptiles even more. The snakes were *terrific.*" We all had a *great* time at the zoo.

This activity, and adaptations of it, can be used as a springboard for children to analyze a piece of their own writing, looking for overworked words and substituting more interesting and precise words.

Many word-processing programs now have a built-in thesaurus. Children can be shown how to use the thesaurus to help find "just the right word" for what they want to say. Teachers can also use the thesaurus to develop exercises in which students must decide which synonyms would fit best in specific contexts, like the following:

Which synonym would you most likely find in a funeral announcement or an obituary?

dead departed extinct

Exercises such as this one are a part of vocabulary instruction that promotes deep and fluent word knowledge.

Antonyms. In addition to matching activities (i.e., where students associate the target words with words that are opposite in meaning) and selecting activities (i.e., where students select the best choice for an antonym from several listed), consider strategies where children are challenged to work with antonyms in various print contexts.

For example, ask children to change the meanings of advertisements: Change the advertisement! Don't sell the merchandise! Children can ruin a good advertisement by changing the underlined words to words that mean the opposite. The following are examples of the antonym-advertisment activity.

Today through Tuesday!

Save now on this quality bedding.

The bigger the size, the more you save.

GREAT truckload sale

Just take your purchase to Checkouts

and Cashiers will deduct 30% from ticketed Price

Similar activities can be developed for a target word in a sentence or several new vocabulary words in a paragraph. You may devise an activity in which children work with sentence pairs. In the first sentence, the target word is underlined. In the second sentence, a child must fill in the blank space with an antonym for the target word.

1. The ship sank to the *bottom* of the ocean.

   The climbers reached the_______________of the mountain.

2. The *joyful* family reunion never had a dull moment.

   The funeral was the most _______________ occasion that I had ever experienced.

Sentence pairs will generate variations of antonyms. Therefore, children should be asked to defend their choices. In the first pair of sentences, *top, peak,* and *highest point* are acceptable antonyms for *bottom. Sad, solemn,* and *depressing* are all possible antonyms for *joyful.*

Multiple-Meaning Words. Words with multiple meanings give children opportunities to see how words operate in context.

The *hall* was so long that it never seemed to end.

The concert took place in a large *hall.*

The Football *Hall* of Fame is located in Canton, Ohio.

In content area textbooks, children frequently run across common words that have different meanings (e.g., mean, table, force, bank, spring). These can lead to confusion and miscomprehension. A strategy for dealing with multiple-meaning words involves prediction and verification.

1. Select multiple-meaning words from a text assignment. List them on the board.
2. Have students predict the meanings of these words and write them on a sheet of paper next to each term.
3. Assign the reading selection, noting the page numbers where students can find each word in the text reading.
4. Ask students to verify their original predicted meanings. If they wish to change any of their predictions, they can revise the meanings based on how each word was used in the selection (Vacca and Vacca, 1989).

Classifying and Categorizing Words

When children manipulate words in relation to other words, they are engaging in critical thinking. Vocabulary strategies and activities should give students the experience of *thinking about, thinking through,* and *thinking with* vocabulary. Working with relationships among words provides this opportunity.

Through the aid of **categorization** and classification strategies, students recognize that they can classify and categorize words that label ideas, events, or objects. Such strategies involve the processes of joining, excluding, selecting, and implying. Children will learn to study words critically and form generalizations about the shared or common features of concepts. Word sorts, categorization, semantic mapping, analogies, paired word sentence generation, the possible sentences strategy, and collaborative learning exercises are all activities that help children conceptualize as well as learn and reinforce word meanings.

Word Sorts. The process of sorting words is integrally involved in concept formation. Word sorting is an unbelievably simple, yet valuable, activity to initiate. Individually or in small groups, children sort through vocabulary terms that are written on cards or listed on an exercise sheet. The object of word sorting is to group words into different categories by looking for shared features among their meanings. The strategies can be used effectively at any grade level.

There are two types of word sorts: the *open sort* and the *closed sort.* In the *closed sort,* students know in advance what the main categories are. In other words, they must select and classify words according to the features they have in common with a category. The closed sort reinforces and extends the ability to classify words. The *open sort,* on the other hand, stimulates inductive thinking. No category or grouping is known in advance of sorting, and students must search for meanings and discover relationships among words.

Fifth-grade students participating in a unit on the newspaper discovered the many functions of a newspaper: to inform and interpret, influence, serve, and entertain. A closed-sort task that children participated in involved the completion of the following worksheet in small groups.

> *Directions:* In your groups, place the topics below under the proper headings. You may use a topic more than once. Base your decisions on class discussions and what is found in today's newspaper.

the largest picture on A-1
Weather Watch
News Watch
the first full-page ad
the first Focal Point story
legal notices
the first letter to the editor
Dear Abby
the astrology column
the crossword puzzle
the Market at a Glance column (business)
the Transitions column (sports)
the Goren on Bridge column
the classified index
display advertising
death notices
the headline on A-1

Informs or interprets	Influences	Serves	Entertains

Ms. Prince introduced a science unit on fish in this way. She had her third graders work in groups to brainstorm and list everything they could think of relating to the word fish. Their list included:

good to eat	fun to catch	slippery
pretty	water	bugs
fins	tail	shiny

While the students were still in groups, she then asked them to come up with one or more categories or groups that two of the words could go in. The students came up with the following categories:

Fins and tail are *parts of a fish's body.*

Pretty, slippery, and shiny describe *how fish look.*

Good to eat and fun to catch tell about *things people like to do with fish.*

After the children had read the chapter on fish, Ms. Prince asked them to find words from the chapter that could go in the category or group that describes *how fish look.* The students very quickly added *scales* and *gills* to this category. In this way, Ms. Prince involved students in an open sort before reading, and a closed sort (i.e., using a category identified by the children) after reading the text.

An excellent use of open sorting is to coordinate it with word banks. Word banks, closely associated with the language experience approach, are collections of word cards a student owns because he or she can recognize them immediately. Word banks will be discussed in Chapter 8.

Categorization. Vocabulary activities involving categorization help students form relationships among words in much the same manner as open and closed sorts. The difference, however, lies in the amount of assistance a child is given. For example, a teacher may give students from two to six words per grouping and ask them to do something with the sets of words. Different formats may be used to "do something" with the word sets. Consider giving the children sets of words and ask them to circle the word in each set that includes the others. This exercise requires them to perceive common attributes or examples in relation to a more inclusive concept and to distinguish superordinate from subordinate terms. Children are involved in the cognitive process of joining.

Directions: Circle the word in each group that includes the others.

generals troops armies warriors	ocean lake water bay	spicy sour taste salty

Other categorization exercises may direct students to cross out the word that does not belong in each set. This format forces students to manipulate words that convey the meanings of common items. In these activities children learn to exclude those words that are not conceptually related to other words.

Directions: Cross out the word in each group that doesn't belong

meat butter oatmeal fish oil	earth ground stable soil	judgment treasure cash price

The younger children are, the more manipulative and directed the categorization activity might be. Word cards may be used instead of worksheets. Working with sets of cards, a teacher may place one set at a time on a worktable and call on a child to remove the card that doesn't belong. The other children around the table must then attempt to explain the child's choice. Moreover, manipulative activities that require cutting, pasting, or drawing work well.

Semantic Mapping. In Chapter 12, we will discuss **semantic mapping,** or webbing, a strategy that shows readers and writers how to organize important information. Semantic mapping can also revolve around vocabulary learning by providing a visual display of how words are related to other words. Earlier in this chapter semantic mapping was used to make distinctions among class, example, and attribute relations. Similarly, students can use semantic mapping to cluster words belonging to categories and to distinguish relationships. According to Smith and Johnson (1980), the procedures for semantic mapping can be varied to suit different purposes.

The first step in the semantic mapping of vocabulary is for the teacher to select a word central to a story or from any other source of classroom interest or activity, and then write this word on the board. From this point, the procedures can vary depending on the objective of the lesson. For example, the teacher can ask the class to think of as many words as they can that are in some way related to the word and jot them down. As students share the words they have written with the class, the words are grouped into categories on the board around the central concept. The students can nominate names for the categories and discuss the category labels, relating their experiences to the words on the board.

Semantic maps can be elaborately developed or kept relatively simple, depending on the sophistication of the class and grade level. In Figure 7.7, a group of beginning readers developed a concept of the five senses through a mapping strategy.

The teacher began the map by writing the target concept, five senses, in the middle of the board. She then presented the class with a familiar situation: "How often have you known that your sister was making a snack even before you got to the kitchen to see or taste it?" The children responded by saying they could smell food cooking or hear a sibling preparing the snack. The teacher praised the student responses and continued, "You

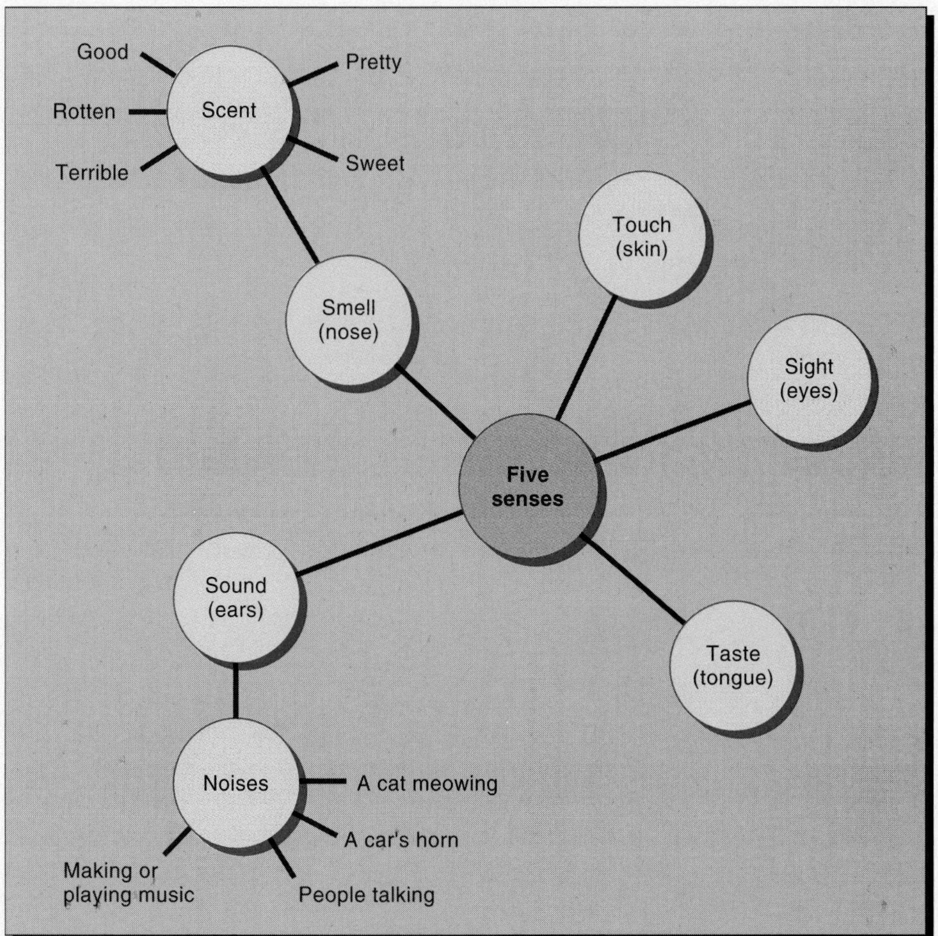

● **FIGURE 7.7** A semantic map of the five senses

were using your senses of smell and sound to know that a snack was being fixed." She then wrote *smell* and *sound* on the board, and connected the words to the central concept.

The children's attention was then directed to the bulletin board display of five children, each enjoying one of the senses. Through a series of questions, the class gradually developed the remainder of the semantic map. For example, when the concept of smell was being developed, the teacher noted, "We call a smell 'scent,'" and connected *scent* to *smell* on the map. She then asked, "How do you think flowers smell?" "What words can you tell me to determine different types of smells?" As the students volunteered words, the teacher placed them on the map. When the teacher asked, "When you think of sound, what's the first thing that comes to your mind?" the children quickly said "noises." The teacher connected *noises* to *sounds.* Further discussion focused on types of noises, both pleasant and unpleasant.

Analogies. An **analogy** is a comparison of two similar relationships. On one side, the words are related in some way; on the other side of the analogy, the words are related in the same way. Analogies probably should be taught to students beginning in the intermediate grades. If they are not familiar with the format of an analogy, they may have trouble reading it successfully. Therefore, give several short demonstrations in which you model the process involved in completing an analogy.

1. Begin by asking students to explain the relationship that exists between two words. For example, write on the board a simple class-example relation:

   apple fruit

   Ask students, "What is the relationship between the two words?" Explanations may vary greatly but arrive at the notion that an apple is a type of fruit.

3. Explain that an analogy is a comparison of two similar sets of relationships. Write on the board:

   Apple is to *fruit* as *carrot* is to ______________.

   Suggest to students, "If an apple is a type of fruit, then a carrot must be a type of ______________." Discuss the children's predictions, and provide additional examples.

5. Note than an analogy has its own symbols:

   apple:fruit::carrot: ______________

   Point out that the symbol : means *is to* and :: means *as.* Walk students through an oral reading of several analogies saying: "An analogy reads like this." (The class reads the analogy in unison following the teacher's lead.)

7. At first provide simple analogies and gradually increase the complexity of the relationships.

8. Develop analogies from vocabulary used in stories, content-area texts, or from topics of interest in the classroom.

Ignoffo (1980) explained the value of analogies this way: "Analogies are practical because they carry an implied context with them. To work the analogy, the learner is forced to attempt various . . . procedures that involve articulation, problem solving, and thinking" (p. 50).

In Box 7.2, we illustrate some of the types of word relationships from which many analogies can be developed.

● **BOX 7.2**

Using Word Relationships to Form Analogies

Directions: Study each type of relationship and for each example given, complete the analogy. Then compare your responses with a classmate or colleague.

1. Purpose Relationship

   Examples

   Teeth:Chew : : Pen: ________________

   Chair:Sit : : Knife: ________________

2. Part to Whole Relationship

   Examples

   Antler:Deer : : Tusk: ________________

   Cat:Feline : : Dog: ________________

3. Synonym Relationship

   Examples

   Small:Tiny : : Create: ________________

   Copy:Imitate : : Large: ________________

4. Antonym Relationship

   Examples

   Black:White : : Day: ________________

   High:Low : : Morning: ________________

5. Place Relationship

   Examples

   Book:Bookcase : : Car: ________________

   Flowers:Vase : : Clothes: ________________

6. Attribute Relationship

   Examples

   Rare:Whale : : Common: ________________

   Detective:Clue : : Scientist: ________________

7. Cause and Effect Relationship

   Examples

   Furnace:Heat : : Freezer: ________________

   Seed:Tree : : Egg: ________________

Paired-Word Sentence Generation. Students often need many exposures to new and conceptually difficult words in order to begin using these words in their speaking and writing vocabularies (Duin and Graves, 1987). After students have classified and categorized words through word sorts or other strategies, **paired-word sentence generation** can spur them into using these words in their speaking and writing.

Simpson (1987) described paired-word sentence generation as a task that could be used to *test* students' understanding of difficult concepts. We have taken her notion of paired-word sentence generation and developed it into a teaching strategy. In using this strategy, the teacher gives the students two related words. The goal of the strategy is to generate *one* sentence that correctly demonstrates an understanding of the words *and* their relationship to each other. However, there are several steps to help elementary students reach this goal. We will describe these steps by illustrating how Mr. Fratello used the strategy with his fifth-grade class as they worked with the concepts *reptile* and *cold blooded.* First, Mr. Fratello had each student write sentences with the words *reptile* and *cold blooded* in them. The class came up with sentences like these:

Reptiles are cold blooded.
Snakes, lizards, and turtles are reptiles.

Cold blooded means that when the air is warm their bodies are warm and when the air is cold their bodies are cold.

Mr. Fratello then led the class in a sentence-combining activity to write a sentence that would give the reader information about what reptiles are and what cold blooded means, as well as how the two concepts are related to each other. The class came up with sentences like:

Reptiles, like snakes, lizards, and turtles, are cold blooded because they are cold when the air is cold and warm when the air is warm.

Snakes, lizards, and turtles are reptiles that are cold blooded, which means they are warm when the air is warm and cold when the air is cold.

Mr. Fratello asked his fifth graders to generate paired-word sentences throughout the school year. They first worked as a whole class and later worked in groups of four made up of both high and low achievers. Finally, they worked alone on devising their own sentences.

Possible Sentences. Another strategy in which children relate concepts to each other is **possible sentences.** To implement this strategy the teacher chooses six to eight vocabulary words plus four or five contrast words. For example, in studying *Meat Eaters, Plant Eaters* using a big book, (Rigby, 1986), third-grade teacher Jane chose the words *bison, herd, reptile, rodent, mammal, coyote.* Then she choose the words *grasses, eagle, alligator, animals, and plants.* Jane wrote these words on the board. She led her class in a discussion concerning the meaning of each of the words, supplying a definition if no one in the class could do so. These definitions were also written on the board. Next, she asked her third graders to think of a *possible sentence* that might be in *Meat Eaters, Plant Eaters* and that contains at least two of these words. All sentences the children supplied were written on the board whether they were accurate or not. The children then read the selection together. Finally, the class discussed each sentence to decide whether it was true on not based on what they had read. Any sentence that they decided was not accurate based on what they learned through reading was rewritten so that it was accurate (Stahl and Kapinus, 1991).

The possible sentences strategy mobilizes students' prior knowledge and allows them to tie together vocabulary words. In addition, the prediction component increases involvement in learning of related vocabulary words.

Collaborative Learning. In addition to working with synonyms, antonyms, different ways of classifying and categorizing words, semantic mapping, analogies, paired word generation, and possible sentences, students can be motivated to devise vocabulary learning activities through collaborative learning grouping. O'Donnell (1990) gave four groups of inner city students a list of five challenging vocabulary terms. She had students number off, thus randomly assigning students to groups so that they were not always with their best friends. Each student in the group had a job, like task master, scribe, discussion leader, and encourager (Kagan, 1992). The groups were asked to prepare a ten-minute lesson for their peers for the purpose of teaching the words. She urged the groups to be creative and think of interesting ways to help class members learn their words. Further, she reminded students that they would be tested on all twenty words at the end of the week. O'Donnell reports that some of the material was so creative that other teachers asked for copies! As the group presentations were given, O'Donnell said, "I sat in the back of the room and noticed, with envy, the rapt attention each group was receiving. . . . They truly wanted to learn from each other." Further, when her students were tested on their knowledge of the vocabulary taught, the test results exceeded her expectations.

Developing Word Meanings Through Stories and Writing

Vocabulary functions differently in literature and in content material. When reading literature, knowing the meaning of a *new* word may not be necessary for understanding the gist of the story. In contrast, content area vocabulary often represents major concepts that are essential for comprehension and learning. For example, children who cannot give a definition of a *stamen* after reading about the parts of a flower have not grasped important content. On the other hand, children can understand a story about a band when they only glean from context that a *tambourine* is a musical instrument but don't know what exactly it is like. Secondly, vocabulary in literature often involves simply learning a new label for a concept already possessed, like learning that *desolate* means *very sad.* In content areas, often the purpose of the text is to teach the concepts as in the example of the second-grade science material labeling the parts of the flower, whereas this is not generally true in reading stories. Finally, in content texts, vocabulary terms often have a high degree of semantic relatedness as do the terms *nectar, pollen, anther, stamen, stigma, and style.* This is less likely to be true of vocabulary terms selected from literature (Armbruster and Nagy, 1992).

Yet, as mapping the story *The Paperbag Princess* illustrates, story grammar can be used to develop word meanings. The following two strategies, semantic analysis to writing and predict 'o gram draw upon insights from story grammar.

Semantic Analysis to Writing. Since authors develop a theme through a series of related incidents, Beyersdorfer and Schauer (1989) reasoned that stories provide a situational context that could be used for rich development of word meanings. When using this strategy, the teacher narrows the selection of words to those semantically related to the theme. Students then develop definitions based on personal schema for the theme.

In using *semantic analysis to writing,*

1. The teacher identifies the theme and composes a question involving critical thinking related to the theme.
2. The teacher selects words used by the author or consults a thesaurus to locate about five words (both synonyms and antonyms) relating to the theme—words that are too closely synonymous are discarded.
3. The teacher constructs a **think sheet** (see Box 7.3) for discussion purposes as well as for writing.

Brad, a sixth-grade teacher who was piloting a literature-based reading program, decided to involve his students in semantic analysis to writing with the thought-provoking book *A Wrinkle In Time* by Madeleine L'Engle. In this story Meg Murry, along with her precocious brother Charles Wallace and their friend Calvin O'Keefe, hope to rescue her father from a mysterious fate. The children travel through time to the planet Camazotz with the assistance of Mrs. Whatsit, Mrs. Who, and Mrs. Which. There they confront IT, the planet's intimidating force for conformity. Meg and friends find her father, but Charles Wallace gets swallowed up in IT. Meg's father cannot rescue Charles Wallace because he has been away so long from him that the familiar ties are too weak: Meg has to go back to IT and rescue Charles Wallace.

Although many themes can be derived from this book, Brad chose to use *self-reliance* in semantic analysis to writing because Meg, the main character, changed in terms of self-reliance through the many incidences in the book. Brad found that the dictionary definition of *self-reliance* was "sure of one's self and one's ability; needing, wishing for, and getting no help from others."

Brad then devised the questions: "Was Meg in *A Wrinkle In Time* self-reliant?" "If so, how?" "What did she do that showed self-reliance?" "If not, what did she do that was not self-reliant?"

In order to make the think sheet, Brad used a thesaurus and chose the following words and phrases:

self-confidence
certainty
trust in oneself
independence
conviction

● BOX 7.3

Think Sheet for Extended Definition of Self-Reliance

Questions you will respond to in an essay:

Was Meg in *A Wrinkle in Time* self-reliant? If so, how? What did she do that showed self-reliance? If not, what did she do that was not self-reliant? Further, did she change during the story?

What is self-reliance? ______________________________

____

Directions:

1. As a class, we will define the terms. Write down the definitions as we do this.
2. To this list add two words (numbers 6 and 7) suggested during brainstorming. Consult your dictionary and record a definition.
3. Decide which of the seven words contribute an essential characteristic to your definition of *self-reliance.*
4. Locate evidence from the story that proves Meg did or did not demonstrate the characteristics. Give the page number and a phrase description of the event.
5. Using the order of importance, rank the essential characteristics.
6. Write an essay. Define self-reliance and support the definition with evidence from *A Wrinkle in Time*.

Term-definition	Essential yes-no	Illustration-story, page number
1. Self-Confidence		
2. Certainty		
3. Trust in oneself		
4. Independence		
5. Conviction		
6. Courage		
7. Determination		

Because he knew the book would prove quite difficult for some of the readers in the class, Brad read the book orally to the class over a two-week period. He knew that some of these same readers would write interesting essays on self-reliance. Each day as he read the chapters, students wrote in a response log (response logs will be described in Chapter 10), and the class had lively discussions comparing their responses.

Students were now prepared for Brad to involve them in the semantic analysis to writing strategy. As a result of the class brainstorming and discussion, the terms *courage* and *determination* were added to the think sheet. Small-group work then began in earnest to find incidents that showed that Meg was or was not self-reliant.

Next, the class had an animated debate about whether Meg was or was not self-reliant, citing evidence for both positions. Many felt that Meg was not self-reliant and supported this with the incident when Meg finds her father and becomes quite disillusioned when her father is not able to get her brother, Charles Wallace, away from IT. Students who felt Meg became self-reliant cited the fact that Meg finally mustered the courage to attempt to save Charles Wallace from IT. Thus, two different beginning statements and story frames were formulated to help students begin writing their first drafts, after they had worked in pairs to rank the importance of their supporting evidence.

I think Meg in *A Wrinkle in Time* ______________________________
WAS/WAS NOT

self-reliant. I think this because ______________________________

______________________________. Further, ______________________________

______________________________. In addition,

______________________________.

In conclusion, ______________________________

______________________________.

Brad took home many stimulating essays to read after his students had eagerly read them to each other. Many students later chose their self-reliant essay from all those accumulated in their writing folder to revise and edit.

Predict 'o Gram. Story elements—like the setting, the different incidents in the plot, characterization, the problem or goal of the character, how the program or goal is resolved, and the theme or larger issue to which the problem or goal relates—can be used to develop students' meaning vocabulary with the predict 'o gram strategy.

In planning for predict 'o gram, teachers choose words from a story that they feel will be challenging to the students. The words and their meanings are discussed and children relate their personal associations with the words. Finally, students work in groups to predict how they think the author might use each term in the story. Would the author use it to

Predict 'o Gram
for
Crow Boy by Taro Yashima

Directions: Discuss with members of your group how you think Taro Yashima would use the vocabulary words below. Would he use them to describe the characters? Or the problem or goal of the character? Or the solution to the problem? Place each word in the appropriate square. Be prepared to tell *why* you think so.

Vocabulary words: forlorn, imagine, interesting, graduation, trudging, attendance, admired, charcoal, announced, rejected

Setting where the story took place	charcoal interesting
Characters the people in the story	forlorn imagine trudging
Problem or goal main character	rejected
Solution to the problem or attainment of goal	graduation attendance announced admired

● **FIGURE 7.8** An example of a predict 'o gram

tell about the setting? The characters? The problem or goal or trouble the characters have? Would the author use the word to tell about how the problem or trouble was solved? Students then read to discover how the author did use the terms.

Mrs. Nowak, a third-grade teacher in the same school as Brad, was also beginning to use a literature-based program with the basal reading program she had used for five years. She was planning for a group of students to read *Crow Boy* by Taro Yashima. The words she thought would be challenging included *forlorn, interesting, trudging, admired, announced, imagine, graduation, attendance, charcoal,* and *rejected.* To get students thinking about the problems in the story she asked them to free-write about their thoughts on "Sometimes kids tease a shy, different classmate." The students shared their free writes. Then Mrs. Nowak told them what was happening at the beginning of the story. She led them in a discussion concerning how the meanings of the terms related to personal experiences and predicting which of the words the author would use for each story element.

Figure 7.8 shows how the group completed the predict 'o gram from *Crow Boy.* The students then read the story looking to see how the author actually used the challenging vocabulary terms. In the final section of this chapter, we suggest ways to help children gain control over their own vocabulary learning.

Developing Independence in Vocabulary Learning

There is no question that wide reading and thus learning the meaning of words from context is an important way for people to extend their vocabularies. Fielding, Wilson, and Anderson (1986) found that the amount of free reading was the best predictor of vocabulary growth between the grades of two and five. Nagy (1988/1989) theorized that after third grade, for children who do read a reasonable amount, reading may be the single largest source of vocabulary growth. Students are also exposed to terms as they listen to teachers, parents, and television.

Next, we will look at the strategies of self-selection and word knowledge rating. These two strategies aid students in monitoring their own growth in vocabulary knowledge as they use context in reading and listening. The *self-selection* strategy helps children become sensitized to the many words that they read and hear in school and at home that they can add to their meaning vocabulary. *Word knowledge rating* helps children develop an awareness of the extent to which they know the words they come across as they read and interact with others.

Self-Selection Strategy. Words for the self-selection strategy can be drawn from basal readers, literature, content-area instruction, or incidental learning experiences. As the name implies, children select the words to be studied. In describing how to use this strategy, Haggard (1986) explained that the first step is to ask students to bring to class one word they believe the class should learn; the teacher also chooses a word. These words are then written on the board and students give the definitions they gleaned from the context in which they found the word. Class members add any information they can to each definition. The students and teacher consult pertinent references like dictionaries, glossaries, and textbooks to add to the definitions that are incomplete or unclear.

At this point, students can explain why they think a word is important to learn. Through this discussion students narrow the list, agreeing to exclude terms that many already know or are not useful enough. The agreed-upon terms and their definitions are recorded in vocabulary journals that are kept throughout the year. Students may also enter into their own vocabulary journal personal words they chose, but that were not chosen by the group. The class list of words is then used in activities like word sorts, analogies, synonym matching, or any of the other activities that have been described. The class-agreed-upon words also become part of end-of-unit tests. By using this strategy, students become aware of many striking words that they see and hear in their daily lives.

Word Knowledge Rating. Word knowledge rating is a way to get children to analyze how well they know vocabulary words. Words chosen by the teacher or by the students in the self-selection strategy are written on a worksheet or on the board. We suggest students rate words using Dale's (1965) continuum to explain the degrees of word cognition.

I've never seen the word.

I've heard of it, but I don't know what it means.

I recognize it in context. It has something to do with _______

I know the word in one or several of its meanings.

After students have rated themselves on their knowledge of the words, lead them in a discussion using questions such as "Which are the hardest words?" "Which do you think most of us don't know?" "Which are the easiest?" "Which do you think most of us know?" (Blachowicz, 1986). The exchange could also involve consideration of the question "Which terms are synonyms for concepts we already know, and which are somewhat or totally new concepts to us?"

Through such discussions, students will begin to make judgments concerning the depth of their knowledge of vocabulary terms that they have encountered, as well as the amount of effort needed to add the term to their meaning vocabulary.

SUMMARY

Vocabulary instruction is one facet of reading instruction about which there is minimal controversy. Educators agree that it is possible to extend students' knowledge of word meanings, and it is important to do so because of the relationship between this knowledge and reading comprehension. This chapter explored that relationship, then delved into the instructional opportunities teachers can provide to expand children's vocabulary knowledge and to develop their interest and motivation to *want* to learn words and to monitor their own vocabulary learning.

Six guidelines for establishing vocabulary programs throughout the elementary grades were presented. Included were numerous strategies for vocabulary and concept development that can be used throughout the school day and that capitalize on children's natural spontaneity, using direct instruction and cooperative learning groups as well as reinforcement activities. These strategies can be adapted for teaching vocabulary through basal readers, literature, or content-area instruction—providing a natural framework for concept development at all ages.

TEACHER-ACTION RESEARCHER

1. Choose any grade level and teach a vocabulary lesson, directing it to a small group consisting of at least four children. The lesson should emphasize one of the following strategies discussed in the chapter: (a) relating experiences to vocabulary learning; (b)

developing word meanings using synonyms, antonyms, or multimeaning words; and (c) classifying and categorizing words. In what ways did the strategy selected work well with the children?

2. Observe a classroom teacher during reading and language arts instruction for several consecutive days. Record the time spent on vocabulary instruction. Look for vocabulary instruction that reflects the aptitude and knowledge hypotheses as well as the instrumental hypothesis. How much time is devoted to vocabulary learning in each category? What kinds of activities have been incorporated into the instruction? What conclusions do you draw from your observations? What implications can you make for further instruction?

3. Discuss with several children a semantic map developed around a key concept. How much do the children already know about the concept? What areas require further development?

KEY TERMS

aptitude hypothesis
knowledge hypothesis
instrumental hypothesis
vocabulary
concepts
class relationships
superordinate
subordinate
vocabulary-building skills
prereading activities
definitional knowledge
synonyms
antonyms
categorization
semantic mapping
analogy
paired-word sentence generation
possible sentences
think sheet

CHAPTER 8

Word Identification

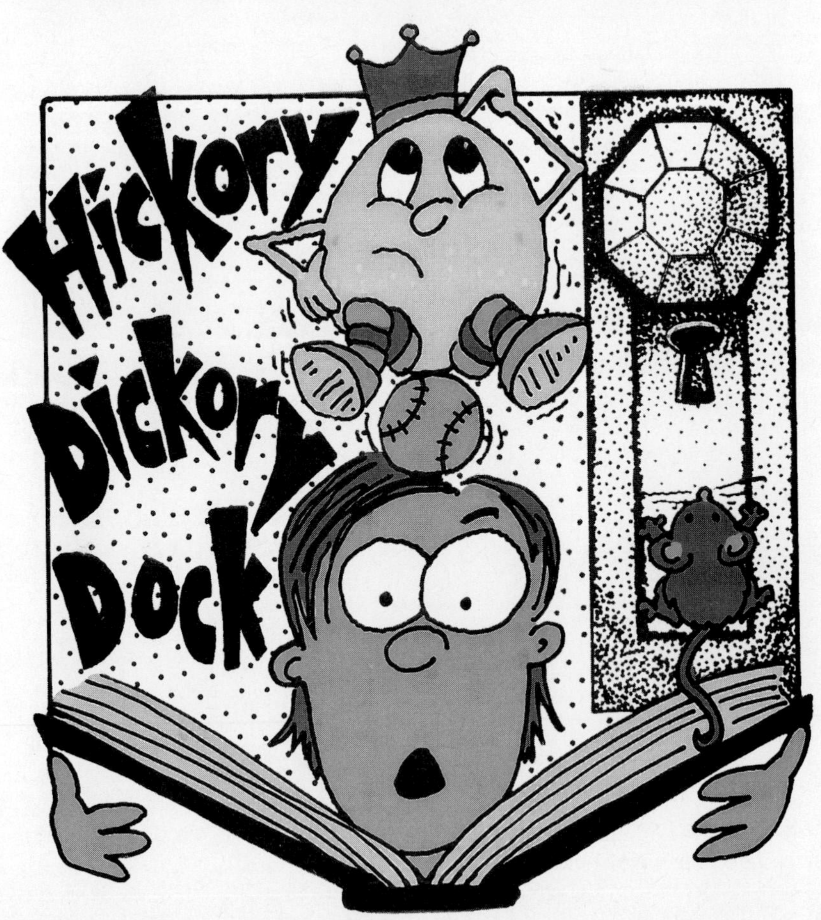

BETWEEN THE LINES

In this chapter you will discover:

- **The philosophical differences that teachers have about how words should be taught.**
- **How skilled readers identify words.**
- **How children acquire word identification abilities.**
- **The role that experience with reading, seeing, discussing, and using and writing words plays in the development of sight words.**
- **How letter-sound knowledge can be taught to support comprehension.**
- **Guidelines for teaching phonics.**
- **What word identification strategies to model with students.**

Steve, 3½ years old, was staring at a gum wrapper with PAL written on it. He said, "This says 'gum.'" Was Steve reading? We like to think so. The roots of literacy have begun to take hold for Steve. He has made the association between speech and print and knows intuitively that reading is supposed to make sense. At his present level of development, Steve makes use of information in his immediate surroundings to determine what print says. This is one way context cues are used by skilled readers. As Steve continues to develop as a reader, he will learn to use other word identification cues, from the context in the flow of print and within words themselves.

Words inevitably enter into the discussion when children are asked to explain what they are doing during the class time they spend on learning to read. Words are what children usually perceive as the meat of instruction in learning to read. Some children report that they are studying words or learning new words. Others explain what they do when they come to a word they don't know: Marcia's strategy is to sound it out, and Lionel tries to come up with a word that makes sense. Either way, children spend a lot of time and energy working with words.

How teachers invest their time in helping readers identify words is an important instructional question and the subject of much debate. While there are differences in practice, it's the philosophical differences that seem to predominate (Stahl, 1992). In some circles, nothing can create a more heated discussion that how words should be taught: "look-say!" or "intensive phonics." Terms such as these have good or bad connotations, depending on one's perspective. Some reading experts feel strongly that words shouldn't be studied in isolation, nor should other units of written language such as individual letters or letter combinations. Others stress that accurate word identification is an important aspect of learning to read, and that learning sound-letter relationships is the most efficient way to achieve accuracy.

We do not see the debate over how words should be taught as fruitful. The authors of *Becoming a Nation of Readers* (1985) made some sense when they wrote, "Based on what we know, it is incorrect to suppose that there is a simple or single step which, if taken correctly, will immediately allow a child to read. Becoming a skilled reader is a journey that involves many steps. Strengthening any one element yields small gains. For large gains, many elements must be in place" (p. 4).

The question of teaching children to identify words is not an either you do or you don't proposition. The time that each of us will invest in teaching children to identify words will depend on what we believe about reading and learning to read. Our own implicit model of reading influences not only the amount of instructional time given to word identification, but also the *type* of instruction we emphasize to help children identify words.

A teacher's instructional beliefs and actions in the classroom are bound to influence children's reading behavior. How? Kraus (1983), for example, studied two first-grade classrooms for the better part of a school year to provide insights into the question. In one first-grade class (Classroom X) the teacher placed much emphasis on learning and using sound-letter relationships. When students came to unfamiliar words as they read, they were told to sound them out or were given help in doing this. In the other class (Classroom Y) the teacher emphasized reading for meaning as a way of identifying words. She taught students to monitor their own reading. When children asked the teacher for help on troublesome words, she would tell them to read on and skip the word, and come back later to see if they could then figure it out. She also emphasized the idea that sometimes a reader can get the gist of the author's message without recognizing every word.

The children in both classrooms were individually interviewed to determine their perceptions of the strategies they use when they come to unrecognized words during reading. Here is how Sue in Classroom X responded to the interviewer's questions:

Interviewer: *What would you do if you were reading by yourself and you came to a word you didn't know?*

Sue: Sound it out.

Interviewer: What would you do if you tried to sound it out and you still couldn't figure it out?
Sue: I'd tell the teacher. She would help me sound it out.
Interviewer: What if you are all alone?
Sue: I'd call my brother. He could tell me the word.
Interviewer: What could you do by yourself to figure it out?
Sue: I'd go next door. Someone there could help me sound the word out.
Interviewer: If no one were around to help you?
Sue: I'd yell, "Anybody come and help me!"
Interviewer: But what if no one heard you yelling for help?
Sue: I'd stop reading.

Sue's response, while quite illustrative, was fairly typical of the responses made by other class members. It appeared that most of the children in Classroom X had developed a single strategy for word identification. If sounding out the word failed, most of the children suggested they would either seek the help of a significant other (e.g., a teacher, parent, older sibling) or just stop reading until help arrived.

In contrast, here is how Bill, a first-grader from Classroom Y, answered the interviewer's questions. This, too, is indicative of the responses made by the children interviewed.

Interviewer: What do you do when you come to a word you don't know?
Bill: I'd skip over the word and then read the next sentence. Then I'd say like, "Is it 'blank'?" I'd look at the letters to see if they are the same as "blank." Then I'd go back to the beginning and see if "blank" makes sense.
Interviewer: What would you do if you were reading and you tried but couldn't figure out a word?
Bill: I'd keep reading. Sometimes one word doesn't matter.

The teacher in Classroom X was operating from a bottom-up, skills perspective of learning to read. Her counterpart in Classroom Y, however, was more interactive in her orientation toward reading. The instructional emphasis in Classroom X rested squarely on learning *sound-letter relationships,* because the teacher believed *phonics* provided the most efficient means for transferring learning from one reading situation to another. On the other hand, the teacher in Classroom Y believed that children should make use of phonic knowledge, but they must also take advantage of other kinds of information while reading.

Two teachers with two different instructional emphases. Yet each had the same instructional goal in mind for word identification: Both teachers wanted their students to achieve independence in word identification while reading. The means, however, by which they started young readers on the road to independence were decidedly different.

Word Identification and the Interactive Model

The teacher in Classroom Y believes that children can make use of not only graphic information, but also other kinds of information as they read. For her, reading is an interactive process. Let's take a closer look at what it means to identify words from an interactive perspective by participating in the following demonstration.

Suppose the following lines were flashed on a screen in half-second intervals, and you were asked to write down what you could remember after each line was flashed.

Line 1	Z\rcO-
Line 2	xmrbacdy
Line 3	boragle
Line 4	institution
Line 5	flour wiggle come stove investigate girl door yell
Line 6	the beautiful girl ran down the steep hill

When we have conducted this experiment in our reading methods classes, here's what usually happens.

Most class members are unable to accurately remember the squiggles on line 1. However, they are able to remember some, but not all, of the letters in line 2. Both the nonword *boragle* in line 3, which follows conventional English letter patterns, and the word *institution* in line 4 are usually recalled. After line 5 is flashed, students are unable to recall all the words in the string, but the whole string of words in line 6, which makes a sentence, is usually recalled.

What can we learn from this demonstration? Frank Smith (1985) tells us human beings can make about four fixations per second with their eyes. When looking at the flashed items, skilled readers use about 50 milliseconds of visual intake, and then use 200 milliseconds to process the intake. During the intake they can probably only attend to about five to seven items. The limit of being able to hold about five to seven items in short-term memory operates in looking at each of the six lines for a half second. What changes line by line is the nature of the items. Skilled readers are able to *chunk* together or to perceive some of the items as a unit.

In line 1, skilled readers are not able to chunk the squiggles into meaningful letter combinations. In line 2, the squiggles are recognized as individual letters. However, within the time constraints, readers cannot chunk all of the letters into meaningful letter combinations, so they have difficulty holding *all* the letters in their short-term memory. In lines 3, 4, and 5, readers can chunk the letter into familiar letter combinations or patterns. *Boragle* and *institution* are recalled, but readers cannot recall all of the words in line 5, because these words cannot be chunked together into a meaningful utterance. Readers stand a greater chance to recall line 6, because this string of words represents a meaningful sentence.

Researchers have studied two basic processes that occur as a reader reads. One of these processes is the *chunking* of individual letters into letter combinations, letter combinations into words, and words into meaningful phrases. The other process involves *prediction.* All efficient skilled readers predict, although not all are conscious of doing so. As readers read, they form hypotheses about what the text is likely to say—perhaps the hypothesis involves the word or phrase that comes next, or what the next few sentences will be about—and then read to see if their predictions are correct. If their predictions are confirmed, they make more hypotheses. If their hypotheses are not confirmed, they may focus more carefully on the text to see what the author does say, and then modify the direction of their predicting in light of this new information.

What cues do readers use to make these predictions? They use knowledge they have about the world, how language works, and sound-letter relationships. This discussion is another way of describing the interactive nature of reading, or how readers use graphic cues from the page and their own knowledge as they process information from print. Neither source of information is focused on exclusively by readers. Interactive models of reading emphasize that skilled readers are able to efficiently *coordinate* the two kinds of information as they read. Let's look more closely at the role of **word identification** in skilled reading.

Word Identification of Skilled Readers

Skilled readers are able to chunk letters together and to chunk words into meaningful units. Let's examine some other word identification abilities of skilled readers through two more experiences. In the first experience, students are divided into two groups, and each group is given a copy of the same sentence with different letters deleted. One group receives:

___ e _ a _ _ a _ _ o ___ ___ e _ oa _.

This group is unable to determine what the sentence says. The other group quickly and successfully decides what the sentence says. This is what they see:

Th _ m _n r _ n d _ wn th _ r _ d.

This version of the sentence can be read with relative ease. This is because consonants (i.e., all the letters *except a, e, i, o,* and *u*) are exceptionally reliable concerning how they relate to specific sounds in the English language. Furthermore, as this experience illustrates, skilled readers are able to determine *any* word in their listening and speaking vocabulary using their knowledge of consonant sound-letter associations *provided the consonants are in a known context.*

A second but related insight into the word identification abilities of skilled readers is demonstrated in the next experience. One group of students is handed List 1 and the other group List 2; both lists contain nonsense words.

List 1	**List 2**
scrass	tblc
sook	gfpv
tolly	oeaiu
amittature	rtbm
lanfication	gdhtaiueo

The group with List 1 easily comes to a consensus on how to pronounce the words on their list, but the group with List 2 finds the task impossible.

Written English has common letter patterns, or *orthographic patterns,* which skilled readers of English are able to associate with sound *extremely rapidly* and *extremely accurately.* Skilled readers know that *scr* is likely to occur in printed language, but that *tblc* is not likely to occur. When skilled readers encounter multisyllable words (or even nonwords that contain common orthographic patterns), they depend on their ability to break these patterns into syllables. This is done by using their knowledge of likely and unlikely sequences of letters. We know that the letters *lan* would go together to pronounce "lan," that *fi, ca,* and *tion* should be treated as a cluster of letters that we chunk together or treat as a group. Laboratory studies prove that skillful readers break words into syllables automatically, *in the course of perceiving letters.* Skilled readers are able to do this because of their knowledge of likely and unlikely sequences of letters, or **orthographic knowledge.** This knowledge is known *extensively,* overlearned so to speak, so that skilled readers do not have to put energy into identifying words (Adams, 1990a).

Before considering one final insight concerning the word identification abilities of skilled readers, it is helpful to understand the linguistic terms which are given below along with their definitions.

> The *alphabetic principle* suggests that letters in the alphabet map to *phonemes* or sounds. English is generally regarded as having forty-four phonemes. Phonemes have no meaning in themselves, and they make up morphemes.
>
> The *lexical system* is the system of meanings. *Morphemes* are the smallest meaningful units in our language. They make up words that convey meanings in complex ways through syntactic and semantic systems, which were discussed in Chapter 1.

With these terms in mind, our next experience will be provided by Don Holdaway (1979).

> We think of the alphabet principle as a wonderful invention BUTWEOVER-LOOKANINVENTIONALMOSTASBRILLIANTANDCERTAINLYMORESIMPLE—namely the visual display of the lexical system as distinctive, perceptual units through the device of spaces. Indeed, written language is perceived as words, not as a series of individual letters. At the perceptual level, and operationally, the written language is largely lexical. It is only perceived as alphabetic for the mature user at rare moments of crisis. (p. 83)

And what are these moments of crisis? They occur when skilled readers meet unrecognized words—which is *rare,* as Holdaway puts it. In other words, skilled readers rapidly identify over 99 percent of the words they come across, and they do this while focusing their attention on grasping the meaning of what they are reading.

Therefore, skilled readers' word identification abilities are quite extensive. By using their knowledge of consonant sound-letter associations and the context of sentences, skilled readers can decode just about anything they can talk about. They can rapidly and accurately identify words by using orthographic or letter patterns. Finally, skilled readers can do this while focusing their attention on what the print is telling them. According to Adams (1990b), in summarizing word-identification studies, "Research indicates that the most critical factor beneath fluent word reading is the ability to recognize words, spelling patterns, and whole words, effortlessly, automatically, and visually. Moreover, the goal of all reading instruction—comprehension—critically depends on this ability" (p. 14).

Implications for Learning to Read

How are word identification abilities acquired as children learn to read?

First, as we stressed in Chapters 3 and 4, children need to have numerous experiences with books before they begin working with words. According to the authors of *Becoming a Nation of Readers* (1985): "The single most important activity for building the knowledge required for eventual success in readers is reading aloud to children." This is most beneficial when the children themselves actively participate—talking about the story, chiming in on familiar refrains, and discussing the meanings of words. Children who come to school without having an abundance of such experiences need ample encounters with oral and printed language as well as early opportunities to begin to write. Sharing books with children, writing down their dictated stories, and engaging them in authentic reading and writing experiences will help to provide a base. Predictable books work especially well for beginning word identification (Bridge, Winograd, and Haley, 1983). Stahl and Miller (1989) find that such programs are effective in kindergarten.

Second, children cannot learn to read through experiences with words alone. They must read texts. Adams (1990b) put it this way, "Children do need explicit instruction in letters and sounds, but such instruction *must* take place in an environment where they are surrounded by print in the form of storybooks, notes, displays, charts, and so forth" (p. 48). Furthermore, engaging children in writing *can* facilitate learning useful phonic knowledge. This is true in situations where children do not feel required to use correct spelling; they can sound out words as they think they are spelled. In this way, students extend their knowledge of letter-sound associations.

Finally, children do not acquire the word identification abilities of the skilled readers described above by being taught *about* language. Rather, they acquire these abilities by *using* language. There are some consistent generalizations or rules in phonics or letter-sound associations that we will discuss later in this chapter. These generalizations apply to consonants, consonant blends, and the orthographic or letter combinations or patterns previously discussed. However, skilled readers do not stop reading to recite a rule when they come to an unrecognized word. Teaching students to do this is unproductive and can be debilitating to their learning to read.

Teachers need to model for students how to use phonic knowledge while reading. Many of the teaching strategies in this chapter will illustrate this. Classroom studies indicate that in the primary grades, the amount of time students are engaged in *teacher-led* instruction in phonics is a strong predictor of their reading achievement (Rosenshine and Stevens, 1984). However, in too many classrooms, the principal way that phonics is taught is through seatwork activities; that is, through activities that require children to complete workbook pages or ditto sheets.

Unfortunately, some teachers assign seatwork activities, not for meaningful learning or reinforcement, but because students need to be kept busy while the teacher works with small groups. In other words, phonic worksheets are used extensively to assist in *classroom management.* We agree with Johnson and Louis (1987) that worksheets need to be kept to a minimum because of:

> the effect an unending stream of such papers has on children's perception of reading and writing. There is an acute danger that they will begin to think of reading and writing as making brief selections among options provided by an outside party. Clearly nothing can be further from the truth. We need to develop teaching activities that stay as close as possible to the way adults use reading and writing in real life. (p. 21)

It is far more meaningful and productive to engage students in real-life reading and writing experiences than in meaningless busywork.

In addition to modeling how word identification strategies can be used, what else can teachers do so that children will begin using phonic knowledge in real reading? Don Holdaway (1980) answers this question by saying that teachers need to induce healthy reading behaviors in beginning readers, and then use these behaviors with meaningful text. What does Holdaway mean by this? Here's how Jean Carson, a first-grade teacher, induces healthy reading behaviors.

Jean has a small group of first graders who are unable to associate the letter *d* with the d sound. She shows the children a picture of a *dog digging* a hole. Jean asks the children to describe what is happening in the picture and writes their ideas on a language experience chart. The group reads the language experience story in unison. Then specific children find the words that start with *d* and read those words. Later, the language experience story is written on the bottom half of a ditto sheet so the students can illustrate the story and practice reading the story in pairs. After several days of rereading the story in unison fashion, as a small group and in pairs, Jean knows each student can read the story without the support of the unison reading. She then has the students take the story home to read to their parents. In this way, Jean induced her beginning readers to read words that begin with *d* and gave them much practice at it.

Traditionally, the teaching of word identification has been organized around the development of **sight words,** the acquisition of phonics or sound-letter association knowledge, structural analysis, and the use of context. These word-identification strategies may be necessary for some students, but should be taught in meaningful ways, as we discuss in the following pages.

The Development of Sight Words

Teaching children to identify words immediately should not necessarily suggest "look-say" or flash-card instructional practices. There is more to immediate word identification than flashing a sight-word card and requiring an instant response. Immediate identification of words is the result of *experience with* reading, seeing, discussing, using, and writing words.

Why Teach Words as Wholes?

Several reasons are usually given for beginning word identification with whole words. One is that students learn to recognize words by their configuration (i.e., their length and general contour or shape). The configuration of a word, however, has been shown to be a low utility cue in word identification (Marchbanks and Levin, 1965). A word's general contour loses its usefulness, because there are many words that have similar configurations.

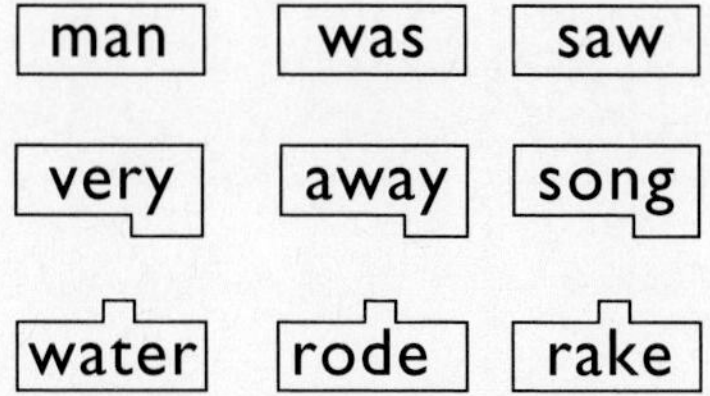

Configuration clues may be more useful for unusual looking words. For example, we may speculate that words such as *elephant* and *McDonald's* are quickly identified by young children because of their distinctive shapes.

Yet we may also argue that words such as these are identified automatically by a child because they are charged with personal meaning. No doubt some combination of the semantic and graphic features of words helps to trigger instant recognition.

Durkin's (1980) rationale for whole word instruction still makes the most sense. She suggested whole word methodology at the outset of reading instruction on the following grounds: Whole word learning allows children to sense "real reading" quickly. It can also be of greatest interest to most children, because they are apt to be familiar with the concept of a *word* rather than linguistic concepts associated with phonics; that is, the child's concept of a *letter* or a *sound.*

Immediate identification of words is the result of experience with reading, seeing, discussing, using, and writing words.

The following two paragraphs illustrate a second reason for teachers to be concerned with sight words:

PARAGRAPH 1:

Once upon a __________ there was a __________ __________ __________ One __________ __________ __________ an __________ in the __________. __________ __________, "An __________ __________ has a __________ of __________ I'll __________ this __________ __________ me to his __________ of __________."

PARAGRAPH 2:

__________ __________ __________ time __________ __________ __________ mean man named Grumble. __________ day Grumble saw __________ elf __________ __________ woods. Grumble said, "__________ elf always __________ __________ pot __________ gold. __________ make __________ elf take __________ __________ __________ pot __________ gold."

Students were divided into two groups, with each group given either Paragraph 1 or 2. The students who read Paragraph 1 were unable to answer questions when asked about the passage. The students who read Paragraph 2 at least knew that the passage was about a mean man named Grumble and an elf. They even figured out that Grumble wanted to take the elf's pot of gold.

Why do two groups comprehend the same passage so differently? Paragraph 1 has only the **function words** from the original paragraph. Function words are gramatically necessary words such as articles, conjunctions, pronouns, verbs of being, and prepositions that bind together information bearing words. These words do much to help a sentence function, but they do not get across the meaning of a passage by themselves. Nouns, action verbs, adjectives, and adverbs are *content words:* they supply the content or information of the topic. The group reading Paragraph 2, containing the content words, could figure out what the author was saying about Grumble and the elf's pot of gold.

How Should Function Words Be Taught?

Function words like *was, there, the, has,* and *of* have been taught as basic sight words early in children's reading instruction. Basic sight words are words that need to be recognized immediately by sight, because they recur over and over in print. Sometimes these words have been called high-frequency words. The rationale for teaching recognition of these words early is this: Beginning readers, who can quickly and accurately identify high-frequency words, will more readily read across *any line of print,* because these words make up 65 percent or more of *all* written material. When readers are able to rapidly identify these common words, they are much more able to use context to help identify words while they read.

Another reason children have been taught high-frequency, function words as sight words is because a large number of them are not phonically regular. Words like *the, one,* and *of* do not conform to predictable sound-letter associations.

High-frequency function words are also troublesome to young readers because of the similarity of their graphic features. Some children frequently become confused, for example, over words beginning with *wh* and *th* (e.g., that, what, then, when, where). Instructional strategies are needed to help children deal with function words to the point of an immediate, automatic recognition.

When a teacher prints on a word card the word *elephant* or *desk* or even *run* or *happy,* beginning readers have a notion of what these words mean. However, when a teacher prints *is* or *because* on a word card, a first-grader is often puzzled. As you could tell from reading the paragraph with only function words above, *function words have very little meaning when they are isolated from the flow of language.* For this reason, function words should be taught in the context of sentences, paragraphs, and stories.

Children are less likely to confuse such words as *was* and *saw* when meaning is being emphasized. After all, when the two words are interchanged *the sentence does not make sense.* Jan Wiggins, a first-grade teacher, knew the usefulness of introducing confusing sight words like *was* and *saw* using predictable patterned language. The day after her class took a fall nature walk, she had her students dictate a caption story in which each caption described something they had seen on the walk.

I *saw* an oak tree.

I *saw* a squirrel.

I *saw* some poison ivy.

Jan and her students first read the story in unison, and then individual students read it aloud. The students then illustrated the sentence that they had contributed to the captioned story.

A week or so later, Jan read *Feelings from A to Z* by Pat Visser. After discussing the feelings of the children and the situations that were described in the book, Jan asked her students to remember a feeling that they had experienced and to draw a picture of the situation that caused them to feel that way. The captions written under their illustrations used the pattern, I was __________ when __________.

I *was* embarrassed when I sat down in green paint.

I *was* scared when I went through a haunted house at Halloween.

I *was* happy when my mother came home from the hospital.

The students then compared the two sets of caption stories they had dictated, framing the words *was* and *saw* in the highly predictable contexts. Once she felt confident that the students could read the stories, she gave them further practice in reading these confusing pairs by sending illustrated copies of the captioned stories home with them to read to their parents.

Words such as *was* and *saw; every* and *very;* and *what* and *that* are *graphically* similar. That is, these words *look alike.* Context-type activities such as the one Jan used sensitize students to minimal differences in words. A beginning reader learns that words that look alike must make sense and sound right in the context of what is being read.

Sometimes young readers will habitually misidentify function words (or content words for that matter) that have minimal graphic differences. A first grader, for instance, may start a sentence that begins with *then* by reading the word *when.* This miscue may occur out of habit, probably for no other reason than a beginner often relies heavily on what is grammatically *familiar.* From a language point of view, a young child is apt to begin more sentences orally with the word *when* than the word *then.* In cases such as this, the child's schema for how language works plus a graphic cue from the word itself contributes to the observed response.

We recommend that children listen to themselves read so that they can develop an ear for the kinds of misidentifications just described. The tape recorder is an invaluable learning resource. As children listen to themselves read aloud, ask, "Does this (the misidentification) sound right?" "Does what you just heard make sense?"

Teaching Key Words

One of the quickest and most interesting ways to ease children into reading is through **key-word teaching.** Key words are a fundamental aspect of language-experience instruction. The concept of key words emerged from the work of Sylvia Ashton-Warner (1959, 1963, 1972).

What are key words? As Veatch and her associates (1979) described them, "From the first moment a child comes into the classroom she has within herself words that have meaning and feeling for her" (p. 19). Key words are charged with personal meaning and feeling, for they come out of the experience and background of the young child. According to Veatch, *key vocabulary* learning initiates a young child into the world of literacy.

Teachers can help students identify words quickly through key-word instruction. Key words become the core of what might be traditionally called sight-word development. Students learn key words through whole word methodology. The emphasis in learning words as wholes is to tie instruction to meaningful activity; that is, through *seeing, discussing, using, defining,* and *writing* words.

Ashton-Warner (1972) suggested that each child keep a file of special personal words drawn both from personal experiences and experiences with literature. The word cards could be used in the following way. A group of children's personal word cards are put together. The children sort out their own word cards and read them to each other before placing them back into their files. Those cards that are not recognized are left out and later discarded. Thus, the words kept by each child retain personal meaning and use. What a powerful way to spark interest in writing.

Working with Key Words. Veatch et al. (1979) advocated many useful strategies for group and individual key-word instructions.

GROUP ACTIVITIES

Retrieving words from the floor. Children's word cards (the word cards of a group or half the class are usually best) are placed on the floor face down. Each child is asked to find a word, hold it up, and tell it to whomever is watching.

Telling stories spontaneously. A child can tell a story about a word; the story does not have to be recorded. Making up a story as a child talks is allowed.

Classifying words. Select a topic according to a classification (e.g., desserts, television characters, funny words, places, scary words). All of the children who have a dessert word, for example, would stand in one area of the room. The teacher might want to label the area with a sheet of paper that says dessert. Children who have words of other classifications also stand in their designated areas. (See word-sorting activities in this chapter.)

Relating words. If one child has the word *cake,* and another the word *knife,* a child might relate the words by saying that "a knife can cut a cake." The teacher should try to get the children to relate words by asking questions such as: "What can my word do to the cake?" "How can my word be used with the cake?" "Is there something that my word can do with the cake?" The teacher can continue this by asking the children, "Does someone else have a word that can be used with the word *cake?*"

Exchanging words. If a child does not know a word, a teacher can say, "That doesn't make any difference. Just put it in the exchange box." Children may go through the exchange box at any time, and if they find a word they want and *know,* they can take that word and add it to their stockpile. If they lose a word and cannot find one to replace it, they may get another one from the teacher.

Learning a partner's words. Each child chooses a partner, and they teach each other their own words.

Coauthorship. Two or more children get together and combine their words or ideas to make longer words or stories from their original words or ideas.

Using two words in story. In groups of two, each child selects one word from a stockpile of favorite words. The children then use the two words to write a silly story, a funny story, a sad story, or a make-believe story.

Acting out words. If the key word is conducive to acting out, a child could dramatize the word for the other children to guess. Examples of good words for acting out are *rabbit, owl, bird, clock,* and *leaf.*

Hiding words. The teacher writes a word on a medium-sized piece of heavy paper (perhaps 4" × 5"). When the children are not in the classroom (e.g., at recess), the word cards are placed around the room in easy-to-spot places. In various ways, the children can find the words.

INDIVIDUAL ACTIVITIES

Making booklets. The teacher or the children make a booklet of words and pictures. The booklet should be designed so that when it is open, both the picture and word can be seen at the same time.

Making alphabet books. After children are confident that they know their words and can claim them for their own, they can record the words in the correct section of an alphabet book divided by initial letter.

Making sentences. Children write their words on a piece of paper or on the board and then proceed to add other words, such as function words, to make sentences of varying length. The following are some examples of sentences written for key words: Get the *lion.* Casper, the *ghost,* can fly.

Illustrating. Children draw a picture about the key word and then dictate to the teacher a caption for the picture.

Inventing words. Children create combination words using two words from the word bank (e.g., *kangaroo* and *rooster* combine to form *kangarooster*). They can illustrate and/or write about the newly created word.

Exploring feelings. Children choose words to describe their present feelings.

Exploring identity. Children choose a self-descriptive word for each letter in their name.

Naming special people. Children select words that describe family members, friends, teachers. A photograph of the person is attached to the name and put on a bulletin board entitled, "Special People."

Personal words and other sight word strategies help children to learn to identify words without having to focus on individual letters and the sounds that are associated with them. Next, we consider a second area of word identification instruction, phonics, the teaching of letter-sound relationships.

Developing Phonic Knowledge

An integral part of the great debate revolves around the extent to which gaining meaning from print entails using speech sounds. Psycholinguistic theorists Kenneth Goodman and Frank Smith have suggested that as mature readers we comprehend directly from the visual cues without any mediation of our knowledge of sound-letter associations. Other theorists Philip Gough (1985) and S. J. Samuels (1986) have held that mature readers very rapidly access meaning through well-learned letter patterns. From an interactive perspective, the answer lies somewhere in between: Skilled readers' ability to comprehend is triggered by *semantic and graphophonic features* (i.e., a single letter or letter cluster).

Phonics instruction, or teaching the relationships between speech sounds and letters, has a place in learning to read. For, "some children," according to Stanovich (1993), "do not discover the alphabetic principle on their own and need systematic direct instruction. . . " (p. 285). Consequently, it is important to examine *how* letter-sound knowledge can be taught to best support comprehension and gain independence in reading ability.

Many children, we have argued, come to school having partial or more fully developed concepts about the *alphabetic* principle. They have developed these concepts implicitly through their own efforts at learning to read. Because they are active participants in a literate culture, some children have organized for themselves a rich pool of phonic information about letters, sounds, words, and so on. Of course, some children enter school with very little knowledge of the relationships between speech and print.

Once children are in school, writing and reading, as well as phonics, can assist them in continuing to discover *and* rediscover their ideas about written language: The continuous flow of speech can be segmented into parts (i.e., words); written symbols called letters represent speech sounds; and words consist of strings of sounds or phonemes. In English, there is not a consistent one-to-one match between each written symbol, grapheme, and each distinct spoken sound, phoneme. Sounds represented by written symbols assist in determining an unknown word. Finally, blending is a process of linking letter sequences with sound sequences. The larger the letter sequence to which a sound sequence can be mapped or attached, the better.

The teacher's job in phonics instruction is to mediate children's language discoveries and rediscoveries by showing them how to use phonic knowledge to assist in the identification of words. Thus the instructional aims of phonics are twofold: (1) to help learners develop and refine a *working knowledge* of how spoken language is coded in writing; and (2) to allow learners to use this knowledge to identify and represent words in print.

Phonics instruction should occur in meaningful language situations. In daily instructional routines, however, phonics has a tendency to get overemphasized in many classrooms. Teachers sometimes find themselves spending an inordinate amount of time on phonics skill sessions that are isolated from continuous, meaningful text. Many lament that they are unable to find time for their students to practice the application of phonic knowledge to relevant reading material. As a result, youngsters can easily form the wrong message about phonics:

Reading = Phonics or Sounding Out Words.

As the Commission on Reading acknowledged, many of the phonics programs available today "fall considerably short of the ideal." This is why the Commission has called for "renewed efforts to improve the quality of instructional design, materials, and teaching strategies" (*Becoming a Nation of Readers,* 1985, p. 43). Moreover, the Commission emphasized that phonics instruction shouldn't drag on beyond a child's second year in school. The instructional questions, then, rest mainly with how phonics should be taught and what teachers must know about the content of phonics in order to teach sound-letter relationships sensibly.

The Content and Language of Phonics

In Chapter 2, we introduced the terms **analytic phonics** and **synthetic phonics** to describe the two major approaches to instruction in sound-letter relationships. The analytic method emphasizes the discovery of sound-symbol relationships through the analysis of known words. Analytic phonics is the preferred approach in most basal programs. The steps of the analytic approach proceed from the whole word to a study of its constituent parts. The sequence of instruction usually involves the following steps:

1. Observe a list of known words with a common phonic element, for example, the initial consonant *t*.

2. Begin questioning as to how the words look and sound the same and how they are different.
3. Elicit the common phonic element and discuss.
4. Have the learners phrase a generalization about the element, for example, all the words start with the sound of the letter *t*. The sound of the letter *t* is /t/ as in top.

The synthetic approach, on the other hand, takes a different route to developing phonic knowledge and skill. It uses a building-block approach to understanding sound-symbol relationships. The sequence of instruction goes something like this:

1. Teach the letter names.
2. Teach the sound(s) each letter represents.
3. Drill on the sound-symbol relationships until rapidly recognized. Discuss rules and form generalizations about relationships that usually apply to words, (when vowels are short or long, for example).
4. Teach the blending together of separate sounds to make a word.
5. Provide the opportunity to apply blending to unknown words.

There are many similarities between these analytic and synthetic phonics. Both approaches address rules, discuss isolated phonic elements, break words apart, and put them back together again. In so doing, the danger of fragmenting word identification from actual text situations is always present. The challenge to both approaches is the ready application of phonic knowledge to a stream of written language.

Most phonic programs, whether they are based on analytic or synthetic methods or a combination of both, single out *phonic elements* for instructional emphasis. These elements help to distinguish the relationships that exist between speech sounds and letters.

Consonants. Consonants are all the sounds represented by letters of the alphabet except *a, e, i, o, u.* Consonants conform faily closely to *one-to-one correspondence*—for each letter there is one sound. This property of consonants makes them of great value to the reader when attempting to sound out an unknown word. There are some consonant anomalies:

The letter *y* is a consonant only at the beginning of a syllable as in *yet.*

The letter *w* is sometimes a vowel as in *flew.*

Sometimes consonants have no sound as in *know.*

The letters *c* and *g* each have two sounds called hard and soft sounds:

Hard *c: cat, coaster, catatonic* (*c* sounds like /k/)

Hard *g: give, gallop, garbage* (*g* sounds like /g/)

Soft *c: city, receive, cite* (*c* sounds like /s/)

Soft *g: giraffe, ginger, gym* (*g* sounds like /j/)

Consonant Blends. *Consonant blends* are two or three consonants grouped together, but each consonant retains its original sound. There are several major groups of blends:

l blends: *bl cl fl gl pl sl*

r blends: *br cr dr fr gr pr tr*

s blends: *sc sk sm sn sp st sw*

3-letter blends: *scr spr str squ*

Consonant Digraphs. When two or more consonants are combined to produce a new sound, the letter cluster is called a *consonant digraph.* The common consonant digraphs are:

ch as in *chin* *ph* as in *phone*
sh as in *shell* *gh* as in *ghost*
th as in *think* *-nk* as in *tank*
wh as in *whistle* *-ng* as in *tang*

Vowels. Vowels are all the sounds represented by the letters *a, e, i, o, u.* The letter *y* serves as a vowel when it is not the initial sound of a word. Sometimes *w* functions as a vowel, usually when it follows another vowel. There is *rarely a one-to-one correspondence* between a letter representing a vowel and the sound of the vowel. Vowel sounds are influenced heavily by their location in a word and the letters accompanying them. Several major types of vowel phonemes are worth knowing about.

A *long vowel* sound is a speech sound similar to the letter name of a vowel. A *macron* (&) is sometimes used to indicate that a vowel is long. *Short vowel* sounds are speech sounds given to vowel letter names. Short sounds are represented by a *brev* (&). The short sound of each vowel letter is evident in the following words:

/a/ as in *apple* or *car*

/e/ as in *exit* or *bed*

/i/ as in *igloo* or *pit*

/o/ as in *octopus* or *hot*

/u/ as in *umbrella* or *hug*

Often when a vowel letter initiates a word, the short sound will be used, for example: *at, effort, interest, optimist,* and *uncle.*

Vowel Digraphs. *Vowel digraphs* are two vowels that are adjacent to one another. The first vowel is usually long and the second is silent. Vowel digraphs include *oa, ee, ea, ai, ay* as in *boat, beet, beat, bait,* and *bay.* There are notable exceptions: *oo* as in *look, ew* as in *flew,* and *ea* as in *read.*

Vowel Diphthongs. *Vowel diphthongs* are sounds that consist of a blend of two separate vowel sounds. These are /oi/ as in *oil,* /oy/ as in *toy,* /au/ as in *taught,* /aw/ as in *saw,* /ou/ as in *out,* and /ow/ as in *how.* Generally children do not need to be taught these formally.

Consonant-Influenced Vowels. The letter *a* has a special sound when followed by an *l* as in *Albert* or *tallow. R*-controlled vowels occur when any vowel letter is followed by an *r: star, her, fir, for,* and *purr.* The power of *r* over vowel sounds is perhaps the most beneficial to point out to children, although in the process of forming their own generalizations about short- and long-vowel sounds children have probably incorporated *r*-controlled vowel notions (Heilman, Blair, and Rupley, 1986).

Phonograms. Phonograms are letter clusters that help to form word families or rhyming words. Letter clusters such as *ad, at, ack, ag, an, ap, ash, ed, et, ess, en, ine,* and *ike* can be used to develop families of words; for example, the *ad* family: *bad, dad, sad, fad,* and so on. Phonograms may be one of the most useful phonic elements to teach, because they encourage children to map speech sounds onto larger chunks of letters.

Syllables. A **syllable** is a vowel or a cluster of letters containing a vowel and pronounced as a unit. Phonograms, for example, are syllables. The composition of the syllable signals the most probable vowel sound. Examine the following patterns:

These patterns underlie the formation of syllables. The number of syllables in a word is equal to the number of vowel sounds. For example, the word *disagreement* has four vowel sounds and thus four syllables. The word *hat* has one vowel sound, and thus one syllable.

Long vowels	CV	be
	CVe	ate like rote
	CVVC	paid boat
Short vowels	VC or CVC	it hot
R-controlled	Vr CVr	art car, her
Digraph/Diphthong Variations	VV	saw, book boil, out

There are three primary syllabication patterns that signal how to break down a word into syllabic units.

The VCCV pattern. When there are two consonants between two vowels, the word is usually divided between the consonants: *hap-pen, mar-ket,* and *es-cape.* However, we do not split consonant digraphs such as *sh* or *th* or *ng* as in *sing-er, fa-ther.* There is a variation of this pattern—the VCCle pattern. A word with this pattern is still divided between the consonants: *sad-dle, bot-tle, rat-tle,* and *pud-dle.*

The VCV pattern #1. When one consonant is between two vowels the division is before the consonant: *re-view, o-pen,* and *be-gin.* Again there is a slight variation with the VCle pattern, but still divide before the consonant; for example: *peo-ple, ta-ble,* and *cra-dle.*

The VCV pattern #2. If using VCV #1 does not result in a familiar word, then divide after the consonant as in *sal-ad* or *pan-el.*

Some Guidelines for Teaching Phonics

All children, regardless of the type of instruction they receive, learn about letter-sound correspondences as part of learning to read. And, according to Stanovich (1993), "direct instruction in alphabetic coding facilities early reading acquisition" (pp. 285–286). Firth (1985) describes three stages which children go through as they learn about words. The first stage is *the logographic stage.* Children in this stage of word identification learn words as whole units, sometimes embedded in a logo, such as a stop sign. The second stage is the *alphabet stage* in which children use individual letters and sounds to identify words. The last stage is the *orthographic stage* in which children begin to see patterns in words and use these patterns to identify words without sounding them out. Generally, children go through these stages and begin to see words orthographically by the end of the first grade. Following the orthographic stage children grow in their ability to recognize words automatically, without having to think consciously about spelling patterns.

Here are some guidelines which work both in classrooms where the basal reader is the core text and in classrooms where reading instruction is centered around the shared readings of literature.

1. Phonics Instruction Needs to Build On a Foundation of Phonemic Awareness and Knowledge of the Way Language Works. In Chapter 4, we emphasized that young children differ in their phonemic awareness of sounds in spoken words. Phonemic segmentation is an important word identification strategy. Juel (1988) finds that children who were in the lower fourth of their class in phonemic awareness in the first grade remained in the lower fourth of their class in reading four years later.

Once children are able to segment sounds, they also need to be shown the *blending* process. *Blending* means joining together the sound represented by letters and letter clusters in a word. Essentially the reader links the sound sequence with the letter sequence. The emphasis should be on directing children to attach sounds to groups of letters. The larger the cluster of letters to which sounds are attached the better. A sight word is an example of a large chunk of letters to which sounds have been attached.

Whenever possible, children should practice segmenting and blending unfamiliar words that are *encountered in meaningful print context.* Remember, phonics instruction is designed to help children approximate the pronunciation of unfamiliar words. When approximations occur within a print context, readers can rely on meaning cues as well as phonic information to assist in word identification.

In addition to differing in phonemic awareness, children also come to phonics instruction with varying degrees of generalizations about the way the written language works. Their generalizations constitute a particular level of linguistic awareness as described in Chapter 4. Teachers might use such tests as the *Concepts About Print Test: Sand and Stones* (Clay, 1979a); *Test of Early Reading Ability* (TERA) (Reid, Hresko, and Hammill, 1981); *Linguistic Awareness in Reading Readiness Test* (Downing, Ayers, and Shaefer, 1982); and *Developmental Spelling Assessment* (Morris and Perney, 1984).

Informally, teachers may engage young children in experiences concerning the notions of word, letter, and alphabet through such activities as cutting language experience stories into strips and asking individual children to cut off the words; having children sort words and letters; discussing the alphabet using alphabet books; and having children look at storybooks and indicate orally the pages, pictures, words, and so on.

2. Phonics Instruction Needs to Be Integrated into a Total Reading Program. Stahl (1992) suggests that at least half of the time devoted to the teaching of reading and probably more should be spent on the actual reading of stories, poems, plays, and trade books. Furthermore, no more than 25 percent of the time, and possibly less, should be spent on phonics instruction and practice.

It is important to show children how to use phonic knowledge taught in actual reading of texts and in this way integrating phonics with real reading. Unfortunately, too many phonics programs are not related to the actual reading children are asked to do. Children seem to learn letter-pattern knowledge best if they observe a pattern appearing in many different words, rather than in repetitions of the same word.

Trachtenburg (1990) proposes a means to integrate phonic skills with reading print. She recommends a "whole-part-whole sequence:"

1. *Whole:* Read, comprehend, and enjoy a whole, quality literature selection.
2. *Part:* Provide instruction in a high utility phonic element by drawing from or extending the preceding literature selection.
3. *Whole:* Apply the new phonic skill when reading (and enjoying) another whole, high quality literature selection.

For example, the teacher would first read orally *Angus and the Cat* and engage the children in a discussion of it. Next, the children could read it chorally together. Then the teacher would provide instruction in *-an* and *-at* phonograms, which are high utility phonic elements. This instruction could include finding the words in the story, the children writing sentences using these words, cloze exercises, as well as sorting words having these elements and reading them to partners. Finally, children could read books such as *The Cat in the Hat* or *Who Took the Farmer's Hat* which also contain many words with these phonic elements. This sequence may span over five or six lessons for beginning readers. Trachtenburg (1990) also provides a list (see Box 8.1) of trade books with a high percentage of common phonic elements.

3. Phonics Instruction Needs to Focus on Reading Print Rather Than on Learning Rules. Skilled readers do not refer to phonics rules but see words in terms of patterns of letters. Adams (1990) points out that they recognize new words by comparing them or spelling patterns within them to words they already know. For example, when Stahl (1992) asked skilled readers to pronounce *minatory,* most people said the first syllable was /min/ as in *minute* or *miniature,* comparing it to a pattern in a word they already know how to pronounce. Phonics instruction should help children do this. Teachers need to first draw their attention to the order of letters in words and then encourage them to examine common patterns in words, through sounding out words and showing similarities between words. There is no need to have children memorize phonics rules. Not only are phonics rules confusing to some children, but Clymer (1963) finds that only 45 percent of the commonly taught phonics rules worked as much as 75 percent of the time. According to

● **BOX 8.1**

Trade Books that Repeat Phonic Elements

SHORT *A*

Flack, Marjorie. *Angus and the Cat.* Doubleday, 1931.
Griffith, Helen. *Alex and the Cat.* Greenwillow, 1982.
Kent, Jack. *The Fat Cat.* Scholastic, 1971.
Most, Bernard. *There's an Ant in Anthony.* William Morrow, 1980.
Nodset, Joan. *Who Took the Farmer's Hat?* Harper & Row, 1963.
Robins, Joan. *Addie Meets Max.* Harper & Row, 1985.
Schmidt, Karen. *The Gingerbread Man.* Scholastic, 1985.
Seuss, Dr. *The Cat in the Hat.* Random House, 1957.

LONG *A*

Aardema, Verna. *Bringing the Rain to Kapiti Plain.* Dial, 1981.
Bang, Molly. *The Paper Crane.* Greenwillow, 1985.
Blume, Judy. *The Pain and the Great One.* Bradbury, 1974.
Byars, Betsy. *The Lace Snail.* Viking, 1975.
Henkes, Kevin. *Sheila Rae, the Brave.* Greenwillow, 1987.
Hines, Anna G. *Taste the Raindrops.* Greenwillow, 1983.

SHORT AND LONG *A*

Aliki. *Jack and Jake.* Greenwillow, 1986.
Slobodkina, Esphyr. *Caps for Sale.* Addison-Wesley, 1940.

(continued)

SHORT *E*

Ets, Marie Hall. *Elephant in a Well.* Viking, 1972.
Galdone, Paul. *The Little Red Hen.* Scholastic, 1973.
Ness, Evaline. *Yeck Eck.* E.P. Dutton, 1974.
Shecter, Ben. *Hester the Jester.* Harper & Row, 1977.
Thayer, Jane. *I Don't Believe in Elves.* William Morrow, 1975.
Wing, Henry Ritchet. *Ten Pennies for Candy.* Holt, Rinehart & Winston, 1963.

LONG *E*

Galdone, Paul. *Little Bo-Peep.* Clarion/Ticknor & Fields, 1986.
Keller, Holly. *Ten Sleepy Sheep.* Greenwillow, 1983.
Martin, Bill. *Brown Bear, Brown Bear, What Do You See?* Henry Holt, 1967.
Oppenheim, Joanne. *Have You Seen Trees?* Young Scott Books, 1967.
Soule, Jean C. *Never Tease a Weasel.* Parents' Magazine Press, 1964.
Thomas, Patricia. *"Stand Back," said the Elephant, "I'm Going to Sneeze!"* Lothrop, Lee & Shepard, 1971.

SHORT *I*

Browne, Anthony. *Willy the Wimp.* Alfred A. Knopf, 1984.
Ets, Marie Hall. *Gilberto and the Wind.* Viking, 1966.
Hutchins, Pat. *Titch.* Macmillan, 1971.
Keats, Ezra Jack. *Whistle for Willie.* Viking, 1964.
Lewis, Thomas P. *Call for Mr. Sniff.* Harper & Row, 1981.
Lobel, Arnold. *Small Pig.* Harper & Row, 1969.
McPhail, David. *Fix-it.* E.P. Dutton, 1984.
Patrick, Gloria. *This is . . .* Carolrhoda, 1970.
Robins, Joan. *My Brother, Will.* Greenwillow, 1986.

LONG *I*

Berenstain, Stan and Jan. *The Bike Lesson.* Random House, 1964.
Cameron, John. *If Mice Could Fly.* Atheneum, 1979.
Cole, Sheila. *When the Tide Is Low.* Lothrop, Lee & Shepard, 1985.
Gelman, Rita. *Why Can't I Fly?* Scholastic, 1976.
Hazen, Barbara S. *Tight Times.* Viking, 1979.

(continued)

BOX 8.1 *(Continued)*

SHORT O

Benchley, Nathaniel. *Oscar Otter.* Harper & Row, 1966.
Dunrea, Olivier. *Mogwogs on the March!* Holiday House, 1985.
Emberley, Barbara. *Drummer Hoff.* Prentice-Hall, 1967.
McKissack, Patricia C. *Flossie & the Fox.* Dial, 1986.
Miller, Patricia, and Iran Seligman. *Big Frogs, Little Frogs.* Holt, Rinehart & Winston, 1963.
Rice, Eve. "The Frog and the Ox" from *Once in a Wood.* Greenwillow, 1979.
Seuss, Dr. *Fox in Socks.* Random House, 1965.

LONG O

Cole, Brock. *The Giant's Toe.* Farrar, Straus, & Giroux, 1986.
Gerstein, Mordicai. *Roll Over!* Crown, 1984.
Johnston, Tony. *The Adventures of Mole and Troll.* G.P. Putnam's Sons, 1972.
Johnston, Tony. *Night Noises and Other Mole and Troll Stories.* G.P. Putnam's Sons, 1977.
Shulevitz, Uri. *One Monday Morning.* Charles Scribner's Sons, 1967.
Tresselt, Alvin. *White Snow, Bright Snow.* Lothrop, Lee & Shepard, 1947.

SHORT U

Carroll, Ruth. *Where's the Bunny?* Henry Z. Walck, 1950.
Cooney, Nancy E. *Donald Says Thumbs Down.* G.P. Putnam's Sons, 1987.
Friskey, Margaret. *Seven Little Ducks.* Children's Press, 1940.
Lorenz, Lee. *Big Gus and Little Gus.* Prentice-Hall, 1982.
Marshall, James. *The Cut-Ups.* Viking Kestrel, 1984.
Udry, Janice May. *Thump and Plunk.* Harper & Row, 1981.
Yashima, Taro. *Umbrella.* Viking Penguin, 1958.

LONG U

Lobel, Anita. *The Troll Music.* Harper & Row, 1966.
Segal, Lore. *Tell Me a Trudy.* Farrar, Straus, & Giroux, 1977.
Slobodkin, Louis. *"Excuse Me—Certainly!"* Vanguard Press, 1959.

Source: Reprinted by permission of P. Trachtenburg, and the International Reading Association. P. Trachtenburg, "Using Children's Literature to Enhance Phonics Instruction." *The Reading Teacher,* 43 (1990): 648–653.

Adams (1990b), "Children cannot become skillful decoders by memorizing generalizations or rules. Rules are useful only as far as they pertain to experience" (p. 83).

Vowel sound-letter associations are often taught with phonics rules. Adams (1990b) points out the vowel letter-sound correspondences are more stable when one looks at rimes than when letters are looked at in isolation. She gives the example that *ea* taken alone is thought of as irregular. However, in the rime *-ead,* it is regular in such words as *bread, read,* and *dead.* Clymer (1963) noted that children generally find it easier to learn to read words by using rhyming phonograms, and recent research (Adams, 1990b) on the relative ease with which children learn differing kinds of phonograms has reinforced this insight.

> Phonograms containing long vowels were learned as easily as phonograms containing short vowels,
>
> Long-vowel phonograms spelled with silent e were no more difficult to learn than long-vowel phonograms containing vowel digraphs,
>
> Phonograms containing vowel variants, including *r-*, *l-*, and *w-* controlled vowels, vowel digraphs, and vowel diphthongs, were almost as easy to learn as those containing long- and short-vowel sounds, and
>
> Phonograms containing one final consonant are easier to learn than phonograms ending in consonant blends. (p. 84)

4. Phonics Instruction Needs to Include the Teaching of Onsets and Rimes. Instead of teaching phonic rules, teach children to use onsets and rimes. An *onset,* or the part of the syllable before the vowel, is a consonant or consonant blend or digraph; a *rime* is the part from the vowel onward. As we have noted earlier, consonant sound-letter associations are fairly consistent. In addition, phonograms or rimes have been found to be generalizable. One study found that of the 286 phonograms that appear in primary-grade tests, 95 percent were pronounced the same in every word in which they were found (Durrell, 1963). In addition, these 272 stable phonograms are contained in 1,437 of the words commonly found in the speaking vocabularies of primary children (Murphy, 1957). Finally, according to Wylie and Durrell (1970), nearly 500 primary-grade words can be derived from the following set of only 37 consistent letter clusters:

> *-ack -all -ain -ake -ale -ame -an -ank -ap -ash -at*
>
> *-ate -aw -ay -eat -ell -est -ice -ick -ide -ight -ill*
>
> *-in -ine -ing -ink -ip -ir -ock -oke -op -ore -or*
>
> *-uck -ug -ump -unk.*

We can safely conclude that phonic information is much easier for young readers to acquire when phonograms are taught than when a one-to-one blending process is taught. Further, phonograms *are* fairly consistent so that young readers can be shown without much confusion how to use phonograms while reading real texts.

However, real texts do not include those texts written with a high proportion of words with the same and similar phonograms: "Ann ran." "A man ran." "A ram ran." These texts are quite difficult to read even for proficient readers reading silently (Baddeley and Lewis, 1981; Perfetti and McCutcheon, 1982). Tongue-twisting texts are not useful for teaching beginning readers.

Many successful reading programs use rime-based phonics instruction (Stahl, 1993). For example, children compare an unknown word to already known words and then use context to confirm predictions (Gaskins, 1988). When encountering *wheat* in a sentence such as, "The little red hen gathered the wheat," a child may compare it to *meat* and say, "If m-e-a-t is *meat,* then this is *wheat.*" This approach teaches decoding effectively but is meaning oriented (Stahl, 1992; Cunningham, 1991).

5. Phonics Instruction Needs to Include Invented Spelling Practice. When young children are encouraged to write and to use **invented spelling** of words as discussed in Chapter 5, they use the phonics they know and in this way "practice phonics principles." Writing with invented spelling improves children's awareness of phonemes, an important precursor to learning to decode. Clarke (1989) found that children in a synthetic phonics program who were encouraged to invent spelling and given time for writing journals were significantly better at decoding and comprehension than children in a traditional spelling program.

6. Phonics Instruction Needs to Develop Independent Word Recognition Strategies, Focusing Attention on the Internal Structure of Words. The purpose of phonics instruction is for children to use consistent sound-letter associations and to notice orthographic patterns in words, using those patterns to recognize words in text. When children blend the sounds in a word, find a word that has the same rime, or write in invented spellings, they have to pay attention to the orthographic patterns in words. In this way children learn to recognize words efficiently (Stahl, 1992).

Phonics instruction needs to support children as they go through the stages described above. Bookhandling experiences, storybook reading, and "Big Book" experiences as discussed in Chapters 3 and 4 facilitate children in the alphabetic stage. Blending sounds into words, working with rimes, and writing with invented spelling aids children as they move into the orthographic stage.

As Stahl and others stress, the overall goal of word identification instruction, including the teaching of phonics, should *not* be for children to learn to sound out words. Rather, we want children to identify words quickly so that their time and attention will be focused on comprehending text as skilled readers do. Ways to help children develop automatic word recognition will be discussed in Chapter 9.

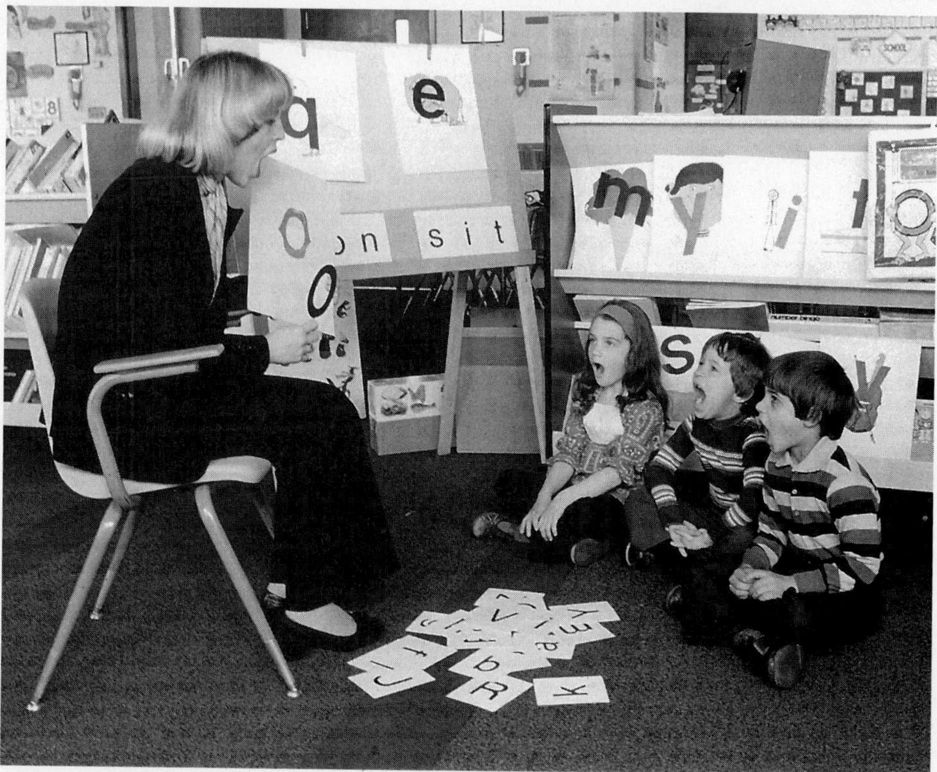

Through phonics instruction, children learn to recognize words in text through orthographic patterns developed by using consistent sound-letter associations.

Putting It All Together for Lowest Achieving Students

Joe is struggling with reading in the first grade. Chances are great that he will remain a low achieving reader for quite a long time (Juel, 1988). Traditionally, Joe may be retained in first or second grade and placed in a remedial program of some kind. Typically, these remedial programs will teach Joe more and more phonics and he will be involved in less and less real reading of texts. Research has shown that the best way to break this cycle of failure is to identify and provide remediation for children as early as possible (Stanovich, 1986).

Two programs which have proven effective are the Early Intervention in Reading (EIR) and the Reading Recovery programs (see Chapter 15). Reading Recovery, while impressively successful, is quite expensive for it involves individual tutoring outside of the regular classroom. Like Reading Recovery, the intent of EIR is to provide quality supplemental instruction early in first grade in order to prevent low-achieving readers from experiencing unnecessary failure. Also like Reading Recovery, the EIR program makes use of quality literature, develops students' phonemic segmentation and blending ability, and teaches students to use phonic and context clues as they read.

In sequencing phonics instruction, there isn't a "best" model to follow. In general, however, the following sequence appears reasonable (Stoodt, 1981; Tanner, 1983):

Begin with the consonant sounds.

Observe initial consonant sound of known words.
Explore initial consonant substitution.
Observe final consonant sound of known words.
Point out the two sounds of *g* and *c*.

Develop an awareness of consonant blends and digraphs.

Observe blends and digraphs in initial positions.
Observe blends and digraphs in final positions.
Continue to encourage substitution strategies.

Develop knowledge of vowel sounds.

Observe the letter patterns associated with common long-vowel sounds.
Observe the letter patterns associated with short-vowel sounds.
Observe vowel digraphs, diphthongs, and *r*-controlled vowels.
Develop blending ability as the coordination of sound sequences with letter sequences.

Develop an awareness of syllables and syllabication patterns.

Direct attention to larger chunks or groups of letters within words.
Continue to develop blending ability by having students coordinate sound sequences with larger letter clusters.

Developing awareness of syllables is considered part of structural analysis, the next skill area we consider.

Structural Analysis

Structural analysis is a way to create awareness of and interest in multisyllable words. Young children might be asked to compare the length of words like hippopotamus and zoo in sentences like, "We saw a hippopotamus at the zoo." Then they can be asked to clap the number of syllables in hippopotamus and zoo. From here children can be involved in the notion of segmenting sounds by taking the syllable "hip" and discussing how many sounds they hear, and matching the syllables in hippopotamus to place holders written on the board as __ __ __ __ __. Children can participate in similar directed investigations using their personal words.

Once students know and use consonant sound-letter association knowledge in independent reading, they are introduced to *vowel*-letter patterns. Students need to be involved in sorting and writing multisyllable as well as single syllable words as they work with vowel-letter patterns. For example, students can work with the pattern *-ad* in the words *mad, lad, had, sad, ladder, admit, paddle, sadness, address,* and even *advantage.* Children can sort words with the same letter cluster and the same number of syllables, as well as the same meaning. These letter-cluster words can be included in dictated spelling exercises. Both word sorting and dictated spelling will be discussed as teaching strategies later in this chapter.

Children can be guided to investigate the length of words, the number of syllables in them, and the number of sounds of phonemes in a separate syllable. Similar directed word study can be focused on affixes, compound words, and vowel-letter patterns. **Affixes** are clusters of letters that are morphological or meaningful structures, rather than phonetic structures, which makes them easier for children to learn. An affix can be a prefix, a group of letters that go in front of a word, or a suffix, a group of letters that go at the end of a word. **Suffixes** often serve grammatical purposes.

For example, after young children have read in unison a favorite like "This old man. He played one. He played nick nack on my thumb. . . " point out that the *ed* at the end of played tells that this happened in the past.

During intermediate elementary school years, deliberate, systematic affix teaching can be limited to nine frequently occurring prefixes and ten frequently occurring suffixes (see Tables 8.1 and 8.2). These affixes cover about 75 percent of the prefixed words and 85 percent of the suffixed words in printed books used in grades 3 through 9. The goal of affix instruction is how to *use* these word-part clues to derive the meaning of unfamiliar words (White, Sowell, and Yanagihara, 1989).

The teaching of **prefixes** should include explicitly defining and presenting examples and nonexamples (Stotdky, 1977). The teacher can write "A prefix is a group of letters that go in front of a word. A prefix changes the meaning of a word. When you peel it off, a word must be left." Prefixed words can be compared with "tricksters" like *uncle* and *reason.* After students have a clear idea of what a prefix is, they can be taught the meanings of specific prefixes. White, Sowell, and Yanagihara (1989) give suggested grade levels at which the specific high utility prefixes can be taught. See Table 8.3 for a suggested sequence of prefix teaching.

Intermediate elementary youngsters should know how to dismantle suffixed words so they can identify familiar and meaningful base words. In addition, they can be explicitly taught about the three major kinds of spelling changes that occur in suffixation: 1) consonant doubling (thinning, swimming, begged); 2) *y* to *i* (worried, flies, busily, reliable, loneliness); 3) deleted silent *e* (baking, saved, rider, believable, refusal, breezy).

● TABLE 8.1

The Most Common Prefixes in Printed School English for Grades 3–9

Rank	Prefix	Number of different words with the prefix*	Percentage
1	*un-*	782	26
2	*re-*	401	14
3	*in-, im-, ir-, il-,* 'not'	313	11
4	*dis-*	216	7
5	*en-, em-*	132	4
6	*non-*	126	4
7	*in-, im-,* 'in or into'	105	4
8	*over-* ,'too much'	98	3
9	*mis-*	83	3

*From John B. Carroll, Peter Davies, and Barry Richman, *The American Heritage Word Frequency Book* (Boston, MA: Houghton Mifflin, 1971.)

In sum, instruction in affixes needs to be explicit, but limited to affixes which occur frequently in texts used in elementary grades. Affix instruction can also be incorporated into the teaching of important content words.

Compound words is another structural analysis topic to focus on in first- and second-grade instruction. Karen Brothers, a second-grade teacher, made a chart for compound words. The chart also had two illustrations: one for the word *butterfly* and the other for the sentence, "Have you ever seen a butterfly?" with an illustration of some butter with wings flying (See Figure 8.1). Whenever her students discovered new compound words they made two illustrations for them and added them to the compound words chart.

Structural analysis instruction, like phonics instruction, needs to be designed to help children approximate the pronunciation of unfamiliar words. *When approximations occur within a print context, readers can rely on meaning cues as well as graphic information to assist in word identification.*

TABLE 8.2

English Suffixes Ranked by Frequency of Occurrence

Rank	Suffix	Number of occurrences in sample	Percentage*
1	*-s, -es*	673	31
2	*-ed*	435	20
3	*-ing*	303	14
4	*-ly*	144	7
5	*-er, -or* (agentive)	95	4
6	*-ion, -tion, -ation, -ition*	76	4
7	*-ible, -able*	33	2
8	*-al, -ial*	30	1
9	*-y*	27	1
10	*-ness*	26	1

*The total actually exceeds 100 percent due to rounding upward on items in ranks 13–20. The sample consisted of the 2,167 suffixed words appearing on 60 randomly selected pages in John B. Carroll, Peter Davies, and Barry Richman, *The American Heritage Word Frequency Book* (Boston, MA: Houghton Mifflin, 1971).

TABLE 8.3

Possible Prefix Lessons, with Suggested Grade Levels

Lesson	Grade level	Content
1	4	The concept of a prefix: instances and noninstances
2	4	Prefixes meaning 'not': *un-; dis-*
3	4	Prefixes meaning 'not': *in-, im-, ir-, non-*
4	5	A prefix meaning 'again' or 'back': *re-*
5	5	Alternative meanings of *un-; dis-; in-, im-*
6	5	Three more useful prefixes: *en-, em-; over-; mis-*

Source: White, Sowell, and Yanagihara, 1989.

● **FIGURE 8.1 A chart illustrating a compound word**

Using Context to Identify Words

As noted in Chapter 3, some preschool children have developed an expectation that print should make sense. They have heard stories frequently read to them and are immersed in a language-rich environment. These young children rely heavily on pictures or other aspects of the immediate situation in deciding what printed words say.

Steve, the 3-year-old at the beginning of this chapter, makes use of information from his immediate surroundings, his *environmental context*. But as he continues to develop as a reader, he will learn to use with greater sophistication various kinds of *contextual information from the print itself.*

Context Analysis

In **context analysis,** readers use context clues to identify words they have heard but may not have experienced visually in print. When readers can combine meaning clues with phonic information, they have developed a powerful tool for word identification. Cloze-type activities help to show readers how to use the context of a sentence or passage.

Modified Cloze Passages. Modified **cloze passages** can be constructed from materials that are at first relatively easy to read. The material used can be stories and poems from basal readers, language-experience stories, other written products of the students, or subject-matter texts. Gradually the difficulty of the reading material can be increased. Note that cloze-type materials are available commercially from publishing companies. However, teachers often produce the most effective cloze passages, because they are in the best position to gear the material to the needs of their students.

Cloze activities can contain as little as one deletion in a sentence or up to ten to twenty deletions in a passage. There are different deletion systems: selective word deletion, systematic word deletion, and partial word deletion. The kind of deletion system used determines what aspects of the passage are focused on as students complete the cloze passages and as they discuss their responses to cloze passages.

Selective Word Deletion. Important nouns, verbs, adjectives, and adverbs can be deleted. These words carry the meaning of the context of what the author is saying. When selected nouns, verbs, adjectives, and adverbs are deleted the focus is on meaningful information from the passage. In addition, vocabulary characteristics of a subject are emphasized. For example, if the subject of a cloze passage is "Going to the zoo," such words as *yak* and *zebra* are discussed in terms of how their meaning contributed to the meaning of the passage.

Systematic Word Deletion. In this deletion system every *n*th word in a passage is deleted. For example, every fifth, tenth, or twentieth word can be deleted. When such a cloze deletion system is used as a *teaching device,* many function words will be deleted; therefore, much of the discussion will consider examples such as "Bill went ________ the hill." Did Bill go up, down, or around the hill? The students must deduce appropriate words from the context of the rest of the passage.

Partial Word Deletion. In this deletion system, every *n*th word or selected word is partially deleted. The following partial deletions can be used: (1) only initial consonants, initial consonant blends, digraphs, or initial vowels are given and all other letters are deleted; (2) the letters mentioned above plus terminal consonants or terminal consonant digraphs are given and all other letters are deleted; and (3) only consonants are given and vowels are deleted.

Cloze passages in which only the initial letters are given help children understand that initial letter(s) serve to reduce the number of meaningful substitutions available. The discussion of this type of cloze would include how useful the content plus some graphic information can be. The more graphic information given, the more certain the reader will be of what the word is. Study the following examples:

SELECTIVE WORD DELETIONS

Slim and Shorty were ________ who lived on a big ranch a long way from town. Slim and Shorty had five mules. One day Slim ________, "We're almost out of ________. We have to go to ________. We'll take the ________ to carry the food home."

SYSTEMATIC WORD DELETIONS

Slim and Shorty began to line __________ the mules. Slim got on the __________at the front of the line. __________ got on the mule at the __________ of the line.

PARTIAL WORD DELETIONS

Then Shorty s__________, "How will we get all five m__________ to town?" Slim said, "You w__________ the mules. That way we don't l__________any."

Cloze with Choices Given When students find it difficult to complete cloze activities, giving choices for the deleted words makes the task easier. Here are some differing procedures to use in devising the choices for the cloze blanks.

1. The incorrect item, or foil, can be a different part of speech as well as different graphically.

   The doctor was __________ that the patient got better so quickly.
   MONKEY/AMAZED

2. The foil can be graphically similar to the correct item and a different part of speech.

   The doctor was __________ that the patient got better so quickly.
   AMAZON/AMAZED

3. The foil and correct answer can be graphically similar and the same part of speech.

   The doctor was __________ that the patient got better so quickly.
   AMUSED/AMAZED

4. Three choices can also be given: the correct response, a word of the same part of speech that is graphically similar, and a word of a different part of speech that is and graphically similar.

   The doctor was __________ that the patient got better so quickly.
   AMAZED/AMUSED/AMAZON

A discussion of these particular cloze examples would include a discussion of why a doctor would be more likely to be *amazed* than *amused* by a patient's progress in getting well. Students would also note that, "The doctor was *amazon* that the patient got better so quickly," makes no sense.

Cryptography and Mutilated Messages. Many children enjoy deciphering codes and writing messages in codes. When something is written in code, something has been done to change the graphic display, so context is used to break the code.

Here are a few ways messages can be mutilated or changed. You and your students can think of more ways. There are also trade books on cryptology that your students can enjoy.

Color names are inserted. (Look red under blue the green table.)

Bottom of letter is covered.

Words are scrambled. (Door the open.)

No spaces are left between words and a letter is inserted between words. (Illustrateathebpoemcondpagedfifty-sixeoffyourgbook.)

Notice that each of these coded messages tells the reader to do something. This is a good way to use codes. Jane Jones, a second-grade teacher, devised some coded messages that led her students on a treasure hunt. Students read directions in coded messages telling them to look specific places, for example, "Look behind the red geraniums." Behind the geraniums was another coded message that told them to look another place. These coded messages finally led them to a treasure.

Using Context to Decide If a Word Is Important

How important is a single word, anyway? This is a question readers need to ask about words they find troublesome. To get this notion across, have students read a somewhat difficult selection. Ask them to put light marks by words that they do not recognize, but tell them *not to try to figure them out.* This is actually hard to do! After students have read the selection, ask them to summarize what the author was saying. Then go back and discuss the words the students have marked. Do they know what these words are now? Many of the words they will know in spite of the fact that they did not actually try to figure them out. What about the words they are still unable to recognize? Students need to decide, "Are these important to understanding the selection?" If students feel the word is important to understanding the selection, decide how meaning cues and sound-letter cues can be used to determine what the word is. The point of this lesson, though, is to realize that often a selection can be read and understood without recognizing every word. Students can categorize difficult words that they think are crucial to understanding the selection and those that are not, and then discuss why they placed particular words in each category.

Lessons such as this one can be structured to convey the idea that some words contribute more to understanding a selection than others. Also, a teacher needs to encourage students informally to ask themselves about unrecognized words they meet as they read; for example, "How important is this word to understanding what the author is saying?"

Watson (1978) devised a teaching strategy that she called "reader selected miscues" to help children see that they are in control of making sense out of print. Children should become aware that they are in control of making sense out of print. Children should become aware that they have a range of options available to them as readers when they encounter words they don't recognize or, for that matter, something they don't understand during reading.

Steps in the Reader-Selected-Miscue Strategy. The following procedures may be adapted to fit a variety of reading situations that may arise during the course of a school day:

1. Children are assigned to read a selection (fiction or nonfiction) silently and without interruption.
2. When a troublesome word is encountered or something is not making sense, a child inserts a bookmark or lightly marks the page to indicate the problem and then continues reading.
3. When the reading is completed, the children review the words or concepts they have marked and select *three* that caused the greatest difficulty.
4. In addition, the children are asked to explain *how* some of the problems or words that they encountered seemed to "solve themselves" as they continued to read.
5. Finally, the students are to examine passages involving the troublesome words or ideas that they had marked and help each other in clarifying them.

What do readers learn from this procedure? For one thing, they learn that everyone makes mistakes; no one reads "word-perfectly." Readers also see that they are the ones to decide what is hard for them and what comes easily. They see that a portion of a text may be quite readable to some readers and less readable for others, but that everyone meets words or concepts that perplex them. Finally, they see from reader selected miscues that with a keep-going strategy, many unknowns will be clarified by the text as they keep reading.

Word Identification in Action

In order to use phonic knowledge while focusing on the meaning of texts, young readers need to begin with familiar texts using substitution strategies. Substitution strategies are an excellent means of involving children in *using word and phonic knowledge while reading meaningful text.* By using familiar texts children can use what they already know to build new skills and abilities. After students have experienced much success with substitution strategies in familiar texts, it's appropriate to model productive word identification strategies with students, involving them in word problem solving while reading unfamiliar but meaningful texts. Next, let's see how Jan Estes, a first-grade teacher, used the substitution strategies called inventions, errors, and spoonerisms (Johnson and Louis, 1987).

Substitution Strategies

Jan's first graders were responding well to the extensions of the shared-book activity. She had also been working on building a sight vocabulary and on developing consonant sound-letter knowledge. Her students had taken many familiar stories home to read to their parents. A group of ten children had independent reading-like behavior developed through unison reading, the shared-book experience extension activities, listening at the *listening center,* and practicing reading the familiar texts. They could read about 15 words as wholes, and knew 7 to 10 consonant sound-letters.

Jan decided to begin modeling word-identification strategies while reading familiar texts to the group. She decided to use the nursery rhyme "Jack and Jill," which the children had already been reading together in unison. They were able to recognize sentences and words in this rhyme. She wrote on chart paper:

Jack and Jill went down the hill
To fetch a pail of water.
Jill fell down
And broke his crown.
And Jack came tumbling after.

She showed the nursery rhyme to the group and said, "It's supposed to say, 'Jack and Jill went up the hill to fetch a pail of water.' Is there anything wrong?" The children quickly joined into the spirit of the game. They noticed it said, "Jack and Jill went down the hill" and "Jill fell down." After many experiences with finding what was wrong with sentences like these, Jan had her students write "inventions" using the nursery rhymes they had been reading together and from which they had been recognizing lines and words. Here are some of the inventions they wrote:

Mary had a little mouse.
Jill and Jack broke their crowns.
The mouse fell down the clock.
Humpty Dumpty sat on a hill.

Jan also put the children's inventions on chart paper, and the children read their inventions to each other. She engaged the children in this activity for a few weeks. Then she began making charts in which consonant and consonant blends were substituted in the nursery rhyme.

Humpty Dumpty sat on a hall.
Humpty Dumpty had a great wall.
All the king's horses and all the king's pen
Couldn't put Humpty together again.

As before, Jan said such things as, "It's supposed to say 'Humpty Dumpty sat on a wall.' Is there anything wrong?" and "It's supposed to say, 'Humpty Dumpty had a great fall.' Is there anything wrong?" Her students responded, "Yes, it says *hall* and it should say *wall.*" When the group was comfortable finding the errors in a guided group setting, she had the students write sentences with "errors" in them. In helping them write these errors, she underlined the words to change to make the errors, which were important content words *and* contained common letter patterns. She used the list of the 37 common letter-cluster patterns on page 336. Some of the sentences containing errors students wrote were:

Hickory Dickory Dock
The mouse ran up the lock.
Humpty Dumpty sat on a ball.

As before, she wrote students' errors on chart paper or the board and the students enjoyed reading and responding to each others' errors.

When the children were proficient at both inventions and errors, Jan added spoonerisms to their repertoire of ways to manipulate familiar texts. In making the spoonerisms, she interchanged initial consonants and consonant blends. Here are some spoonerisms she created for her students:

Lary had a little mamb.
Her sneese were white as flow.
And everywhere that Lary went, her mamb was sure to go.

In discussing these spoonerisms, she pointed out that there were two "tricks" in them. She asked students to read them carefully and tell what the sentence *should* say and what it *does* say. She had one student tell how to correct the line, and another student change the letters to make it correct. As she worked with spoonerisms with small groups, she had the students take more and more responsibility for finding the mistakes and correcting them (Johnson and Louis, 1987).

After many experiences with all three **substitution strategies**—inventions, errors, and spoonerisms—Jan decided to begin to show students how to use word identification strategies when they come across a hard word in unfamiliar texts.

Modeling and Using Word Identification

Jan began working with meaningful texts that were *not* familiar. She had a group of beginning readers in her class who could identify the names of four or five animals in print. She showed the group the word *carrot.* The students did not recognize it, and Jan did not tell them what the word was. They then played the action riddle game. She showed the children a chart that said:

Be a rabbit.
Hop like a rabbit.
Eat a carrot.

The beginning readers were able to read and act out what the chart said. They knew the word carrot because it made sense and began with a /c/ sound like the beginning of the word *cat.* She involved them in other action riddles like:

Be a dog.
Bark like a dog.
Eat some dog food.

In this case, students used the context to determine the word *bark.* Jan began using activities like this with unfamiliar texts more and more in her group extensions of the shared-book experiences. As with the substitution activities, the children devised action riddles in writing using invented spellings and shared them with their classmates when they met in teacher-directed groups.

As the school year continued, Jan's first graders knew most of the consonant and consonant blend sound-letter associations, and could easily respond when sounds were transposed in a spoonerism. She decided to begin modeling for her children how to use context to predict what unrecognized words might be and then use phonics to confirm the predictions. She involved her students in directed group word problem-solving activities like a game we call "Gugglefunk." The first few times they played Gugglefunk, Jan was "it." She used an overhead projector to display the text of *Bony-Legs* by Joanna Cole, and used paper to cover content words that she felt her students were not able to recognize by sight.

Bony-Legs was a _____________, bad witch.

She could run very fast on her bony old legs.

Her teeth were made of _____________, and she liked to eat little children. . . .

She read the text aloud, saying Gugglefunk in the blank. Next, she had her students predict what word could be in the first blank. The students' predictions were written on the board. She responded to their predictions by saying, "Could be," "That's a good guess," and "That makes sense, doesn't it?" Then she began giving information about the graphic-sound features of the first covered word, beginning by giving the initial consonant. "It begins with an *h,*" and she wrote an *h* on the board. She said, "It has three syllables like this," and she clapped three times. "The first syllable is *hor,*" and she wrote *hor* on the board. The children came up with *horrible* and she showed them that this was the word that had been covered up.

She followed a similar procedure with the second word. She told them the first letter was *i,* it had two syllables, and that the last letter was *n.* The students came up with the word that the author had chosen, *iron,* only after all the letters were given. While modeling how to play this game, she emphasized that readers can figure out words by using the context or sense of the print plus letter-sound knowledge. She emphasized that often words can be figured out in context with the initial letters and the final letters only. In addition, consonants are usually very useful in determining what word makes sense and has those letters. When working with multiple-syllable words, she would point out common letter patterns in syllables as the *or* in horrible.

Once children had some experiences with Gugglefunk with Jan as the leader, she asked individual children to prepare passages to present to the rest of the group. For example, Antonio made this Gugglefunk passage from the same book, *Bony-Legs.* Antonio actually did not recognize the words that he had covered.

"You ____________ cat!" yelled Bony-Legs. "Why did you trick me?"

"You never fed me. But Shasha gave me ____________ to eat."

Antonio then was "it" and for the first Gugglefunk told the students the word began with an *sn,* ended with a *y,* had an *ea* in the middle and a *k* after the *ea.* Each of these letters were written on the board as Antonio said them. The students were able to come up with *sneaky* using this word problem-solving strategy.

Jan played this game throughout the rest of the school year with groups of students. They began to see how skilled readers focused on what made sense in the passage, and then used consonant and letter-pattern knowledge to confirm what the printed word is.

Jan's students became very capable at determining hard words through these problem-solving word games. Jan also engaged her students in activities that we call working with words. These strategies will be presented in the next section.

Word-Bank Strategies

Word banks are simply boxes of word cards that individual students are studying. Word banks are a natural extension of the language experience approach in which students learn to read words from dictated stories. Students make word cards from the words in their language experience stories and study them. A quick way of helping children begin a word bank without using dictation is to have students read a selection that is fairly easy for them. The students underline words that they could not immediately recognize and words that they cannot figure out, as well as words that they consciously used context or mediated strategies to figure out. The students then write each of these words on word cards. Words for word banks can be gleaned from basal readers, trade books, signs, labels, and print with which the children are involved. Words in the word banks can then be used in writing activities and sorting activities.

Wall Word Banks. Another way to extend phonic knowledge is through wall word banks. Wall word banks are begun when students notice words that rhyme, but are not spelled with the same letter patterns. For example, in Susan Valenti's second-grade classroom the class read in a shared-book experience Shel Silverstein's "Enter This Deserted House," in which the poet rhymes the words *do, too, blue,* and *few* as he creates for readers young and old the eerie feeling of entering a deserted house.

As Susan shared the poem, the children noticed that *do, too, blue,* and *few* all rhymed, but were not spelled with the same letter pattern. So Susan and her class started a wall word bank for this sound. The wall word bank was strips of shelf paper hung on the wall. Students were asked to find words for each of the spellings of the sound /oo/. The following are some of the words they found:

do	*too*	*blue*	*few*
tool	clue	dew	
fool	sue		

Word wall banks can also be made for collecting words that begin with affixes like *dis.* Susan's class made one with the following words: *disagree, disadvantage, distinct,* and *disappear.*

Sorting. Earlier we stated that the best clues for recognizing a word are its total context and the word's graphic similarity to words that are already known. In sorting words, students look for similarities in words, including graphic similarities.

Classifying stimuli into classes according to their common properties is one of the most basic and powerful operations of human thinking, and is responsible for much of a child's natural learning ability. This is why the sorting activity is so suitable for studying words.

There are two kinds of **sorting activities:** (1) open sorts and (2) closed sorts. In both open and closed sorts, children are guided toward *discovering* similarities in words, rather than *being told* how they are alike.

The following steps for open sorts are suggested:

1. Each child in a small group has a word bank. Sorting activities can be done with children seated on the floor or at a table.
2. The children are asked to go through their word banks and group together some words that go together in some way.
3. After grouping words together, each child tells what words they have grouped together. Then another student reads their minds by telling how the group of words is alike.
4. In open sorts, there is no one correct answer. Students just have to be able to explain why they grouped words as they did. For example, Jill grouped top, tickle, to, and terrible together because they all begin with the letter *t.* John sorted tomato, potato, tomorrow, and butterfly together because they all have three syllables. Sue sorted mother, father, sister, and brother together because they are all members of a family. Helen classified pretty, ugly, green, and fat together because they all describe something.

   Notice students can sort words by attributes concerning letter-sound relationships, by attributes referring to the meaning of the words, or by attributes referring to how they function in sentences.

In closed sorts, the students search to group words according to a specific attribute the teacher has in mind. There is a correct way to sort the words in closed sorts. The students figure out what that correct way is.

The ability to generalize from the known to the unknown is a fundamental aspect of all word analysis. The closed sort is an excellent way to get students to think about letter patterns in words. As students are learning the consonants and consonant blends, they can sort pictures of objects beginning with the consonants and consonant blends.

Also, students can group words by letter patterns. *In having students sort words into groups of those with the same letter patterns, you are teaching the process of looking for letter patterns; you are not just teaching individual letter patterns.* Just as skilled readers have not learned to recognize 50,000 plus words instantly by sight by studying 50,000 word cards, skilled readers have not learned English letter patterns by studying them in isolation. They have learned how English letters are patterned by reading and writing. So the purpose in having students sort words by letter patterns is to encourage children to look for graphic similarities in words. Students can be given word cards with letter patterns that are not similar.

sad pad glad ladder radish tadpole advertise

dip rip lip zipper tulip hippopotamus shipwreck

A harder task is to have students sort word cards with letter patterns that are somewhat similar.

sad glad admit admiration

made grade lemonade

Students can also be asked to sort words with inflectional endings.

plays wishes played wished

Notice that these words could be sorted by the words with the same roots or by the words with plural versus past tense endings.

We do not advocate that phonic or syllabication rules be taught as students describe why a group of words are alike. The purpose is to have students get the notion of looking for graphic similarities in words, not to teach phonic rules.

One final note about when *not* to use closed sorts for graphic similarities. Suppose you note that John is confused about a sound-letter relationship like the soft *c* in *city* and *cent* and the hard *c* in *cat, cot,* and *cup.* This is *not* the time to have John sort the above words into groups. Rather, John needs to read these words in predictable contexts as we previously described in the section on the development of sight words. Having John focus on the phonic elements of hard and soft *c* in words devoid of context is likely to confuse him more concerning when *c* goes with the /k/ sound and when it goes with the /s/ sound. However, John will have little difficulty reading and understanding how the *city mouse* has to beware of house cats and has great cheese, while the *country mouse* must eat nasturtium seeds and lives under less stress.

The Importance of Self-Monitoring

The central importance of self-corrective behavior, *even at the earliest stages of development,* is crucial in learning to read. When a teacher places a high premium on students' word-perfect oral reading performance, young developing readers are at risk of not developing a healthy self-monitoring system. Such readers become dependent on the teacher or other able readers to help them when they meet a hard word. One of the reading teacher's main goals is to encourage children to self-monitor their reading by encouraging **self-corrections.**

What do we know about the influence of immediate and delayed teacher correction on children's self-corrections and reading proficiency? McNaughton (1981) studied not only what happened during reading instructional time, but also during independent reading aloud situations. He defined an immediate teacher correction as one that occurred within five seconds of a child's oral reading error. A delayed teacher correction occurred after five seconds or when the reader completed reading a sentence.

Second-grade readers *self-corrected fewer of their own reading errors* when they received immediate help as opposed to children who received delayed help. They were also less accurate in their initial identification of words than children receiving delayed instruction. McNaughton also found that in independent oral reading situations that took place at different times of the day, children who were corrected immediately during reading instructional time continued not to self-correct miscues and were less accurate in word identification than children who were given delayed teacher help. Apparently, these children transferred certain reading behaviors stemming from immediate correction to independent reading activity.

McNaughton's research illustrates that immediate correction may interfere with the development of strategies to monitor meaning during reading. When readers assume the bulk of responsibility for correcting, they seem to be better able to maintain and modify strategies for anticipating meaning and overcoming word identification obstacles.

Teaching Readers to Self-Correct

The reader who miscues in oral reading and corrects without being prompted demonstrates an important reading behavior. Self-correction may reliably predict the reader's ability to retell and comprehend text. Good readers consistently correct higher percentages of miscues than poor readers. Classroom teachers need to be aware of ineffective reading strategies that inhibit or discourage corrective reading behaviors.

Therefore, D'Angelo (1982) suggested the following dos and don'ts for encouraging children to self-correct oral reading miscues. These suggestions can be incorporated in oral reading situations.

Don't overemphasize speed or rate in oral reading. This discourages both corrections and comprehension.

Don't immediately supply the correct response or allow prompting from peers.

Don't overemphasize accuracy or pronunciation.

Don't ignore corrections a reader makes. They indicate which cueing systems are being used or disregarded.

Do encourage regressions when miscues occur.

Do provide think-time for reprocessing of information.

Do urge attempts to correct, successful or not.

Do ask whether or not miscues fit and make sense.

Do reward, praise, and positively reinforce corrections.

Another way to help children self-monitor is to discuss with them what to do when they come to unknown words. When children attempt to figure out unknown words in text, encourage them to use semantic, grammatical, and sound-letter information. Direct the process by fostering a search for information cues as described in the previous section. Help children monitor their searches by using a chart similar to the one in Figure 8.2. Explain the procedures listed on the chart and give children practice using them.

SUMMARY

The underlying premise of this chapter is that *how* teachers help children with word identification is extremely important and these hows are related to their beliefs about reading. We looked at word identification abilities of both skilled readers and those successfully learning to read. We took a look at four traditional word identification skill areas: sight words, phonics, structural analysis, and using the context.

When readers can combine meaning cues with phonic cues, they have developed a powerful tool for word identification. This is why readers must learn how to use contextual information to recognize words. Various kinds of contextual activities can be designed to help students coordinate semantic, syntactic, and phonic information. These activities involve cloze-type passages in which target words are deleted from the text. These words can be deleted selectively or systematically depending on the teacher's purposes. Readers must also become aware that a text selection can be read and understood without identifying every word. Context-centered activities such as the reader selected miscue strategy can help students in this respect.

We then discussed some overriding procedures that integrate these skill areas into real reading. Finally, we presented teaching strategies and our thoughts on how to sequence the use of these strategies.

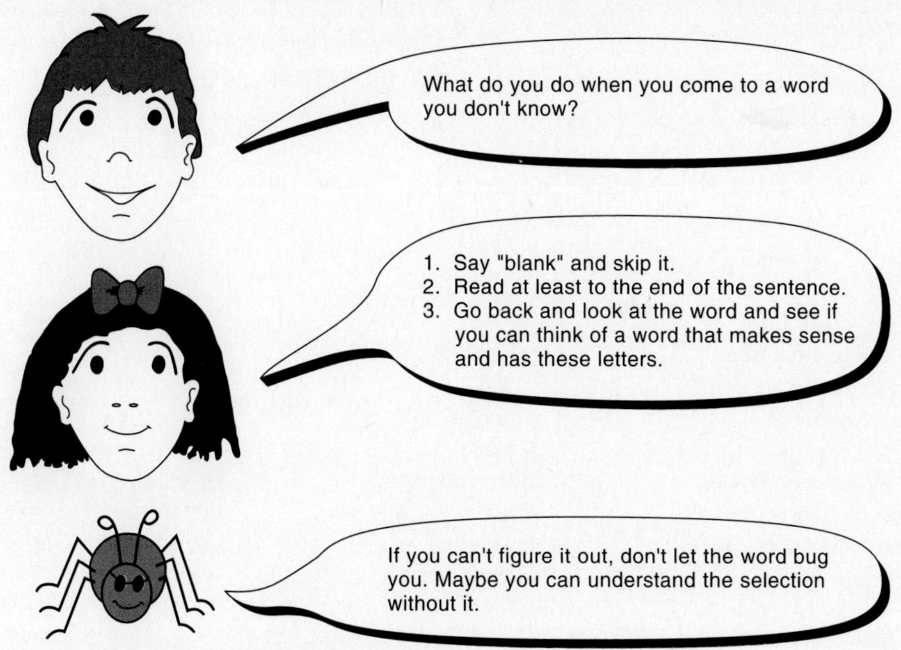

● **FIGURE 8.2** A chart for monitoring an unknown word

TEACHER-ACTION RESEARCHER

1. Arrange to visit a first-or second-grade classroom during a lesson involving word identification skill areas: sight words, phonics, structural analysis, or using the context. Observe *how* the teacher helps children with word identification. What does the teacher's approach reveal about his or her beliefs about reading? To what extent are the observed approaches and activities integrating aspects of word identification into real reading? Arrange to observe in another classroom, preferably in another district, and ask the same kinds of questions.

2. Prepare and teach a word identification lesson to a small group of second or third graders. Make provisions in the lesson to combine phonics or structural analysis with context usage and application so that the focus of the lesson is not on learning rules but is focused on reading print. Describe the reactions and interactions of the children during the lesson. How would you change the lesson if you were to work with the same group of children tomorrow? How would you extend the lesson?

3. Collect several samples of writing from a child in primary school. Analyze the writing to determine the child's phonic knowledge. Then interview the child's teacher to determine his or her perceptions of the child's strengths and gaps in phonic knowledge. Does your analysis match the teacher's perceptions? Why or why not?

4. Prepare a list of words found in a picture book and have a child read the list to you. Note which words are read correctly. Have the same child read the picture book itself while you note how the child reads the words. Did you discover any differences in the child's ability to read the words in the list as compared to the same words in the book? What did the reader seem to know about the relationship of sound to print? How do you explain your findings?

KEY TERMS

word identification
orthographic knowledge
sight words
function words
key-word teaching
phonics instruction
analytic phonics
synthetic phonics
consonants
vowels
phonograms
syllable
invented spelling
structural analysis
affixes
suffixes
prefixes
compound words
context analysis
cloze passages
substitution strategies
word banks
sorting activities
self-correction

CHAPTER 9

Reading Fluency

BETWEEN THE LINES

In this chapter you will discover:

- **The importance of developing fluency in young readers.**
- **What classroom routines, strategies, and reading materials help foster fluency development during oral reading.**
- **Why a program of sustained silent reading (SSR) is so critical for independent reading.**

Jamie, a first grader, labored as she read out loud. Word by word, she started, then stopped, then started again. Haltingly slow. Disjointed. She read the story in a monotone, as if the words from the story were on a list rather than a conversational flow of sounds in oral language.

"Jamie, read the story with expression, like you're talking to us," Mrs. Leonardo said in a supportive voice. Teachers like Mrs. Leonardo often encourage the reading beginner to be expressive. Perhaps they have known intuitively that which researchers are beginning to thoroughly investigate and understand: reading with expression is a sign of progress, a sign that a child is reading fluently and with comprehension.

In the delightful book, *The Wednesday Surprise* by Eve Bunting, Anna, a 7-year-old, teaches her grandmother to read by reading together with her on Wednesday evenings. Anna says, "I sit beside her on the couch and she takes the first picture book from the bag. We read the story together, out loud, and when we finish one book we start a second." When asked by her mother, "When did this wonderful thing happen?" Anna explains, "On Wednesday nights. . . . And she took the books home, and practiced."

Anna's a smart 7 year old. The role of practice in learning to read is extremely important. As the authors of *Becoming a Nation of Readers* (1985) suggest: "No one would expect a novice pianist to sight read a new selection every day, but that is exactly what is expected of the beginning reader" (p. 52). A budding pianist practices a piece over and over to get a feel for the composition, to gradually develop control over it, and to become competent and confident with it.

And so it is with young readers. In this chapter, we underscore the value of having readers develop fluency in oral and silent reading situations. Practice and rereading are essential aspects in the development of reading fluency that cannot be overlooked nor neglected. Rereading a selection over and over can lead to rapid word recognition that makes fluent reading with comprehension possible. Let's explore why and how.

Defining Oral Reading Fluency

The term *fluent* is often associated with doing something easily and well. When applied to reading, **fluency,** in everyday terms, means reading easily and well. With this ability comes a sense of control and confidence, and often a knowledge of what to do when the reader gets bogged down or entangled in a text. Allington (1983a) equates fluent oral reading with *prosody* or prosodic reading. Prosody is a linguistic concept that refers to such features in oral language as *intonation, pitch, stress,* and the *duration* placed on specific syllables, as well as the *pauses.* These features signal some of the meaning conveyed in oral language.

Have you ever sat in a class or served on a committee with a person who used few prosodic cues while speaking? Sometimes it's difficult to focus on what the person is trying to say or what the person means. In the same way, reading with expression, or using prosodic features while reading orally, has the potential of conveying more meaning than reading without expression. In addition, prosodic cues convey moods and feelings. Children generally know instantly when a parent is irritated with them. A mother's tone of voice (intonation) is usually enough to signal, "Mom is mad."

In learning to understand oral language, children rely on prosodic features. Similar conditions appear to be necessary in learning to understand written language. Schreiber (1980) find that students learned how to put words together in meaningful phrases, *even though a written text provides few phrasing cues and uses few graphic signals for prosodic features in print.* When Mrs. Leonardo asked Jamie to read with expression or as if she were talking to others, she was suggesting to Jamie that she rely on her intuitive knowledge or prosodic features in oral language, not only to help convey meaning to others, but also to help her understand what she was reading.

Instruction in fluent oral reading produces readers who move from word-by-word reading to more efficient phrase reading (Chomsky, 1976; Samuels, 1979). Fluency instruction has also resulted in improved reading achievement, assessed through measures of comprehension (Dowhower, 1987).

In this chapter, we look closely at both oral and silent fluency and explain how fluent reading may be fostered and developed in young readers or, for that matter, at-risk readers. But first, it is essential that the concepts of *immediate* word identification and *automaticity* be explored.

Immediate Word Identification

The term **immediate word identification** is often used to describe rapid recognition. Keep in mind, however, that the process of immediate word identification is far more complicated than recognizing words on flash cards. When a word is retrieved rapidly from long-term memory, the process is often triggered by well-developed schema that the reader has developed for a word. In immediate word identification, semantic or physical features in a word (e.g., a single letter or a letter cluster) trigger quick retrieval of that word.

Immediate word identification is the strategy used by skilled readers on 99 percent of the printed words they meet. It is also the method used by children when they identify their first words. Often one of the first words children learn to identify in print is their name. Jessica, a 4-year-old, can recognize her printed name, but may not attend to each individual letter. She recognizes her name, because some distinctive feature triggers rapid retrieval from long-term memory.

In the previous chapter, we looked at children acquiring phonic knowledge as one tool in identifying words. We also considered how to help children analyze syllabic and/or meaning-bearing units in unfamiliar words. Both phonic and structural analysis involve *mediated word identification.* Mediation implies that the reader needs more time to retrieve words from long-term memory. Readers use mediating strategies when they don't have in place a well-developed schema for a word: The schema is lacking in either semantic or physical features sufficient for rapid retrieval.

How do skilled readers reach a point where they don't have to rely on mediated word identification strategies? Reading researchers are finding that *repetition is extremely important in learning to recognize words.* The amount of repetition needed for beginning readers to be able to recognize words immediately has not been appreciated. *Traditionally, repetition of reading texts has not been systematically included in reading instruction.*

As mature readers, we are able to immediately identify or read by sight thousands and thousands of words. How did we learn to identify these words? Did we use flash cards to learn each one? Did we first sound out each word letter by letter? Probably not.

In the past few years, the effects of developing oral reading fluency in meaningful texts have been studied with impressive results (Chomsky, 1976; Samuels, 1979; Allington, 1983a; Dowhower, 1987; Koskinen and Blum, 1986).

Automaticity

J. Samuels (1988) argues that word recognition needs to be accurate and *automatic.* To explain the term **automaticity** an analogy is often made to driving a car. Most of the time, a skilled driver will focus little attention or use little mental energy while driving. Skilled drivers frequently daydream or ponder happenings in their lives as they drive, yet they still manage to drive in the appropriate lane at an appropriate speed (most of the time!). They drive on automatic pilot. Nevertheless, when the need arises, a driver can swiftly focus attention on driving as, for example, when a warning light goes on or when weather conditions suddenly change. In other words, most of us drive with automaticity, with little use of mental energy, but when necessary, we're able to rapidly attend to what we're doing as drivers.

When readers are accurate but not automatic, they put considerable amounts of mental energy into identifying words as they read. When readers are both accurate and automatic they recognize or identify words accurately, rapidly, easily, and with little mental energy. Like the skilled driver, the skilled reader can rapidly focus attention on a decoding problem, but most of the time will put energy into comprehending the text.

Fluency strategies are also one way of getting rid of the "uh, ohs," which are a part of learning any new skill. When taking tennis lessons, the beginner often makes mental comments such as "Uh, oh. I need to hit in the middle of my racket." "Oh, what a crummy backhand shot." Each hit is judged as either good or bad. Children are also prone to struggle with the "uh, ohs" when learning to read. This especially happens when they think about which words they can and cannot identify. As with the beginning tennis player, the reading beginning often gets anxious because the "uh, ohs" interfere with constructing meaning from the text. Developing automaticity is one way to give beginning readers a feel for reading without anxiety.

Developing Oral Reading Fluency

Children learn to become fluent in an environment that supports oral reading as communication. In mindless situations where children take turns reading in round-robin fashion, little constructive is accomplished. In round-robin reading, children often do not view their role as tellers of a story or as communicators of information. Instead, their role is to be word perfect. Accuracy, not automaticity or comprehension, permeates round-robin reading. While we are strong proponents of oral reading in classrooms, the emphasis during oral reading must be on communication and comprehension, not word-perfect renderings of a reading selection. Let's take a closer look at several classroom routines, strategies, and reading materials that can help to foster and develop fluency during oral reading.

Repeated Readings and Predictable Texts

Repeated readings, as defined in earlier chapters, mean simply having a child reading a short passage from a book, magazine, or newspaper more than once with differing amounts of support. Samuels (1979) propose the method of repeated readings as a strategy to develop rapid, fluent oral reading. Here are several steps suggested by Samuels when using the method of repeated readings:

1. Students choose short selections (50 to 200 words) from stories that are difficult enough that they are not able to read them fluently.
2. Students read the passage over several times silently until they are able to read it fluently.

3. The teacher can involve students in a discussion of how athletes develop athletic skills by spending considerable time practicing basic movements until they develop speed and smoothness. Repeated reading uses the same type of practice.

4. Samuels suggests that students tape-record their first oral rendition of the passage as well as their oral rendition after practice so that they can hear the difference in fluency.

Adapting Repeated Readings. Lauritzen (1982) proposes modifications to the repeated-reading method that make the method easier to use with groups of children. Mrs. Leonardo, a first-grade teacher, used the repeated-reading method in this way. She began by reading aloud to her students and discussing what happened in the story, *Love You Forever,* written by Robert Munsch and illustrated by Sheila McGraw. It begins:

> A mother held her new baby and very slowly rocked him back and forth, back and forth. And while she held him, she sang:
>
> I'll love you forever, I'll like you for always,
>
> As long as I'm living my baby you'll be. . . .

However, when the baby grew and pulled all the food out of the refrigerator and took his mother's watch and flushed it down the toilet, sometimes his mother would say, "This child is driving me crazy!"

> But at night, while she rocked him she sang:
>
> I'll love you forever, I'll like you for always,
>
> As long as I'm living my baby you'll be.

After this initial reading by the teacher, Mrs. Leonardo read it with the children in *choral-reading* fashion. She and individual children next took turns reading parts of the passage with the children reading the refrain with repetitive language: "I'll love you forever, I'll like you for always, As long as I'm living my baby you'll be." Then Mrs. Leonardo asked the children how they thought the mother felt when she was rocking her son at night, and how they could read the refrain to show that feeling. She also asked how the mother felt when she said, "This child is driving me crazy!" and how she showed this with her voice.

Finally, each child chose a passage in the book, and read the passage silently and then several times orally to a partner. Some of the children also read along while listening to a tape-recorded version of the story. These activities were continued until each child was able to read the passage with accuracy and fluency.

Studies on repeated readings have fallen into two categories: *assisted* repeated readings in which students read along with a live or an audiotaped model of the passage, and *unassisted* repeated readings in which the child engages in independent practice (Dowhower, 1989). In both assisted and unassisted repeated readings students reread a meaningful passage until oral production is accurate, smooth, and resembles spoken language. Notice how Mrs. Leonardo used both assisted and unassisted readings in order to develop reading fluency, beginning initially with assisted reading. First, she read the passage and the students listened and discussed the story. Then she gradually assisted students less as they continued to repeatedly reread the story.

When teachers discuss the repeated-reading strategy, they frequently ask, "Don't students find repeated-readings of the same story boring?" To the contrary, teachers who have used repeated readings find that young children actually delight in using the strategy. Children plead to have their favorite bedtime story read over and over. In the same vein, they get very involved in practicing a story with the goal of reading it accurately and fluently, and are eager to share their story with their parents and classmates.

Some upper-grade children continue to need to read the same material repeatedly to increase fluency. Bidwell (1990) suggests engaging upper elementary-school children in drama. Upper-grade children will enthusiastically rehearse a part many times in preparing to present it to an audience.

Using Predictable Literature for Repeated Readings. Children delight in repeated readings, especially when *predictable literature* is used. Rhodes (1981) has delineated several characteristics of predictable stories. In Box 9.1, some criteria for predictable literatures are outlined.

Love You Forever has many of the characteristics of predictable books. It has *a context or setting which is familiar or predictable* to most young children. *The pictures are*

● **BOX 9.1**

Characteristics of Predictable Stories

1. Is the context (setting) one which is familiar or predictable to the reader?
2. Are the pictures supportive and predictable given the text?
3. Is the language natural? That is, does the author use common language patterns?
4. Is the storyline predictable (the transitions clear) after the book has been started?
5. Does the language "flow"?
6. Does the book reflect creativity, capture an interesting thought, or communicate something worthwhile, worthy of the title literature?
7. Is there repetition of specific language?
8. Are there cumulative episodes in the plot?
9. Is there rhyme?

supportive of the text, that is, there is a good match between the text and the illustrations. The language is natural, that is, *common language patterns* are used. The *storyline is predictable.* There is a *repetitive pattern* of the mother rocking the child at night regardless of the trials during the day. There is also *repetitive language* in the refrains. Further contributing to the predictability of the book is the *rhyme of language.*

Other characteristics of predictable books delineated by Rhodes (1981) but not exemplified in *Love You Forever,* are rhyme and the use of *cumulative patterns* as in *The Great Big Enormous Turnip:*

The black dog pulled the granddaughter.
The granddaughter pulled the old woman.
The old woman pulled the old man.
The old man pulled the turnip.
And they pulled—and pulled again.
But they could not pull it up.

Predictable texts are particularly helpful in developing fluency, because children can rely on these characteristics of predictability. With predictable stories less able readers can use intuitive knowledge of language and sense rather than rely on mediated techniques that draw on their mental energy. Using predictable texts, readers can develop fluency by repeatedly reading them with less and less assistance.

Choral Reading

Telling students to read with expression is not enough for many developing readers. Rather, many children need to listen to mature readers read with expression, and interpret and practice different ways of orally reading selections. **Choral reading** is an enjoyable way to engage children in listening and responding to the prosodic features in oral language in order to read with expression. In essence, through the use of choral reading techniques, students consider ways to get across the author's meaning using prosodic cues like pitch, loudness, stress, and pauses.

Choral reading is defined as the oral reading of poetry that makes use of various voice combinations and contrasts to create meaning or to highlight the tonal qualities of the passage (Arbuthnot, 1961). McCauley and McCauley (1992) extend this definition to include sound effects, exclamatory words, crowd noises, asides, as well as simple movements like exaggerated raising of the eyebrows. Further, primary children enjoy choral reading combined with puppetry. For example, with the cumulative story, *An Invitation to the Butterfly Ball,* by Jane Yolen (1976), children can use paperbag puppets representing ten different kinds of animals invited to a dance by a tiny elf. The story begins, "One little mouse in great distress looks all around for a floor-length dress," and adds two moles, three rabbits and so on, up to ten porcupines (Walley, 1993).

In preparing for a choral reading of a text, the teacher models one way the selection can be read while the children listen. Then students identify how the teacher reads the passage. Did he or she read parts loudly or softly? What kind of tempo did he or she use? Did he or she emphasize particular syllables? Was his or her voice pitched higher or lower in different parts of the passage? Students are then invited to try different ways of reading or interpreting a part, and may want to respond to the mood or feeling that each interpretation imparts (Cooper and Gray, 1984).

Choral reading increases reading fluency (Bradley and Talgott, 1987; Chomsky, 1976; Dowhower, 1987; Samuels, 1979; Schrieber, 1980). In addition, it provides a legitimate, fun way for children to practice and reread a text which leads to a decreased number of oral reading miscues (Herman, 1985).

There are four major types of choral reading: refrain, line-a-child, dialogue, and unison. Each type works well with different kinds of selections (Miccinati, 1985).

Mrs. Leonardo used the *refrain* type of choral reading with *Love You Forever;* that is, she read the stanzas and the children chimed in on the refrain. The refrain is the easiest type of choral reading to model and to learn.

Mrs. Leonardo used the *line-a-child* type of choral reading with "Five Little Chickens," an old jingle from *Sounds of Powwow* by Bill Martin and Peggy Brogan.

Said the first little chicken with a queer little squirm,
I wish I could find a fat little worm.
Said the second little chicken with a queer little squirm,
I wish I could find a fat little bug. . . .

After the five little chickens have spoken:

Said the old mother hen from the green garden-patch,
If you want any breakfast, just come here and scratch!

She had the whole group read the lines that began with *said,* and individual children read what the little chicken and the mother chicken said. The line-a-child format can be easily used on selections in which there are different characters who have lines to speak. When using this type of choral reading, children learn that listening for one's cue is essential or the choral reading breaks down.

Mrs. Leonardo's children giggled when she read to them "The Deaf Woman's Courtship."

Old woman, old woman, will you do my washing?
Speak a little louder, sir; I'm rather hard of hearing.
Old woman, old woman, will you do my ironing?
Speak a little louder, sir; I'm rather hard of hearing.
Old woman, old woman, can I come a-courting?
Speak a little louder, sir; I think I almost heard you.
Old woman, old woman, marry me tomorrow.
GOODNESS GRACIOUS MERCY SAKES! NOW I REALLY HEARD YOU!

Then the class discussed and practiced the *dialogue* type of choral reading with the boys reading the male part and the girls reading the old woman's responses. This selection was also useful to discuss with the children when to use soft and loud voices and when to pitch their voices high or low.

A fourth type of choral reading is the *unison* choral reading, which is often used by teachers who work on oral reading fluency. Yet from a choral reading perspective, this is the most difficult because the entire group speaks all the lines and responds to the prosodic cues simultaneously. Timing, parallel inflections, and consistent voice quality are of prime importance, otherwise there is a sing-song effect. This points to the need for the teacher to model how to read a selection with expression and to discuss how to use stress, pitch, intonation, and loudness when reading in unison. Otherwise, students may get the idea that oral reading should be done in a sing-song fashion.

The Oral Recitation Lesson

Hoffman's (1985) **Oral Recitation Lesson (ORL)** provides a useful structure for working on fluency in daily reading instruction (see Box 9.2). ORL has two components: *direct instruction* and *student practice.* In direct instruction, the teacher models fluency by reading

● BOX 9.2

Steps in the Oral Recitation Lesson

Direct-Instruction Component

Phase 1

1. The teacher reads selection to class or a group modeling fluency.
2. The teacher discusses the selection with the students summarizing. The Directed Listening-Thinking Activity followed by orally completing story frames work well here.

Phase 2

3. The teacher and students talk about how to read the selection fluently and expressively. The use of choral-reading techniques and how to get the author's intended meaning across to the listeners are discussed.
4. Students select and orally read portions with class members providing positive feedback.

Student-Practice Component

Paired repeated reading of the material used in the direct-instruction component

Pairs of students:

1. Read a personally selected portion of the selection silently.
2. Read to partner three times.
3. Self-evaluate each repetition.
4. Evaluate improvement in smoothness, word accuracy, and expression.

a story to the class. The reading is followed by a discussion of the story and students are asked to summarize what happened.

As a variation, the children can predict what will happen as the story unfolds. Hoffman emphasizes that predictable stories should be used in the ORL.

Next, the teacher and students talk about what expressive oral reading is like—that it is smooth, not exceedingly slow, and that it demonstrates an awareness of what punctuation marks signal. Students then read in *chorus* and individually, beginning with small text segments and gradually increasing the length of the segment. Finally, individual students select and orally read a portion of the text for their classmates. Other class members provide positive feedback to students concerning the aspects of expressive oral reading discussed.

We suggest that choral-reading techniques be used in this phase of the ORL. This can show students how prosodic cues facilitate meaning for listeners.

The second component of the ORL, student practice, permits children to practice reading orally the same text used in the direct-instruction component. The goal for the students is to achieve oral reading fluency. Hoffman suggests that second graders should reach the goal of reading 75 words per minute with 98 percent accuracy before moving to another story. This component takes from 10 to 15 minutes, with students doing soft or whisper reading. The teacher checks on individual mastery and maintains records of students' performance on individual stories.

Paired repeated readings as delineated and researched by Koskinen and Blum (1986) provide some useful ways to set up student practice so that children will be involved in sustained practice in this component of the ORL.

Paired Repeated Readings

In paired repeated readings, students select their own passage from the material with which they are currently working. The passage should be about 50 words in length. Students, grouped in pairs, should each select different passages, which makes listening more interesting and discourages direct comparison of reading proficiency. The material should be predictable and at a level where mastery is possible.

When working together, the students read their own passage silently, and then decide who will be the first reader. The first reader then reads his or her passage out loud to a partner three different times. Readers may ask their partner for help with a word. After each oral reading the reader self-evaluates his or her reading. A self-evaluation sheet might ask the reader, "How well did you read today?" Responses to be checked might range from fantastic to good to fair to not so good. The partner listens and tells the reader how much improvement was made after each rendition of the reading; for example, if the reader knew more words and read with more expression during the final reading. A listening sheet can be used to help a partner evaluate a fellow partner's reading (see Figure 9.1). The partners then switch roles.

Another way to organize fluency practice is to use a **paired reading** strategy with peer tutoring. This is a particularly useful strategy in second and third grade where differences between the most fluent and the least fluent readers become evident.

Reading 3

How did your partner's reading get better?

He or she read more smoothly __________

He or she knew more words __________

He or she read with more expression __________

Tell your partner one thing that was better about his or her reading.

● **FIGURE 9.1** A listening sheet

Topping (1989) notes that the collaborative work of children in pairs has enormous potential, but teachers must be able to organize and monitor this activity carefully. He advocated structured pair work between children of *differing ability* in which a more able child (tutor) helps a less able child (tutee) in a cooperative learning environment.

Teachers often recognize the value of extra reading practice in a paired reading situation for less able children, but sometimes express concern about the worth of the activity for more able students. Research reviews on the effectiveness of peer tutoring with paired reading have shown that the more able reader accelerates in reading skill at least as much as the less able reader (Sharpley and Sharpley, 1981).

For growth in fluent reading to be maximized, the teacher needs to pair students carefully. One way to do this is to match the most able tutor with the most able tutee. This procedure seems to aid in matching pairs with an appropriate *relative competence* to each other, which maximizes the success of using this technique. As in any collaborative learning group, do not group best friends or worst enemies. You also need to consider how to handle absences.

Here's a general plan for paired reading with peer tutoring. The tutee chooses a book that has been read to the children or used in direct instruction. The book needs to be within the tutor's readability level (i.e., 95 to 98 percent accuracy level). The tutor and the tutee discuss the book initially and throughout the reading. They read together aloud at the tutee's pace. If the tutee happens to make a word error, the tutor says the word correctly. The pair continues reading together. When the tutee wants to read alone, he or she signals nonverbally; for instance, with a tap on the knee. The tutor praises the tutee for signaling, then is silent and the tutee reads alone. The tutor resumes reading when requested by the tutee. If the tutee makes an error or does not respond in five seconds, they use the same correction procedure described above and then the pair continues to read together. At the conclusion, the pair discusses the story based on questions developed by the tutor before the session.

This procedure allows for tutees to be supported through the text with higher readability levels than they would attain by themselves. The text level also ensures stimulation and participation for the tutor, who promotes discussion and questioning on the content of the text.

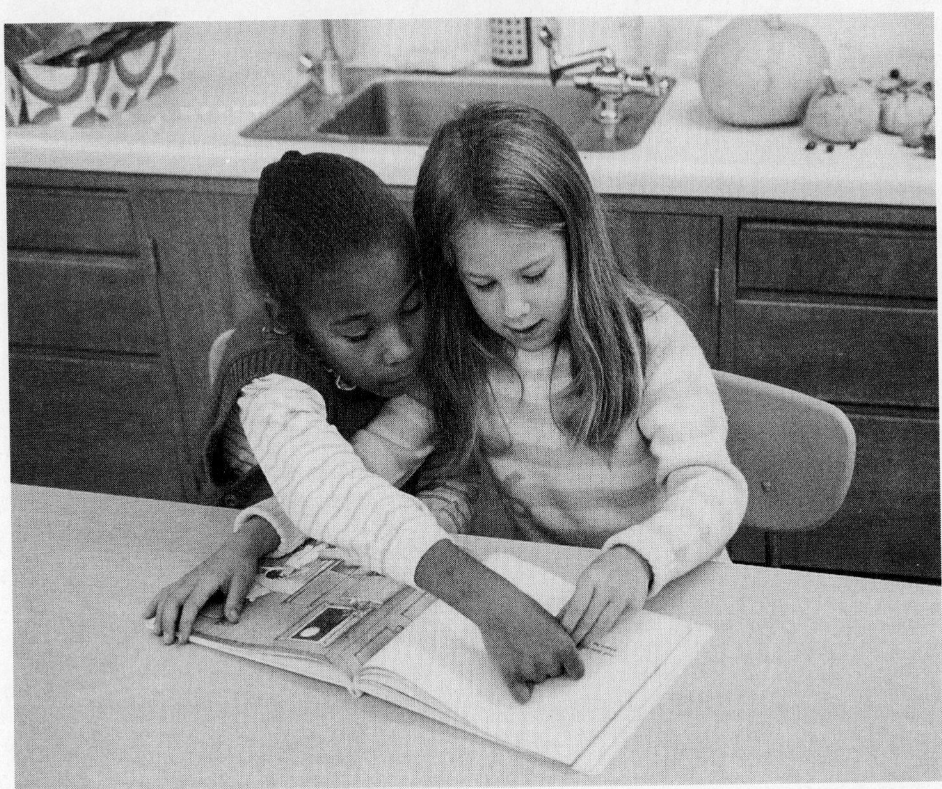

Paired reading is a useful strategy for developing reading fluency.

Parents and Paired Reading. The subject of reading is often perceived by parents as too complicated for them to teach to their children. All too often, attempts at "teaching" word attack skills end in frustration for both child and parents. Paired reading offers the possibility of making parental involvement in the reading growth of their children easy, effective, and enjoyable (Rasinski and Fredericks, 1991). Several years ago, teachers in the Akron (Ohio) Public Schools decided to emphasize at parent meetings that paired reading is easy to learn and do, works with all ages of children using texts from books to newspapers, takes only a few minutes a day, and is proven to improve reading fluency. After reading teachers were introduced to paired reading, Chapter I parents were asked to participate in paired reading with their children for five minutes each day. Many did and, at the end of the school year, a mother of a Chapter 1 child reported, "At first I thought this was silly and that it couldn't make much difference in Katie's reading. Then I saw the improvement myself. We both had fun together, and she was reading. I now believe in the program and really enjoy it" (p. 515).

Sylvia, a whole language teacher in a multigrade class of kindergarten, first-, and second-grade inner-city students, has developed a home reading program which includes activities like paired reading (Vacca and Rasinski, 1992). The children may take home classroom books that have been coded (one dot for "easy"). Their parents are "expected to read to or with their children or listen to their children read" (p. 83). Parents reading daily with children can be most effective.

Cross-Age Reading

Labbo and Teale (1990) claimed that a primary problem with many struggling readers in the upper-elementary grades is that they are weak in fluency. Cross-age reading provides these readers with a lesson cycle that includes modeling by the teacher, discussing the text, and allowing for opportunities to practice fluency.

Cross-age reading also provides upper-grade youngsters with a legitimate reason for practicing for an oral reading performance. In short, cross-age reading seems to be a powerful way to provide upper-elementary students with purposeful activities to develop reading fluency, as well as to provide younger students with valuable literary experiences.

The cross-age reading program described by Labbo and Teale (1990) has four phases: preparation, prereading collaboration, reading to kindergartners, and postcollaboration. In the preparation phase, the older students are helped by their teacher to prepare for a storybook-sharing session in three specific ways. First, the teacher helps select appropriate books. Students can be guided to select books they personally like, that have elements in the story that the kindergarten students can identify with, and that have illustrations that complement the story.

Second, the teacher helps the students prepare by having them engage in repeated readings of the text. Students may be paired with partners who can give each other positive feedback concerning growth in fluency and expressiveness of oral reading. Students should also rehearse on their own to gain control over and confidence with a story.

Third, as part of preparation, the teacher helps the students to decide how their books will be introduced, where to stop in their books to discuss the story, and what questions to ask to ensure the kindergartner's involvement in the story.

The purpose of the prereading collaboration phase is to ensure that the students are ready to share their books orally. In a 15- to 20-minute session a few days before the actual reading to the kindergartners, the older students set personal goals concerning their reading, report on and try out their ideas for involving the kindergartners, and receive and give feedback in a positive, supportive environment. Once the readers are prepared, they go as a group with the teacher to the kindergarten classroom and read their prepared story to small groups. Labbo and Teale (1990) summarized the enthusiasm generated by this occasion by a kindergartner who clung to a sixth-grade reader and called to her teacher when it was time for the upper-grade students to depart, "Mrs. Smith, when is this lady gonna get to come back and read some more to me? That was fun!" (p. 366).

The postreading collaboration is an opportunity for the students to share and reflect on the quality of the storybook reading interactions. Furthermore, the reflective nature of these postreading discussions can be used to help students develop strategies to improve subsequent readings.

In an urban district in Texas, fourth graders regularly read to kindergartners and first graders in a cross-age reading program. Yet, soon after the program began, the fourth-grade teachers realized they were not able to provide sufficient support to help their students read fluently and lead the younger children through a Directed Listening-Thinking Activity. Some children needed more encouragement to practice the book enough to become fluent themselves—particularly since teachers expected the fourth graders to be able to ask the younger children for predictions about a reading as well as answers to simple comprehension questions. To help solve the problem, fourth-grade teachers enlisted the aid of high school students. Soon, the fourth graders were paired with high school buddies. Once a week each pair met to practice fluency and to prepare ways to engage the kindergartners and first graders in making predictions at different junctures in the story.

Automated Reading

In an **automated reading** program, Simultaneous listening and reading (SLR), a procedure suggested by Carol Chomsky (1976), is used. In the SLR procedure a child reads along with a tape recorder or a record. The steps in SLR include the following:

1. Students listen individually to tape-recorded stories, simultaneously following along with the written text. They read and listen repeatedly to the same story until they can fluently read the story.
2. Students choose the book or a portion of the book in which they want to work. When they are making their selections, the teacher explains that they will continue listening to the same story until they are able to read it fluently by themselves. Students need to choose a book that is too hard to read right away, but not so hard that it is out of range entirely.
3. Students are to listen to their books every day, using earphones and following along in the text as they listen. They need to listen to the whole story through at least once; then they can go back and repeat any part they choose to prepare more carefully. They can also record themselves as they read along with the tape or tape-record themselves as they read aloud independently.
4. Every three or four days the teacher listens to the students read orally as much as they have prepared. Students are encouraged to evaluate themselves on how fluently they read the selection they have prepared.
5. Sometimes it takes students a while to get accustomed to working with tape recorders, and at the beginning they can keep losing their place in the book. It takes practice to coordinate their eyes and ears in following along with the text. Once students become familiar with a story, keeping their place is not a problem.
6. Chomsky reported that when students first begin using this method, it may take as long as a month before they are able to read a fairly long story aloud fluently. Stu-

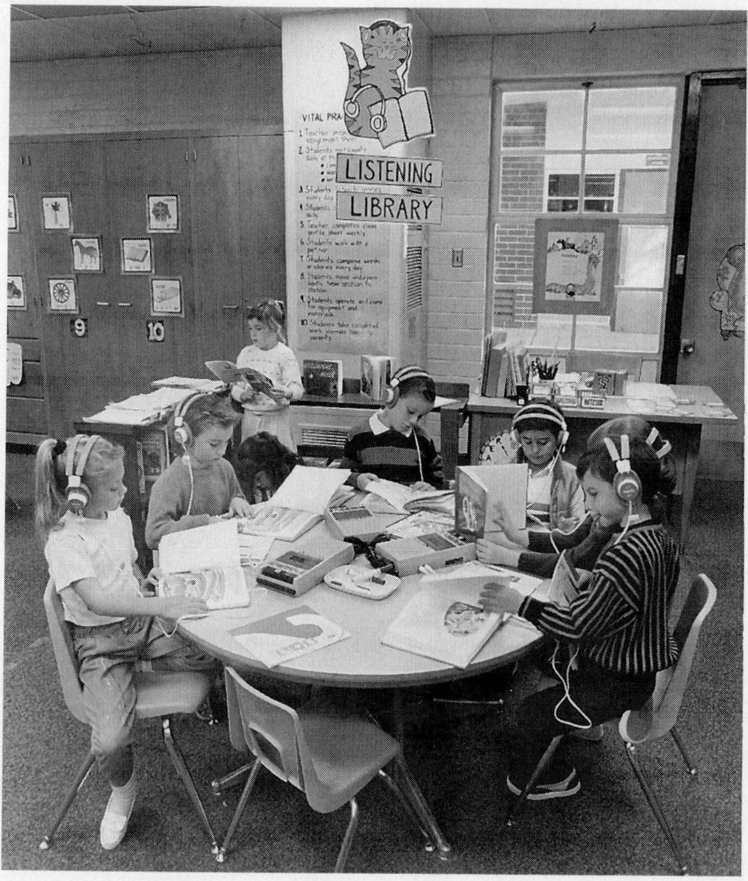

In simultaneous listening and reading, children listen individually to recorded stories while following along with the written text.

dents begin taking a much shorter time period, maybe two or three weeks, to be able to read a fairly long story fluently as they become more proficient with SLR.

When students are able to read the story fluently without the aid of the tape, they need to be given opportunities to read the story to their parents, the principal, or fellow students. Students using this strategy could not present the story without having a book to follow so they have not really memorized the book. However, a combination of memorization and reading enables students to have an experience of successful, effective, fluent reading.

Several schools in Madison, Wisconsin, use SLR in an automated reading program (Dowhower, 1989). Children are sent to the library to choose a book with an audiotape, which is not too easy or too hard for them to read. The criteria for selecting tapes for the automated reading program includes high interest, appropriate pacing, language patterns, clear page-turning cues, and lack of cultural biases. To monitor the difficulty level of books chosen, each child takes a test by reading a list of 20 words from the story. If the child knows more than 15 words, the book is probably too easy; if they know 8 or fewer words, the book may be too hard. Another way to monitor book difficulty level is for the child to read a short section orally, with a teacher, librarian, or aid keeping a running record of miscues made. Dowhower (1989) indicated that on the first reading a child should read with 85 percent accuracy or better before starting to practice, otherwise the text is too hard.

Once a book is selected, a child then reads along with an audiotape several times daily until the story can be read smoothly and expressively. When children are ready, they read the whole book, or several pages if the book is too long, to an adult.

The SLR strategy as used in automated reading can be another useful way for students to develop fluency through practice reading. It is important, however, that students be involved in experiences in which expressive oral reading is modeled and texts are discussed, in addition to having the opportunities for practice that SLR provides. With this word of caution, we will next turn to the question of how to monitor the development of fluency.

Monitoring Oral Reading Fluency

How does a teacher know if students are developing fluency? There are no formal tests that measure automaticity in reading.

Nevertheless, there is a simple, informal procedure a teacher can use to check students' ability to read fluently. First, the student reads orally from a passage that he or she has not previewed or practiced. After reading, the student retells everything that he or she remembers about the passage. The teacher can follow up with questions that probe comprehension, if the child does not provide enough information.

This informal test gives the teacher two indications of automaticity. First, does the child read with few hesitancies and with expression? *Lack of expression is an indicator of a disfluent reader.* The second indicator is the quality of the child's retelling of the story and/or ability to answer the questions. *If the child can read orally and comprehend the text at the same time, as these task conditions demand, the decoding had to be automatic* (Samuels, 1988).

In addition to developing oral reading fluency, students also need time in class to develop fluency in silent reading, where comprehension is the sole reason for reading. Next, let's concern ourselves with the silent reading program.

The Silent Reading Program

At the beginning of this chapter, we defined fluent reading as reading easily and well with a sense of confidence and knowledge of what to do when things go wrong.

Fluent readers are seasoned readers, just as some individuals are considered to be seasoned runners. A seasoned runner has knowledge of what it is like to run for long periods of time. Although seasoned runners have developed patterns of running, they choose when, where, and how far to run. They have gained much knowledge about themselves, on how to assess how they feel so they do not run too far (or that they run far enough) and what they can do to protect themselves from a running injury. Self-knowledge contributes to self-confidence as a runner. In short, seasoned runners have *metacognition* for running; that is, they have knowledge of the task of running, knowledge about themselves as runners, and the ability to monitor themselves during running.

Fluent readers are seasoned readers in that they are able to sustain reading for longer periods of time. They know that productive silent reading means accomplishing as much silent reading as possible during a period of time. In order to do this they know that they must keep their mind on the ideas, responding to high-potency words and sentences and giving less attention to ideas of lesser importance. Although there are distinct patterns in their reading, they choose daily what they are going to read, for what purposes, and how long they need to read in order to suit those purposes. They know that on some days, and with some reading materials, they probably won't be able to concentrate as well as on other days.

Similar to seasoned runners, fluent readers develop a metacognition for reading. They have knowledge of the task of reading, they have knowledge of themselves as readers, and they are able to self-monitor their reading. Fluent readers perceive themselves as able readers. They engage in a reading task with confidence that they will succeed.

Fluent readers grow in leaps and bounds from silent-reading experiences. A *sustained silent reading* program, where children read materials they chose themselves, is extremely important to the development of reading fluency.

Sustained Silent Reading

As explained by Hunt (1970), **sustained silent reading (SSR)** is a structured activity in which students are given fixed-time periods for reading self-selected materials silently. Here are the essential steps.

1. Each student must select his or her own book.
2. Each student must read silently without interruption for a fixed period of time.
3. The teacher reads along with the students and permits no interruptions.
4. Students are not required to answer content-related questions or give reports or their reactions to what they have read during SSR.

A major reason why a structured reading activity like SSR is so important is that, despite teacher encouragement, many students *do not choose to read* on their own. SSR provides for all students the kind of reading experience in school that avid readers get on their own—the chance to read whatever they want to read without being required to answer questions or read orally. In other words, reading for the sake of reading should not be reserved for only the good readers.

The overall goals of SSR are (1) to produce students who choose to read *over other activities;* and (2) to encourage students to voluntarily read material selected *by themselves* for information or pleasure. For students to enjoy reading and seek it as an activity we believe they need to participate in structured silent reading during regular class time. Through SSR experiences they begin to see that they can read for extended periods of time and that it is an enjoyable activity.

Even the most reluctant reader will read when a structured period of silent reading is provided. Levine (1984) found that special education high school students who read six to eight years below grade level became engrossed in reading during SSR. In fact, children who say they do not like to read and who disrupt classes will read during SSR.

Learning to read independently is a major benefit. Without SSR, some students may never obtain independence and self-direction in reading and in choosing what they would like to read. Students will read if they are given time to read, if they are permitted to choose their own reading selections, and if what they read does not have to be discussed, labeled, or repeated back to the teacher.

McCracken and McCracken (1978), who have contributed much to the concept of SSR, identified seven positive messages about reading that children learn by participating in SSR.

1. *Reading books is important.* Children develop a sense of what the teacher values by noting what the teacher chooses to have them do. Children who spend most of their time completing ditto sheets will perceive completing this work as important. Children who read only basal-reader-length stories will perceive reading stories five to ten pages in length as important. If teachers want their students to choose to read fully developed pieces of literature, they must provide time for children to reach such materials.

2. *Reading is something anyone can do.* Since no one watches them, poor readers can make mistakes without worrying. Able readers are "relieved they do not have to prove that they are bright every time they read something" (McCracken, 1971, p. 582). When one is allowed to choose one's own material and read at one's own rate, reading is something *everyone* can do.

3. *Reading is communicating with an author.* Reading is often perceived by students as communicating with a teacher if it is only done in situations where short snatches of material are read with reactions then elicited by the teacher. One of the most exciting reactions to SSR we have observed in students is their individual responses to an author's message.

4. *Children are capable of sustained thought.* Many teachers are concerned that students "have short attention spans" and that they "don't stick to a task for very long." Students, however, have relatively little trouble sustaining their reading for long periods of SSR. They actually look forward to the extended peacefulness.

5. *Books are meant to be read in large sections.* If basal reading is the main way students participate in reading, they often get the notion that reading involves reading three- to ten-page segments, not whole selections of literature. In SSR, students get to read larger chunks of material.
6. *Teachers believe that pupils are comprehending.* It is neither possible nor desirable for teachers to know what each student has learned and felt about every story or book read. Students take something away from every reading experience. One way teachers can show students they trust them to learn from reading is not to question them about what they read during SSR.
7. *The teacher trusts the children to decide when something is well written.* When SSR programs are functioning, students are not requested by the teacher to report on what they have read. What often happens is that students will want to spontaneously share what they have read and feel is worth sharing (p. 408).

Classrooms without voluntary, sustained reading often foster the idea that reading is something one does when forced and only for short periods of time. Each of these positive messages about reading is an important notion to get across if we want students to choose reading over other activities.

Putting SSR into Action

When beginning SSR with your class, talk over with students the reasons for having it and the rules: (1) Everyone reads; (2) Everyone is quiet; (3) Everyone stays seated (Hilbert, 1993). If they are near the end of a book, they need to have a second choice at hand. Many teachers allow students to sit in places other than their desks, but students must decide where to sit *before* SSR begins. A "Do Not Disturb" sign outside the classroom door is often helpful.

Initially, begin with short periods of SSR, perhaps 5 to 10 minutes for first and second graders and 10 to 15 to 20 minutes for third through sixth graders. Gradually extend the time to 30 to 45 minutes for the upper-elementary grades. Hilbert (1993) suggests beginning the timing when the last child has actually begun to read.

During SSR children read books of their own choosing. At first many reluctant readers choose comics, joke books, and other short books with pictures. Often, as the year goes on, children begin selecting more challenging pieces of literature as well as nonfiction selections (Hilbert, 1993). This is particularly true when SSR is combined with other strategies such as literature circles as explained in Chapter 10. It often takes a month of daily SSR for the more reluctant, restless reader to get into reading for a sustained period of time.

SSR for Beginning Readers and Less Able Readers

The standard procedures for SSR imply that students must already have some degree of reading proficiency before they can participate fully. Nevertheless, it's very important to establish and nurture the habit of sustained attention to a self-selected book in children's *earliest* classroom reading experiences. Hong (1981) has described some procedures for adapting SSR for younger readers in what she called booktime. Booktime was used with a group of first graders who had been placed in the lowest reading group in their class. Characterized by their teacher and the reading specialist as having exceptionally short attention spans, the children appeared uninterested in reading and lacked a basic sight vocabulary and word identification skills. Here are the procedures for booktime, which Hong says "evolved gradually as the children made clear what they need and want in their reading environment."

1. Booktime is held at the same time each day so that children come to expect this period as a permanent part of their routine. Repetition of instructions quickly becomes unnecessary. Younger and slower readers will probably have to begin with one to five minutes. With these readers, an eventual ten- to fifteen-minute session should be sufficient each day.
2. The reading group for booktime consists of five to seven students, rather than a whole class. This contributes to a certain intimacy and allows some sharing without getting too noisy and hectic.
3. Introduction and accessibility of books are critical factors. Booktime assumes the teacher regularly reads aloud to the children. After books are read to the group, they should be placed in the classroom library. The library gradually will accumulate a set of books, each of which will have been introduced to the group in an earlier reading aloud session. This avoids the problem of an individual trying to select a book from a collection of unknown ones. New titles constantly will be added to the library while the less popular or overly familiar ones can be removed.
4. Children select just one book. They may go through several books in one period, but they must peruse only one at a time. And there is no saving books by tucking them under one's arm or sitting on them while reading another book.
5. Because children may go through more than one book in a given session, booktime is best conducted with children sitting on the floor near the book collection, rather than each child taking a book back to his or her seat. There should be little or no people traffic through the reading area. If possible, larger, noisier activities are set on the opposite side of the room.
6. The teacher reads with the children as in standard SSR. But in this situation she or he may also respond to children's questions about print such as, "What's this word?" "Does this say *wait?*" This gives children feedback on their hypotheses about print. They feel encouraged when they hear they've successfully decoded a new word, and they know when they have to revise their conclusions. On the other hand, teachers will want to avoid becoming word machines, spewing out every unknown word. Children should be encouraged to read as best they can and to try to figure out words on their own.

As in SSR, teachers don't interrogate children either during or after the reading; teachers only respond. With such a limited teacher role, other individuals can help with booktime.

7. Children may read in pairs and talk to each other quietly. The sharing of a book avoids the fuss that comes when two children want the same book. The quiet talk also has educational benefits. It can be quite helpful in reviewing a story (i.e., for comprehension and sense of story), exchanging reactions and feelings (i.e., a response to literature), and figuring out some of the text (i.e., word identification skills).
8. Children are guided toward treating books with respect. That is, there should be no throwing or rough handling of books. This reinforces the sense of books as something special.

Hong reports that the success of booktime depends upon the quality of the books that are presented. A major criterion is that the plot be clear, well paced, and predictably sequential. The language should be whole, using complete, natural sentences that create a flow and rhythm. Predictable, patterned books are excellent choices for booktime.

As the children described by Hong participated in booktime, they became more accustomed to it. They began by focusing their attention on specific books, then developed favorites to which they often returned. The children progressed from a merely general interest and a focus on illustrations toward paying more specific attention to the features of print. After several weeks of booktime, it was not unusual to see the children spend an entire session on the first few pages of a single book, attempting to read the text using a combination of context clues and decoding.

Parents and SSR

Often parents want to help students with their academic progress. However, helping students with workbook pages or with oral reading can become frustrating for both the child and the parents. Encouraging parents to have short, sustained silent reading times with their children is one way for parents to do something specific that assists their child's school progress but limits the activities to low-pressure, pleasurable interactions. Spiegel (1981a) suggests the following schedule for sending a series of newsletters to parents to acquaint them with the recreational reading program of which SSR is a major part.

Newsletter 1 (day 1): Explain what a recreational reading program is and how it will work in your class, and include a schedule of what information will be contained in subsequent newsletters.

Newsletter 2 (day 3): Present a rationale for having a recreational reading program, with emphasis on how it fits into the basic curriculum. Include a short statement of support from the principal and reading teacher.

Newsletter 3 (day 5): Make suggestions about how parents can help support the program through their efforts at home.

Newsletter 4 (day 7): Make a list of the ways parents can volunteer their time in the classroom to support the program.

To prepare parents for what to expect, some teachers begin the school year with a letter sent home. Vacca and Rasinski (1992) write about Gay, a third-grade teacher, who sends a letter to parents highlighting her philosophy toward literacy. She explains in the communique that "children learn to read and write by reading and writing" (pp. 159–160). Informal chats, formal conferences, and telephone calls to parents in the evenings are other ways to keep parents informed about how their children are doing and *why* they are spending time on such activities as SSR.

There is one other person whose support parents and teachers can enlist to promote independent sustained reading—the principal. Explain to the principal the importance of a recreational reading program and the need for a large supply of books. The principal can also be invited to participate in classroom SSR, and thus be an important model. This is a good way to convey the idea that reading is important.

Teaching Sustained Silent Reading

We believe sustained silent reading can be taught. Productive reading can be strengthened by helping readers to realize that success means learning to sustain themselves with print for longer periods of time. Children can keep track of the amount of silent reading accomplished during the reading period through charts (see Figure 9.2) or graphs (see Figure 9.3). Such demonstrations of growth are particularly important for lower-achieving or at-risk readers.

After a silent reading session, the teacher can build the climate for productive silent reading and self-evaluation by discussing individually, in small groups, or with the whole class, the students,' as well as the teacher's, responses to these questions:

Name ____________________

Title of Book ____________________

Monday	Tuesday	Wednesday	Thursday	Friday
____ pages	____ pages	____ pages	____ pages	____ pages

Date ____________________

● **FIGURE 9.2** A chart for sustained silent reading

2. Interview both a primary and an upper-grade teacher who use sustained silent reading (SSR) regularly. Use the questions below and/or devise questions of your own. Then compare interview responses with those of your classmates:
   a. How often do you conduct SSR?
   b. How do you think your students benefit from SSR?
   c. Can you think of an instance in which specific children have changed in their behavior over a period of time because of their participation in SSR? Describe the change.
   d. Have you seen any changes in the behavior of restless, reluctant readers over a period of time?
   e. Does your principal or other school personnel participate in SSR? If so, what effect do you think this has?

KEY TERMS

fluency
immediate word identification
automaticity
repeated readings
predictable text
choral reading
Oral Recitation Lesson (ORL)
paired reading
automated reading
sustained silent reading (SSR)

CHAPTER 10

Bringing Children and Literature Together

BETWEEN THE LINES

In this chapter you will discover:

- **That literacy is personal and readers benefit from a supportive environment.**
- **What it means to bring children and books together in a literature-based program.**
- **How to choose literature and involve children through activities.**
- **Ways to organize classes around books.**
- **Major strategies for encouraging readers to respond to literature.**

Imagine the expression on Laura Pils' face when she received a brightly colored, handmade Valentine's Day card in the shape of a heart from Michael, a friend of one of Laura's first-grade students. In purple letters, the card read, "Happy Valentine's Day. I love you Miss Piss" (Pils, 1993).

"It's so fitting," Laura thought of Michael's card. "It is these first attempts at literacy that are so wonderful . . . all the parts are not in place yet but the soul is there, speaking loud and clear while trying to find its own voice" (Pils, 1993, p. 653). Laura's first-grade class in Middleton, Wisconsin personifies the type of literate community where all of the students, including those who fall behind the others in their literacy development and are not particularly anxious to learn, feel that they are valued members of the class and that they have something to offer the rest of the children. Dan is a case in point. So is Michael.

Michael is Dan's friend. Although Laura never had Michael as a student, she came to know him through Dan. Now Dan was one of the more needy students in Laura's class who had been struggling from the beginning of the school year with reading and writing. His language skills were limited; he had difficulty expressing himself other than through crying, acting out, and sometimes getting into verbal and physical fights with his classmates.

Dan's story is not unlike that of students in other schools and in other classrooms whose path to literacy, for one reason or another, is rough and uncertain. Yet within the literacy community that is Laura's classroom, there is an air of confidence that all of the children will find their way to literate activity. "But how to reach them?" That is the challenge that she faces. Twenty-five years of teaching experience with literacy beginners helps Laura to realize that she must first establish a level of trust in the classroom and then find a "hook" that will connect literacy to the lives of the children. For many teachers, like Laura, literature is the hook.

Her attempts to reach Dan eventually were realized when Laura learned that his grandparents, with whom Dan spent summers near the ocean, were visiting from Connecticut. She arranged in advance for the grandparents to make a surprise visit to the classroom as "mystery readers." Throughout the year, mystery readers are invited into the classroom, unannounced to the children, to share in a surprise reading of a child's favorite book. Open invitations are extended to parents, grandparents, and older brothers and sisters to visit and read to the class. On the day that his grandparents visited the classroom, Dan "stood proudly next to his grandma and grandpa and introduced them. As they read, they stopped often and had Dan assist in the telling of the story. We took their picture with Dan and tacked it to the Mystery Reader board" (Pils, 1993, p. 652). On that eventful day, Dan took a giant step forward in his journey toward literacy; he felt, perhaps for the first time, that he had something of himself to give to the other students. Throughout the remainder of the year, he made steady progress and contributed to the community through the stories that he wrote and shared with others.

Dan is now in the third grade and he is still making an impact on the community of readers and writers in Miss Pils first-grade class. He helps select books for her class: "Knowing that I like pigs, he checked out every pig book in the library. He came into the room beaming when he found a pig story that had just arrived; he was teaching me about a new book" (Pils, 1993, p. 653). And Michael, who once declared his love for Miss Pils, also helps to select books for her class. Dan and Michael even were invited to participate in reading to the class books that they had liked "when they were little." As Laura Pils explains: "We took their pictures and put them on the Mystery Reader board. We wrote them thank-you notes. Their teacher said they were so proud. I was proud too."

The story of Dan and Michael illustrates convincingly that at its best, literacy is a personal and self-engaging activity. Children who view themselves as contributing members of a classroom of readers and writers develop a sense of self-worth and commitment. Bringing children and books together in a literate community not only fosters the ability to think better but also to feel and to imagine.

Reading literature requires children to respond to books affectively as well as cognitively. Children respond emotionally to the literary text as a whole. These feelings, by and large, are unique and tied to each reader's life experiences. Emphazing personal involvement in literature develops in children an imagination, a sense of wonder, and an active participation in the literary experience. To our mind, bringing children and literature together is one of the highest acts of humanity in the classroom.

Supporting a Community of Readers

There are long-term benefits implicit in bringing children and books together on a regular basis. First, reading expands children's experiential backgrounds. Children who have never milked a cow and been awakened by a rooster, or lived in a tenement apartment and played in the alley of a big city can expand their world through reading. Second, literature provides children with good models of writing. These models are invaluable in children's own writing development, and will do much to teach them about the unique characteristics of written language. Third, children learn to read by reading, a theme we have repeated throughout this book. When they are encouraged to read books regularly, children are more likely to develop patience with print. In this way, they gain valuable practice in reading. Fourth, when the prime purpose for reading is enjoyment and pleasure, children want to understand what they are reading and are likely to select books with familiar topics, themes, or characters. Natural reading situations are created that will promote students' use of reading strategies. And fifth, wide reading provides opportunities for children to develop vocabulary knowledge. Readers learn the meaning of words by meeting them again and again in a variety of contexts in which they are usually able to construct meanings.

Literature-based reading programs have the potential for much success with all types of students, but particularly with readers like Dan and Michael who can easily "slip through the cracks" without a supportive environment for literacy development. Simply defined, a **literature-based reading program** may be viewed in the context of instructional practices and student activities using literature, books, novels, short stories, magazines, plays, and poems that have not been rewritten for instructional purposes. Furthermore, children's literature often *supplants, not supplements,* a basal reading program.

Studies have been conducted in classrooms where literature-based programs were beginning to be used with populations that traditionally had not been successful in literacy learning in school. A landmark study, conducted by Cohen (1968) and later replicated by Cullinan, Jaggar, and Strickland (1974) with New York City second graders from low-socioeconomic neighborhoods, compared the growth of two groups of children in reading. One group was taught from a basal reader program, while the other participated in a literature-based program. The literature group showed significant increases over the basal reader group in word knowledge, comprehension, and quality of vocabulary. Also, children who speak limited English have made great gains in reading when immersed in real literature (Larrick, 1987; Roser, Hoffman, and Farest, 1990). The reading ability of emotionally handicapped children also increased significantly through a literature-based reading program (D'Alessandro, 1990).

Reading achievement studies of literature-based reading programs also report significant shifts in the children's attitudes toward reading. Tunnell and his colleagues (1988), for example, found that with mainstreamed learning-disabled children in a literature-based program, "negative attitudes toward books and reading virtually disappeared as self-concept in relation to literacy rose" (p. 473). Literature-based programs seem to affect children's conceptions of reading, also. Rasinski and DeFord (1985) asked children from classrooms using different types of reading programs questions like, "What is reading?" and "What happens when you read?" The responses from children in the different classrooms were dramatically different. Children in the literature-based classroom conceived reading to be more of a meaning-related activity than did the children from a basal reading classroom and the children from a mastery learning classroom.

No wonder recent reports such as *Becoming a Nation of Readers* call for reading programs that provide children with many, varied opportunities to read high-quality literature (Anderson et al., 1985).

The real value of literature-based reading programs is that they create a **community of readers.** Hepler and Hickman (1982) proposed the idea of a community of readers to characterize how children, in alliance with their friends and teacher, work together in classrooms in which school reading becomes like adult reading, where adults are motivated to read. In these classrooms, children informally and spontaneously talk over their experiences with books and recommend books to each other. In Hepler's (1982) yearlong study of a fifth- and a sixth-grade classroom, she found it common for children who discovered something of particular appeal to read that passage aloud to a friend, offer the book to a friend for approval, or simply nudge the nearest person and point out "the good part."

Hansen (1987) has expanded this idea into "a community of readers and writers." She explained that students should help each other learn, not out of a sense of duty, but because they know each other as people. Children sharing their thoughts on what they have read helps make this happen. In book-sharing talks, sometimes children have similar thoughts about a book, but often they have unique contributions to make to the discussions. The teachers who have worked with Hansen have come to realize that each child has something to share; that everyone knows something that others will find interesting. This attitude encourages students to have confidence in themselves and to take risks by eliminating the fear of not knowing the right answer. Hansen suggested, "When words, whether our own written words or our verbal responses to someone else's, give us a place in the group, print acquires a new dimension for us. Learning is usually social, we learn very little entirely on our own. Without a community, people have less desire to write or read" (p. 64).

Classrooms where children support each other as readers and writers are not without design. Rather, "they are carefully structured environments that reflect a teacher's commitment to literature as a natural medium for children's reading and language learning as well as a source of fun and satisfaction" (Hickman, 1983, p.1). In these classrooms children's responses to literature are livelier and more positive than in the average classroom, and their choices of books seem to be made with more care.

Hooking children on books helps them realize their literacy potential. Table 10.1 outlines some of the hooks that we explore in this chapter, all of which support a community of readers in the elementary classroom.

● TABLE 10.1

Hooking Students on Books

Immerse students in literature	Use instructional time to show the value of reading	Help students find and share books they want to read
Create a classroom climate in which literature is an integral component.	Find classroom time for students to read books of their choice.	Help students to find books of interest at the appropriate level.
Use many genres of children's books, including folktales, poetry, realistic fiction, historical fiction, and informational books.	Model reading behavior and become a reader of children's books.	Tell or read the beginning of interesting stories.
Select and organize a classroom collection of books.	Encourage students to respond to the aesthetic dimensions of literature.	Develop annotated lists of books worth reading.
Read and tell stories. Show films and filmstrips of literature selections.		

Surrounding Children with Literature

One thing that sets these classrooms apart is that the teachers are enthusiastic about children's literature. Teachers who make a point of talking about their own favorite books or stories or are themselves engrossed in a new book often find their students wanting to read those same books for themselves. These teachers also show personal interest in books in other ways. Some teachers share autographed copies of books from their own collections or display book-related items such as ceramic or stuffed toy characters, or posters designed by a picture-book artist.

Jill, a first-grade teacher, showed a stuffed rabbit with a blue jacket as she read Beatrix Potter's *Peter Rabbit.* Another teacher told the story of "Little Red Riding Hood" using a doll on which one end was Red Riding Hood and the upside-down end was a wolf wearing grandmother-type spectacles. Whatever way the teacher's enthusiasm is expressed, it helps to create a setting where children know that attention to the world of books is legitimate and desirable.

Selecting a Classroom Collection of Books

A major classroom characteristic that brings children and books together is many carefully selected books. These books come from different sources—the teacher's personal collection, the school library, the public library, and paperback book clubs. While the core collection is permanent, many of the borrowed titles change frequently, so there is always something new to encourage browsing.

Not just any old book is in this collection for the sake of quantity. These books are carefully chosen for a variety of reasons as illustrated by Hickman (1983).

> One teacher of a fourth- and fifth-grade group, for example, often includes many picture books. She chooses some like Mizumura's *If I Were a Cricket* and Foreman's *Panda's Puzzle* for the special purpose of comparing the artists' way with watercolor; others, like Wagner's *The Bunyip of Berkeley's Creek,* all chosen just because they are good stories and the teacher thinks the children will enjoy them. The teacher is sensitive to children's interests and books that will have immediate appeal; thus the presence of *Tales of a Fourth Grade Nothing* by Blume, *How to Eat Fried Worms* by Rockwell, and *The Mouse and the Motorcycle* by Cleary. The teacher also recognizes that the students need some books that will stretch their imaginations and abilities, stories of sufficient depth to bear rereading and reflection. Some of the titles chosen for this purpose are Babbitt's *Tuck Everlasting,* Cooper's *The Dark Is Rising,* and Steig's *Abel's Island.* Still others, like Konigsburg's *From the Mixed-Up Files of Mrs. Basil E. Frankweiler,* are available in multiple copies so that small groups can read and discuss them. (p. 2)

One notable feature of book selection is that each title bears some relationship to others in the collection. There may be multiple books by an author or an illustrator or several books that represent a genre such as folktales. Other connections may be based on a content theme such as spooky books, nature books, or survival books.

Choosing Classroom Literature. To be able to choose literature for classroom collections and to give guidance to students as they choose books to read, a teacher needs to be familiar with children's literature. Because children's literature has expanded extensively in the last 20 years, this is a formidable task.

There are several strategies that can be used to help choose classroom literature. Here are some tips on how to avoid being overwhelmed as you become familiar with children's literature.

1. *Read and enjoy children's books yourself.* The best way to become familiar with children's books is not to read anthologies or reviews, but to read the books themselves. It

The extensive expansion of available childrens' literature makes choosing a classroom literature collection a formidable task.

is a good idea to keep a card file on the books you have read to jog your memory later. This card file can be used with children to help them in choosing books to read. It can also be used as you share your feelings about particular books with other teachers.

2. *Read children's books with a sense of involvement.* Only by reading books thoroughly can you prepare yourself to share them honestly with children.

3. *Read a variety of book types.* There are various classifications of genres or types of books. By being familiar with specific books in each of the different genres, you can be more helpful when children ask for such things as "a scary mystery" or "something true to life."

4. *Read books for a wide variety of ability levels.* Children at any grade level vary tremendously in their reading abilities and interests. For example, Haywood's *B is for Betsy* is read avidly by some second and third graders. Other children at the same grade level will read somewhat more difficult books such as Sobol's *Encyclopedia Brown Lends a Hand* and Blume's *Tales of a Fourth Grade Nothing.* Still others may

benefit from spending time with picture books such as Sendak's *Where the Wild Things Are* or Emberley's *The Great Thumbprint Drawing Book.*

5. *Share how your students respond to particular books with other teachers or other university students.* In the San Antonio, Texas, school district, a book-reporting system was developed recently. Anyone who read a book and used it with children filled out a review card, which included a brief summary, a rating, comments on the book's unique value, and recommendations for suggested ability levels. No card was turned in unless the book was used with children. Teachers used these cards to help select books for their classrooms. Not unexpectedly, with this teacher-sharing system in place, the children read more along with their teachers.
6. *Start by reading several books that are considered by many to be of "good" quality.* Appendix C lists the Newbery and Caldecott award-winning books. As you read these and begin using them with children, you will begin to know books to which children in your class will respond favorably.

Determining Good Literature. Stewig (1980) explained that the appellation *good* for books for children is a "fragile raft of opinion on the shifting quicksand of taste." A teacher's first priority is to choose books that children will like and will read. In order to choose such a collection of books, teachers must be knowledgeable and enthusiastic about children's literature. Through reading children's literature and talking about books with children, teachers learn which books to use in their classrooms. A second consideration is to use accepted ways to judge books according to plot, theme, characterization, and setting. In addition, there are a few criteria to use in building a *balanced* collection of books.

1. *The collection needs to contain modern, realistic literature as well as more traditional literature.* In the last few years, some critics have voiced concern about the appropriateness of realism in some of the recent children's literature. Other observers feel realism is justified, because it depicts problems children must face while growing up. Each teacher and school must decide whether to include books that deal with divorce, death, and drug use—issues that touch the lives of many of today's children. Traditional literature, which children have delighted in for many years, should also be a part of the classroom collection of books.
2. *The collection needs to contain books that represent different ethnic and minority groups as well as mainstream Americans. The collection also needs to contain stories that depict nontraditional families.* See Chapter 11 for specific criteria useful in evaluating books for stereotyping.
3. *The collection needs to contain books with different types of themes and books of varying difficulty.* The classroom library needs traditional literature, fantasy, poetry, historical fiction, nonfiction, and picture books. Even upper-grade classroom collec-

tions should have some picture books. Picture books often have a good story plot and provide a way to get less enthusiastic students into reading.

There is one more consideration when compiling the classroom collection: the science, art, social studies, and music curricula. Include books on topics that will be studied in these subject areas. Again, make materials on specific topics available in a wide range of reading levels, because of the different reading abilities of students in the same grade level.

Designing the Classroom Library. As a classroom collection develops, care must be given to the area of the classroom that houses the classroom library. There are a number of physical features of classroom libraries that increase children's voluntary use of books (Morrow, 1985; Morrow and Weinstein, 1982; Routman, 1991; Fractor et. al., 1993). Such a classroom library is highly visible. Thus, it is obvious that it is an important part of the classroom. There are clear boundaries which set the library area apart from the rest of the classroom. The library is a quiet place for five or six children to read away from the rest of the classroom. The library affords some comfortable seating—maybe carpet pieces, beanbags, or special chairs. The classroom library holds five to six books per child. Multiple copies of favorites are included. A variety of genres and reading levels are available. The library has both open shelves to display attractive covers and shelves to house many books with the spine out. Books in the library are organized and labeled by genre, theme, topic, author, reading level, content area, or some combination of these features. The library has literature-oriented displays like flannel boards, puppets, book jackets, and posters.

Once the classroom library is in place, the literature program itself needs attention. A major part of the program includes reading aloud and telling stories to children.

Listening to Literature

According to Stewig (1980), "most elementary school teachers understand the values that accrue as a result of sharing literature with children" (p. 8). Teachers naturally seem to know that there is no better way for children to become interested in the world of books than through listening to stories and poems. In this way, children learn that literature is a source of pleasure. When they listen to literature, children are exposed to stories and poems they can not, or will not, read on their own. Often, once children are excited by hearing a selection, they want to read it for themselves. One study found that reading aloud to fifth graders for 20 to 30 minutes per day affected both the quantity and quality of their voluntary reading (Sirota, 1971).

Through hearing stories and poems children develop a positive disposition toward books. Cumulative experiences with hearing stories and poems are likely to improve reading comprehension and vocabulary development. A study by Cohen (1968) reports that 7-year-olds who were read to for 20 minutes each day gained significantly in vocabulary and reading comprehension. Listening to stories and poems also can provide a basis for group discussion, which often leads to shared meanings and points of reference.

For these reasons, literature listening time can be one of the most productive times in the school day. Sharing literature with children is not a "frill." Most primary teachers include time for reading aloud in their schedules; upper-elementary teachers spend less time reading stories to students. Chow Loy Tom (1969) finds that about 40 percent of third- and fourth-grade teachers read aloud to students, while only 26 percent of sixth-grade teachers read to their students. Among the reasons teachers gave for not reading aloud was lack of time.

A recent national study of readaloud practices shows that teachers tend to read to children for a period of 10 to 20 minutes a day (Hoffman and Roser, 1993). However, only 34 percent of the time spent on these readalouds is related to units of study. Further, the amount of book talk following readalouds often lasts fewer than five minutes. Children rarely engage in exploring their response to literature during a readaloud.

Although teachers may read aloud to students to fill odd moments between a completed activity and the bell or to schedule reading aloud as a calming-down activity, it is important to note that sharing literature is not a time killer. It is too serious and central to the reading program as a whole to be treated in an offhand way. Reading aloud needs to be incorporated into all aspects of the curriculum.

Choosing Literature to Read Aloud. What kind of thought and planning go into deciding what literature to share? Why not go to the library, pull some books from the shelf, and, when reading-aloud time arrives, pick up a book and read? In classrooms where students become enthusiastic about literature, the teachers have carefully selected which books to read. They have considered the age of the children and what will interest them. They also present different types of literature. Often books read aloud are related to each other in some way. For example, a second-grade teacher read several books by Keats: *The Snowy Day, Dreams,* and *Boggles.* The students soon could recognize a Keats book by its illustrations.

Hickman (1983) notes the example of a fourth-grade teacher who thought her students would be excited by characters that were transformed magically from one type of being to another. She read to her students tales of magical changes such as "Beauty and the Beast" in Peace's version and Tresselt's retelling of Matsutani's "The Crane Maiden." Her class also heard Perrault's version of the familiar "Cinderella" and a native American myth, "The Ring in the Prairie," by Schoolcraft. Last, she read "A Stranger Came Ashore" by Hunter, a fantasy story with magical transformation that is more difficult to understand than the transformations in the preceding stories.

Another teacher might focus on books to demonstrate an assortment of character types.

> In planning experiences with characterization, the teacher chooses books that present a wide variety of characters: male and female, young and old, rich and poor, real and imaginary. The books are read to children and savored. Sometimes the selections are discussed; at other times they are not. Reading occurs each day; the teacher is aware that children may be assimilating unconsciously

> some of the aspects of successful characterizations exemplified in what they are hearing. (Stewig, 1980, pp. 62–63)

Folktales in which the plot is generally very important can be read to illustrate simple characterization. Other authors give vivid physical descriptions. Consider this description from Judy Blume's *Are You There God? It's Me, Margaret.*

> When she smiles like that she shows all her top teeth. They aren't her real teeth. It's what Grandmother calls a bridge. She can take out a whole section of four top teeth when she wants to. She used to entertain me by doing that when I was little. . . . When she smiles without her teeth in place she looks like a witch. But with them in her mouth she's very pretty. (pp. 15, 18)

Teachers can also share with children books in which authors show what the characters are like by describing what they do and how they interact with others. Even books for the very young do this. For example, in *Sam* by Ann Herbert Scott, Sam tries to interact with his mother, brother George, sister Marcia, and his father, all of whom are too preoccupied with their own concerns. Finally, the family responds. The characters all are developed skillfully by the author and portrayed in subtle monochromatic illustrations by Symeon Shimin. In hearing and discussing such books, children gain an awareness of how authors portray characters.

In classrooms where children get into literature, teachers carefully choose which books to share with their students and have a reason for reading a particular book to their class. Often they read a series of books that are related in some way.

Preparing to Read Aloud. Teachers need to prepare for story time. First, before reading a book aloud to the class they should be familiar with the story's sequence of events, mood, subject, vocabulary, and concepts.

Second, teachers must decide how to introduce the story. Should the book be discussed intermittently as it is read, or should there be discussion at the conclusion of the reading? Furthermore, what type of discussion or other type of activity will follow the reading?

Setting the Mood. Many teachers and librarians set the mood for literature sharing time with a story-hour symbol. One librarian used a small lamp: When the lamp was lit, it was time to listen. Deliberate movement toward the story-sharing corner in the classroom may set the mood for story time. Some teachers create the mood with a record or by playing a piano. As soon as the class hears a specific tune, they know that it is time to come to the story-sharing corner. Norton (1980) describes using a small painted jewelry box from Japan. As she brings out the box, Norton talks with the children about the magical stories contained in it. She opens the box slowly while the children try to catch the magic in their hands. The magic is wonderful so they hold it carefully while they listen. When the story ends, each child carefully returns the magic to the box until the next story time.

Introducing the Story. There are numerous ways to introduce stories. The story-sharing corner could have a chalkboard or easel with a question relating to the literature to be shared, or a picture of the book, which can quickly focus the children's attention. Many teachers effectively introduce a story with objects. For example, a stuffed rabbit may be used to introduce *The Velveteen Rabbit* by Williams. A good way to introduce folktales is with artifacts from the appropriate country.

Other ways to introduce a story would be to ask a question, to tell the students why you like a particular story, or to have the students predict what will happen in the story using the title or the pictures. You might tell them something interesting about the story's or author's background. It is advantageous to display the book, along with other books by the same author or with books on the same subject or theme. Introductions, however, should be brief and vary from session to session.

Activities After Reading Aloud. Once the stage is set for literature sharing, the teacher needs to read expressively and clearly. There are many different ways to encourage children to respond after hearing a piece of literature. These will be discussed later in this chapter. After some selections, the teacher simply can allow children to react privately to what they have heard. Davis (1973, pp. 19–21) calls this the *impressional approach.* The basic idea is that children will take from an experience whatever is relevant to them; therefore, each child will take something from the listening experience. There is no particular reason for the teacher to know precisely what each child gets from each listening experience. Teachers should probably strike a balance between these two approaches. Too many discussions and other follow-up activities may diminish interest; too little will result in a lessened impact of the literature listening.

Allow Others to Present Literature. In addition to teachers reading literature aloud daily, Trelease (1989) suggested that another way to promote the importance of reading aloud is to set up guest reader programs in which the principal, parents, the superintendent, and local sports and news personalities read literature favorites to children. Children, too, can present literature to children. In Chapter 9, we described a cross-age tutoring program where older elementary children can be shown how to select and prepare for reading to younger children. A word of caution: An important part of these read-ins by school and community leaders is the selection of the books to be read and the preparation of how the selection will be presented. Don't let the reader do this without guidance!

Readers' Theatre. Another way to involve children in presenting literature to other children is through **readers' theatre.** McCaslin (1990) defines readers' theatre as the oral presentation of drama, prose, or poetry by two or more readers. Readers' theatre differs from orally reading a selection in that several readers take the parts of the characters in the story or play. Instead of memorizing or improvising their parts as in other types of theatre productions, the players read them. Since the emphasis is on what the audience *hears* rather than sees, selection of the literature is very important. Readers' theatre scripts generally contain a great deal of dialogue and often are adapted from a piece of literature. An example of a readers' theatre script for Kraus's *Leo the Late Bloomer* is illustrated in Box 10.1.

During a readers' theatre program, the members of the audience use their imagination to visualize what is going on, because movement and action are limited. Although there is

● BOX 10.1

A Readers' Theatre Script: Leo the Late Bloomer

by Robert Kraus

CHARACTERS: (5) Narrator 1 (N–1)
Narrator 2 (N–2)
Father
Mother
Leo

N–1: (Each person should turn around, then back, as they are introduced.) This is the story of a tiger, Leo the Late Bloomer. I am the first narrator. Next to me is the second narrator. The characters are father, mother, and Leo.

N–2: Leo couldn't do anything right.

N–1: He couldn't read.

N–2: He couldn't write.

N–1: He couldn't draw.

N–2: He was a sloppy eater.

N–1: And, he *never* said a word.

Father: What's the matter with Leo?

Mother: Nothing! Leo is just a late bloomer.

Father: Better late than never.

N–1: Every day Leo's father watched him for signs of blooming.

N–2: And every night Leo's father watched him for signs of blooming.

Father: Are you sure Leo's a bloomer?

Mother: Patience! A watched bloomer doesn't bloom.

N–1: So Leo's father watched television instead of Leo.

N–2: The snows came. Leo's father wasn't watching. But Leo still wasn't blooming.

N–1: The trees budded. Leo's father wasn't watching. But Leo still wasn't blooming.

All: Then one day, in his own good time, Leo bloomed!

N–1: He could read!

N–2: He could write!

Father: He could draw!

Mother: He ate neatly!

N–1: He also spoke. And it wasn't just a word.

N–2: It was a whole sentence. And that sentence was . . .

Leo: I made it!

All: The end.

no one correct arrangement of the cast in presenting a readers' theatre, an effective procedure to have the student readers stand in a line facing away from the audience and then turn toward the audience when they read their part.

In preparing for a readers' theatre, students read the selection silently, then they choose parts and read the selection orally. Students need to practice reading expressively. Props and scenery may be used, but should be kept simple. As with oral reading of literature, an introduction and the setting of the mood before the presentation are important.

After students have presented several readers' theatres using teacher- or commercially prepared scripts, students can write their own scripts, either adapting literature they enjoy or using stories they have written. Here's how to guide students to develop their own scripts: Once children have read a story, they transform it into a script through social negotiation. The writing of a story into a script requires much rereading as well as knowledge and interpretation of the text. Once the script is written, the children formulate, practice, and refine their interpretations. Finally, the readers' theatre is presented to an audience with hand-held scripts (Shanklin and Rhodes, 1989).

Story Telling

There are three significant reasons for including story telling in the curriculum.

1. *An understanding of the oral tradition in literature.* Young children in many societies have been initiated into their rich heritage through story telling; today, few children encounter such experiences.
2. *The opportunity for the teacher to actively involve the children in the story telling.* When the teacher has learned the story, he or she is free from dependence on the book and can use gestures and action to involve the children in the story.
3. *The stimulus it provides for children's story telling.* Seeing the teacher engage in story telling helps children understand that story telling is a worthy activity and motivates them to tell their own stories (Stewig, 1980).

Each of these reasons is important. Children are sure to be spellbound by a well-told story. Close eye contact, the storyteller's expressions, ingenious props, and the eliciting of the children's participation contribute to the magic. Although we cannot expect everyone to acquire a high level of expertise for a large number of stories, story telling is a skill one can master with practice, a story at a time.

Selecting the Story to Tell. Beginning storytellers should choose selections they like and with which they feel comfortable. Simpler stories are often the most effective for story telling. Stories with which many children are familiar and can help with the dialogue are excellent choices to prepare for story telling to younger children. "The Three Bears," "The Three Little Pigs," and the "Three Billy Goats Gruff" fit in this category. Since ancient and modern fairy tales usually appeal to children ages 6 through 10, consider stories like

"The Elves and the Shoemaker," "Rumpelstiltskin," and "The Bremen Town Musicians." Older elementary children frequently prefer adventure; so myths, legends, and epics like "How Thor Found His Hammer," "Robin Hood," "Pecos Bill," and "Paul Bunyan" tend to be popular choices.

You might select several stories about a certain topic. For example, Norton (1980) suggests telling two stories about "forgetting": "Icarus and Daedalus," a Greek legend in which Icarus forgets that his wings are wax, and "Poor Mr. Fingle" (Gruenberg, 1948), who wanders about a hardware store for years because he forgot what he wanted to buy. Bauer's *Handbook for Storytellers* includes an annotated bibliography of stories arranged by subject as well as recommendations for single stories.

One of the purposes of story telling is to give children an understanding of oral tradition. Even very young children can understand that today stories are usually passed down in books, whereas many years ago they were orally handed down.

An effective way to help children gain this understanding is to tell stories that are similar in plot, such as "The Pancake" from Norse tales included in Sutherland's *Anthology of Children's Literature,* and *The Bun* by Brown. All of these stories have some kind of personified edible goodie chased by a series of animals and eaten by the most clever animal. Jane, a kindergarten teacher, read these three stories to her class, then guided her students in making a chart showing how the three stories were alike and different. The class then dictated a story entitled "The Pizza." In the class's story, the Pizza rolled and was chased by the school nurse, some first graders, and the principal. Its fate, of course, was to be gobbled by the kindergartners. Through their experiences, the kindergarten class developed a story using elements from their school life, just as storytellers in the oral tradition did from their personal experiences.

Preparing a Story for Telling. The task of memorizing a story may seem formidable. How can teachers or children prepare for telling a story in front of others? Actually, stories do not need to be memorized. In fact, the telling is often more interesting if the story unfolds in a slightly different way each time. The following steps are helpful in preparing to tell a story.

1. Read the story two or three times to get it clearly in your mind.
2. List the sequence of events in your mind or on paper, giving yourself an outline of the important happenings. Peck (1989) suggested mapping the story by considering the setting, the characters, the beginning event, the problem and attempts at solving it, and the solution. This structure enabled her students to tell stories they had devised without stilted memorization of lines.
3. Reread the story, taking note of the events you didn't remember. Also determine sequences you do need to memorize, such as "Mirror, mirror, on the wall, who's the fairest of them all?" from *Snow White.* Many folk and fairy tales include elements like this, but such passages are not difficult to memorize.
4. Go over the events again and consider the details you want to include. Think of the meaning of the events and how to express that meaning, rather than trying to memo-

rize the words in the story. Stewig (1980) recommends jotting down the sequence of events on notecards; he reviews the cards whenever he has a few free minutes. He reports that with this technique it seldom takes longer than a few days to fix the units of action of a story in your memory.

5. When you feel you know the story, tell the story in front of a mirror. After you have practiced it two or three times, the wording will improve and you can try changing vocal pitch to differentiate among characters. Also, try changing your posture or hand gestures to represent different characters.

Now that you have prepared the story, decide how to set the mood and introduce it, just as you would before reading a piece of literature. Effective story telling does not require props, but you may want to add variety and use flannel boards and flannel board figures or puppets. These kinds of props work well with cumulative stories containing a few characters. Jessica, a first-grader, told how her teacher had a puppet of "The Old Lady Who Swallowed a Fly" with a plastic see-through window in her stomach. As the story was told, the children delighted in seeing the different animals in the old lady's stomach and helping the teacher tell the repetitive story.

Helping Children Select Books

One trait of independent readers is the ability to select books they can enjoy and from which they can get personally important information. In fact, Anderson, Higgins, and Wurster (1985) finds that good readers know how to select literature relevant to their interest and reading level, while poor readers do not. More often than not, a teacher will hear a child moan, "I can't find a book I want to read." Comments like this usually reveal that students do not feel confident in finding good books by themselves. Earlier we alluded to ways for students to become acquainted with specific books: Teachers can tell exciting anecdotes about authors, provide previews of interesting stories, show films or filmstrips about stories, suggest titles of stories that match students' interests, or compile teacher- and/or student-annotated book lists. To be able to do these things well, teachers need to be well versed in children's literature and know their students.

Beyond this, children need to be shown how to choose books. Hansen (1987) proposes that children be asked to choose and read books of three different difficulty levels. Children should have an "Easy Book" on hand to encourage fluent reading and the "I-can-read" feeling. Second, children need a "Book I'm Working On," in which they can make daily accomplishments by working on the hard spots. Finally, children need a "Challenge Book," which they can continue to go back to over a period of time. This helps them gain a sense of growth over a long period. By letting children know we expect them to read at all levels, children learn to judge varying levels themselves and to give honest appraisals of how books match with their reading ability.

For independent readers, book choice is related to reading purposes and intentions as they read the book. Rick may decide to read *A Wind in the Door,* because he liked *A Wrin-*

kle in Time by the author Madeleine L'Engle. When he begins to read, he compares the two books. As he becomes engrossed in the book, he reads to see how the story unfolds. Children need to discuss with each other and their teacher why they chose a specific book and what they are thinking about as they read it.

In addition to their teacher, an even more persuasive source that can help children decide what books to read is their classmates. Peer recommendations make the act of choosing a book more efficient and less risky. Recommendations from friends are the primary way adult readers decide what books to read. For many adults, the next best thing to reading a good book is telling someone else about it.

The use of **dialogue journals** is another effective tool used by teachers to get to know how students feel about their reading and to guide students to "the right book." Jan, a fifth-grade teacher, has her students write daily in a journal. One of her students wrote, "I like it when the whole class reads together. I think it makes me want to read more." Jan responded with, "I'm glad." Another student made the following journal entry: "My favorite book was *Florence Nightingale.* I liked it because of the way she improved the hospitals and made them stay clean. Also she acted differently than any other person I've read about" (Smith, 1982, p. 360). In response to this journal entry, Jan suggested the student read other biographies of courageous women.

Dialogue journals seem to work well at the beginning of the school year in providing a response to children concerning their thoughts and feelings about the books they are choosing and reading. Later in the year, buddy journals can be instituted as was explained in Chapter 5. Sometimes students will begin recommending books to each other in their buddy journals.

There is another understanding in the world of adult readers that is communicated to students in classrooms where students are into reading: If an adult reader does not like a particular book, he or she doesn't finish it. It is common for an adult to say, "I just couldn't get into that book," or "I never finished that biography." Here is some advice by Lewis Smith (1982) to a classroom of readers concerning what to do about books they have difficulty getting through.

> Mark mentioned that he didn't like his version of *Dan Boone*—it didn't pick up his interest, so he stopped reading. That's okay. You should read books you like, because if you spend too long trying to read one you don't like, it may make you doubt reading itself. Jamie asked about this too—she gets discouraged because she reads so slowly. Her mom told her she would get better as she reads more. You do learn to read by reading and by choosing books that interest you. The books should have some new words, but not so many that they discourage you. (p. 359)

Smith also encouraged children to ask for suggestions about which books are interesting. But each child needs to decide for him- or herself if a book is too hard, too easy, or interesting enough to be read cover to cover. Of course, there are times when students need to be nudged to finish a book or to make the next "Book I'm Working On" a bit more challenging.

Organizing for Literature-Based Instruction

Organizational patterns for literature-based instruction vary from structured whole class studies of **core books** to independent reading of self-selected books in **literature circles** and **reading workshops.** Just as time, response, and choice are important in writing, these factors are also critical to the success of literature-based reading programs.

Core Books

Sometimes teachers will organize literature around the study of core books. In some schools a set of core books forms the nucleus of the reading program at each grade level (Routman, 1991). A curriculum committee comprised of district-wide teachers is often assigned to develop a collection of books at each grade that is judged to be age appropriate and of high quality. Figure 10.1, for example, represents some of the books that are part of the core book curriculum in the Shaker Heights School District in Ohio.

Core books are taught within the framework of whole class study. Students have little or no choice in the selection of core books. As part of a whole class study, teachers assign various activities and use a variety of instructional strategies to support students' interactions with the texts. Many of the comprehension, vocabulary, word identification, and fluency strategies discussed in the previous section of this book are easily adapted to the study of core books.

Often teachers use core books as springboards for independent reading in which children choose books with related themes and situations or decide to read other works by an author that they have studied. Brenda Church, for example, is an inner-city fifth-grade teacher in Akron who introduces a unit on survival by having her students do a whole-class study of Jean George's *Julie of the Wolves* (Harper and Row, 1959). As the unit evolves, the students also read novels in groups. They select a novel from the choices that Brenda gives them from the Survival Tales Book List shown in Figure 10.2 (Vacca and Rasinski, 1992).

The major problem with a core book approach is to guard against "basalizing" literature; that is to say, core books and novels should not be treated like basal textbooks whose major purpose is to organize instruction around the teaching of reading skills. Basalization often results in students completing worksheets, responding to literal comprehension questions, and engaging in round-robin reading (Zarrillo, 1989).

Literature Units

Teachers also organize instruction around **literature units.** Literature units usually have a unifying element such as the study of a genre, an author, or a conceptual theme. With literature units, a teacher usually chooses the theme (or negotiates one with the students) and

Grade 1	Grade 2	Grade 3
Alexander and the Terrible, Horrible, No Good, Very Bad Day by Judith Viorst, illustrated by Ray Cruz. New York: Atheneum, 1972. (Aladdin)	*The Adventures of Spider* by Joyce Cooper Arkhurst, illustrated by Jerry Pinkney. Boston: Little, Brown, 1964. (Scholastic)	*Amazing Spiders* by Alexandra Parsons, photographs by Jerry Young. New York: Knopf, 1990. (Knopf)
Amos & Boris by William Steig. New York: Farrar, Straus & Giroux, 1971. (Sunburst)	*Sidney Rella and the Glass Sneakers* by Bernice Myers. New York: Macmillan, 1986.	*The Comeback Dog* by Jane Resh Thomas, illustrated by Troy Howell. Boston: Houghton Mifflin, 1981. (Bantam Skylark)
Chickens Aren't the Only Ones by Ruth Heller. New York: Grossett & Dunlap, 1981. (Scholastic)	*The Courage of Sarah Noble* by Alice Dalgliesh, illustrated by Leonard Weisgard. New York: Scribner, 1954. (Aladdin)	*The Cricket in Times Square* by George Selden, illustrated by Garth Williams. New York: Farrar, Straus & Giroux, 1981. (Dell Yearling)
Every Time I Climb a Tree by David McCord, illustrated by Marc Simont. Boston: Little, Brown, 1967. (Little Brown)	*Dr. De Soto* by William Steig. New York: Farrar, Straus & Giroux, 1982. (Sunburst)	*I'll Meet You at the Cucumbers* by Lilian Moore, illustrated by Sharon Woodring. New York: Atheneum, 1988. (Skylark)
Frog and Toad Together by Arnold Lobel. New York: Harper & Row, 1971. (Harper Trophy)	*How Much is a Million?* by David M. Schwartz, illustrated by Steven Kellogg. New York: Lothrop, Lee & Shepard, 1985. (Scholastic)	*Koko's Kitten* by Francine Patterson, photographs by Ronald H. Cohn. New York: Scholastic, 1985. (Scholastic)
Henry and Mudge by Cynthia Rylant, illustrated by Sucie Stevenson. New York: Macmillan, 1987. (Aladdin)	*I Want a Dog* by Dayal Kaur Khalsa. New York: Crown, 1987. (Scholastic)	*Miss Rumphius* by Barbara Cooney. New York: Viking, 1982. (Puffin)
Ira Sleeps Over by Bernard Waber. Boston: Houghton Mifflin, 1972. (Sandpiper)	*Lon Po Po: A Red-Riding Hood Story from China* by Ed Young. New York: Philomel, 1989. (Scholastic)	*Mufaro's Beautiful Daughters* by John Steptoe. New York: Lothrop, Lee and Shepard, 1987. (Harper)
Little Bear by Else Holmelund Minarik, illustrated by Maurice Sendak. New York: Harper & Row, 1957. (Harper Trophy)	*Owl Moon* by Jane Yolen, illustrated by John Schoenherr. New York: Philomel, 1987. (Scholastic)	*Ramona Quimby, Age 8* by Beverly Cleary, illustrated by Alan Tiegreen. New York: Morrow, 1981. (Dell Yearling)
Little Red Hen by Paul Galdone. New York: Clarion Books, 1974. (Scholastic)	*The Patchwork Quilt* by Valerie Flournoy, illustrated by Jerry Pinkney. New York: Dial, 1985.	*Stone Fox* by John R. Gardiner, illustrated by Marcia Sewell. New York: Crowell, 1980. (Harper Trophy)
Wiley and the Hairy Man by Molly Bang. New York: Macmillan, 1976. (Aladdin)	*Sam, Bangs, and Moonshine* by Evaline Ness. New York: Holt, 1966. (Holt)	*The Stories Julian Tells* by Anne Cameron, illustrated by Ann Strugnell. New York: Knopf, 1981. (Knopf)

● **FIGURE 10.1** Core books for grades 1–6, Shaker Heights School District

Grade 4	Grade 5	Grade 6
Beauty and the Beast by Michael Hague. New York: Holt, 1989. (Holt)	*A Blue-Eyed Daisy* by Cynthia Rylant. New York: Bradbury, 1985. (Dell Yearling)	*The Dark is Rising* by Susan Cooper, illustrated by Alan Cober. New York: Atheneum, 1973. (Aladdin)
Bunnicula by Deborah and James Howe. New York: Atheneum, 1971. (Camelot)	*Bridge to Terabithia* by Katherine Paterson, illustrated by Donna Diamond. New York: Crowell, 1977. (Harper Trophy)	*Dicey's Song* by Cynthia Voigt. New York: Atheneum, 1983. (Fawcett)
Every Living Thing by Cynthia Rylant, illustrated by S.D. Schindler. New York: Bradbury, 1985. (Aladdin)	*Dear Mr. Henshaw* by Beverly Cleary, illustrated by Paul O. Zelinsky. New York: Morrow, 1983. (Dell Yearling)	*The Great Gilly Hopkins* by Katherine Paterson. New York: Crowell, 1978. (Harper Trophy)
The Hundred Penny Box by Sharon Bell Mathis, illustrated by Leo and Diane Dillon. New York: Viking Penguin, 1975. (Puffin)	*Door in the Wall* by Marguerite de Angeli. New York: Doubleday, 1949. (Dell Yearling)	*Hatchet* by Gary Paulsen. New York: Penguin, 1987. (Puffin)
Knots on a Counting Rope by Bill Martin, Jr., and John Archambault, illustrated by Ted Rand. New York: Holt, 1987. (Holt)	*The Fighting Ground* by Avi. New York: Lippincott, 1984. (Harper Trophy)	*Homesick: My Own Story* by Jean Fritz, illustrated by Margot Tomes. New York: Putnam, 1982. (Dell Yearling)
The Lion, the Witch and the Wardrobe by C.S. Lewis. New York: Macmillan, 1950. (Collier)	*My Side of the Mountain* by Jean Craighead George. New York: Dutton, 1975. (Puffin)	*Lincoln: A Photobiography* by Russell Freedman. New York: Clarion Books, 1987. (Clarion)
The Real Thief by William Steig. New York: Farrar, Straus & Giroux, 1973. (Sunburst)	*On My Honor* by Marion Dane Bauer. Boston: Houghton Mifflin, 1986. (Dell Yearling)	*Mrs. Frisby and the Rats of Nimh* by Robert C. O'Brien, illustrated by Zena Bernstein. New York: Atheneum, 1971. (Aladdin)
Sarah, Plain and Tall by Patricia MacLachlan. New York: Harper & Row, 1985. (Harper Trophy)	*The Pinballs* by Betsy Byars. New York: Harper & Row, 1977. (Harper Trophy)	*Roll of Thunder, Hear My Cry* by Mildred Taylor, illustrated by Jerry Pinkney. New York: Dial, 1976. (Bantam)
A Taste of Blackberries by Doris Buchanan Smith, illustrated by Charles Robinson. New York: Crowell, 1973. (Harper Trophy)	*Spin a Soft Black Song* by Nikki Giovanni, illustrated by George Martins. New York: Farrar, Straus & Giroux, 1985. (Sunburst)	*The Sign of the Beaver* by Elizabeth Speare. Boston: Houghton Mifflin, 1983. (Dell Yearling)
Trouble for Lucy by Carla Stevens, illustrated by Ronald Himler. Boston: Houghton Mifflin, 1981. (Clarion)	*Tuck Everlasting* by Natalie Babbitt. New York: Farrar, Straus & Giroux, 1975. (Sunburst)	*Where the Red Fern Grows* by Wilson Rawls. New York: Doubleday, 1961. (Bantam)

● **FIGURE 10.1** *(continued)*

Survival Tales: Book List

1. Holman, Felice, *Slake's Limbo*. New York: Charles Scribner's Sons, 1974.
2. Sperry, Arnstron. *Call It Courage*. New York: Macmillan, 1940.
3. Aurembou, Renee. *Snowbound*. New York: Abelard-Schuman, 1965.
4. Byars, Betsy. *Trouble River*. New York: Viking Press, 1969.
5. Christopher, John. *The White Mountains*. New York: Macmillan, 1967.
6. Collier, James and Christopher Collier. *Jump Ship to Freedom*. New York: Delacorte Press, 1981.
7. Farley, Walter. *The Black Stallion Legend*. New York: Random House, 1983.
8. George, Jean. *Julie of the Wolves*. New York: Harper & Row, 1959.
9. George, Jean. *My Side of the Mountain*. New York: E. P. Dutton, 1959.
10. Hamilton, Virginia. *The Planet of Junior Brown*. New York: Macmillan, 1971.
11. Konigsburg, E. L. *From the Mixed-up Files of Mrs. Basil E. Frankweiler*. New York: Atheneum, 1967.
12. O'Dell, Scott. *Island of the Blue Dolphins*. Boston: Houghton Mifflin, 1960.
13. O'Dell, Scott. *Sarah Bishop*. Boston: Houghton Mifflin, 1980.
14. O'Dell, Scott. *Sing Down the Moon*. Boston: Houghton Mifflin, 1970.
15. Spears, Elizabeth. *The Sign of the Beaver*. Boston: Houghton Mifflin, 1983.
16. Taylor, Mildred. *Roll of Thunder, Hear My Cry*. New York: Dial Press, 1976.

● **FIGURE 10.2** Survival tales book list

Source: R.T. Vacca and T.R. Rasinski, *Case Studies in Whole Language* (Fort Worth, TX: Harcourt Brace, 1992), p. 227. Reprinted with permission.

pulls together a collection of books relating to the theme; the children, however, have options as to what books to choose from the collection and what activities they might pursue. Successful literature units, as we show in the next chapter, strike a balance between whole-class, small-group, and individually selected activities.

The self-selection of books usually supplements core book and literature unit approaches. Other organization patterns, those that make use of literature circles and reading workshops, place more emphasis on literature self-selection. Let's take a closer look.

Literature Circles

Teachers who have children meet in literature circles believe in the importance of self-selection. They rely on cooperative learning strategies that show children how to work together and discuss books based on personal response to what they have read. Literature circles promote critical thinking. Jamie, a third grader, views her experience with literature circles this way: "Literature circles take the ideas out of your head rather than keeping all the ideas in your head. In literature circles, you get to know a person better and how that book relates to their life and how you and them relate" (Short and Klassen, 1993).

Gay, a third-grade teacher, organizes literature circles (also known as literature study groups) in her classroom. Each Friday, Gay introduces to the class potentially worthwhile books for discussion. If a book is fictional, she builds interest in the story by overviewing its plot, acquainting the students with characters, and reading parts of the story aloud. If the book is informational, she also builds anticipation for ideas by overviewing the content, reading aloud, and showing the students several illustrations from the text. The students then select books, which are to be read by the following Friday. Teams form, not by ability level, but by the titles children select for the following week's workshop (Vacca and Rasinski, 1992).

Teams usually vary in size from two to six students. During the week each team member reads the book. Gay encourages the students to help one another with difficult words or if they experience any other problems while reading. On Friday, the study groups meet for book discussions. As children participate in the study groups, Gay circulates around the room. When teams complete their discussion, the whole class gets together for a debriefing and sharing time. Each team tells about their book and what they learned from the experience. Gay also introduces several new titles for next week's literature study groups. The children then make new selections and form new teams based on their choices.

When a teacher has children choose which books they want to read and discuss in literature circles, they sometimes choose books they cannot yet read independently. These students usually can read books with a partner or by listening and reading along with a tape. The most important aspect of literature circles is the focus on sharing meaning through discussion. Children incorporate reading strategies and build fluency as they read for meaning. The whole premise behind the use of literature circles is that children can learn from each other. As Hansen (1987) puts it, "The test of a well-structured classroom is whether children can read books, get help from others, and share books in small and large groups with and without the teacher" (p. 126).

In order to show children how to work collaboratively, Keegan and Shrake (1991) suggest that teachers model discussion techniques at the beginning of the school year. Various techniques include attending to the topic, participating actively, asking questions for clarification, piggybacking off others' comments, learning to disagree constructively, giving all members opportunities for input, and supporting opinions with evidence. They also recommend that children learn gambits or appropriate ways of interacting with one another. For example, one gambit for disagreeing constructively might be phrased this way, "I disagree with you, John. Instead, I think that. . . " Through explicit instruction and modeling, children learn to use this gambit rather than saying, "John is wrong." As the year continues, teachers need to emphasize other social skills such as encouraging one another, responding to ideas, using eye contact, and sharing feelings.

Literature circles are an excellent way for students to study *multicultural literature,* also discussed in Chapter 15. In Charlene Klassen's (1993) classroom, for example, a literature group read and discussed *A Jar of Dreams* by Yoshiko Uchida in which a Japanese girl struggles to find acceptance in a new country. During the discussion, a Laotian boy commented that it was important to "believe in yourself and keep trying." A Hmong girl said, "When I was in kindergarten, I was lonely and shy." Another student extended the discussion by commenting on the conflict between ethnic groups in the book and the hope that Hmongs and Laotians would find peace. At other times in the discussions one student asked the group to clarify the word "suicide" and another child felt confident enough to admit she did not know where Japan was located. The differences in personal histories of these children provided a wide range of topics for conversation.

Reading Workshops

Nancy Atwell (1987) originated the reading workshop as a way to integrate the language arts around literature. Reading workshops provide an organizational framework that allows readers to demonstrate their use of reading strategies by responding to books and sharing meaning with others. Reutzel and Cooter (1991) describe how Atwell's reading workshop, with several modifications, can work with elementary school children.

The reading workshop has several key features:

Sharing Time. The teacher shares literature. Reutzel and Cooter (1991) provide an example of a teacher reading about vampires and ghouls from Jack Prelutsky's collection of poetry called *Nightmares: Poems to Trouble Your Sleep* (1976) while showing overhead transparencies of some of the book's spooky pen and ink sketches. In this way, the teacher sparks interest in various literary genres for free reading.

Minilessons. The teacher takes several minutes after sharing time to demonstrate a reading strategy through explicit teaching. The focus of a minilesson is often drawn from the observed needs of students, at times discovered during individual reading conferences.

Status-of-the-Class Report. A status-of-the-class chart helps both the teacher and the students to monitor their responsibilities and progress in a reading workshop. The teacher briefly surveys the class to determine how each student plans to use his or her time during sustained silent reading time and/or group activity. The teacher records students' responses on a chart and, as a result, has a record of each child's commitment for the day. Once children are familiar with the status-of-the-class report, the process takes no more than about five minutes per day to complete.

Sustained Silent Reading. During SSR, everyone, including the teacher, reads! This free reading phase varies from classroom to classroom but represents a significant amount of class time as children select and read books of their own choosing. They also keep up-to-date logs recording time spent reading, titles of books read, and when they plan to have individual conferences with the teacher.

Individual Reading Conferences. Each day the teacher meets with one or more students for an individual reading conference. Children make appointments on a sign-up board at least one day prior to the conference. Many teachers require that each student have at least three conferences per grading period. During the reading conferences, the teacher and the child discuss the book the child is currently reading. Questions such as the following can be used to guide the conference:

- What part did you find particularly interesting? Funny? Thrilling? Why?
- Did a happening in the book bring to mind an experience you have had? What was it? How was it similar and/or different from what happened in the story? Why do you think the author wrote this book?

Conferences generally last from five to eight minutes.

Sharing Time. At the end of a reading workshop, the class comes together for ten minutes or so to share the books they are engaged in and the activities they have been working on.

Whether you organize instruction around core book studies, literature circles, or reading workshops, a common thread that runs throughout literature-based programs is the reader's response to the text. How teachers encourage children's aesthetic response to literary texts is an important feature of literature-based instruction.

Encouraging Response to Literature

After reading a book or seeing a movie, we may share the experience by briefly describing the plot. Most often, though, we tell how we felt and why. We point out something in the film or text and/or our personal histories that made us feel the way we did. We give examples from our lives and retell parts of the story. Yet when discussion shifts to the classroom, what usually happens? Often teachers ask questions to elicit a "right answer." Because we have often tried to evaluate what and how much students have understood about the text, teachers spend little time helping students explore, defend, or elaborate on ideas. In this section, we explore the need to lead students in classroom experiences in which they analyze their *personal* reactions to what they have read. Such action supports a **reader-response theory.** In other words, it supports a theory that proclaims that *the reader is crucial to the construction of the literary experience.*

Louise Rosenblatt (1982) was one of the earliest proponents of a reader-response theory. She stated:

> Reading is a transaction, a two-way process, involving a reader and a text at a particular time under particular circumstances. . . . The reader, bringing past experiences of language and of the world to the task, sets up tentative notions of a subject, of some framework into which to fit the ideas as the words unfurl. If the subsequent words do not fit into the framework, it may have to be revised, thus opening up new and further possibilities for the text that follows. This implies a constant series of selections from the multiple possibilities offered by the text and their synthesis into an organized meaning. (p. 268)

Rosenblatt took her analysis of reading one step further into implications for classroom literature discussions. In any reading event, the reader adopts one of two stances: the *efferent stance* or the *aesthetic stance.*

When a reader approaches a reading event with an *efferent stance,* attention is focused on accumulating what is to be carried away from the reading. Readers using this stance may be seeking information, such as in a textbook; they may want directions for action, as in a driver's manual; or they may be seeking a logical conclusion, as in a political article. In an *aesthetic stance,* however, readers shift their attention inward to center on *what is being created during the reading.* Reading is driven by personal feelings, ideas, and attitudes that are stirred up by the text.

In most reading situations, there is both an efferent and aesthetic response to the text. In reading a newspaper article, for example, a reader may take a predominantly efferent stance, but there may be an accompanying feeling of acceptance or doubt about the evidence cited. Although one stance usually predominates over the other in most reading events, the text itself does not dictate a reader's stance. A text is chosen because it satisfies a reader's intended purpose. Rosenblatt's description of what happens in predominately aesthetic reading situations holds direct implications for bringing children and literature together.

> In aesthetic reading, we respond to the very story or poem that we are evoking during the transaction with the text. In order to shape the work, we draw on our reservoir of past experience with people and the world, our past inner linkage of words and things, our past encounters with spoken or written texts. We listen to the sound of the words in the inner ear; we lend our sensations, our emotions, our sense of being alive, to the new experience which, we feel, corresponds to the text. We participate in the story, we identify with the characters, we share their conflicts and their feelings. (p. 270)

Teachers create responsive environments in their classrooms by inviting children to react to literature through various symbol systems and modes of expression: art, movement, music, creative drama, talk, writing. Alternative forms of communication, such as art or movement, are especially appealing for students who may have difficulty expressing their feelings and thoughts in words. When children connect drawing with reading, for example, their artwork often helps them to discover and shape their response to a story. Various visual arts media—pencil drawings, chalk, markers, crayons, paint, cardboard and paper construction—can be used to encourage responses to literature. In addition, students can design book jackets, mobiles, posters, or comic strips to capture the personal appeal or meaning that texts evoke.

● **FIGURE 10.3** Jessica's drawing for Grimbold's Other World

Jessica's drawing in Figure 10.3 illustrates her personal involvement and understanding of Nicholas Gray's *Grimbold's Other World.* Jessica's teacher encouraged her to talk about the drawing in relation to the story. Later, the drawing became the basis for a book jacket, displayed prominently in the classroom with other student-created book jackets, to "advertise" books to classmates.

Drawing, creative drama, and role playing often serve as springboards for oral and written response. Children, especially at the primary level, gravitate naturally to drawing or dramatically performing a story before they talk or write about it.

Sparking Discussion with Book Talks

Whole class study of core books, reading workshops, and literature circles provide numerous opportunities for children to talk about books. Having **book talks** is a great way to evoke children's responses to literature. Here are some suggestions to spark book talk discussions:

1. Depending on the text, ask questions such as, "Did anything especially interest you? Frighten you? Puzzle you? Seem familiar? Weird?" Have children tell which parts of

Literature Across Cultures

The People Could Fly, told by Virginia Hamilton and illustrated by Leo and Diane Dillon (New York: Knopf, 1985)

In a multicultural society bound together by diverse groups who maintain their own cultural traditions and experiences, books help us to celebrate our distinctive differences and understand our common humanity. Culturally diverse books in the United States typically tell the stories of people of color—African-Americans, Native-Americans, Asian-Americans, and Hispanic-Americans. These stories are told through poems, folklore, picture books, realistic and historical fiction, biography, and nonfiction.

Mrs. Katz and Tush, by Patricia Polacco (New York: Bantam, 1992), page 3

In addition to Yakota's questions, the following checklist is designed by Cullinan and Galda (1994) to help teachers select quality multicultural literature.

Checklist for Evaluating Culturally Diverse Literature

- **Are characters from different cultures portrayed as individuals without stereotyping?**
- **Does the work qualify as good literature in its own right?**
- **Is the culture accurately portrayed from the point of view of someone inside the cultural group?**
- **Are issues presented in their true complexity as an integral part of the story—not just a focus on problems or social concerns?**
- **Does the dialogue maintain the natural melodies of the native language or dialect without making it difficult to read?**
- **Do the books show the diversity within as well as across human cultures?**
- **Do the illustrations contain accurate, authentic representations of people and scenes from different cultural groups?**
- **Do people of color lead as well as follow? Do they solve their own problems or do they depend on white benefactors?**

Source: B. Cullinan and L. Galda. *Literature and the Child* (3rd ed.). (Fort Worth, TX: Harcourt, Brace, 1994) p. 345. Reprinted with permission.

Appendix D contains a partial listing of children's books representative of African-American, Asian-American, Hispanic-American, and Native-American cultures. These books, and many others, may easily be incorporated into a literature-based classroom, discussed in Chapter 10.

Printed as a special insert to accompany Jo Anne L. Vacca, Richard T. Vacca, and Mary K. Gove's *Reading and Learning to Read, Third Edition* (1995).

Grateful acknowledgment is made to the publishers who granted special permission to reprint the illustrations included in this insert.

HarperCollins College Publishers
10 East 53rd Street
New York, NY 10022

the text caused these reactions and have them compare these experiences to their real-life experiences (Rosenblatt, 1982, p. 276).

2. Have children tell about the most memorable incident, character, or setting of the book. Children share with each other the specific parts of the text they recalled most clearly after hearing or reading a story (Benton, 1984, pp. 268–269).
3. Ask students to tell about the part of the story or character they remember most vividly. For example, "How did the character(s) feel in this part of the story?" "Have you ever felt like this?" "Describe the situation you were in."
4. Read the opening of a story. Immediately afterward, tell students to jot down what was going on in their heads—pictures, memories, thoughts—during the reading. The jottings should be in a stream-of-consciousness style. Then share the responses and distinguish the common responses from the idiosyncratic ones. This shows students that reading has shared elements as well as highly individual ones and that sharing reactions is a valid way of talking about literature (Benton, 1984, p. 269).
5. Ask students, "What pictures do you get in your mind's eye of this character, setting, or event?" "If character *X* were to come through the door now, what would he or she look like?" "If you went to the place where the story occurred (i.e., setting), what would you see?" "Why do you say so?"
6. Ask, "What do you feel about this character? This setting? This event? Why?"
7. Ask, "What opinions do you have of this character? Setting? Incident? The way the story was told? Why?"

Book talks encourage children to go beyond a literal retelling of a story. They can be used in concert with a **free response** heuristic to help students discover and shape their responses to literature. A heuristic, by its nature, is any kind of a prompt that stimulates inquiry and speculation.

Engaging in Free Response

Free response encourages active involvement in reading and an integration of children's background knowledge with the selection's meaning. The technique generates a spirited discussion going far beyond the recall of information. Inferential, evaluative, and analytical thinking are the rule when children's free responses are discussed (Santa, Dailey, and Nelson, 1985).

Free response works well with literature selections that generate diversity of opinion as well as emotional reactions from readers. The first time a group of children is guided through free response, they hear a section of a narrative and then stop to respond in writing. Lower-grade students, for example, might be given three minutes to respond in writing, and upper-grade students five minutes. Thinking through the story structure of a particular story is useful in determining where to make the breaks for students to respond.

Mrs. Nowak used a free-response heuristic with her second-grade class with *Thomas' Snowsuit* by Robert Munsch and illustrated by Michael Martchenko. This story is a humorous treatment of power struggles between Thomas, who does not want to wear his new snowsuit, and his mother. The power struggle concerning whether he should wear his snowsuit or not continues with his teacher and the principal at school.

Mrs. Nowak introduced the story to her class by asking if they could recall not wanting to wear some clothing they were supposed to wear. A lively discussion ensued. Then Mrs. Nowak asked what they thought *Thomas' Snowsuit* would be about, and the children had no difficulty predicting that Thomas didn't want to wear his snowsuit. Mrs. Nowak then began reading.

> One day Thomas' mother bought him a nice new brown snowsuit. When Thomas saw that snowsuit, he said, "That is the ugliest thing I have ever seen in my life. If you think I am going to wear that ugly snowsuit, you are crazy!"
>
> Thomas' mother said "We will see about that."
>
> The next day, when it was time to go to school, the mother said, "Thomas, please put on your snowsuit," and Thomas said, "NNNNNO."

Mrs. Nowak stopped reading and asked her students to write down their reactions to what they just heard. She emphasized that "Any thought related to the story is correct; there are no wrong responses." After several segments of reading and responding, Mrs. Nowak led a discussion in which the children shared their free responses. When she asked their reactions to Thomas telling his mother, "NNNNNO," Jeremy said, "He's going to get into trouble!" Sue said, "I wouldn't want to wear an old brown snowsuit, either." To each response, Mrs. Nowak probed, "Why do you think so?" Mrs. Nowak remained impartial, and the children's responses became a catalyst for discussion.

When students are freely responding independently, Santa, Dailey, and Nelson (1985) recommend that teachers develop with their students criteria for free response, which are then displayed in the classroom.

> Things that I like or dislike about a character or event.
>
> Questions about things I do not understand.
>
> Comments about what I think an unfamiliar word might mean.
>
> Events from my life that come to mind as I read.
>
> Situations or events with which I do not agree.
>
> Can I make predictions? What will happen next? Is the author giving me a clue here?

The heuristic situations above prompt students to view reading as a problem-solving activity. As such, free response is easily incorporated into the use of reading journals that help students to explore and clarify their response to text. Various kinds of reading journals, as we explored in Chapter 5, encourage children to solve problems as they respond to meaning during reading. Response journals, in particular, invite children to respond to literature freely and personally. Their responses vary from monitoring understanding to plot and character involvement to literary evaluation.

Exploring Response Options in Literature Journals

Literature journals provide children with the freedom to express their feelings and thoughts about literary texts. The potential for students to do more than summarize the text is omnipresent when they are invited to write freely as they engage in reading. Research on the content of literature journals shows that readers often expand their ways of thinking about a text beyond retelling when they write journal entries or literary letters on a regular basis (Hancock, 1993a and 1993b; Wells, 1993).

Teachers can enhance the variety of reader response by making children aware of the various options for response in a literature journal. As Hancock (1993) explains: "The classroom teacher plays a vital role in the expansion and enrichment of student response to literature. The teacher serves as a catalyst for encouraging exploration [of response options]. . . . Striving to awaken new modes of response within the reader is the responsibility of the teacher in the role of facilitator and response guide" (p. 470).

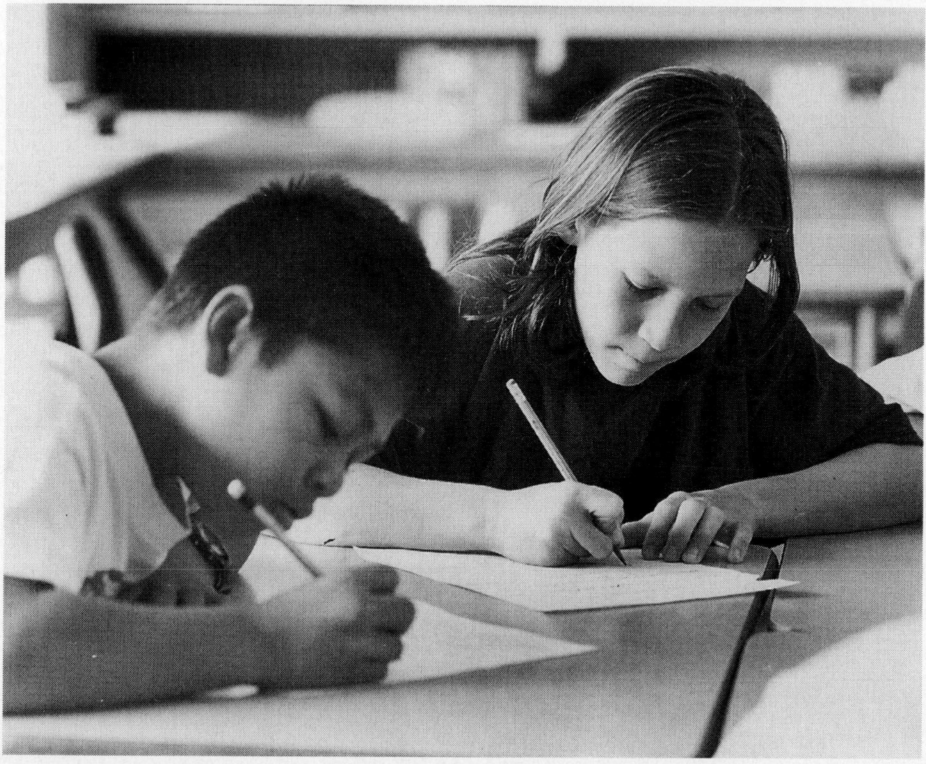

Literature journals give children the freedom to express their thoughts and feelings about literary texts.

Hancock (1993b) explores the journal responses of sixth-grade students to several award winning books: *Hatchet* (Paulsen, 1987), *One-Eyed Cat* (Fox, 1984), *The Great Gilly Hopkins* (Paterson, 1978), and *The Night Swimmers* (Byars, 1980). As a result of her analysis of the content of the students' literature journals, Hancock identified three categories of response: *personal meaning-making; character and plot involvement;* and *literary evaluation.* Table 10.2 outlines eight response options that are available to students within these three categories.

Options for personal meaning-making encourage students to make sense of the emerging plot and characters. Journal entries might reflect the student's attempts to monitor understanding of the story; make inferences about characters; make, validate, modify, or invalidate predictions about the plot; and express wonder or confusion by asking questions or raising uncertainties.

Options for character and plot responses engage students in character identification, character assessment, and personal involvement in the unfolding events of the story. For example, some students will identify strongly with the goals and problems associated with the main character of the story; they put themselves in the character's shoes. As a result, there is a strong sense of empathy expressed by the reader for the character's predicament. Readers will also judge the actions of character within the framework of their own moral standards and value systems. Moreover, students' responses suggest that they become personally involved in the story, expressing satisfaction or dissatisfaction as they become entrenched in the plot.

Finally, readers take on the role of literary critic as they evaluate authors or make comparisons with other books that they have read.

A crucial step in becoming a catalyst for student response is to share guidelines, such as those suggested in Chapter 5, for writing in literature journals. In the guidelines, establish an environment for response by encouraging students to react freely and informally without fear of making mechanical writing errors. Also suggest different response options as outlined in Table 10.2.

In addition, one of the most effective ways to extend response options is to state a dialogue with students in their journals. A teacher's comments in response to a journal entry will help students to reexamine their responses to the text. When responding to journal entries, it is best to be nonjudgmental, encouraging, and thought provoking. Once a supportive comment is written, the teacher may decide to direct a child toward an unexplored area of response. Hancock (1993a) shows how Michael wrote many responses (about 40 percent) relating why he did or did not like the book he was reading. He was mainly using his journal as a place to express his *literary evaluations.* Here is one such entry:

> This is getting real boring because the author is writing so much about one thing. The author keeps going back to the same thing "Mistakes" this is getting boring (p. 472).

His teacher wrote back the following comments:

> I really appreciate your efforts to critique *Hatchet.* It seems that you are a bit disillusioned with some of Brian's actions. You've been attributing that dissatisfaction to the author. Have you thought of sharing your advice with Brian?

● TABLE 10.2

Response Options for Literature Journals

Response Option	Example
Personal Meaning-Making	
Monitoring understanding	In this story, Brian has divorced parents. (*Hatchet*) Ned's really taking the gun being put away really hard. (*One-Eyed Cat*) Oh, now I get it. The door is too heavy for the animals to open. (*Hatchet*) These past few pages show how one lie can lead to a whole series of lies. (*One-Eyed Cat*)
Making inferences	I think Gilly is jealous of W.E. because Trotter loves him. (*The Great Gilly Hopkins*) Brian must be very very hungry to eat a raw egg. (*Hatchet*) Ned probably doesn't mean he wants the cat to die. (*One-Eyed Cat*) Retta seems a little like Gilly Hopkins—rebellious and different. (*The Night Swimmers*)
Making predictions	I think the Secret was his mom's dating another man. (*Hatchet*) I was right about the Secret! (*Hatchet*) I bet Gilly's mother won't show up. (*The Great Gilly Hopkins*) I didn't think she'd steal the money. (*The Great Gilly Hopkins*)
Expressing wonder or confusion	I wonder if Gilly is so mean because she wasn't brought up by her own mother. (*The Great Gilly Hopkins*) The author is telling so many things . . . I got lost on p. 28. (*Hatchet*) Is that cat supposed to be playing the role of some sort of sign? (*One-Eyed Cat*) Bowlwater plant? Are these people really cheap or what? TV Ping Pong? (*The Night Swimmers*)

(*continued*)

TABLE 10.2 *(continued)*

Response Option	Example
Character and Plot Involvement	
Character identification	If I were Ned, I'd want to get the thought out of my head. (*One-Eyed Cat*) Poor Gilly. I guess that's the way it is if you're a foster kid. (*The Great Gilly Hopkins*) Johnny is like my brother. Roy is like my sister. I'm like Retta, not so bossy. (*The Night Swimmers*) He shouldn't waste time waiting for the searchers he should get food. (*Hatchet*)
Character assessment	Brian is stupid for ripping a $20 bill. (*Hatchet*) It's really mean of Gilly to use W.E. in a plan to run away. (*The Great Gilly Hopkins*) I don't think I like Mrs. Scallop. She is sort of mean and has crazy ideas like that Ned's mother got sick because Ned was born. (*One-Eyed Cat*) Brian is getting better and having less self-pity on himself. (*Hatchet*)
Story involvement	Eyes rolling back in his head until it is white showing. How gross! (*Hatchet*) The scenery sounds so pretty. (*One-Eyed Cat*) I wish Ned hadn't shot that poor cat. He did though. (*One-Eyed Cat*) I can't wait to get on with my reading. I hope Shorty asks Brendelle to marry him. (*The Night Swimmers*)
Literary Evaluation	
Literary criticism	These were boring pages because all they talked about were fish. (*Hatchet*) I don't think the author should have Gilly use swear words. (*The Great Gilly Hopkins*) I like this author because she has some suspense like the spy. (*The Night Swimmers*) This is fun reading this part because it's like *My Side of the Mountain.* (*Hatchet*)

Based on research by Marjorie R. Hancock, "Exploring and Extending Personal Response Through Literature Journals," *The Reading Teacher,* 46: 6 (1993) 466–474.

> Although he can't really hear you, your suggestions for plot changes may be directed to the main character as well as to the author. You may even find your involvement in the book will increase if you feel you can talk to Brian. Give this a try and see if you feel comfortable with this mode of response (p. 472).

Interactive comments such as these help students to refocus and redirect their responses to a literary text; they pave the way to personal meaning-making.

SUMMARY

Capturing children's interest and bringing them together in a literate community where they can be immersed in books, is a top priority goal of most reading and language arts teachers. In this chapter we have offered a variety of ways for teachers to develop students who will choose to read.

As children learn to work together in a community of readers and writers, they talk over their experiences with books and recommend books to each other. Teachers, in turn, facilitate an environment supportive of literature by carefully structuring the classroom, selecting a collection of books, and creating settings and predictable routines. Literature-based reading programs, hooking students on books, story telling, classroom libraries, and readers' theater all assist children in reading more both in and out of the classroom.

Organizing for literature-based instruction revolves around: (1) studies of core books (a collection at each grade level judged to be age appropriate and of high quality); (2) literature units (around a theme); (3) literature circles (which lend themselves to the study of multicultural literature); and (4) reading workshops (integrating language arts and literature in responding and sharing).

Finally, we explored strategies for responding to literature, such as book talks and response journals, when encourage children to extend their individual thoughts and feelings about books they read through a variety of response options.

TEACHER-ACTION RESEARCHER

1. Think of a child or adolescent whom you would characterize as an avid reader. (Avid readers are enthusiastic about books, empathize with characters, and talk about books with their friends, sharing their reactions and feelings.) Develop a profile of the avid reader you selected. Describe how this child or adolescent exhibits behaviors associated with avid readers. Discuss ways in which you could help this reader further develop these habits and behaviors.

2. Interview several elementary- or middle-school librarians or media-center directors. In what ways do they support the reading development of children and assist the classroom teacher? Compile their ideas, summarizing them, and report your findings to the class.

3. Work with a group of children and guide them in dramatizing a story after they have read it or heard it read aloud. The selection could be from either a basal reader or a trade book.
4. Collaborate with a classroom teacher to set up a book display that would interest children in reading. Decide on a general theme and introduce the children to books related to that theme. Observe what happens and make notes on the experience. If possible, return to the classroom in a week to observe during language-arts time. Talk with the teacher about the ways the students have used the book display.
5. Prepare a bibliography of children's literature that would be appropriate for a particular grade level's classroom library. Use the school librarian, classroom teachers' recommendations, and bibliographies from journals such as *Language Arts* and *The Reading Teacher* as resources. What books would be the core of the library? What books could be added over time? Include annotation that would explain why each book was chosen. For example, which books would be useful in content area instruction? Which books would help teach sound-symbol correspondence?

KEY TERMS

literature-based reading program
community of readers
readers' theatre
dialogue journals
core books
literature units
reading workshop
literature circles
reader-response theory
book talks
free response
literature journals

CHAPTER 11

Basal Readers and Instructional Materials

BETWEEN THE LINES

In this chapter you will discover:

- **The history of basal reading programs.**
- **What the authors of three major reading programs have to say about trends of the 1990s, such as literature-based instruction.**
- **An overview of the terminology, components, and characteristics of programs.**
- **How types of instructional decisions and reading materials relate to belief systems.**

"See Dick wave bye-bye. See Jane wave bye-bye. See Dick and Jane walk hand in hand into the sunset. Yes, our little friends, Dick and Jane, are gone." This quote, taken from an article in the *Chicago Sun Times* (Currie, 1993) about the demise of basal reading books was premature. As Mark Twain said, "Reports of my death are greatly exaggerated." Basal readers are not disappearing, but they are changing rather significantly. While children's literature and information-type books have become exceedingly popular and are helping many children and teachers discover the rewards of reading, the basal reading program is still the material that is most widely used for reading instruction in this country. Elementary students at all grade levels read stories from readers and/or anthologies and write in the accompanying workbooks and/or journals.

While the Dick and Jane of our childhood are no longer present, new basal reading program characters, characteristics, and trends are still important parts of understanding and teaching reading. Basal reading programs are indeed what many children and parents think about when they think of reading instruction. And, many teachers who are becoming increasingly knowledgeable, comfortable, and adept at integrating trade books (fact and fiction) into the overall reading program are also using basal readers on a daily basis. Teachers with implicit and explicit theories about reading make hundreds of decisions daily about reading instruction in their classrooms. Many of these decisions require teachers to be familiar with basal readers.

In spite of continued popular support for teacher-directed, basal reader textbooks as the traditional method of teaching reading by teachers and administrators, there is a growing unease among many teachers who feel required to use them. Unfortunately, "because of highly resistant forces and well-established traditions, teachers have sometimes come to disregard their own feelings, intuitions, and expertise as professionals" (Reutzel and Cooter, 1992, p. 4). Teachers then, need to understand basal reading programs—how they can work in the classroom—while developing a perspective about their use.

Knowing and understanding how these sets of materials can support students' literacy development is essential for teachers, given the prominence of basals in our schools. Teachers need to judge the educational opportunities which basals do or do not offer and be able to look for other reading and skill activities without fear of reprisal and without undue concern about students' performance on standardized tests. Furthermore, teachers need to recognize options for reorganizing and consolidating basal offerings (Wepner and Feeley, 1993).

In order to do this, teachers will need assistance in these areas: (1) judging what reading material should be assigned and when supplementary materials are needed; (2) determining which basal teachers' guide suggestions should be omitted, followed, or modified; and (3) evaluating student responses to questions (Barr & Sadow, 1989).

In this chapter we examine basal reading programs and the instructional concepts that have come to be associated with them. How long have basal readers been used in classrooms? How have they changed over the years? The basal reading programs published today are comprehensive; they are based on information about new developments in education as well as the changing population in the schools. It is essential to study their rationale, organization, components, and lesson frameworks. Most importantly, it is necessary to reflect on how one's beliefs about reading can help teachers plan or modify lessons in the basal program.

While systematic instruction in basals based on identified goals and objectives can be helpful, teachers do not necessarily need to follow the basal in a prescribed, lockstep fashion with every child learning in a specific order (Spiegel, 1992). Teachers do need to create the necessary conditions to satisfy the demands of their students.

Ironically, the pervasive use of basal readers has not put an end to the problem of insufficient supplementary materials. Principals purchase a reading program and sometimes discover they don't have enough materials for students who want to *read.* This reveals two basic lessons regarding materials for reading instruction: (1) supplementary materials are perceived as important to the reading program; and (2) what some teachers think of as supplemental may be the heart of instruction to other teachers, and vice versa.

Hence, we devote the last section of this chapter to an analysis of instructional materials, beginning with the *types* of materials available. We will determine how different types of materials correspond to our *belief systems.* Several ways of evaluating and selecting commercial materials for classroom use will be suggested. Finally, we'll look into the development of successful teacher-made materials.

Historical Background

Young newspaper readers in the greater Cleveland area were treated to a historical tour of their basal reading books in a news article written especially for elementary-age students and featuring "McGuffey and His Readers." Pictures of William McGuffey, his birthplace, and his writing desk accompanied an actual page reproduction with a story about Bess and her two goats from Lesson XXXIII in the *McGuffey Primer,* the very first book in a series used for reading instruction.

Here's how basal readers were described in the news article so that children could understand what they are all about.

> There are many different kinds of basal texts.
>
> How and when words are introduced are carefully planned by experts.
>
> The books come in a series.
>
> The words and stories get longer and harder as the child moves from one level to the next.

Moreover, children were informed that McGuffey first published his series in 1836, and that the readers began with the *Primer* and ended with the *Sixth Reader.* As far as the content of the basal readers was concerned, stories were about everyday life and the rewards of good behavior. Does the content sound somewhat familiar? It should. According to a study by Aaron and Anderson (1981), a remarkable number of values appearing in the readers of the early 1900s appear in today's basals. Although the stories may have changed, Aaron and Anderson acknowledge that "the same virtues are there waiting to be taught" (p. 312).

Just as the young Cleveland readers found insightful differences and similarities between their reading material today and the *McGuffey Readers,* teachers also benefit from such comparisons. A page from an 1878 reader is shown in (Figure 11.1).

1683: A Strong Bottom-Up Approach

The New England Primer, published for American colonists in the late 1600s, followed a strong bottom-up model of instruction. The alphabet was taught first; then vowels, consonants, double letters, italics, capitals, syllables, and so on were presented for instruction in that order. There was, however, no such thing as a controlled vocabulary. Words were not introduced systematically in basal readers until the mid-1800s. Colonial children might meet anywhere from twenty to one hundred new words on one page!

By the mid-1800s, the word method, silent reading, and reading to get information from content were introduced in basals. The classics, fairy tales, and literature by American authors became the first supplementary reading materials. Colored pictures, attention

28 SECOND READER.

LESSON XV.

drĕss	hēard	ŭn′-cle	her-sĕlf′
knīfe	wĭshed	lăd′-der	stō′-ries
wrŏng	strānge	fĭn′-ger	lo͝ok′-ing

WILLIE'S STORY.

One day, when Willie had been reading in his new book, his mother wished him to tell her what he had read in it, and Willie said:

"I read about a little girl who wanted to do just as she liked for one whole day.

"Her mother said she could. So the little girl cut her own bread and butter; but she let the knife slip, and cut her finger.

"Then she ate so much candy that she made herself sick. Then she put on her prettiest dress to play in the garden, and tore it.

"And then she went up a ladder, which her mother never would let her climb, and when she was up very high she heard a noise in the garden.

SECOND READER. 29

"It was the dog barking at a strange cat, mamma; and while the little girl was looking around to see what it was, she put her foot on the wrong part of the ladder.

"I mean, mamma, she only put her toe on the round; so her foot slipped, and she fell, and was almost killed.

"That was the end of her day of doing just as she liked."

Write a sentence having in it the word knife.
Write a sentence having in it the word ladder.

● **FIGURE 11.1** Sample page from *The Appelton Reader* (1878)

to children's interests, and the teacher's manual all appeared by the 1920s. It was then that the work pad was used for seatwork and skills practice in grades one through three.

Basal Readers as We Knew Them

The reading series used in schools in the 1990s are a far cry, both in appearance and substance, from the first readers. Nevertheless, current readers retain many features that were considered at one time or another innovative. Basal reading series have grown noticeably in size and in price. While not necessarily prescribing the bottom-up teaching approach that was used in the 1600s, today's teacher's manual presents a much more serious dilemma for classroom teachers: It often purports to include everything that any teacher will ever need to teach reading.

Publishing companies began to expand and add many new components or features to their basal reading programs around 1925. The preprimer, for example, was added to the basal program to introduce beginning readers to the series and build a beginning reading vocabulary (i.e., words recognized at sight). Inside illustrations and outside covers also became increasingly colorful. Word lists such as Thorndike's became the standard for choosing readers' vocabulary.

As the major author for the Scott, Foresman program, William S. Gray was probably responsible for much of the structure associated with the reading instruction that we experienced as children. Workbooks accompanied our reader. First, we worked on skills; then we read for enjoyment. Each book had a different title and much of the story content was supposed to be "realistic" narrative. Whether it was, or is, realistic content is an issue publishers and classroom teachers continue to deal with in this decade.

As the concept of reading readiness became more popular, teacher's manuals contained more detail and readiness books provided opportunities to practice prerequisite skills. One preprimer multiplied to two, three, or even four preprimers.

Instruction in basal reading programs depended in part on strict adherence to the scope and sequence of reading skills (see Figure 11.2 for a sample from a 1993 program). This terminology evolved from the 1948 *Ginn Basic Reader's* objective which was to provide a *vertical* arrangement of skill development and to ensure continuity in skill development (Smith, 1965, p. 285). Teacher's editions were keyed to the children's books, and diagnostic and achievement tests such as those in the *Sheldon Basic Reading Series* were developed. Clearly, basal reading programs had become more sophisticated and, to many teachers, *unwieldy*. How would they manage the basal reading program?

Until the 1960s, books in reading series were arranged according to grade placement. Grades turned into levels (anywhere from fifteen to twenty) or, as it became known, the management system. By the 1970s, teachers and curriculum committees in general sought clarification about levels in relation to grades. As a result, publishers used the term *level* and cross-referenced this with its traditional grade equivalent. In Table 11.1 there is a listing of the various texts, by level, from Houghton Mifflin's *The Literature Experience* (1991).

As can be seen in Table 11.1, there is sometimes more than one level (and book) per grade. To help decide the book level for pupils entering the program guidelines were suggested. These included Pupil placement tests and an informal tryout of a book using a one-hundred-word selection.

Management systems became necessary when publishers significantly overhauled their reading series in the 1970s. The majority of textbook publishers added new components, particularly in the area of assessment, such as pre- and postskill tests, section tests, and end-of-book tests.

The Dick, Jerry, Jane, and Alice that some of us grew up with in the 1950s, 1960s, or 1970s are now part of the past. Today's basal is often labeled literature-based, a term that has taken hold in the nineties.

HBJ Treasury of Literature
Scope and Sequence

Grade/Level	1–1	1–2	1–3	1–4	1–5	1–6	2	3	4	5	6	7	8
STRATEGIC READING													
Active Reading Strategies													
Read Fiction (Narrative Text)													
Read Nonfiction (Expository Text)													
Analyze Details													
Synthesize Ideas/Information													
Make Inferences													
Decoding Strategy: Use phonetic/structural analysis plus context to unlock pronunciation.													
Vocabulary Strategy: Use phonetic/structural/contextual clues to determine meanings.													
Use Self-Assessment Strategies													
COMPREHENSION													
Cause-Effect							●	●	●	●	●	●	●
Classify/Categorize		●					●						
Compare and Contrast								●	●	●	●	●	●
Draw Conclusions							●	●	●	●	●	●	●
Fact-Fantasy/Nonfact				●			●						
Author's Purpose											●	●	●
Author's Viewpoint											●	●	●
Fact-Opinion								●	●	●	●	●	●
Main Idea (Global Meaning)/Details						●	●	●	●	●	●	●	●
Make Generalizations											●	●	●
Make Judgments											●	●	●
Paraphrase								●	●	●	●		
Make Predictions					●		●	●	●	●	●	●	●
Referents													
Sequence			●				●	●	●	●	●	●	●
Summarize								●	●	●	●	●	●
VOCABULARY													
Key Words/Selection Vocabulary	●	●	●	●	●	●	●	●	●	●	●	●	●
Synonyms/Antonyms													
Multiple-Meaning Words											●	●	●
Homophones/Homographs													
Context Clues					●		●	●	●	●	●	●	●
Vocabulary Strategy: Use phonetic/structural/contextual clues to determine meanings.													
Analogies													
Connotation/Denotation													
Glossary													
Dictionary (for Word Meaning)								●	●	●	●	●	●
DECODING													
Phonics													
Initial/Medial/Final Consonants	●	●	●	●									
Phonograms													
Short Vowels/Long Vowels		●	●	●	●	●							
Consonant Clusters/Digraphs (Initial/Final)			●	●	●	●							
R-Controlled Vowels							●						
Vowel Diphthongs/Vowel Digraphs/Variant Vowels							●						
Schwa													
Decoding Stragegy: Use phonetic/structural analysis plus context to unlock pronunciation.													
Structural Analysis													
Inflected Forms (With Verbs), With and Without Spelling Changes		●	●	●	●	●	●						
Possessives, Comparatives, Superlatives													
Contractions			●	●									
Compound Words													
Syllabication													
Suffixes/Prefixes							●	●	●	●	●	●	●
Greek and Latin Roots									●	●	●	●	●

● **FIGURE 11.2** Program scope and sequence chart

● TABLE 11.1

Houghton Mifflin Reading Texts (1991)

BOOK/LEVEL	
Level K1	*Level 2+*
ALL ABOUT ME	COME ONE, COME ALL
Level K2	*Level 3*
LET'S BE FRIENDS	JUST LISTEN
Level A	*Level 3+*
TOO BIG	GOLDEN THREADS
Level B	*Level 4*
DREAM A STORY	DINOSAURING
Level C	*Level 5*
BEARS DON'T GO TO SCHOOL	FAST AS THE WIND
Level 1	*Level 6*
WITH A CRASH AND A BANG!	BEYOND THE REEF
Level 1+	*Level 7*
BOOKWORM	BRIGHT GLORY
Level 2	*Level 8*
SILLY THINGS HAPPEN	WORLDS APART

Source: From *The Literature Experience,* Teachers' Edition, 1991, Houghton Mifflin Company.

Basal Programs of the Nineties

Trends that are characteristic of basal readers developed and used in the 1990s are found in most reading programs sold by various publishers. An increase in instruction designed to help children become aware of and control their own comprehension process is one such trend. More strategy lessons as compared to isolated skill instruction followed by practice is another major trend. Also, more programs are organized thematically and include children's literature, stories by well-known children's authors, and non-fiction selections.

What better way to investigate these trends than to talk with the senior authors of three of the major basal reading programs today? Following in Box 11.1 are the conversations that we had with Dr. Patricia Edwards, Dr. Jeanne Paratore, and Dr. Lyndon Searfoss at the 1993 Annual Convention of the International Reading Association in San Antonio, Texas.

Most reading series on the market today attempt to satisfy every consumer's appetite when it comes to reading instruction. In order to do that, publishing companies, as the authors quoted in Box 11.1 say, take great care to include certain major components.

Before we look closer at basal reading series and discuss their major components, we should understand several concepts germane to basal instruction.

The terms in Box 11.2 will vary from one series to the next, but it is safe to say that certain components will be found in most programs. A brief overview of some of the major components that are part of almost every basal series follows.

1. *The readiness program.* Big books and workbooks are designed to introduce and develop basic concepts in language, letter-sound relationships, sense of context, following directions, and listening comprehension. Both the HBJ and Scott Foresman (1993) kindergarten programs are thematically organized and include a variety of support materials.

   The HBJ kindergarten program in the Treasury of Literature (1993) series includes: Big books, little big books, theme books, picture books, a readaloud anthology, literature posters, literature and music cassettes, picture/word cards, an assessment package, and a teacher's edition.

2. *Beginning Reading.* New basic sight words are introduced; high-frequency sight words accumulate. Vocabulary and readability are controlled, and experience charts are used to help word recognition. Traditionally, an eclectic phonics approach is favored (e.g., sight words, phonic analysis, context analysis, structural analysis). As many as six levels may be completed by children at the end of the first grade.

3. W*orld Identification Strand.* Skill lessons are provided to teach sight vocabulary and phonics, structural analysis, and the use of context. Students are exposed to new skills, systematically and sequentially, and are tested on them for mastery. Skills may then be retaught and reinforced through additional skill exercises. Some basals, however, do *not* connect the topics of stories in the readers with the word-identification program.

4. *Comprehension Strand.* Beginning at the early levels, most basal series set specific objectives for comprehension instruction. There are numerous comprehension questions, usually following a routine that continues throughout the book. Questions typically inquire into purpose, motives and acts of main characters, recall of details, and vocabulary usage. There is an effort to incorporate three levels or types of comprehension, from literal to interpretive to critical (especially in the intermediate and upper levels). This decade has brought an increase in questions that encourage prediction making.

● BOX 11.1

A Conversation With Three Authors

Jo Anne Vacca spoke with three authors, Patricia A. Edwards, Jeanne R. Paratore, and Lyndon W. Searfoss, about contemporary issues in basal reading programs. Edwards, a professor at Michigan State University, is an author with the ScottForesman Reading Series. Paratore is the director of the Center for the Assessment and Design of Learning/Intergenerational Literacy Project at Boston University and an author with the Silver Burdett and Ginn Reading Series. Searfoss is a professor at Arizona State University and an author with the D.C. Heath and Company Reading Series.

Vacca: *Why did you become a basal author? What particular contribution do you make?*

Edwards: In the past, basal reading materials have addressed the home-school component in a hit or miss fashion. Teachers need to look through the lenses of children and include materials that represent multiple home environments. I stress the importance of finding an answer to a question like "when you're teaching in somebody else's village, what do you need to know?"

Patricia Edwards. . . *When you're teaching in somebody else's village, what do you need to know?*

(continued)

BOX 11.1 *(continued)*

Edwards: Basals have tried to incorporate authentic literature which reflects the multiple student populations. Basal companies have listened to the whole language movement. Entertaining is not teaching. There is a continuing need for balancing. Teachers need control of theory in order to be decision makers. This has been emphasized in the last five years.

Vacca: *A recent criticism is that the packaging and terminology of basal materials have changed, especially in relation to whole language, but the contents have not. How valid is this criticism?*

Searfoss: This criticism is not valid. If you watch teachers teach and students learn in today's classrooms, with a basal based on literature, you do not see or hear the same dialogue you heard ten years ago. There is interaction between and among teachers and students, cooperative learning, and reading and writing for genuine purposes. Coupled with strategy instruction that shows kids how to *use* skills, we have a new day for the basal in classrooms.

Edwards: Newly-trained teachers are not prepared to make all decisions about instruction. They need structure. Young teachers graduating from college with approximately three courses in reading and language arts need assistance when they are first teaching. They typically have been placed in difficult situations. For example, a new first-grade teacher whom I had worked with was having tremendous difficulty. I went to her school and met with her principal and supervisor saying, "You need to give Sarah some support." Basal instruction is one way to provide support for teachers who can then make connections.

Paratore: I don't believe that it is at all valid. There have been some important changes, as outlined above, driven by improved understandings about literacy learning. The shift to unedited text; the availability and integration of trade books with the anthology; emphasis on coreading and rereading of text and emphasis on teacher and student choices are changes in both materials and in practices that grow out of what some have termed the whole language movement. Other aspects long associated with basal reading programs remain. We have intentionally and deliberately kept a strong instructional component in the basal reading program in both phonics and comprehension because of the belief among the team of authors that at least some children will fail to become successful readers without such instruction.

(continued)

Searfoss: The biggest change in basal materials is represented by respect for teacher as decision-maker. Given an array of choices, how do teachers make decisions? Thematic units, for example, are great but teachers who have only several hours of built in in-service a year have very little time to plan them. For example, there is a need to learn how to incorporate reading and writing into instruction across the curriculum. Well-written teachers' manuals have traditionally been the only in-service many teachers receive in a new reading program.

Lyndon Searfoss. . . *We have a new day for the basal in classrooms.*

Paratore: There have been several important changes over the last five years: (1) a shift from edited to unedited literature; (2) integration of language arts, particularly writing; (3) an emphasis on teacher and student choices; and (4) numerous changes in assessment including the inclusion of portfolios and process-based tests. Although it's fair to say that none of these changes has been complete or fully achieved, in each there have been important steps forward.

(continued)

● **BOX 11.1** *(continued)*

Edwards: Basals have tried to incorporate authentic literature which reflects the multiple student populations. Basal companies have listened to the whole language movement. Entertaining is not teaching. There is a continuing need for balancing. Teachers need control of theory in order to be decision makers. This has been emphasized in the last five years.

Vacca: *A recent criticism is that the packaging and terminology of basal materials have changed, especially in relation to whole language, but the contents have not. How valid is this criticism?*

Searfoss: This criticism is not valid. If you watch teachers teach and students learn in today's classrooms, with a basal based on literature, you do not see or hear the same dialogue you heard ten years ago. There is interaction between and among teachers and students, cooperative learning, and reading and writing for genuine purposes. Coupled with strategy instruction that shows kids how to *use* skills, we have a new day for the basal in classrooms.

Edwards: Newly-trained teachers are not prepared to make all decisions about instruction. They need structure. Young teachers graduating from college with approximately three courses in reading and language arts need assistance when they are first teaching. They typically have been placed in difficult situations. For example, a new first-grade teacher whom I had worked with was having tremendous difficulty. I went to her school and met with her principal and supervisor saying, "You need to give Sarah some support." Basal instruction is one way to provide support for teachers who can then make connections.

Paratore: I don't believe that it is at all valid. There have been some important changes, as outlined above, driven by improved understandings about literacy learning. The shift to unedited text; the availability and integration of trade books with the anthology; emphasis on coreading and rereading of text and emphasis on teacher and student choices are changes in both materials and in practices that grow out of what some have termed the whole language movement. Other aspects long associated with basal reading programs remain. We have intentionally and deliberately kept a strong instructional component in the basal reading program in both phonics and comprehension because of the belief among the team of authors that at least some children will fail to become successful readers without such instruction.

(continued)

Vacca: *What is the most important thing a preservice or beginning teacher needs to know about basal instruction?*

Paratore: Perhaps one of the greatest misconceptions about basal readers is that they represent *the* reading program. I don't believe that's the case. Instead, I view the basal as one component of a total program. A beginning teacher should come to his or her classroom with a basic instructional plan in mind and view the basal reader as one means for operationalizing that plan. As she or he pages through the many suggestions in the teacher's editions, decisions must be made about which parts of the lesson plan fit into the teacher's instructional design, and which parts do not; what pieces meet the needs of particular students and which ones do not; which elements link particularly well to the focus in other areas of the curriculum and so on. The strength of the basal reading program is in its range of options. The weakness is in the suggestion that everything in the teacher's edition is of equal importance for every child.

Edwards: Don't take any one piece of material as "The Bible." Look at the plan, the structure provided, the scope, and sequence. Then, think about your region of the country, your students. Draw from literature that would best fit their needs. You can adapt, reconstruct for localized needs. Ask, "What do I need to know?"

Searfoss: New teachers need a good background in children's and adolescent literatures. To expect teachers to use literature to drive instruction is realistic; to ask teachers with limited knowledge of literature for children and adolescents to do so is unrealistic.

Vacca: *What is the most important thing an experienced teacher needs to know about basal instruction?*

Paratore: I'm not sure it's different. It seems that years ago teachers were taught to use the basal reader in a linear fashion, going from lesson to lesson and task to task. They are no longer planned to be used in that way. Teachers, experienced and new, need to be flexible in their use of a basal reading program, using it when appropriate, but choosing from other sources to build a diverse and effective program.

Searfoss: Experienced teachers, some of whom are operating on 20–25 years of experience, were certified without a course in children's literature. They also may not have access to libraries on site or near their schools. Therefore, they would find it difficult to implement literature-based series.

(continued)

● **BOX 11.1** *(continued)*

Edwards: A veteran teacher has had numerous experiences; therefore, I would suggest doing a profile of your experiences with basal reading materials. Summarize the positive and negative experiences. Experienced teachers need to update. Keep what you know and, like the beginning teacher, look at who is in your classroom. Keep one foot in the door and one foot in the future.

Vacca: *How effective are basal materials in providing a range of materials suitable for culturally diverse populations in schools?*

Edwards: Basal companies have tried to select good literature and form authoring teams to incorporate a wide range of literature and characters. Yet, some materials still miss the mark and don't really appeal to minority children. For too long, multicultural education has focused on artifacts. We need a lens to enable us to learn things about other people's culture.

Searfoss: In current classrooms using basal materials, children are exposed to a broader range of materials than in some classrooms where the reading materials are entirely teacher-selected. Multicultural children's literature is not something most teachers are familiar with. They may even tend to avoid this responsibility if it is placed entirely in their hands. The next wave of basals will need an even better array of resources to provide for better exposure to a broader range of materials.

Paratore: This can be a strength of a basal reader. It is important that all children, minority and majority, read about people who represent their cultures and their understandings. In a good basal reading program, a systematic and deliberate effort has been made to represent the full range of cultural and linguistic groups represented in our classrooms and in our communities.

5. *Literature.* Basal reading programs are now available that are literature-based, that is, the majority of the stories in each reader are excerpted or adapted from actual children's literature or are specially written by popular children's authors for inclusion in the student anthologies. The quality of the adaptations varies, however. A welcome trend is the availability of supplemental classroom libraries, which serve an important role in helping children learn the value of reading real literature beyond the basal selections. As the tradebooks offered by the basal publishers can be expensive, Wepner and Feeley (1993) suggest teachers supplement their classroom libraries with offer-

● BOX 11.2

The Language of Basal Instruction

CODE EMPHASIS The emphasis of programs from the beginning is on decoding. The content and sequence in teaching sound-symbol correspondence is controlled so children can learn quickly how to transform unfamiliar printed words into speech.

CLASSROOM LIBRARIES Supplemental children's literature books that are related by theme or genre to the stories in the student anthologies and are offered in addition to anthologies.

COMPUTER MANAGEMENT SYSTEM Systems that allow teachers to use microcomputers to score tests, store skill-progress information, and prepare status reports for reading groups, classes, or grade levels.

CONTINUOUS PROGRESS Teachers are encouraged to teach students at their reading levels, not necessarily at their grade levels. The instructional materials in a series are prepared for about 17 to 20 levels ranging from readiness materials in kindergarten and first grade to advanced reading materials in seventh and eighth grades. Instead of using one reader in each grade, students may be working in different readers at different levels in the same classroom.

CONTROLLED VOCABULARY The number of "new" words that students encounter in each reading lesson is controlled. Three ways in which publishing companies control vocabulary in their reading program are: (1) Many high-interest words are used first, followed by the introduction of more abstract words; (2) high-frequency words appear in the beginning, with low-frequency words gradually inserted in the text; and (3) words that follow regular spelling patterns are used first, then words with some irregular spelling patterns are used. Words introduced in lower-level readers are repeated often in subsequent readers.

CRITERION-REFERENCED TESTS Informal tests devised by either the publishing company or teacher to measure individual student attainment in skills associated with phonics, vocabulary, and comprehension. The teacher sets the criterion (e.g., 8/10) for adequate performance. The purpose is to assess a reader's performance, regardless of how that performance compares to others taking the same test.

(continued)

● **BOX 11.2** *(continued)*

EXTENSION OR INTEGRATING ACROSS THE CURRICULUM	After the story is read and the main parts of the suggested lesson framework are completed, many teachers continue the lesson by using additional activities. Art, music, and writing are catalysts to extend ideas and concepts initiated during the lesson. Questioning at the interpretive and applied levels extends comprehension through group discussion.
INFORMAL ASSESSMENT OPPORTUNITIES/ NOTES	Suggestions in the teacher's manual for noticing children's strengths and weaknesses as they read and write. Some go so far as to recommend a teachable moment.
INSTRUCTIONAL AIDS	Charts, workbooks, ditto masters, skill packs, cards, game boxes, and so on are available at various levels of reading series. They are intended to help teachers who are too busy to make their own instructional devices.
KINDERGARTEN PROGRAM	Literature-based basal program's first level for beginning or nonreaders. Includes big books, individual big books, a readaloud anthology. (Most of the readiness programs are now labeled *K*).
LEVELS	Each level provides a sequential arrangement of student books (readers), teacher's editions, and ancillary materials and is built upon those that come before it; each corresponds to grade levels. This ensures more than one book for some grade levels and makes continuous progress possible. By grade four, most literature-based series have only one level (book) per grade.
LITERATURE-BASED READING PROGRAMS	Basal series that use selections from children's literature that may or may not have been revised to control readability. Most try to include activities that reflect current best practice based on research including cooperative learning, writing process, and modeling comprehension strategies.

(continued)

MANAGEMENT	The testing program provides teachers with a system to arrange or manage the placement of pupils in different levels of the program. Also initial placement tests for "move-ins" are provided. Tests also help identify skills that students need to acquire or strengthen. In addition, tests may indicate that students have mastered skills at one level and should proceed to the next level. Management combines two major elements: behavioral objectives and criterion-referenced tests.
MEANING EMPHASIS	Programs in which reading is taught as a communication process rather than as a series of subskills. They emphasize comprehension more than decoding skills, providing for a variety of word identification methods in different combinations. Meaningfulness of the story content, meaningful ways for children to respond, and integration of language arts activities are some obvious features of this emphasis.
PRIMER	Commonly used in the first grade, this is the book given to children before their first readers. This term is now rarely used.
READERS'/ WRITERS' JOURNALS OR NOTEBOOKS	Children practice reading and phonics skills in workbooks that supplement lessons in the text with independent activities. Writer's journals may vary, but most ask comprehension questions rather than act as guides for response.
READING PROGRESS CARDS/RUNNING RECORDS	Provide an informal assessment record, an individualized record-keeping system to track a student's progress through the entire reading program.
REINFORCEMENT	To ensure that skills have been learned, exercises involving similar and contrasting examples are used to reinforce the learning. This reteaching cycle includes the use of extension activities.
SCOPE AND SEQUENCE	This refers to the general plan in basal reading programs for the introduction of skills in a sequential or vertical arrangement and with expanding or horizontally conceptualized reinforcement. Students move up through the levels and across within each level (see Figure 11.2).

(continued)

● **BOX 11.2** *(continued)*

SKILL BUILDING	Skills (e.g., basic sight vocabulary, conceptual development, listening facility, comprehension) are not presented only once. They are introduced at one level, then repeated and reinforced at subsequent levels with increasing depth. Instruction begins with simpler subskills and follows this design: introduction of a skill, reinforcement of the skill, and review of the skill.
SKILL MAINTENANCE	Recently learned skills are reviewed as necessary to form the base for new learning to occur.
STRANDS	Areas of skills that are developed at increasingly higher levels throughout the program are grouped into strands. Some popular strands of instruction are word identification, vocabulary development, comprehension, reading-study skills, and language arts.
VOCABULARY DEVELOPMENT	To assist them in becoming skillful readers, teachers work to increase students' vocabularies. In order to develop a large number of sight words, new words are introduced, repeated often in the text selections, and more new words are introduced. Phonics and other word analysis skills and meaning-getting strategies using context are employed to continue vocabulary development.
WHOLE WORD METHOD	Words, rather than letters or syllables, are the main instructional unit. Teachers work on the recognition of words, not on sounding out the words.
WORKBOOKS	Children practice reading skills in workbooks that supplement lessons in the text with independent activities. Their purpose is to reinforce skills and concepts that teachers have already taught during the lesson framework with the reader.

ings from vendors such as Scholastic and Trumpet Book Clubs as well as the school library.

6. *Language Arts.* Listening, writing, composing, grammar, spelling, punctuation, dictionary work, library work, dramatization, and so forth are found in basal programs. These features sometimes appear in connection with another component; for exam-

ple, a writing assignment accompanies a reading comprehension lesson. Frequently, language arts activities are suggested under enrichment or extension. There may be separate language exercises; language development may also be a separate strand. Many basal series combine reading and language enrichment activities in their upper-level books.

7. *Management.* The systematic instruction of the basal reading program, based on identified goals and objectives, requires systematic assessment in order to determine the students' progress toward meeting those identified goals and objectives (Spiegal, 1992). To this end, basal reading programs offer lesson plans, pacing suggestions, training and in-service programs, informal and formal assessment components, and record-keeping aids.
8. *Assessment.* More and more basal programs offer support for portfolio assessment. The Houghton Mifflin "literature experience" (1991) gives teachers suggestions for types of formal and informal evaluations that can be included in each student's portfolio. Each lesson includes various assessment options, including samples of student journals, writing center assignments, and independent reading logs. As Greer (1992) notes, basal assessments now provide a wider range of question types and response formats; they no longer rely on skills tests as the sole means of evaluation. But the goal of successful assessment is still to inform the teacher's instructional decision making and the students' understandings of their progress toward their own goals.

Characteristics of Basal Readers

More significant than similarities and differences among basal reading programs are the improvements in certain components. The overall physical appearance, literary variety, and reduction of stereotyping deserve special recognition. Other components have become more complex, or thorough, depending on one's viewpoint.

Appearance

Pupils books, anthologies, teacher's editions (often spiral-bound), supplementary paperbacks, journals, workbooks, ditto masters, activity books, self-correcting boxed materials, videos, and phonics picture cards are just some of the physical components now available. Many hard-cover pupil readers are identical in cover design and title to the corresponding supplemental materials at that level.

Illustrations

Illustrations reveal an important growth in the quality of basal reading material. One trend is the use of the actual illustrations as reproduced from the original children's literature selection. Many companies intersperse in-house illustrations with some from original sources. Ginn was one of the first companies to feature real children as characters in the stories with accompanying photographs. First graders could read about Jim and Beth and Ana and Sara and Ken going to visit a book van or taking a trip to Sea World. This is now common practice.

Teachers remain the most important element in terms of critically evaluating and deciding what is appropriate and valuable for their classes to read. When the experience of their culture isn't addressed in the illustrations or text of a basal series, children may not become engaged in meaningful learning. Culturally relevant teaching (Ladson-Billings, 1992) celebrates and builds on the cultural background of students as they move into literacy. Such teaching helps students to critically examine their reading, asking "How does this compare to my experiences? My knowledge? My feelings?" The validity and logic of what we read in school can be assessed in terms of how it fits the values not only of our own beliefs and assumptions, but also of those with different world views from our own.

Stereotyping

The illustrations and content of basal readers have made strides in guarding against stereotyping, tokenism, and life-style oversimplifications. Nevertheless, teachers should continue to be sensitive to these issues as they evaluate and use reading materials, especially basal readers. Some distinctions in terminology are in order.

1. *Stereotyping* is an oversimplified generalization about a particular group, race, or sex, with derogatory implications.
2. *Tokenism* is a minimal, or token, effort to represent minorities. Look for nonwhite characters whose faces look like white ones tinted or colored in.
3. *Life-style oversimplifications* show an unfavorable contrast between minority characters and their setting with an unstated norm of white middle-class suburbia. Look for lack of appropriateness and for exaggerations of reality, such as "primitive" living.

Some studies have shown a distinct improvement in the basal reading programs' depiction of gender roles (Klebacher, 1984; Hitchcock and Tompkins, 1987), Native Americans, Hispanics, and African-Americans (Garcia and Florez-Tighe, 1986; Reyhner, 1986). Yet other studies showed few positive depictions of the elderly (Gutknect, 1991) and no third-grade-level, nonwhite main characters (Reimer, 1992).

Mem Fox (1993), an educator and children's author, warns that books serve to construct our selves as we read them, by presenting us with an image of ourselves. Recently, textbooks written to celebrate the 1492 voyage of Christopher Columbus to the Americas called native peoples "savages." Cultural stereotypes, she notes, are easily and unthinkingly reinforced in even our favorite books. Teachers need to be aware of the politically loaded messages in literature and textbooks so that all students can be affirmed by reading books that are not boring yet celebrate diversity.

Slapin (1992), in an effort to help teachers and students choose books with undistorted views and nonracist histories offers these suggestions: (1) look at how ethnic groups are portrayed in illustrations and in picture books; (2) look for stereotypes; (3) look for loaded words; (4) look for tokenism; (5) look for distortion of history; (6) look at lifestyles; (7) look at dialogue; (8) look for standards of success; (9) look at the role of women; (10) look at the role of elders; (11) look at the authors or illustrator's background. Reimer (1992) suggested that more literature by, rather than about, people of color needs to be made available in classrooms.

Language Style

The style of written language found in basal readers has been an interest of researchers for decades. Ruth Strickland (1962) was among the first to verify that children's command of oral language surpassed the language appearing in their basal readers. Reading and language researchers of the 1980s and 1990s continued to find out more about *basalese,* a pejorative term for the language style used in basal readers.

As more and more basal reading programs attempt to incorporate children's literature in their reading anthologies, the demands of readability (controlled vocabulary and sentence length) can lead to a stilted, unnatural, and bland language known as *basalization* (Goodman, 1988) or *primerese* (Ammon, Simons and Elster, 1990).

Since controlled vocabulary for beginning readers is a hallmark of basal programs, overreliance on pictures, dialogue, and short sentences to carry meaning can lead young readers to picture dependence, hindering reading acquisition (Simons and Elster, 1990). Additionally, primerese discouraged top-down, knowledge-based processing in a study of first-grade readers, with disadvantages becoming more pronounced as readers' word recognition increased (Ammon, et al.). Unfortunately, a study of reading selections in first-grade basal readers showed that most stories in basals are either specially written or adapted versions of children's literature with controlled vocabulary and sentence length (Wepner and Feeley, 1993). Goodman (1989) argues that children learn language, including written language, most easily when it is authentic and functional. However, when basal readers are written to meet readability standards rather than to include authentic meaningful language, students are denied the opportunity to rely on what makes sense as a guide to meaningful reading.

By the fourth-grade level, and depending on the publisher, more stories are included from original sources. Teachers need to be aware of which basals have the highest quality stories that best serve the needs of their students, and to choose their stories accordingly.

Teachers should accept the children's natural language and encourage spontaneous conversation. The idea is to build on children's language strengths.

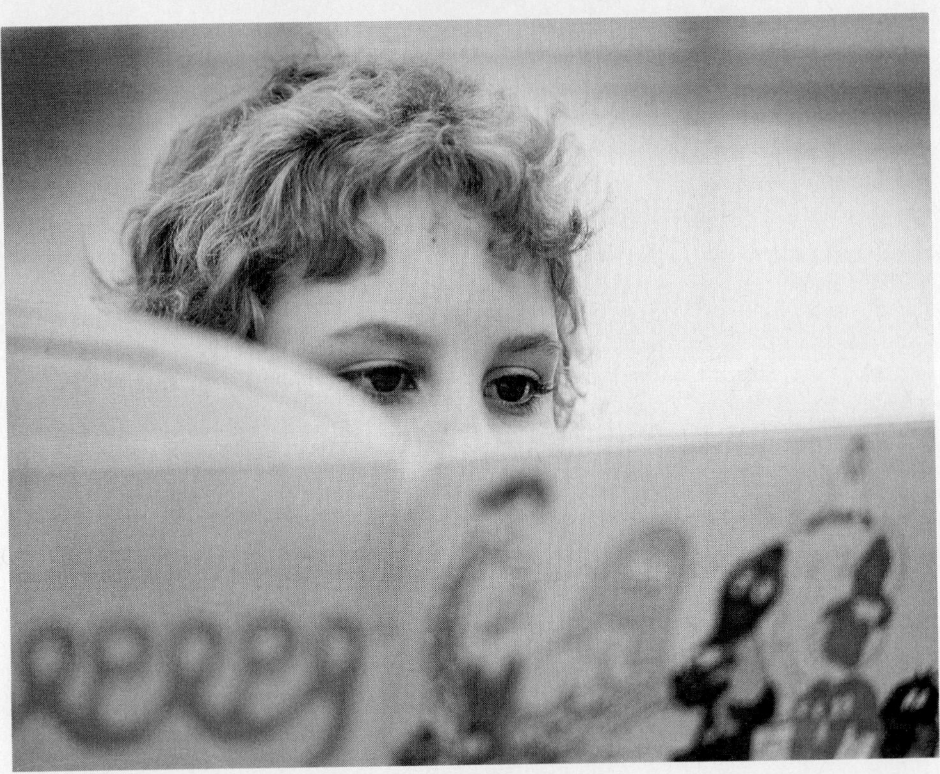

Overreliance on pictures, dialogue, and short sentences to carry meaning can lead young readers to picture dependence, thus hampering reading acquisition.

Workbooks

Many of the workbooks that go along with the basal readers are called reader's journals or writer's journals. Yet the content remains much the same as yesterday's workbooks: practice on phonics or decoding skills in the primary grades and comprehension or study skills practice in the intermediate grades. While opinions vary as to the appropriate number of pages to assign (some teachers and administrators strictly adhere to a policy requiring every page to be completed, yet few publishing company sales representatives would advocate this), one aspect of workbook practice is undeniable—it takes classroom time away from actual reading.

If the task demands of workbook items are analyzed, that is, if the type of response the activity requires the student to make is categorized, little actual reading is required. Jachym (1992) found that over 60 percent of all items in first-grade workbooks asked students to select and mark the response or to transcribe a single word. Only 5 percent of items in one series required students to supply or compose a word in an open-ended response. Equally troubling is the nature of the exercises that allowed students to arrive at the wrong answer for the right reason or the right answer for the wrong reason. Mastery of the skill being practiced bore little relation to correct or incorrect response.

Workbooks may or may not be related to the textbook selections students are reading. The most important consideration for teachers should be how workbooks are used. Wepner and Feeley (1993) suggest that teachers become aware of time spent completing trivial or inappropriate workbook tasks that could be spent on actual reading.

A fourth-grade teacher we know, comparing his district's decision not to purchase the workbooks or skillbooks that accompanied their new literature anthologies to a nearby district's acquisition of the entire program, commented on the freedom he felt to allow his students time for reading. "There is too much to do in terms of workbook activity to ever get as much reading done as you'd like. And those teachers who have the workbooks feel as if they have to use them." Teachers must take an active role in deciding the appropriate use of workbooks in their classrooms.

We suggest the following guidelines, adapted from Osborn (1984), for elementary teachers who are interested in evaluating the effectiveness of workbooks used in the classrooms. To be effective, workbooks should have the following characteristics:

1. They should reflect the most important aspects of what is being taught in the reading program.
2. The level of vocabulary in workbooks should relate to the rest of the program and to the students.
3. Workbooks should have instructional language consistent with that used in the rest of the lesson and workbook.
4. Instructions in workbooks should be brief and unambiguous.
5. Workbooks should provide opportunities to practice component tasks before performing discriminatory tasks.
6. Workbooks should contain accurate and precise content.
7. Workbooks should provide consistent response modes from task to task that involve reading and writing.
8. Pictures in workbooks should be consistent with the content.
9. Workbooks should be accompanied by brief explanations of purpose.

Lesson Framework

Nearly all basal reading programs organize instruction around some variation of the directed reading activity (DRA) first described by Betts in 1946. While the sequence and suggested activities are relatively standard, enough variation in strategies and emphasis exists to give each publisher's version a unique feel.

The newest basal programs incorporate lessons and activities that are designed to promote strategic reading and to foster students' metacomprehension (Schmitt and Hopkins,

1990). However, lesson plans in the teachers' manuals can be overwhelming. One publisher devotes 20 pages to a 46-word story; another series has a 42-page lesson plan for a 20-page story. While some lessons have suggestions marked "teacher's choice," Reutzel and Hollingsworth (1991) note that many teachers are afraid to leave out any of the workbook, skill sheets, or suggested instruction for fear students will perform poorly on reading comprehension skills tests, even though testing gains from reading books was equivalent to gains from skill practice. The confusing nature of so many options could be overwhelming to novice teachers.

Most basal lessons are organized in four phases.

Motivation and Background Building. This aspect of the lesson involves getting ready to read. It is sometimes referred to as the prereading phase of instruction. The teacher attempts to build interest in reading, set purposes, and introduce new concepts and vocabulary. Several procedures may include:

1. Predicting, based on title, pictures, and background knowledge, what the story might be about.
2. Teacher thinkalouds to model prediction, set purposes, and share prior knowledge.
3. Discussion of pronunciation and meaning of new words; review of words previously taught.
4. Location of geographical setting if important (map and globe skills).
5. Development of time concepts.
6. Review of important reading skills needed in doing the lesson.

Guided Reading (Silent and Oral). Depending on the grade level, the story is often read on a section-by-section basis (primary grades) or in its entirety. Following silent reading, children may be asked to read the story aloud or orally read specific parts to answer questions. The guided reading phase of the lesson focuses on comprehension development through questioning. Considerable improvement in lessons and activities that promote strategic reading, including explicit strategy instruction and comprehension skill instruction, are included in many newer basals (Schmitt and Hopkins, 1990). Teachers, however, may adapt questions from the manual or they may generate their own questions during a DRA (Shake, 1988). Stopping the student's reading to ask comprehension questions or even to have students predict what will come next may interfere with the joy of reading and the involvement of a reader in an engaging piece of literature. Teachers need to be aware of ruining a literature experience with inopportune questions (Larrick, 1991).

Skill Development and Practice. Skill development and practice activities center around direct instruction of reading skills, arranged according to "scope and sequence" and taught systematically. Sometimes this phase of the DRA involves oral rereading, always for a specific skills purpose. Activities and exercises from workbooks that accompany the basal story are used to reinforce skills in broad areas: word analysis and recognition, meaning vocabulary, comprehension, and study skills.

Follow-up and Enrichment. There are many possibilities for follow-up and enrichment activities. These are often called integrating across the curriculum and they are usually related to art, music, writing, home economics, or drama. Truly integrated math, science, or social studies curriculum ideas are so rare as to be nonexistent. Follow-up and enrichment may include specific procedures such as:

1. Creative activities—dramatization, writing about personal experiences related to the lesson, or the preparation of original projects.
2. Workbook assignments to strengthen specific skills that children may appear to be weak in. (This involves use of an independent practice workbook to supplement the practice workbook discussed in the previous section.)
3. Additional vocabulary practice.
4. The interpretation of a related experience such as reading a poem or another story on a similar theme.
5. Related reading in other texts and library books.

Making Instructional Decisions

The basal lesson can be a tool at our command, or it can command our classroom actions. According to the authors we interviewed (see Box 11.1), teachers who rely solely on their teacher's manual are not following best practice.

Basal programs have certain physical similarities but a more careful content analysis "reveals that there are significant differences among programs" (Dole and Osborn, 1989, p. 5). Teachers must make informed decisions about using, not using, and/or supplementing basal reading programs. They need to address how whole language and the more traditional use of basal readers can complement each other; how children's literature, technological software innovations, and anthologies can each contribute to good instruction.

Let's consider how two experienced fourth-grade teachers handle their teacher's manuals. Barbara has been teaching for seven years. She follows the lessons in her basal assiduously, lesson-by-lesson and page-by-page from the teacher's manual. Her compliance, she suggests, is based on a couple of factors. First, the basal program was put together by reading experts "who know far more than I ever will about reading." We concurred that her observation may in fact be the case but added, "Do these experts know your students as well as you do? Do they know your children's learning and reading strategies? Their needs? Their fears? Or their personal triumphs?" Barbara replied, "Perhaps not. But the lessons must be good or they wouldn't be included in the manual and, besides, they save me hours of planning time."

By contrast, Karen, a fourth-grade teacher with 12 years of experience, follows basal lessons but "reorganizes parts to fit what I think should be taught in my class." We inquired whether her lesson modification required much planning time. Karen replied, "I guess it does, but it's time well spent. I keep what I think is worthwhile and skip some activities because they don't make sense to me. These decisions take very little time. Planning time is consumed when I decide to do something on my own, like develop my own worksheets or devise a game to reinforce skills."

A decision either to adhere closely to the teacher's manual or to modify lessons should be a conscious one. The more teachers become aware of and reflect about *why* and *how* they use basals, the better. Although we avoid putting value judgments on either teacher's attitude, we believe that the process of becoming aware enables teachers to use their knowledge and skills more fully and effectively. Modifications of basal lessons allow teachers to rely on their own strengths as well as those of their students. In the final analysis, teachers should not be faced with an either/or dilemma in using basals to teach reading. Rather, they need to decide where to place instructional emphasis.

It is not unusual to discover very different kinds of reading instruction going on in the same elementary school. Even using just one basal reading program, instructional emphasis often varies from teacher to teacher. It is clearly impossible to teach every activity suggested in a basal reading lesson. There isn't enough time in the day; moreover, we wonder whether a teacher would need to do so to produce proficient readers. From an instructional point of view the question is not "Am I going to do everything as suggested in the teacher's manual?" The more appropriate question was posed this way by an elementary teacher: "If I'm going to skip parts in the teacher's manual or modify the lesson, I have to have the courage to believe that what I am emphasizing is instructionally worthwhile. So I ask myself, 'What do I need to replace or adapt in the lesson to make it work for me?'"

Designing Alternative Lessons

As teachers of reading become more familiar with instructional options available from this text and others, they are going to try them in their classrooms. However, they will use alternative strategies *in conjunction with their basal texts.* Furthermore, they may even prefer to follow the basic procedure or steps of the traditional lesson framework and incorporate some alternatives into this structure.

Designing alternative lessons personalizes reading instruction for teachers and students. Consequently, all the whys and hows of designing alternative lessons cannot and probably should not be uncovered. Nevertheless, based on numerous conversations with teachers over the years, there are three major reasons why teachers design alternative reading lessons: (1) the nature of their students as readers; (2) the type of reading material; and (3) the desire to teach comprehension.

Students. Teachers at all grade levels voice concern about two sets of readers in particular: (1) the so-called reluctant readers on one end, and (2) gifted readers on the other. Teachers empathize with a third-grade teacher who said it is important that "poorer readers do not become bogged down in working on isolated skills. These readers need to spend time on comprehension, too." Gifted students need challenging activities, especially creative activities and those involving higher-level thinking skills. Creative problem solving can and should be used with all groups of readers. In fact, it is just as appropriate for poor readers to partake in problem-solving activities.

Material. Different material makes different demands on the reader. It also provides countless opportunities for teachers to exercise creative judgment. For certain reading groups the objectives of a lesson might actually be better met by omitting parts of the lesson. Sometimes expansion of a component is necessary. If material seems too difficult, it's up to the teacher to facilitate easier management, perhaps with some content-area prereading strategies such as those mentional in Chapter 12. Stories with some suspense, which lend themselves to making predictions, are of particular value to teachers who regularly alternate the DRA with an alternative lesson structure, the Directed Reading-Thinking Activity (DR-TA).

Comprehension. As more teachers and administrators become aware of the importance of teaching as well as testing comprehension, there is increasing interest in finding new strategies. There has been a definite receptivity on the part of teachers taking in-service workshops and graduate coursework to learn additional strategies for improving their students' comprehension. It seems that more instructional time is spent in college classrooms on the topic of comprehension. As teachers begin to accumulate strategies, they pilot them in their own classrooms and settle on several that work particularly well.

Instructional Materials

Due to the proliferation of reading materials, it is virtually impossible to offer teachers a comprehensive list of current instructional materials in reading. It's not an exaggeration to say that such a list would be out of date before the ink was dry. Teachers must select materials discerningly, for, it is *their* role, "not of instructional methodologies, to teach" (Smith, 1992, p. 440). Furthermore,

> Teachers must find materials of interest to each individual in their classrooms, ensuring that each child is both helped to read and protected from boredom, anxiety, and failure—all matters that distant instructional designers and educational planners cannot attend to. (Smith, 1992, p. 435)

There are a number of factors to consider when selecting instructional materials. Talmage (1985) described the process as one of screening, matching needs, and decision making. Table 11.2 arrays three major kinds of reading materials: basic instructional programs, supplementary materials, and trade books. Basic materials such as a comprehensive reading program will be used by most children. Supplementary programs incorporating technology will be used as an enrichment for some children and a reinforcement of

● TABLE 11.2

Types of Reading Materials

Type	Label	Purpose
I. Basic instructional literature-based programs and materials	Basal readers and anthologies of literature from a wide range of genres	Intended to provide the majority of reading instruction to the majority of students
II. Supplementary programs	Software packages; skills kits; high-interest, low-vocabulary series	Intended to meet special needs such as enrichment; reinforcement of skills; the needs of particu-lar groups such as the gifted, bilingual-bicultural, and learning disabled
III. Trade books	Library books; popular fiction and nonfiction paperbacks for children and adolescents	Individual titles suited to children's interests. Intended for independent reading rather than direct instruction

basic skills for others. They are much less likely to be scrutinized by selection committees. Trade books, such as library hardcover and paperback books, will be chosen by individual children from the collection selected by librarians, specialists, and the classroom teacher. Literature programs are increasingly replacing basic instructional programs for the most able readers.

Examples of the types of reading materials listed in Table 11.2 can be added as you come into contact with the materials. Take some time now to think of examples of basic materials; supplementary high-interest, low-vocabulary materials; trade books; and software. When you finish the chapter, add others that you may already be familiar with or from new materials you are researching.

Classrooms differ as to the predominant types of reading material they supply. For example, there are some rooms in which the only visible reading materials are textbooks for reading, science, social studies, and so on. Other rooms evidence racks of paperback books; still others display sturdy cardboard kits with student record books piled nearby. Few classrooms, if any, have the same mix of types of reading materials.

One explanation for this phenomenon might be grade level. Lower grades work on different objectives than upper grades. Does this account for the use of one type of material over another? Another explanation might be the reading program of the school district; it's plausible that type of material would be influenced by program. Certainly, one's use of the basal reading program is closely connected to district curriculum. These are valid explanations, but neither accounts for the teacher's belief system in making decisions about materials.

Beliefs About Reading and Instructional Materials

How do teachers' beliefs about reading correspond to their selection and use of instructional materials for reading? There is no definitive answer to this question. There are many complicating factors that prevent teachers from exercising complete freedom of choice and, hence, prevent us from knowing why certain materials are present in any given classroom. Nevertheless, we believe it is important to consider the relationship between materials used to deliver instruction and the beliefs teachers hold about reading instruction. In other words, it makes sense to assume there is a relationship between what we do and why we do it

Figure 11.3 illustrates the major types of reading materials across the continuum of beliefs from bottom-up (on the left) to top-down (on the right). Basal reading programs take up the middle (or moderate) sections of the continuum whereas programmed, prescriptive materials and children's literature books correspond to the bottom-up and top-down quarters, respectively. Supplementary materials span several sections, from flash and skill cards to workbooks to high-interest, low-vocabulary materials.

Differences in beliefs about unit of language to be emphasized are super-imposed in the next layer. Letter-sound emphasis corresponds to materials found in prescription programs with a heavy word analysis component. Whole language emphasis corresponds to materials such as library books and paperbacks without arbitrary skill divisions. This unit of language emphasis is illustrated further by a dotted boundary line for context. Materials involving minimal use of context are on the left whereas materials involving maximal use of context are on the right.

A third layer that we might add is instructional strategy corresponding to these materials. We have initiated this with several basic strategies discussed in other chapters. For example, the DRA corresponds to most basal programs, whereas the DR-TA corresponds to many basal reader stories and other stories found in literature and high-interest, low-vocabulary materials. Sustained silent reading (SSR) corresponds to magazines and trade books; that is, personalized rather than prescriptive materials. What other strategies would you place in one spot or move to several points on this continuum?

Unfortunately, often by the time we step back, look at the types of instructional materials we are using, and relate them to our beliefs and priorities, the materials are already in place. How were they selected in the first place?

Selecting Reading Materials

Many classroom teachers have served on textbook selection committees. A bit of probing reveals the sophistication of the effort: Did teachers use different rating scales for various groups such as parents, teachers, and administrators? Were there presentations by com-

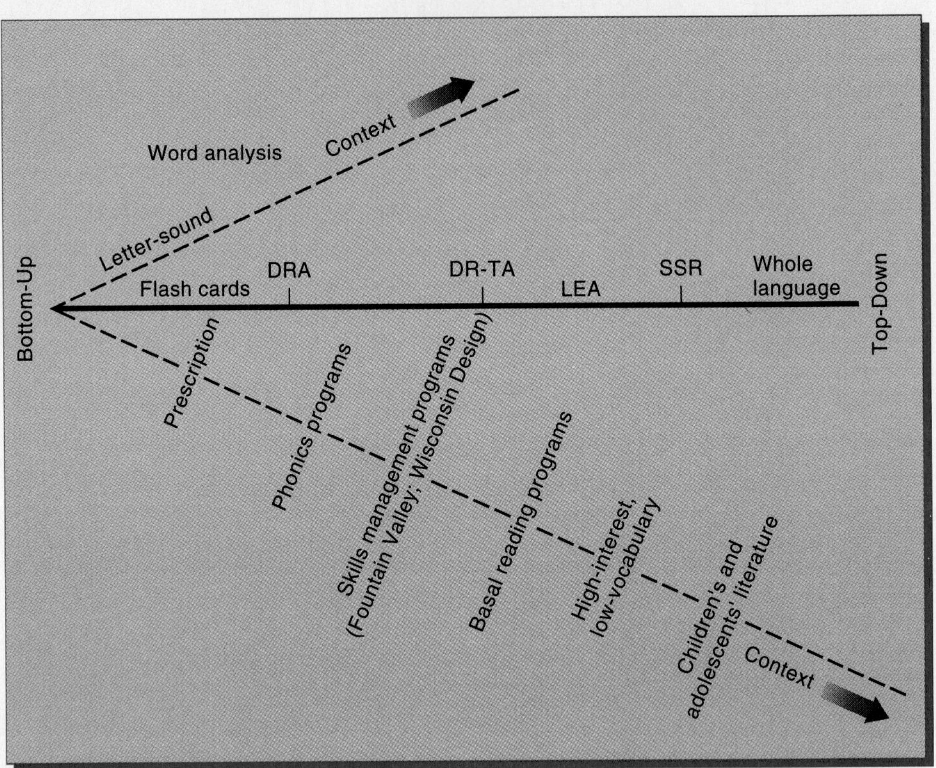

● **FIGURE 11.3** Reading instructional materials according to belief systems

pany representatives? Was there piloting of one or two finalists in classrooms over a period of time?

Social trends such as treatment of women and minorities, return to basics, and increasing involvement of parents have varying degrees of impact on curriculum development and materials selection. Depending on the community, other issues need to be considered. Censorship is probably the most pervasive issue because it deals with people's values. The *act of examining publications for objectionable matter* is not the intended mission of most educational materials selection committees. Yet there is a fine line between examining materials for their contribution to instructional goals and banning materials for their conveyance of implicit or explicit messages to students.

A spin-off on the volatile issue of censorship is the increase in media attention given to reading and materials. The morning news, for example, might feature a middle-school librarian and her program to bring parents, their adolescent children, and adolescent novels together. After reading the novels, parents and children get together to discuss the books. That evening, the newspaper carries an article about parents objecting to several books on astrology and numerology that were given to their children as part of a grant-funded program.

Trends and issues are important as they directly or indirectly influence curriculum materials selection. We need to keep them in perspective. The next time you are asked to assist in selecting materials, consider these critical questions as guides or criteria to get your committee started.

1. Have you personally evaluated the content of the materials in terms of accuracy of content, level of presentation, and use of level of language? Have you found the materials acceptable in these areas?
2. Does the field testing data reveal on whom the materials were field tested? How many students were involved in the use of the materials? In what geographic location were these tests conducted? What were the results?
3. Are authors and publishers readily identifiable within the content of the material?
4. Is there an accompanying instructional guide and, if so, are the curriculum aims, objectives, and instructional strategies presented?
5. Have these materials been used on pupils similar to the pupils in your reading programs? If so, what results were achieved by using these materials?
6. Do you feel you will present these materials with honesty and objectivity?
7. Have members of your district formulated specific ways or methods these materials can be used?
8. Will these materials complement the other instructional messages of your reading programs?
9. Does the material's content present information in a fair and nonbiased manner?
10. Are important concepts reinforced so that there is sufficient repetition of major points?

Evaluating Reading Materials

Reading programs, the most prevalent type of instructional material, are also the most likely to be evaluated by teachers and other groups. Publishing companies have become so attuned to this process that they gear high-power, professional presentations to convince school districts to adopt their particular program. School districts in turn have developed extensive evaluation forms to keep track of and compare the programs' elements.

The brief evaluation form in Box 11.3 illustrates the components that are usually examined and reported on at some length. Note that additional information at the bottom reflects expectations for fair and realistic treatment of people of different races, sexes, ages, cultures, and physical conditions. This evaluation format applies to textbooks in other subject areas as well as reading and to secondary as well as elementary and middle levels.

Checklists designed to evaluate reading materials of a supplementary nature may be criticized as rather shallow analysis. Their benefits, however, far outweigh this criticism. Checklists are relatively easy to construct; teachers are more willing to spend the short

● BOX 11.3

Textbook Evaluation Profile Chart

TITLE OF TEXTBOOK	Excellent	Good	Acceptable	Poor	Not included	Not applicable
I. Authorship						
II. Learner verification and revision						
III. General characteristics						
IV. Physical and mechanical features						
V. Philosophy						
VI. Organization of material						
VII. Objectives						
VIII. Subject-matter content						
IX. Readability						
X. Teaching aids and supplementary material						
XI. Teacher's edition or manual						
Total number in each rating classification for all categories						

Additional Information:

purpose	interest level	sexism
age level	readability	ageism
grade level	racism	diversity

Statement	Yes	No	Unsure
1. Reading materials are consistent with philosophy and goals of the program.	______	______	______
2. Materials are adequate for various phases of the program:			
a. Oral language development	______	______	______
b. Listening comprehension	______	______	______
c. Word recognition	______	______	______
d. Reading comprehension	______	______	______
e. Study skills	______	______	______
f. Recreational reading	______	______	______
g. Literature appreciation	______	______	______
3. The materials are			
a. Interesting and stimulating	______	______	______
b. Easy for children to use	______	______	______
c. Readily available	______	______	______
d. Durable	______	______	______
e. Well organized	______	______	______
f. Cost-effective	______	______	______
4. The materials accommodate the range of reading abilities.	______	______	______
5. A variety of cultures is depicted in illustrations and text content.	______	______	______
6. I feel adequately prepared to use all materials available.	______	______	______

Teacher's Name: ______________________________ Grade Level: ______________

● **FIGURE 11.4** Sample checklist for examining the potential effectiveness of materials

amount of time it takes to develop a list to help them examine materials. Figure 11.4 gives a sample checklist for examining the potential effectiveness of materials; it is one informal evaluation designed by teachers of elementary reading/language.

The evaluation form shown is brief, to the point, deals with teachers' own programmatic goals, and will yield useful information. Unlike more elaborate and lengthy commercial evaluation instruments, such checklists can be used by those who actually select and use materials.

With the proliferation of software in the 1990s and increased efforts to develop multicultural, diverse, and authentic materials, teachers need to be more aware than ever about what they are using in instruction. Here are some questions to think about before buying additional materials: Does the material actually contain what its advertisement claims? Are the skill areas that are emphasized really important to literacy? Are the materials likely to hold the interests of the students in your class? Is there sufficient time devoted to reading in relation to other activities? Are thinking and metacognitive strategies included? Is writing integrated in a meaningful way?

Teacher-Made and Student-Produced Materials

Have you ever walked into an elementary classroom that resembled an attraction at Disney World? The teacher is, to put it mildly, creative and talented at making materials. Many of us are not this gifted, yet we want to generate supplementary materials of the teacher-made variety for our own students. This is a good reason for becoming involved in designing and producing materials. A second and even more practical reason is to help solve a real problem: The classroom is deficient in materials and there is little or no financial support available. *What would you do in a similar situation?*

If teacher-made materials are to retain one of their major attributes—ease in construction—it's important to avoid unnecessary complications. Thus to begin designing and producing your own materials, know the three C's: concepts, content, and clients.

What are the major *concepts* you want (and need) to teach?

How complex is the *content* and how is it organized?

What is its value to your student *clients* and how familiar are they with it?

With knowledge of these criteria at your fingertips, you should be able to design appropriate materials in any of the categories that follow.

Games. One obvious benefit that comes with playing instructional games in the classroom is instant motivation. Games provide a change of pace, even in the classroom where Wheel of Fortune or Jeopardy is played every Friday morning from ten to eleven. Games also provide skill practice. Combining these two thoughts produces a good answer to the question "Why are games so popular?" Students reinforce their own skills and have a good time doing it.

The most typical type of game over the years has probably been flash cards or game board plus word cards. Card games and spin-the-dial or shake-the-dice board games are used to assist students in categorizing, reviewing vocabulary meanings, and sequencing.

The cost of teacher-made games is not necessarily less than commercial materials if durability and professional appearance are taken into consideration (Snyder, 1981). Changing a familiar commercial game or favorite old game into a new one is easier to do than starting from scratch. Perhaps more than any other factor, teacher time must be considered. If the game is worthwhile to your students, it's worth spending some time making it. How can you judge the relative importance of the concept being practiced to your students' learning?

One illustration of this is a teacher who holds a top-down belief about reading and is concerned about what she perceives is an overemphasis on phonics in many commercial materials in her classroom. Her goal was to help her students practice translating visual symbols into meaning. She decided it was worth the time and developed a whole language reading game for her second graders.

Newspapers. For years, teachers at all levels and in virtually all subject areas have made instructional use of the newspaper. Whether it's looking at classified ads, cutting out comic strips, or actually obtaining a classroom subscription to a major newspaper, students have been exposed to the newspaper as part of their school experience.

Newspapers, like games, generate enthusiasm in the classroom. They also provide a good resource to develop, reinforce, and refine reading-related skills, especially in vocabulary and comprehension. As a bonus, newspapers are a good way to communicate with parents when homework assignments are based on newspapers (Criscuolo, 1981).

Two efficient methods for designing newspaper activities are (1) to begin with a particular competency your students need to work toward and select different parts of the paper for the activities, and (2) to begin with the various parts of the paper and develop activities according to your students' competency needs.

The advantages of newspapers range from their minimal cost and constantly renewed supply of ideas to their different reading levels and wide appeal. As the teaching ideas above illustrate, writing instruction as well as reading can be highlighted. One final important benefit of newspapers in the classroom is their natural appeal to the multiple cultures in our society; teachers can use newspapers to help bridge cultural differences (Shields and Vondrak, 1980).

SUMMARY

We examined basal reading programs and other types of instructional materials in this chapter, emphasizing the need for teachers to understand and use materials wisely. Beginning with the predominant vehicle for reading instruction in elementary classrooms, we reminisced about the origins of basals and some instructional concepts that have been associated with their use throughout the years.

After recalling the books of the Dick, Jane, Jerry, and Alice era, we devoted a section to investigating current reading series by talking with several authors of current reading programs.

Basal programs of the nineties, best described as comprehensive, have come a long way. Consequently, we investigated their concepts, language or terminology, and major components. Rather than assigning pros and cons to basal reading programs, we concentrated on the significant improvements made in several areas. Their appearance, organization, illustrations, and attempts at improving literature selection and reducing stereotypes represent strides made by the publishers. What teachers do with basal readers during instructional time is another matter.

Despite institutional expectations and peer pressure brought to bear in using a basal reading program, it's the teacher who provides the reading instruction. Teachers who make daily decisions about children and who elect to spend more class time on vocabulary or whole language or decoding are molding their own reading program. Teachers who become aware and reflect about why and how they use basals make a list of pros and cons obsolete. They consciously emphasize one strategy over another as they take control of reading instruction. Often, and in conjunction with their basal series, teachers modify lessons to individualize for a particular group of students, to capitalize on a type of written material, or to emphasize a skill area. These are teachers who strengthen and take ownership of their basal reading program.

When we considered next the wide assortment of other instructional materials, one question persisted: How do teachers analyze the abundance of classroom materials available for reading instruction? There are current trends and issues that teachers need to consider in relation to materials. They need to differentiate among the types of commercial reading material and to assimilate criteria for evaluating them. The selection and use of commercial and teacher-made materials affords teachers still another opportunity to choose what is instructionally worthwhile in reading and learning to read.

Materials, including basal programs, are only the vehicles for instruction. Someone needs to sit in the driver's seat with a clear route in mind, and take control of the vehicle. That someone is the classroom teacher.

TEACHER-ACTION RESEARCHER

1. Select a teacher who consistently uses basal reader instruction. Interview the teacher about his or her attitude toward basal instruction. How closely is the teacher's manual followed? How does the teacher use the basal workbooks? In what ways, if any, does the teacher deviate from the suggested steps in the manual? What reasons does the teacher give for making modifications?

2. Arrange to teach a basal lesson to a group of children following the guidelines suggested in the teacher's manual. Reflect on the experience. In what ways were the guidelines effective or ineffective for this particular group of children? How would you amend the lesson to better fit their instructional needs?

3. Create an original lesson for a basal story without consulting the teacher's manual. Then try out the lesson with a group of children. Reflect on the experience. Consult the manual and compare the original lesson you developed with the suggested one. What did you learn from the experience?

4. Compare some selections in a literature-based basal to the actual works. What changes (if any) were made to the authors' original texts? How were your responses to the stories changed? What instructional decisions might a teacher need to make if the literature selections in her basal series were adapted from children's literature rather than being actual whole texts?

KEY TERMS

code emphasis
classroom libraries
computer management system
continuous progress
controlled vocabulary
criterion-referenced tests
extension (integrating across the curriculum)
informal assessment opportunities (notes)
instructional aids
kindergarten program
levels
literature-based reading programs
management
meaning emphasis
primer
reader's/writer's journals (notebooks)
reading progress cards (running records)
reinforcement
scope and sequence
skill building
skill maintenance
strands
vocabulary development
whole word method
workbooks

CHAPTER 12

Making the Transition to Content-Area Texts

BETWEEN THE LINES

In this chapter you will discover:

- **Why content-area textbooks are difficult for students.**
- **Factors that help determine textbook difficulty.**
- **How using literature across the curriculum benefits teaching and learning.**
- **How to integrate trade books, inquiry-centered projects, and other strategies into units of study.**
- **A variety of learning strategies for students to use before and during reading and writing.**

Shirley and Ingrid were sitting at the table in the teachers' workroom, reviewing their new fourth graders' portfolios from last year. "Why is it," Ingrid asks, "that some kids seem to do so well in reading in third grade and then, when we get them, they seem to go into a slump?" "I'm not certain," replies Shirley, "but it may be that it's just too difficult for some students—like Eric—to switch gears from learning to read to reading to learn."

This unnecessary dichotomy between learning to read and reading to learn may actually stand in the way of a child's literacy development. Even before entering school, most children who have had book experiences at home expect print to be meaningful. From as early as age 2, children can be observed engaging in a process of making sense—negotiating meaning—of an author's message (Harste, Woodward, and Burke, 1984). Our contention throughout this book is that children should be learning to read *as* they are reading to learn and to enjoy.

Nonetheless, the problems associated with the transition students make to content-area texts, where reading to learn is at a premium, are real. The marked difference in reading ability of good and poor readers known as "the fourth-grade slump" can be attributed to students who find expository texts difficult to read and understand (Chall, Jacobs, and

Baldwin, 1990). The Commission on Reading, in preparing *Becoming a Nation of Readers* (1985), recognized that for many children the transition to content-area texts leads to their first difficulties with reading. Content-area texts are inherently difficult. Take, for example, an elementary textbook. It's often devoid of narrative writing; a textbook doesn't tell stories. Most children, of course, are weaned on narrative writing and come to school with a developing, if not well-developed, schema for stories. They're on terra firma with the storybook.

A textbook, on the other hand, relies heavily on an expository style of writing—description, classification, and explanation. By its very nature, a textbook often is dry and uninteresting to the novice reader. As Brozo and Tomlinson (1986) put it, when children first encounter content-area texts in school, it is the beginning of a "journey into the uncharted sea of exposition" (p. 289).

In this chapter you'll explore some of the factors that make content-area textbooks difficult, as well as the role of a teacher of reading within the context of content-area instruction. Elementary teachers often view their responsibilities in a reading program primarily in terms of skill and strategy development. Their actions are motivated by the question, "How can I help children become more skillful and strategic as readers?" Their main concern, then, is with *process* or how to guide children's reading development. Yet a concern for the *content* of the reading program should be as important a matter for elementary teachers as a concern for process.

The resurgence of children's literature in the 1980s underscores the importance of meaningful content and authentic texts in elementary classrooms. When a classroom reading program is content rich, the slump alluded to earlier becomes more apocryphal than real. In literature-based classrooms, children make the transition to content-area texts naturally. Although conceptual demands are placed on the students, they learn to approach and appreciate many kinds of texts. They also understand the value of fiction in developing concepts identified for study in content areas. And from a reading-to-learn perspective, children become aware of and use a variety of strategies as they engage in content-area activities.

Why Are Content-Area Textbooks Difficult?

Content-area textbooks are an integral part of schooling. In most classrooms, textbooks blend into the physical environment, much like desks, bulletin boards, and chalkboards. Even a casual observer expects to see textbooks in use in the elementary classroom. Yet teachers often remark that children find textbooks difficult. When students have trouble reading texts, we are acutely aware of the mismatch between the reading abilities students bring to text material and some of the difficulties of the text.

To compensate for this, some teachers avoid textbook assignments. Instruction revolves around lecture and other activities instead of the textbook. Some teachers abandon difficult materials, sidestepping reading altogether as a vehicle for learning.

In lieu of either abandoning difficult materials or avoiding reading altogether, we need to get answers to some very basic questions. How does the textbook meet the goals of the curriculum? Is the conceptual difficulty of the text beyond students' grasp? Does the author have a clear sense of purpose as conveyed to this audience? How well are the ideas in the text organized? With answers to these and other questions, teachers have some basis upon which to make decisions about text-related instruction, exercising their professional judgment.

Factors in Judging the Difficulty of Textbooks

The difficulty of text material is the result of factors residing in both the reader and the text. Therefore, to judge well, you need to take into account several different types of information. A primary source of information is the publisher. Consider the publisher-provided descriptions of the design, format, and organizational structure of the textbook along with grade level readability designations. A second source is your knowledge of students in the class. A third source is your own sense of what makes the textbook useful in learning a particular subject.

The first order of business is to define how the textbook will be used. Will it be used as the sole basis for information or as an extension of information? Will it be used in tandem with informational books and other forms of children's literature? Is it to provide guided activities?

Students in a university reading methods class were curious as to how elementary teachers compensated for difficult or confusing content-area textbooks. For a research project, they surveyed over 40 elementary teachers. The college students were surprised that more than 80 percent of the teachers did not think that content textbooks were too difficult. What was even more surprising to the students, however, was the fact that the teachers *did not expect* that the elementary students would learn from the textbooks. One comment summed up most responses: "The students learn the facts and ideas they need when we talk about what is important during class discussions." So while the elementary teachers did not think the textbook was too difficult, they didn't expect students to learn by reading it either! Most elementary teachers, however, continue to use textbooks to teach content subjects, especially those subjects they feel less prepared and confident to teach, like science, even if they believe the textbooks are often difficult for students to read (Barman, 1992).

How Difficult Is the Text to Understand? This question might be recast into a set of subsidiary questions: How likely are students to comprehend the text? How difficult are the concepts in the text? Has the author taken into consideration the prior knowledge that students bring to the text? The ability to understand the textbook, to a large extent, will be influenced by the match between what the reader already knows and the text itself. Background knowledge and logical organization of **expository texts** are crucial factors for comprehending new information (Beck and McKeown, 1991).

Irwin and Davis (1980) suggested that teachers analyze a text, using questions such as the following:

Are the assumptions about students' vocabulary knowledge appropriate?

Are the assumptions about students' prior knowledge of this content area appropriate?

Are the assumptions about students' general experiential backgrounds appropriate?

Are new concepts explicitly linked to the students' prior knowledge or to their experiential backgrounds?

Does the text introduce abstract concepts by accompanying them with many concrete examples?

Does the text introduce new concepts one at a time with a sufficient number of examples for each one?

Does the text avoid irrelevant details?

How Usable Is the Text? To determine how usable a text is, you will need to consider its organizational features and its presentation of material. Your responses to the following questions will help you to decide whether a textbook is **considerate** or *inconsiderate*. For example, your responses may reveal the extent to which relationships among ideas in the text are clear, the logical organization between ideas, and the use of *signal words* (connectives) to make relationships explicit. To determine if a text is *user friendly* consider these questions (Irwin and Davis, 1980).

Does the table of contents provide a clear overview of the contents of the textbook?

Do chapter headings clearly define the content of the chapter?

Do chapter subheadings clearly break out the important concept in the chapter?

Do topic headings provide assistance in breaking the chapter into relevant parts?

Does the glossary contain all the technical terms used in the textbook?

Are graphs and charts clear and supportive of the textual material?

Are illustrations well done and appropriate to the level of the students?

Are lines of text an appropriate length for the level of the students who will use the textbook?

Are important terms in italics or boldface type for easy identification by readers?

Are end-of-chapter questions on literal, interpretive, and applied levels of comprehension?

Is an adequate context provided to allow students to determine meanings of technical terms?

Are the sentence lengths appropriate for the level of students who will be using the text?

How Interesting Is the Text? Textbooks should appeal to students. The more relevant the text, the more interesting it will be to children. Illustrations and pictures should have appeal, and they will, when they depict persons that students can relate to. Does the cover design and other artwork convey up-to-date, refreshing images? Are type sizes and faces varied? Does the boldface lettering of headings contrast with lightface lettering of the main narrative? Italics and numbering of words and phrases in lists are two other devices that can help make the printed page come alive for elementary students. In addition to the questions just raised, consider these as you analyze a textbook for interest.

Is the writing style of the text appealing to the students?

Are the activities motivating? Will they make the student want to pursue the topic further?

Does the book clearly show how the knowledge being learned might be used by the learner in the future?

Does the text provide positive and motivating models for both sexes as well as for all racial, ethnic, and socioeconomic groups?

Does the text help students generate interest as they relate experiences and develop visual and sensory images?

Perhaps because textbooks need to cover so many subjects for state and local curriculum guidelines, nonfiction, expository writing becomes confused in our minds with textbook writing. While it's true that textbooks and nonfiction are different from narratives and fiction, children, even first graders, can be taught to recognize the difference between fantasy or fiction and actual, fact-based explanatory prose.

Once the information accrues about factors contributing to textbook difficulty, you are in a position to use professional judgment. How the more traditional readability formula can be a complement to a teacher's judgment instead of a substitute for it warrants a closer look.

Readability

When elementary teachers judge instructional content-area materials, they frequently assess **readability.** Readability formulas can help to *estimate* textbook difficulty, but they are not intended to be precise indicators. Of the many readability formulas available, the most popular ones are relatively quick and easy to calculate. They typically involve a measure of sentence length and word difficulty to ascertain a grade-level score for text materials. This score supposedly indicates the reading achievement level students would need to comprehend the material. You do, however, need to be aware of limitations associated with using readability formulas.

Limitations. Readability formulas yield scores that are simply estimates, not absolute levels, of text difficulty. These estimates are often determined along a single dimension of an author's writing style: vocabulary difficulty and sentence complexity, measured by word and sentence length, respectively. These are two variables most often used to predict the difficulty of a text. Nevertheless, they only *indirectly* assess vocabulary difficulty and sentence complexity. Are long words always harder to understand than short ones? Are long sentences necessarily more difficult than short ones?

Keep in mind that a readability formula doesn't take into account the experience and knowledge that even young readers bring to content material. The reader's emotional, cognitive, and linguistic backgrounds aren't included in readability estimates. Hittleman (1973) maintained that readability is actually a moment in time in which a reader's human makeup interacts with the topic, the purposes for reading, and the semantic and syntactic structures in the material. This makes good sense because formulas are not designed to expose the variables operating within the reader. Thus several factors that contribute to a reader's ability to comprehend text are not dealt with: purpose, interest, motivation, emotional state, and environment. This is an important limitation.

Suggestions. Formulas in and of themselves need not be a liability if you follow Nelson's (1978) suggestions for using them.

> Learn to use a simple readability formula as an aid in evaluating text material for student use.
>
> Don't assume automatic comprehension will result from matching readability level of material to reading achievement level of students.
>
> Don't assume that automatic reading ease will result from text materials rewritten according to readability criteria. (Leave the rewriting of text material to the linguists, researchers, and editors who have time to analyze and validate their manipulations.)
>
> Do provide materials containing essential facts, concepts, and values of the subject at varying levels of readability within the reading range of your students.

> Do recognize that using a readability formula is no substitute for instruction. The elementary teacher still needs to prepare students to read the assignment, guide them in their reading, and reinforce new concepts through rereading and discussion (pp. 624–25).

Fry Readability Graph. One fairly quick and simple readability formula is the Fry Readability Graph developed by Edward Fry (1968, 1977). Fry used two variables to predict difficulty and determine grade-level scores for materials from grade one through college: sentence length and word length. The total number of sentences in a sample passage determines sentence length, while the total number of syllables in the passage determines word length.

Three 100-word samples from the selected reading material should be used to calculate its readability. Grade-level scores for each passage can then be averaged to obtain an overall readability level. The readability graph in Box 12.1 is useful in predicting the difficulty of material within one grade level when the accompanying directions for the Fry Formula are followed.

In 1990, Fry noted that for short passages of between 100 to 300 words in length, a formula for readability should account for difficulty of words and difficulty of sentences, as shown in Box 12.2. Using the contextual meaning of difficult words and their corresponding grade level gives a more accurate reading level than sentence complexity alone. For example, the word *convention* has three meanings with three levels of difficulty. As a *meeting,* it is a sixth-grade-level word; as a *custom,* it is a tenth-grade-level word; as a *diplomatic agreement,* it is a twelfth-grade-level word. Its use in the particular passage affects the readability of the passage.

Early in their academic lives, students need to develop a healthy respect for textbooks as resources and reference tools. Although they may sometimes find textbooks to be formidable in size, appearance, and writing style, children shouldn't view them as *the source* of information, but rather one of many informational sources. Their misperceptions develop when textbooks become the exclusive domain of learning in content areas. As teachers, we can make the transition to textbook study less difficult by creating opportunities for learning that capitalize on a variety of informational sources.

Sue Mathieson, a first-grade teacher in a rural Pennsylvania school district, focuses her reading instruction around content-area subject matter. Her students read and write about science. "They want to know about their world and how it works. They study animals with such enthusiasm! But to my amazement, they are equally as interested in photosynthesis and how plants grow!" Such natural interest in the working of the world helps Sue design intrinsically motivating reading lessons.

Alternative sources of information—biographies, informational books, picture books, realistic and historical fiction, manuals, magazines, pamphlets, and reference books—help children to recognize that learning in content areas requires exposure to many genres in literature. When teachers integrate textbook study with children's literature, they extend and enrich the curriculum. As Alfonso (1987) suggested, content-area learning becomes "a significant event" in the lives of children.

● BOX 12.1

Fry Readability Graph

Graph For Estimating Readability—Extended

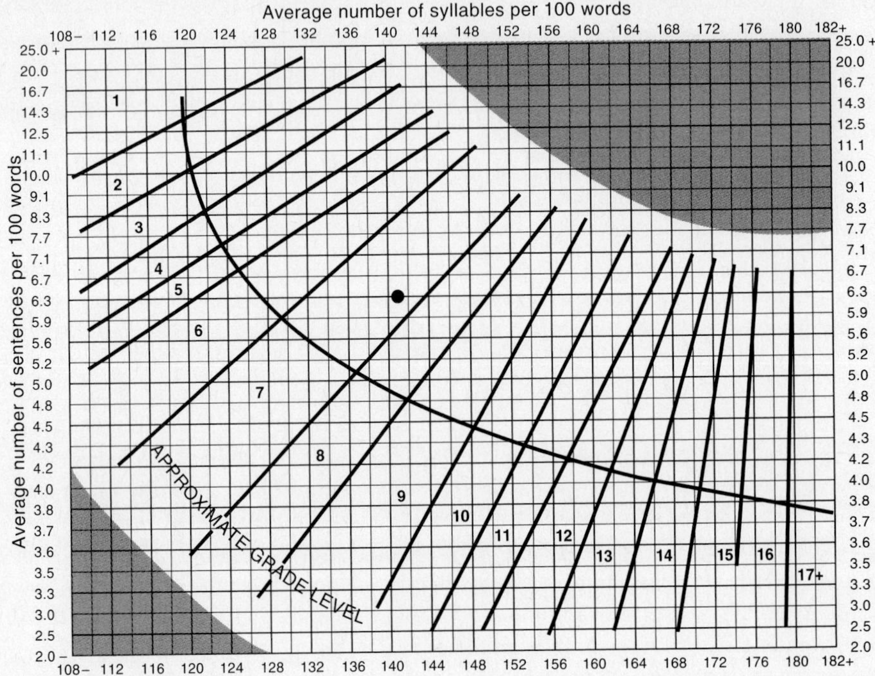

Expanded Directions for Working Readability Graph

1. Randomly select three sample passages and count out exactly 100 words each, beginning with the beginning of a sentence. Do count proper nouns, initializations, and numerals.

2. Count the number of sentences in the 100 words, estimating length of the fraction of the last sentence to the nearest one-tenth.

3. Count the total number of syllables in the 100-word passage. If you don't have a hand counter available, an easy way is to simply put a mark above every syllable over one in each word, then when you get to the end of the passage, count the number of marks and add 100. Small calculators can also be used as counters by pushing numeral 1, then pushing the + sign for each word or syllable when counting.

(continued)

4. Enter graph with *average* sentence length and *average* number of syllables; plot dot where the two lines intersect. The area where the dot is plotted will give you the approximate grade level.
5. If a great deal of variability is found in syllable count or sentence count, putting more samples into the average is desirable.
6. A word is defined as a group of symbols with a space on either side; thus, *Joe, IRA, 1945,* and *&* are each one word.
7. A syllable is defined as a phonetic syllable. Generally, there are as many syllables as vowel sounds. For example, *stopped* is one syllable and *wanted* is two syllables. When counting syllables for numerals and initializations, count one syllable for each symbol. For example, *1945* is four syllables, *IRA* is three syllables, and & is one syllable.

Reprinted with permission from Edward Fry, *Elementary Reading Instruction* (New York: McGraw-Hill, 1977).

Using Literature Across the Curriculum

The use of children's literature in elementary classrooms extends and enriches information provided in content-area textbooks. Often, textbooks cannot treat subject matter with the breadth and depth necessary to fully develop ideas and concepts. Literature, as discussed in Chapter 10, has the potential to capture children's interest and imagination in people, places, events, and ideas. And it has the potential to develop in-depth understandings in ways that textbooks aren't equipped to do.

Nonetheless, having a wide array of literature available for content-area learning is necessary but not sufficient to ensure that children make good use of trade books. Teachers must plan for their use by weaving literature into meaningful and relevant instructional activities within the context of content-area study. In this section, the focus is not only on the uses and benefits of **literature across the curriculum,** but also on the preparation of units of study to help you identify concepts, select literature, and develop activities.

Some Uses and Benefits of Literature

There are many benefits to using literature across the curriculum. For one, **trade books** provide students with intense involvement in a subject; for another, they are powerful schema builders. Trade books and informational texts also may be used to accommodate a

● BOX 12.2

Fry Short Passage Readability Formula

Rules

1. Use on a passage that is at least three sentences and forty words long.
2. Select at least three key words that are necessary for understanding the passage. You may have more key words.
3. Look up the grade level of each key word in *The Living Word Vocabulary.**
4. Average the three hardest key words. This gives you Word Difficulty.
5. Count the number of words in each sentence and give each sentence a grade level using the sentence length chart (Table 12.1).
6. Average the grade level of all sentences. This gives you Sentence Difficulty.
7. Finally, average the Sentence Difficulty (Step 6) and the Word Difficulty (Step 4). This gives you the Readability estimate of the short passage.

Formula

$$\text{Readability} = \frac{\text{Word Difficulty} + \text{Sentence Difficulty}}{2}$$

Cautions

1. This method should be used only when a long passage is not available. With anything 300 words or longer, use the regular Readability Graph.
2. This method was developed on passages at least three sentences and 40 words long. With anything shorter than that, use the formula at your own risk. It may be better than nothing, but certainly has less reliability.
3. Be careful when looking up the grade level of the key words that you get the grade level for the same meaning as the meaning of that key word as it is used in the passage.
4. The range is grade levels 4–12. In reporting any score 4.0 or below, call it "4th grade or below" and any score above 12.9 call "12th grade or above."

TABLE 12.2

Sentence Length (Difficulty) Chart

Words per sentence	Grade level estimate
6.6 or below	1
8.6	2
10.8	3
12.5	4
14.2	5
15.8	6
18.2	7
20.4	8
22.2	9
23.2	10
23.8	11
24.3	12
25.0	13
25.6	14
26.3	15
27.0	16
Above 27	17

For use with the Fry Short Passage Readability Formula, 1989.

wide range of student abilities and interests. When literature is used in tandem with textbooks, there's something for everyone. Children may choose from a variety of topics for intensive study and inquiry. One benefit for the teacher, of course, is that literature may be used instructionally in a variety of ways.

Trade Books Provide Intense Involvement in a Subject. A textbook compresses information. Intensive treatment gives way to extensive coverage. As a result, an elementary textbook is more likely to mention and summarize important ideas, events, and concepts rather than develop them fully or richly. Brozo and Tomlinson (1986) underscored this point by illustrating the content treatment of Hitler, the Nazis, and the Jews in a fifth-grade social studies textbook.

> Hitler's followers were called Nazis. Hitler and the Nazis built up Germany's military power and started a campaign against the Jews who lived in that country. Hitler claimed that the Jews were to blame for Germany's problems. He took away their rights and property. Many Jews left Germany and came to live in the United States. The Nazis began to arrest Jews who stayed in Germany and put them in special camps. Then the Nazis started murdering them. Before Hitler's years in power came to an end, six million Jews lost their lives. (p. 289)

A textbook, as you can surmise from the preceding paragraph, often condenses a subject to its minimum essentials. The result often is a bland and watered-down treatment of their subjects, which is particularly evident in today's history textbook (Sewell, 1987). The paragraph on Hitler's treatment of the Jews is a vivid example of "the principle of minimum essentials" in textbook practice. The passage represents the extent of the text relating to the Holocaust in Houghton Mifflin's *America: Past and Present* (1980). While it may be accurate, it takes one of the most tragic and horrifying events in world history and compresses it into a series of summarizing statements.

Greenlaw (1988) noted that most textbooks are written to be "noncontroversial" and have "little style or dramatic flair." What is the alternative to bland and lifeless texts? Greenlaw provides an answer: "Many fine trade books have been published in recent years. . . . We can locate stimulating informational books on almost any topic for almost any level. These books should not become a substitute for the text, but should become an appealing means for students to pursue interests relating to the core topic" (p. 18).

Intense involvement in a subject is one of the major benefits of trade books as a vehicle for content study. What better way to bring to life the realities and horrors of World War II than to have fifth or sixth graders enrich their textbook study by reading (or listening to) some of the trade books suggested in Box 12.3.

A favorite story of many middle-grade students involving the German occupation of Europe during World War II is *In Winter When Time Was Frozen* (Pelgrom, 1980). The story is about a young girl, Noortje, and her life as an evacuee on the Everingen's farm in Holland. Brozo and Tomlinson (1986) reported that after hearing her teacher read the story aloud, one fifth grader responded: "This book describes the life of these people so well you'd think the Everingens and the other people were a part of your own family." According to Brozo and Tomlinson, "Were it not for stories like these, most historical events of national and international scope and most notable human achievements and tragedies would remain for many American children distant or even mythical notions with no emotional connections" (p. 290).

Trade Books Are Schema Builders. Intense involvement in a subject generates background knowledge and vicarious experience, which will make textbook concepts easier to grasp and assimilate. As a result, one of the most compelling uses of trade books is as schema builders for subjects under textbook study. Trade books build background

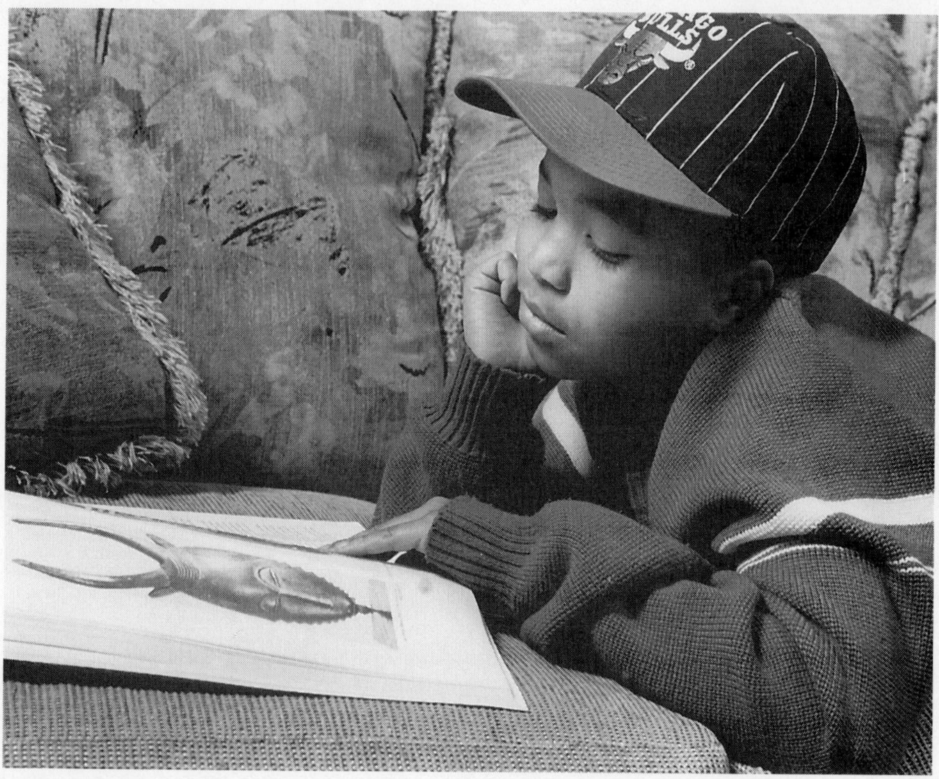

Trade books and informational texts provide students with intense involvement in a subject.

knowledge and provide children with vicarious experiences that they are not likely to encounter in textbooks.

The transition to content-area reading is smoother when students bring a frame of reference to textbook study. Reading literature strengthens the reading process, because reading about a topic can dramatically improve comprehension of related readings on the same topic (Crafton, 1983). Natural reading experiences in trade books generate background knowledge, which will help students comprehend related discourse.

Not only do trade books help to bridge knowledge gaps, they also create interest and arouse curiosity in areas such as science, health, social studies, and history. Heinly and Hilton (1982), for example, encouraged the use of historical and realistic fiction in social studies, noting that when children read stories about people in historical contexts, it helps them with cause-effect relationships and chronological order. Dole and Johnson (1980), likewise, noted that trade books in science can provide background knowledge for science concepts covered in class and can help students relate these concepts to their everyday lives.

● BOX 12.3

Something to Think About: M. Jean Greenlaw on Using Literature to Extend the Curriculum

In a middle-school social studies text, 19 of 848 pages are devoted to World War II. What possible depth of knowledge can be developed in reading 19 pages and answering two pages of questions on the topic? From some arid, single paragraphs in a textbook, however, can come an intense involvement with a subject, as expanded by the reading of trade books.

People, emotion, and commitment are missing from textbooks. A paragraph states that Benito Mussolini dreamed of restoring the power of the ancient Roman Empire to Italy by building up the army and air force. He was proud of his forces and was eager to see them in action. Compare this with Erik Haugaard's *The Little Fishes,* in which Guido, a 12-year-old orphan, experiences the war in Italy. Begging, stealing, lying, protecting his friends, watching them die—this was Guido's war—a far cry from Mussolini's dream!

Another paragraph describes the police state set up by Hitler and notes that in a police state, people are forced to obey. In *Ceremony of Innocence,* James Forman writes of four German young people who did not obey. Hans and Sophie Scholl and two friends defied the Gestapo and wrote and distributed leaflets decrying the "Nazi cancer." Hans and Sophie died for their beliefs, but they are remembered. A recent biography, *The Short Life of Sophie Scholl* by Herman Vinke, provides additional information by revealing portions of her diary and presenting interviews with family and friends.

(continued)

Trade Books Accommodate Abilities and Interests. When teachers use trade books in tandem with textbooks, there's something for everyone. A teacher can provide students with trade books on a variety of topics related to a subject under investigation. Books on related topics are written at various levels of difficulty. Greenlaw (1988) maintained that one of the benefits of trade books is that children can select books on a reading level appropriate to their abilities and interests. Self-selection may range from picture books to books written for adults: "All selections should be valued, and students should be encouraged to share the information they have gleaned in creative ways" (p. 18).

Trade Books Are Resources in Instructional Units. When planning to incorporate trade books in a unit of study, Brozo and Tomlinson (1986) defined several steps in a teaching strategy.

Identify salient concepts that become the content objectives for the unit.

What are the driving human forces behind the events?

The horror of German concentration camps is covered in one brief paragraph in the textbook. It is little wonder that many citizens question the continuing pursuit of Nazi war criminals, when the only knowledge of the camps they have is through sterile materials. How much more eloquent is *I Never Saw Another Butterfly,* a book of poems and drawings by Jewish children from the Terezin concentration camp. This collection, edited by Hana Volavkova, reflects both the horror and the hope of the camp's inmates.

As a final example, one paragraph is devoted to the bombing of Japan. Compare this with Eleanor Coerr's moving story, *Sadako and the Thousand Paper Cranes,* the story of a child who died from the delayed effects of radiation and who became a symbol for all who suffered. Also, experience that horrible moment and the aftereffects with Toshi Maruki, who writes of a child who lived through it and who, as an adult, has finally been able to express her pain, in *Hiroshima No Pika.*

Conclusion

There is not a subject covered in textbooks that could not be enhanced in the way I have suggested. Whether it is magnetism, the solar system, the Middle Ages, or drugs, there are good trade books available and students who can be motivated to read them. It will take more time to teach in this fashion, as subjects will be considered carefully rather than skimmed over. Discussion will take place rather than rote answer-giving. We even run the risk that students will become interested in what they have learned!

What patterns of behavior need to be studied?
What phenomena have affected ordinary people or may affect them in the future?

Identify appropriate trade books to help teach concepts.
Read and become familiar with a variety of children's books.
Use children's literature textbooks and subject guide reference indices such as *The Best in Children's Books* (Sutherland, 1980).

Teach the unit.
Use textbook and trade books interchangeably.
Use strategies such as a readaloud in which a trade book becomes a schema builder before reading the textbook.
Use trade books to elaborate and extend content and concepts related to the unit.

Follow up.
Engage students in strategies and activities that involve collaboration, inquiry, and various forms of expression and meaning construction.

Evaluate students' learning by observing how they interpret and personalize new knowledge.

As part of the unit, trade books make excellent resource material. An attractive display of children's books is a great way to launch a unit (Chan, 1979). Also, trade books and other forms of print and nonprint materials can be used in interest centers or as resource material for student projects and inquiries. Vacca and Vacca (1993) outlined procedures for guiding individual or group inquiry projects (see Box 12.4).

Developing Units of Study

A unit of study organizes instruction around multiple sources of information within the context of meaningful and relevant classroom activity. You can integrate various content areas around reading and writing strategies and the study of different types of narrative and informational books in ways that will give students a real sense of freedom and continuity in what they are learning.

Getting Started. The title of the unit reflects the topic or theme to be studied. One of the first steps in planning the unit, as was suggested earlier, involves identifying salient concepts to be learned as a result of participation in unit activities. Once the concepts are identified, selecting information sources and developing activities are next in order.

Webbing. Often, constructing a **literature web** for the unit helps you to envision the integration of content with activities and/or informational sources (Huck, Hepler, and Hickman, 1987).

A literature web shows the relationships that exist among the major components of the unit. Study Box 12.5 and Box 12.6; each illustrates a web, one developed by a second-grade teacher for a unit on communities and the other developed by a sixth-grade teacher for a unit on the Middle Ages.

In the sixth-grade web, the teacher elects to organize activities and information sources within the various content areas that will be integrated into the unit. In the second-grade web, the teacher organizes trade books around the types of communities that children will be exploring. Either organizational strategy is useful.

Putting a Unit to Work. "The heart of a unit," according to Coody and Nelson (1982), "is children's day-to-day learning experiences in the classroom" (p. 23). This couldn't be more the case than in Ms. Mark's third-grade class, where students participated in a four-week science unit on birds. Here's how Ms. Mark described the unit, "Birds Are Special Animals":

> "Birds Are Special Animals" is intended for a class of third-grade students. The unit will require approximately four weeks of daily sessions. For the first three weeks, the focus will be on activities planned for the entire class. During the last week of the unit, the focus will be on small group and individual projects. The students will use *The Life of Birds,* edited by Donald Moyle, as their main reading source. Supplemental readings from other sources will be assigned throughout the unit. Audiovisual materials will be

● BOX 12.4

Guiding Inquiry-Centered Projects in Units of Study

PROCEDURES FOR GUIDING INQUIRY-CENTERED WRITING PROJECTS

Raise questions, identify interests, organize information
- Discuss interest areas related to the unit of study
- Engage in goal setting
  - Arouse curiosities
  - Create awareness of present level of knowledge
- Pose questions relating to each area and/or subarea
  - "What do you want to find out?"
  - "What do you want to know about ____________?"
  - Record the questions or topics
  - "What do you already know about ____________?"
- Organize information; have students make predictions about likely answers to gaps in knowledge
  - Accept all predictions as possible answers
  - Encourage thoughtful speculations in a nonthreatening way

Select materials
- Use visual materials
  - Books and encyclopedias
  - Magazines, catalogues, directories
  - Newspapers and comics
  - Indexes, atlases, almanacs, dictionaries, readers' guides, card catalog
  - Films, filmstrips, slides
  - Videotapes, television programs
- Use nonvisual materials
  - Audiotapes
  - Records
  - Radio programs
  - Field trips
- Use human resources
  - Interviews
  - Letters
  - On-site visitations
- Encourage self-selection of materials
  - "What can I understand?"
  - "What gives me the best answers?"

(continued)

BOX 12.4 *(continued)*

Guide the information search
- Encourage active research through
  - Reading
  - Listening
  - Observing
  - Talking
  - Writing
- Facilitate with questions
  - "How are you doing?"
  - "Can I help you?"
  - "Do you have all the materials you need?"
  - "Can I help you with ideas you don't understand?"

Have students keep records
- Keep a learning log that includes plans, procedures, notes, rough drafts, etc.
- Keep book-record cards
- Keep a record of conferences with the teacher

Consider different forms of writing
- Initiate a discussion of sharing techniques
- Encourage a variety of writing forms
  - An essay or paper
  - A "lecture" to a specific audience
  - A case study
  - Story, adventure, science fiction, etc.
  - Dialogue, conversation, interview
  - Dramatization through scripts
  - Commentary or editorial
  - Thumbnail sketch

Guide the writing process
- Help students organize information
- Guide first-draft writing
- Encourage responding, revising, and rewriting
- "Publish" finished products
  - Individual presentations
  - Classroom arrangement
  - Allow for class interaction

"Procedures for Guiding Research" from Richard T. Vacca and Jo Anne L. Vacca, *Content Area Reading,* 4th ed. (New York: HarperCollins Publishers 1993).

● BOX 12.5

A Second-Grade Teacher's Literature Web for a Unit on Communities (Some Sample Titles)

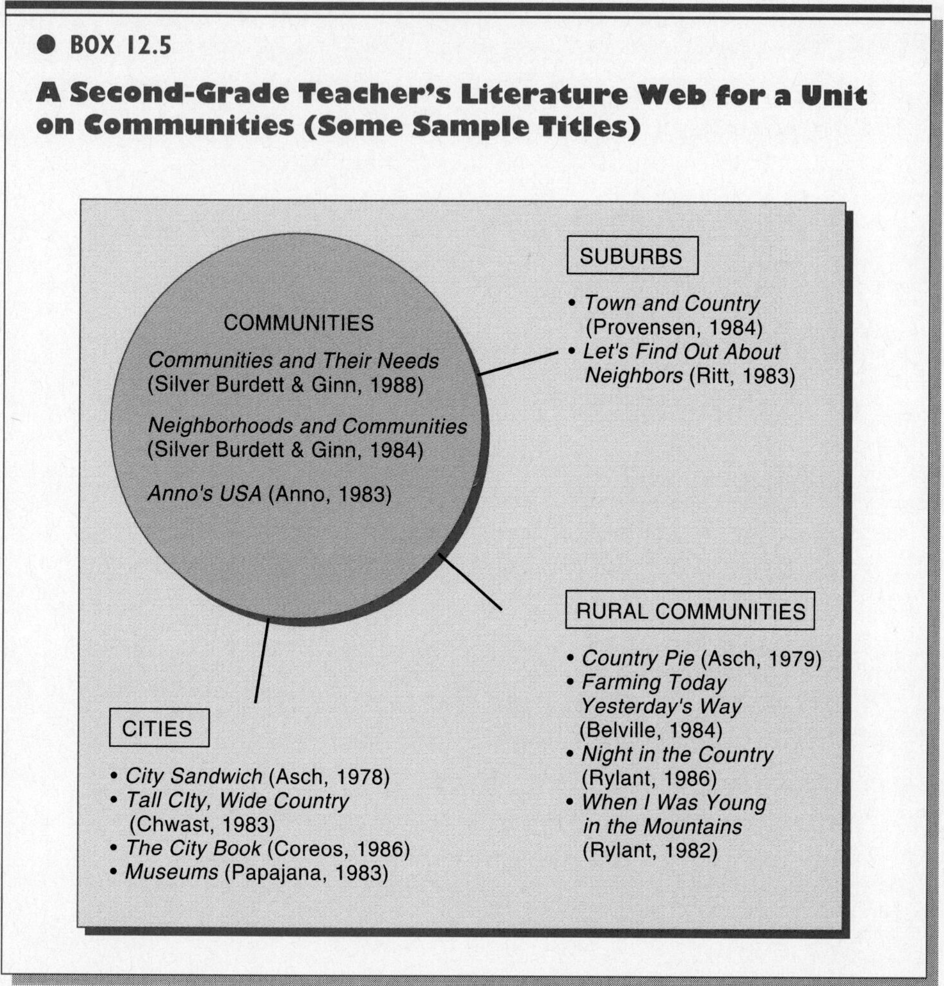

> used as needed to introduce and reinforce concepts. Students will also have access to a variety of materials with which they can explore areas of individual interest. During this unit, the students will have the opportunity to investigate many aspects of ornithology including the evolution of birds, the adaptation of birds to their habitats, and the interrelation of birds and people.

As stated in her description of the unit, *The Life of Birds* was the class's central source of information; it helped form the basis by which students "branched out" into a variety of information sources—both fiction and nonfiction. For example, Ms. Mark used *Mr. Popper's Penguins* by Atwater as a read-aloud to introduce children to the study of penguins. *A Chick Hatches,* another readaloud, was used in conjunction with an experiment on the incubation of an egg. Ms. Mark read different sections of the

BOX 12.6

A Sixth-Grade Teacher's Literature Web for a Unit on the Middle Ages

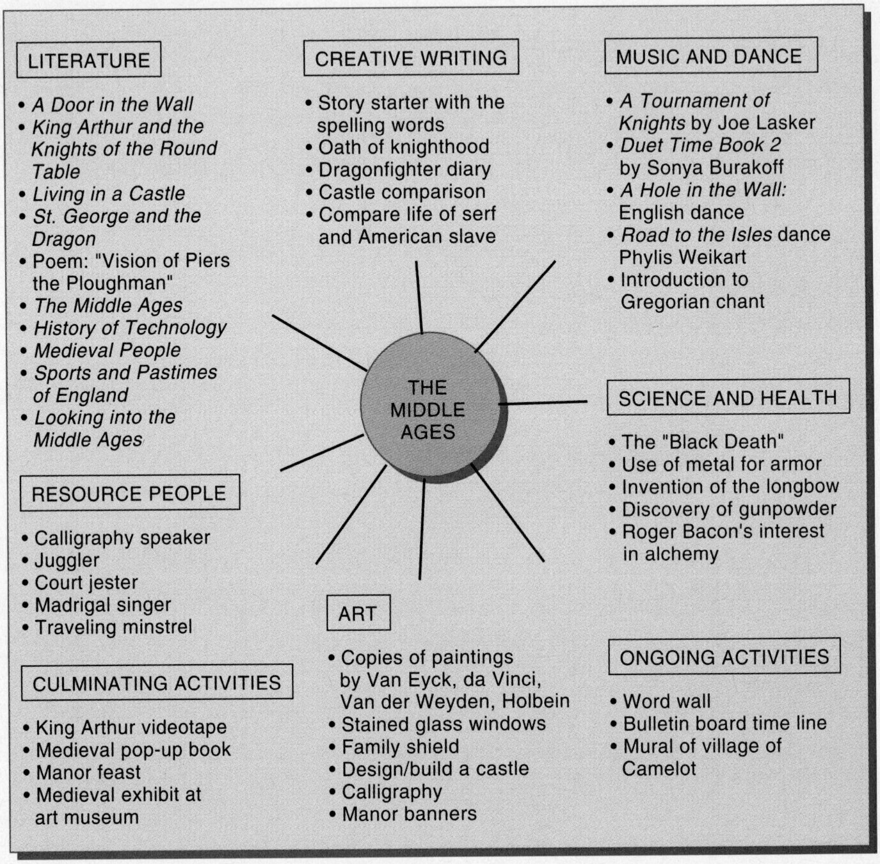

book during the course of the unit, as children observed the egg's hatching and different stages of the chick's development.

The last two weeks of the unit contained equally rich and varied activities but emphasized more writing than the initial assignments. For example, Ms. Mark capitalized on the classroom experiment of hatching a live chick with the following writing activity.

Our Chick Has Hatched!

After the chick has hatched and the class has decided on its name, each student will write an announcement to his family about the new arrival. The announcement will consist of two parts: (1) statistics of the hatching, and (2) a personal note.

To help the students write the first part, actual samples of birth announcements were brought in by students and the teacher. These were read aloud and posted on the bulletin board. The teacher used these samples to walk the students through the process of announcing birth statistics, including name, date, weight, and length.

When the students had some practice with the first part of the assignment, some additional guidelines were given for writing the personal note. The personal note was not to be longer than one page and it was to focus on the one aspect of the incubation process that most impressed the student.

Developing a unit of study involves deliberate teacher planning to set a tone for students to actively engage in learning around a content theme or topic. It allows a rich opportunity to make reading useful by bridging the gap between children and content-area textbooks.

The activities used in a unit of study evolve from your knowledge of reading, writing, discussion, and listening strategies. The strategies that follow are designed to help students learn from texts. They are appropriate with expository writing, but in most cases can be adapted to stories. These strategies, when combined with the strategies presented in previous chapters, bridge the gap between students and potentially difficult texts.

Strategies Before Reading

The strategies in this section augment those found in Chapter 6. For learning to occur, there must be a point of contact between the reader's knowledge of the world and the ideas communicated by the textbook author. As we explained in Chapter 6, what students know, feel, and believe is a major factor in learning; it helps determine the extent to which they will make sense out of any situation. Thus an instructional goal worth pursuing is to help students make contact through a variety of learning strategies that build and activate background knowledge. Such strategies involve prereading preparation.

We noted in Chapter 6 that you can help students learn new ideas by giving them a frame of reference as they get ready to read. A frame of reference is actually an anchor point; it reflects the cognitive structure students need to relate new information to existing knowledge. Helping students organize what they know and showing them where and how new ideas fit is essential for learning to take place.

Previewing and Skimming

A good way to start previewing with a group of children is to model some questions that all readers ask to prepare for reading. **Previewing,** after all, should help students become aware of the purposes for a reading assignment. "What kind of reading are we going to do?" "What is our goal?" "Should we try to remember details or look for the main ideas?" "How much time will this assignment take?" "What things do we already know about . . . (the solar system, for example)?" "What do we still need to find out?" These questions prepare children for what's coming. Raising questions and setting purposes is the beginning of efficient processing of information. It calls for further explicit instruction in previewing.

First, select a subject area in which your textbook contains aids that are obviously visual. The textbook writer has incorporated a number of organizational and typographic aids as guideposts for readers. Point out how the table of contents, preface, chapter introductions or summaries, and chapter questions can give readers valuable clues about the overall structure of a textbook or the important ideas in a unit or chapter. Previewing a table of contents, for example, not only creates a general impression, but also helps readers of all ages to distinguish the forest from the trees. The table of contents give students a feel for the overall theme or structure of the course material so that they may get a sense of the scope and sequence of ideas at the very beginning of the unit. You can also use the table of contents to build background and discuss the relatedness of each of the parts of the book. Model for students the kinds of questions that should be raised. "Why do the authors begin with ______________ in Part One?" "If you were the author, would you have arranged the major parts in the text differently?" "Why?"

To illustrate how you might use the table of contents, study how a fourth-grade teacher introduced a unit on plants in the environment. Ms. Henderson asked her students to open their books to Part One in the table of contents. "What do you think this part of the book ["Plant Competitors"] is about?" "Why do you think so?" Key words or terms in the table of contents led to these questions: "What do you think the author means by *unwanted plants?*" "What does *parasite* mean?" "What do parasites have to do with *nongreen plants?*" Open-ended questions such as these helped Ms. Henderson keep her fourth-graders focused on the material and on the value of predicting and anticipating content.

As these students get into a particular chapter, they will learn how to use additional organizational aids such as the chapter's introduction, summary, or questions at the end. These aids should create a frame of reference for the important ideas in the chapter. They can also survey chapter titles, headings, subheadings, words and phrases in special type, pictures, diagrams, charts, and graphs.

Here are some rules or steps to follow when previewing as Ms. Henderson's students did.

Read the title, converting it to a question. ("What are plant competitors in man's environment?")

Read the introduction, summary, and questions, stating the author's main points. ("All living things compete with each other; the competitors of useful plants become man's competitors; weeds are unwanted plants; nongreen plants living in or on other plants and animals are parasites; people try to control plant competitors.")

Read the heads and subheads; then convert them to questions. (Competition; weeds; nongreen plant competitors; controlling plant competitors. "How are plant competitors controlled?")

Read highlighted print. ("Competitors; nongreen plants; parasites; smut; chemical sprays are very poisonous.")

Study visual materials; what do pictures, maps, and so on tell about a chapter's content? (Pictures of mustard plants, destroyed ears of corn, a white pine attacked by tiny nongreen plants, a helicopter spraying a truck farm.)

Until Ms. Henderson's fourth-graders were able to do this somewhat independently, she walked them through the steps many times. She also selected one or two pages from the assigned reading and developed transparencies with some questions her students should ask while previewing. Showing the overhead transparencies to the whole class, she explained her reasons for the questions. Then the students opened their books to another section of the chapter, taking turns asking the kinds of questions she had modeled. Soon they raised some of their own questions while previewing.

Skimming. Learning how to skim content material effectively is a natural part of previewing. *Skimming* involves intensive previewing of the reading assignment to see what it will be about. To help elementary students get a good sense of what is coming, have them read the first sentence of every paragraph (often an important idea). The fourth graders about to study plant competitors read these first sentences.

If you had two pet cats and gave one of them some tuna fish, what would happen?

Plants, of course, don't know they are competing.

Even green plants compete with one another for energy sources.

Plants are often weakened by the parasites growing on them.

Many states passed laws to help with the control of weeds.

An effective motivator for raising students' expectations about their assigned text material is to direct them to skim the entire reading selection rapidly, taking no more than two minutes. You might even get a timer and encourage the children to zip through every page. When time is up, ask the class to recall everything they've read. Both the teacher and the students will be surprised by the quantity and quality of the recalls.

Previewing and skimming are important strategies for helping children develop knowledge of textbook aids and for surveying texts to make predictions. They help get at general understanding as students learn how to size up material, judge its relevance to a topic, or gain a good idea of what a passage is about.

Organizers

To prepare children conceptually for ideas to be encountered in reading, help them link what they know to what they will learn. An **organizer** provides a frame of reference for comprehending text precisely for this reason—to help readers make connections between their prior knowledge and new material. Swaby (1983) defined organizers as involving teacher-directed attempts to clarify and organize students' thinking "in such a way that they know what information they already have that will be important and helpful in comprehending incoming information. . . . Any effort by a teacher to prepare students conceptually for incoming information by hooking the major concepts of the new information to the concepts already possessed by the learners can be interpreted as an advance organizer" (p. 76).

There's no one way to develop or use an organizer. Organizers may also be developed as *written previews* or as *verbal presentations.* Whatever format you decide to use, an organizer should highlight key concepts and ideas to be encountered in print. These should be prominent and easily identifiable in the lesson presentation. Another key feature of an organizer activity should be the explicit links made between the children's background knowledge and experience and the ideas in the reading selection.

An organizer may be developed for narrative or expository text. It can be used for difficult text selections, when the material is unfamiliar to students because of limited schema. An organizer can be constructed by following these guidelines:

Analyze the content of a reading selection, identifying its main ideas and key concepts.

Link these ideas directly to children's experiences and storehouse of knowledge. Use real-life incidents, examples, illustrations, analogies, or anecdotes to which student readers can relate.

Raise questions in the organizer that will pique interest and engage students in thinking about the text to be read.

Study the advance organizer in Box 12.7 on page 437 and then read the selection that follows:

UNDERSTANDING THE LANGUAGE OF A DOG

Dogs may not use words to tell how they feel, but they do use parts of their bodies to talk. This is called "body language." When you wave to someone, you are using body language. When a dog wags its tail, it is using body language, too.

Most dogs have a strong sense of *territoriality.* This means they are protective of things that belong to them, including their living space. A dog may feel quite

● BOX 12.7

Organizer for the Reading Selection "Understanding the Language of a Dog"

MAIN IDEA OF PASSAGE TO BE READ	Dogs and human beings are alike in an important way. We both use "language" to communicate messages to others. A dog uses a unique language.
BUILDING AND SHARING PRIOR KNOWLEDGE AND EXPERIENCES	When you think of our "language," what comes to mind immediately? *Probably words.* Using words in speaking and writing is one way to communicate a message to someone else. But try to think about how you sit or stand when you're angry or pouting. Can someone get the message you're trying to communicate just by looking at you? How about when you're nervous or excited? How else do we show others what we're feeling or thinking about without using words? (Discuss the other elements of body language.) Can anyone ever tell what your pet is thinking or feeling? How? (Discuss student responses. Compare examples.)
MAKING THE CONNECTION BETWEEN PRIOR KNOWLEDGE AND THE PASSAGE TO BE READ	Use what we have just discussed to read the passage for today. Look for specific ways in which a dog can communicate with you, or with other animals.

strongly about its bed, a favorite toy, or the backyard. And it is the dog's sense of territoriality that makes it communicate through its body.

A dog may use its body to say many things. By bowing down, wagging its tail, barking, or holding out one front paw, the dog may be saying, "Let's play." When the dog crouches down and rolls over on its back, it means, "Come closer." And if the dog scratches at you with a paw, it may mean, "I want something."

> A dog may use body language to warn you away from its territory. To do this, the dog may show its teeth, stick its ears up, growl, or hold its tail out stiffly. This means, "Stay away." The dog may growl, crouch, lower its tail, and flatten its ears against its head. This means, "Better stay away. I'm not sure about you."

As we already suggested, the key to a successful organizer lies in the discussion that it initiates. Children must participate actively in making the links between what they know and what they will learn. Much will be lost if they are assigned to read (or listen or view) an organizer without the opportunity to act upon it within the context of their own experiences.

Graphic Organizers. Key concepts or main ideas in the material being studied can also be displayed as a **graphic organizer,** where key technical terms are arranged to show their relationships to each other.

Ms. Mark designed a graphic organizer to show her third graders vocabulary in relation to more inclusive vocabulary concepts they would meet in their study of birds. Before constructing this activity, Ms. Mark listed the key concepts in her four-week unit, "Birds Are Special Animals." She then followed the steps suggested by Barron (1968) for developing an organizer and introducing it to her students.

Analyze vocabulary and list important words. Ms. Mark found these key terms in *The Life of Birds,* edited by Donald Moyle:

prehistoric birds	protection
development	language
behavior	ornithology
migration	difference

Arrange the concepts to be learned. Ms. Mark first chose the word "ornithology" as the most inclusive concept, superordinate to all the others. Next, she classified the terms immediately *under* the superordinate concept and coordinated them with each other.

Add any other vocabulary terms that you believe students understand. Ms. Mark added terms like protect, animals, and help.

Evaluate the organizer. The interrelationships among the key terms looked like Figure 12.1 and made sense to Ms. Mark and her third graders.

Introduce students to the learning task. Ms. Mark created as much discussion as possible among her third graders as she presented the vocabulary terms. She drew on their understanding and previous experiences with birds as well as on class activities over the previous few days that introduced the unit (e.g., some preassessment and an anticipation guide).

As you complete the learning task, relate new information to the overview. Using this overview as a study guide throughout the bird unit, Ms. Mark encouraged students to

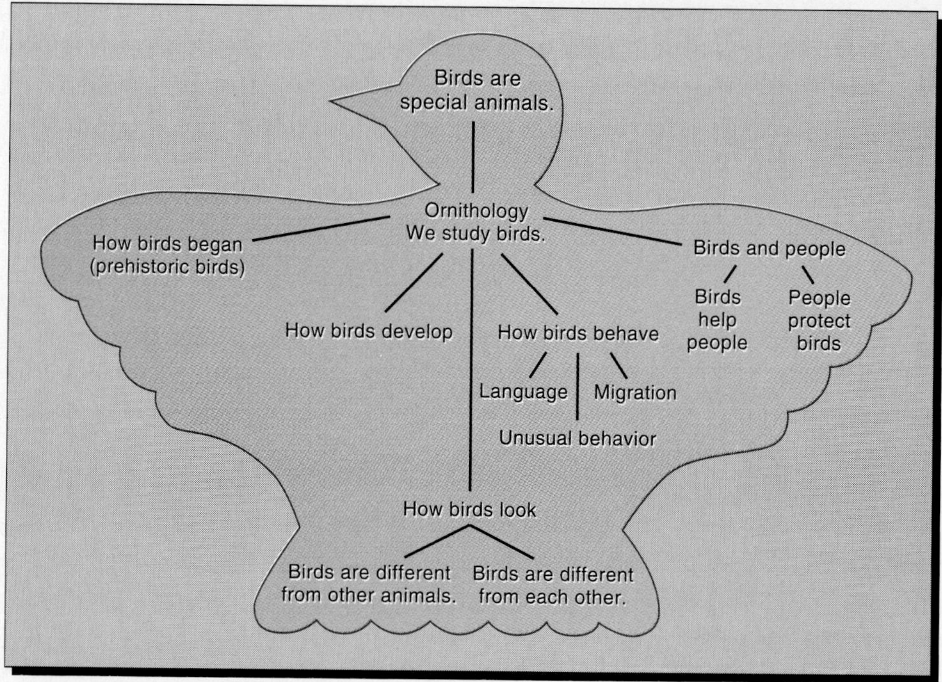

● **FIGURE 12.1** Graphic organizer

discuss what information was still needed and where it might best be located on the graphic organizer.

Anticipation Guides

By creating anticipation about the meaning of what will be read, teachers facilitate student-centered purposes for reading. An **anticipation guide** is a series of oral or written statements for individual students to respond to before they read the text assignment. The statements serve as a springboard into discussion. Students must rely on what they already know to make educated guesses about the material to be read: They must make predictions.

Let's go back to the fourth-grade class studying about plants in the environment. The teacher, Ms. Henderson, wanted to help students discuss what they knew and believed about the unit in order to raise their expectations about the content matter before reading the text. Above all, she was determined to involve students actively. Here are the guidelines that Ms. Henderson followed in constructing and using anticipation guides.

Analyze the material to be read. Determine the major ideas, implicit and explicit, with which students will interact.

Write those ideas in short, clear declarative statements. These statements should in some way reflect the world that students live in or know about. Therefore, avoid abstractions whenever possible.

Put these statements into a format that will elicit anticipation and prediction making.

Discuss readers' predictions and anticipations prior to reading the text selection.

Assign the text selection. Have students evaluate the statements in light of the author's intent and purpose.

Contrast readers' predictions with the author's intended meaning.

Using these guidelines, Ms. Henderson pinpointed several major concepts, put them in the form of short statements, and wrote each one on the board. After some initial discussion about what students might already know about plants in the environment, Ms. Henderson distributed two three-by-five-inch pieces of construction paper (one green and one yellow) to each child and explained:

> On the yellow paper write "unlikely" and on the green paper write "likely." I will read each of the statements on the board; you will think about it and decide whether it is "likely" or "unlikely." Then, after fifteen seconds, I will say "Go" and you will hold up either your yellow *or* your green card.

The anticipation guide for the above activity included several statements.

> A dandelion is always a weed.
>
> All plants make their own food.
>
> All living things in the environment compete with one another.

The information in each of the statements was developed in two short chapters in the students' text. After each statement or pair of statements, Ms. Henderson encouraged the children to discuss the reasons for their responses with questions such as "Why?" "Why not?" or "Can you give an example?"

An interesting example of how an anticipation guide may be used in conjunction with a four-day lesson is contained in Box 12.8. It was designed for use with third graders as an introduction to a unit on primates revolving around the book, *The Story of Nim, the Chimp Who Learned Language* by Anna Michel.

After the small group discussion, the whole class discusses the trends and ideas that emerged in the groups. These ideas are written on the board in a place where they can remain for a day or two. The book is then assigned in its entirety to be read before the next day's class. Next day, students consider each statement on the anticipation guide again and discuss in small groups the ideas that emerged from reading the text. They compare these with the prereading ideas on the board to identify similarities and differences in the

● BOX 12.8

Anticipation Guide for The Story of Nim, the Chimp Who Learned Language

Directions: Read the statements below and place a check next to those that you agree with. Discuss your choices in small groups and explain why you agreed with the statements you checked.

________1. Chimpanzees can imitate what humans do, but attach no meaning to their actions.

________2. Language can be learned by animals in the same way and sequence in which a child learns language.

________3. Once language is learned, a chimpanzee will forget it and those who taught him, given an absence from one or both.

________4. Scientists undertake projects with animals in order to better understand humans.

________5. Relationships between animals and people aren't as close as those between people and people or animals and animals.

Developed by Elizabeth Martin and reprinted with permission.

two sets of ideas. Reasons for ideas should be given by students and controversial issues arising might then lead to a debate. For example, "What is the real meaning in a chimpanzee's language acquisition compared with a human child's?"

Brainstorming

This prereading activity, **brainstorming,** is especially helpful in getting students to generate ideas they can use to think about the upcoming reading material. The brainstorming procedure involves two basic steps: (1) identifying a broad concept that reflects the main topic to be studied in the assigned reading, and (2) having students work in small groups to generate a list of words related to the broad concept within a specified length of time.

Brainstorming sessions are valuable not only from an instructional perspective, but from a diagnostic one as well. Observant teachers discover what knowledge their students possess about the topic to be studied. It also helps students become aware of how much they know, individually and collectively, about the topic.

Some teachers assign hypothetical problems to be solved before reading a selection, or a real-life school-related problem. Others simply select a major concept in the reading material and get students actively involved in brainstorming. Mr. Davis, a sixth-grade teacher, used the latter model to develop a brainstorming activity for a story by Robert Zacks, "The Nest."

Mr. Davis began by telling his sixth graders they would soon be reading a story called "The Nest." But first, he said, they would work with one of the major concepts of the story, *restrictions.* He divided the class into small groups, using an alphabetical scheme. (Other times he may choose the groups or let students form their own groups.) Once the groups were formed, Mr. Davis used a three-step brainstorming activity.

> In your groups, brainstorm as many ideas as possible in three minutes that relate to the concept *restrictions.* Have one member of your group record your ideas.
>
> As a group, put the ideas into categories (groups) wherever they seem to be related. Be prepared to explain the reasons behind the grouping of ideas.
>
> Following class discussion on how ideas were grouped, examine your own work again and, using these ideas and others gained from the other groups, make predictions on what you believe the story might be about. Be sure to consider the title of the story somewhere in your predictions.

The activity took about twenty minutes and required intermittent teacher direction. Mr. Davis, for example, followed Step 1 with a brief oral direction for Step 2. Before moving on to Step 3, he initiated a class discussion in which groups shared their ideas for grouping ideas into categories and the logic behind the categories. This gave both individuals and groups a chance to react to the varied categories. Although a teacher may offer some suggestions to a group that has bogged down in the categorizing process, we caution that this be done sparingly and only to keep the process going.

After Step 3 of the brainstorming activity is complete and predictions have been generated, the story is usually assigned. It would, however, also be possible to extend the prereading phase. To illustrate, Mr. Davis might have asked students to complete a survey of parents, grandparents, and other adults about restrictions they were faced with in a different generation and which ones bothered them the most.

Strategies to Guide and Model Reading

There are numerous strategies that can be used to guide reading and writing in content areas (Vacca and Vacca, 1993). Certainly those suggested in Chapters 5, 6, and 7 may be adapted for textbook study. In this section, strategies are explained that help children learn from expository text. They not only guide the reading process, but also model for students how a skilled reader might approach and study a text selection.

Helping Students Recognize Text Structure

Since understanding concepts and ideas in content-area texts is easier when students can determine the main ideas and distinguish which are the major and minor supporting details, helping students learn how authors of content text organize information helps them learn the information.

Hess (1991) had students brainstorm questions as they began a unit on animal study. Students wrote questions ("I wonder. . . ") on strips of paper. This seemed to help students set a purpose for reading. Classifying and sorting the questions into groups helped students determine the type of information they needed. Hess notes "once students had categorized their own questions, they easily recognized the structure of expository text" (p. 230).

To help students determine the relationship of major ideas and supporting details, Maria Valeri-Gold (1993) used words from science and social studies textbooks to help students determine the relationship of words and concepts by having students arrange the words into outline form.

Teach students how to outline:

A visual representation

Numbers, letters and space represent importance of ideas—the further an idea is indented, the less important it is.

Write words on a transparency or give students words on a worksheet with blank outline.

Ask students: Which words fit together in groups? Which words describe categories? Which word explains the whole topic?

Students unscramble words onto blank outline.

Students can create their own lists and challenge other students.

Reciprocal Teaching

Reciprocal teaching, as devised by Palincsar and Brown (1984), helps students to understand how to study and learn from text. The success of a reciprocal teaching lesson depends on the teacher's ability to model how an expert reader uses four comprehension activities to understand a text selection: (1) raising questions about a text segment; (2) predicting what the segment is about; (3) summarizing the important points; and (4) clarifying difficult vocabulary and concepts.

In reciprocal teaching, the teacher begins the lesson by modeling each of the four comprehension activities while leading a discussion of the text. During this phase of the lesson, the quality of the dialogue between teacher and students depends on how explicit the teacher is in demonstrating each of the comprehension activities.

After observing the teacher, students are invited to share or add to what the teacher has stated and then to teach the remaining sections of the text selection. For example, a student assumes the role of the teacher and proceeds to model one or more of the comprehension activities on the next segment of text. If the student runs into trouble with any of

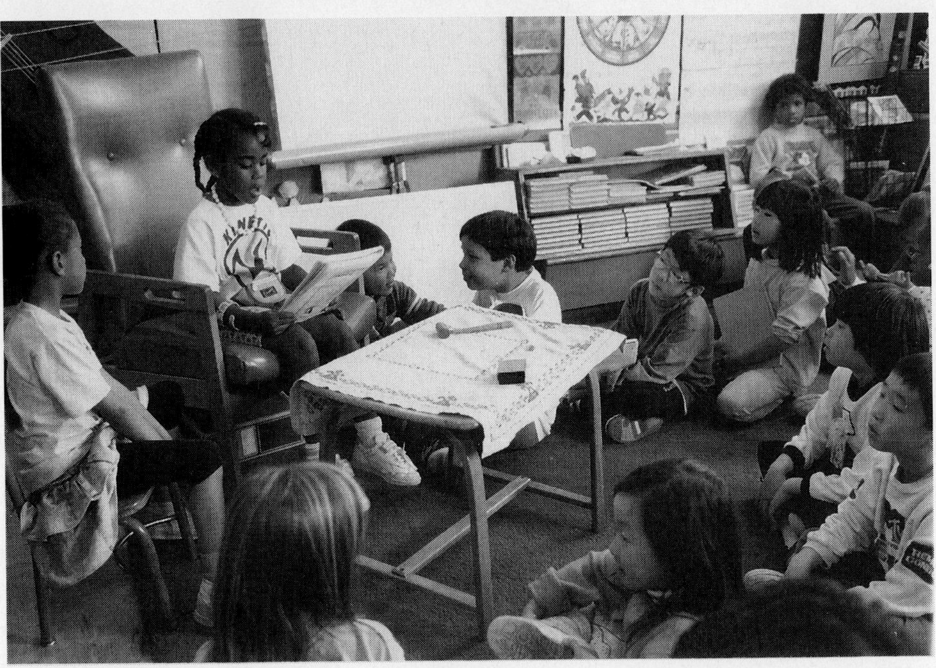

In reciprocal teaching, a student assumes the role of the teacher and models one or more comprehension activities from a text.

the activities, the teacher recenters the lesson to provide support by adjusting the demands of the task. Gradually, the teacher withdraws support and the student continues teaching the lesson.

Planning is the key to reciprocal teaching. Herrmann (1988) suggested that teachers plan a lesson in two phases. In the first phase, you should become familiar with the text selection. This entails the following:

Identify which text segments will be used to demonstrate the four comprehension activities.

Identify salient questions in the selection and generate additional questions about the material.

Generate possible predictions about each text segment.

Underline summarizing sentences and generate possible summaries for each text segment.

Circle difficult vocabulary or concepts.

The second phase of planning requires two additional decisions on the part of the teacher. First, you will need to decide to what extent students already use the comprehension activities. Which activities do they use effectively? What will they need to help them better comprehend? And second, decide on the level of support that various students require to eventually lead each of the activities.

In Box 12.9, Herrmann (1988) provides an excellent model of a reciprocal teaching lesson.

Reciprocal teaching helps students to think more strategically about reading. Our experience with the procedure suggests that it is a complicated strategy; teachers will need to work with it several times before they feel accomplished with its implementation. Nevertheless, if used often enough students will begin to approach learning from text knowing what to do and how to do it.

● **BOX 12.9**

Model of a Reciprocal Teaching Lesson

1. Read the text title and have the students tell what they expect or would like to learn from the selection. Summarize the group's predictions and, if appropriate, add a few of your own. Note how the lesson begins in the following lesson excerpt.

T: What's the title of our new passage?
S: "The Miracle of Butterflies."
T: Right. What's the miracle of butterflies? In your own words, what would you predict this is going to be about?
S: How butterflies fly?
T: Oh, that's a good prediction!
S: What they do.
S: What season they come out, like summer.
T: Okay. Those are some excellent predictions. Let's begin.

2. Read a small portion of the text aloud, paragraph by paragraph.
3. Ask a question about the content. Invite the group to answer the question. Invite individuals to share additional questions generated while they read the selection.

T: My question is: What have the people of Butterfly City, U.S.A., done to protect the butterflies?
S: They made a law making it illegal.
T: To do what?
S: To kill butterflies.
T: Exactly. Does anyone else have a question?

(continued)

BOX 12.9 *(continued)*

4. Summarize what has been read by identifying the gist of the segment and explain how you arrived at this summary. Invite the group to comment on the summary. Note how the teacher summarized in the following lesson excerpt.

   T: My summary is that this is about the migration of monarch butterflies. I thought of that summary because the authors introduced the story with a good topic sentence. That was a good clue. Do you have anything that should be added to my summary?

5. Lead a discussion to clarify any words or ideas that are unclear or confusing.

   T: Let me ask you something here. Is there an unclear meaning in this paragraph?
   S: Yes. Where it says "scrawls in wavy light."
   T: Now, does the sun ever write a message in the sky?
   S: No.
   T: No. What is the author doing here?
   S: Making up the whole thing in his mind.
   T: All right. It doesn't really happen but the author is using this expression to say that the sun sends us a message and that it can be used as an energy source. But certainly you will never look at the sky and see a message written by the sun.

B. A. Herrmann, "Two Approaches for Helping Poor Readers Become More Strategic," *The Reading Teacher,* 42 (1988) p. 27. Reprinted by permission of the International Reading Association.

SUMMARY

Elementary children often experience their first difficulties with reading when they encounter textbooks in content areas. The transition to content-area reading should not pose major obstacles, although textbooks are inherently difficult for most students. In literature-centered classrooms, children make the transition to content-area texts naturally. They learn to approach and appreciate many genres of books, including the textbook.

To understand what makes a textbook difficult, several factors that contribute to the readability of a text were explained. Also, we explored the uses and benefits of using literature across the curriculum. Literature provides children with intense involvement in a subject through many kinds of texts (e.g., biography, historical and realistic fiction, informational books). Literature is also a schema builder and can be used to accommodate different reading abilities and interests in the classroom. Moreover, units of study provide teachers with the structure needed to coordinate literature study within the context of meaningful activity.

Various strategies were presented to show how teachers can facilitate textbook study and learning. Some strategies to implement before reading included previewing, organizers, anticipation guides, and brainstorming. Other strategies were recommended for guiding and modeling children's reading.

TEACHER-ACTION RESEARCHER

1. Plan a content-area lesson using a reading selection from a social studies or science textbook. What prereading strategies will you use? How will you guide reader-text interactions? What follow-up or post-reading strategies will you decide upon? Teach this lesson to a small group of children. Evaluate the lesson asking: What concepts did the children acquire through the reading? How well did you establish purpose and activate a schema for reading? Did you sustain motivation throughout the lesson? What was the most effective part of the lesson? What was the least effective part?

2. Construct a graphic organizer using the procedures suggested in this chapter. In a lesson, try out the graphic organizer that you developed. Evaluate your use of this activity.

3. Observe a lesson taught to students in a content area other than reading, such as math, science, health, or social studies. Note all the instructional strategies that the teacher uses to help students learn with texts. How are the students involved in the lesson? Think about the ways that reading to learn played or didn't play a role in the lesson. What alternative instructional strategies might have been used?

KEY TERMS

expository text
considerate text
readability
literature across the curriculum
trade books
literature web
previewing
organizers
graphic organizer
anticipation guide
brainstorming

CHAPTER 13

Assessing Reading Performance

BETWEEN THE LINES

In this chapter you will discover:

- **The reasons to use authentic assessments in making decisions about instruction.**
- **Purposes for formal, standardized assessments.**
- **Purposes for informal, alternative assessments.**
- **Techniques for using miscue analysis, running records, kidwatching, anecdotal notes, checklists, and interviews.**
- **Essential elements of portfolios.**

It was springtime, and Sue Latham smiled as she looked through a folder with assessment information on John, a "low" reader in her third-grade classroom. How her assessment of him had changed from early fall to now! She noted that on a *formal,* **standardized reading test,** given in October, John had scored in the 32nd percentile, which meant that he was below average in comparison to other third graders. Although she did not think this score was particularly useful to her *in deciding how to work with John,* Mrs. Latham knew that her principal examined these scores. She also noted that on an assessment, more *informal* in nature, related to his attitude toward reading John viewed himself positively. He also did well on a section from another informal reading assessment in which he picked questions from a list that he thought would help a person understand the important ideas about a selection. This reminded her of yesterday's social studies lesson on explorers. John and other students had raised some insightful questions as the class previewed the chapter, and created a class list of questions that might be answered as they worked on the chapter.

At the start of the school year, Mrs. Latham had decided to work with John in a second-grade basal reader along with four other students. Her decision initially was based on a conversation with John's second-grade teacher and her review of the *skill mastery tests* administered as part of the basal reader program. One of these tests assessed students' ability to associate the hard and soft sound of the letter *g*. John didn't reach mastery of this particular skill. In other words, he didn't score correctly on 80 percent of the items related to the skill objective; in fact, he answered only six out of ten items correctly. This puzzled Mrs. Latham because just the day before John had shared a part of a book he was reading about a visit to the zoo, which included seeing *g*iraffes and petting *g*oats. John didn't experience difficulty reading passages containing words with soft and hard *g* sounds. Later in October, she had a miscue analysis compiled from a **running record** of John's oral reading during small group instruction. She had noted no difficulties in his reading of either soft or hard sounds.

Mrs. Latham decided back then to capitalize on John's strength of raising questions about material read both in his reading group and in social studies and science units. She decided *not* to use additional instructional time working on the soft and hard sound of *g*, even though he had not achieved mastery for this objective on the basal reader test. In fact, in November, she thought that John was functioning well enough in the second-grade basal reader to reassign him to the third-grade reader. The bottom line is that Mrs. Latham considered information from informal and formal tests *and* her observations of John in actual reading situations. She then *made decisions based on multiple data sources.* Corroborating her instructional decisions was John's **portfolio** of work in progress: some stories and poems he was working on in response to their literature theme unit on tall tales and his personal reading list for sustained silent reading. By using examples of John's actual reading and actual writing, Sue Latham had made an **authentic assessment** of John's *performance in literacy*—a reason to smile.

In this chapter, we emphasize the importance of making decisions about instruction using multiple ways to authentically assess the *processes* students are engaged in as they read and learn. Diagnostic testing *and* teaching allow you to gather information in order to make inferences about children's reading ability and performance. Tests provide one perspective for becoming knowledgeable about a student's performance; actual teaching situations provide another perspective; and portfolios of student work provide still another. The information gathered from several situations and sources helps to strengthen decisions. Let's examine why.

Toward a Corroborative Framework for Decision Making

The process that Sue Latham used to develop an authentic assessment of John is another example of how teachers screen and filter information about children's performance through their concepts and beliefs about reading and learning to read. Mrs. Latham holds an interactive view of the reading process. She believes that reading acquisition involves coordinating and integrating many skills during actual reading situations. A child learns to read the way Mrs. Latham first learned to use a stick shift in a car with manual transmission. What needed to be learned was how to coordinate the use of the clutch pedal, gas pedal, brake, and stick in shifting from gear to gear. A beginner may practice pushing the clutch pedal in and out in isolated drill or simulate shifting from gear to gear. However, actually experiencing stick shifting in traffic makes the difference in learning how to coordinate and integrate the skills.

And so it is with John in his learning to become a fluent reader. When contrasting his performance on the test with his performance in a real reading situation, Mrs. Latham chose to weigh the information from the teaching situation more heavily than the score on the test. Because her students keep portfolios of their work in reading and writing, they too understand their progress in literacy and are learning to evaluate their own strengths and weaknesses in various reading and writing tasks. Portfolios also helped Mrs. Latham plan the kinds of instruction that would move her students toward more mature reading and writing. The student portfolios, works-in-progress in literacy, are a record of the process of learning in reading and writing for each student. They hold valuable data about growth and progress in literacy performance, and, where weaknesses exist, they are useful in planning the instructional next step. Portfolios have become an important aspect of authentic assessment of literacy performance.

Casey Stengel, manager of the New York Yankees in the 1950s and later, of the New York Mets, was as renowned for his wonderful use of language as he was for winning baseball games. On one occasion after losing a hard-fought game, Stengel was quoted as saying, "You can know the score of the game and not know the real score." The real score involves understanding and appreciating the dynamics of what happens on the playing field during the game regardless of the outcome. In our estimation, the real score in reading always involves understanding and appreciating *how* children interact with print in authentic reading situations and *why*. Authentic assessment, according to Wiggins (1989), involves asking our students to actually perform a task that represents the type of "thoughtful knowhow" (p. 705) that demonstrates sufficient knowledge and understanding in a subject to do it well.

We advocate using *multiple indicators* of student performance for assessment. Any single indicator—whether it involves commercially prepared or teacher-made tests or observation—provides a perspective, one means of attesting to the accuracy of the score or phenomenon under examination. Multiple indicators, however, build a *corroborative framework* that strengthens decision making. As teachers we are constantly faced with making decisions. Multiple indicators of reading strengthen decision making, because information from one data source builds on or is contrasted with information from other data sources. The result is a rich knowledge base for understanding how and why students perform in reading.

Because reading takes place inside the head, the process is not directly observable and, therefore, not directly measurable. Yet, one of the important functions of reading tests, whether formal or informal, should be to help teachers understand a human process that is essentially hidden from direct examination. What are some national trends impacting on assessment? To what extent do standardized, criteria-referenced, informal, and teacher-made tests play a constructive role in the classroom? Why is keeping a running record an invaluable part of authentic classroom assessment? How can portfolio assessment be used to show parents, students, and administrators growth that students have made in reading and writing? Let's read to find out answers to these broad but important questions.

Trends in Assessment

The growing demand for reliable, comprehensive, understandable, and up-to-date information about assessment is unrelenting. Two major trends are directly associated with this demand: (1) the public's call for assurance that students will leave school well prepared, and (2) educators' search for first-hand process indicators of student performance to evaluate their progress.

Proficiency Testing

As our nation's education system moves closer to the year 2000, state legislators are enacting laws that require students to pass proficiency exams before they can graduate. The premise is that, if a student attains a certain score on a test that all other students across the state take, then he or she has demonstrated competence in that body of knowledge (math, reading, writing, etc.). This **proficiency testing** provides the public with a *guarantee* that students can perform at a level necessary to function in society. Unfortunately, there are no real guarantees on any test, especially based on a one-time performance. Yet, this is a good example of what Roger Farr sees as public dissatisfaction with education, and the continuing focus on standards and testing (1992a).

Compounding this demand for more standardized testing is the problem that the tests themselves are not adequate, given what we now know about literacy. The new standardized achievement tests do not help us understand students' reading as a process of constructing meaning in context. As Ravitch (1993) notes, new standardized achievement tests should reflect knowledge that is worthwhile and useful, for "standards will be meaningless if students continue to be tested without regard to them" (p. 772). And, Farr's analysis of reading-test content has led to the "conclusion that the reading required on most tests is not much like the reading behavior that our new understanding describes" (p. 31).

Johnston (1992), however, argues that our preoccupation with testing in the United States is based on a faulty notion that "if we just work hard enough, we can make a really good reading test that will be a good measure of real reading—a more valid test" and that—as a consequence—reading instruction will improve (p. 340). More problematic is our unexamined use of massive testing and the side effects of this testing on the educational system in terms of wasted time and talent.

Authentic Assessment

The second major trend in assessment is the movement toward authentic assessment of literacy—determining what exactly students can and can't do in real-life reading and real-life writing. This allows teachers to assess students in the type of situations that Wiggins (1989) calls "performance of exemplary tasks" (p. 703). Performance samples, whether formally or informally produced, teacher observation using anecdotal records and checklists, interviews and conferences designed to uncover students' thinking processes as they approach a reading or writing task, and folders or portfolios of student work all contribute to a teacher's data collection about student reading and writing practices. In each of these areas, the input of the student is essential to understanding and developing a picture of literacy achievement that matches the complexity of the reading and writing process.

Today's teachers want to know more about factors that contribute to their students' literacy achievement. Perhaps most important for teachers to consider is how they will use

Authentic assessment of literacy—determining what exactly students can and can't do in real-life reading and writing—is one of the major trends in assessment.

the information they will gather. Farr (1992b) points out that different audiences (the public, school administrators, teachers, students, and parents) have different reasons for assessing student literacy. No one test, state mandated or not, or assessment vehicle will answer every question asked about students' strengths and weaknesses as they become literate.

Will test results help the teacher to plan classroom instruction? Will they guide students to become self-reflective? Can they assess the strengths and weaknesses of a district-wide reading program? In each case, the information that is gathered will need to be analyzed, interpreted, and shared appropriately so as to be meaningful and useful.

Teachers often understand that the answer to the question "How is Johnny doing in reading?" is "It depends." They know that the contextual and constructive nature of reading demands a multidimensional way of looking at students' literacy performance. Yet teachers also realize that often they are judged by how their students perform on standardized achievement tests that give a linear, one-dimensional view of reading and writing. Ravitch notes that teachers, caught in a bind, "know that they will be judged by test results, and they will continue to teach to the tests by which they are judged" (1993, p. 772).

Formal Assessment

Pressures for accountability have led many school districts and states to use formal reading tests as a means of assessment. Formal tests may be norm referenced or criteria referenced. Many of the recent standardized tests give *both* norm-referenced and criteria-referenced results of students' performance. Norm-referenced test results, in particular, appear to fill the bill for evaluating effectiveness through comparison.

Standardized Tests

Standardized tests are machine scorable instruments that sample reading performance based on a single administration. Standardized test scores are useful in making comparisons among individuals or groups at the local, state, or national level. A norm-referenced test is constructed by administering it to large numbers of students in order to develop **norms.** It's inefficient and difficult, if not impossible, to test every student in an entire population. Norms, therefore, represent average scores of a sampling of students selected for testing according to factors such as age, sex, race, grade, or socioeconomic status. Once norm scores are established, they become the basis for comparing the performance of individuals or groups to the performance of those who were in the norming sample. These comparisons allow you to determine whether a child or group is making "normal" progress or performing in "normal" ways.

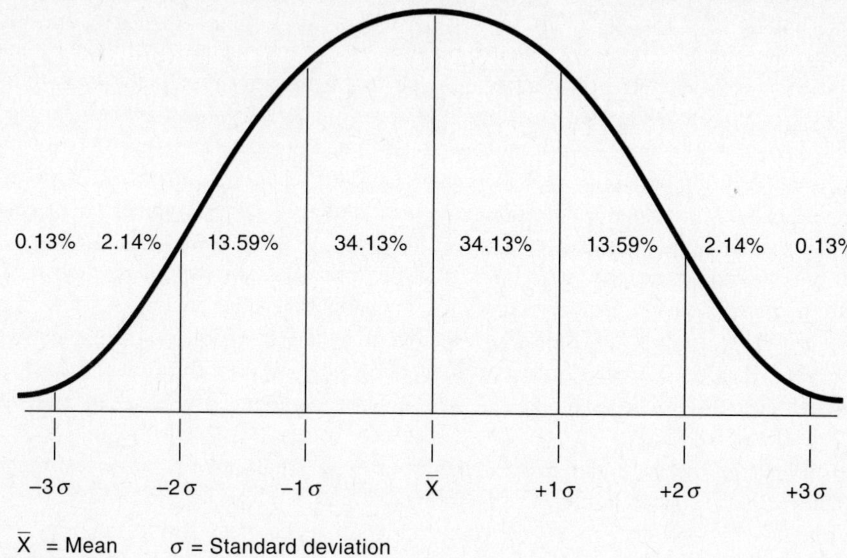

● **FIGURE 13.1** A bell curve

Normal progress or performance, of course, depends on the *representativeness* of the norming sample. Therefore, the norms of a test should reflect the characteristics of the population. Moreover, *it's important to make sure that the norming sample used in devising the tests resembles the group of students tested.* Some norm-referenced tests provide separate norms for specific kinds of populations (e.g., urban students). The technical manual for the test should contain information about the norming process, including a description of the norming group.

In developing norm-referenced tests, the scores in the norming sample are distributed along a *normal*, or *bell-shaped, curve.* That is to say, scores cluster symmetrically about the *mean,* the average of all scores. In Figure 13.1, notice that the majority of the scores (about 68 percent) are concentrated within one *standard deviation* above or below the mean. The standard deviation is an important measure, because it represents the variability or dispersion of scores from the mean. The standard deviation, roughly speaking, can help you interpret a child's performance. You can judge how well a child performed on a test by examining a score in relation to the standard deviation. A score that falls more than one standard deviation below the mean on a reading test would *probably* raise a red flag or be a cause for concern. Recognize, however, that standardized tests aren't error free: There are measurement problems with any test. Some tests, without question, are better than others in helping teachers to interpret performance. The more *valid* and *reliable* the reading test, the more likely it is to measure what it says it does.

Reliability refers to the stability of the test. Does the test measure an ability consistently over time or consistently across equivalent forms? The reliability of a test is expressed as a correlation coefficient. Reliability coefficients can be found in examiner's manuals and are expressed in numerical form with a maximum possible value of +1.0. A reliability coefficient of +1.0 means that students' scores were ranked exactly the same on a test given on two different occasions or on two equivalent forms. If students were to take a test on Monday and then take an equivalent form of the same test on Thursday, their scores would be about the same on both tests, if they were indeed reliable. A test consumer should examine reliability coefficients given in the examiner's manual. A reliability coefficient of +0.85 or better is considered good, whereas a reliability coefficient below +0.70 suggests that the test lacks consistency.

A statistic tied to the idea of reliability is the *standard error of measurement.* The standard error of measurement represents the range within which a subject's *true score* will likely fall. A true score is the score a test taker would have obtained if the test were free of error. Suppose the standard error of measurement was 0.8 for a reading test. If a student achieved a score of 4.0 on the test, then his or her true score would fall somewhere between 3.2 and 4.8. Rather than assume that a score received by a student is exactly accurate, the teacher should identify the standard error of measurement in the test manual and interpret each score as falling within a range.

Validity is probably the most important characteristic of a test. It refers to how well a test measures what it is designed to measure. A test developer will validate a test for general use along several fronts. First, the test should have *construct validity.* To establish construct validity, the test developer must show the relationship between a theoretical construct such as *reading* and the test that proposes to measure the construct. Second, the test should have *content validity.* Content validity reflects how well the test represents the domain or content area being examined. Are there sufficient test items? Are the test items appropriate? Third, the test should have *predictive validity.* In other words, will it accurately predict future performance?

Types of Test Scores. To make interpretations properly you need to be aware of differences in the type of scores reported on a test. The raw, or obtained, score reflects the total number of correct items on a test. Raw scores are converted to other kinds of scores so that comparisons among individuals or groups can be made. A raw score, for example, may be converted into a *grade equivalency score.* This type of conversion provides information about reading performance as it relates to students at various grade levels. A grade equivalency score of 4.6 is read as "fourth grade, sixth month in school." Therefore a student whose raw score is transformed into a grade equivalency of 4.6 is supposedly performing at a level that is average for students who have completed six months of the fourth grade.

The idea behind a grade equivalency score is not flawless. When a score is reported in terms of grade level, it is often prone to misinterpretation. For example, don't be swayed by the erroneous assumption that reading growth progresses throughout the school year at a constant rate—that growth in reading is the same from month to month. Based on what is known about human development generally and language growth specifically, such an assumption makes little sense when applied to a human process as complex as learning to read.

One of the most serious misinterpretations of a grade equivalency score involves making placement decisions. Even though a child's performance on a test or subtest is reported as a grade level, this doesn't necessarily suggest placement in materials at that level. Suppose a student received a grade equivalency score of 2.8 on a comprehension subtest. The score may represent information about his or her ability to comprehend, but it doesn't mean that the student should be placed at the second grade, eighth month of basal reading or library materials. First, the standard error of the test indicates that there is a range within which 2.8 falls. Second, the test's norms were in all likelihood not standardized against the content and level of difficulty of the basal reading curriculum in a particular school or of library books. In 1981, the International Reading Association passed a resolution cautioning teachers on the misuse of grade equivalents and advocated the abandonment of grade equivalent scores for reporting students' performance. In place of grade-level scores, the use of *percentile scores* and *standard scores* such as *stanines* provides a more appropriate vehicle for reporting test performance.

Percentiles refer to scores in terms of the percentage of a group the student has scored above. If several second graders scored in the 68th percentile of a test, they scored as well as or better than 68 percent of the second graders in the norming population. Whereas grade equivalency scores are normed by testing children at various grade levels, percentile norms are developed by examining performance only within a single grade level. Therefore, percentile scores provide information that helps teachers interpret relative performance within a grade level only. For this reason, percentiles are easily interpretable.

Stanine is one of several types of standard score. A standard score is a raw score that has been converted to a common standard to permit comparison. Because standard scores have the *same* mean and standard deviation, they allow teachers to make direct comparisons of student performance across tests and subtests. Specifically, stanine refers to a *sta*ndard *nine*-point scale. When stanines are used to report results, the distribution of scores on a test is divided into nine parts. Therefore, each stanine represents a single digit that ranges from 1 to 9 in numerical value. A stanine of 5 is the midpoint of the scale and represents average performance. Stanines 6, 7, 8, 9 indicate increasingly better performance; stanines 4, 3, 2, and 1 represent decreasing performance.

Types of Tests. Different norm-referenced tests have different purposes. Two broad types of tests are frequently used in schools. An assessment that is based on a **survey test** represents a measure of general performance only. It does not yield precise information about an individual's reading abilities. Survey tests are often used at the beginning of the school year as screening tests to identify children who may be having difficulties in broad areas of instruction. A survey test may be given to groups or individuals.

A standardized **diagnostic test,** on the other hand, is a type of formal assessment that is intended to provide more detailed information about individual students' strengths and weaknesses. The results of a diagnostic test are often used to profile a student's strengths and weaknesses of reading performance. Some diagnostic tests are individual; others are designed for group administration.

Most diagnostic tests are founded on a bottom-up, subskills view of reading. Therefore, diagnostic tests are characterized by a battery of subtests that uses large numbers of items to measure specific skills in areas such as phonics, structural analysis, word knowledge, and comprehension.

Although survey and diagnostic tests are designed to be informative, teachers need to know *why* they want to use tests and *for what* they are testing (Farr and Carey, 1986). Because there is more formal testing and more attention to informal, alternative assessments, we need to be clear about the bottom line (Farr, 1992b): *does it help students?*

In general, much controversy has surrounded the use of standardized achievement tests in American education, especially as they apply to culturally diverse populations. In the field of reading, the uses and misuses of standardized tests have also been debated.

Uses of Standardized Test Results. Critics of formal testing tend to argue against the uses to which the standardized test information is put. As noted earlier, scores from formal testing shouldn't be used as the *only* source of information considered in making instructional decisions. But they often are. Another inappropriate use of standardized test scores is in the evaluation of teachers.

Some critics call into question whether there is any worth at all to formal testing. For example, Goodman (1975) argued that such tests are mainly measures of intelligence and don't assess that which can be construed as reading. He contended that the reading measured on reading tests isn't the same as most "real-world" kinds of reading. Seldom in real life would someone read a short passage and then be required to answer a series of questions about it. As mentioned earlier, test makers of the "new breed" of tests are increasing passage length and using formats different from answering multiple-choice questions. How the test makers of the 1990s are applying knowledge of the reading process in constructing tests is shown in Figure 13.2 which highlights some changes at the state level.

Most test developers assert that their tests can provide accurate and reliable information about groups of 25 or more. From this perspective, scores can show schoolwide trends and differences among groups within a school. Standardized test results can also be used to get an idea of how students in a school compare to other students across the country when assumptions about representatives have been met. In addition, they will indicate if the school as a whole is increasing or decreasing in general reading achievement.

Standardized test scores are increasingly being used to evaluate the effectiveness of a district, a school, or a program. Michael Kirst, codirector of Policy Analysis for California Education and former president of the California State Board of Education, said in an interview that he found norm-referenced tests to be useful in piecing together a more complete picture of pupil performance statewide. Using several tests, Kirst said he and his staff were able to identify problem areas in education. In California today, the results are used to produce a "public report card on *each school,*" according to Kirst (McClellan, 1988). As statewide testing becomes more prevalent, publicizing of norm-referenced scores in a report card of district and school effectiveness may become more common.

Norm-referenced test scores are being used to make school-by-school and district-by-district comparisons. The next step is provisions for *state-by-state* comparisons of fourth-graders' achievement in both *reading* and mathematics by the National Assessment of Educational Progress (NAEP), which has served as "the nation's report card." The International Reading Association (IRA), long concerned with the issue of assessment in reading instruction, reaffirmed a resolution in 1990 "that where large-scale assessments are conducted for the purpose of monitoring outcomes, results should not be reported for individual pupils, classes, or schools."

Changes in Reading Tests

Test Passages
Use full-length stories or articles (500 to 2,000 words) that are taken from classroom materials such as children's magazines, literature, and content area textbooks.
Comprehension
Use inferential questions requiring synthesis of information across a complete passage. Focus on information central to understanding the theme or main purpose of the passage.
Reading Strategies
Assess the students' knowledge of the reading process (for example: strategies for understanding the passaage and awareness of literary devices).
Personal Attitudes and Interests
Assess students' interest in the content of the passage and how difficult they thought it was.
Prior Knowledge
Assess how much students already know about the topics or concepts discussed in the passage.
Scoring
Use multidimensional scores: a primary score based on how well students understood what they read, along with subscores that can help explain the primary score and be used to shape instruction for each student.

● **FIGURE 13.2**

Adapted from Charles W. Peters and Karen K. Wixson, "Smart New Reading Tests Are Coming," *Learning 89,* April 1989, p.44. ©1989 Springhouse Corporation, 1111 Bethlehem Pike, Springhouse, PA 19477. Reprinted with permission.

Despite criticisms, such as those inherent in IRA's resolution, the use of standardized tests is very widespread, with results being used as report cards that judge the effectiveness of programs, individual schools, and school systems, as well as the education in individual states and across the nation. Despite their pervasive use, there is much misunderstanding of standardized test results.

A phenomenon surrounding the massive use of norm-referenced tests is "the Lake Wobegon effect." Garrison Keillor tells stories about Lake Wobegon, where "the women are strong, the men are good looking, and all the children are above average." Writing about the "Lake Wobegon effect," John Pikulski (1989) reported a survey done by a West Virginia physician. He found that 82 percent of 3,503 school districts and 100 percent of the 32 states surveyed with mandated testing programs reported that the average score for students in that district or state was "above average." However, as Pikulski points out, if we are involved in the concept of "average," only 50 percent of the population are above average and the other 50 percent are below average. Consider the "Lake Wobegon effect" in districts where children come from affluent homes. Teachers and administrators in these districts boast that the average scores for students on their standardized tests are "above average," yet we know that the variable that accounts for the most variance in standardized test scores is socioeconomic status of the test takers. We can only speculate on why the "Lake Wobegon effect" is so prevalent, but it very clearly demonstrates a misconception concerning norm-referenced testing.

Criterion-referenced testing is another kind of testing conducted in schools, and the assumptions underlying it are different from those of norm-referenced testing. Rather than comparing a student's test performance to that of a norming sample, performance on a criterion-referenced test hinges on mastery of specific reading skills. Let's examine criterion-referenced assessment and how test information is used in classroom decision making.

Criterion-Referenced Tests

Criterion-referenced tests have been used in formal situations for districtwide purposes, in classroom situations, and more recently, in statewide testing. The major premise behind criterion-referenced testing is that the mastery of reading skills should be assessed in relation to specific instructional objectives. Test performance is measured against a criterion, or acceptable score, for each of the objectives. Suppose, for example, that there are ten test items for each skill objective. Eight to ten correct items on the test would suggest a level of mastery as specified by the objective. A score of six or seven correct items would signal that additional practice and review of the skill under examination are needed. Fewer than six correct items would mean that a student is probably deficient in the skill and needs extensive reteaching to reach criterion or mastery.

Unlike a norm-referenced situation, performance on a criterion-referenced test is judged by what a student can or can't do with regard to the skill objectives of the test. The test taker isn't compared to anyone else. The rationale for assessment, then, is that it will indicate strengths and weaknesses in specific skill areas. Whereas norm-referenced test scores are used to screen students and to make general grouping decisions, results from a criterion-referenced assessment are used to make instructional decisions about reading-skills development. For this reason, criterion-referenced tests have become part of the standard operating procedure of the reading skill management systems described in Chapter 2.

Reliability and Validity of Criterion-Referenced Tests. The reliability and validity of criterion-referenced tests have been called into question (Pearson and Johnson, 1978). It has been argued that test makers have tended not to establish statistical reliability and validity for criterion-referenced tests as they do for norm-referenced tests. As a result, users of criterion-referenced tests need to be aware of some of the important issues of reliability and validity surrounding the use of such tests.

Criterion-referenced tests often measure students' performance on a large number of objectives. Because the number of objectives tested is large, the number of items testing each objective may be as low as four or five. Such a practice leads to questions of how *reliable* the measurement of each skill can be with such a small number of items. It's possible that students who perform poorly on a criterion-referenced test won't perform poorly in another situation that assesses the same skill. For example, will a child who cannot count syllables in a word be unable to break down similar words into pronounceable parts when reading orally? Will a child who cannot answer inferential questions as directed on a test be unable to make inferences from a story in an oral retelling?

Test makers assume that mastery of specific skills leads to better reading ability. This is at best a tenuous assumption. A teacher must ask, "Do test items really measure what they are supposed to measure?" Smith and Johnson (1980) pointed out the problem in this respect.

> Test purchasers rightly assume that the tests provided for measuring attainment of objectives are valid indices of the skills at issue. However, if a test uses a paper-and-pencil task, then it ought, at the very least, to validate those measures by administering group and individual tests to a small sample of students. We are not convinced that identifying the initial consonant *f* from the distractor set *f, t, v, r* when given an oral stimulus is the same as saying /f/ when seeing *f,* or reading sentences which contain words starting with *f.* (p. 169)

Smith and Johnson's point is well taken, as is their concern for questions related to the concept of mastery. What does mastery performance mean on a criterion-referenced test? For example, are comprehension skills ever mastered? Or, as Smith and Johnson (1980) asserted, "We hope that no child could 'test out of' main ideas, or sequence . . . for if conceptual difficulty of words or contextual relationships were increased, the same child could fail to show mastery" (p. 170). Comprehension is an ongoing, developing process, as we have maintained throughout this book. To test for mastery of a comprehension skill would provide a teacher with misleading information at best.

Criterion-referenced tests are similar to standardized diagnostic tests in the sense that both attempt to identify strengths and weaknesses in specific skill areas. As is the case with diagnostic tests, criterion-referenced tasks are part of a strong bottom-up approach to reading and learning to read. The teacher must recognize, however, that a criterion-referenced test provides only one perspective for understanding children's reading performance. Other indicators of reading should be weighed carefully in planning instruction.

Informal Assessment

Informal measures of reading such as *reading inventories, miscue analyses,* and *running records* yield useful information about student performance. As the name implies, an **informal assessment** doesn't compare the performance of a tested group or individual to a normative population. Instead, informal tests may be given throughout the school year to individuals or groups for specific instructional purposes.

Informal reading tests gauge performance in relation to the student's success on a particular reading task or a set of reading tasks. In this respect, they are similar to criterion-referenced measures. One of the best uses of informal tests is to evaluate how students interact with print in oral and silent reading situations. In the following sections, we explore how these measures can be used to inform decision making and strengthen inferences about children's reading behavior and performance.

Informal Reading Inventories

The **informal reading inventory (IRI)** is an individual administered reading test. It usually consists of a series of graded word lists, graded reading passages, and comprehension questions. The passages are used to assess how students interact with print orally and silently. Johns (1985) claimed that learning how to use an IRI is an important part of a teacher's preparation. With the information gathered from an IRI you will be able to place students in appropriate instruction materials with some degree of confidence. Moreover, an analysis of oral reading miscues helps you to determine the *cueing systems* that students tend to rely on when reading. In short, IRI information can lead to instructional planning that will increase children's effectiveness with print.

IRIs are commercially available, although teachers can easily construct one. Selections from a basal reading series may be used to make an IRI. If you decide to make and use an IRI at least three steps are necessary:

1. Duplicate 100- to 200-word passages from basal stories. Select a passage for each grade level from the basal series, preprimer through grade eight. Passages should be chosen from the middle of each basal textbook to ensure representativeness.

2. Develop at least five comprehension questions for each passage. Be certain that different types of questions (based on question-answer relationships discussed in Chapter 6) are created for each graded passage. Avoid the following pitfalls:

    Questions that can be answered without reading the passage (except for on-your-own questions).
    Questions that require yes-no answers.
    Questions that are long and complicated.
    Questions that overload memory by requiring the reader to reconstruct lists (e.g., "Name four things that happened. . . ").

3. Create an environment conducive to assessment. Explain to the student before testing why you are giving the assessment. In doing so, attempt to take the mystery out of what can be a worrisome situation for the student.

Administering an IRI. Commercially published IRIs have graded word lists that can be used for several purposes: (1) to help determine a starting point for reading the graded passages; (2) to get an indication of the student's sight word proficiency (e.g., the ability to recognize words rapidly); and (3) to get an indication of the student's knowledge of sound-letter relationships to attack unfamiliar words.

When giving the IRI, the teacher may simply estimate placement in the graded passages instead of using word lists. Select a passage from the inventory that you believe the student can read easily and comprehend fully, for example, a passage two grade levels below the student's present grade. If the passage turns out to be more difficult than anticipated, ask the student to read another one at a lower level. However, if the student reads the passage without difficulty, then progress to higher grade level passages until the reading task becomes too difficult.

Oral reading is usually followed by silent reading. In both oral and silent reading situations, the student responds to comprehension questions. However, an excellent variation is to first require students to retell everything that they recall from the reading. Note the information given and then follow up with aided-recall questions such as the following:

What else can you tell me about ______ and ______?

What happened after ______ and ______?

Where did ______ and ______ take place?

How did ______ and ______ happen?

Why do you think ______ and ______ happened?

What do you think the author might have been trying to say in this story?

Do not hurry through a retelling. When asking a question to aid recall, give the student time to think and respond.

Recording Oral Reading Errors. During the oral reading of the passage, the teacher notes reading errors such as mispronunciations, omissions, and substitutions. As the student reads, the teacher also notes how fluent the reading is. Does the student read in a slow, halting, word-by-word fashion? Or does he or she read rapidly and smoothly? Errors are recorded by marking deviations from the text on a copy of the passages read by the student. By *deviation,* we mean any difference that is observed between what the student says and the words on the page.

The following coding system can be used to mark errors:

1. *Omissions.* An omission error occurs when the reader omits a unit of written language; that is, a word, several words, parts of words, or a sentence(s). Circle the omitted unit of language.

Example Jenny was (still) at school. She never played (after school.)

2. *Substitutions.* A substitution error is noted when a real word (or words) is substituted for the word in the text. Draw a line through the text word and write the substituted word above it.

Example The ~~lion~~ [monkey] looked lonely.

3. *Mispronunciation.* A mispronunciation miscue is one in which the word is pronounced incorrectly. Follow the same procedure as a substitution error, writing the phonetic spelling above the word in text.

frag

Example Because he was a frog, we called him Hoppy.

4. *Insertion.* The insertion miscue results when a word (or words) is inserted in the passage. Use a caret (^) to show where the word was inserted and write the word.

quickly

Example She ^ ran away.

5. *Repetition.* In repetition, a word or phrase is repeated. Treat the repetition of more than one word as a single unit, counting it as one miscue. Underline the portion of text that is repeated.

Example This is a tale about a man who is blind.

6. *Reversal.* The reversal error occurs when the order of a word (or words in the text) is transposed. Use a transpositional symbol (a curved mark) over and under the letters or words transposed.

Example He went no his trip.

"See you later," Sue said.

7. *Pronunciation.* A word (or words) is pronounced for the reader. Place the letter *P* over the word pronounced.

p

Example This was a startling development in his life

In addition to marking errors, you should also code the reader's attempts to correct any errors made during oral reading. Self-correction attempts result in repetitions, which may have one of three outcomes:

1. *Successful correction.* The reader successfully corrects the error. Correct miscues are coded in the following manner:

(c) why

Example I did not know where I was going.

2. *Unsuccessful correction.* The reader attempts to correct an error but is unsuccessful. Unsuccessful correction attempts are coded in the following manner:

(uc) 1. complied 2. completed

Example He felt compelled to leave.

3. *Abandoned correct form.* The student reads the text word or words correctly, but then decides to abandon the correct form for a different response. Code this behavior in the following manner:

(AC) wandered

Example Mike wondered if the tracks were made by a bear.

Familiarity with a coding system is important in marking oral errors. To ensure accurate coding, tape-record the student's reading. You can then replay the student's reading to check whether all errors are recorded accurately. Moreover, tape-recording will help in analyzing the student's responses to comprehension questions or a retelling of the material.

Determining Reading Levels. The following reading levels can be determined for individual students by administering an IRI.

Independent level: The level at which the student reads fluently with excellent comprehension. The independent level has also been called the recreational reading level, because not only will students be able to function on their own, but they often have high interest in the material.

Instructional level: The level at which the student can make progress in reading with instructional guidance. This level has been referred to as the teaching level, because the material to be read must be challenging but not too difficult.

Frustration level: The level at which the student is unable to pronounce many of the words or is unable to comprehend the material satisfactorily. This is the lowest level of reading at which the reader is able to understand. The material is too difficult to provide a basis for growth.

Listening capacity level: The level at which the students can understand material that is read aloud. This level is also known as the potential level, because if students were able to read fluently, they would not have a problem with comprehension.

The criteria used to determine reading levels have differed slightly among reading experts who have published IRIs. However, the most recommended over the years have been the "Betts criteria," so named for Emmett Betts (1946), who is generally considered to be the "father" of the IRI.

In making decisions about a student's reading level, teachers should be cognizant of two powerful correlates that determine whether children will find material difficult or not. First, there is a strong relationship between a student's interest in a topic and reading comprehension. Estes and Vaughan (1973), for example, found that children's reading levels fluctuated consistently between frustration and instructional levels depending upon their interest in the passage content of graded selections. Second, a strong case has been built throughout this book for the relationship that exists between background knowledge and reading comprehension. If children do poorly on a particular passage because they have limited knowledge or schema for its content, it's easy to err by underestimating reading level.

The point to remember is that reading levels are not chiseled in stone. Levels do fluctuate from material to material depending on a child's schema and interest in the passage content. The placement information that an IRI yields gives a "ball park" figure, an "indication." Therefore, placement decisions should rest on corroborative judgment, with IRI results providing one important source of information.

Analyzing Oral Reading Miscues

Oral reading errors are also called miscues. The terms *error* and *miscue* essentially describe the same phenomenon—a deviation or difference between what a reader says and the word on the page. Goodman (1973a) believed that the term *error* signals something that is wrong or undesirable. In its place, he popularized the word *miscue* to reinforce a positive view of error in the reading process. A miscue provides a piece of evidence in an elaborate puzzle. Differences between what the reader says and what is printed on the page are not the result of random errors. Instead, these differences are "cued" by the thought and language of the reader, who is attempting to construct what the author is saying.

Miscues can be analyzed *quantitatively* or *qualitatively.* A quantitative analysis involves counting the number of errors; it pivots around a search for *deficits* in a student's ability to read accurately. A quantitative analysis is used, for example, to determine the reading levels previously discussed. In addition, a tallying of different types of errors has traditionally been a strategy for evaluating the strengths and weaknesses of a child's ability to analyze words. For example, does the reader consistently mispronounce the beginnings of words? An analysis based on this question helps to pinpoint specific difficulties. Does the reader consistently have trouble with single consonants? Consonant clusters?

In a quantitative analysis, each miscue carries equal weight, regardless of the contribution it makes to a child's understanding of the material read. A qualitative miscue analysis, on the other hand, offers a radically different perspective for exploring the strengths of students. A qualitative miscue analysis is a tool for assessing what children do when they read. It is not based on deficits related to word identification, but rather on the *differences* between the miscues and the words on the page. Therefore some miscues are more significant than others.

A miscue is significant if it affects meaning—if it doesn't make sense within the context of the sentence or passage in which it occurs. Johns (1985) explained that miscues are generally significant when:

1. The meaning of the sentence or passages is significantly changed or altered and the student does not correct the miscue.
2. A nonword is used in place of the word in the passage.
3. Only a partial word is substituted for the word or phrase in the passage.
4. A word is pronounced for the student.

Miscues are generally *not* significant when:

1. The meaning of the sentence or passage undergoes no change or only minimal change.

2. They are self-corrected by the student.
3. They are acceptable in the student's dialect (e.g., "goed" home for "went" home; "idear" for "idea").
4. They are later read correctly in the same passage. (p. 17)

We agree with Johns that only significant miscues should be counted in determining reading levels according to Bett's criteria. He recommended subtracting the *total* of all *dialect miscues,* all *corrected miscues,* and all *miscues that do not change meaning* from the total number of recorded miscues.

Miscue analysis can be applied to graded passages from an IRI or to the oral reading of a single passage that presents the student with an extended and intensive reading experience. In the case of the latter, select a story or informational text that is at or just above the student's instructional level. The material must be challenging, but not frustrating.

Through **miscue analysis,** teachers can determine the extent to which the reader uses and coordinates graphic-sound, syntactic, and semantic information from the text. To analyze miscues, you should ask at least four crucial questions (Goodman and Burke, 1972).

1. *Does the miscue change meaning?* If it doesn't, then it's *semantically acceptable* within the context of the sentence or passage. Some examples of semantically acceptable miscues are:

   back
   I want to bring him home.

   shop
   Steve went to the ~~store.~~

   to
   His feet are firmly planted ~~on~~ the ground.

   Mom
   ~~Mother~~ works on Wall Street.

   Some examples of semantically unacceptable miscues are:

   court
   Bill went to ~~camp~~ for the first time.

   leaped
   The mountain ~~loomed~~ in the foreground.

   quiet
   The summer had been a ~~dry~~ one.

2. *Does the miscue sound like language?* If it does, then it's *grammatically acceptable* within the context of a sentence or passage. Miscues are grammatically acceptable if they sound like language and serve as the same parts of speech as the text words. The above examples of semantically acceptable and unacceptable miscues also happen to be syntactically acceptable. Two examples of syntactically unacceptable miscues are:

   carefully
   Bill ~~reached~~ for the book.

to
I have a good idea.

In each example, the miscue doesn't sound like language when the text is read aloud.

3. *Do the miscue and the text word look and sound alike?* Substitution and mispronunciation miscues should be analyzed to determine how similar they are in approximating the graphic and pronounciation features of the text words. *High graphic-sound similarity* results when two of the three parts (beginning, middle, and end) of a word are similar, as in the miscue below.

   going
   He was ~~getting~~ old.

   Some *graphic-sound similarity* is present when one of three word parts is alike.

4. *Was an attempt made to self-correct the miscue?* Self-corrections are revealing because they demonstrate that the reader is attending to meaning and is aware that the initial miscuing did not make sense.

A profile can be developed for each reader by using the summary sheet in Figure 13.3. Study the following passage that has been coded and then examine how each miscue was analyzed on the summary sheet.

walk
~~works~~ Ⓒ lean
Sheep dogs ~~work~~ hard on a farm. They must learn to take the sheep from place to
Ⓒ mostly these Ⓒ always mostly
place. They must see that the sheep do not run away. And they ~~must~~ see (that) the
loose and
sheep do not get ~~lost or~~ killed.
~~Something~~ trying ~~works~~ ⓊⒸ learn
Sometimes (these) dogs are ~~trained~~ to do other kind(s) of farm work. They earn
helps
the right to be called good ~~helpers~~, too.
another working ~~coot~~
Can you think of ~~one other~~ kind of ~~work~~ dog? He does not need a coat or
doesn't ~~leave~~ and sleep
strong legs like the sheep do(g's). He does not learn to work ~~with~~ a sled in the
doesn't ~~leave~~
deep, cold snow. He ~~does not~~ learn to be a farm worker.

Text	Miscue	Context: Semantically Acceptable	Context: Syntactically Acceptable	Self-Corrections	Graphic/Sound Similarity: Begin-ing	Graphic/Sound Similarity: Middle	Graphic/Sound Similarity: Ending	Graphic/Sound Summary
work	walk	*no*	*yes*		X		X	high
learn	lean	—	—	*yes*				
must	mostly	—	—	*yes*				
the	these	*yes*	*yes*		X	X		high
away	always	—	—	*yes*				
that		*yes*	*yes*					
lost	loose	*no*	*yes*		X			some
or	and	*no*	*yes*					none
these		*yes*	*yes*		X	X	X	XXX
trained	trying	*no*	*yes*		X			some
kinds	kind	*yes*	*yes*		X	X		high
earn	learn	*no*	*yes*	*no*		X	X	high
helpers	helps	*yes*	*yes*		X	X		high
one other	another	*yes*	*yes*			X	X	
work	working	*yes*	*yes*		X	X		high
dog's	dog	*yes*	*yes*		X	X		high
learn	leave	—	—	*yes*				
with	and	*no*	*no*					none
sled	sleep	*no*	*yes*		X			some
does not	doesn't	*yes*	*yes*					

Percentage of semantically acceptable miscues = 53 percent
Percentage of syntactically acceptable miscues = 88 percent
Percentage of successful self-corrections = 80 percent
Percentage of miscues with high graphic-sound similarity = 58 percent
Percentage of miscues with some graphic-sound similarity = 25 percent

FIGURE 13.3 Qualitative Miscue Analysis Summary Sheet

To determine the percentage of semantically acceptable miscues, count the number of yes responses in the column. Then count the number of miscues analyzed. (Do not tally successful self-corrections.) Divide the number of semantically acceptable miscues by the number of miscues analyzed and then multiply by 100.

To determine the percentage of syntactically acceptable miscues, proceed by counting the number of yes responses in the column. Divide that number by the number of miscues analyzed (less self-corrections) and then multiply by 100.

To determine the percentage of successful self-corrections, tally the number of yes responses in the column and divide the number by the number of self-correction attempts and then multiply by 100.

To determine the percentage of higher or some graphic-sound similarity, analyze mispronunciations and substitutions only. Divide the total of high-similarity words by the number of words analyzed and then multiply by 100. Follow the same procedure to determine whether some similarity exists between the miscues and text words.

One final piece of information can be tabulated. Determine the number of miscues that were semantically acceptable or that made sense in the selection *and* the number of successful self-corrections. Divide this number by the total number of miscues. This percentage gives you an estimate of the extent to which the reader reads for meaning.

Inferences can be made about oral reading behavior once the miscues are charted and the information summarized. Although the reader of the passage miscued frequently, his strengths are apparent: He reads for meaning. More than half of the miscues were semantically acceptable. When attempting to self-correct, the reader was successful most of the time. Over 60 percent of his miscues were semantically acceptable or were successfully self-corrected; most of his miscues sounded like language. Moreover, the great majority of his substitution and mispronunciation miscues reflected knowledge of graphic-sound relationships.

Seven significant miscues were made on the passage (which was slightly over 100 words long). This indicates that the material bordered on frustration and probably is not appropriate for instruction. However, the reader has demonstrated strategies that get at meaning.

Miscue analysis is time consuming. However, when you want to know more about a student's processing of print, miscue analysis is very useful. If you are pressed for time, but you still have a need to know how well a student is processing print, use miscue question number one, "Does the miscue change meaning?" and look to see if the student self-corrects and how successfully. Extensive experience with miscue analysis has led Goodman and Burke, the authors of the Reading Miscue Inventory, to suggest the following correlations about reading proficiency (Weaver, 1980). The following chart gives a quick measure of the percentage of effectiveness in using reading strategies by adding the number of miscues that did not change the meaning of the passage, *and* the number of miscues that were successfully self-corrected over the total number of miscues.

Effectiveness in using reading strategies	Miscues that did not change the meaning of the passage *and* miscues that were successfully self-corrected
Highly effective	**60 to 100%**
Moderately effective	**40 to 79%**
Somewhat effective	**15 to 45%**
Ineffective	**no more than 14%**

Throughout this chapter, we have emphasized the point that *multiple measures* are important; we should not rely on one test score concerning a child's progress in becoming literate. Furthermore, assessments need to *show that a student has grown,* not just compare the student to other students of similar age. This is particularly important to students who are at risk in reading. Some teachers prefer to keep track of students' progress by using a running record.

A Running Record

Keeping track of students' growth in reading, their use of the cueing systems of language—semantics, syntax, and graphophonics—can help teachers understand the process that goes on in readers' heads. For, when readers try to construct meaning as they read aloud, we can begin to see the relationship between the miscues they make and comprehension. We realize that not all deviations from the text are equal in importance, and one miscue is not as informative as a series of miscues.

Rhodes and Shanklin (1993) describe five methods for collecting and analyzing miscues. Each method varies in the time it takes to administer, and in the depth and type of knowledge it reveals about the reader. However, one method differs significantly from the others in that it does not require a separate copy of the text in order to keep track of the reading. The running record developed by Marie Clay and explained in her book *The Early Detection of Reading Difficulties* (1985) can be done with only a blank sheet of paper, making it especially good for collecting data about a child's reading during regular classroom activities. To take a running record, the teacher marks a check for each word a child says correctly, matching the number of checks on a line of her paper with the number of words in a line of the text being read. Deviations from print are marked in much the same way as in other miscue analysis procedures. For example:

Correct word	✓
Insertion	*word spoken*
Omission	-
Substitution	*word spoken*
Self-correction	sc

Detailed explanations of conducting a running record are available in Clay (1985), Johnston (1992), and Kemp (1987). Teachers of beginning readers (who read aloud more often, who read slowly and read shorter, less complicated texts) often prefer to take a running record because it does not require special preparation or disrupt the flow of the classroom lesson. However, as students read faster, and read more complicated texts, running records become more difficult to take.

The approximate reading level suggested by an IRI along with information on how a reader uses the cueing systems of language to construct meaning while reading as gathered in a miscue analysis or running record can help teachers understand a child's progress in becoming literate.

It's equally important for *students* to have feedback on their efforts and learn how to self-assess. By graphically monitoring changes in measures that show that students' efforts have paid off, teachers can help low achievers maintain a keep-trying attitude.

While not a panacea, using graphs is a way to graphically demonstrate to parents and students progress on the factors that contribute to growth in literacy learning.

For example, a graph can be made to display Louisa's growth in reading texts of increasing difficulty as in Figure 13.4. The number of books read per month in voluntary reading programs may also be graphed. Figure 13.5 graphically shows both the number of books Susan read each month and the total number of books she read (Flood and Lapp, 1989). In addition, students like Leroy can be interviewed at different periods, and their responses can be compared to show changes in perception or attitude as in Figure 13.6.

Keeping a running record need not become an overwhelming task. A folder for each child or a notebook with a page for each child that contains a collection of information about his or her literacy learning helps teachers organize the information they collect for assessment. Assessment folders or notebooks could contain information from informal reading tests, miscue analyses, and observational data. Because it is difficult to remember classroom events, we recommend writing down anecdotal records or using a checklist to record important incidents.

The assessment folder that teachers keep for their own use, or to share with parents or students, is one type of portfolio. As the interest in developing authentic assessment to match our understanding of the constructive nature of the reading process grows, portfolios have emerged as important avenues of assessment.

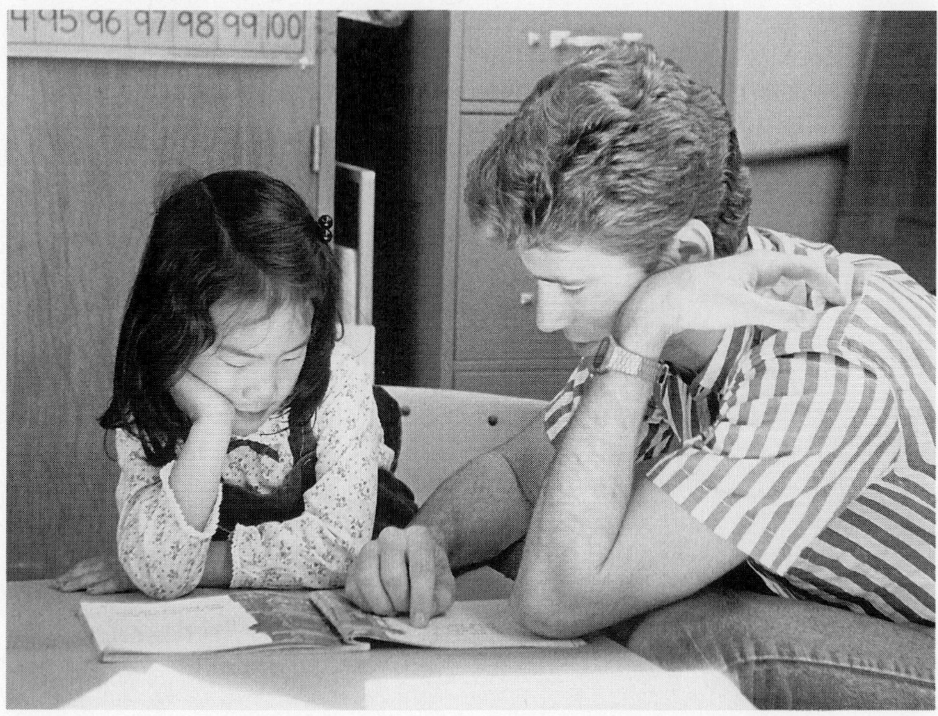

Students need feedback on their efforts to learn how to self-assess their reading progress.

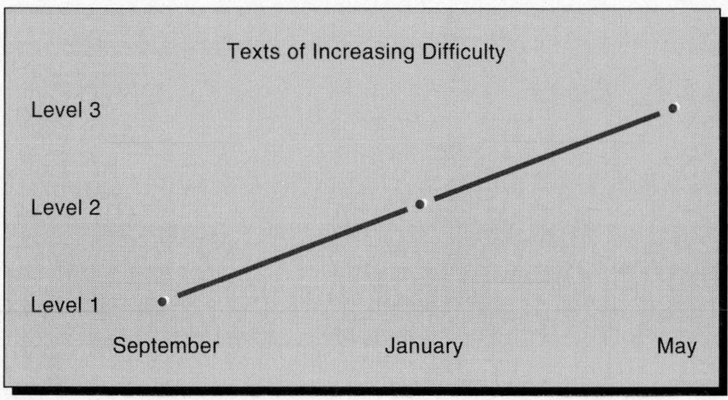

● **FIGURE 13.4** Louisa's growth in reading

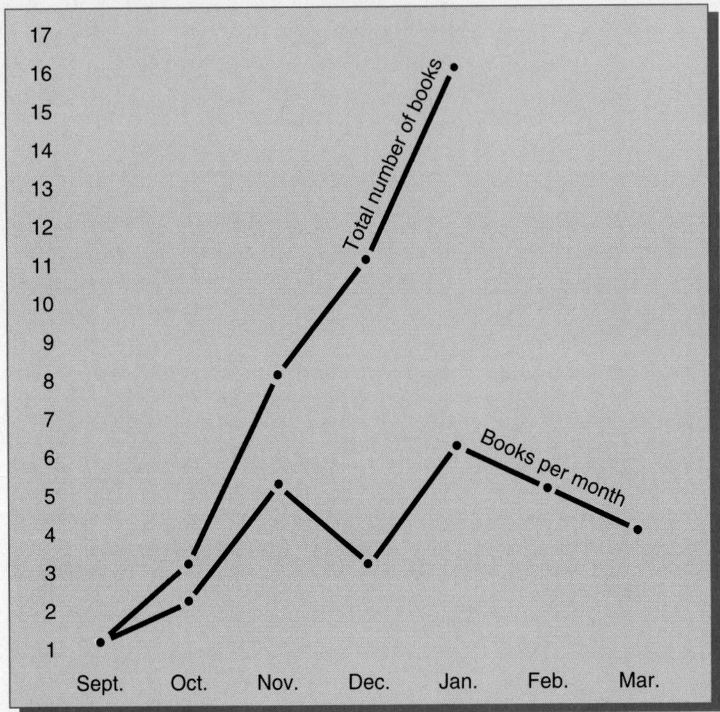

● **FIGURE 13.5** Susan's growth in voluntary reading

What do you do when you come to a word you don't know?

September: I ask someone.

April: I read the rest of the sentence. Then I try to think of a word that has those letters and makes sense in the story.

● **FIGURE 13.6** Leroy's responses to an interview question

Portfolio Assessment

Teachers are discovering that through the process of portfolio assessment of student work they are becoming more aware of students' individual behaviors. A portfolio is intended to "document the literary development of a student" and includes "evidence of student work in various stages" (Noden and Vacca, 1994). Portfolios have become a national and local trend within the whole language approach. **Portfolio assessment** has become synonymous with a process of involving students in reflecting on and making decisions about their work. Evidence that goes into student portfolios is collaboratively chosen by teachers and students and is more likely to represent a process or activity than a product. Read the vignette in Box 13.1 to learn about two teachers' experiences with portfolios.

Portfolios vary according to the purpose they serve. As a way of planning future instruction and for organizing and managing the classroom, portfolios can be invaluable to the teacher, as we discuss in Chapter 14. For the purpose of assessment, that is, of ascertaining how students perform in a real literacy situation, portfolios should be records of growth and progress. The information they contain needs to be analyzed, interpreted, and shared appropriately in order to be meaningful and useful.

Essential Elements of Portfolios

Although portfolios differ from each other in that each one reflects a literacy profile or picture of a different learner and a different classroom, they share several points in common that keep them from simply being a storage of work done in the classroom. Whether they contain *work-in-progress,* one type of portfolio; *best-efforts,* another type; or a combination of both, portfolios usually include:

- Work completed over time
- Several examples of varying types of work—written responses to reading as well as artistic response, writing in several genres, and teacher-assigned as well as student self-generated work
- An introduction, summary, and/or self-reflection by the student as to the nature of a piece or what it demonstrates about his or her literacy
- Collaboration between teacher and student in terms of work assigned and chosen

Reflecting our understanding of reading as a process of constructing meaning, reading folders may contain writing or artwork done in response to reading; poems, stories, or plays written by the student; research conducted about an author, a genre, or a historical time period; writing or reading done in response to science, math, or social studies; notes made about insights and ideas for future use in writing; notes from a writing or reading conference with the teachers or with peer groups; a reading log or a response journal; or a growing list of books read.

One of the most essential elements of the portfolio is the students' self-evaluation of their work. Working with peers and with the teacher, the work-in-progress portfolio becomes the best-work portfolio. Students, usually with the teacher's input, decide which work best evidences growth in literacy. For some students, if left entirely on their own, the selection of best work may seem overwhelming or they leave out work the teacher considers essential. Laurie Voss, a first-grade teacher, found that her students responded best to a system in which she and the student would have to agree on one of three portfolio selections (Voss, 1992).

● BOX 13.1

Class Works

Changing View

Two elementary school teachers in a team from a small town in Ohio teach a cohort of first and second graders. Last summer, Lori Taylor and Diana Jones explained to a graduate class of education majors how using portfolios has changed not only their view of literate behavior in their students, but their approach to teaching and assessment.

"Before portfolios, when we allowed students to choose and explain a project they were especially proud of, we would have limited ourselves to judgments about students' reading ability based on the basal end of unit tests, or oral reading during small group instruction. We would have never noticed how Joshua responded to reading," Lori told the class. "Or, if we had noticed him," Diana added, "it would have been because he was fidgety during oral reading, never knowing when it was his turn to read, or because his score on the basal mastery test was low."

"We were totally surprised that the project Josh was proudest of, the one he wrote about for his reading response portfolio, was something he had done at *home.* After a unit on inventions and machines, Josh had gone home, dissected an old vacuum cleaner and created some sort of invention. We invited Josh to bring it to school, and it actually worked. Josh keeps most of his portfolio entries on a table in the back of the room, because they're mainly 3-D and don't fit into the portfolio all that well.

"We could include a picture, but Josh gets a big kick out of having space on the table. At any rate, the history of his inventions and the directions he writes to explain how they work are excellent, much more sophisticated than his lackluster oral reading would indicate.

"Now, we always try to think of meaningful activities, ones that will help our students with the real problems they have in reading or writing to create their portfolios. Our map unit, which culminated in a trip to City Hall and an audience with the mayor to see the huge map of the city, had us knee-deep in geography, math, history, civics, and spelling.

"We don't have time for worksheets anymore. They just don't add anything to our portfolios."

REFLECTIVE INQUIRY

- How have Lori Taylor and Diana Jones' views of the nature of literate behavior changed?
- In what ways are teaching and assessment directly connected in their first/second grade classroom?
- What does this vignette suggest about how to use portfolios for assessment in the classroom?

A critical aspect of literacy is learning to monitor and evaluate one's own efforts. This need for self-reflection is nurtured as students explain what contributed to the success of the pieces they choose for inclusion in the best-work portfolio. They demonstrate their personal values and their insights into their own learning. As they measure themselves against their own standards, they must work together with their teachers to explore the possibilities for growth during everyday classroom experiences.

Portfolios provide an excellent way for teachers, students, and parents to explore together what students have learned. Mike Milliken, a fifth-grade teacher noted that portfolios allowed him to create stronger ties between home and school. "Because the portfolios helped enhance communication with parents by offering a clear picture of school, they became a vital link between children's home and school lives" (Milliken, 1992, p. 43).

Portfolio assessment changes grading from a meaningless *A, B,* or *C* on a report card to a collection of artifacts, a clear record of growth and literacy development over time. In determining how to assign letter grades to portfolios, Grace (1993) suggests that grades may be higher than usual because students are so involved with the process. She suggests grading based on "effort, improvement, commitment to the task, mechanics, and volume" (p. 27).

A fourth-grade teacher we know in a rural school district was especially pleased by the ease with which parents understood what students were accomplishing in the new literature-based reading program his district had recently adopted. After Lyle shared the students' portfolios with their parents, he said, "at first they were confused because skill and drill worksheets weren't coming home. But parents clearly saw what their children were writing, and the amount of writing they did in response to our reading, and the list of books they were reading during silent reading time. They were amazed at how good some of the work was. And parents also understood that a barren folder showed a problem or a lack of effort. What surprised me most, though," Lyle continued, "was they weren't angry about a *C* grade. They wanted to know how they could encourage their child to read more or write more. They wanted to get in on the process as helpers. That was a first for me."

The contents of the portfolio are viewed and reviewed periodically, helping students, teachers, and parents or others who are interested and have a stake in students' literacy growth to see evidence of growth and change.

When a student's work is judged by its ability to show growth and positive change, and when students have a role in self-evaluation of their reading and writing process and products, the teacher's role in assessment is apt to change.

During a three-year study on assessment of giftedness in grades K–3, teachers reported positive and negative effects of portfolio assessment (Shaklee, 1992). According to Beverly Shaklee, the principal investigator, the teachers had always observed their students, but not systematically. They also reported finding out more about the "quiet child" through heightened observation skills and anecdotal record keeping. Instead of overlooking certain children, they now found themselves asking, "What is he thinking? How can I relate this to tomorrow's reading lesson?" Perceived drawbacks to the portfolio assessment process centered almost exclusively on the amount of time it takes to collect information and analyze outcomes. Yet, one of the most powerful assessment strategies used by teachers is observation or **kidwatching.**

Kidwatching While Teaching

Observing how children interact with print while being taught is what portfolio assessment is all about. The term *kidwatching* has been coined to dramatize the powerful role of observation in helping children grow and develop as language users. Yetta Goodman (1978) maintained that teachers screen their observations of children through their concepts and beliefs about reading and language learning.

In many classrooms, kidwatching is an ongoing, purposeful activity. Because language learning is complex, it's impossible to observe everything that happens in the classroom. The first essential, therefore, in observing children's reading and language use is to decide what to look for in advance. Clearly teachers need to watch for behaviors that are significant to growth in reading behavior. For example, probably the clearest indicator of word identification difficulties is failure to self-correct. Consequently, this is a behavior that the teacher as an expert process evaluator would take note of as students read orally.

Because it is unobtrusive and does not interfere with ongoing activities, kidwatching enables teachers to catch students in the act, so to speak, of literate behaviors. But knowing what it is that we see and what it means in terms of our students takes practice and good judgment. As Rhodes and Shanklin (1993) note, good anecdotal records and observations depend on teachers who "must understand the developmental nature of reading and writing, the processes of reading and writing, and how both might vary in different literacy contexts" (p. 28).

Dolores Fisette (1993) describes the informal reading conference as the ideal place to kidwatch. While her students choose a book and read it to her, and then translate the story into their own words, she notes which reading behaviors and strategies each student evidences, as well as how completely a student has comprehended the story as evidenced in the retelling. She can then use this information, recorded on a checklist, to plan instruction. What do students know how to do well? What do they need to learn or to practice?

Anecdotal Notes. Teachers write short **anecdotal notes** that capture the gist of an incident that reveals something the teacher considers significant to understanding a child's literacy learning. Anecdotal notes are intended to safeguard against the limitations of memory. Record observations in a journal, on charts, or on index cards. These jottings become your "field notes" and will aid you in classifying information, inferring behavior, and making predictions about individual students or instructional strategies and procedures.

Post-it notes and other small pieces of paper that are easily carried about and transferred to a child's folder are perfect for writing on-the-spot anecdotal records.

It isn't necessary or even realistic to record anecdotal information every day for each student especially in classes with 25 or 30 children. However, over a period of time, focused observations of individual children will accumulate into a revealing and informative record of literacy and language learning.

Charts are particularly useful for keeping anecdotal records. Charts can be devised to record observations in instructional situations that are ongoing: participation

Mrs. Carter
Grade 2
Time Period: March 27–April 2

Name	Date	Behavior	Date	Behavior
George	3/27	Frequently asks for assistance with spelling.	4/2	Appears to be writing more independently but still worries about correct spelling of words.
Henry	3/27	Revising draft of April Fool's story; has lots of ideas.	3/29	Writes fluently; ready to publish.
Helen	3/28	Copied a recipe from a cook book.	4/2	Wrote first original story; was very anxious to have story read; wanted to begin another story.
Maxine	3/29	Draws pictures to rehearse before writing; concentrates on handwriting and neatness.	4/1	Wrote a riddle; wants to share it with class.

● **FIGURE 13.7** An observational chart for journal writing

in reading and writing activities, small and large group discussions, book sharing, silent and oral reading. For example, the chart in Figure 13.7 was developed to record observations of children's participation in journal-writing sessions.

In addition, charts can be used to record certain behaviors across instructional activities. Examine the chart in Figure 13.8, devised to monitor and record evidence of risk taking.

A good strategy for developing a permanent record for each child in class is to cut observations apart from the individual charts. Then you can glue each student's anecdote into a permanent growth record. These can be used during conferences with students or with parents.

Mrs. Metzger

Grade 4

Week: October 11–October 15

Name	Date	Evidence of Risk Taking
Tony	10/11	Showed more willingness to try to spell independently.
Betty	10/12	Volunteered to be the recorder for Radio Reading.
Marie	10/11	Declined to reread portion of story being discussed; reluctant to participate in discussion.
Holly	10/13	Self-corrected miscues during oral reading; wasn't afraid to take guesses at unknown words.

● **FIGURE 13.8** A risk-taking chart

Some teachers find that writing anecdotal information can be unwieldy and time consuming, expecially if they are observing students over long stretches of time. An alternative to ongoing anecdotal notes is the use of checklists.

Checklists. Using a **checklist** is somewhat different from natural, open-ended observation. A checklist consists of categories that have been presented for specific diagnostic purposes.

Checklists vary in scope and purpose; they can be relatively short and open-ended, or longer and more detailed. To be useful, checklists should guide teachers to consider and notice what students can do in terms of their reading and writing strategies. The DR-TA checklist in Figure 13.9 can reveal how a group of students interacts with a text. Collaboratively designed checklists serve the added purpose of helping teachers develop and refine their beliefs about what constitutes important literacy performance. Johnston (1993) notes that such communally designed checklists have certain constraints that teachers should consider:

> —the possible list can be extremely long
>
> —a workable list must be reasonably brief
>
> —everyone will have different priorities
>
> —a checklist has implications for practice
>
> —checklists should always be thought of as drafts. (p. 137)

When Mrs. Cartwright began using an open-ended checklist designed to show evidence of creative thinking and leadership skills on the part of her second graders, she noticed an unanticipated benefit. "It was easy for me to overlook quiet students who were more peer centered or who kept to themselves but out of trouble. But, if I didn't have an annotation for a particular student for a few days, I had to stop and ask myself, why? What did I need to do to make sure that all of my students were included in activities? I'm more aware of who I watch, and why I watch them."

Interviewing. Through **interviewing** you can discover what children are thinking and feeling. Periodic student interviews can lead to a better understanding of (1) reading interests and attitudes; (2) how students perceive their strengths and weaknesses; and (3) how they perceive processes related to language learning.

Cecile Kraus (1983) studied the perceptions of first graders toward reading. She found that 6- and 7-year olds not only could verbalize their personal constructs of reading, but that their perceptions reflected the way in which they interacted with print. Here are some of the questions that Krause asked the students in individual interviews.

1. Suppose someone from another planet happened to land on earth, saw you reading, and said to you, "What are you doing?" You would probably answer, "I'm reading." Then that person might ask, "What is reading?" How would you answer?
2. What would you do to teach someone to read?
3. Who is the best reader you know? What makes her or him the best reader?
4. How did you learn to read?
5. What did your teacher do to help you learn?
6. If you are reading all by yourself and you come to a word you don't know, what do you do? Why? What do you do if that doesn't help? Why?
7. What should the teacher do when a person is reading out loud and says a word that is not the same as the word in the story?

Teacher: Mr. Niece

Grade: 5

Time Period: Fourth Period

Group: Niece's Nikes

	Student Name					
	Joe	Fred	JoAnne	Mary	Rich	Emma
Reading Behavior During DRTA						
Reading Title of a Selection						
1. Participates in predicting/is cooperative.	√	√			√	√
2. Makes some predictions with coaxing.	√	√				
3. Initiates own predictions eagerly after prompting with title.	√					
4. Low risk taking/reluctant.		√		√		
5. Predictions are numerous.			√			
After Reading Sections of a Selection						
1. Retelling is accurate.	√		√		√	
2. Retelling is adequate.		√				√
3. Retelling is minimal.				√		
4. Confirms or refutes past predictions.	√		√			√

● **FIGURE 13.9** A Directed Reading-Thinking Activity checklist

8. Is it important for the teacher to teach you the new words before you read a story? Why or why not? *(If a conditional answer is given:)* When would it be important?

Interviews provide a rich source of information. When coupled with observations made during teaching, interviews strengthen data from formal and informal tests of student performance. Moreover, interviews may reveal information that will not be provided by more traditional means of assessment.

SUMMARY

Reading is a process that takes place inside the head; it isn't directly observable or measurable. Observation and interview; informal reading inventories; miscue analysis; standardized, norm-referenced tests; and criterion-referenced tests all contribute to helping teachers understand a human process that's essentially hidden from direct examination. This is why, in order to make an authentic assessment, teachers need to base their decisions on multiple indicators of reading performance.

Trends in reading evaluation are in a state of flux. We discussed statewide testing programs leading the way in developing and implementing standardized tests that reflect an interactive model of reading and that legitimize informal measures of reading performance.

Norm-referenced and criterion-referenced tests are widely used in schools. In this chapter we examined how to interpret test scores and considered issues related to reliability, validity, and the uses of such tests. By way of contrast, we studied informal tests, whether commercially prepared or teacher made. For example, informal reading inventories can be useful in matching children with appropriate materials and in determining how children interact with print in oral and silent reading situations.

Oral miscue analysis provides insight into the reading strategies children use to make sense out of text. Miscue analysis can be applied to any oral reading situation and, therefore, may be used in conjunction with informal reading inventories.

Throughout this chapter we have recommended caution toward any single indicator of reading performance. Portfolio assessment is a way to overcome the emphasis on norm-referenced scores and grades in the eyes of parents and students and to demonstrate the growth occurring in students' reading. With the emphasis on self-reflection, portfolio assessment often involves observation, or kidwatching. It allows teachers to become more aware of students' individual behaviors as they engage in reading and learning activities within the context of classroom instruction. Anecdotal notes, checklists, and interviews are some of the techniques by which to better understand what children do, and why.

TEACHER-ACTION RESEARCHER

1. Plan a reading lesson with an elementary- or middle-school teacher, then arrange to be the teacher's "eyes" and "ears." Watch what happens during the lesson, taking notes and focusing on how much children are involved in learning. Discuss your notes with the teacher. What instructional decisions would you and the teacher make for the next lesson?

2. Do a miscue analysis with a student to find out more about the student's processing of print. Follow the procedures in this chapter and administer the miscue analysis to determine the percentage of semantically acceptable miscues, etc. Analyze to what extent the reader was able to use and coordinate graphic sound and syntactic information from the text.

3. Discuss the results you obtained and your general observations with the child's classroom teacher. How does the child's reading behavior observed in classroom instruction coincide with the results of your analysis?

4. Develop a method of portfolio assessment that you believe would serve to show students' growth in literacy. What would be the essential elements of all of the portfolios? What elements would you leave open to student selection? Design a cover sheet that would serve to organize and explain the portfolio's contents. Determine the criteria you would use to evaluate the contents of the portfolio and how you would explain your evaluation standards to students, parents, and administrators.

KEY TERMS

standardized reading test
running record
portfolio
authentic assessment
proficiency testing
norms
reliability
validity
survey test
diagnostic test
criterion-referenced tests
informal assessment
informal reading inventory (IRI)
miscue analysis
portfolio assessment
kidwatching
anecdotal notes
checklist
interviewing

CHAPTER 14

Managing and Organizing an Effective Classroom

BETWEEN THE LINES

In this chapter you will discover:

- **What features make up a cooperative learning centered classroom environment.**
- **The teacher's role(s) in facilitating interactive literary experiences.**
- **How individualized instruction influences effective reading instruction.**
- **Characteristics of classroom communities.**
- **Ideas for organizing and managing the classroom through learning centers, recordkeeping, and portfolio systems.**

A third-grade teacher in a suburban Cleveland elementary school decided to make a change from basal driven reading instruction to a literature-based instruction program. Mrs. Fawcett had done some reading about using collaborative learning and natural texts to teach children to want to read as well as how to read. The more she read and the more she chatted with her colleague Donna, also taking graduate courses at a nearby university, the more determined Mrs. Fawcett became to pilot her idea.

One spring, a visit to Mrs. Fawcett's classroom found the students in the middle of reading-language arts time. They had finished reading a selection and were in the midst of a cooperative group assignment.

Children relied on one another for interpreting instruction and for solving problems. Although Mrs. Fawcett circulated among the groups and was available to offer assistance, the children preferred to collaborate in their groups and only resorted to asking the teacher for help when they continued to be confused or unsure.

Quincy: I need Mrs. Fawcett.
Santos: No, you don't. I'll show you how to do it.
Quincy: I don't think she wants you to write them down.

Santos: Yeah, that's what these (lines) are for.
Quincy: What are details?
Santos: Little tiny things. Not the main idea, but little things that make you think of it.
Quincy: Characteristics of a whale. What are characteristics of a whale?
Santos: I'll go get a dictionary. What do we need to look up?
Quincy: Characteristics of whales.
Maylee: C-H, you need C-H-A. Use the guide words.
LaWanda: Yeah, use the guide words, you guys!
Santos: Here it is! I found it!

Most surprising was the patience and the respect with which children who were not friends and who might avoid one another on the playground or in other settings worked together happily and productively in this setting. Individual friendships, preferences, and gender differences did not appear to affect the collaborative group dynamics. The most able readers were not consistently group leaders. Children of all ability levels were observed participating in the reading activities on an equal basis. The collaborative nature of the project appeared to provide a low-risk setting where children felt comfortable and confident to participate in reading and reading-related activities. In this environment for learning, children's ability levels were not obvious; they did not appear to be a factor in cooperative learning.

When reading teachers like Mrs. Fawcett take control of the physical arrangement of their classrooms, the grouping of students for instruction, and the way they approach activities and select and use materials, they are managing the classroom. Images of how teachers view their role (technician, expert, learner, etc.) vary depending on how they view the reading process and, in turn, their instructional beliefs, concerns, and emphases. What, then, do teachers need to consider in order to effectively manage their classrooms? Teachers must conceptualize and organize classroom instruction, select classroom materials, approaches, and activities, and achieve a physical organization in which all the pieces fit together.

To manage and organize effective classrooms, teachers deserve relevant, up-to-date information, as well as traditional practices. We believe that the confluence of *new* or newly verified information with *old* or long-standing ideas provides an intelligent rationale for making classroom management decisions. We begin this chapter with efforts to improve instruction through collaborative learning and social context, used effectively by Mrs. Fawcett to create the climate in her third-grade classroom.

Improving Instruction

Teachers struggle to incorporate performance assessment, authentic texts and contexts, and learners with diverse needs into an instructionally effective program, because most want to improve their instructional practice. Knowing how to individualize and socialize classroom instruction is basic to this goal.

Collaborative and Cooperative Learning

Since reading is a communication skill, one must consider the social aspect of learning to read. **Collaborative learning** is one way to build cooperation while stimulating student interest. Classroom management and organization must begin to prepare students to be flexible so that they can recognize and adapt to competitive, cooperative, and individualized interaction situations (Kagan, 1989). We, therefore, define the term *collaborative learning as a cooperative learning environment in which students work together to complete tasks.*

The same features that characterize a cooperative learning centered classroom—feelings of safety, acceptance, support and belonging—also characterize environments that encourage creativity and intrinsic motivation (Baloche and Platt, 1993). Vygotsky's (1978) studies on how we internalize language and thinking as we interact with each other socially have given us new ways to look at the importance of the social context of learning. According to Vygotsky, the best role for the teacher is to mediate between what students are able to do on their own and what they are able to do with support, prompting, and encouragement. Teachers can use this understanding of the role of the social context of thinking and learning to help them organize classroom instruction which will support learners as they construct new meanings through reading and writing.

Teachers are renewing their focus on creating authentic classroom situations that help children become active learners and gain competence in reading and writing. Collaboration and interaction among children during classroom literacy instruction gives them rich opportunities to practice and to refine new literacy learning. Mandel and Sharkey (1993) describe a literature-based program that was designed to foster the social as well as the co-operative aspects of literacy learning. The program, in urban schools that serve mostly students from minority backgrounds, consisted of three components: literacy centers, teacher-guided activities, and time for students to work together on independently chosen reading or writing activities. This program of literacy instruction was designed to increase student motivation and maintain student interest in literacy by alternating teacher modeling during whole-group instruction with opportunities for students to work cooperatively on self-directed yet socially defined activities. The increased participation in meaningful reading and writing led to improved performance. Teachers noted that children needed to make choices about the type of work they would do. They negotiated small groups, made rules and delegated tasks to the groups, and decided on appropriate outcomes. The motivation and enthusiasm for learning came from the opportunities the students had to make their own choices about tasks and to work together to read, to listen to a book or tape, or to engage in writing activities. They practiced strategies the teacher had modeled, often assisting and coaching each other as they worked.

The advantages of collaborative learning are numerous and well documented: (1) higher motivation to learn and greater intrinsic motivation; (2) academic improvement in both tutor and tutee; (3) increased self-esteem; (4) more positive perceptions about the intentions of others; (5) decrease of negative competition; (6) greater acceptance of differences; (7) decreased dependence on the teacher; and (8) higher achievement test scores (Wood in Jongsma, 1990).

Collaborative work is not always smooth and without conflict, both social and cognitive. How do you decide which group member will be responsible for which task? How can the group decide, if research data conflicts, which source is accurate? Both Mandel and Sharkey (1993) and Shanahan, Robinson, and Schneider (1993) note that the type of discussion, thinking, reading, and writing that students must do to resolve their disagreements often leads to greater levels of student learning.

Cooperative Learning and the Teacher's Role. Developing social skills for successful group work is a prerequisite when collaborative learning is a new experience for students. The classroom teacher needs to create activities that encourage and model (1) getting to know and trust group members; (2) communicating accurately and unambiguously; (3) accepting and supporting one another; and (4) constructively resolving conflicts to make mutual achievement of the goals possible (Johnson and Johnson, 1989/1990). The teacher's role may change to that of facilitator when operating the classroom collaboratively.

When the teacher is not the sole authority for interpretation in the classroom, when children are assisted in constructing their own reading and writing processes, students learn to connect their life experiences with literacy activities in expanded ways. Pearson (1993) found that even young students can engage in self-directed discussions about books and reading that cover all aspects of comprehension, and can evaluate the quality of their writing and their comprehension without direct teacher supervision.

Sometimes readers bring experiences from their own lives to their reading, giving them a logical and valid response that may be different from the teacher's or from other students' responses. If the teacher's experiences and interpretations totally shape school literacy experiences, students with different cultural and academic backgrounds may find they have little or no opportunity to connect their own experiences with their reading and writing.

For example, Cynthia Lewis (1993) describes how a student in her class understood how to do the kind of close reading of texts required in school, but who used his own "interpretive lens" to build meaning. His view helped him to construct a response that did not fit Lewis' cultural expectations, as he sympathized with the klutzy and bumbling guest in the story while showing disdain for the rich but insincere host. Lewis notes that teachers must be aware of how social identity informs our communication and our interpretations. Reading and writing in school should involve helping children learn ways to stretch the boundaries of the familiar and already known, but teachers also need to legitimize the knowledge and experience that students of diverse backgrounds bring to literacy tasks.

Direct Instruction

Both direct and indirect teaching occur in many reading classrooms. For example, "conventional classrooms can contain elements of whole language instruction, while direct teaching can occur in whole language classrooms" (Slaughter, 1988, p. 30). The question becomes a pragmatic one for each teacher. How is instruction delivered? How are students grouped together and for what purpose? Being a whole language teacher does not mean that one abandons direct instruction.

The *key* to **direct instruction,** we believe, is not that teachers consistently prefer small or large groups but rather they remain *flexible* in forming and disbanding groups and display a willingness to deliver teacher-centered or teacher-facilitated instruction. For example, teachers who guide a Directed Reading-Thinking Activity are adept at assuming a more facilitating role and taking a back seat as their students begin to take charge of questioning and answering.

It is important to remember that even with literature-based reading instruction teachers still play an important role in helping children to learn to read and to learn how to be proficient readers. While focusing on constructing meaning as the primary goal of all reading instruction, teachers need to be sure to incorporate direct teaching of certain reading strategies that their students need. Spiegel (1992) explains that direct teaching and systematic instruction can be important components of whole language classrooms. She describes direct instruction this way: "student and teacher are focused on a goal or objective, on what is to be learned; students are aware of why it is important to learn the task at hand; and students are explicitly taught how to do a particular process through teacher modeling and explanation" (p. 41).

Direct instruction in a meaning-centered classroom is not about isolated phonics drills and worksheets to teach and test skills knowledge. Rather, teachers focus direct instruction on the strategies that proficient readers and writers use to make sense of texts, modeling not only the strategies themselves, but ways to think about using them flexibly in actual reading and writing situations.

Teachers make, verify, and reassess numerous decisions about instruction. Learning more about teachers and their decision making, therefore, is central to understanding many factors in an effectively managed and organized classroom.

Classroom Teachers of Reading

The classroom teacher of reading, in addition to providing sound daily instruction in reading, performs several other roles and interacts with other essential personnel. According to Wepner, Feeley, and Strickland (1989), there are three basic categories of skills required for leadership in reading in schools: technical knowledge, interpersonal skills, and management skills. Examine Table 14.1 (adapted from Wepner, 1989) to focus on some of the major responsibilities associated with the role of classroom teacher of reading.

Analysis of the rather complex role of classroom teacher of reading provides a useful common ground for principals and teachers and prospective teachers to talk to each other. Teachers' attitudes and behaviors, as perceived by students, also seem to have a noticeable effect on a student's self-concept. Since our self-concept affects how we feel about a situation, in this case a learning situation, it's important to think about teachers' behaviors. Harris, Rosenthal, and Snodgrass (1986) reported that better student outcomes were positively associated with such variables as task orientation, explanation, nonverbal warmth, and praising (p. 173).

● TABLE 14.1

Skills of Classroom Teacher of Reading

TECHNICAL KNOWLEDGE SKILLS	
Evaluator	Evaluates how reading programs work in class. Evaluates students' reading progress.
Instructor/Trainer	Stimulates, extends, and reinforces learning. Demonstrates appropriate reading strategies.
Diagnostician	Uses informal and formal data to assess students' strengths and weaknesses.
Consultant	Works with parents to improve reading performance. Works with paraprofessionals.
INTERPERSONAL SKILLS	
Advisor	Assists students, parents, and administrators with effective reading practices.
Collaborator	Works with other teachers and principals to establish roles, expectations, and rewards for student control.
Communicator	Models appropriate reading behavior. Encourages student interaction. Communicates realistic student expectations. Communicates enthusiasm, warmth, and expectations, and provides good classroom climate.
MANAGEMENT SKILLS	
Coordinator	Coordinates all facets of the reading program in the classroom. Works with other teachers for grouping and teaching.
Leader	Creates effective reading environments. Leads in-service sessions.
Organizer	Develops lists of budgetary items for reading. Provides appropriately planned instruction. Organizes classroom for recreational reading.

Students know that their teachers are more important than the techniques, approaches, and materials used. Teachers' expectations for their students' success or lack of it are often revealed in their general behaviors in the classroom. Teacher expectations are lived up to—or down to—by students. Yet these are intangibles; they are not obvious. How can teachers, closest to their own behaviors and role responsibilities, deal with students constructively? More important, do students observe and assess teachers' behaviors and classroom assignments in ways that are consistent with the teacher's intentions?

There are several ways in which classroom teachers of reading can benefit from introspection through reflection.

First, as teachers who are expected to possess numerous technical, personal, and management skills, we can *examine our role* in relation to these skills, the roles we must assume, and the other essential school personnel and external persons with whom we interact. We need to *seize opportunities to interact with other teachers to talk about mutual problems and to share the latest developments,* whether about working with at-risk children developing insights into a new technique to implement some aspect of whole language in the classroom.

Second, as teachers we need to *analyze our own attitudes and behaviors* to find out whether or not they are conducive to forming positive attitudes in students. What verbal and nonverbal signals do we send? What is the environment like in our classroom? What are the expectations that we may be in fact communicating?

Third, teachers need to *identify basic instructional practices in reading.* Basic in this case means in positively affecting students' attitudes through the important combination of interest plus needs. What classroom instructional practices in Box 14.1 are you already implementing? Check *yes* for those; check *perhaps* if you are interested in finding ways to implement the suggestion; check *no* if you are not now implementing it and are not interested in finding ways to do it.

Fourth, teachers need to realize that many times it is the overwhelming pressures of factors outside school that win out. In spite of the care we take to examine the educational and attitudinal factors as well as our own reflections, our efforts at creating a responsive, well-organized, effective classroom won't always pay off. Relationships in families, nutrition, illness, abuse, addictions, economic hardship, and community pressures can and do override school factors. They are not, however, excuses for inaction. The important point for us as teachers is to *make certain that we keep our expectations high and provide as many quality opportunities as necessary for students to reach.*

Individualizing Instruction

The term *individualizing,* more than *individualized,* connotes the process of providing differentiated instruction to students. It reflects the accumulation of previous knowledge and direct experiences in reading classrooms over the years. We believe that most teachers of

● BOX 14.1

Instructional Practices Inventory

	Yes	Perhaps	No
1. I am aware of my students' attitudes toward certain aspects of reading			
2. I plan reading activities that students tend to like.			
3. I use reading materials in which my students can succeed.			
4. I use materials related to the interest and needs of my students' norm group.			
5. I provide situations where the usefulness of reading is apparent, such as reading that is necessary in order to do a certain desired project or activity.			
6. I model reading, either orally or silently, so that my students can see that I value reading.			
7. I provide for recreational reading in my classroom.			
8. I use reading material found in the students' everyday life.			
9. I encourage *parents* to improve attitudes toward reading by reading to their children, providing reading materials, and being examples themselves by reading in front of their children.			
10. I avoid using reading as a punishment.			
11. I use bibliotherapy; I guide my students into books that deal with their problems and relate to their world.			
12. I am enthusiastic when I teach reading.			
13. I am positive in my approach; I emphasize students' abilities instead of constantly referring to their errors and inadequacies.			

reading still ascribe to this process, which originated as the individualized instruction approach.

Individualized instruction has to be one of the all-time ten most misunderstood terms in education. Naturally, it means different things to different people. To some, it means programmed, prescriptive instruction; to others, it means one-to-one teaching or tutoring; to yet others, it means flexible grouping for instruction. Often educators disagree over the definitions of terms, but the disagreement doesn't cause any harm.

What Is Individualized Instruction in Reading?

This is the key question for those interested in classroom organization because it can help clarify the major ways we choose to deliver reading instruction: in small groups, whole class, or one-to-one.

Individualized instruction evolved out of a 150-year-old American goal of providing free schooling for everyone. Its biggest impetus came with the development of reading tests in the early part of the twentieth century. It spawned many experiments in education such as ability grouping, flexible promotions, and differentiated assignments. Many of the plans followed the ideas outlined in the Dalton and the Winnetka plans, which allowed children to work in reading and content areas at their own pace (Smith, 1965, p. 194).

Gradually, individualized instruction went beyond children's learning rates and reading achievement. The child's interest in reading, attitude toward reading, and personal self-esteem and satisfaction in reading expanded the goal of instruction (Smith, 1965, p. 378). Terms associated with individualization ranged from *individual progression* in the 1920s to *individualized instruction in reading,* to *self-selection in reading,* to *personalized reading.* Today, we might add *objective-based* and *prescriptive* learning.

An interesting irony is that originally, procedures used in individualized classrooms did not vary widely, whatever the adopted term. Read the following classic description; does it conjure up a reasonable picture of individualized instruction in your mind?

> Each child selects a book that he wants to read. During the individual conference period the teacher sits in some particular spot in the room as each child comes and reads to her. As he does so, she notes his individual needs and gives him appropriate help. Finally she writes what the child is reading, his needs, and strengths on his record card. Then another individual conference is held, and so on. If several children need help on the same skills, they may be called together in a group for such help. (Smith, 1965, p. 379)

This scenario does, after all, seem like a plausible description of individualized instruction. How it's actually *applied* in reading classrooms around the country is another matter entirely. In practice, two variations of the original individualized approach to instruction are often found in today's classroom: (1) Individualized procedures are one part of the total program (i.e., one day a week); or (2) Parts of individualized reading are integrated into another reading approach (i.e., self-selection during free reading). Individualization can refer to instruction that is appropriate for the student regardless of whether it occurs within a one-to-one, small group, or a whole-class setting. According to Yanok (1988), individualization is a process of personalizing teaching to provide instruction that recognizes and responds to the unique learning needs of each child.

While individualized instruction as an approach to or a program for reading instruction is not as widespread as others, its *influence* on reading teachers has been pervasive. *Teacher assessment of individual readers' strengths and weaknesses* is at the very core of effective reading instruction. This is not peculiar to individualized instruction, but is a tenet that cuts across the delivery of reading instruction, regardless of the organization pattern used.

Influences of Individualized Instruction

The term *individualized instruction* in reading has waxed and waned. Models of prescriptive and of personalized individualized programs such as skills management systems and literature-thematic units have come and gone. What are we left with? What historical influences of the individualized instruction movement have helped shape the delivery of reading instruction today?

As Gates stated in a 1964 correspondence, "I have always believed that if one accepts the theory that the basal reading program must be used it should be adjusted to individual needs and each child should be encouraged to move on into wider and more advanced material as rapidly as possible" (Smith, 1965, p. 240). Individualization of instruction is not contrary to basal reader programs. However, it has gone beyond the traditions of ability grouping.

Durrell, in the 1950s, suggested as much when he challenged teachers of reading to provide for individual differences of students. Teachers should be "providing suitable materials; individual conferences; extensive individual silent reading; long-range assignments; workbooks, standard test lessons, and other self-administering materials; small grouping of 5 to 6 pupils" (Smith, 1965, p. 294).

Let's examine further two major ramifications of individualizing instruction in reading that evolved out of a long tradition, yet still coincide with effective classroom management.

Groups. The concept of creating and disbanding groups of differing sizes, abilities, and interests for the purpose of providing specific instruction is germane to effective classroom instruction. Yet, while **grouping** is used to organize the teaching of content subjects (such as math and social studies), reading instruction is historically associated with grouping. The reading group or circle is indigenous to reading.

Can you remember your old reading group? We might joke about having been a bluebird, robin, eagle, maybe even a buzzard. Whether such memories are amusingly nostalgic or painful, few of us ever lose them completely. It's probably just as well that we do remember, because reading groups today are as prevalent as they ever were. One of the reasons for this lack of change, according to Goodlad (1983), is that "the circumstances of teaching make it difficult for teachers to do other than what they have already learned to do" (p. 469).

Consequently, we observe daily reading circles or, for other purposes, small groups may gather for story discussions and questions. Large groups of whole classes may stay intact for silent reading and writing; books may be reported in individual conferences.

What are some consequences of placing students in groups? As we discussed earlier, under direct instruction, teachers' behaviors toward children assigned to "low" groups differ from their behaviors toward those assigned to the "high" group. Teachers are less likely to ask the lower group to answer higher-level comprehension questions (Allington in Good, 1982, p. 27). In addition to how group placement affects students' performance, "we need to understand much more thoroughly the consequences of placing students into groups" as it affects students' expectations.

A corollary to grouping and collaborative learning is awareness of the *physical environment* of the classroom. What do the space, materials, and decision-making capabilities of students and teachers reveal about the classroom as a place for learning? If someone took a photograph of your classroom, how would you describe the composition of student groups and the nature of activities in progress?

Classroom climates or **classroom environments** are distinct and the recognition that a classroom is the total of all its organizational components has grown through the years. Furthermore, we have come to acknowledge that this physical environment embodies the goals of the classroom and the teacher's role. Teachers have learned to combine their knowledge about reading and learning to read to create as conducive a learning environment as possible.

Materials. The endorsement of a wide variety of reading **materials** has become accepted practice across school districts, as we discussed in Chapter 11. Originally provided for the purpose of matching students with materials on their reading level, the concept of material variety quickly expanded. Now there are diverse materials to meet students' interests and to provide instructional variety as well. Reference books, catalogs, paperback books, and magazines are found in corner shelves for free and silent reading. Skill cards from kits, along with workbook pages and dittos, are self-checked by students; hardcover basal readers and softcover high-interest, low-vocabulary series move from the shelf to circled readers to desks and back again to the shelf.

Materials are involved in most of the instructional day. When many reading teachers speak about presenting a skill, reinforcing the skill, testing for its mastery, and perhaps reteaching the skill, they are assuming that *materials* accompany each one of these steps. They are probably right. Teachers at the other end of the spectrum, those whose programs revolve around independent reading of personally selected books, short stories, and poems, have a much different concept of materials.

This raises a major issue related to materials: *recordkeeping* and the amount of teacher time required to keep records. Recordkeeping refers to the necessity of keeping records on individual readers' total and daily performance in relation to skill needs and reading strategies; materials used; completed and projected activities; assigned groups;

grades and test scores received; and recommendations for future instructional placement. Teachers are always seeking efficient ways of accumulating, recording, and synthesizing this kind of information. Publishing companies frequently promote built-in recordkeeping components for both students and teachers.

We have established that many materials are a must for reading teachers. They are also something of a paradox. If you manage individual reading, you need a variety of materials. On the other hand, if you have a lot of materials, you need to effectively manage and organize your classroom.

Putting It All Together: Organizing a Classroom Community

We have considered a number of factors necessary to manage classroom reading instruction. Getting the classroom under control, grouping students for instruction, and examining our own behaviors and expectations help us deal with the task of organization. The ramifications of individualizing instruction, along with the basic need to orchestrate children and materials and our beliefs with some degree of efficiency, bring us to a final consideration—putting the pieces together.

The social nature of reading and writing and the importance of contextual factors in literacy instruction call for teachers to organize their classrooms into nurturing and supportive **communities of learners.** Literacy becomes a useful tool for thinking and learning and for enjoyment when reading and writing are the activities students (and the teacher, too) use every day to learn about themselves and about the larger world they inhabit.

What are the qualities that comprise a learning community? Rosaen and Hazelwood (1993) offer these guidelines:

1. The classroom culture is focused on collaborative inquiry.
2. Each group shares responsibilities collaboratively.
3. The teacher and each student are personally involved in and are committed to learning.
4. The teacher both participates in and acts as facilitator in the collaborative context.
5. Knowledge is socially constructed—evidence rather than authority determines validity.

When teachers organize a classroom community through reading and writing, the classroom can take varying shapes with varying activities since the needs of the learners drive instructional practices. Nevertheless, these classroom communities will share some of the following characteristics:

1. The focus is on authentic reading and writing activities.
2. Risk taking is encouraged by viewing errors as a natural and normal aspect of learning.
3. Learners are given options (which books to read, which topics to write on, how long a project might take).
4. Learners are trusted as teachers give up some control.
5. Decisions concerning routines, rules, and activities are made collaboratively.
6. The teacher's role is as facilitator, participant, and/or guide rather than as transmitter of facts.
7. Emphasis is on the social nature of learning and knowing.
8. Reflection and inquiry are essential to learning and to teaching.
9. Power relationships among students and teachers change as teaching and learning become the valued work of all members of the classroom. (Adapted from Clyde and Condon, 1993, p. 92.)

Creating such communities means that teachers must think of classrooms as learning places rather than as workplaces. But moving to such a community takes time. The teacher must help students by planning and setting up routines. Students need to be initiated into the kind of inquiry and collaborative work this definition of learning requires. Teachers need to help students value "thinking, questioning, discussion, learning from mistakes, trying new ideas, responding and challenging ideas, and appreciating diversity."

What does a classroom community look like? The creation of a functional classroom usually entails creatively making do with what is already there. Hence, we have a potpourri of elementary classroom designs ranging from traditional row after row to open modular groupings to cozy carpets and cubbyholes.

Creating a Physical Environment

What actually goes on in the classroom once the door is closed? Any experienced teacher will acknowledge that, within the confines of one's own classroom, there is a certain degree of autonomy that outside pressures don't penetrate. The physical arrangement of the classroom, given an understanding custodian, is one expression of a teacher's autonomy. The way the furniture is arranged contributes to the reading program's organization.

Arranging desks, chairs, materials, and so forth can contribute a great deal to the organization of an entire semester or year-long reading program. The *physical structure* put into place by the reading teacher can support the goals or underlying structure of the reading program. It can work for the teacher as much as if not more than any other component in the total program and total classroom environment.

Experienced teachers realize this eventually. Perhaps, if more prospective and practicing teachers were exposed to philosophies such as Herbert Kohl's in his classic, *The Open Classroom* (1969), they would do even more behind the classroom door.

> The placement of objects in space is not arbitrary, and rooms represent in physical form the spirit and souls of places and institutions. A teacher's room tells us something about who he is and a great deal about what he is doing.
>
> It is important for teachers to look at the spatial dimensions of their classrooms, to step back so they may see how the organization of space represents the life within it. (p. 35)

Stepping Back. When you do step back and look carefully at your reading classroom, what do you see?

A classroom's physical structure can support the goals or underlying structure of a reading program.

One perspective to take as you look around the room is to examine it for *space usage,* or books, nooks, and crannies. For example, do you see a space suitable for a reading loft? Such a loft might hold four or five readers on top and house a minilibrary underneath. Is there any room for a reading fort made of empty carpet-roll tubes? How about creating student "offices" by using partitions to divide a table into three or four separate areas? If these aren't feasible ways to use space, you might consider establishing several special reading spots, such as a chair, carpet, cupboard, or sofa.

Still another scan of your classroom might be made with *storage techniques* in mind. Boxes, labeled shelves, bulletin boards, and pegboards are multipurpose and inexpensive. Boxes make good filing cabinets; students, too, might like their own filing drawers. Thorough and visible labeling helps students know where to return materials in the room. Interactive and integrative bulletin boards may help students develop positive attitudes toward reading according to Frager and Valentour (1984). One of the most unusual storage techniques observed was three rows of eight ten-gallon cardboard ice cream containers! They were sturdy and, if nothing else, contributed to positive student attitudes (or memories)!

We asked a fifth-grade teacher whose classroom we admired and whose teaching always seemed to be carried out with purpose and reflection this question: "What do you *call* your arrangement, Wanda?" She responded, "I don't know; it doesn't really have a name, but it works." We asked her to describe why and how her reading classroom is organized. Read Wanda's description of her classroom and how it came into being in Box 14.2.

The physical environment teachers of reading create can set the stage for a productive reading program. Children's literature programs and the use of literature in the elementary and early childhood classroom have been studied and serve to illustrate the connection between physical environment and program. Morrow (1982) reported a definite relationship between children's frequency of use of literature and physical design or program characteristics. Yet library corners were neither carefully designed nor valued as an important area of the classroom (p. 344).

Teachers who make books accessible to children by making changes in time and physical design of their classroom are contributing to the development of readers. Huck, Hepler, and Hickman (1987) suggest that books should be such a natural part of the classroom environment that there should be "no argument as to whether to have a classroom collection of books or a library media center." Both are necessary (p. 641). And, children develop more interest in books when they share in the planning of a reading center (p. 642).

Ideas for Getting Organized

Ideas for getting your classroom organized run the gamut from deciding to establish learning centers to developing a portfolio system. Some pertain to the classroom as a whole and others to individual students in selected activities. They are all ways of bringing order and organization to the classroom community.

● **BOX 14.2**

Class Works

Wanda's Description of Her Classroom

A fascinating experience in class arrangement took place in my classroom one year—all because a father of one my students worked for a cardboard box factory.

He came to me one day with the free offer of 50 heavy-duty, double-strength cardboard boxes approximately two-by-two-by-two-feet in size. Could I use them? The price was right, so of course I said, yes.

Now, how could I use this terrific gift? And then the answer came to me one day when a student said, "Mrs. Rogers, I haven't sat in my own seat since the first five minutes of today!" I gave this some thought and realized that with the flexible grouping we were constantly using, the children actually did spend very little time at their own desks. So I asked, "Why not do away with desks?" And we did.

Each student was given a box that was to house books, supplies, and so on. We stacked the boxes two tall and they provided instant dividers to make separate spaces in the room for small groups to meet.

Much of our class instruction was done in small groups with different groupings for each subject. By removing "desk ownership," we eliminated territorial problems. No more did we hear, "Jim wrote all over my desk during reading class." "You can't sit here. I don't want your cooties all over my desk." "Mrs. Rogers, Judy stole my pencil out of my desk when she was sitting there."

Desks were viewed as workbenches and storage areas for learning activities equipment and materials. By removing student-desk associations, the desks themselves became more flexible for rearranging to meet different organizational needs.

An unexpected benefit was that students became more involved. Because they no longer had a desk for retreat where they could while away time unproductively or daydream, they tended to "find something to do" when they finished a task; kibbitz in on another group of students, use the library or resource center, take a book to a corner, or involve themselves in a listening or hands-on activity in special areas set up for that purpose. They learned to move themselves from one task to another, rather than "sit in *their* seats" and wait to be told what to do by the teacher.

One of the best advantages was that it opened new vistas of classroom organization for me as a teacher. I found myself less restricted and more creative and efficient. I could arrange the management of an activity without the confines of "desk ownership."

REFLECTIVE INQUIRY

- Why did Wanda feel more creative when she changed the way desks were used?
- How closely connected are classroom organization and management?

Developed by Wanda Rogers; reprinted with permission.

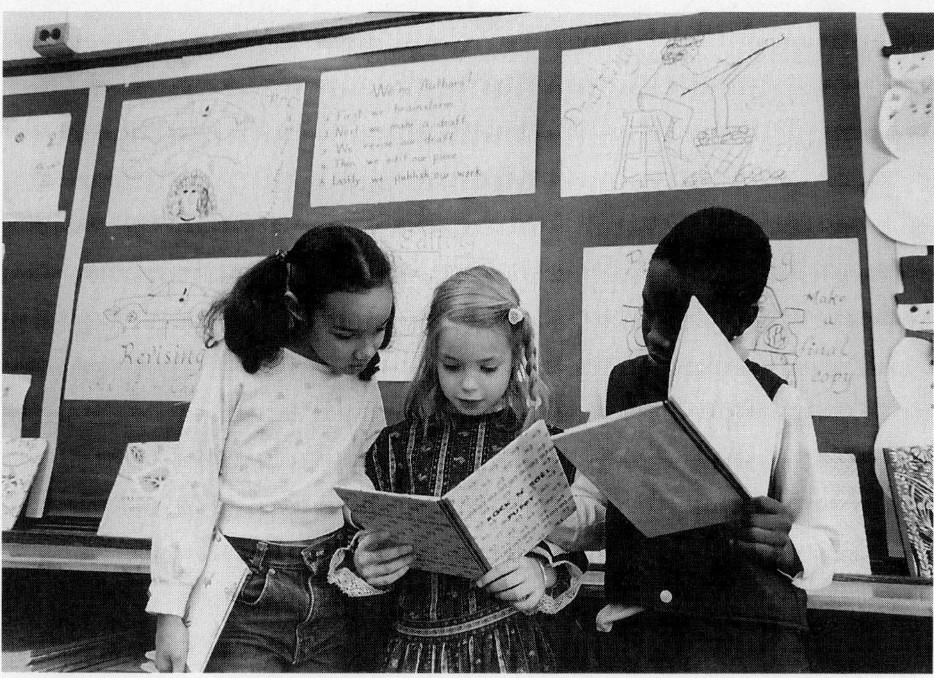

Classroom learning centers allow more diverse opportunities for students to work alone or in groups, establishing choices, commitment, and responsibility.

Learning Centers. Several advantages to setting up **learning centers** are that they allow more pupil movement, more and diverse opportunities for pupils to work in small groups or independently, and more pupil choice, commitment, and responsibility.

Why teachers choose to use learning centers is important, because their purpose should determine the type of center. Provisions for flexible grouping, individual work, research, and group or committee work are essential for centers in classrooms that foster optimal literacy development for each student (Lapp and Flood, 1993). Such an environment encourages collaborative and social aspects of literacy learning and allows the teacher to plan for various reading and writing activities. Even in the smallest of classrooms, a center for quiet reading and research and a center for groups to meet and talk can usually be arranged, if only by placing desks together to make collaborative work areas.

Supplementing textbooks and basal readers with dictionaries, encyclopedias, newspapers and magazines, comic books, children's literature, nonfiction tradebooks, art supplies, books on tape, and students' own previously published writing gives students sources for varied reading and writing ideas. These sources can be located in centers organized in a variety of ways:

Subject:	Language arts, math, social studies, science, music
	____________________
Interest:	Sports, records, insects, food, rocks, cultures, airplanes
	____________________
Inquiry:	"Are camels still used on the desert?"
	____________________
Problem solving:	"You're visiting a friend overnight. You wake up and smell smoke; what do you do?"
	____________________
Theme:	Appearance and reality ("Is Wilbur, in reality, a terrific pig?")
	____________________
Construction:	Building models, making films ("Construct a six-petal flower using LOGO turtle graphics.")
	____________________

We've added a blank line to each type above. Can you add another example to each?

Room Diagrams. One of the most useful ideas for organizing any classroom, whether you have learning centers or other formats, is a diagram of the classroom. A room diagram serves three simple yet essential purposes: (1) it helps the teacher keep track of where and how various activities are taking place and with whom; (2) it helps parents and other teachers acclimate to your classroom whether they are visiting or presiding over another class or study hall (it becomes a handy seating chart); and (3) it gives students an opportunity to see what is available for them to do now and anticipate what other activities are in store for them.

Room diagrams are just as useful to the teacher who is beginning to use optional activities or centers as they are to the teacher who has scrapped traditional formats completely. To illustrate, the rooms outlined in Figure 14.1 are traditional elementary classrooms in which learning centers are separated from regular instructional areas either around the periphery or off to one side. While classrooms that have distinct areas for diverse activities tend to have certain days or times set aside for their use, other classrooms have alternatives integrated into their daily routines.

Figure 14.2 outlines a room in which learning or activity areas are conducive to collaborative learning. Interestingly, there is research to suggest that desk arrangement is important in keeping students on task. For example, students seated in circles are found to engage in more on-task behavior than those in rows, and students seated in clusters engage

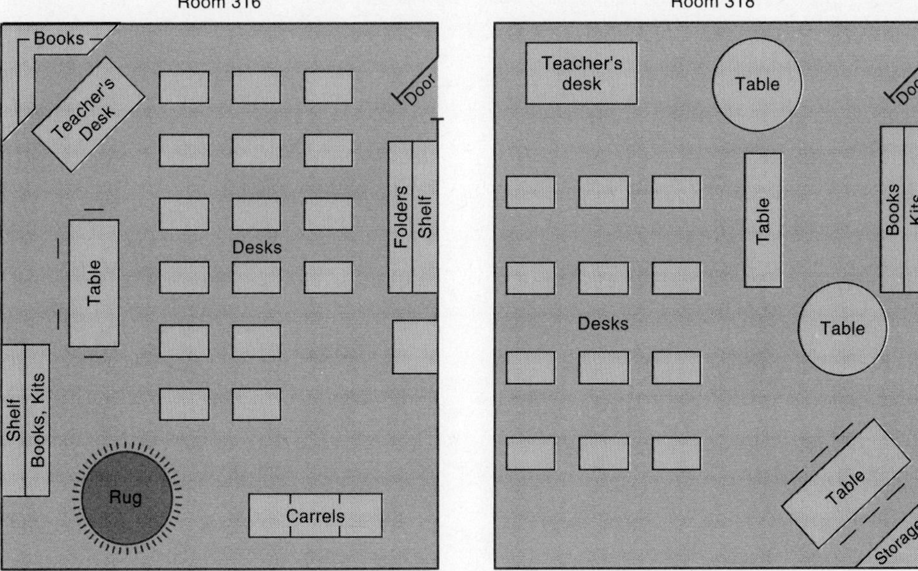

● **FIGURE 14.1** Traditional classrooms with activity centers

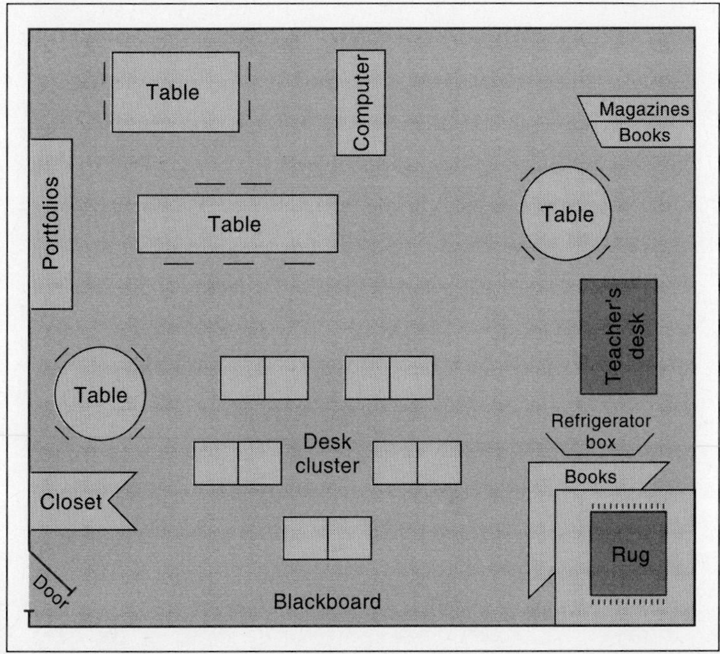

● **FIGURE 14.2** A learning center classroom

Schedule (January 4 to February 1)			Name Julie A.		
Special Comments: Use time at Station 2 to finish the introduction to your portfolio.					
Week	**Monday**	**Tuesday**	**Wednesday**	**Thursday**	**Friday**
A	—	1	2	3	7
B	7	3	9	5	5
C	8	1	4	5	5
D	6	4	4	8	5
E	9	8	1	4	3

● **FIGURE 14.3** Individual student unit schedule

in more on-task behavior than those in rows but less than those in circles (Rosenfield et al., 1985).

Student Schedules. The secret to effective implementation of classroom learning centers is teacher organization and the scheduling of students to designated activities. Arranging **student schedules** is time consuming. In order to develop an *individual schedule* (see Figure 14.3 for a five-week unit), teachers need to consider where and when and in what combinations they want students at the various stations. A student who needs extensive work in a particular area, such as composition or listening, is given more time at that numbered station. All students, regardless of their strengths and weaknesses, usually want equal time at certain popular areas, such as games or free-reading stations.

In addition to, or instead of, individual student schedules, teachers may develop *small group schedules* to rotate groups of students to different stations. This type of schedule is often called *rotational.* Figure 14.4 illustrates a schedule designed for second graders to follow during their language-arts hour each morning for a week to ten days.

The names of stations that the teacher believes are important enough to merit a block of time during language arts are put in the outer, stationary circle. Names of students are listed in the inner circle, which can be rotated daily or more or less frequently. In some cases, teachers let the students decide when to go to the next station or center.

A third way of scheduling students is through *contracting.* Ideally, this is a contractual agreement between student and teacher in which the student makes a commitment to assume responsibility for a learning experience. The amount of teacher input needed varies from student to student. Independent students will more readily participate in this kind of decision making than other, more dependent ones.

Successful contracting is looked at as a process that begins during teacher-student conferences. First, the interests of the student are uncovered through discussion or observation and discussion. Next, the teacher confers with the student about what will be needed to follow up on the interest, and a contract is drawn up and signed. Materials are searched out and organized as the student carries out the plan of study. Then the teacher helps as needed by answering questions and giving direct instruction as needed. The process continues and the contract is completed when the student achieves his or her goals.

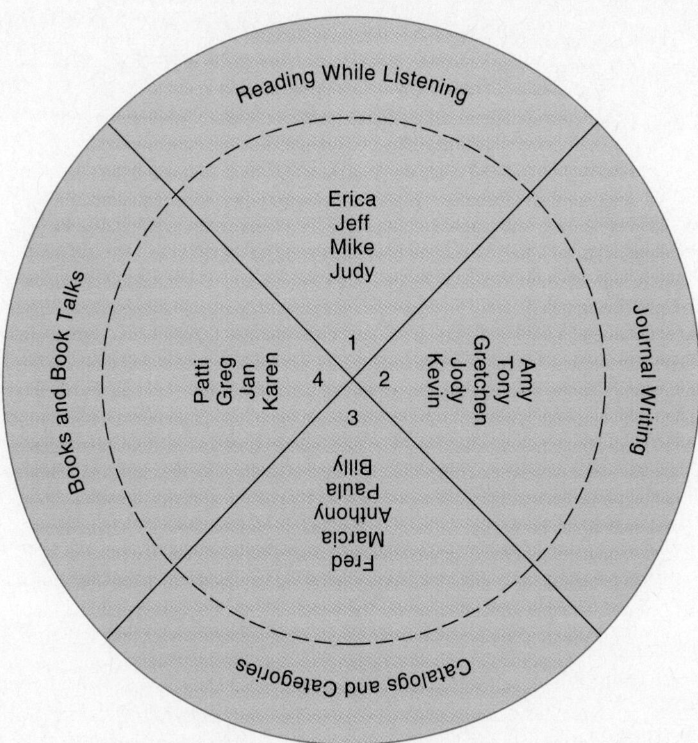

● **FIGURE 14.4** Small group student schedule

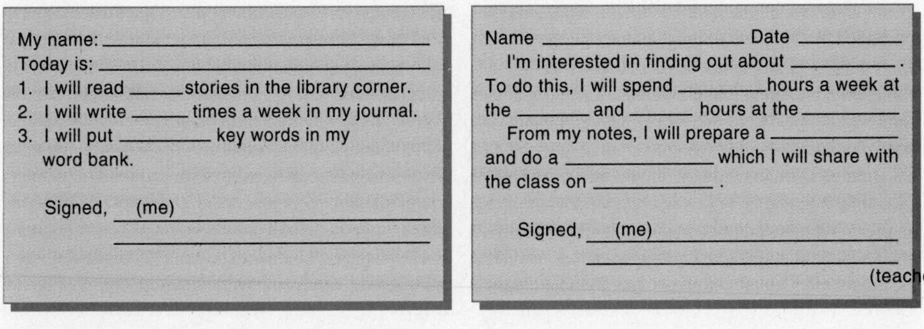

My name: ______________________
Today is: ______________________
1. I will read _____ stories in the library corner.
2. I will write _____ times a week in my journal.
3. I will put _______ key words in my word bank.

Signed, (me) ______________________
____

Name ______________________ Date __________
I'm interested in finding out about __________.
To do this, I will spend ________ hours a week at the _______ and _______ hours at the ________.
From my notes, I will prepare a __________ and do a ______________ which I will share with the class on __________.

Signed, (me) ______________________
____
(teach

● **FIGURE 14.5** Individual student contracts

Contracts, then, are potentially the most individual and personal of schedules. They should not be done en masse. Two contracts are illustrated in Figure 14.5, the one on the left for a second grader and the one on the right for a fifth grader.

Recordkeeping. Keeping track of books and stories read by students and materials used by students, or **record keeping,** is a problem for many teachers. It is not feasible for

WHAT HAVE I BEEN READING?				
Date	Title	Author	+ rating –	# pp.
Mar. 13	Lon Po Po: A Red-Riding Hood Story from China	Ed Young	+	87
Apr. 2	Mufaro's Beautiful Daughters	John Steptoe	+	206

● **FIGURE 14.6** Individual reading chart

teachers to take on the task of recording who read what, in what level, and what was it all about. Parent volunteers and teacher aides are ideal assistants. However, the most valuable assets to any organized classroom are the students themselves.

Any classroom that has a reading-library corner or that includes sustained silent reading in its reading program should also have a system to record what students are reading. One system is to have cards or charts attached to the inside back cover of a student folder (or portfolio or reading journal) as shown in Figure 14.6.

When students work on multiple drafts of writing and self-selected reading materials, keeping track of information in an uncomplicated and understandable manner is essential. Just as students might keep a record of their ongoing literacy growth using portfolios for documentation and assessment, teachers can also use a portfolio system to assess their teaching effectiveness and to plan and organize instruction.

Portfolio Systems

Collecting student work in a **portfolio system** as described in Chapter 13 can serve several purposes in the classroom. When students are evaluated not just on the number of correct answers they give, but on their willingness to stretch their thinking, their improvement in problem solving and communication skills, and their attitudes towards themselves as learners, portfolios have the capacity to reinforce curricular goals way beyond acquisition of basic skills.

Crowley (1993) notes that portfolios can serve as a vehicle for teachers to evaluate students' strengths and weaknesses as learners. Using portfolios in this way transforms them from a way to assign grades into tools to refine instructional decision making based on students' unmet needs. In one study, when a group of teachers was supported in implementing and reflectively interpreting portfolio assessment in their classrooms, these teach-

Negative Indicators	Alternate behaviors
a. Segregated groups	________
b. Rude remarks	________
c. Slurs	________
d. Misconceptions	________
Positive Skills Observed	**Examples**
a. Caring	________
b. Teamwork	________
c. Initiative	________
d. Effort	________
e. Problem solving	________
Community Services Performed	**Examples**
a. Graffiti cleanup	________
b. Little Brothers and Sisters	________
c. Publish booklet, "Fighting Prejudice at	________
Our School"	________

● **FIGURE 14.7** A sample page from a teacher log

Source: Flood, J., Lapp, D., and Nagel. G., "Assessing Student Action Beyond Reflection and Response," *Journal of Reading,* 36:5 (February 1993) 422.

ers noted a new excitement about teaching and a fundamental change in the ways in which they organized their teaching based on a new awareness of students' literacy behaviors (Viechnicki, Barbour, Shaklee, Rohrer, and Ambrose, in press). Portfolio assessment led to a "blending of instruction and management." Noticing each student and reflecting on what student behaviors meant in terms of learning and teaching inspired teachers to rethink their teaching, to share ideas collaboratively with other teachers, and to include parents in learning about what was happening in the classroom through portfolio assessment. Thus, portfolios became a link between parents and the school, and between teachers and their colleagues.

While student work makes up the bulk of a student-generated assessment portfolio, a *teacher's portfolio* needs to include other types of information as well. A loose-leaf binder with a page for each student and room for adding other pertinent data and artifacts should have a place for anecdotal records, observations during lessons, and perhaps surveys from parents, peers, or self about attitudes and aptitudes. If the teacher keeps self-adhesive labels handy, she can easily write notes about a child as needed and transfer them later to a notebook page or an observation form.

A similar idea to the teacher's portfolio is the **teacher's log** organized especially for assessment, with several pages for each student in which to record observations and narratives (Flood, Lapp, and Nagel; 1993). Teachers can uses such logs to record not only reading and writing activities, but social behaviors as well. A sample page from a teacher log that focused on student responses to a unit on multicultural literature and appreciating diversity of cultural heritage shows how students are progressing in ways that go beyond basic facts to critical thinking. See Figure 14.7.

Name ______________________
Date ________________

Directions: Answer Yes or No in each box.

		Centers										
		1	2	3	4	5	6	7	8	9	10	11
1.	Did I improve in this activity?											
2.	Did I understand and follow directions?											
3.	Did I write neatly and accurately?											
4.	Did I do as much as I could?											
5.	Did I learn anything new?											

6. The activities I did my best work on were ____________________ and ____________.

   It was my best work because ____.

7. The activities that I had difficulty with were ____________________ and ____________.

   They were difficult because ____.

8. The activity I like most is ____.

9. The activity I dislike most is ____.

Comments about my portfolio: ____

● **FIGURE 14.8** Self-evaluation form

Part of the process of keeping such records is making sure that each child has a note or observation and that a sample of the child's work has been collected at least once a week. This makes it possible to reflect on *patterns* that emerge about children's learning and the impact of instruction.

Finally, both student and teacher could fill out a self-evaluation form (see Figure 14.8). They might do this individually and then compare their responses in a conference. The form could be oriented toward the actual classroom activities or serve as a summative statement placed at the end of a student's portfolio.

SUMMARY

In this chapter, we considered what teachers need to do in order to effectively manage and organize their classrooms for reading instruction. A great deal that we do to manage reading instruction and to organize our classrooms and materials can be traced back through the evolution of individualized instruction. Collaborative learning, the social nature of reading and writing, and the teacher's role in creating a classroom community introduced new information, but the goal of reading instruction remains constant: to produce independent readers. We paid close attention to the role of the classroom teacher as central to understanding all other factors in an effective classroom. How a teacher organizes and manages a classroom while attempting to individualize instruction depends heavily on the teacher's daily decisions.

To this end, we considered the ways in which teachers put everything together, creating an environment, a climate, an overall sense of structure or togetherness that you feel when you enter a classroom. This, too, is a changeable area; most teachers want to create a classroom environment conducive to learning. How they schedule students, balance activities and materials, and test and keep records differs from teacher to teacher. Just as teachers individualize in various ways, their classroom environments vary from straight-row traditional to flexible-seating open arrangements. Learning centers—how to organize this type of classroom and materials—were illustrated along with room diagrams, schedules, recordkeeping, and portfolio systems.

Whatever the students, the priorities, the reading program, or the instructional approach, each individual teacher must manage her or his classroom. The way we orchestrate all these variables and use our physical environment often determines our effectiveness as teachers.

TEACHER-ACTION RESEARCHER

1. First describe how you would organize your classroom to support the goals of your reading program. Develop a room diagram to illustrate how you would arrange furniture, materials, student activities, storage, and so on. Label the diagram and share it with another colleague or student in the class.

2. Visit several elementary schools with different physical facilities and room arrangements. Select an organizational plan that you find most effective and efficient and explain why. Then select another that you observed and believe to be less effective and efficient. Why do you believe this is the case?

3. Interview several elementary- or middle-school teachers preferably from different schools asking them how they group children for instruction in reading and language arts. Compare the results and ascertain what are the most prevalent reasons given for grouping students for the purposes of reading instruction.

4. Visit a classroom where the teacher uses portfolio assessment. How does the use of portfolios affect instruction in this class? What kinds of ongoing observations about students' literacy learning does the teacher make? How are the observations recorded? Note what types of instructional decisions are based on information the teacher gains from ongoing assessment of student progress and keeping portfolios.

KEY TERMS

collaborative learning
direct instruction
individualized instruction
grouping
classroom environments
materials
communities of learners
learning centers
student schedules
record keeping
portfolio system
teacher's log

CHAPTER 15

Meeting the Literacy Needs of Diverse Learners

BETWEEN THE LINES

In this chapter you will discover:

- **Linguistic, cultural, cognitive, and academic factors that influence individual diverse learners.**
- **Issues about learning to read and write in relation to definitions of literacy and diversity.**
- **Illustrations of linguistic, dialectical, cultural, and academic and cognitive diversity in instructional situations.**
- **Ways to plan and implement strategies to differentiate instruction, building on students' background knowledge and experiences.**

Beth Arnold's elementary school in a midwestern city school district has been given the task of teaching students whose first languages are Spanish, Arabic, or French, as well as teaching the neighborhood children who speak a dialect of English known as BEV (Black English Vernacular). On a tour of the school during Community Day, visitors might see the school librarian sharing picture books and children's literature written in the students' first language with parents, or see classes taught in Spanish. They might chat with an African-American child who learned to speak and read in Arabic from listening to instruction for students with limited English proficiency (LEP) who are taught some of their content-area subjects in his classroom. As the principal of the school, Beth, an energetic African-American woman, works hard to keep every student and every parent feeling involved and part of the school community.

"Our job here isn't just to teach students to speak English," Ms. Arnold says. "Part of our job is also to help these students *feel welcome* in school. Feeling welcome is essential for learning, and feeling welcome can't happen if no one understands you nor can you understand anyone. Our language is totally connected to our sense of who we are. If no one values our language, can they value us?"

In a rural school district, a first-grade teacher, Arlene, takes great pride in the tenderness and care her students give the class mascot, a rabbit named Nibbles. "At the beginning of the year I saw a class filled with students who weren't ready to learn in the way that I might have expected with another kind of class. My students came to school with worries about parental abuse. They got their only healthy meals from the school's breakfast and lunch program. They had learned to survive in a world that was hostile and tough, but one at odds with the kind of cooperation and focus that reading instruction takes. Together, we learned to care for Nibbles, we learned to care for ourselves and each other, and *then* we were ready to take care about learning to read."

In an economically and racially mixed district, Jennifer, another first-grade teacher, noticed that one of her students was disruptive and inattentive while the rest of the class was eagerly reading the Henry and Mudge series by Cynthia Rylant and writing and sharing their responses in collaborative reading groups. "Ira was quiet, and spoke with a slight impediment," she remembers. "He seemed very ordinary. Yet when I was giving Individual Reading Inventories to the students in October, he read passages at the third-grade level. And even though he seemed to substitute words while reading aloud in the higher graded passages, he could answer the comprehension questions I asked him with perfect accuracy. I noted that Ira's miscues didn't change meaning. I was chagrined to think I was asking such a gifted reader to sit quietly when the instructional materials I had chosen did not match his needs at all. Now he is reading Cynthia Rylant books with interest too, but he chooses titles that match his reading level more closely."

These stories illustrate some of the factors that influence diverse learners as they approach the task of becoming literate, and the challenging decisions that principals like Beth and teachers like Arlene and Jennifer must make about content, materials, and teaching in order to meet the learning needs of all their students. Scores of factors that potentially influence an individual's success in learning to read have been identified and researched, but most fall under three categories:

Linguistic diversity—the language the student feels most comfortable communicating in, the first or home language, is not the language of instruction in the school;

Cultural diversity—the student's home, family, socioeconomic group, culture, and/or society is different from the predominate (middle-class) culture of the school;

Cognitive and academic diversity—the child learns more slowly, more quickly, or differently from the pace and style of learning expected at school.

These factors influence how, when, and under what circumstances students will best learn to read and write. What happens when the optimal conditions for certain students' acquisition of literacy do not match what happens in particular classrooms? Such students may be labeled at risk for reading failure. *Diverse learners exhibit diverse needs. In order to learn successfully, their needs must be met. Teachers need to be aware of the nature of diversity and what it means for teaching reading to students who are linguistically, culturally, or academically diverse.* These topics are addressed in this chapter.

The Complexity of Diversity in Literacy Classrooms

Complicating the choices teachers must make in helping students learn to read and write are the differing definitions both of literacy and of diversity. Kameenui (1993) notes that reading research refers to "critical literacy," "occupational literacy," "pragmatic literacy," as well as "literacy as cultural form." Each definition of literacy implies a different purpose for becoming literate and the appropriate instructional strategy suited for that purpose.

Further complicating the choices teachers must make in the classroom is the complex nature of diversity (Garcia, Pearson, and Jimenez, 1990). The range of needs in learning to read is reflected by the range of children who compose our classrooms. There is no one African-American experience just as there is no one Hispanic-American experience or European-American experience. Neither are students alike who are identified with learning disabilities. Chall and Curtis (1991) describe such diverse factors contributing to reading disability as neurological irregularities, motor coordination, auditory sequencing and blending, memory, attention, perception, and oral language development. Additionally, socioeconomic background, geographic location, levels of parental education, cultural heritage, verbal skill, and adequacy of teaching have all been identified as factors influencing student success or lack of it in learning to read.

Beliefs and values about what it means to be literate and who may appropriately become literate lend an emotional and political layer to the diversity issue. Literacy is power, and certain groups have historically been denied access to this power. For example, slaves in the United States were denied access to literacy, with the risk of punishment by owners or slavebreakers for those who struggled to become literate (Harris, 1993). For better or for worse, this appreciation of the power of literacy continues today, with competing views of the appropriateness of both the content and the availability of reading and writing instruction common among educators and theorists. Gadsden (1992) raises the issue of access to literacy by asking: Who controls access? How is it achieved? How do the learners themselves and the classroom situations they are in contribute to learning and developing access to literacy?

Literacy and Social and Cultural Values

A heightened understanding in recent years of the nature of literacy as shaped by cultural and societal influences rather than as a neutral vehicle for expression (c.f. Heath, 1982; Ogbu, 1993) has led to a reexamination among teachers and administrators of the ways in which we describe the diversity among learners. Traditionally, school programs were not designed to fit the needs of special learners. Rather, learners were expected to fit into the needs of the school. Some of the definitions and changing terminology used in describing diversity are explained in Table 15.1.

● **TABLE 15.1**

Terminology Related to Diversity

DEFINITIONS	
LEP	Limited English proficiency
ESL	English as a second language
Chapter I	Federally-funded program to provide extra reading instruction to children from poor families
Title VII	Federally-funded program for children whose first language is not English
CHANGES IN THE WAY WE TALK ABOUT READERS	
At risk	Of promise
Language deficient	Language minority
Culturally deprived	Culturally different
Cultural assimilation	Cultural pluralism

Fillmore and Wong (1992) note that although the United States has a long history of non-English speaking immigrant children attending public school, only recently have attempts to design large-scale bilingual education programs seen support. The "melting pot," wherein minority students would become more like the majority, giving up or adjusting whatever linguistic or cultural differences interfered with schooling, served as the metaphor that guided the role of linguistic, cultural, and other minorities in the United States throughout the twentieth century (Mann, 1979; Ogbu, 1993). The underlying basis of the melting pot is the ojective to assimilate minorities into the larger society, accompanied by a sacrifice of language and culture for the minority group.

These assimilationist objectives still underlie many educational programs. When students were viewed as unable to enter the mainstream, they received remedial or compensatory education. Federal monies that funded programs designed to improve the education of language minority students or those with low socioeconomic status (Title VII of the Elementary and Secondary Education Act for bilingual students, Title 1 of the same act revised as Chapter I of the Education, Consolidation and Improvement Act for reading, Headstart for disadvantaged preschoolers) originated on the assumption that students were deficient and needed to master basic skills before they could be expected to achieve in regular classrooms (Fillmore and Wong, 1992; Strickland and Ascher, 1992).

Linguistic research has helped us to understand that language variation is to be expected, and is not good or bad, logical or illogical, in and of itself. Social norms create language options that users of that language choose systematically. Language variations are not random. This view, that language and cultural diversity result from difference rather than deficiency, is paramount to the changed view of how best to teach reading and writing in today's changed and changing classrooms.

In a very real sense, language variations face all readers. No one talks like books are written. The conventions of oral language differ from the conventions of written language. Very few published materials are simply "talk written down." In addition, we've all read authors like Mark Twain and Shakespeare, though none of us talks like Huck Finn or Hamlet. As readers, we can understand different language forms, even though we might never use them in our own speech. In other words, we don't need to abandon our oral language patterns in order to read. The same is true of our students, of course. When making decisions about reading instruction for linguistically diverse learners, it's wise to remember that one doesn't have to talk like a book in order to read one.

Instructional Beliefs and Diverse Learners

The emphasis on meeting students' needs as much as possible in the regular classroom means that classroom teachers are now expected to work with students who may previously have been sent to a specialist or taught in a resource room (McAlloon, 1992/93). As the number of languages spoken by immigrants to the United States and Canada rises, teachers may also find (especially in outlying areas or in small districts) that there isn't an available teacher who is fluent in a particular child's home language. Teachers who believe they are unprepared to meet the challenges of **inclusion** (teaching diverse learners in the classroom), may feel frustrated and stressed. Worksheets, isolated exercises, and other skill-related instruction that is not helpful to particular learners may be chosen because it seems easier, even when a specialist is available for in-class or pull-out remediation (Bean, Cooley, Eichelberger, Lazar, and Zigmond, 1991). How teachers react to these instructional challenges depends to a large extent on how they believe students become literate and the best ways to meet those needs in the classroom.

The traditional response to remedial reading was to give students with reading difficulty more intense instruction through skill and drill, especially in sound/symbol correspondences, or phonics (Chall and Ascher, 1991; Zucker, 1993). Allington (1977) noted that remedial readers were less likely to read connected text or to work on constructing meaning from print than were readers who were considered more able. **Bilingual learners** are often instructed using primary level worksheets, even when their age or conceptual development means that such work is inappropriate (Freeman and Freeman, 1993).

What is good reading instruction? For all readers, research and theory points to instruction that focuses on reading as a meaning-making activity, with opportunities for practice in connected and meaningful texts, and the opportunity for sufficient and meaningful feedback. Since language activities are based on communicative competence, it is important for all learners to determine how effective their communicative, meaning-making attempts are in the particular contexts in which they find themselves.

For low-achieving, gifted, and linguistically and culturally diverse students, reading remains a process of constructing meaning using both the learner's background knowledge about reading and his or her life experiences with the syntactic, semantic, and graphophonemic cues of the text. When the process breaks down at any point, whether in terms of background knowledgeable about what it means to read or what a particular word might mean, knowledgable teachers develop opportunities to expand their students' repertoires of successful strategies for making meaning. Shirley Brice Heath (1991) reminds us that helping students exhibit literate behavior removes the onus associated with focusing on literacy skills, which may not be the true measure of a students' understanding if they are nonnative speakers, or their potential, if (for example) they have culturally different expectations for meaning or literacy. Yet, as Stansberry (1986) notes, more of the same instruction that failed the beginning reader in the first place is unlikely to produce good results no matter how intensely it is taught. In fact, Allington (1983a) attributes the majority of reading failures to poor instruction rather than to any inherent problem in the readers themselves.

A kindergarten study of two bilingual, ethnic minority children by Schmidt (1993) concluded that, "schools may actually interfere with children's literacy learning, if educators do not work to understand the diverse cultural backgrounds of the children in classrooms (p. 226)." She recommends instruction based on connections with homes of ethnic-minority students to help parents and children understand, for example, the holidays and celebrations in the school. For connections to be made, the school must reach out to the parents whose difficulties in communicating with the teacher often prevent them from initiating contact.

Linguistic Diversity in Literacy Classrooms

What works in terms of the language and literacy development in first languages is also what works for second language acquisition (Fitzgerald, 1993). Although the most dramatic examples of linguistic diversity are students whose first language is not English, linguistic diversity is evidenced among native English speakers as well. Geographic location, socioeconomic status, and educational levels as well as gender, age, and occupation all affect the way we speak. In the past, these dialectical variations were thought to be confounding factors in certain groups' ability to learn to read.

Dialectical Diversity

We all speak a dialect of English, although it is much easier for us to see our own speech as natural, and the speech of everyone else as the dialect. Depending on how old you are, where you were born or grew up, whether you are male or female, and your economic level, your speech will vary. What do you call a sandwich with many kinds of sliced meats and cheese on a large oblong bun? A "hoagie?" "Grinder?" "Sub?" What would you call something wonderful and out of the ordinary? "Neat?" "Cool?" "Fly?" "Superb?" Would you explain where something "is at" or where "it is?" How would you form the past tense of "to dive?" Whether you say dived, dive, duv, or dove will depend on your geographic region and social class. To a person from the Northeast, a southerner's pronunciation of *drink* sounds more like his own pronunciation of *drank,* while the rest of the country pronounces final *r*s that the Boston native most likely does not.

Those language variations and countless others are examples of the natural evolutions of spoken language, proof of the changing nature of living languages. Latin, a language no longer spoken by people in a communicative and social function, is considered a dead language. It doesn't change. So change and variation within and among languages are natural, and linguists have shown that all languages are equally effective for expressing the needs of its speakers, equally complete, and equally rule-governed, or systematic. **Dialects** are likewise rule-governed (Labov, 1985).

The difficulties associated with dialectal and linguistic differences in the classroom is the *value* assigned to language, to the perceived goodness or badness of a particular speech variation. Roberts (1985) emphasizes that in and of themselves, language variations are neither good nor bad, and that such judgments are often about the people who speak them rather than about clarity or precision (which are also value-laden judgments!).

Dialects and Reading Strategies

How do language variations and associated values affect the instructional job of literacy teachers? For a time it was thought that beginning readers who spoke a variation of Standard Edited English, the dialect of English found in most textbooks, would read poorly because the language was different from their own. In response to this concern, readers were written in BEV (Black English Vernacular), supposedly remedying the effects of dialectical interference for children whose dialect was unlike the school form.

Dialectical Miscues. When reading aloud, children often substitute one word for another. Such errors, or miscues, often help teachers understand the manner in which a child is or isn't constructing meaning from a text. Language choices are not random; miscues help a teacher decide which of the cueing systems of written language a reader is using to comprehend the text. When a child substitutes a word (or words) in oral reading that would be in his speaking dialect for the word printed on the page (for example, reading *he don't* for *he doesn't*), the miscue probably shows that the reader is indeed reading the text for meaning. Such a substitution, of a word in the child's dialect, would be impossible if the reader had not comprehended the text.

As more research on reading is done in the classroom, we learn that reading revolves around the experiences that the reader brings to the text to actively make sense of it. Reading is only partly about the marks on the page. This, in turn, is changing the way we think about dialects and decoding, and how reading teachers should address dialectical differences.

Teachers need to help their students make the sound/symbol correspondences in beginning reading, but they also need to help students grow in their understanding that writing is not just speech written down. In fact, writing is like another dialect of English. For example, at the end of a particularily grueling semester of reading and writing, a student complained that his friends kept remarking that he was talking like a book. They had noticed that he had adjusted his speech so that it matched written texts. Appropriate vocabulary and syntax for writing seems stilted and unnatural if we use it in face-to-face conversation. Once we learn about book language, with its different rules for conveying meaning, we do not need to see our spoken dialect in print in order to understand a written text.

Using Language Experience. Helping beginning readers discover the connection between spoken and written language is one of the most important aspects in teaching beginning readers. For beginning readers, and especially students who have linguistic variations from school language, the **language experience approach (LEA)** is a good way to help make the connection between speech and writing concrete. Most importantly, LEA gives students the kind of reading material that they can most easily read—predictable, meaningful, and contextually complete—because they dictate or write it.

LEA, described in Chapters 2 and 4, begins with ample time for *discussion* of whatever topic interests the students. Rigg (1989) suggests stories that have interest for all students, even students with limited proficiency in English. Discussions leading to stories about pets, recipes, interviews with the class VIP-for-a-day, retellings of a story that has been read aloud, stories patterned after other stories, advice to students in next year's class, and a newcomer's reaction to life in the United States are all popular with children.

The next step, *dictating,* involves the teacher (or a student acting as a peer scribe) writing down the exact words dictated by class members. The scribe rereads each sentence, repeating it to help students remember what they had to say and to help beginning readers back what is written. While the scribe writes down exactly what the children say, it is important to use conventional spelling and not to try to reproduce phonetically what children say. Riggs (1989) notes that the focus is on students' ideas and not on adult grammatical forms. In fact, she notes that copies of LEA dictations help provide running records of student progress in mastering standard forms of English.

Students can revise the LEA text after rereading, either in groups, individually, or as a class with the author's permission. Then, the text can be prominently displayed or copies can be made for individuals so that the students can use it for rereading, illustrating, or for story starters.

Learning the Language of Books. Teachers permit students to grow as readers by helping them understand the different patterns of language that give meaning and structure to writing. Reading aloud to children and encouraging wide reading in the classroom and at home can help beginning readers develop an ear for the stylistic conventions of books and written language. Predictable and patterned books, fairy tales, and folklore and books with rich illustration help all students learn the conventions of written language because contextual clues help carry the meaning of the text. These books help all beginning readers, but they offer the extra support that children with limited experience speaking English need.

Special Concerns of ESL Readers

We know that children who receive instruction in their native language learn to read English more easily (Collier, 1989; Cummins, 1989; Hudelson, 1987). Children transfer the knowledge of what it means to read readily from one language to another. What it means to read Spanish is the same as what it means to read in English, and a native Spanish speaker can use all the cueing systems of language—syntax, semantics, and graphophonemic correspondence—to learn to read in Spanish.

Although the ideal development of second language literacy would have each nonnative speaker receiving instructional support in her home language while she learned mastery of English, the reality is often quite different. But that does not mean that the regular classroom teacher cannot offer the ESL student rich and meaningful language-based literacy experiences. *The same principles that guide language and literacy learning in a first language should guide literacy learning in a second language.*

Supporting students' first languages and offering them resources to help them develop proficiency with written language is possible even without special or bilingual language classes. Many activities that teachers may already use in their reading classrooms to teach literacy to native speakers are especially useful for second-language learners. Freeman and Freeman (1993) offer suggestions for support in a first language for ESL learners well within the means of all:

1. Include environmental print from the student's first language in the classroom.
2. Make sure that the classroom and school libraries have books in languages other than English.
3. Help students to publish and share their writing in their first language.
4. Enlist the help of bilingual aides—other students, parents, teacher's aides, or community volunteers.
5. Use commercial or student-produced videotapes to support language learning and to improve self-esteem.

Authentic Communication. It seems logical that a nonnative speaker of English immersed in a literate environment would easily develop competence in reading and writing English. Language learning does not take place, however, without an active, communicative process at work. An example of the primacy of social communication in learning a language is underscored by the case of the hearing child of deaf parents. The

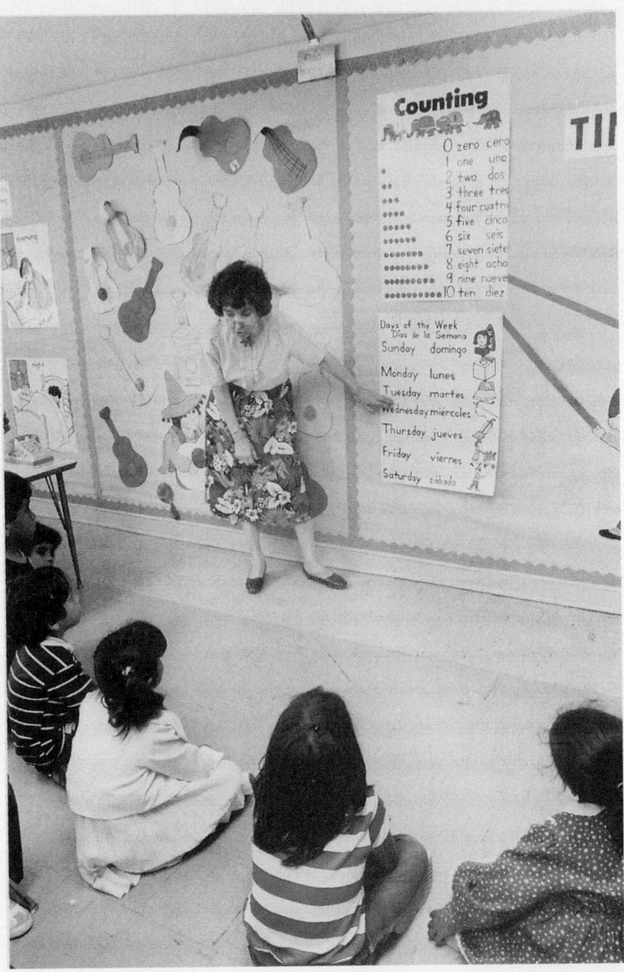

The same principles that guide language and literacy learning in a first language should guide literacy learning in a second language.

child's parents used only American Sign Language, but they exposed the child to the television every day. Although by age of 3 he could sign fluently, he did not understand or speak English (Moskowitz, 1985). Television is one-way communication; it asks without answering; it offers no response. Without active communication, language learning suffers.

A similar situation is encountered by the child who speaks little or no English and suddenly finds herself in a classroom where almost none of what she hears makes sense. Without sufficient understanding of English, it is difficult for the nonnative speaker of English to take the active role necessary for constructing meaning. Language learning must involve **authentic communication.**

Freeman and Freeman (1993) note that second-language learners may seem to have shorter attention spans than native speakers, when in actuality they are suffering from the fatigue of struggling to make sense out of a language they barely know. Because they cannot easily express what they do know, nonnative speakers may do poorly on tests. They may remain quiet and uninvolved in the classroom because it takes them longer to process a response or because they are self-conscious about failure. They may lack background knowledge or they may not understand which features of the language they hear or see are the features essential for constructing meaning. Second-language learners need to be involved in activites that require communication. It is essential these learners receive feedback on whether or not their communication works.

Using Dialogue Journals. **Dialogue journals** help ESL students understand the conventions of writing while engaged in authentic communication. The student writes in the journal to the teacher; the teacher responds, but never corrects errors. Teachers often consciously repeat a misspelled word or usage error correctly in their response, modeling for the student the conventional form. Edlesky (1989) notes that for dialogue journals to be successful, they must remain authentic communication, and not become writing for the sake of completing an assignment. She finds the most successful entries are those where student and teacher get to know each other, or when students let off steam, complain, or otherwise get a chance to communicate concerns or questions not addressed otherwise during class time. Less successful are journals that substitute for diaries because language in the usually-secret diary often turns into contrived writing when it is to be shared. Additionally, such writing may lead to a greater chance for clashes of cultural expectations.

Group Reading Conferences. When the teacher reads a story to six or so students who then have a chance to share their responses, ESL students have a chance to hear others' responses while they practice formulating their own. Allen (1989) tells the story of several Southeast Asian students comparing Cinderella books.

> These girls had several versions of Cinderella spread out on the floor. They were moving back and forth between the books and looking at the pictures with much attention. As the teacher listened in, she heard them working hard to decide in which book Cinderella wore the most beautiful dress, in which book the prince was the handsomest, and in which the stepmother was ugliest. No lesson on the construction of the comparative and the superlative could have provided such enthusiastic and extensive practice! (p. 59).

Content Area Activities. Learning with language is easier than learning about language; that is, using language meaningfully to explore, share, decide, react, label, and question helps students develop not only academic concepts, but literacy concepts as well. Hudelson (1989) suggests five principles for developing activities in content areas that will also help ESL students with English language skills.

1. Students will learn both content and language more easily when they are active participants in activities that require oral and written language directly related to specific

content. Filling out charts individually or in small groups, making notes in a learning log, interviewing family members or peers, conducting experiments and noting results—all these activities can be designed to engage students in both language and content.

2. Students learn content and language when they are interacting with either students or adults who provide feedback, ideas, and reasons for communication.
3. Language processes (speaking, reading, writing, listening) are interrelated. Using all of these processes helps students become more adept language users. Activities that give students the opportunity to discuss in whole-class and small-group format, to write, and to act out concepts help them to learn English as they understand the material being studied.
4. That literacy is acquired through use, not through the learning of isolated skills, is as true of a second language as of a first. Students need to read and write whole, authentic texts.
5. Background knowledge facilitates comprehension. Activities involving all the language process (not just the textbook) can help to build background. Semantic webs or maps of what students already know, brainstorming activities, demonstrations, and discussions help students begin reading with a clear focus on the content and the purpose for reading.

(Adapted from Hudelson (1989), pp. 140–141)

Cultural Diversity in Literacy Classrooms

When the norms for using language, when the learner's and the teacher's expectations about appropriate behavior, differ, communication may not be straightforward. Intended cues to meaning may not bring about intended results. Purpose and context also affect our meaning making, as this story of a young theology student delivering a children's sermon illustrates:

> All of the children were called to the front of the church and the pastor began his sermon:
>
> "Children, I'm thinking of something that is about five or six inches high; that scampers across the ground; that lives in either a nest in the tree or makes its

home in the hollowed-out portion of a tree's trunk. The thing I'm thinking about gathers nuts and stores them in winter; it is sometimes brown and somethimes gray; it has a big bushy tail. Who can tell me what I'm thinking of?"

Knowing the proper church behavior, the children remained quiet and reserved. No one ventured an answer. Finally, Robert, age 6, slowly and ever so tentatively raised his hand. The pastor, desperate for a response so he could go on with the sermon, said with some relief, "Yes, Robert, what do you think it was?"

"Well," came the response, "ordinarily I'd think it was a squirrel, but I suppose you want me to say it was Jesus." (Harste, Woodward, and Burke, 1984).

Closely related to language and linguistic diversity is cultural diversity. Because native speakers learn language in social settings, they also learn their culture's norms for language use. Native speakers are able to deliberately shift their language to fit their audience, the context, and the purpose of their communication. Different social groups also develop different norms for language use. The subtle cues about meaning in language use become invisible to us, however, and we often take for granted our own knowledge about language as "natural." But language is a shared system; the rules are always culturally defined and culturally specific. Different cultures have different rules.

Because rules for using language are so culturally specific, it is easy for teachers not to recognize that language rules are indeed in effect for speakers of other dialects, or speakers with different cultural norms for communicating. Delpit (1986, 1988) argues that teachers need to recognize the strengths of the language of minority children, but then to move beyond—to help those children acquire the norms, the rules, for communication in the language of school. Direct teaching of language norms within a meaningful and communicative context, she maintains, can help students who come to school without the background knowledge of the meaning of literacy and school language conventions.

Heath and Mangiola (1989) remind us of the affective dimension of language and schooling. When acceptable means of displaying knowledge clash with cultural means, passivity and disinterest may result. They tell of Alicia, who did not want to be a "schoolgirl." To be a schoolgirl, head in a book, not interested in dances or going out, always doing homework, did not interest Alicia. But to be involved in dynamic and collaborative activities that required the knowledge in books—tutoring younger students, writing social studies texts for them, or composing scripts for the school's radio shows—then Alicia was interested. When she saw literacy as useful and compelling, Alicia was eager to be literate.

Teaching Strategies

If teachers are aware of the possibilities for cultural incongruence, they can make adjustments in their teaching methods and classroom organization to accomodate difference. For example, in some Hispanic situations, it is considered polite to spend a few minutes in small talk about health and home before beginning actual business. Children accustomed to this pattern may be disoriented by abrupt teacher talk about task, student response, and more teacher talk (Cazden, 1988). Hawaiian children seemed to learn better when their teachers used the pattern of interaction known as "talk-story" that followed conversational pattern in the students' homes (Au and Mason, 1983).

Determining Cultural Expectations. How can a teacher decide if cultural misunderstandings are interfering with learning in the classroom? Several things to look for include:

1. Lessons that continually go awry
2. Extended lack of student progress
3. Lack of student involvement

Teachers can observe the interactions of students as they work and play together, read about cultural differences as well as cultural similarities, and maintain communication with parents and family in order to determine appropriate classroom changes (adapted from Fitzgerald, 1993, p. 642).

A kindergarten teacher in Patricia Schmidt's 1993 study had not asked the two ethnic-minority children in her class about their own families' holiday celebrations. Yet, they were totally confused by Christmas, St. Patrick's Day, and Easter. So much so, that "Peley drew bunnies using red and green as the predominant colors." Finding out about holidays around the world and introducing games and literature to reinforce holiday themes can help teachers turn cultural misunderstandings into student involvement.

Validating Each Child's Experience. Since we use our previous knowledge of the world to help us construct the meaning of our reading and writing, it is only sensible that students with different experiences will have different readings of books and texts. Our cultural schemata, the beliefs we hold about how the world is organized, influence comprehension. In a study of proficient readers, Pritchard (1990) found that retellings of the story were significantly more complex and contained fewer distortions when the reader was reading a culturally familiar text. Background knowledge that may be common and familiar for a suburban American child may be unknown and confusing to a child from a center city or a rural farm area, and even more confusing to a child recently emigrated to the United States.

Helping students build background knowledge before reading remains an important task for teachers in classrooms with students with culturally diverse experiences. However, cultural groups are difficult to define (Yakota, 1993). Asian students will have varying experiences and languages depending on their home country (China, Cambodia, Vietnam) as well as their social class and geographic region within that country. The Hispanic experience is not only Mexican-American, but Puerto Rican and Central American as well. Jewish Americans often consider themselves a cultural minority as well as a religious minority.

Choosing Quality Multicultural Literature. Teachers choosing to use multicultural literature in the classroom help students to recognize the unique contributions of each culture and the similarities of the human experience across cultures. Additionally, they help nonmainstream cultures to appreciate and value their heritage and give all students the benefits of understanding ways of knowing about the world that are different from

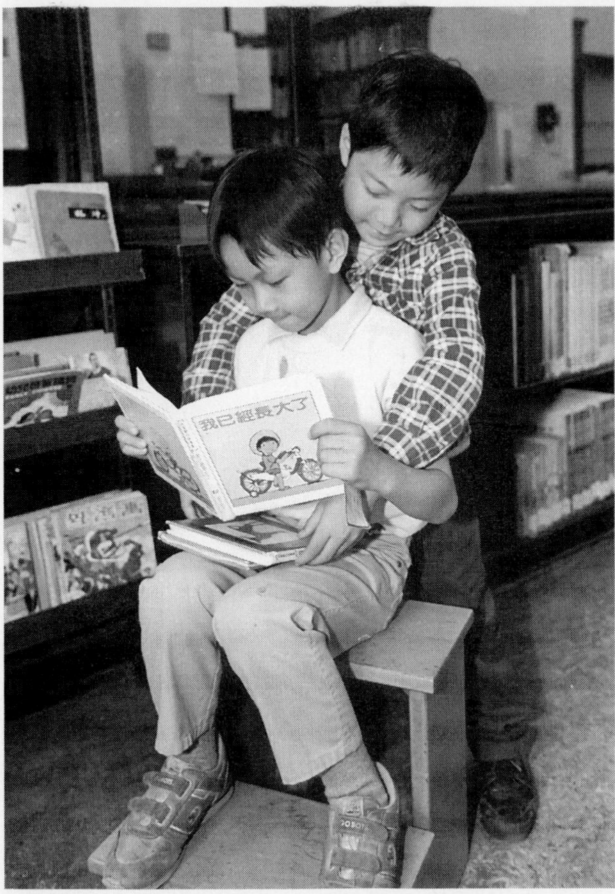

By using multicultural literature in the classroom, teachers help nonmainstream students appreciate and value their heritage.

their own. Asking several questions can help teachers choose which books will be most useful to them in their classrooms.

1. **Is this book good literature?** Is the plot strong? Is characterization true to experience? Are setting, theme, and style well developed?
2. **Is this book culturally accurate?** Will it help readers gain a true sense of the culture?
3. **Is the book rich in cultural details?** Do details that give readers insight as to the nuances of daily life enhance the story? Or is the culture overgeneralized?
4. **Are dialogue and relationships culturally authentic?** For example, *Pacific Crossing* (Soto, 1992), about Mexican-American students who go to Japan as exchange students, deals with both cultures authentically.

5. **Are cultural issues presented with enough depth and realism for readers to get a true sense of how culture affects the lives of people?**

6. **Are members of a minority included for a purpose, or could the story be told as easily about any cultural group?** Otherwise, minority characters are only a "quota" and do not add a sense of their unique, culturally-rooted experience.

(Adapted from Yokota, 1993, pp. 159–160)

Choosing books that reflect the insider's perspective not only helps students from nonmainstream cultures read about and validate it own experiences, it helps children understand diverse experiences of groups other than their own.

Academic and Cognitive Diversity in Literacy Classrooms

As human beings, we make sense of our experiences by putting them into categories and giving the categories labels. While this ability to categorize and label is essential to help us sort through the amount of information we accumulate, it's of little use as we attempt to describe the diversity of experience and ability we face in our students. Labels can never fully represent the range of experiences that students bring to the task of learning to become literate.

Nonetheless, especially in programs funded by the federal government, such as Chapter 1 remedial math and reading programs, and for special education service in most school districts, labeling becomes an essential for inclusion in the program. Identifying students who may need different or more instruction is an essential yet sticky problem. For example, standardized tests are often used as measures of student ability, even though they are less likely than grades to predict future success (Ascher, 1990) and do not give teachers useful guidance as to what the instructional needs of their students might be. Occasionally, a district may focus on a curriculum solely designed to raise test scores, leading to instruction focusing on basic skills that do not translate well into reading as a meaning-based activity (Strickland and Ascher, 1992). Legitimate ways of knowing are often not measured by standardized tests; gifted students and linguistically and culturally diverse students often do not test as well as their actual ability would suggest (Tuttle, 1991).

Reading failure is an emotional issue. Among students, parents, and educators alike, the belief that reading is the key to academic as well as personal success is strong. Research indicates that students who experience early reading difficulty maintain or increase below-level performance (Stanovich, 1986). The prestige and power associated with cultural and societal definitions of literacy adds further to the sense of the importance of helping students become literate. However, certain categories can be used to describe learners and their needs that will help us plan the classroom activities that can help all of our students grow as readers and writers, including those with linguistic and cultural differences, those with learning disabilities, young readers having difficulties, and gifted readers.

Planning Instruction for Readers Having Difficulty

The instruction teachers give to students who experience reading difficulty should be much like the instruction they give to other students. No one aspect of the language cueing system should be emphasized over any other. While phonics-only was at one time touted as the way to help poor readers, we know that especially poor readers need to use their decoding skill in the construction of meaning. Sacrificing *real* reading gives students the wrong idea about reading—that it is about pronouncing words, that it is not supposed to make sense.

Activities that require students to be actively involved in constructing meaning, using all the cueing systems of written language, are especially appropriate for struggling readers. These activities, and their benefits for readers, are discussed in previous chapters and include strategies of choral reading, repeated readings, reading aloud to students, QAR, summary writing, and reader's theater.

Because students with diverse needs often need extra instruction in order to catch up with more able-reading peers, time is always a problem for classroom teachers when dealing with students with special needs. Such teachers need to teach as much as possible with the limited amount of instructional time available. Kameenui (1993) suggests that teachers keep the following instructional framework in mind as they plan instruction for diverse learners:

1 Instructional time is limited: teach reading strategies, concepts, or problem-solving analysis in the most efficient manner possible.

2. Intervene and take remedial measures as quickly as possible, and as often as necessary, providing:

    Frequent opportunities to read connected texts.

    Activities that require all learners them to be active participants in reading (small-group or partner reading).

    Opportunities to develop phonemic awareness and letter recognition as early as possible.

3. Teach less, but teach it well:

    Select essential objectives and the most important strategies.

    Additionally, Spiegel (1992) notes that instruction must be sustained and focused enough for all students to learn strategies and concepts effectively.

4. Communicate reading strategies clearly and effectively, especially during the beginning phases of instruction:

For students who come to school without experiences with or knowledge of the language of school, and who have not internalized the rules of that language, direct instruction can be helpful (Delpit, 1988; Speigel, 1992).

Since language is learned best in communicative and social situations, direct instruction is most effective when used within the context of connected, meaningful reading and writing.

5. Reading instruction must be guided strategically by the teacher:

   Teacher-directed and student-centered activities must all have as their goal not only the improvement of reading, but helping students who have difficulties to catch up with their more able-reading peers.

   The ultimate goal of all reading instruction is for students to direct their own learning.

6. Effectiveness of instruction and materials should be evaluated during instruction by measuring student performance:

   Instruction should focus on what students need to learn as well as on how well they are learning it.

(Adapted from Kameenui, 1993)

Early Intervention for Low Achieving Readers

Because early reading success is so important for later reading success, and because early reading failure is likely to haunt a student for many years (Stanovich, 1986), **early intervention** *to help lower-than-expected achievers in reading catch up with able reading peers is essential.* A program designed especially for students in first grade who are experiencing difficulties with reading is Reading Recovery (Clay, 1985; Pinnell, Fried, and Estice, 1990).

Reading Recovery. A program begun in New Zealand and brought to the United States by Marie Clay, **Reading Recovery** focuses on low-ability readers who work in the program receiving daily, individual instruction for about 15 weeks and catch up to their peers in 70 to 80 percent of cases.

Several of the principles of Reading Recovery are useful for the regular classroom, helping teachers support learners as they acquire word identification strategies:

1. Use books with illustrations and predictable language to help keep word identification in the context of creating meaning.
2. Read and reread words and stories to develop fluency.
3. Keep a running record of children's reading of text. By doing so, the teacher has a way to determine how children are making meaning with text.

4. Teach words in connection with the whole text. Talk about stories before reading the book; help children understand the big ideas.

5. Help children develop self-monitoring strategies by helping them to problem-solve about what the words are and what they mean.

6. Use writing activities in connection with reading as writing and reading develop concurrently.

Reading Recovery, because it involves intense tutor training, individual tutoring, and pulling students out of the regular classroom, is an expensive option that schools may not be able to provide. An alternate program, one that involves supplemental in-class instruction by the regular classroom teacher, is known as **Early Intervention in Reading or EIR** (Taylor, Short, Fry, and Shearer, 1992).

Early Intervention in Reading. EIR involves small-group tutoring for the lowest five or so students in a class with the idea that early supplemental instruction can help to prevent the cycle of reading failure with its far-reaching effects on student achievement. Students can be selected for inclusion in the program on the basis of readiness tests, ability to segment words into sounds (phonemic awareness), and sight word and vocabulary knowledge. Materials needed include picture books with strong appeal for first graders, teacher-made summaries of the books on a chart and in booklets for teacher-student reading, and other short, easy-to-read picture books for independent reading. Box 15.1 outlines the procedures for EIR instruction.

Gifted Readers

Students who have wide vocabularies, read two or more years above grade level, have excellent memory for story details, understand complex concepts and ideas, and learn quickly and with minimum structure the skills and strategies necessary for reading sophisticated texts may be classified as gifted readers (Davis and Johns, 1991). While it is important to remember that **gifted readers** do not automatically learn without instruction, because they learn quickly they may not be sufficiently challenged by reading instruction aimed at average readers.

Classroom teachers can differentiate instruction for highly able readers by using modifications: compacting instruction and modifying curriculum by adapting content and processes (Dooley, 1993).

1. Compacting Instruction
   a. Identify needs of readers through pretest of strategy or skill that will be taught.
   b. Students do not receive instruction for material they have already mastered.
   c. For strategies or concepts that need to be taught, the students can join regular instruction, or they can use structured inductive or "discover" learning materials to master the strategy or concepts.

2. Modifying Curriculum

● BOX 15.1

Early Intervention in Reading Instruction

Day 1

The teacher begins the session by reading a picture book aloud to the students, modeling fluent reading and appropriate book-reading behaviors. The teacher then reads the summary of the book from the chart. The teacher helps students identify contextual, graphophonemic, and syntactic clues that help identify words. The students practice separating words into their component sounds by writing several words from the story in the back of their booklets. Each word chosen for this kind of practice is written in boxes already duplicated on the page. For example, the student could write the word *that* th/a/t or *cat* c/a/t.

Days 2 and 3

The children, with the teacher's help, reread the summaries. The teacher encourages and instructs the use of reading strategies that help the children identify words. The children also write a sentence in their booklet that is related to the story. The teacher encourages the students to write down the sounds they hear in the words, only supplying letters the children cannot produce by themselves.

Fluency is encouraged throughout the EIR program. Students also reread their summaries, either independently or in pairs with an aide. After the third day, the children take a copy of the booklet home to read to their parents, and another story is begun.

Transition to Independent Reading

Four to six months into the program, the children begin to read 50–150-word picture books they have not read previously while working with the teacher on 90–150-word summaries. As the children read new books, the teacher listens to the child read and encourages uses of strategies when the children come to difficult words. Eventually, usually about six months into the program, the students begin to read 200-word picture books with teacher assistance. Again, repeated readings and teacher instruction and encouragement with reading strategies help the students gain fluency.

a. Adapting content
   (1) Have students read longer and more in-depth selections.
   (2) Have students select reading materials that reflect their own needs and interests in an in-depth study of a particular theme, genre, or author.
   (3) Add an interdisciplinary approach to the topic.

b. Adapting process
   (1) Have students analyze and evaluate their reading.
   (2) Focus on critical reading strategies through the use of reading guides which include pre-, during-, and after-reading activities.
   (3) All students should be encouraged to think critically, but highly able readers may need less instruction and less structure to do so.

Identifying Gifted Students in Diverse Settings

Shaklee (in press) notes that students who are most likely to be identified as gifted are those from middle- and upper-middle-class backgrounds. Children of poverty are often just as able, but their creative abilities may go unrecognized. A classroom teacher may need to readjust her ways of seeing her students so that all students can be given the kind of challenging instruction that will help them best grow as readers and learners.

Teachers may wish to keep an *observational portfolio* (see also Chapters 13 and 14) based on the following:

1. Parents' survey—what are your child's strengths? etc.
2. Anecdotal records—what does the child self-select to read? What activities does the child choose for him- or herself? Does the child initiate? Explain? Facilitate for others? Show evidence of new and different ways to solve problems?
3. Observations of lessons
4. Examples of student work
5. Peer nomination—who do other students say knows something special or useful?

SUMMARY

Understanding and accepting children's differences has been a common thread throughout this chapter. Diversity among learners is a fact of life in classrooms. Ignoring this creates unnecessary difficulties and frustrations for both students and teachers. Embracing it, on the other hand, leads to effective instructional adaptations in reading.

Adapting instruction to meet the needs of diverse learners was at the core of this chapter. Three types of learner diversity were explored: linguistic, cultural, and academic and cognitive.

Linguistic diversity in the classroom may be the result of a variety of factors. Dialects differ from each other in phonology, syntax, and lexicon. Rather than viewing linguistic diversity as a disadvantage or barrier, teachers and students must understand and value linguistic diversity. Children should have many natural opportunities to use language so that they can experiment with language and discover their options as language users. Teachers must recognize that children may read in their own dialect patterns, but these dialect miscues seldom interfere with the child's quest for meaning. Instruction for linguistically diverse learners should capitalize on children's strengths in comprehension and expression. Our goals for children should center upon language growth and flexibility, not change. The same principles that guide language and literacy learning in a first language should guide literacy learning in a second language.

Cultural diversity is closely related to language and linguistic diversity. Teachers need to help children acquire the norms for communication in the language of the school. They need to make adjustments in teaching strategies to accommodate difference, turning cultural misunderstandings into student involvement.

Children with learning disabilities, young readers having difficulties, and gifted readers also benefit from instructional adaptations for their *academic* or *cognitive diversity.* Teachers often need to provide extra instruction in order to actively involve struggling readers in constructing meaning. Strategies for supplemental in-class instruction are useful for differentiating teaching as well as for pull-out programs such as Reading Recovery.

Teachers who adopt instruction effectively use their understanding of children's needs and their beliefs about reading to make instructional decisions. They recognize that whatever the adaptation, meaning must be at the heart of reading instruction. They also facilitate meaningful interaction among all students whenever possible. Finally, their decisions convey the uniqueness and value of each individual in the classroom. Their classroom libraries contain books that reflect the diversity among us all. Their reading to children, discussions with them, and instructional choices help children grow as readers and grow in their understanding of those around them.

TEACHER-ACTION RESEARCHER

1. Find out about the language and culture of minority groups that live in your community. Explore the resources available, concentrating on children's books about or from these cultures. Prepare an annotated bibliography of some of the books that could be used during instruction with children from these cultures and their classmates.

2. Observe in an urban or a suburban classroom containing students from various cultures, including limited English proficiency students. Or select a classroom with predominantly gifted students or others with special needs. Keep a running record of children's opportunities to interact with each other throughout the school day. Afterward, evaluate the interactions and decide on other times when interaction might have been encouraged.

3. Research booklists and annotated bibliographies of books that would be appropriate for readers with special needs, who read English as a second language or who wish to learn about other cultures. Some journal sources include *Booklist, Language Arts,* and *The Reading Teacher.* Read one (or more) of the recommended books with a student.

Reflect on the student's response to the book(s). How does reading these books differ from reading other children's literature?

4. Listen to a child who speaks BEV (Black English Vernacular) or another dialect of English read aloud. Does the child make miscues that fall into a pattern based on dialectical differences? How can you determine if miscues are dialectically based? Interview classroom teachers about their views on dialectical substitutions in oral reading. Do you agree with the teachers? What evidence about reading and language would you use to support your views?

KEY TERMS

linguistic diversity
cultural diversity
cognitive and academic diversity
inclusion
bilingual learners
dialects
language experience approach (LEA)
authentic communication
dialogue journals
early intervention
Reading Recovery
gifted readers

APPENDIX A

Beliefs About Reading Interview

If you are a preservice teacher studying reading for the first time, you may find it difficult to answer some of the questions in Form A. However, we encourage you to respond to all of the questions based on whatever sources of knowledge and beliefs you currently hold about the reading process and how it should be taught. Knowledge sources may include your own school experiences, observations in the field, experiences as a reader, and previous study. Toward the end of the semester, you may wish to respond to the interview questions again. This will provide a good measure of the growth you have made in thinking about reading and learning to read. Team up with a partner, if possible, and take turns interviewing one another. Study the directions and respond to Form A or Form B of the Beliefs About Reading Interview.

BOX A.1

Beliefs About Reading Interview

Directions: Select *Form A* of the interview if you are preparing to become a teacher. Select *Form B* of the interview if you are presently a teacher. Respond to each question, thinking in terms of *your own* classroom: whether it is the one in which you plan to teach or the one in which you now teach. As you respond to each question, explain *what* you (would) do and *why* you (would) do it.

FORM A: PRESERVICE TEACHERS

1. You have just signed a contract for your first teaching position in an elementary school. Which goals for reading instruction do you feel most confident in making progress in during the school year?
2. Suppose a student is reading orally in your class and makes an oral reading error. What is the first thing you will probably do? Why?

(continued)

● BOX A.1 *(continued)*

3. Another student in your class is reading orally and doesn't know a word. What are you going to do? Why?
4. You have read about and probably tried out different kinds of strategies and activities for teaching students to read. Which ones do you feel will be the *most* important in your classroom? Why?
5. What kinds of activities do you feel your students should be involved in for the *majority* of their reading instructional time? Why?
6. Here are the typical steps in the Directed Reading Activity (DRA) as suggested in basal reader manuals: (1) introduction of vocabulary; (2) motivation or setting purposes; (3) reading; (4) questions and discussion after silent reading; and (5) skills practice for reinforcement.

   Rank these steps in order from *most* important to *least* important (not necessarily in the order you will follow them).
7. Is it important to introduce new vocabulary words *before* students read a selection? Why or why not?
8. Suppose your new students will be tested to give you information to help you decide how to instruct them in reading. What would this diagnostic test include and what kind of information would you hope that it gives you about your students?
9. During silent reading, what do you hope your students will do when they come to an unknown word?
10. Look at the oral reading mistakes, which are underlined below, on these transcripts of three readers. Which of the three readers would you judge as the best or most effective reader (Harste and Burke, 1977)?

channel ... *channel*
READER A I live near this canal. Men haul things up and down the canal in big boats.

2. candle
1. ca ... *candle*
READER B I live near this canal. Men haul things up and down the canal in big boats.

2. candle
1. ca ... *cannel*
READER C I live near this canal. Men haul things up and down the canal in big boats.

(Continued)

FORM B: INSERVICE TEACHERS

1. Of all the goals for reading instruction that you have in mind as a teacher, which one(s) do you think you have made good progress toward accomplishing this year? Explain why.
2. What do you usually do when a student is reading orally and makes an oral reading error? Why?
3. What do you usually do when a student is reading orally and doesn't know a word? Why?
4. You probably use different kinds of strategies and activities in teaching reading. Which ones do you feel are the *most* important for your students? Why?
5. What kinds of activities do you feel students should be involved in for the *majority* of their reading instructional time? Why?
6. Here are the typical steps in the Directed Reading Activity (DRA) as suggested in basal reader manuals: (1) introduction of vocabulary; (2) motivation or setting purposes; (3) reading; (4) questions and discussion after silent reading; and (5) skills practice for reinforcement.

   Rank these steps in order from *most* important to *least* important (not necessarily in the order you follow them).
7. Is it important to introduce new vocabulary words *before* your students read a selection? Why or why not?
8. Suppose your students were tested to provide you with information that helped you decide how to instruct them in reading. What did diagnostic testing include and what kind of information did it give you about your individual students?
9. During silent reading, what do you hope your students do when they come to an unknown word?
10. Look at the oral reading mistakes that are underlined on the transcripts of three readers. (These are the same as on item 10 of the preservice form.) Which of these three readers do you judge as the best or most effective reader?

Determining Your Beliefs About Reading

In order to determine your beliefs about reading, study the sample responses on pages 546–550. Then compare each answer to the interview questions to the samples given. Each response should be judged to be *bottom-up* (BU), *top-down* (TD), or *not enough information* (NI) given to clearly determine if it is bottom-up or top-down.

Ask yourself as you judge your responses, "What unit of language did I stress?" For example, if you said that your major instructional goal "is to increase students' ability to associate sounds with letters," then the unit of language emphasized suggests a bottom-up (BU) response. Bottom-up responses are those that emphasize *letters* and *words* as the predominant units of language.

One the other hand, a top-down (TD) response would be appropriate if you had said that your major instructional goal is to "increase students' ability to read library books or other materials on their own." In this response, the unit of language involves the entire selection. Top-down responses emphasize sentences, paragraphs, and the selection itself as the predominant units of language.

An example of a response that does not give enough information (NI) is one in which you might have said, "I tell the student to figure out the word." Such a response needs to be probed further during the interview by asking, "How should the student figure out the word?"

The following rating sheet will help you to determine roughly where you lie on the continuum between bottom-up and top-down belief systems.

■ Rating Your Beliefs About Reading

After you have judged each response to the interview questions, check the appropriate column on the rating sheet for each interview probe.

An overall rating of your conceptual framework of reading is obtained from the following chart and shows where you fall on the beliefs about reading continuum in Figure 2.2, page 42.

Rating Chart

STRONG BOTTOM-UP:	Gave zero or one top-down response (the rest of the responses are bottom-up or not enough information)
MODERATE BOTTOM-UP:	Gave two to three top-down responses
INTERACTIVE OR MODERATE TOP-DOWN:	Gave two to three bottom-up responses
STRONG TOP-DOWN:	Gave zero or one bottom-up response

● TABLE A.1

Rating Sheet for Conceptual Framework of Reading Interview

	RATING SCALE		
Interview Probe	BU	TD	NI
1. Instructional goals			
2. Response to oral reading when reader makes an error			
3. Response to oral reading when a student does not know a word			
4. Most important instructional activity			
5. Instructional activities reader should be engaged in most of the time			
6. Rank ordering of steps in a reading lesson			
7. Importance of introducing vocabulary words before students read			
8. Information from testing			
9. How a reader should respond to unfamiliar words during silent reading			
10. Rationale for best reader			

Guidelines for Analyzing Beliefs About Reading Interviews

Directions: Use the following summary statements as guidelines to help analyze your responses to the questions in the interview.

Question 1: Main Instructional Goals

BOTTOM-UP RESPONSES:

Increase children's ability to blend sounds into words or ability to sound out words.

Increase knowledge of phonetic sounds (sound-letter associations).

Build sight vocabulary.

Increase ability to use word attack skills.

TOP-DOWN RESPONSES:

Increase students' ability to read independently by encouraging them to read library or other books that are easy enough for them on their own.

Increase enjoyment of reading by having a lot of books around, reading aloud to children, and sharing books I thought were special.

Improve comprehension.

Increase ability to find specific information, identify key ideas, determine cause-and-effect relationships, and make inferences. (Although these are discrete skills, they are categorized as top-down because students use higher-order linguistic units—phrases, sentences, paragraphs—in accomplishing them.)

■ Question 2: Teacher Responses When Students Make Oral Reading Errors

BOTTOM-UP RESPONSES:

Help students sound out the word.

Tell students what the word is, and have them spell and then repeat the word.

TOP-DOWN RESPONSES:

Ask "Does that make sense?"

Don't interrupt; one word doesn't "goof up" the meaning of a whole passage.

Don't interrupt; if students are worried about each word, they won't be able to remember what is read.

Don't correct if the error doesn't affect the meaning of the passage.

If the error affects the meaning of the passage, ask students to reread the passage, tell students the word, or ask "Does that make sense?"

■ Question 3: Teacher Responses When Students Do Not Know a Word

BOTTOM-UP RESPONSES:

Help students sound out the word.

Help them distinguish smaller words within the word.

Help them break the word down phonetically.

Help them sound the word out syllable by syllable.

Tell them to use word attack skills.

Give them word attack clues; for example, "The sound of the beginning consonant rhymes with ______________."

TOP-DOWN RESPONSES:

Tell students to skip the word, go on, and come back and see what makes sense.

Ask "What makes sense and starts with ______________?"

Questions 4 and 5: Most Important Instructional Activities

BOTTOM-UP RESPONSES:

Working on skills.

Working on phonics.

Working on sight vocabulary.

Vocabulary drill.

Discussing experience charts, focusing on the words included and any punctuation needed.

Tape-recording students' reading and playing it back, emphasizing accuracy in word recognition.

TOP-DOWN RESPONSES:

Actual reading, silent reading, and independent reading.

Comprehension.

Discussion of what students have read.

Book reports.

Tape-recording students' reading and playing it back, emphasizing enjoyment of reading or comprehension.

Question 6: Ranking Parts of the Directed Reading Procedure

BOTTOM-UP RESPONSES:

The following are most important:

Introduction of vocabulary

Activities to develop reading skills

The following are least important:

Setting purposes for reading

Reading

Reaction to silent reading

Introduction of vocabulary, when the teacher stresses students' using word attack skills to sound out new words

TOP-DOWN RESPONSES:

The following are most important:

Setting purposes for reading

Reading

Reaction to silent reading

The following are least important:

Introduction of vocabulary

Activities to develop reading skills

■ Question 7: Introducing New Vocabulary Words

BOTTOM-UP RESPONSES:

Introducing new vocabulary is important because students need to know what words they will encounter in order to be able to read a story.

Previewing new vocabulary isn't necessary; if students have learned word attack skills, they can sound out unknown words.

Introducing new words is useful in helping students learn what words are important in a reading lesson.

Vocabulary words should be introduced if students don't know the meanings of the words; otherwise it isn't necessary.

TOP-DOWN RESPONSES:

Vocabulary words need not be introduced before reading because students can often figure out words from context.

Question 8: What a Reading Test Should Do

BOTTOM-UP RESPONSES:

Test word attack skills.

Test ability to name the letters of the alphabet.

Test sight words.

Test knowledge of meanings of words.

Test ability to analyze letter patterns of words missed during oral reading.

Test visual skills such as reversal.

TOP-DOWN RESPONSES:

Test comprehension: Students should be able to read a passage orally, look at the errors they make, and use context in figuring out words.

Test whether students are able to glean the meanings of words from context.

Answer questions like the following: Do students enjoy reading? Do their parents read to them? Do their parents take them to the library?

Have students read passages and answer questions.

Have students read directions and follow them.

Question 9: What Students Should Do When They Come to an Unknown Word During Silent Reading

BOTTOM-UP RESPONSES:

Sound it out.

Use their word attack skills.

TOP-DOWN RESPONSES:

Look at the beginning and the end of the sentence and try to think of a word that makes sense.

Try to think of a word that both makes sense and has those letter sounds.

Skip the word; often students can understand the meaning of the sentence without knowing every word.

Use context.

Question 10: Who Is the Best Reader?

Reader A	Reader B	Reader C
Miscue is similar both graphically and in meaning to the text word.	Miscue is a real word that is graphically similar but not meaningful in the text.	Miscue is a nonword that is graphically similar.

BOTTOM-UP RESPONSES:

Reader C, because *cannel* is graphically similar to *canal.*

Reader B, because *candle* is a real word that is graphically similar to *canal.*

TOP-DOWN RESPONSES:

Reader A, because *channel* is similar in meaning to *canal.*

APPENDIX B

The DeFord Theoretical Orientation to Reading Profile (TORP)

Name ______________________________

Directions: Read the following statements, and circle one of the responses that will indicate the relationship of the statement to your feelings about reading and reading instruction. SA = strongly agree; SD = strongly disagree.

(Select *one* best answer that reflects the strength of agreement or disagreement.)

	SA	2	3	4	SD
1. A child needs to be able to verbalize the rules of phonics in order to assure proficiency in processing new words.	1 SA	2	3	4	5 SD
2. An increase in reading errors is usually related to a decrease in comprehension.	1 SA	2	3	4	5 SD
3. Dividing words into syllables according to rules is a helpful instructional practice for reading new words.	1 SA	2	3	4	5 SD
4. Fluency and expression are necessary components of reading that indicate good comprehension.	1 SA	2	3	4	5 SD
5. Materials for early reading should be written in natural language without concern for short, simple words and sentences.	1 SA	2	3	4	5 SD
6. When children do not know a word, they should be instructed to sound out its parts.	1 SA	2	3	4	5 SD

7. It is a good practice to allow children to edit what is written into their own dialect when learning to read. — 1 2 3 4 5 (SA … SD)

8. The use of a glossary or dictionary is necessary in determining the meaning and pronunciation of new words. — 1 2 3 4 5 (SA … SD)

9. Reversals (e.g., saying "saw" for "was") are significant problems in the teaching of reading. — 1 2 3 4 5 (SA … SD)

10. It is a good practice to correct a child as soon as an oral reading mistake is made. — 1 2 3 4 5 (SA … SD)

11. It is important for a word to be repeated a number of times after it has been introduced to ensure that it will become a part of sight vocabulary. — 1 2 3 4 5 (SA … SD)

12. Paying close attention to punctuation marks is necessary to understanding story content. — 1 2 3 4 5 (SA … SD)

13. It is a sign of an ineffective reader when words and phrases are repeated. — 1 2 3 4 5 (SA … SD)

14. Being able to label words according to grammatical function (e.g., nouns, etc.) is useful in proficient reading. — 1 2 3 4 5 (SA … SD)

15. When coming to a word that's unknown, the reader should be encouraged to guess upon meaning and go on. — 1 2 3 4 5 (SA … SD)

16. Young readers need to be introduced to the root form of words (e.g., run, long) before they are asked to read inflected forms (e.g., running, longest). — 1 2 3 4 5 (SA … SD)

17. It is not necessary for a child to know the letters of the alphabet in order to learn to read. — 1 2 3 4 5 (SA … SD)

18. Flash-card drills with sight words is an unnecessary form of practice in reading instruction. — 1 2 3 4 5 (SA … SD)

19. Ability to use accent patterns in multisyllable words (pho´ to graph, pho to´ gra phy, and pho to gra´ phic) should be developed as part of reading instruction. — 1 2 3 4 5 (SA … SD)

20. Controlling text through consistent spelling patterns (e.g., The fat cat ran back. The fat cat sat on a hat.) is a means by which children can best learn to read.	1 SA	2	3	4	5 SD
21. Formal instruction in reading is necessary to ensure the adequate development of all the skills used in reading.	1 SA	2	3	4	5 SD
22. Phonic analysis is the most important form of analysis used when meeting new words.	1 SA	2	3	4	5 SD
23. Children's initial encounters with print should focus on meaning, not upon exact graphic representation.	1 SA	2	3	4	5 SD
24. Word shapes (word configuration) should be taught in reading to aid in word recognition.	1 SA	2	3	4	5 SD
25. It is important to teach skills in relation to other skills.	1 SA	2	3	4	5 SD
26. If a child says "house" for the written word "home," the response should be left uncorrected.	1 SA	2	3	4	5 SD
27. It is not necessary to introduce new words before they appear in the reading text.	1 SA	2	3	4	5 SD
28. Some problems in reading are caused by readers dropping the inflectional endings from words (e.g., jump*s*, jump*ed*).	1 SA	2	3	4	5 SD

Source: "Validating the construct of theoretical orientation in reading instruction" by Diane DeFord, *Reading Research Quarterly 20,* Spring 1985. Reprinted by permission of the International Reading Association.

■ Determining Your Theoretical Orientation

To determine your theoretical orientation, tally your total score on the TORP. Add the point values as indicated on each item, *except for the following items:*

5, 7, 15, 17, 18, 23, 26, 27

For these items, reverse the point values by assigning five points for strongly agree (SA) to one point for strongly disagree (SD):

5 SA	4	3	2	1 SD

Once your point totals have been added, your overall score on the TORP will fall in one of the following ranges:

Theoretical Orientation	Overall Score Range
Phonics	0–65
Skills	65–110
Whole language	110–140

APPENDIX C

Children's Book Awards

The Newbery Medal

Named in honor of John Newbery (1713–1767), the first English publisher of children's books, this medal has been given annually (since 1922) by the American Library Association's Association for Library Service to Children. The recipient is recognized as author of the most distinguished book in children's literature published in the United States in the preceding year. The award is limited to citizens or residents of the United States.

1922 *The Story of Mankind* by Hendrik Willem van Loon, Liveright
Honor Books: *The Great Quest* by Charles Hawes, Little; *Cedric the Forester* by Bernard Marshall, Appleton; *The Old Tobacco Shop* by William Bowen, Macmillan; *The Golden Fleece and the Heroes Who Lived Before Achilles* by Padraic Colum, Macmillan; *Windy Hill* by Cornelia Meigs, Macmillian

1923 *The Voyages of Doctor Dolittle* by Hugh Lofting, Lippincott
Honor Books: No record

1924 *The Dark Frigate* by Charles Hawes, Atlantic/Little, Brown
Honor Books: No record

1925 *Tales from Silver Lands* by Charles Finger, Doubleday
Honor Books: *Nicholas* by Anne Carroll Moore, Putnam; *Dream Coach* by Anne Parrish, Macmillan

1926 *Shen of the Sea* by Arthur Bowie Christman, Dutton
Honor Book: *Voyagers* by Padraic Colum, Macmillan

1927 *Smoky, The Cowhorse* by Will James, Scribner's
Honor Books: No record

1928 *Gayneck, The Story of a Pigeon* by Dhan Gopal Mukerji, Dutton
Honor Books: *The Wonder Smith and His Son* by Ella Young, Longmans; *Downright Dencey* by Caroline Snedeker, Doubleday

1929 *The Trumpeter of Krakow* by Eric P. Kelly, Macmillan
Honor Books: *Pigtail of Ah Lee Ben Loo* by John Bennett, Longmans; *Millions of Cats* by Wanda Gág, Coward; *The Boy Who Was* by Grace Hallock, Dutton; *Clearing Weather* by Cornelia Meigs, Little; *Runaway Papoose* by Grace Moon, Doubleday; *Tod of the Fens* by Elinor Whitney, Macmillan

1930 *Hitty, Her First Hundred Years* by Rachel Field, Macmillan
Honor Books: *Daughter of the Seine* by Jeanette Eaton, Harper; *Pran of Albania* by Elizabeth Miller, Doubleday; *Jumping-Off Place* by Marian Hurd McNeely, Longmans; *Tangle-Coated Horse and Other Tales* by Ella Young, Longmans; *Vaino* by Julia Davis Adams, Dutton; *Little Blacknose* by Hildegarde Swift, Harcourt

1931 *The Cat Who Went to Heaven* by Elizabeth Coatsworth, Macmillan
Honor Books: *Floating Island* by Anne Parrish, Harper; *The Dark Star of Itza* by Alida Malkus, Harcourt; *Queer Person* by Ralph Hubbard, Doubleday; *Mountains Are Free* by Julia Davis Adams, Dutton; *Spice and the Devil's Cave* by Agnes Hewes, Knopf; *Meggy Macintosh* by Elizabeth Janet Gray, Doubleday; *Garram the Hunter* by Herbert Best, Doubleday; *Ood-Le-Uk the Wanderer* by Alice Lide and Margaret Johansen, Little

1932 *Waterless Mountain* by Laura Adams Armer, Longmans
Honor Books: *The Fairy Circus* by Dorothy P. Lathrop, Macmillan; *Calico Bush* by Rachel Field, Macmillan; *Boy of the South Seas* by Eunice Tietjens, Coward; *Out of the Flame* by Eloise Lownsbery, Longmans; *Jane's Island* by Marjorie Allee, Houghton; *Truce of the Wolf and Other Tales of Old Italy* by Mary Gould Davis, Harcourt

1933 *Young Fu of the Upper Yangtze* by Elizabeth Foreman Lewis, Winston
Honor Books: *Swift Rivers* by Cornelia Meigs, Little; *The Railroad to Freedom* by Hildegarde Swift, Harcourt; *Children of the Soil* by Nora Burglon, Doubleday

1934 *Invincible Louisa* by Cornelia Meigs, Little
Honor Books: *The Forgotten Daughter* by Caroline Snedeker, Doubleday; *Swords of Steel* by Elsie Singmaster, Houghton; *ABC Bunny* by Wanda Gág, Coward; *Winged Girl of Knossos* by Erik Berry, Appleton; *New Land* by Sarah Schmidt, McBride; *Big Tree of Bunlahy* by Padraic Colum, Macmillan; *Glory of the Seas* by Agnes Hewes, Knopf; *Apprentice of Florence* by Anne Kyle, Houghton

1935 *Dobry* by Monica Shannon, Viking
Honor Books: *Pageant of Chinese History* by Elizabeth Seeger, Longmans; *Davy Crockett* by Constance Rourke, Harcourt; *Day on Skates* by Hilda Van Stockum, Harper

1936 *Caddie Woodlawn* by Carol Brink, Macmillan
Honor Books: *Honk, The Moose* by Phil Stong, Dodd; *The Good Master* by Kate Seredy, Viking; *Young Walter Scott* by Elizabeth Janet Gray, Viking; *All Sail Set* by Armstrong Sperry, Winston

1937 *Roller Skates* by Ruth Sawyer, Viking
Honor Books: *Phebe Fairchild: Her Book* by Lois Lenski, Stokes; *Whistler's Van* by Idwal Jones, Viking; *Golden Basket* by Ludwig Bemelmans, Viking; *Winterbound* by Margery Bianco, Viking; *Audubon* by Constance Rourke, Harcourt; *The Codfish Musket* by Agnes Hewes, Doubleday

1938 *The White Stag* by Kate Seredy, Viking
Honor Books: *Pecos Bill* by James Cloyd Bowman, Little; *Bright Island* by Mabel Robinson, Random; *On the Banks of Plum Creek* by Laura Ingalls Wilder, Harper

1939 *Thimble Summer* by Elizabeth Enright, Rinehart
Honor Books: *Nino* by Valenti Angelo, Viking; *Mr. Popper's Penguins* by Richard and Florence Atwater, Little; *"Hello the Boat!"* by Phillis Crawford, Holt; *Leader by Destiny: George Washington, Man and Patriot* by Jeanette Eaton, Harcourt; *Penn* by Elizabeth Janet Gray, Viking

1940 *Daniel Boone* by James Daugherty, Viking
Honor Books: *The Singing Tree* by Kate Seredy, Viking; *Runner of the Mountain Tops* by Mabel Robinson, Random; *By the Shores of Silver Lake* by Laura Ingalls Wilder, Harper; *Boy with a Pack* by Stephen W. Meader, Harcourt

1941 *Call It Courage* by Armstrong Sperry, Macmillan
Honor Books: *Blue Willow* by Doris Gates, Viking; *Young Mac of Fort Vancouver* by Mary Jane Carr, T. Crowell; *The Long Winter* by Laura Ingalls Wilder, Harper; *Nansen* by Anna Gertrude Hall, Viking

1942 *The Matchlock Gun* by Walter D. Edmonds, Dodd
Honor Books: *Little Town on the Prairie* by Laura Ingalls Wilder, Harper; *George Washington's World* by Genevieve Foster, Scribner's; *Indian Captive: The Story of Mary Jemison* by Lois Lenski, Lippincott; *Down Ryton Water* by Eva Roe Gaggin, Viking

1943 *Adam of the Road* by Elizabeth Janet Gray, Viking
Honor Books: *The Middle Moffat* by Eleanor Estes, Harcourt; *Have You Seen Tom Thumb?* by Mabel Leigh Hunt, Lippincott

1944 *Johnny Tremain* by Esther Forbes, Houghton
Honor Books: *These Happy Golden Years* by Laura Ingalls Wilder, Harper; *Fog Magic* by Julia Sauer, Viking; *Rufus M.* by Eleanor Estes, Harcourt; *Mountain Born* by Elizabeth Yates, Coward

1945 *Rabbit Hill* by Robert Lawson, Viking

Honor Books: *The Hundred Dressed* by Eleanor Estes, Harcourt; *The Silver Pencil* by Alice Dalgliesh, Scribner's; *Abraham Lincoln's World* by Genevieve Foster, Scribner's; *Lone Journey: The Life of Roger Williams* by Jeanette Eaton, Harcourt

1946 *Strawberry Girl* by Lois Lenski, Lippincott
Honor Books: *Justin Morgan Had a Horse* by Marguerite Henry, Rand; *The Moved-Outers* by Florence Crannell Means, Houghton; *Bhimsa, The Dancing Bear* by Christine Weston, Scribner's; *New Found World* by Katherine Shippen, Viking

1947 *Miss Hickory* by Carolyn Sherwin Bailey, Viking
Honor Books: *Wonderful Year* by Nancy Barnes, Messner; *Big Tree* by Mary and Conrad Buff, Viking; *The Heavenly Tenants* by William Maxwell, Harper; *The Avion My Uncle Flew* by Cyrus Fisher, Appleton; *The Hidden Treasure of Glaston* by Eleanore Jewett, Viking

1948 *The Twenty-one Balloons* by William Pène du Bois, Viking
Honor Books: *Pancakes-Paris* by Claire Huchet Bishop, Viking; *Li Lun, Lad of Courage* by Carolyn Treffinger, Abingdon; *The Quaint and Curious Quest of Johnny Longfoot* by Catherine Besterman, Bobbs; *The Cow-Tail Switch, and Other West African Stories* by Harold Courlander, Holt; *Misty of Chincoteague* by Marguerite Henry, Rand

1949 *King of the Wind* by Marguerite Henry, Rand
Honor Books: *Seabird* by Holling C. Holling, Houghton; *Daughter of the Mountains* by Louise Rankin, Viking; *My Father's Dragon* by Ruth S. Gannett, Random; *Story of the Negro* by Arna Bontemps, Knopf

1950 *The Door in the Wall* by Marguerite de Angeli, Doubleday
Honor Books: *Tree of Freedom* by Rebecca Caudill, Viking; *The Blue Cat of Castle Town* by Catherine Coblentz, Longmans; *Kildee House* by Rutherford Montgomery, Doubleday; *George Washington* by Genevieve Foster, Scribner's; *Song of the Pines* by Walter and Marion Havighurst, Winston

1951 *Amos Fortune, Free Man* by Elizabeth Yates, Aladdin
Honor Books: *Better Known as Johnny Appleseed* by Mabel Leigh Hunt, Lippincott; *Gandhi, Fighter Without a Sword* by Jeanette Eaton, Morrow; *Abraham Lincoln, Friend of the People* by Clara Ingram Judson, Follett; *The Story of Appleby Capple* by Anne Parrish, Harper

1952 *Ginger Pye* by Eleanor Estes, Harcourt
Honor Books: *Americans Before Columbus* by Elizabeth Baity, Viking; *Minn of the Mississippi* by Holling C. Holling, Houghton; *The Defender* by Nicholas Kalashnikoff, Scribner's; *The Light at Tern Rock* by Julia Sauer, Viking; *The Apple and the Arrow* by Mary and Conrad Buff, Houghton

1953 *Secret of the Andes* by Ann Nolan Clark, Viking

Honor Books: *Charlotte's Web* by E. B. White, Harper; *Moccasin Trail* by Eloise McGraw, Coward; *Red Sails to Capri* by Ann Weil, Viking; *The Bears of Hemlock Mountain* by Alice Dalgliesh, Scribner's; *Birthdays of Freedom,* Vol. 1 by Genevieve Foster, Scribner's

1954 . . . *and now Miguel* by Joseph Krumgold, T. Crowell
Honor Books: *All Alone* by Claire Huchet Bishop, Viking; *Shadrach* by Meindert DeJong, Harper; *Hurry Home Candy* by Meindert DeJong, Harper; *Theodore Roosevelt, Fighting Patriot* by Clara Ingram Judson, Follett; *Magic Maize* by Mary and Conrad Buff, Houghton

1955 *The Wheel on the School* by Meindert DeJong, Harper
Honor Books: *The Courage of Sarah Noble* by Alice Dalgliesh, Scribner's; *Banner in the Sky* by James Ullman, Lippincott

1956 *Carry on, Mr. Bowditch* by Jean Lee Latham, Houghton
Honor Books: *The Secret River* by Marjorie Kinnan Rawlings, Scribner's; *The Golden Name Day* by Jennie Lindquist, Harper; *Men, Microscopes, and Living Things* by Katherine Shippen, Viking

1957 *Miracles on Maple Hill* by Virginia Sorensen, Harcourt
Honor Books: *Old Yeller* by Fred Gipson, Harper; *The House of Sixty Fathers* by Meindert DeJong, Harper; *Mr. Justice Holmes* by Clara Ingram Judson, Follett; *The Corn Grows Ripe* by Dorothy Rhoads, Viking; *Black Fox of Lorne* by Marguerite de Angeli, Doubleday

1958 *Rifles for Watie* by Harold Keith, T. Crowell
Honor Books: *The Horsecatcher* by Mari Sandoz, Westminster; *Gone-Away Lake* by Elizabeth Enright, Harcourt; *The Great Wheel* by Robert Lawson, Viking; *Tom Paine, Freedom's Apostle* by Leo Gurko, T. Crowell

1959 *The Witch of Blackbird Pond* by Elizabeth George Speare, Houghton
Honor Books: *The Family Under the Bridge* by Natalie S. Carlson, Harper; *Along Came a Dog* by Meindert DeJong, Harper; *Chucaro: Wild Pony of the Pampa* by Francis Kalnay, Harcourt; *The Perilous Road* by William O. Steele, Harcourt

1960 *Onion John* by Joseph Krumgold, T. Crowell
Honor Books: *My Side of the Mountain* by Jean George, Dutton; *America Is Born* by Gerald W. Johnson, Morrow; *The Gammage Cup* by Carol Kendall, Harcourt

1961 *Island of the Blue Dolphins* by Scott O'Dell, Houghton
Honor Books: *America Moves Forward* by Gerald W. Johnson, Morrow; *Old Ramon* by Jack Schaefer, Houghton; *The Cricket in Times Square* by George Selden, Farrar

1962 *The Bronze Bow* by Elizabeth George Speare, Houghton
Honor Books: *Frontier Living* by Edwin Tunis, World; *The Golden Goblet* by Eloise McGraw, Coward; *Belling the Tiger* by Mary Stolz, Harper

1963 *A Wrinkle in Time* by Madeleine L'Engle, Farrar
Honor Books: *Thistle and Thyme* by Sorche Nic Leodhas, Holt; *Men of Athens* by Olivia Coolidge, Houghton

1964 *It's Like This, Cat* by Emily Cheney Neville, Harper
Honor Books: *Rascal* by Sterling North, Dutton; *The Loner* by Esther Wier, McKay

1965 *Shadow of a Bull* by Maia Wojciechowska, Atheneum
Honor Book: *Across Five Aprils* by Irene Hunt, Follett

1966 *I, Juan de Pareja* by Elizabeth Borten de Trevino, Farrar
Honor Books: *The Black Cauldron* by Lloyd Alexander, Holt; *The Animal Family* by Randall Jarrell, Pantheon; *The Noonday Friends* by Mary Stolz, Harper

1967 *Up a Road Slowly* by Irene Hunt, Follett
Honor Books: *The King's Fifth* by Scott O'Dell, Houghton; *Zlateh the Goat and Other Stories* by Isaac Bashevis Singer, Harper; *The Jazz Man* by Mary H. Weik, Atheneum

1968 *From the Mixed-Up Files of Mrs. Basil E. Frankweiler* by E. L. Konigsburg, Atheneum
Honor Books: *Jennifer, Hecate, Macbeth, William McKinley, and Me, Elizabeth* by E. L. Konigsburg, Atheneum; *The Black Pearl* by Scott O'Dell, Houghton; *The Fearsome Inn* by Isaac Bashevis Singer, Scribner's; *The Egypt Game* by Zilpha Keatley Snyder, Atheneum

1969 *The High King* by Lloyd Alexander, Holt
Honor Books: *To Be a Slave* by Julius Lester, Dial; *When Shlemiel Went to Warsaw and Other Stories* by Isaac Bashevis Singer, Farrar

1970 *Sounder* by William H. Armstrong, Harper
Honor Books: *Our Eddie* by Sulamith Ish-Kishor, Pantheon; *The Many Ways of Seeing: An Introduction to the Pleasures of Art* by Janet Gaylord Moore, World; *Journey Outside* by Mary Q. Steele, Viking

1971 *Summer of the Swans* by Betsy Byars, Viking
Honor Books: *Kneeknock Rise* by Natalie Babbitt, Farrar; *Enchantress from the Stars* by Sylvia Louise Engdahl, Atheneum; *Sing Down the Moon* by Scott O'Dell, Houghton

1972 *Mrs. Frisby and the Rats of NIMH* by Robert C. O'Brien, Atheneum
Honor Books: *Incident at Hawk's Hill* by Allan W. Eckert, Little; *The Planet of Junior Brown* by Virginia Hamilton, Macmillan; *The Tombs of Atuan* by Ursula K. Le Guin, Atheneum; *Annie and the Old One* by Miska Miles, Atlantic/Little; *The Headless Cupid* by Zilpha Keatley Snyder, Atheneum

1973 *Julie of the Wolves* by Jean George, Harper

Honor Books: *Frog and Toad Together* by Arnold Lobel, Harper; *The Upstairs Room* by Johanna Reiss, Crowell; *The Witches of Worm* by Zilpha Keatley Snyder, Atheneum

1974 *The Slave Dancer* by Paula Fox, Bradbury
Honor Book: *The Dark Is Rising* by Susan Cooper, Atheneum/McElderry

1975 *M. C. Higgins, the Great* by Virginia Hamilton, Macmillan
Honor Books: *Figgs & Phantoms* by Ellen Raskin, Dutton; *My Brother Sam Is Dead* by James Lincoln Collier & Christopher Collier, Four Winds; *The Perilous Gard* by Elizabeth Marie Pope, Houghton; *Philip Hall Likes Me, I Reckon Maybe* by Bette Greene, Dial

1976 *The Grey King* by Susan Cooper, Atheneum/McElderry
Honor Books: *The Hundred Penny Box* by Sharon Bell Mathis, Viking; *Dragonwings* by Laurence Yep, Harper

1977 *Roll of Thunder, Hear My Cry* by Mildred D. Taylor, Dial
Honor Books: *Abel's Island* by William Steig, Farrar; *A String in the Harp* by Nancy Bond, Atheneum/McElderry

1978 *Bridge to Terabithia* by Katherine Paterson, Crowell
Honor Books: *Anpao: An American Indian Odyssey* by Jamake Highwater, Lippincott; *Ramona and Her Father* by Beverly Cleary, Morrow

1979 *The Westing Game* by Ellen Raskin, Dutton
Honor Book: *The Great Gilly Hopkins* by Katherine Paterson, Crowell

1980 *A Gathering of Days: A New England Girl's Journal, 1830–32* by Joan Blos, Scribner's
Honor Book: *The Road from Home: The Story of an Armenian Girl* by David Kherdian, Greenwillow

1981 *Jacob Have I Loved* by Katherine Paterson, Crowell
Honor Books: *The Fledgling* by Jane Langton, Harper; *A Ring of Endless Light* by Madeleine L'Engle, Farrar

1982 *A Visit to William Blake's Inn: Poems for Innocent and Experienced Travelers* by Nancy Willard, Harcourt
Honor Books: *Ramona Quimby, Age 8* by Beverly Cleary, Morrow; *Upon the Head of a Goat* by Aranka Siegel, Farrar

1983 *Dicey's Song* by Cynthia Voigt, Atheneum
Honor Books: *The Blue Sword* by Robin McKinley, Greenwillow; *Dr. De Soto* by William Steig, Farrar; *Graven Images* by Paul Fleischman, Harper; *Homesick: My Own Story* by Jean Fritz, Putnam; *Sweet Whispers, Brother Rush* by Virginia Hamilton, Philomel

1984 *Dear Mr. Henshaw* by Beverly Cleary, Morrow

Honor Books: *The Sign of the Beaver* by Elizabeth George Speare, Houghton; *A Solitary Blue* by Cynthia Voigt, Atheneum; *Sugaring Time* by Kathryn Lasky, Macmillan; *The Wish Giver* by Bill Brittain, Harper

1985 *The Hero and the Crown* by Robin McKinley, Greenwillow
Honor Books: *Like Jake and Me* by Mavis Jukes, Knopf; *The Moves Make the Man* by Bruce Brooks, Harper; *One-Eyed Cat* by Paula Fox, Bradbury

1986 *Sarah, Plain and Tall* by Patricia MacLachlan, Harper
Honor Books: *Commodore Perry in the Land of the Shogun* by Rhoda Blumberg, Lothrop; *Dogsong* by Gary Paulsen, Bradbury

1987 *The Whipping Boy* by Sid Fleischman, Greenwillow
Honor Books: *On My Honor* by Marion Dane Bauer, Clarion; *Volcano: The Eruption and Healing of Mount St. Helens* by Patricia Lauber, Bradbury; *A Fine White Dust* by Cynthia Rylant, Bradbury

1988 *Lincoln: A Photobiography* by Russell Freedman, Clarion/Houghton
Honor Books: *After the Rain* by Norma Fox Mazer, Morrow; *Hatchet* by Gary Paulsen, Bradbury

1989 *Joyful Noise: Poems for Two Voices* by Paul Fleischman, Harper
Honor Books: *In the Beginning: Creation Stories from Around the World* by Virginia Hamilton, Harcourt; *Scorpions* by Walter Dean Myers, Harper

1990 *Number the Stars* by Lois Lowry, Houghton
Honor Books: *Afternoon of the Elves* by Janet Taylor Lisle, Orchard; *Shabanu: Daughter of the Wind* by Suzanne Fisher Staples, Knopf; *The Winter Room* by Gary Paulsen, Orchard

1991 *Maniac Magee* by Jerry Spinelli, Little, Brown
Honor Book: *The True Confessions of Charlotte Doyle* by Avi, Orchard

1992 *Shiloh* by Phyllis Reynolds Naylor, Atheneum
Honor Books: *Nothing But the Truth,* by Avi, Orchard; *The Wright Brothers: How They Invented the Airplane,* Holiday House

1993 *Missing May* by Cynthia Rylant, Orchard
Honor Books: *The Dark Thirty: Southern Tales of the Supernatural* by Patricia McKissack, ill. by Brian Pinkney, Knopf; *Somewhere in the Darkness,* by Walter Dean Myers, Scholastic; *What Hearts* by Bruce Brooks, Harper

1994 *The Giver* by Lois Lowry, Houghton
Honor Books: *Crazy Lady* by Jane Leslie Conly, Harper; *Dragon's Gate* by Lawrence Yep, Harper; *Eleanor Roosevelt: A Life of Discovery* by Russel Freedman, Clarion

The Caldecott Medal

Since 1938, the Association of Library Service to Children of the American Library Association has annually awarded the Caldecott Medal to the illustrator of the most distinguished picture book published in the United States in the preceding year. The recipient must be a citizen or resident of the United States. The medal is named in tribute to the well-loved English illustrator Randolph Caldecott (1846–1886).

1938 *Animals of the Bible* by Helen Dean Fish, ill. by Dorothy P. Lathrop, Lippincott
Honor Books: *Seven Simeons* written and ill. by Boris Artzybasheff, Viking; *Four and Twenty Blackbirds* by Helen Dean Fish, ill. by Robert Lawson, Stokes

1939 *Mei Li* written and ill. by Thomas Handforth, Doubleday
Honor Books: *The Forest Pool* written and ill. by Laura Adams Armer, Longmans; *Wee Gillis* by Munro Leaf, ill. by Robert Lawson, Viking; *Snow White and the Seven Dwarfs* written and ill. by Wanda Gág, Coward; *Barkis* written and ill. by Clare Newberry, Harper; *Andy and the Lion* written and ill. by James Daugherty, Viking

1940 *Abraham Lincoln* written and ill. by Ingri and Edgar Parin d'Aulaire, Doubleday
Honor Books: *Cock-A-Doodle Doo . . .* written and ill. by Berta and Elmer Hader, Macmillan; *Madeline* written and ill. by Ludwig Bemelmans, Viking; *The Ageless Story,* ill. by Lauren Ford, Dodd

1941 *They Were Strong and Good* written and ill. by Robert Lawson, Viking
Honor Book: *April's Kittens* written and ill. by Clare Newberry, Harper

1942 *Make Way for Ducklings* written and ill. by Robert McCloskey, Viking
Honor Books: *An American ABC* written and ill. by Maud and Miska Petersham, Macmillan; *In My Mother's House* by Ann Nolan Clark, ill. by Velino Herrera, Viking; *Paddle-to-the-Sea* written and ill. by Holling C. Holling, Houghton; *Nothing at All* written and ill. by Wanda Gág, Coward

1943 *The Little House* written and ill. by Virginia Lee Burton, Houghton
Honor Books: *Dash and Dart* written and ill. by Mary and Conrad Buff, Viking; *Marshmallow* written and ill. by Clare Newberry, Harper

1944 *Many Moons* by James Thurber, ill. by Louis Slobodkin, Harcourt
Honor Books: *Small Rain: Verses from the Bible* selected by Jessie Orton Jones, ill. by Elizabeth Orton Jones, Viking; *Pierre Pigeon* by Lee Kingman, ill. by Arnold E. Bare, Houghton; *The Mighty Hunter* written and ill. by Berta and Elmer Hader, Macmillan; *A Child's Good Night Book* by Margaret Wise Brown, ill. by Jean Charlot, W. R. Scott; *Good Luck Horse* by Chih-Yi Chan, ill. by Plao Chan, Whittlesey

1945 *Prayer for a Child* by Rachel Field, ill. by Elizabeth Orton Jones, Macmillan

Honor Books: *Mother Goose* ill. by Tasha Tudor, Walck; *In the Forest* written and ill. by Marie Hall Ets, Viking; *Yonie Wondernose* written and ill. by Marguerite de Angeli, Doubleday; *The Christmas Anna Angel* by Ruth Sawyer, ill. by Kate Seredy, Viking

1946 *The Rooster Crows . . .* (traditional Mother Goose) ill. by Maud and Miska Petersham, Macmillan
Honor Books: *Little Lost Lamb* by Golden MacDonald, ill. by Leonard Weisgard, Doubleday; *Sing Mother Goose* by Opal Wheeler, ill. by Marjorie Torrey, Dutton; *My Mother Is the Most Beautiful Woman in the World* by Becky Reyher, ill. by Ruth Gannett, Lothrop; *You Can Write Chinese* written and ill. by Kurt Wiese, Viking

1947 *The Little Island* by Golden MacDonald, ill. by Leonard Weisgard, Doubleday
Honor Books: *Rain Drop Splash* by Alvin Tresselt, ill. by Leonard Weisgard, Lothrop; *Boats on the River* by Marjorie Flack, ill. by Jay Hyde Barnum, Viking; *Timothy Turtle* by Al Graham, ill. by Tony Palazzo, Viking; *Pedro, the Angel of Olvera Street* written and ill. by Leo Politi, Scribner's; *Sing in Praise: A Collection of the Best Loved Hymns* by Opal Wheeler, ill. by Marjorie Torrey, Dutton

1948 *White Snow, Bright Snow* by Alvin Tresselt, ill. by Roger Duvoisin, Lothrop
Honor Books: *Stone Soup* written and ill. by Marcia Brown, Scribner's; *McElligot's Pool* written and ill. by Dr. Seuss, Random; *Bambino the Clown* written and ill. by George Schreiber, Viking; *Roger and the Fox* by Lavinia Davis, ill. by Hildegard Woodward, Doubleday; *Son of Robin Hood* ed. by Anne Malcolmson, ill. by Virginia Lee Burton, Houghton

1949 *The Big Snow* written and ill. by Berta and Elmer Hader, Macmillan
Honor Books: *Blueberries for Sal* written and ill. by Robert McCloskey, Viking; *All Around the Town* by Phyllis McGinley, ill. by Helen Stone, Lippincott; *Juanita* written and ill. by Leo Politi, Scribner's; *Fish in the Air* written and ill. by Kurt Wiese, Viking

1950 *Song of the Swallows* written and ill. by Leo Politi, Scribner's
Honor Books: *America's Ethan Allen* by Stewart Holbrook, ill. by Lynd Ward, Houghton; *The Wild Birthday Cake* by Lavinia Davis, ill. by Hildegard Woodward, Doubleday; *The Happy Day* by Ruth Krauss, ill. by Marc Simont, Harper; *Bartholomew and the Oobleck* written and ill. by Dr. Seuss, Random; *Henry Fisherman* written and ill. by Marcia Brown, Scribner's

1951 *The Egg Tree* written and ill. by Katherine Milhous, Scribner's
Honor Books: *Dick Whittington and His Cat* written and ill. by Marcia Brown, Scribner's; *The Two Reds* by William Lipkind, ill. by Nicolas Mordvinoff, Harcourt; *If I Ran the Zoo* written and ill. by Dr. Seuss, Random; *The Most Wonderful Doll in the World* by Phyllis McGinley, ill. by Helen Stone, Lippincott; *T-Bone, the Baby Sitter* written and ill. by Clare Newberry, Harper

1952 *Finders Keepers* by William Lipkind, ill. by Nicolas Mordvinoff, Harcourt

Honor Books: *Mr. T. W. Anthony Woo* written and ill. by Marie Hall Ets, Viking; *Skipper John's Cook* written and ill. by Marcia Brown, Scribner's; *All Falling Down* by Gene Zion, ill. by Margaret Bloy Graham, Harper; *Bear Party* written and ill. by William Pène du Bois, Viking; *Feather Mountain* written and ill. by Elizabeth Olds, Houghton

1953 *The Biggest Bear* written and ill. by Lynd Ward, Houghton
Honor Books: *Puss in Boots* by Charles Perrault, ill. and tr. by Marcia Brown, Scribner's; *One Morning in Maine* written and ill. by Robert McCloskey, Viking; *Ape in a Cape* written and ill. by Fritz Eichenberg, Harcourt; *The Storm Book* by Charlotte Zolotow, ill. by Margaret Bloy Graham, Harper; *Five Little Monkeys* written and ill. by Juliet Kepes, Houghton

1954 *Madeline's Rescue* written and ill. by Ludwig Bemelmans, Viking
Honor Books: *Journey Cake, Ho!* by Ruth Sawyer, ill. by Robert McCloskey, Viking; *When Will the World Be Mine?* by Miriam Schlein, ill. by Jean Charlot, W. R. Scott; *The Steadfast Tin Soldier* by Hans Christian Andersen, ill. by Marcia Brown, Scribner's; *A Very Special House* by Ruth Krauss, ill. by Maurice Sendak, Harper; *Green Eyes* written and ill. by a A. Birnbaum, Capitol

1955 *Cinderella, or the Little Glass Slipper* by Charles Perrault, tr. and ill. by Marcia Brown, Scribner's
Honor Books: *Book of Nursery and Mother Goose Rhymes,* ill. by Marguerite de Angeli, Doubleday; *Wheel on the Chimney* by Margaret Wise Brown, ill. by Tibor Gergely, Lippincott; *The Thanksgiving Story* by Alice Dalgliesh, ill. by Helen Sewell, Scribner's

1956 *Frog Went A-Courtin'* ed. by John Langstaff, ill. by Feodor Rojankovsky, Harcourt
Honor Books: *Play with Me* written and ill. by Marie Hall Ets, Viking; *Crow Boy* written and ill. by Taro Yashima, Viking

1957 *A Tree Is Nice* by Janice May Udry, ill. by Marc Simont, Harper
Honor Books: *Mr. Penny's Race Horse* written and ill. by Marie Hall Ets, Viking; *1 Is One* written and ill. by Tasha Tudor, Walck; *Anatole* by Eve Titus, ill. by Paul Galdone, McGraw; *Gillespie and the Guards* by Benjamin Elkin, ill. by James Daugherty, Viking; *Lion* written and ill. by William Pène du Bois, Viking

1958 *Time of Wonder* written and ill. by Robert McCloskey, Viking
Honor Books: *Fly High, Fly Low* written and ill. by Don Freeman, Viking; *Anatole and the Cat* by Eve Titus, ill. by Paul Galdone, McGraw

1959 *Chanticleer and the Fox* adapted from Chaucer and ill. by Barbara Cooney, T. Crowell
Honor Books: *The House That Jack Built* written and ill. by Antonio Frasconi, Harcourt; *What Do You Say, Dear?* by Sesyle Joslin, ill. by Maurice Sendak, W. R. Scott; *Umbrella* written and ill. by Taro Yashima, Viking

1960 *Nine Days to Christmas* by Marie Hall Ets and Aurora Labastida, ill. by Marie Hall Ets, Viking
Honor Books: *Houses from the Sea* by Alice E. Goudey, ill. by Adrienne Adams, Scribner's; *The Moon Jumpers* by Janice May Udry, ill. by Maurice Sendak, Harper

1961 *Baboushka and the Three Kings* by Ruth Robbins, ill. by Nicolas Sidjakov, Parnassus
Honor Book: *Inch by Inch* written and ill. by Leo Lionni, Obolensky

1962 *Once a Mouse* . . . written and ill. by Marcia Brown, Scribner's
Honor Books: *The Fox Went Out on a Chilly Night* written and ill. by Peter Spier, Doubleday; *Little Bear's Visit* by Else Holmelund Minarik, ill. by Maurice Sendak, Harper; *The Day We Saw the Sun Come Up* by Alice E. Goudey, ill. by Adrienne Adams, Scribner's

1963 *The Snowy Day* written and ill. by Ezra Jack Keats, Viking
Honor Books: *The Sun Is a Golden Earring* by Natalia M. Belting, ill. by Bernarda Bryson, Holt; *Mr. Rabbit and the Lovely Present* by Charlotte Zolotow, ill. by Maurice Sendak, Harper

1964 *Where the Wild Things Are* written and ill. by Maurice Sendak, Harper
Honor Books: *Swimmy* written and ill. by Leo Lionni, Pantheon; *All in the Morning Early* by Sorche Nic Leodhas, ill. by Evaline Ness, Holt; *Mother Goose and Nursery Rhymes* ill. by Philip Reed, Atheneum

1965 *May I Bring a Friend?* by Beatrice Schenk de Regniers, ill. by Beni Montresor, Atheneum
Honor Books: *Rain Makes Applesauce* by Julian Scheer, ill. by Marvin Bileck, Holiday; *The Wave* by Margaret Hodges, ill. by Blair Lent, Houghton; *A Pocketful of Cricket* by Rebecca Caudill, ill. by Evaline Ness, Holt

1966 *Always Room for One More* by Sorche Nic Leodhas, ill. by Nonny Hogrogian, Holt
Honor Books: *Hide and Seek Fog* by Alvin Tresselt, ill. by Roger Duvoisin, Lothrop; *Just Me* written and ill. by Marie Hall Ets, Viking; *Tom Tit Tot* written and ill. by Evaline Ness, Scribner's

1967 *Sam, Bangs & Moonshine* written and ill. by Evaline Ness, Holt
Honor Book: *One Wide River to Cross* by Barbara Emberley, ill. by Ed Emberley, Prentice

1968 *Drummer Hoff* by Barbara Emberley, ill. by Ed Emberley, Prentice
Honor Books: *Frederick* written and ill. by Leo Lionni, Pantheon; *Seashore Story,* written and ill. by Taro Yashima, Viking; *The Emperor and the Kite* by Jane Yolen, ill. by Ed Young, World

1969 *The Fool of the World and the Flying Ship* by Arthur Ransome, ill. by Uri Shulevitz, Farrar

Honor Book: *Why the Sun and the Moon Live in the Sky* by Elphinstone Dayrell, ill. by Blair Lent, Houghton

1970 *Sylvester and the Magic Pebble* written and ill. by William Steig, Windmill
Honor Books: *Goggles!* written and ill. by Ezra Jack Keats, Macmillan; *Alexander and the Wind-Up Mouse* written and ill. by Leo Lionni, Pantheon; *Pop Corn & Ma Goodness* by Edna Mitchell Preston, ill. by Robert Andrew Parker, Viking; *Thy Friend, Obadiah* written and ill. by Brinton Turkle, Viking; *The Judge* by Harve Zemach, ill. by Margot Zemach, Farrar

1971 *A Story—A Story* written and ill. by Gail E. Haley, Atheneum
Honor Books: *The Angry Moon* by William Sleator, ill. by Blair Lent, Atlantic/Little; *Frog and Toad Are Friends* written and ill. by Arnold Lobel, Harper; *In the Night Kitchen* written and ill. by Maurice Sendak, Harper

1972 *One Fine Day* written and ill. by Nonny Hogrogian, Macmillan
Honor Books: *If All the Seas Were One Sea* written and ill. by Janina Domanska, Macmillan; *Moja Means One: Swahili Counting Book* by Muriel Feelings, ill. by Tom Feelings, Dial; *Hildilid's Night* by Cheli Duran Ryan, ill. by Arnold Lobel, Macmillan

1973 *The Funny Little Woman* retold by Arlene Mosel, ill. by Blair Lent, Dutton
Honor Books: *Anansi the Spider* adapted and ill. by Gerald McDermott, Holt; *Hosie's Alphabet* by Hosea, Tobias, and Lisa Baskin, ill. by Leonard Baskin, Viking; *Snow-White and the Seven Dwarfs* translated by Randall Jarrell, ill. by Nancy Ekholm Burkert, Farrar; *When Clay Sings* by Byrd Baylor, ill. by Tom Bahti, Scribner's

1974 *Duffy and the Devil* by Harve Zemach, ill. by Margot Zemach, Farrar
Honor Books: *Three Jovial Huntsmen* written and ill. by Susan Jeffers, Bradbury; *Cathedral: The Story of Its Construction* written and ill. by David Macaulay, Houghton

1975 *Arrow to the Sun* adapted and ill. by Gerald McDermott, Viking
Honor Book: *Jambo Means Hello* by Muriel Feelings, ill. by Tom Feelings, Dial

1976 *Why Mosquitoes Buzz in People's Ears* retold by Verna Aardema, ill. by Leo and Diane Dillon, Dial
Honor Books: *The Desert Is Theirs* by Byrd Baylor, ill. by Peter Parnall, Scribner's; *Strega Nona* retold and ill. by Tomie dePaola, Prentice

1977 *Ashanti to Zulu: African Traditions* by Margaret Musgrove, ill. by Leo and Diane Dillon, Dial
Honor Books: *The Amazing Bone* written and ill. by William Steig, Farrar; *The Contest* retold and ill. by Nonny Hogrogian, Greenwillow; *Fish for Supper* written and ill. by M. B. Goffstein, Dial; *The Golem* written and ill. by Beverly Brodsky McDermott, Lippincott; *Hawk, I'm Your Brother* by Byrd Baylor, ill. by Peter Parnall, Scribner's

1978 *Noah's Ark* ill. by Peter Spier, Doubleday
Honor Books: *Castle* written and ill. by David Macaulay, Houghton; *It Could Always Be Worse* retold and ill. by Margot Zemach, Farrar

1979 *The Girl Who Loved Wild Horses* written and ill. by Paul Goble, Bradbury
Honor Books: *Freight Train* written and ill. by Donald Crews, Greenwillow; *The Way to Start a Day* by Byrd Baylor, ill. by Peter Parnall, Scribner's

1980 *Ox-Cart Man* by Donald Hall, ill. by Barbara Cooney, Viking
Honor Books: *Ben's Trumpet* written and ill. by Rachel Isadora, Greenwillow; *The Garden of Abdul Gasazi* written and ill. by Chris Van Allsburg, Houghton

1981 *Fables* written and ill. by Arnold Lobel, Harper
Honor Books: *The Grey Lady and the Strawberry Snatcher,* ill. by Molly Bang, Four Winds; *Truck* ill. by Donald Crews, Greenwillow; *Mice Twice,* written and ill. by Joseph Low, Atheneum; *The Bremen-Town Musicians,* ill. by Ilse Plume, Doubleday

1982 *Jumanji* written and ill. by Chris Van Allsburg, Houghton
Honor Books: *Where the Buffaloes Begin* by Olaf Baker, ill. by Stephen Gammell, Warne; *On Market Street* by Arnold Lobel, ill. by Anita Lobel, Greenwillow; *Outside Over There* by Maurice Sendak, Harper; *A Visit to William Blake's Inn* by Nancy Willard, ill. by Alice and Martin Provensen, Harcourt

1983 *Shadow* by Blaise Cendrars, tr. and ill. by Marcia Brown, Scribner's
Honor Books: *When I Was Young in the Mountains* by Cynthia Rylant, ill. by Diane Goode, Dutton; *A Chair for My Mother* by Vera B. Williams, Greenwillow

1984 *The Glorious Flight: Across the Channel with Louis Blériot* by Alice and Martin Provensen, Viking
Honor Books: *Ten, Nine, Eight* by Molly Bang, Greenwillow; *Little Red Riding Hood* retold and ill. by Trina Schart Hyman, Holiday House

1985 *St. George and the Dragon* retold by Margaret Hodges, ill. by Trina Schart Hyman, Little, Brown
Honor Books: *Hansel and Gretel* retold by Rika Lesser, ill. by Paul O. Zelinsky, Dodd; *Have You Seen My Duckling?* by Nancy Tafuri, Greenwillow; *The Story of Jumping Mouse* by John Steptoe, Lothrop

1986 *The Polar Express* written and ill. by Chris Van Allsburg, Houghton
Honor Books: *The Relatives Came* by Cynthia Rylant, ill. by Stephen Gammell, Bradbury; *King Bidgood's in the Bathtub* by Audrey Wood, ill. by Don Wood, Harcourt

1987 *Hey, Al!* by Arthur Yorinks, ill. by Richard Egielski, Farrar
Honor Books: *The Village of Round and Square Houses* written and ill. by Ann Grifalconi, Little, Brown; *Alphabetics* written and ill. by Suse MacDonald, Bradbury; *Rumpelstiltskin* retold and ill. by Paul O. Zelinsky, Dutton

1988 *Owl Moon* by Jane Yolen, ill. by John Schoenherr, Philomel
Honor Book: *Mufaro's Beautiful Daughters* written and ill. by John Steptoe, Lothrop

1989 *Song and Dance Man* by Karen Ackerman, ill. by Stephen Gammell, Knopf
Honor Books: *The Boy of the Three Year Nap* by Allen Say, Houghton; *Free Fall* by David Wiesner, Lothrop; *Goldilocks and the Three Bears* adapted and ill. by James Marshall, Dial; *Mirandy and Brother Wind* by Patricia McKissack, ill. by Jerry Pinkney, Knopf

1990 *Lon Po Po: A Red Riding Hood Story from China* adapted and ill. by Ed Young, Philomel
Honor Books: *Bill Peet: An Autobiography* by Bill Peet, Houghton; *Color Zoo* by Lois Ehlert, Lippincott; *Hershel and the Hanukkah Goblins* by Eric A. Kimmel, ill. by Trina Schart Hyman, Holiday House; *The Talking Eggs* by Robert D. San Souci, ill. by Jerry Pinkney, Dial

1991 *Black and White* written and ill. by David Macaulay, Houghton Mifflin
Honor Books: *Puss in Boots* by Charles Perrault, tr. by Malcolm Arthur and ill. by Fred Marcellino, Farrar; *"More, More, More," Said the Baby* by Vera B. Williams, Greenwillow

1992 *Tuesday* written and ill. by David Wiesner, Clarion
Honor Book: *Tar Beach* written and ill. by Faith Ringold, Crown

1993 *Mirette on the High Wire* written and ill. by Emily Arnold McCully, Putnam
Honor Books: *Seven Blind Mice* written and ill. by Ed Young, Philomel; *The Stinky Cheese Man and Other Fairly Stupid Tales* by Jon Scieszka, ill. by Lane Smith, Viking; *Working Cotton* by Sherley Anne Williams, ill. by Carole Byard, Harcourt

1994 *Grandfather's Journey* written and ill. by Allen Say, Houghton
Honor Books: *Peppe the Lamplighter* by Elisa Bartone, ill. by Ted Lewin, Lothrop, Lee, and Shepard; *In the Small, Small Pond* written and ill. by Denise Fleming, Holt; *Owen* written and ill. by Kevin Henkes, Greenwillow; *Raven: A Trickster Tale from the Pacific Northwest* written and ill. by Gerald McDermott, Harcourt; *Yo! Yes?* written and ill. by Chris Raschka, Orchard

APPENDIX D

Recommended Books for Multicultural Reading Experiences

African-American Books

Folklore

Aardema, Verna. *Bimwili and the Zimwi.* (P)
———. *Bringing the Rain to Kapiti Plain.* (P)
———. *Oh, Kojo! How Could You!* (I)
———. *Why Mosquitoes Buzz in People's Ears.* (P-I)
Bryan, Ashley. *All Night, All Day: A Child's First Book of African American Spirituals.* (P-I-A)
———. *What a Morning! The Christmas Story in Black Spirituals.* (P-I)
Grifalconi, Ann. *The Village of Round and Square Houses.* (P)
Hamilton, Virginia. *The People Could Fly.* Illus. Leo and Diane Dillon. (I)
Keats, Ezra Jack. *John Henry.* (I)
Lester, Julius. *How Many Spots Does a Leopard Have?* (I)
———. *The Tales of Uncle Remus: The Adventures of Brer Rabbit.* (P-I)
San Souci, Robert D. *Sukey and the Mermaid.* Illus. Brian Pinkney. (P-I)
Steptoe, John. *Mufaro's Beautiful Daughters.* (P)

Poetry

Adoff, Arnold. *All the Colors of the Race.* (I)
———. *Black Is Brown Is Tan.* (P)

P = primary, I = intermediate, A = adolescent

———. *In for Winter, Out for Spring.* (P-I)
———. *My Black Me: A Beginning Book of Black Poetry.* (P)
Brooks, Gwendolyn. *Bronzeville Boys and Girls.* (P-I)
Bryan, Ashley. *Sing to the Sun.* (P-I)
Clifton, Lucille. *Some of the Days of Everett Anderson.* (P)
———. *Everett Anderson's Goodbye.* (P)
———. *Everett Anderson's Nine Month Long.* (P)
Giovanni, Nikki. *Spin a Soft Black Song.* (P-I)
Greenfield, Eloise. *Honey, I Love and Other Love Poems.* (P-I-A)
Price, Leontyne. *Aīda.* Illus. Leo and Diane Dillon. (A)

Picture Books

Clifton, Lucille. *Boy Who Didn't Believe in Spring.* (P)
———. *Everett Anderson's Christmas Coming.* (P)
———. *Three Wishes.* Illus. Michael Hays. (P)
Crews, Donald. *Bigmama's.* (P)
Daly, Nikki. *Something on my Mind.* (P)
Greenfield, Eloise. *Grandpa's Face.* (P)
———. *She Come Bringing Me That Little Baby Girl.* (P)
Grifalconi, Ann. *Darkness and the Butterfly.* (P)
———. *Osa's Pride.* (P)
Hamilton, Virginia. *Drylongso.* Illus. Jerry Pinkney. (I)
Hoffman, Mary. *Amazing Grace.* Illus. Caroline Binch. (P)
Howard, Elizabeth Fitzgerald. *Aunt Flossie's Hats (and Crab Cakes Later).* Illus. James Ransome. (P)
Johnson, Angela. *One of Three.* Illus. David Soman. (P)
———. *Tell Me a Story, Mama.* Illus. David Soman. (P)
McKissack, Patricia C. *Flossie and the Fox.* (P)
———. *Mirandy and Brother Wind.* Illus. Jerry Pinkney. (P-I)
Pinkney, Gloria Jean. *Back Home.* Illus. Jerry Pinkney. (P)
Polacco, Patricia. *Chicken Sunday.* (P)
———. *Mrs. Katz and Tush.* (P-I)
Ringgold, Faith. *Tar Beach.* (P-I)
Steptoe, John. *Stevie.* (P)
Williams, Sherley Anne. *Working Cotton.* Illus. Carole Byard. (P)
Wilson, Beth P. *Jenny.* Illus. Dolores Johnson. (P)

Novels

Davis, Ossie. *Just Like Martin.* (I)
Greenfield, Eloise. *Koya DeLaney and the Good Girl Blues.* (I)
Hamilton, Virginia. *Cousins.* (I)
———. *M. C. Higgins, the Great.* (I-A)
———. *Planet of Junior Brown.* (I-A)
———. *Zeely.* (I)

Myers, Walter Dean. *Fast Sam, Cool Clyde, and Stuff.* (I-A)
———. *The Young Landlords.* (A)
———. *Hoops.* (A)
———. *Motown and Didi.* (A)
———. *Somewhere in the Darkness.* (A)
———. *Won't Know Till I Get There.* (A)
Smothers, Ethel Footman. *Down in the Piney Woods.* (I-A)
Taylor, Mildred. *The Road to Memphis.* (A)
———. *Roll of Thunder, Hear My Cry.* (A)
Yarbrough, Camille. *Cornrows.* (P)

Nonfiction

McKissack, Patricia, and Frederick McKissack. *A Long Hard Journey: The Story of the Pullman Porter.* (I)
Myers, Walter Dean. *Now Is Your Time!: The African-American Struggle for Freedom.* (I-A)

Biography

Freedman, Florence B. *Two Tickets to Freedom: The True Story of Ellen and William Craft, Fugitive Slaves.* (I-A)
Hamilton, Virginia. *Anthony Burns: The Defeat and Triumph of a Fugitive Slave.* (I-A)
Haskins, James. *Bill Cosby: America's Most Famous Father.* (I)
———. *Diana Ross, Star Supreme.* (I)
Lester, Julius. *To Be a Slave.* (I-A)

Asian-American Books

Folklore

Birdseye, Tom. *A Song of Stars.* Illus. Ju-Hong Chen. (P)
Demi. *The Empty Pot.* (P)
Louie, Ai-Ling. *Yeh-Shen: A Cinderella Story from China.* Illus. Ed Young. (P-I)
Yacowitz, Caryn. *The Jade Stone: A Chinese Folktale.* Illus. Ju-Hong Chen. (I)
Yep, Laurence. (reteller).
The Bufferfly Man. (I)
———. *The Rainbow People.* (I)
———. *Tongues of Jade.* Illus. David Wiesner. (I)

Poetry

Baron, Virginia Olsen. *Sunset in a Spider Web: Sijo Poetry of Ancient Korea.* (I-A)
Behn, Harry. *Cricket Songs.* (I-A)
Demi. *In the Eyes of the Cat: Japanese Poetry for All Seasons.* Tze-si Huang. (P-I-A)

Picture Books

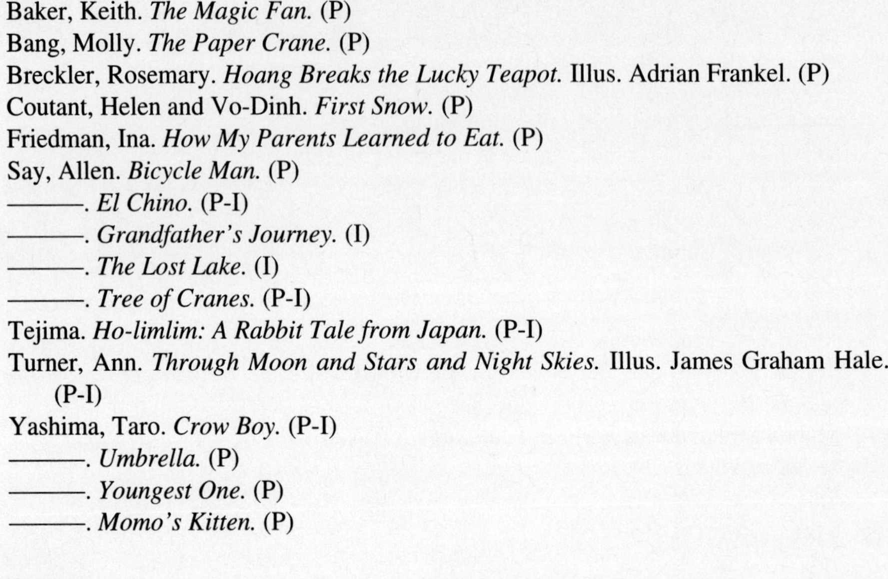

Baker, Keith. *The Magic Fan.* (P)
Bang, Molly. *The Paper Crane.* (P)
Breckler, Rosemary. *Hoang Breaks the Lucky Teapot.* Illus. Adrian Frankel. (P)
Coutant, Helen and Vo-Dinh. *First Snow.* (P)
Friedman, Ina. *How My Parents Learned to Eat.* (P)
Say, Allen. *Bicycle Man.* (P)
———. *El Chino.* (P-I)
———. *Grandfather's Journey.* (I)
———. *The Lost Lake.* (I)
———. *Tree of Cranes.* (P-I)
Tejima. *Ho-limlim: A Rabbit Tale from Japan.* (P-I)
Turner, Ann. *Through Moon and Stars and Night Skies.* Illus. James Graham Hale. (P-I)
Yashima, Taro. *Crow Boy.* (P-I)
———. *Umbrella.* (P)
———. *Youngest One.* (P)
———. *Momo's Kitten.* (P)

Novels

Merrill, Jean. *The Girl Who Loved Caterpillars.* Illus. Floyd Cooper. (I)
Namioka, Lensey. *Yang the Youngest and His Terrible Ear.* (I)
Uchida, Yoshiko. *A Jar of Dreams.* (I)
———. *The Best Bad Thing.* (I)
———. *The Happiest Ending.* (I)
———. *The Invisible Thread.* (I)
Yep, Laurence. *Dragonwings.* (I-A)
———. *Sea Glass.* (I-A)
———. *Child of the Owl.* (I-A)
———. *Mountain Light.* (I-A)

Nonfiction

Banish, Roslyn. *A Forever Family.* (I)
Brown, Tricia. *Lee Ann.* Photos by Ted Thai. (I)
Hoyt-Goldsmith, Diane. *Hoang Anh: A Vietnamese-American Boy.* Photos by Lawrence Migdale. (I)
McMahon, Patricia. *Chi-Hoon: A Korean Girl.* (P-I)
Meltzer, Milton. *The Chinese Americans.* (A)
Schlein, Miriam. *The Year of the Panda.* Illus. Kam Mak. (P-I)
Waters, Kate, and Madeline Slovenz-Low. *Lion Dancer: Ernie Wan's Chinese New Year.* (P-I)
Wolf, Bernard. *In the Year of the Tiger.* (I)

Biography

Huynh, Quang Nhuong. *The Land I Lost: Adventures of a Boy in Vietnam.* (I)
Lord, Bette Bao. *In the Year of the Boar and Jackie Robinson.* (I)

Hispanic-American Books

Folklore

Aardema, Verna. *Borreguita and the Coyote.* Illus. Petra Mathers. (Mexico) (P-I)
———. *The Riddle of the Drum: A Tale from Tizapan, Mexico.* (P-I)
Alexander, Ellen. *Llama and the Great Flood.* (Quechua story from Peru) (I)
Belpre, Pura. *Once in Puerto Rico.* (I)
———. *The Rainbow-Colored Horse.* (Puerto Rico) (P-I)
de Paola, Tomie. *The Lady of Guadalupe.* (Mexico) (P-I)
de Sauza, James. *Brother Anansi and the Cattle Ranch.* (Nicaragua) (P)
Joseph, Lynn. *A Wave in Her Pocket: Stories from Trinidad.* Illus. Brian Pinkney. (I)
Kurtycz, Marcos. *Tigers and Opossums: Animal Legends.* (Mexico) (I)
Schon, Isabel. *Doña Blanca and Other Hispanic Nursery Rhymes and Games.* (P-I)
Vidal, Beatriz. *The Legend of El Dorado.* Adapted by
Wolkstein, Diane. *Banza: A Haitian Story.* Illus. Marc Tolon Brown. (P)

Poetry

de Gerez, Toni. *My Song Is a Piece of Jade: Poems of Ancient Mexico in English and Spanish.* (I-A)
Delacre, Lulu. *Arroz Con Leche: Popular Songs and Rhymes from Latin America.* (P-I)
Soto, Gary. *A Fire in My Hands.* Illus. James M. Cardillo. (I)
———. *Neighborhood Odes.* Illus. David Diaz. (I)

Picture Books

Belpre, Pura. *Santiago.* Illus. Symeon Shimin. (P)
Cruz, Martel. *Yagua Days.* (P)
Czernicki, Stefan, and Timothy Rhodes. *The Sleeping Bread.* (P)
Dorros, Arthur. *Abuela.* Illus. Elisa Kleven. (P)
Ets, Marie Hall, and Aurora Latastida. *Nine Days to Christmas, a Story of Mexico.* (P)
Garza, Carmen Lomas. *Family Pictures. Cuadros de Familia.* (P-I)
Havill, Juanita. *Treasure Nap.* Illus. Elivia Savadier. (Mexico) (P)
James, Betsy. *The Dream Stair.* (P)
Politi, Leo. *Pedro, the Angel of Olvera Street.* (P)
Roe, Eileen. *Con Mi Hermano: With My Brother.* (P)
Tompert, Ann. *The Silver Whistle.* Illus. Beth Peck. (P)

Novels and Short Stories

Cameron, Ann. *The Most Beautiful Place in the World.* Illus. Thomas B. Allen. (P-I)
Carlson, Lori M., and Cynthia L. Ventura (editors). *Where Angels Glide at Dawn: New Stories from Latin America.* Illus. José Ortega. (I)
Mohr, Nicholasa. *Felita.* (I)
———. *Going Home.* (I-A)
———. *El Bronx Remembered.* (A)
———. *In Nueva York.* (A)
———. *Nilda.* (A)
Soto, Gary. *Baseball in April and Other Stories.* (I)
———. *Taking Sides.* (I-A)

Nonfiction

Ancona, George. *Bananas: From Manolo to Margie.* (P-I)
Anderson, Joan. *Spanish Pioneers of the Southwest.* (P-I)
Brown, Tricia. *Hello, Amigos!* Photos by Fran Ortiz. (P-I)
Brusca, Maria Christina. *On the Pampas.* (I)
Emberley, Rebecca. *My House: A Book in Two Languages/Mi Casa: Un Libro en Dos Lenguas.* (I)
McDonald's Hispanic Heritage Art Contest. *Our Hispanic Heritage.* (P)
Meltzer, Milton. *The Hispanic Americans.* (A)
Perl, Lila. *Pinatas and Paper Flowers, Holidays of the Americas in English and Spanish.* (I-A)
Shalant, Phyllis. *Look What We've Brought You from Mexico.* (I)
Zak, Monica. *Save My Rainforest.* Illus. Bengt-Arne Runnerstrom. Trans. Nancy Schimmel. (I)

Biography

Codye, C. *Luis W. Alvarez.* (I-A)
de Treviño, Elizabeth Borten. *I, Juan de Pareja.* (A)
———. *Juarez, Man of Law.* (A)
———. *El Guero.* (I-A)
Gleiter, Jan. *David Farragut.* (A)
———. *Diego Rivera.* (A)
Shorto, R. *David Farragut and the Great Naval Blockade.* (A)

Native-American Books

Folklore

Bierhorst, John. *The Ring in the Prairie: A Shawnee Legend.* (I)
———. *Doctor Coyote.* (I)

de Paola, Tomie. *The Legend of the Bluebonnet.* (P)
Dixon, Ann. *How Raven Brought Light to People.* Illus. James Watts. (P-I)
Goble, Paul. *Beyond the Ridge.* (P-I)
———. *Buffalo Woman.* (P-I)
———. *Crow Chief: A Plains Indian Story.* (I)
———. *Death of the Iron Horse.* (P-I)
———. *Her Seven Brothers.* (P-I)
———. *Iktomi and the Boulder: A Plains Indian Story.* (P-I)
———. *Iktomi and the Berries: A Plains Indian Story.* (P-I)
———. *Iktomi and the Ducks: A Plains Indian Story.* (P-I)
———. *Iktomi and the Buffalo Skull: A Plains Indian Story.* (P-I)
———. *Star Boy.* (P-I)
Harris, Christie. *Once Upon a Totem.* (I-A)
Highwater, Jamake. *Anpao: An American Indian Odyssey.* (I-A)
MacGill-Callahan, Sheila. *And Still the Turtle Watched.* Illus. Barry Moser. (P)
Martin, Rafe. *The Rough-Face Girl.* Illus. David Shannon. (P-I)
Monroe, Jean Guard, and Ray A. Williamson. *They Dance in the Sky.* Illus. Edgar Stewart. (I-A)
Oughton, Jerrie. *How the Stars Fell into the Sky.* Illus. Lisa Desimini. (P-I)
Rodanas, Kristina. *Dragonfly's Tale.* (P-I)
Siberell, Anne. *The Whale in the Sky.* (P-I)
Taylor, C. J. *How Two-Feather Was Saved from Loneliness.* (P-I)

Poetry

Baylor, Byrd. *The Other Way to Listen.* (P-I)
Bierhorst, John. *A Cry from the Earth: Music of the North American Indians.* (P-I)
Bruchac, Joseph, and Jonathan London. *Thirteen Moons on Turtle's Back: A Native American Year of Moons.* Illus. Thomas Locker. (P-I)
Clark, Ann Nolan. *In My Mother's House.* Illus. Velino Herrera. (P-I)
Jones, Hettie. *The Trees Stand Shining: Poetry of the North American Indians.* Illus. Robert Andrew Parker. (P-I)
Wood, Nancy. *Many Winters.* (I-A)

Picture Books

Baker, Olaf. *Where the Buffaloes Begin.* Illus. Stephen Gammell. (P)
Baylor, Byrd. *Hawk, I'm Your Brother.* (P-I)
Buchanan, Ken. *This House Is Made of Mud.* Illus. Libba Tracy. (P-I)
Steptoe, John. *The Story of Jumping Mouse: A Native American Legend.* (P)
Yolen, Jane. *Sky Dogs.* Illus. Barry Moser. (P)

Novels

Hobbs, Will. *Bearstone.* (I-A)
O'Dell, Scott, and Elizabeth Hall. *Thunder Rolling in the Mountains.* (A)

Rohmer, Harriet, Octavia Chow and Morris Vidaure. *The Invisible Hunters.* Illus. Joe Sam. (I-A)

Spinka, Penina Keen. *Mother's Blessing.* (I)

Strete, C. K. *Big Thunder Magic.* (P-I)

———. *When Grandfather Journeys Into Winter.* (I)

Wosmek, Frances. *A Brown Bird Singing.* (I)

■ Nonfiction

Freedman, Russell. *Children of the Wild West.* (I-A)

———. *Indian Chiefs.* (I-A)

Hoyt-Goldsmith, Diane. *Pueblo Storyteller.* Photos Lawrence Migdale. (I)

Kendall, Russ. *Eskimo Boy: Life in an Inupiaq Eskimo Village.* (I)

Regguinti, Gordon. *The Sacred Harvest: Ojibway Wild Rice Gathering.* Photos by Dale Kakkak. (I-A)

Yolen, Jane. *Encounter.* (P-I-A)

■ Biography

Ekoomiak, Normee. *Arctic Memories.* (Inuit in Arctic Quebec) (I)

Freedman, Russell. *Indian Chiefs.* (I-A)

Glossary

active comprehension Using prior knowledge, schemata, and metacognition to construct textual meaning, fostered by using questioning during reading.

affixes Clusters of letters that form morphological or meaningful structures rather than phonetic structures; prefixes and suffixes can be affixes.

alphabetic principle Principle that suggests that letters in the alphabet map to phonemes, the minimal sound units represented in written language.

analogy A comparison of two similar relationships.

analytic phonics Basal program approach to phonics teaching that emphasizes the discovery of sound-symbol relationships through the analysis of known words.

anecdotal notes Brief, written observations of revealing behavior that a teacher considers significant to understanding a child's literacy learning.

anticipation guide A series of written or oral statements for individual students to respond to before reading text assignments.

antonyms Words opposite in meaning to other words.

approaches to reading Instructional beliefs and practices derived from the three theoretical models for reading instruction—top-down, bottom-up, and interactive.

aptitude hypothesis Suggests that vocabulary and comprehension reflect general intellectual ability.

assisted reading Strategy combining all features of home-centered learning—reading with children, sharing books, repeating favorite stories, memorizing text, and providing needed assistance.

audience The reader; children should be encouraged to write with their audience in mind.

authentic assessment Asking students to actually perform tasks that demonstrate sufficient knowledge and understanding of a subject.

authentic communication An essential component of language learning requiring active communication and participation.

automated reading Program where students listen individually to tape-recorded stories while reading along with the written text.

automaticity The automatic, almost subconscious, recognition and understanding of written text.

basal reading A major approach to reading that occupies the central and broadest position on the instructional continuum. Built on scope and sequence foundations and traditionally associated with bottom-up theory, basal programs have been modified in recent years with the inclusion of language experience and literature activities.

belief systems Theoretical orientations and philosophical approaches to the teaching of reading.

beliefs about reading See *belief systems.*

big books Enlarged versions of children's storybooks, distinguished by large print and illustrations, and designed to offer numerous opportunities for interaction.

bilingual learners Students whose first language is different from the language of instruction in the school and who may or may not be fluent in the language of instruction.

book talks Discussion opportunities for children to engage in conversations about their responses to reading books from class core study, reading workshops, or literature circles.

bottom-up Reading models that assume the process of translating print to meaning begins with the printed word, a process initiated by decoding graphic symbols into sound.

brainstorming Prereading activity that identifies a broad concept reflecting the main topic to be studied in an assigned reading and organizes students in small groups to generate a list of words related to the topic.

buddy journal Written conversations between children in a journal format; promotes student interaction, cooperation, and collaboration.

categorization Critical manipulation of words in relation to other words through the labeling of ideas, events, or objects.

checklists Number of categories presented for specific diagnostic purposes.

choral reading Oral reading, often of poetry, that makes use of various voice combinations and contrasts to create meaning or highlight the tonal qualities of a passage.

class relationships Conceptual hierarchies organized according to the superordinate and subordinate nature of the concepts.

classroom environments Recognition that a classroom is the total of all its organizational and physical components, embodying its learning goals and the teacher's role.

classroom libraries Collection of children's literature and tradebooks designed to supplement textbooks. May be teacher-created or part of a basal reading series.

cloze passages One or more word deletions within a sentence; used to elicit responses from students.

code emphasis From the beginning, basal reading programs emphasize decoding, or the transformation of unfamiliar printed words into speech.

cognitive and academic diversity Results when children learn faster than, slower than, or differently from what is expected at school.

collaborative learning A cooperative learning environment in which students work together to complete tasks.

communities of learners Concept that enhances the classroom as a nurturing and supportive environment.

community of readers Effect created by literature-based reading programs. Children, in alliance with their friends and teacher, work together in classrooms in which school reading imitates adult reading.

compound words Words formed by the union of two or more distinct words.

comprehending Analyzing text for context and meaning to develop understanding.

computer management system Systems that allow teachers to use computers to score tests, record skill progress information, and prepare status reports.

concepts A mental image of anything grouped together by common features or similar criteria; synonymous with the formation of categories.

considerate text Textbook distinguished by its user-friendliness, particularly in regard to organizational features and presentation of material.

consonants All sounds represented by letters of the alphabet except *a, e, i, o, u.*

constructivism Learning theory associated with Jean Piaget that describes meaning-making as cognitively constructing knowledge by using prior knowledge and experience in interaction with the environment.

context analysis The use of context clues by readers to identify words they may have heard but not experienced visually.

continuous progress Teaching reading at students' individual reading levels, not grade levels.

controlled vocabulary Controlling the number of new words students will encounter in each reading lesson.

core books Collection of books that form the nucleus of a school reading program at each grade level; usually selected by a curriculum committee.

criterion-referenced tests Informal tests devised to measure individual student achievement according to a specific criterion for performance (e.g., eight words out of ten spelled correctly).

cultural diversity Results when a student's home, family, socioeconomic group, culture, and society is different from the predominate culture of the school.

decoding The conscious or automatic processing and translating of the printed word into speech.

definitional knowledge The ability to relate new words to known words; can be built through synonyms, antonyms, and multiple-meaning words.

developmental stages of spelling The gradual recognition and understanding of spelling rules, from letter-sound associations to vowels, transitional spelling, and conventional spelling.

developmentally appropriate practice The matching or gearing of the reading curriculum to children's developing abilities.

diagnostic test Formal assessment intended to provide detailed information about individual students' strengths and weaknesses.

dialects Rule-governed variations and linguistic diversity within a language.

dialogue journal Written conversation between child and teacher that emphasizes meaning while providing natural, functional experiences both in writing and reading.

direct instruction Teacher-centered or teacher-facilitated instruction.

Directed Reading-Thinking Activity (DR-TA) Builds critical awareness of the reader's role and responsibility in interacting with the text through the process of predicting, verifying, judging, and extending thinking about text material.

Discussion Webs Cooperative learning strategy that requires students to explore both sides of issues during postreading discussions before drawing conclusions; uses graphic aids to guide children's thinking.

double-entry journal Journal that gives students an opportunity to identify passages from texts and explore in writing why those passages are interesting or meaningful.

dramatic play Unstructured, spontaneous, and expressive classroom activities requiring little planning.

early intervention Crucial strategy to help lower-than-expected achievers catch up with able reading peers.

emergent literacy Concept that explains children's literacy learning as developmental with no clear beginning or end, rather than as proceeding in distinct sequence. Thus, children begin to develop literacy through everyday experiences with print long before they enter school.

explicit Stated assumptions; meaning created from a written work (or situation) based mainly on given information.

expository text Books (particularly textbooks) that rely heavily on discourse distinguished by description, classification, and explanation.

extension (integrating across the curriculum) Additional activities, including art, music, and writing, that are used as catalysts to extend ideas and concepts initiated during the formal lesson.

family literacy How family interactions influence the language development of young children and provide the context in which they learn to read and write.

fluency The ability to read easily and well.

free response Active involvement or participation in reading through discussion or writing that includes inferential, evaluative, and analytical thinking about a book based on the reader's response.

function words Grammatically necessary words such as articles, conjunctions, pronouns, verbs of being, and prepositions that bind information bearing words.

gifted readers Students who have wide vocabularies, read two or more years above grade level, have excellent memory for story details, understand complex concepts and ideas, and learn skills and strategies quickly and with minimum structure.

graphic organizer Display of key concepts or main ideas in a manner that shows their relationships to each other.

group share session Discussion period intended to help students reflect on the day's work. As part of a writing workshop plan, the session focuses on specific writing concerns.

grouping Concept related to the creation and disbanding of groups of differing sizes, abilities, and interests for the purpose of providing specific instruction.

Head Start Federal government-funded program developed in communities throughout the United States to provide a nursery school environment that can compensate for developmental differences between poor children and their more advantaged counterparts.

images of teachers Perceptions of what it means to be a teacher drawn from personal experience, professional study, classroom work, and, to some extent, the depiction of teachers in the media.

immediate word identification The rapid recognition of words, a process often triggered by a reader's well-developed schema for different words.

implicit Unstated assumptions; the association of meaning to written works (or situations) based on prior knowledge in conjunction with given information.

inclusion Incorporating the diverse needs and abilities of all students into classroom instruction.

individualized instruction Term with various definitions; in essence, any strategy or instructional plan that allows students to work at their own pace and level.

Inferential Strategy Elementary student strategy built around prereading questions and postreading discussion.

informal assessment Informal measures of reading that yield useful information about student performance without comparisons to the performance of a normative population.

informal assessment opportunities (notes) Suggestions in basal program teacher's manuals for noticing children's strengths and weaknesses as they write.

informal reading inventory (IRI) Individually administered—and informal—reading test usually consisting of graded word lists, graded reading passages, and comprehension questions that assess how students orally and silently interact with print.

informational texts Reference materials such as magazines, newspapers, dictionaries, and encyclopedias.

instructional aids Charts, workbooks, ditto masters, skill packs, cards, game boxes, and other devices intended to help teachers who are too busy to create their own aids.

instructional strategies The tactics, plans, and practices that are the keys to reading instruction.

instrumental hypothesis Establishes a causal chain between vocabulary knowledge and comprehension; that is, if comprehension depends in part on the knowledge of word meanings, then vocabulary instruction should influence comprehension.

interactive Reading models that assume that translating print to meaning involves using both prior knowledge and print, and that the process is initiated by the reader making predictions about meaning and/or decoding graphic symbols.

interactive writing Shared writing element where children are invited to volunteer to write parts of a story.

intergenerational literacy Often used in connection with family intervention programs designed to break the cycle of illiteracy from one generation to the next. See *family literacy.*

interviewing Periodic communication with individual students to assess reading interests and attitudes, self-perceptions, and understanding of the language learning process.

invented spelling Beginning stages of children's developmental spelling as they associate letters to sounds in writing.

K-W-L (What do you *know?* What do you *want* to find out? What did you *learn?*) Three-step teaching model designed to guide and motivate children as they read to acquire information from expository texts.

key-word teaching Helping young children identify words quickly and easily through the use of words that are charged with personal meaning and feeling.

kidwatching See *observation.*

kindergarten program Literature-based basal program's first level for beginning or nonreaders.

knowledge hypothesis Suggests that vocabulary and comprehension reflect general knowledge rather than intellectual ability.

language experience activities Using the natural language of children and their background experiences to share and discuss events; listen to and tell stories; dictate words, sentences, and stories; and write independently.

Language experience approach (LEA) See *language experience.*

language experience This major approach to reading, located on the holistic side of the instructional continuum, is tied closely to interactive or top-down theory. Often considered a beginning reading approach, connections between reading and writing are becoming more prevalent in classrooms.

learning centers Classroom areas set aside to offer students more and diverse opportunities to work in small groups or independently and more student choice, commitment, and responsibility.

levels Sequential arrangement of readers, teacher's editions, and ancillary materials for each grade level in basal reading programs.

linguistic awareness Understanding of the technical terms and labels needed to talk and think about reading.

linguistic diversity Results when a student's first language, or language of communication at home, is not the language of instruction in the school.

literacy club Term dramatizing many of the theoretical developments and research findings related to literacy learning and defining the group of written language users with whom a child interacts.

literacy development The stages of language experience.

literacy event Powerful, authentic use of language to convey meaning and understanding between a writer and reader.

literacy play center Designated classroom areas designed around familiar contexts or places and furnished with props to provide an environment where children may play with print on their own terms.

literary letters Response technique popularized by Nancy Atwell (1987). Students correspond with each other and with teachers by writing letters about literary texts.

literate environment An environment that fosters and nurtures interest in and curiosity about written language and supports children's efforts to become readers and writers.

literature across the curriculum Weaving an array of literature into meaningful and relevant instructional activities within the context of content-area study.

literature Any written text that can be used as a model of good writing for children.

literature circles Collaborative strategy involving self-selection; children select books, assemble in groups based on the titles selected, and form study or discussion groups.

literature response journal Invites readers to freely respond to literary texts; less structured than reading logs and other journals.

literature units Instruction organizational technique for arranging book collections by unifying elements such as genre, author, or conceptual theme.

literature web Illustrates the relationships that exist among the major components in units of study.

literature based A major approach to reading that encourages students to personally select their own trade books, with the sessions followed by teacher-student conferences where students may be asked to read aloud from their selections. Used by teachers who want to provide for individual student differences in reading abilities while focusing on meaning, interest, and enjoyment.

literature-based programs Reading programs based on instructional practices and student activities using literature, books, novels, short stories, magazines, plays, and poems that have not been rewritten for instructional purposes.

macrocloze stories Stories given to students with passages deleted from the text; students read the stories and discuss the missing text either orally or in writing.

management Testing program that provides a system for arranging or managing the placement of pupils in different levels of basal reading programs.

materials Diverse array of reference books, catalogs, paperback books, magazines, and ancillaries provided in the classroom to meet students' interests and to offer instructional variety.

meaning emphasis Basal reading programs that teach reading as a communication process rather than as a series of subskills.

metacognition Awareness of one's own cognitive processes including task knowledge and self-monitoring of activity.

minilesson A brief, direct instructional exchange between teacher and students to address specific, observed learning needs of students.

miscue analysis Informal assessment of oral reading errors to determine the extent to which readers use and coordinate graphic-sound, syntactic, and semantic information.

norms Average scores of a sampling of students selected for testing according to factors such as age, sex, race, grade, or socioeconomic status; basis for comparing the performance of individuals or groups.

observation Informal assessment technique used by classroom teachers to document growth in learning by watching and recording students' literate behaviors.

Oral Recitation Lesson (ORL) Structure that makes use of direct instruction and student practice, including reading in chorus, as a means of incorporating fluency into daily reading instruction.

organizers A frame of reference established to prepare children conceptually for ideas to be encountered in reading.

orthographic knowledge Overlearned knowledge of common letter patterns that skilled readers use rapidly and accurately to associate with sounds.

paired reading Theory that structured collaborative work involving pairs of children of the same or different reading ability fosters reading fluency.

paired-word sentence generation Teaching strategy that asks students to take two related words and create one sentence that correctly demonstrates an understanding of the words and their relationship to each other.

patterned stories Highly predictable, enjoyable, and repetitious stories that naturally attract children.

phonemic awareness An understanding that speech is composed of a series of written sounds; a powerful predictor of children's later reading achievement.

phonics instruction Teaching the relationships between speech sounds and letters.

phonograms Letter clusters that help form word families or rhyming words.

portfolio assessment Informal testing that assesses a compilation of reading and writing work documenting the literacy development of a student; seen as widely representative of the reading and writing process.

portfolio Compilation of individual student's work in reading and writing devised for students to understand their literacy progress and evaluate their strengths and weaknesses.

possible sentences Concept-relation strategy where students use vocabulary words and contrast words to generate sentences; usually involves classroom discussion.

predictable texts Literature that is distinguished by familiar or predictable characteristics of setting, storyline, language patterns, or rhyme and that can help to develop fluency.

prefixes Groups of letters arranged in front of words that change the meaning of those words.

prereading activities Designed to help students activate prior knowledge, set purpose, and/or engage their curiosity before reading.

prereading skills Related to the idea that beginning readers need to master certain prerequisite skills before formal reading instruction can take place and that these skills should be developed through carefully sequenced instruction.

prescriptive Individualized reading instruction favored by teachers who devote large sections of reading periods to phonics or linguistics work, focusing on sound-letter relationships.

pretend play Spontaneous creation of stories—including setting, characters, goal, plot, and resolution—during children's play.

previewing Purposes and priorities established before reading to help students become aware of the goals of a reading assignment.

primer Rarely used term for a first-grade-level book given to children before their first readers.

professional knowledge Knowledge acquired from an ongoing study of the practice of teaching.

proficiency testing Standardized testing designed to determine "guaranteed" competency ratings for students across the nation.

psycholinguistics The suggestion that readers act upon and interact with written language in an effort to make sense of an author's text.

Question-Answer Relationships (QARs) Enhance children's ability to answer comprehension questions by teaching them how to find the information they need to answer questions.

readability An assessment of the level and difficulty of textbooks. Sentence length and word difficulty are often among the assessed elements used in formulas that assign grade-level scores for text materials.

reader-response theory Responsibility for constructing textual meaning resides primarily with the reader and depends to a great extent on the reader's prior knowledge and experience.

readers' theater The oral presentation of drama, prose, or poetry by two or more readers.

readers/writers' journals (workbooks) Can be teacher-created means of incorporating authentic writing situations and responses to reading; however, some basal workbooks designed as independent skill and phonics practice activities are labeled this way.

reading log Structured journal used in conjunction with literary texts. After a period of sustained reading, teachers often use prompts to guide students' written responses to the text in their logs.

reading progress cards (running records) Informal assessment records and individualized recordkeeping systems that track student progress in basal reading programs.

reading readiness The implication that children need to reach a certain physical, mental, and emotional maturity level to benefit from reading instruction.

Reading Recovery Early intervention program begun in New Zealand; focuses on low-ability readers who receive intense, individual instruction daily over a 15-week period.

reading workshops Nancy Atwell's 1987 method for integrating the language arts around literature through an organizational framework that allows readers to demonstrate reading strategies by responding to books and sharing meaning with their peers.

reading-writing connection The natural links between reading and writing. Evidence suggests that writing and reading develop together and should therefore be nurtured together.

recordkeeping Tracking the books and stories read by students; can be maintained by teachers or students.

reinforcement Exercises involving similar and contrasting examples that are used to reinforce learning in basal programs.

reliability Consistency of test results over time and administrations.

repeated readings Children reading short passages of text more than once, with different levels of support, to develop rapid, fluent oral reading.

ReQuest Reciprocal questioning; encourages students to ask their own questions about read material.

running records Method for marking miscues of beginning readers while they read. Also, see *reading progress cards.*

schema The technical term used by cognitive psychologists to describe how humans organize and construct meaning.

scope and sequence General plan in basal reading programs for the introduction of skills in sequential or vertical arrangement accompanied by expanding or horizontal conceptual reinforcement.

scrambled stories Stories separated into parts and jumbled; students read the stories and reorder them.

scribbling One of the primary forms of written expression; the fountainhead for writing which occurs from the moment a child grasps and uses a writing tool.

self-correction Important behavior necessary at all levels of learning to read and best developed through delayed teacher correction.

semantic mapping Webbing strategy that shows readers and writers how to organize important information.

shared-book experience Strategy allowing all children in a classroom or small group to actively participate in the reading of a story, usually through the use of a big book with large print and illustrations.

shared reading Teachers and children reading books together, collaborating to construct meaning and enjoy stories.

shared writing Teachers and children collaborating to create a text together, demonstrating some of the important uses of written language and showing children what reading is all about.

sight words Identification strategy that relies on the recognition of a word's contour or shape rather than on linguistic concepts.

skill building Introduction, repetition, and reinforcement of skills at all levels of basal reading programs.

skill maintenance Review of recently acquired skills to form foundation for new learning in basal reading programs.

skills view The basis for the dominant approaches to reading instruction in the twentieth century, where it is assumed that learning to read successfully presumes the acquisition of a finite but sizable number of skills and specific abilities.

sociolinguisitics The exploration of the everyday functions of language and how interaction with others and the environment aid language comprehension and learning.

sorting activities Vocabulary development through categorization activities with groups of words.

stages in the writing process Defined in various ways, these stages include rehearsing, drafting, revising and editing, and publishing.

standardized reading test Formal test of reading ability given according to specific, unvarying directions; usually norm-referenced and machine-scored.

story frames Skeletal paragraphs represented by a sequence of spaces tied together with transition words and connectors signaling lines of thought; frames can emphasize plot summary, setting, character analysis, character comparison, and problem.

story grammar The basic elements that make up a well-developed story, such as plot and setting.

Story Impressions Prereading strategy that helps students anticipate what stories could be about using content fragments to make predictions.

story map An analysis of a story's organizational elements; used to strengthen instructional decisions.

story schema The underlying structure and relationships in a story that act as catalysts for constructing meaning and distinguishing important ideas and events.

storybook experiences Readalouds, readalongs, shared reading, shared writing, rereadings of favorite texts, and independent reading and writing.

strands Areas of skills developed at increasingly higher levels throughout basal reading programs.

structural analysis Means of creating awareness of and interest in multisyllable words where young children compare word lengths and segment sounds.

student schedules Organization of individual student activities in different learning-center areas based on the student's strengths, weaknesses, and interests.

subordinate Concept that is inferior in rank, class, or status.

substitution strategies Inventions, errors, or spoonerisms designed to involve children in using word and phonic knowledge while reading meaningful text.

superordinate Concept that is superior in rank, class, or status.

survey test Broad type of test that measures general performance only.

sustained silent reading (SSR) Structured activity where children are given fixed time periods for reading self-selected materials silently.

syllable A vowel or a cluster of letters containing a vowel and pronounced as a unit.

synonyms Words similar in meaning to other words.

synthetic phonics Uses a building block approach to foster the understanding of sound-symbol relationships and develop phonic knowledge and skill.

teacher's log Observational record of student reading and writing activities and social behaviors organized especially for assessment.

Theoretical Orientation to Reading Profile (TORP) A survey instrument designed by Diane DeFord (1985) that uses three belief systems—phonics, skills, and whole language—to determine teacher beliefs about practices in reading instruction.

think sheets Means of generating responses to questions about texts for discussion purposes.

top-down Models of reading that assume the reading process depends on the prior knowledge and experience of the reader in order to create textual meaning.

trade books Literature and informational books widely available in bookstores; used by teachers to supplement or replace sole dependence on textbooks in reading or content-area instruction.

units of language Categories of written language, ranging from the smallest units, letters, to the largest unit, the whole text selection, that are emphasized for instructional purposes.

uses of oral language Language functions that can and should be adapted to print at the beginning of instruction.

validity How well a test measures what it is designed to measure; most important characteristic of a test.

vocabulary development Introduction and repetition of words for reinforcement in basal reading programs.

vocabulary The breadth and depth of the words we use, recognize, and respond to in meaningful acts of communication.

vocabulary-building skills Allow children to seek clues to word meanings on their own.

vowels All sounds represented by the letters *a, e, i, o, u.*

whole language view The integration of all language arts—reading, writing, speaking, and listening—to create child-responsive environments for learning that are supported by literature-based instruction and curriculum integration.

whole word method Technique where word recognition, rather than letters or syllables, is the main instructional unit.

word banks Boxes of word cards compiled by students that form a natural extension of the language experience approach in which students learn to read words from dictated stories.

word identification Determination of any word in a reader's listening and speaking vocabulary resulting from experience with reading, seeing, discussing, using, and writing words.

word processor Computers add a public quality to writing that encourages sharing and communication, while demonstrating the flexibility and malleability of text, increasing teacher involvement and student independence.

workbooks See *readers/writers' journals.*

writing process Model to describe what writers do as they create texts; writing process activities can be used as a powerful but subtle way to teach reading and extend literary acquisition.

writing workshop Classroom writing time where students are given the structure and direction they need to understand, develop, or use specific writing strategies in planning and revising drafts.

Your Own Questions Self-questioning strategy that helps students set purposes for reading and directs their reading behavior by generating questions and searching the reading situation for answers.

Bibliography

Aaron, R. L., & Anderson, M. K. (1981). A comparison of values expressed in juvenile magazines and basal reader series. *The Reading Teacher, 35,* 305–313.

Adams, M. J. (1990a). *Beginning to read.* Cambridge: MIT Press.

Adams, M. J. (1990b). *Beginning to read: Thinking and learning about print. A summary.* Urbana, IL: University of Illinois, Center for the Study of Reading.

Afflerbach, P. (1993). STAIR: A system for recording and using what we observe and know about our students. *The Reading Teacher, 47*(3), pp. 260–263.

Agnew, A. T. (1982). Using children's dictated stories to assess code consciousness. *The Reading Teacher, 34,* 448–452.

Alfonso, R. (1987). Modules for teaching about young people's literature—Module 6: Informational books. *Journal of Reading, 30,* 682–686.

Allen, R. V. (1976). *Language experiences in communication.* Boston: Houghton Mifflin.

Allington, R. (1977). If they don't read, how they gonna get good? *Journal of Reading, 21,* pp. 57–61.

Allington, R. (1980). Poor readers don't get much in reading groups. *Language Arts,* 57, 872–876.

Allington, R. L. (1983a). Fluency: The neglected reading goal. *The Reading Teacher, 36,* 556–561.

Allington, R. L. (1983b). The reading instruction provided readers of differing reading abilities. *The Elementary School Journal, 83,* 548–559.

Allington, R. L. (1984). Oral reading. In D. D. Pearson (Ed.), *Handbook of reading research* (pp. 829–864). New York: Longman.

Alvermann, D. E. (1991). The discussion web: A graphic aid for learning across the curriculum. *The Reading Teacher, 45,* 2, 92–99.

Ammon, P., Simons, H., & Elster, C. (1990). Effects of controlled, primerese language on the reading process. Technical Report No. 45. Center for the Study of Writing, Berkeley, CA, Center for the Study of Writing, Pittsburgh, PA, ERIC Document Reproduction Service, No. ED 334542.

Anders, P., & Bos, C. (1986). Semantic feature analysis: An interactive strategy for vocabulary development and text comprehension. *Journal of Reading,* 29, 610–616.

Anderson, R. C., & Freebody, P. (1981). Vocabulary knowledge. In J. T. Guthrie (Ed.), *Comprehension and teaching: Research perspectives.* Newark, DE: International Reading Association.

Anderson, R. C., Hiebert, E. H., Scott, J., & Wilkinson, I.A.G. (1985). *Becoming a nation of readers.* Washington, DC: The National Institute of Education.

Anderson, R. C., Higgins, G. D., & Wurster, S. R. (1985). Differences in the free reading books selected by high, average, and low-achievers. *The Reading Teacher, 39,* 326–330.

Angeletti, S. R. (1993). Group writing & publishing: Building community in a second grade classroom. *Language Arts, 70*(6), pp. 494–499.

Argyle, S. B. (1988). *Becoming a teacher of reading: An ecological inquiry.* Ph.D. diss, Kent State University.

Armbruster, B. B., Echols, C., & Brown, A. L. (1982). The role of metacognition in reading to learn: A developmental perspective. *Volta Review, 84,* 45–56.

Armbruster, B. B., & Nagy, W. E. (1992). Vocabulary in content area lessons. *The Reading Teacher, 45*(7), (pp. 550–551).

Artley, A. S. (1975). Words, words, words. *Language Arts, 52,* 1067–1072.

Artley, A. S. (1980). Reading: Skills or competencies? *Language Arts, 57,* 546–549.

Ashton-Warner, S. (1959). *Spinster.* New York: Simon & Schuster.

Ashton-Warner, S. (1963). *Teacher.* New York: Simon & Schuster.

Ashton-Warner, S. (1972). *Spearpoint: Teachers in America.* New York: Knopf.

Atwell, N. (1985). Everyone sits at a big desk: Discovering topics for writing. *English Journal, 74,* 35–39.

Atwell, N. (1987). *In the middle: Writing, reading, and learning with adolescents.* Portsmouth, NH: Boynton/Cook/Heinemann.

Atwell, N. (1993). Forward to *Teachers are researchers.* In Patterson, L., Santa, C., Short, K., & Smith, K. (Eds.). *Teachers are researchers.* Newark, DE: International Reading Association.

Au, K., & Mason, J. (1983). Cultural congruence in classroom participation: Achieving a balance of rights. *Discourse Processes, 6,* 145–167.

Augustine, D. K., Gruber, K. D., & Hanson, L. R. (1989/1990). Cooperation works! *Educational Leadership, 47*(4), 4–7.

Aukerman, R. C. (1981). *The basal reader approach to reading.* New York: Wiley.

Aulls, M. W. (1978). *Developmental and remedial reading in the middle grades.* Boston: Allyn & Bacon.

Aulls, M. W. (1982). *Developing readers in today's elementary school.* Boston: Allyn & Bacon.

Avery, C. (1990). Learning to research/researching to learn. In M. Olson (Ed.), *Opening the door to classroom research.* Newark, DE: International Reading Association.

Baddeley, A. D., & Lewis, V. (1981). Inner active processes in reading: The inner voice, the inner ear, and the inner eye. In C. A. Perfetti & A. M. Lesgold (Eds.), *Interactive processes in reading,* Hillsdale, NJ: Erlbaum Associates.

Bailey, D. (1984). *Influences on beliefs about reading and learning to read and instructional behavior of student teachers.* Ph.D. diss., Kent State University.

Baker, R. (1979). A publisher views the development and selection of reading programs. In T. Hatcher & L. Erickson (Eds.), *Indoctrinate or educate.* Newark, DE: International Reading Association.

Baloche, L., & Platt, T. J., Sprouting magic beans: Exploring Literature Through Creative Questioning & Cooperative Learning. *Language Arts, 70,* pp. 264–271.

Barman, C. R. (1992). An evaluation of the use of a technique designed to assist prospective elementary teachers using the learning cycle with science textbooks. *School Science and Mathematics, 92*(2), pp. 59–63.

Barnitz, J. G. (1980). Black English and other dialects: Sociolinguistic implications for reading instruction. *The Reading Teacher, 33,* 779–786.

Barnitz, J. G. (1982). Orthographies, bilingualism and learning to read English as a second language. *The Reading Teacher, 35,* 560–567.

Barr, R. & Sadow, M. W. (1989). Influence of basal programs on fourth-grade reading instruction. *Reading Research Quarterly, 24,* 44–71.

Barron, R. (1968). The use of vocabulary as an advance organizer. In H. Herber & P. Sanders (Eds.), *Research in reading in the content areas: First report.* Syracuse, NY: Syracuse University Reading and Language Arts Center.

Bean, R., Cooley, W., Eichlenberger, R., Lazar, M., & Zigmond, N. (1991). Inclass or pullout: Effects of setting on the remedial reading program. *Journal of Reading Behavior, 23,* pp. 445–463.

Beck, I., & McKeown, M. G., Research directions social studies texts are hard to understand: Mediating some of the difficulties. *Language Arts, 68*(6), pp. 482–490.

Beck, I. L., & McKeown, M. G. (1983). Learning words well: A program to enhance vocabulary and comprehension. *The Reading Teacher, 36,* 622–625.

Beck, I. L., McKeown, M. G., & McCaslin, E. (1983). All contexts are not created equal. *Elementary School Journal, 83,* 177–181.

Beck, I. L., McKeown, M. G., McCaslin, E., & Burket, A. (1979). *Instructional dimensions that may affect reading comprehension: Examples of two commercial reading programs.* Pittsburgh: University of Pittsburgh Language Research and Development Center.

Beck, I. L., McKeown, M. G., & Omanson, R. (1987). The effects and uses of diverse vocabulary instructional techniques. In M. McKeown & M. Cartis (Eds.), *The Nature of vocabulary acquisition.* Hillsdale, NJ: Erlbaum.

Beck, I. L., Perfetti, C. A., & McKeown, M. G. (1982). Effects of long-term vocabulary instruction on lexical access and reading comprehension. *Journal of Educational Psychology, 74,* 506–521.

Becoming a nation of readers: The report of the commission on reading (1985). Washington, DC: The National Institute of Education.

Benton, M. (1984). The methodology vacuum in teaching literature. *Language Arts, 61,* 265–275.

Berliner, D. C. (1981). Academic learning time and reading achievement. In J. Guthrie (Ed.), *Comprehension and teaching: Research reviews.* Newark, DE: International Reading Association.

Betts, E. A. (1946). *Foundations of reading instruction.* New York: American Book Company.

Beyersdorfer, J. M., & Schauer, D. K. (1989). Semantic analysis to writing: Connecting words, books, and writing. *Journal of Reading, 32,* 500–508.

Bidwell, S. (Sept., 1990). Using drama to increase motivation, comprehension, and fluency. *Journal of Reading, 343*(1), 38–41.

Bissex, G. (1980). *GNYS AT WRK: A child learns to write and read.* Cambridge, MA: Harvard University Press.

Blachowicz, C. L. (1986). Making connections: Alternatives to the vocabulary notebook. *Journal of Reading, 29,* 643–649.

Blanchard, J. S. (1985). *Computer base and reading assessment instruments.* Dubuque, IA: Kendall/Hunt.

Bloom, B. (1956). *Taxonomy of educational objectives: Cognitive domain.* New York: McKay.

Bloomfield, L., & Barnhart, C. (1961). *Let's read.* New York: Holt, Rinehart & Winston.

Blume, J. (1970). *Are you there, God? It's me, Margaret.* New York: Dell.

Bonds, C. W., & Bonds, L. T. (1983). Reading and the gifted student. *Roper Review, 5,* 4–6.

Boothby, P. R. (1980). Creative and critical reading for the gifted. *The Reading Teacher, 33,* 674–676.

Borko, H., Shavelson, R., & Stern, P. (1981). Teacher decisions in the planning of reading instruction. *Reading Research Quarterly, 16,* 450–466.

Bower, B. (1993). *Science News,* Vol. *14*(4), p. 132.

Bradley, J. M., & Talgot, M. R. (1987). Reducing reading anxiety. *Academic Therapy, 22*(4), 349–358.

Brandt, R. (1989/1990). On cooperative learning: A conversation with Spencer Kagan. *Educational Leadership, 47*(4), 8–11.

Bransford, J. D., & Johnson, M. K. (1973). Considerations of some problems of comprehension. In W. C. Chase (Ed.), *Visual information processing.* New York: Academic.

Bredekamp, S. (1987). *Developmentally appropriate practice.* Washington, D.C.: National Association for the Education of Young Children.

Bridge, W., & Haley, S. (1983). Using predictable materials vs. preprimers to teach beginning sight words. *The Reading Teacher, 36,* 884–891.

Bristow, P. S. (1985). Are poor readers passive readers? Some evidence, possible explanations and potential solutions. *The Reading Teacher, 39,* 318–329.

Bromley, K. (1989). Buddy journals make the reading writing connection. *The Reading Teacher, 43,* 122–129.

Brown, A. L. (1985). Metacognition: The development of selective attention strategies for learning from texts. In H. S. Singer & R. B. Ruddell (Eds.), *Theoretical models and processes of reading* (3rd ed.). Newark, DE: International Reading Association.

Brozo, W. G., & Tomlinson, C. M. (1986). Literature: The key to lively content courses. *The Reading Teacher, 40,* 288–293.

Bruckerhoff, C. (1977). What do students say about reading instruction? *The Clearing House,* 51, 103–107.

Brutton, D. (1974). How to develop and maintain student interest in reading. *English Journal,* 63, 74–77.

Bullough, R. V. (1989). *First year teacher: A case study.* New York: Teachers College Press.

Bunting, E. (1989). *The Wednesday surprise.* New York: Clarion Books.

Butler, A. (1988). *Shared book experience.* Crystal Lake, IL: Rigby.

Calkins, L. M. (1983). *Lessons from a child.* Portsmouth, NH: Heinemann Educational Books.

Calkins, L. M. (1986). *The art of teaching writing.* Portsmouth, NH: Heinemann Educational Books.

Cambourne, B. (1984). Language, learning, and literacy. In Butler, A. & Turbill, J. *Towards a reading/writing classroom.* Portsmouth, NH: Heinemann.

Cardarelli, A. F. (1992). Teachers under cover: Promoting the personal reading of teachers. *The Reading Teacher, 45,* 9, 664–669.

Carey, R. (1984). *Selecting a test for the state testing program.* Providence, RI: Rhode Island Department of Education.

Carey, R. (1985). *Program evaluation as ethnographic research.* Providence, RI: Rhode Island Department of Education.

Carr, K. S. (1984). What gifted readers need from reading instruction. *The Reading Teacher, 38,* 144–146.

Cassidy, J. (1979, January). What about the talented reader? *Teacher,* 76–80.

Cassidy, J., & Vukelich, C. (1980). Do the gifted read early? *The Reading Teacher, 33,* 578–582.

Chall, J., Jacobs, E., & Baldwin, L. (1990). *The reading crisis: Why poor children fall behind.* Cambridge, MA: Harvard University Press.

Chall, J., & Curtis, M. (1991). Responding to individual differences among language learners: Children at risk. In J. Flood, J. Jensen, D. Lapp, & J. Squire, (Eds.), *Handbook of research on teaching the English language arts.* NY: Macmillan.

Chan, J. (1979). *Tradebooks: Uses and benefits for content area teaching.* (ERIC Document Reproduction Service No. ED 182 465).

Chaplin, M. T. (1982). No more reading "reading." *Reading World, 21,* 340–346.

Charles, C. M. (1980). *Individualizing instruction* (2nd ed.). St. Louis: C. V. Mosby.

Chenfield, M. (1978). *Teaching language arts creatively.* New York: Harcourt Brace Jovanovich.

Chomsky, C. (1970). Reading, writing, and phonology. *Harvard Educational Review, 40,* 287–309.

Chomsky, C. (1976). After decoding: What? *Language Arts, 53,* 288–296, 314.

Chomsky, C. (1979). Approaching reading through invented spelling. In L. B. Resnick & P. A. Weaver (Eds.), *Theory and practice of early reading,* Vol. 2. Hillsdale, NJ: Erlbaum.

Clark, C., & Yinger, R. (1980). Teacher thinking. In R. Peterson & H. Walberg (Eds.), *Research and teaching: Concepts, findings and implications.* Berkeley, CA: McCutchan.

Clarke, L. K. (1988). Invented versus traditional spelling in first graders' writing: Effects on learning to spell and read. *Research in the Teaching of English, 22,* 281–309.

Clark, M. M. (1976). *Young fluent readers.* London: Heinemann.

Clay, M. M. (1966). *Emergent reading behavior.* Ph.D. diss. University of Auckland, New Zealand.

Clay, M. M. (1979a). *Concepts about print test.* Portsmouth, NH: Heinemann.

Clay, M. M. (1985). *The early detection of reading difficulties: A diagnostic survey with recovery procedures.* Portsmouth, NH: Heinemann.

Clay, M. M. (1979c). *Reading: The patterning of complex behavior* (2nd ed.). Auckland, New Zealand: Heinemann Educational Books.

Clay, M. M. (1979d). *Stones.* Portsmouth, NH: Heinemann.

Clay, M. (1985). *The early detection of reading difficulties: A diagnostic survey with recovery procedures.* Portsmouth, NH: Heinemann.

Clay, M. M. (1988). Exploring with a pencil. *Reading Today, 6,* 20.

Clyde, J. A. and Condon, M. W. F. (1992). Collaborating in coursework and classrooms: An alternative for strengthening whole language teacher preparation cultures. In Weaver, (Ed.), *Supporting Whole Language: Stories of Teacher & Instructional Change.* Portsmouth, NH: Heinemann.

Clymer, T. (1963). The utility of phonic generalizations in the primary grades. *The Reading Teacher, 16,* 252–258.

Cohen, D. (1968). The effect of literature on vocabulary and reading achievement. *Elementary English, 45,* 209–213, 217.

Cole, J. (1983). *Bony-Legs.* New York: Four Winds/ Macmillan.

Collier, V. (1989). How long? A synthesis of research on academic achievement in a second language. *TEOSOL Quarterly, 23,* pp. 509–532.

Connelly, F. M., & Clandinin, D. J. (1988). *Teachers as curriculum planners: Narrative of experience.* New York: Teachers College Press.

Coody, B., and Nelson, D. (1982). *Teaching elementary language arts.* Belmont, CA: Wadsworth.

Cooper, P., & Gray, P. (1984). *Teaching listening as an interactive process.* Paper presented at The International Reading Association Annual Convention, Atlanta, GA.

Crafton, L. (1983). Learning from reading: What happens when students generate their own background knowledge. *Journal of Reading, 26,* 586–593.

Crafton, L. (1991). *Whole language: Getting started . . . Moving forward.* Katonah, NY: Owen Publishers.

Cramer, R. L. (1975). Reading to children: Why and how. *The Reading Teacher, 28,* 460–463.

Cramer, R. L. (1978). *Children's writing and language growth.* Columbus, OH: Merrill.

Criscuolo, N. P. (1977). Book reports: Twelve creative alternatives. *The Reading Teacher, 30,* 893–895.

Criscuolo, N. P. (1979). Twenty-five ways to motivate the reluctant reader. *School and Community, 65,* 13–16.

Criscuolo, N. P. (1981). Creative homework with the newspaper. *The Reading Teacher, 34,* 921–922.

Criscuolo, N. P. (1984). Reaching remedial readers successfully. *Academic Therapy, 19,* 613–617.

Crowley, J. (October, 1991). Joy of big books. *Instructor.*

Crowley, Mary L. (1993). Student mathematics portfolio: More than a display case. *The Mathematics Teacher, 86*(7), pp. 544–546.

Cullinan, B., Jaggar, A., & Strickland, D. (1974). Language expansion for black children in primary grades: A research report. *Young Children, 29,* 98–112.

Cummins, J. (1989). *Empowering minority students.* Sacramento, CA: Association of Bilingual Education.

Cunningham, P. (1975–76). Investigating a synthesized theory of mediated word recognition. *Reading Research Quarterly, 11,* 127–143.

Cunningham, P. (1981). A teacher's guide to materials shopping. *The Reading Teacher, 35,* 180–184.

Cunningham, P. M. (1991). *Phonics they use: Words for reading and writing.* New York: HarperCollins.

Cunningham, R. T. (1971). Developing question-asking skills. In J. Weigand (Ed.), *Developing teacher competencies.* Englewood Cliffs, NJ: Prentice Hall.

Dale, E. (1965). Vocabulary measurement: Techniques and major findings. *Elementary English, 42,* 895–901.

Dale, E. (1969). *Audiovisual methods in teaching* (3rd ed.). New York: Holt, Rinehart & Winston.

Dale, P. S. (1972). *Language development.* Hinsdale, IL: Dryden.

D'Alessandro, M. (1990). Accommodating emotionally handicapped children through a literature-based reading program. *The Reading Teacher,* 44, 288–293.

Daniele, V. A., & Aldersley, S. F. (1988). Implications of time-on-task research for teachers of the hearing impaired. *American Annals of the Deaf, 133,* 208–211.

D'Angelo, K. (1982). Correction behavior: Implications for reading instruction. *The Reading Teacher, 35,* 395–398.

Davis, D. C. (1973). *Playway: Education for reality.* Minneapolis: Winston.

Davis, F. B. (1944). Fundamental factors of comprehension in reading. *Psychometrika, 9,* 185–197.

Davis, S., & Johns, L. (1991). Identifying and challenging gifted readers. *Illinois Reading Council Journal, 19,* pp. 34a–34d.

DeFord, D. E. (1985). Validating the construct of theoretical orientation in reading instruction. *Reading Research Quarterly, 20,* 366–367.

Degler, L. S. (1978). Using the newspaper to develop comprehension skills. *Journal of Reading, 21,* 339–342.

DeHaven, E. P. (1983). *Teaching and learning the language arts* (2nd ed.). Boston: Little, Brown.

Deighton, L. (1970). *Vocabulary development in the classroom.* New York: Teachers College Press.

Delpit, L. (1988). The silenced dialogue: Power and pedagogy and educating other people's children. *Harvard Educational Review, 58,* pp. 280–298.

Dillon, J. T. (1983). *Teaching and the art of questioning.* Bloomington, IN: Phi Delta Kappa Educational Foundation.

Dishaw, M. (1977). *Descriptions of allocated time in content areas for the A-B period* (Beginning Teachers Evaluation Study Tech. Note 4-2a). San Francisco, CA: Far West Regional Laboratory for Educational Research and Development.

Dole, J. A., & Johnson, V. R. (1980). Beyond the textbook: Science literature for young people. *Journal of Reading, 24,* 579–582.

Dole, J. A., & Osborn, J. (1989). *Reading materials: Their selection and use* (Tech. Rpt. No. 457). Urbana, IL: University of Illinois, Center for the Study of Reading. (ERIC Document Reproduction Service No. 305 592).

Dooley, C. (1993). The challenge: Meeting the needs of gifted readers. *The Reading Teacher, 46,* pp. 546–551.

Dowhower, S. (1987). Effects of repeated reading in second grade transitional readers' fluency and comprehension. *Reading Research Quarterly, 22,* 389–406.

Dowhower, S. L. (1989). Repeated reading: Research into practice. *The Reading Teacher, 43,* 502–507.

Downing, J. (1979). *Reading and reasoning.* New York: Springer-Verlag.

Downing, J. (1982). Reading: Skill or skills? *The Reading Teacher, 35,* 534–537.

Downing, J., Ayers, D., & Shaefer, B. (1982). *Linguistic awareness in reading readiness (LARR) test.* Slough, Berks.: NFER-Nelson.

Duin, A., & Graves, M. (1987). Intensive vocabulary instruction as a pre-writing technique. *Reading Research Quarterly, 22,* 311–330.

Dupuis, M. M., & Snyder, S. L. (1983). Develop concepts through vocabulary: A strategy for reading specialists to use with content teachers. *Journal of Reading, 26,* 297–305.

Durkin, D. (1966). *Children who read early.* New York: Teachers College Press.

Durkin, D. (1978–79). What classroom observations reveal about reading comprehension instruction. *Reading Research Quarterly, 14,* 481–538.

Durkin, D. (1980). *Teaching young children to read* (3rd ed.). Boston: Allyn & Bacon.

Durrell, D. D. (1958). Success in first-grade reading. *Journal of Education,* 1–8.

Durrell, D. D. (1963). *Phonograms in primary grade words.* Boston: Boston University.

Edelman, M. W. (1988). Adolescent pregnancy prevention: What can schools do? In Council of Chief State Officers, *Success in students at-risk: Analysis and recommendations of the Council of Chief State Officers.* Orlando, FL: Harcourt Brace Jovanovich.

Edwards, P. (1989). Supporting lower SES mothers' attempts to provide scaffolding for book reading. In Allen, J. B., & Mason, J. M. (Eds.). *Risk-makers, risk-takers, risk-breakers: Reducing risks for young literary learners.* Portsmouth, NH: Heinemann.

Elbow, P. (1973). *Writing without teachers.* New York: Oxford University Press.

Elbow, P. (1981). *Writing with power: Techniques for mastering the writing process.* New York: Oxford University Press.

Eldredge, J. L., & Butterfield, D. (1988). Alternatives to traditional reading instruction. *The Reading Teacher, 40,* 32–37.

Elkind, D. (1989). Developmentally appropriate practice: Philosophical and practical implications. *Phi Delta Kappan, 71*(2), 113–117.

Elkonin, D. B. (1973). Methods of teaching reading: USSR. In J. Downing (Ed.), *Comparative reading: Cross-national studies of behavior and processes in reading and writing.* New York: Macmillan.

Elley, W., & Mangubhai, F. (1983). The impact of reading on second-language learning. *Reading Research Quarterly, 19,* 53–67.

Estes, T. H., & Vaughan, J. L., Jr. (1973). Reading interest and comprehension: Implications. *The Reading Teacher, 27,* 149–152.

Fagan, W. T. (1989). Empowered students; empowered teachers. *The Reading Teacher, 42,* 8, 572–579.

Farnan, Nancy & Kelly, Patricia (1991). Keeping track: Creating assessment portfolios in reading and writing. *Journal of Reading & Writing Disabilities, 7,* pp. 255–269.

Farr, R., & Carey, F. (1986). *Reading: What can be measured?* (2nd ed.). Newark, DE: International Reading Association.

Farr, R., & Roser, N. (1979). *Teaching a child to read.* New York: Harcourt Brace Jovanovich.

Farr, R. (1992). Putting it all together: Solving the reading assessment puzzle. *The Reading Teacher, 46*(1), pp. 26–37.

Fawcett, G. (1990). Literacy vignette: The gift. *The Reading Teacher, 43,* 504.

Feeley, J. (1974). Television and reading in the seventies. Paper presented at the annual meeting of the International Reading Association, New Orleans, LA.

Fielding, L. G., Wilson, P. T., & Anderson, R. C. (1986). A new focus on free reading: The role of trade books in reading instruction. In T. Raphael (Ed.), *The contexts of school-based literacy.* New York: Random House.

Firth, U. (1985). Beneath the surface of developmental dyslexia. In K. E. Patterson, K. C. Marshall & M. Coltheart (Eds.), *Surface dyslexia: Neuropsychological and cognitive studies of phonological reading.* Hillsdale, NJ: Erlbaum.

Fisette, D. (1993). Practical authentic assessment: Good kid watchers know what to teach next! *The California Reader, 26*(4), pp. 4–9.

Fitzgerald, G. G. (1979). Why kids can read the book but not the workbook. *The Reading Teacher, 32,* 930–932.

Fitzgerald, J. (1993). Literacy and students who are learning English as a second language. *The Reading Teacher, 46,* (pp. 638–647).

Flood, J., & Lapp, D. (1989). Reporting reading progress: A comparison portfolio for parents. *The Reading Teacher, 42,* 508–514.

Flood, J. and Lapp, D. (1993). Are there "real" writers living in your classroom? Implementing a writer-centered classroom. *The Reading Teacher, 48*(3), pp. 254–258.

Flood, James, Lapp, Diane, and Nagel, Greta (1993). Assessing student action beyond reflection and response. *Journal of Reading, 36*(5), pp. 420–423.

Fowler, G. L. (1982). Developing comprehension skills in primary students through the use of story frames. *The Reading Teacher, 36,* 176–179.

Fractor, J. S., Woodruff, M. C., Martinez, M. G., & Teale, W. H. (March, 1993). Let's not miss opportunities to promote voluntary reading: Classroom libraries in the elementary school. *The Reading Teacher, 46*(6), 476–484.

Fox, M. (1993). Politics and literature: Chasing the "isms" from children's books. *The Reading Teacher, 46*(8), pp. 654–658.

Frager, A., & Valentour, J. (1984). Beyond book jackets: Creative bulletin boards to encourage reading. *Reading Horizons, 24,* 259–262.

Freeman, D., & Freeman, Y. (1993). Strategies for promoting the primary languages. *The Reading Teacher, 46,* (pp. 551–558).

Fry, E. B. (1968). A readability formula that saves time. *Journal of Reading, 11,* 513–516, 575–578.

Fry, E. B. (1977). Fry's readability graph: Clarifications, validity and extension to level 17. *Journal of Reading, 21,* 242–252.

Fry, E. B. (1980). The new instant word list. *The Reading Teacher, 34,* 284–290.

Fry, E. (1990). A readability formula for short passages. *Journal of Reading, 33*(8), pp. 594–597.

Gadsden, V. (1992). This issue (literacy and the African-American learner: The struggle between access and denial). *Theory Into Practice, 31,* pp. 274–275.

Galda, L., Cullinan, B., & Strickland, D. (1993). *Language, literacy, and the child.* Fort Worth, TX: Harcourt Brace Jovanovich.

Gambrell, L. B. (1985). Dialogue journals: Reading-writing interactions. *The Reading Teacher, 38,* 512–515.

Gans, R. (1963). *Common sense in teaching reading.* New York: Bobbs-Merrill.

Garcia, J., & Florez-Tighe, V. (1986). The portrayal of Blacks, Hispanics, & Native Americans in recent basal series. *Equity & Excellence, 22*(4), pp. 72–76.

Garcia, G., Pearson, P., & Jimenez, R. (1990). *The at-risk dilemma: A synthesis of reading research.* Champaign, IL: Reading Research and Education Center.

Gaskins, I. W., Downer, M. A., Anderson, R. C., Cunningham, P. M., Gaskins, R. W., Schomner, M., & the teachers of Benchmark School. (1988). A metacognitive approach to phonics: Using what you know to decode what you don't know. *Remedial and Special Education, 9,* 36–41.

Gaskins, R. W. (1988). The missing ingredients: Time on task, direct instruction, and writing. *The Reading Teacher, 41,* 750–755.

Gensley, J. (1975). Let's teach the gifted to read. *The Gifted Child Quarterly, 19,* 21–22.

Gentry, J. R., & Henderson, E. H. (1980). Three steps to teaching beginning readers to spell. In E. H. Henderson & J. W. Beers (Eds.), *Developmental aspects of learning to spell: A reflection of word knowledge.* Newark, DE: International Reading Association.

Giff, P. R. (1980). *Today was a terrible day.* New York: Viking.

Gillet, J., & Kita, M. J. (1979). Words, kids and categories. *The Reading Teacher, 32,* 538–542.

Gillet, J., & Temple, C. (1990). *Understanding reading problems* (3rd ed.). Glenview, IL: Scott, Foresman.

Gipe, J. P. (1980). Use of relevant context helps kids learn new word meanings. *The Reading Teacher, 33,* 398–402.

Gonzales, P. C. (1980). What's wrong with the basal reader approach to language development? *The Reading Teacher, 33,* 668–673.

Good, T. (1982). How teachers' expectations affect results. *American Education, 18,* 25–32.

Goodlad, J. (1983). A study of schooling: Some findings and hypotheses. *Phi Delta Kappan, 64,* 465–470.

Goodman, K. S. (1973a). *Miscue analysis: Application to reading instruction.* Urbana, IL: National Council of Teachers of English.

Goodman, K. S. (1973b). Psycholinguistic universals in the reading process. In F. Smith (Ed.), *Psycholinguistics and reading.* New York: Holt, Rinehart & Winston.

Goodman, K. S. (1975). Do you have to be smart to read? Do you have to read to be smart? *The Reading Teacher, 28,* 625–632.

Goodman, K. (1986). *What's whole in whole language?* Portsmouth, NH: Heinemann.

Goodman, K. S. (1986a). Basal readers: A call for action. *Language Arts, 63,* 358–363.

Goodman, K. S. (1986b). *What's whole in whole language?* Ontario: Scholastic-TAB.

Goodman, K. S., & Buck, C. (1973). Dialect barriers to reading comprehension revisited. *The Reading Teacher, 22,* 6–12.

Goodman, Y. M. (1978). Kid-watching: An alternative to testing. *National Elementary Principal, 10,* 41–45.

Goodman, Y. M., & Burke, C. L. (1972). *Reading miscue inventory manual: Procedure for diagnosis and evaluation.* New York: Macmillan.

Gordon, C. J., & Braun, C. (1983). Using story schemata as an aid to reading and writing. *The Reading Teacher, 37,* 116–121.

Gough, P. (1985). One second of reading. In H. Singer and R. Ruddell (Eds.), *Theoretical models and processes of reading* (3rd ed.). Newark, DE: International Reading Association.

Grace, M. (1993). Implementing a portfolio system in your classroom. *Reading Today,* June/July, 1993, p. 27.

Granger, R. C. (1976). The nonstandard speaking child: Myths past and present. *Young Children, 31,* 479–485.

Graves, D. (1975). An examination of the writing processes of seven-year-old children. *Research in the Teaching of English, 91,* 227–241.

Graves, D. (1979). Research update: What children show us about revision. *Language Arts, 56,* 312–319.

Graves, D. (1983). *Writing: Teachers and children at work.* Portsmouth, NH: Heinemann Educational Books.

Graves, M. F. (1985). *A word is a word ... or is it?* New York: Scholastic.

Greenlaw, M. J. (1988). Using informational books to extend the curriculum. *The Reading Teacher,* 18.

Greer, E. A. (1992). Basal assessment systems: "It's not the shoes." *The Reading Teacher, 45*(8), pp. 650–652.

Gruenberg, R. (1948). Poor Mr. Fingle. In *More favorite stories.* New York: Doubleday.

Guilford, J. P. (1956). The structure of intellect. *Psychological Bulletin, 53,* 267–293.

Guthrie, J. T. (1982). Effective teaching practices. *The Reading Teacher, 35,* 766–768.

Gutknect, B. (1991). Mitigating the effects of negative stereotyping of aging and the elderly in primary grade reading instruction. *Reading Improvement, 28*(1), pp. 44–51.

Haggard, M. R. (1986). The vocabulary self-collection strategy: Using student interest and world knowledge to enhance vocabulary growth. *Journal of Reading, 29,* 634–642.

Halliday, M.A.K. (1975). Learning how to mean: Exploration in the development of language. London: Arnold.

Hancock, M. R. (1992). Literature response journals: Insights beyond the printed page. *Language Arts, 69,* 36–42.

Hancock, M. (1993). Exploring and extending personal response through literature journals. *The Reading Teacher, 46*(6), (pp. 466–474).

Hancock, M. R. (1993). Exploring the meaning-making process through the content of literature response journals: A case study investigation. *Research in the Teaching of English, 27,* 4, 335–369.

Hansen, J. (1981). An inferential comprehension strategy for use with primary children. *The Reading Teacher, 34,* 665–669.

Hansen, J. (1987). *When writers read.* Portsmouth, NH: Heinemann.

Harris, A. J. (1980). An overview of reading disabilities and learning disabilities in the U.S. *The Reading Teacher, 33,* 420–425.

Harris, L. A., & Smith, C. B. (1980). *Reading instruction: Diagnostic teaching in the classroom* (3rd ed.). New York: Holt, Rinehart & Winston.

Harris, M. J., Rosenthal, R., & Snodgrass, S. E. (1986). The effects of teacher expectations, gender, and behavior on pupil academic performance and self-concept. *Educational Research, 79,* 173–179.

Harris, V. (1993). Bookalogues: Multicultural literature. *Language Arts, 70*(3), pp. 215–217.

Harste, J. C., & Burke, C. L. (1977). A new hypothesis for reading teacher research. In P. D. Pearson & J. Hansen (Eds.), *Reading: Theory, research and practice.* Clemson, SC: National Reading Conference.

Harste, J. C., Burke, C. L., & Woodward, V. A. (1982). Children's language and world: Initial encounters with print. In J. Langer & M. Smith-Burke (Eds.), *Bridging the gap: Reader meets author.* Newark, DE: International Reading Association.

Harste, J. C., Short, K. G., & Burke, C. (1988). *Creating classrooms for authors: The reading-writing connection.* Portsmouth, NH: Heinemann.

Harste, J. C., Woodward, V. A., & Burke, C. L. (1984). *Language stories and literacy lessons.* Portsmouth, NH: Heinemann.

Heath, S. (1982). What no bedtime story means; Narrative skills at home and at school. *Language and Society, 11,* 49–77.

Heath, S., (1991). The sense of being literate: Historical and crosscultural features. In R. Barr, M. Kamil, P. Mosenthal, & P. Pearson (Eds.), *Handbook of Reading Research, 2,* pp. 3–25. NY: Longman.

Heath, S., & Mangiola. (1991). *Children of promise: Literate activity in linguistically and culturally diverse classrooms.* Washington, DC: NEA.

Heathington, B. S., & Alexander, J. E. (1984). Do classroom teachers emphasize attitudes toward reading? *The Reading Teacher, 37,* 484–488.

Heilman, A. W. (1977). *Phonics in proper perspective* (3rd ed.). Columbus, OH: Merrill.

Heilman, A. W., Blair, T. R., & Rupley, W. H. (1986). *Principles and practices of teaching reading.* (6th ed.). Columbus, OH: Merrill.

Heimberger, M. J. (1980). *Teaching the gifted and talented in the elementary classroom.* Washington, DC: National Education Association.

Heinly, B. F., & Hilton, K. (1982). Using historical fiction to enrich social studies courses. *The Social Studies, 73,* 21–24.

Henderson, E. H., & Beers, J. W. (Eds.) (1980). *Developmental and cognitive aspects of learning to spell: A reflection of word knowledge.* Newark, DE: International Reading Association.

Henk, W. A. (1985). Assessing children's reading abilities. In L. W. Searfoss & J. E. Readence (Eds.), *Helping children learn to read.* Englewood Cliffs, NJ: Prentice Hall.

Henning, K. (1974). Drama reading: An on-going classroom activity at the elementary school level. *Elementary English, 51,* 48–51.

Henry, G. (1974). *Teaching reading as concept development.* Newark, DE: International Reading Association.

Hepler, S. I. (1982). Patterns of response to literature: A one-year study of a fifth- and sixth-grade classroom. Ph.D. diss., Ohio State University.

Hepler, S. I., & Hickman, J. (1982). The book was okay. I love you—Social aspects of response to literature. *Theory into Practice, 21,* 278–283.

Herber, H. L. (1978). *Teaching reading in content areas* (2nd ed.). Englewood Cliffs, NJ: Prentice Hall.

Herman, P. A. (1985). The effect of repeated readings on reading rate, speech, and word recognition. *Reading Research Quarterly, 20*(5), 553–565.

Herrmann, B. A. (1988). Two approaches for helping poor readers become more strategic. *The Reading Teacher, 42,* 24–28.

Hess, M. L. (1991). Understanding non-fiction: Purpose classification response. *Language Arts, 68*(7), pp. 228–232.

Heymsfeld, C. R. (1989). Point/counterpoints: The value of basal readers. *Reading Today, 7*(1), pp. 1, 18.

Hibert, S. B. (1993). Sustained silent reading revisited. *The Reading Teacher, 46*(4), Dec. '92/Jan. '93, (pp. 354–356).

Hickman, J. (1983). Classrooms that help children like books. In N. Roser & M. Frith (Eds.), *Children's choices.* Newark, DE: International Reading Association.

Hiebert, E. H. (1983). An examination of ability grouping for reading instruction. *Reading Research Quarterly, 18,* 231–255.

Hitchcock, M. E., & Tompkins, G. E. (1987). Basal readers: Are they still sexist? *The Reading Teacher, 41,* 288–292.

Hittleman, D. (1973). Seeking a psycholinguistic definition of readability. *The Reading Teacher, 26,* 783–789.

Hoffman, J. V. (1985). *The oral recitation lesson: A teacher's guide.* Austin, TX: Academic Resource Consultants.

Hoffman, J. V., Rosen, N. L., & Battle, J. (1993). Reading aloud in classrooms: From the modal to a "model." *The Reading Teacher, 46*(6), 496–503.

Holdaway, D. (1979). *The foundations of literacy.* Portsmouth, NH: Heinemann Educational Books.

Holdaway, D. (1980). *Independence in reading* (2nd ed.). Sydney: Ashton-Scholastic.

Holdaway, D. (1982). Shared book experience: Teaching reading using favorite books. *Theory into Practice, 23,* 293–300.

Hong, L. K. (1981). Modifying SSR for beginning readers. *The Reading Teacher, 34,* 888–891.

Hood, W. (1989). Whole language: A grassroots movement catches on. *Learning, 17,* 60–62.

Hopper, G. (1977). Parental understanding of their child's test results as interpreted by elementary school teachers. *Measurement and Evaluation in Guidance, 10,* 84–89.

Hornbeck, D. W. (1988). Introduction. In Council of Chief School Officers, *School success for students at-risk: Analysis and recommendations of Council of Chief School Officers.* Orlando, FL: Harcourt Brace Jovanovich.

Hornsby, D., Sukarna, D., & Parry, J. (1986). *Read on: A conference approach to reading.* Portsmouth, NH: Heinemann.

Hoskisson, K. (1975). The many facets of assisted reading. *Elementary English, 52,* 312–315.

Hough, R. A., Nurss, J. R., & Enright, D. S. (1986). Story reading with limited English speaking children in the regular classroom. *The Reading Teacher, 39,* 510–514.

Huck, C. S., Hepler, S., & Hickman, J. (1987). *Children's literature in the elementary school* (4th ed.). New York: Holt, Rinehart & Winston.

Hudelson, S. (1989). Teaching English through content area activities. In J. Flood, J. Jensen, D. Lapp, & J. Square (Eds.), *Handbook of research on teaching the English language arts.* NY: Macmillan.

Hunt, L. C. (1970). Effect of self-selection, interest, and motivation upon independent, instructional, and frustrational levels. *The Reading Teacher, 24,* 146–151.

Huttar, E. (October, 1991). Do-it-yourself big books. *Instructor.*

Hymes, D. (1974). *Foundations in sociolinguistics: An ethnographic approach.* Philadelphia: University of Pennsylvania Press.

Hymes, J. L. (1958). *Before the child reads.* Evanston, IL: Row, Peterson.

Ignoffo, M. (1980). The thread of thought: Analogies as a vocabulary building method. *Journal of Reading, 23,* 519–521.

Irwin, J. W., & Davis, C. A. (1980). Assessing readability: The checklist approach. *Journal of Reading, 24,* 124–130.

Isakson, M. B., & Boaty, R. M. (1993). Hard questions about teaching research. In Patterson, L., Santa, C., Short, K., & Smith, K. (Eds.). *Teachers are researchers.* Newark, DE: International Reading Association.

Jachym, N. (1992). Task characteristics of first grade reading workbooks. *Reading Improvement, 29*(2), pp. 110–119.

Jacobson, M. L., & Freeman, E. B. (1981). A comparison of language use in basal readers and adolescent novels. *Reading World, 21,* 50–58.

Jaramillo, M. L. (1973). Cultural differences in the ESOL classroom. *TESOL Quarterly, 7,* 51–60.

Johns, J. L. (1985). *Basic reading inventory.* (3rd ed.). Dubuque, IA: Kendall-Hunt.

Johnson, B., & Lehnert, L. (1984). Learning phonics naturally: A model for instruction. *Reading Horizons, 24,* 90–98.

Johnson, D., & Pearson, P. D. (1984). *Teaching reading vocabulary* (2nd ed.). New York: Holt, Rinehart & Winston.

Johnson, D. W., & Johnson, R. T. (1989/1990). Social skills for successful group work. *Educational Leadership, 47*(4), 29–33.

Johnson, T. D., & Louis, D. R. (1987). *Literacy through literature.* Portsmouth, NH: Heinemann.

Johnston, P. (1983). *Reading comprehension assessment: A cognitive basis.* Newark, DE: International Reading Association.

Johnston, P. (1987). Teachers as evaluation experts. *The Reading Teacher, 40,* 744–748.

Johnston, P. H. (1992). *Constructive Evaluation of Literate Activity.* New York: Longmann.

Jongsma, K. S. (1990). Collaborative learning. *The Reading Teacher, 43,* 346–347.

Judy, J. E., Alexander, P. A., Kulikowich, J. M., & Willson, V. L. (1988). Effects of two instructional approaches and peer tutoring on gifted and non-gifted sixth-grade students' analogy performance. *Reading Research Quarterly, 23,* 236–256.

Judy, S., & Judy, S. (1980). *The gifts of writing.* New York: Scribners.

Juel, C. (1988). Learning to read and write: A longitudinal study of fifty-four children from first through fourth grade. *Journal of Educational Psychology, 80,* 437–447.

Juel, C., & Roper-Schneider, D. (1985). The influence of basal readers on first grade reading. *Reading Research Quarterly, 20,* 134–152.

Kagan, S. (1989). *Cooperative learning: Resources for teachers.* San Juan Capistrano, CA: Resources for Teachers.

Kagan, S. (1989/1990). The structural approach to cooperative learning. *Educational Leadership, 47*(4), 12–15.

Kamii, C. (1991). What is constructivism? In Kamii, C., Manning, M., & Manning, G. (Eds.). *Early literacy: A constructivist foundation for whole language.* Washington, DC: National Education Association.

Kamil, M. L., & Pearson, P. D. (1979). Theory and practice in teaching reading. *New York University Education Quarterly,* 10–16.

Kameenui, E. (1993). A special issue on innovations in literacy for a diverse society. *The Reading Teacher, 46,* p. 539.

Kameenui, E. (1993). Diverse learners and the tyranny of time: Don't fix blame; fix the leaky roof. *The Reading Teacher, 46,* (pp. 376–383).

Keegan, B., & Shrake, K. (April, 1991). Literature study groups: An alternative to ability grouping. *The Reading Teacher, 44*(8), (pp. 542–547).

King, D., & Anderson, C. (1980). *America: Past and present.* Boston: Houghton Mifflin.

King, M. (1908). *Language exercises.* New York: Schuster & Sons.

Kirby, D., Latta, D., & Vinz, R. (1988). Beyond interior decorating: Using writing to make meaning in the elementary school. *Phi Delta Kappan, 69,* 10, 718–724.

Kirby D., & Liner, T. (1981). *Inside out: Developmental strategies for teaching writing.* Montclair, NJ: Boynton/Cook.

Kirk, S. A., Kliebhan, J. M., & Lerner, J. W. (1978). *Teaching reading to slow and disabled learners.* Boston: Houghton Mifflin.

Klein, M. L. (1985). *The development of writing in children: Pre-K through grade 8.* Englewood Cliffs, NJ: Prentice Hall.

Kohl, H. (1969). *The open classroom: Teaching in elementary schools.* West Nyack, NY: Parker.

Koskinen, P., & Blum, I. (1986). Paired repeated reading: A classroom strategy for developing fluent reading. *The Reading Teacher, 40,* 70–75.

Kramer, C. J. (1989). Do children accept literature in the reading class? *The Reading Teacher, 42,* 343–344.

Kraus, C. (1983). The influence of first-grade teachers' conceptual frameworks of reading on their students' perceptions of reading and reading behavior. Ph.D. diss., Kent State University.

Kraus, R. (1971). *Leo the late bloomer.* New York: Windmill Books.

Labbo, L., & Teale, W. (1990). Cross-age reading: A strategy for helping poor readers. *The Reading Teacher, 43,* 362–369.

Laberge, D., & Samuels, S. J. (1976). Toward a theory of automatic information processing in reading. In H. Singer & R. Ruddell (Eds.), *Theoretical models and processes of reading* (2nd ed.). Newark, DE: International Reading Association.

Labov, W. (1970). *The study of nonstandard English.* Urbana, IL: National Council of Teachers of English.

Labov, W. (1985). The study of nonstandard English. In V. Clark, P. Escholz, & A. Rosa (Eds.), *Language,* (4th ed.). NY: St. Martin's Press.

Labuda, M., & James, H. J. (1985). Fostering creativity in children who differ. In M. Labuda (Ed.), *Creative reading for gifted learners* (2nd ed.). Newark, DE: International Reading Association.

Ladson-Billings, G. (1992). Reading between the lines and beyond the pages: A culturally relevant approach to literacy teaching. *Theory Into Practice, 28*(4), pp. 312–320.

Lamme, L. L. (1984). *Growing up writing.* Washington, DC: Acropolis.

Larrick, N. (1987). Illiteracy starts too soon. *Phi Delta Kappan, 69,* 184–189.

Larrick, N. (1991). Give us books! . . . But also . . . give us wings! *The New Advocate, 4*(2), pp. 77–83.

Lass, B. (1982). Portrait of my son as an early reader. *The Reading Teacher, 36,* 20–29.

Lass, B. (1983). Portrait of my son as an early reader II. *The Reading Teacher, 36,* 508–517.

Lauritzen, C. (1982). A modification of repeated readings for group instruction. *The Reading Teacher, 35,* 456–458.

Leinhardt, G., Zigmond, N., & Cooley, W. W. (1981). Reading instruction and its effects. *American Educational Research Journal, 18,* 343–361.

Levine, S. G. (1984). USSR: A necessary component in teaching reading. *Journal of Reading, 27,* 394–400.

Lewis, Cynthia (1993). "Give people a chance:" Acknowledging social differences in reading. *Language Arts, 10*(6), pp. 454–461.

Liberman, I. Y., Shankweiler, D., Fisher, F. W., & Carter, B. (1974). Explicit syllable and phoneme segmentation in the young child. *The Journal of Experimental Child Psychology, 18,* 201–212.

Liberman, I. Y., Shankweiler, D., Liberman, A., Fowler, C., & Fischer, F. (1977). Phonetic segmentation and recoding in the beginning reader. In A. Reber & D. Scarborough (Eds.), *Toward a psychology of reading.* Hillsdale, NJ: Erlbaum.

Lindemann, E. (1982). *A rhetoric for writing teachers.* New York: Oxford University Press.

Macchiarola, F. (1988). Values, standards and climate in schools serving students at risk. *School success for students at risk: Analysis and recommendations of the Council of Chief State School Offices.* Orlando, FL: Harcourt Brace Jovanovich.

Maeroff, G. T. (1989). *The school-smart parent.* New York: Times Books.

Mandler, J., and Johnson, N. (1977). Remembrance of things parsed: Story structure and recall. *Cognitive Psychology, 9,* 111–151.

Mangieri, J. M. (1980). Characteristics of an effectively organized classroom. In D. Lapp (Ed.), *Making reading possible through effective classroom management.* Newark, DE: International Reading Association.

Mann, A. (1979). *The one and the many: Reflections on American identify.* Chicago: University of Chicago Press.

Manna, A. L., & Misheff, S. (1987). What teachers say about their own reading development. *Journal of Reading, 31,* 160–169.

Manzo, A. V. (1969). The request procedure. *Journal of Reading, 11,* 123–126.

Manzo, A. V., & Shirk, J. K. (1972). Some generalizations and strategies for guiding vocabulary learning. *Journal of Reading Behavior, 4,* 78–89.

Marchbanks, G., & Levin, H. (1965). Cues by which children recognize words. *Journal of Educational Psychology, 56,* 57–61.

Maring, G. H., Furman, G. C., & Blum-Anderson, J. (1985). Five cooperative learning strategies for mainstreamed youngsters in content area classrooms. *The Reading Teacher, 39,* 310–313.

Mashler, C., & Smallengury, H. (1963). Effects of testing programs on the attitudes of students, teachers, parents, and the community. In N. H. Henry & H. G. Richey (Eds.), *The Impact and Improvement of School Testing Programs, Part 2: 62nd Yearbook of the National Society for the Study of Education.* Chicago: University of Chicago Press.

Mason, G. E., Blanchard, J. S., & Daniel, D. B. (1983). *Computer applications in reading* (2nd ed.). Newark, DE: International Reading Association.

McAllon, N. (1992/1993). Our role in mainstreaming. *The Reading Teacher, 36,* (pp. 328–329).

McCanley, J. D., & McCanley, P. S. (March, 1992). Using choral reading to promote language learning for ESL students. *The Reading Teacher, 45*(7), (pp. 526–533).

McCaslin, N. (1990). *Creative drama in the classroom* (5th ed.). White Plains, NY: Longman.

McClellan, M. C. (1988). Testing and reform. *Phi Delta Kappan, 69,* 768–771.

McCracken, R. A. (1971). Initiating sustained silent reading. *Journal of Reading, 14,* 521–524, 582–583.

McCracken, R. A., & McCracken, M. J. (1978). Modeling is the key to sustained reading. *The Reading Teacher, 31,* 406–408.

McDonald, F. J. (1965). *Educational psychology.* Belmont, CA: Wadsworth.

McDonnell, G. M., & Osburn, E. B. (1978). New thoughts about reading readiness. *Language Arts, 55,* 26–29.

McGee, L. M., & Richgels, D. J. (1990). *Literacy beginnings: Supporting young readers and writers.* Boston: Allyn & Bacon.

McGinley, W. J., & Denner, P. R. (1987). Story impressions: A pre-reading/writing activity. *Journal of Reading, 31,* 3, 248–253.

McLeod, B. (1976). The relevance of anthropology to language teaching. *TESOL Quarterly, 10,* 211–219.

McNaughton, S. (1981). Low progress readers and teacher instructional behavior during oral reading: The risk of maintaining instructional dependence. *The Exceptional Child, 28,* 167–176.

McNeil, J. D. (1974). False prerequisites in the teaching of reading. *Journal of Reading Behavior, 6,* 421–427.

McTighe, J., & Lyman, F. T. (1988). Cueing thinking in the classroom: The promise of theory-embedded tools. *Educational Leadership, 45,* 7, 18–24.

Meyer, L. A., Greer, E. A., & Crummey, L. (1987). An analysis of decoding, comprehension, and story text comprehensibility in four first-grade reading programs. *Journal of Reading Behavior, 19,* 69–98.

Meyers, J. (1989). Making invitations that encourage active learning. *Journal of Reading, 32,* 562–565.

Mezynski, K. (1983). Issues concerning the acquisition of knowledge: Effects of vocabulary training on reading comprehension. *Review of Educational Research, 53,* 258–279.

Miccinati, J. L. (1985). Using prosodic cues to teach oral reading fluency. *The Reading Teacher, 39,* 206–212.

Mickelson, N. (1989). Point/counterpoint: The value of basal readers. *Reading Today, 7*(1), pp. 1, 18.

Milliken, M. (1992). A fifth grade class uses portfolios. (See Graves/Sunskin below). (pp. 33–44).

Moffett, J. (1975). An interview with James Moffett. *Media and Methods, 15,* 20–24.

Moller, B. (1984). An instructional model for gifted advanced readers. *Journal of Reading, 27,* 324–327.

Moorehead, M. (1990). Leslie Anne learns to read. *The Reading Teacher, 44,* 4, 332.

Morphett, M. V., & Washburne, C. (1931). When should children begin to read? *Elementary School Journal, 31,* 496–503.

Morris, D., & Perney, J. (1984). Developmental spelling as a predictor of first-grade reading achievement. *The Elementary School Journal, 84,* 441–457.

Morrow, L. M. (1982). Relationships between literature programs, library corner designs and children's use of literature. *Journal of Educational Research, 75,* 339–344.

Morrow, L. M. (1985). *Promoting voluntary reading in school and home* (Fastback 225). Bloomington, IN: Phi Delta Kappa Educational Foundation.

Morrow, Lesley M., & Sharkey, Evelyn A. (1993). Motivating independent reading and writing in the primary grades through social cooperative literacy experience. *The Reading Teacher, 47*(2), pp. 402–464.

Morrow, L. M., & Weinstein, C. S. (1982). Increasing children's use of literature through program and physical design changes. *Elementary School Journal, 83,* 131–137.

Moskowitz, B. (1985). The Acquisition of language. In V. Clark, P. Escholz, & A. Rosa (Eds.), *Language,* (4th ed.). NY: St. Martin's Press.

Mossburg, J. (1982). First-grade teachers love their reading workbooks. *The Reading Teacher, 35,* 842–843.

Munsch, R. (1985). *Thomas' snowsuit.* Toronto: Annick Press Ltd.

Munsch, R. (1989). *Love you forever.* Toronto: Firefly Books.

Murphy, H. A. (1957). The spontaneous speaking vocabulary of children in primary grades. *Journal of Education, 146,* 1–105.

Nagy, W. (1988/1989). *Teaching vocabulary to improve reading comprehension.* Urbana, IL: National Council of Teachers of English.

Neckerman, K. M., & Wilson, W. J. (1988). Schools and poor communities. In Council of Chief School Officers, *School success for students at risk: Analysis and recommendations of the Council of Chief State Officers.* Orlando, FL: Harcourt Brace Jovanovich.

Neisser, U. (1976). *Cognition and reality: Principles and implications of cognitive psychology.* San Francisco: Freeman.

Nelson, J. (1978). Readability: Some cautions for the content area teacher. *Journal of Reading, 21,* 620–625.

Neuman, S. B. (1982). Television viewing and leisure reading: A qualitative analysis. *Journal of Educational Research, 75,* 299–304.

Neuman, S. B. (1988). The displacement effect: Assessing the relation between television viewing and reading performance. *Reading Research Quarterly, 23,* 414–440.

Neuman, S. B., & Roskos, K. (1990). Play, print, and purpose: Enriching play environments for literacy development. *The Reading Teacher, 44,* 214–221.

Nolte, R. Y., & Singer, H. (1985). Active comprehension: Teaching a process of reading comprehension and its effects on reading achievement. *The Reading Teacher, 39,* 24–28.

Norton, D. E. (1980). *The effective teaching of language arts.* Columbus, OH: Merrill.

Ogbu, J. (1992). Adaptation to minority status and impact on school success. *Theory Into Practice, 31,* pp. 287–295.

Ogle, D. M. (1986). K-W-L: A teaching model that develops active reading of expository text. *The Reading Teacher, 39,* 564–571.

Ohnmacht, D. C. (1969, April). The effects of letter knowledge on achievement in reading in the first grade. Paper presented at the annual meeting of the American Education Research Association, Los Angeles.

Olson, L. (1985, January 11). Programs for the gifted fragmented, inadequate, study says. *Education Week, 4,* 5.

Osborn, J. (1984). *Evaluating workbooks.* Reading Education Report No. 52. Urbana, IL: University of Illinois Center for the Study of Reading.

Owens, R. E. (1988). *Language development,* 2nd Edition. Columbus, OH: Merrill.

Padak, N. D. (1981). The language and educational needs of children who speak Black English. *The Reading Teacher, 35,* 144–151.

Palincsar, A., & Brown, A. L. (1984). Reciprocal teaching of comprehension-fostering and comprehension-monitoring activities. *Cognition and Instruction, 1,* 117–175.

Patterson, L., Santa, C., Short, K., & Smith, K. (Eds.) (1993). *Teachers are researchers.* Newark, DE: International Reading Association.

Pearson, P. D. (1982). *Asking questions about stories.* Needham, MA: Ginn.

Pearson, P. D. (1984). Guided reading: A response to Isabel Beck. In R. C. Anderson, J. Osborn, & R. Tierney (Eds.), *Learning to read in american schools: Basal readers and content texts.* Hillsdale, NJ: Lawrence Erlbaum Associates.

Pearson, P. D. (1993). Teaching & learning reading: A research perspective. *Language Arts, 70*(6), pp. 502–511.

Pearson, P. D., & Gallagher, M. (1983). The instruction of reading comprehension. *Contemporary Educational Psychology, 8,* 317–344.

Pearson, P. D., & Johnson, D. (1978). *Teaching reading comprehension.* New York: Holt, Rinehart & Winston.

Peck, J. (1989). Using storytelling to promote language and literacy development. *The Reading Teacher, 43,* 138–141.

Pelgrom, E. (1980). *The winter when time was frozen.* New York: Morrow.

Perfetti, C. A., & McCutcheon, P. (1982). Speech processes in reading. In N. Lass (Ed.), *Speech and language: Advances in basic research and practice.* New York: Academic Press.

Peters, C. W., & Wixson, K. (1989). Smart new reading tests are coming. *Learning, 17,* 42–44, 53.

Peterson, P. (1979). Direct instruction: Effective for what and for whom? *Educational Leadership, 36,* 46–48.

Piaget, J. (1973). *The language and thought of the child.* New York: World.

Pieronek, F. T. (1980). Do basal readers reflect the interests of intermediate students? *The Reading Teacher, 33,* 408–412.

Pikulski, J. (1989). Questions and answers. *The Reading Teacher, 7,* 533.

Pils, L. (1993). I love you, miss piss. *The Reading Teacher, 468,* 648–653.

Pinnell, G., Fried, M., & Estice, R. (1990). Reading recovery: Learning how to make a difference. *The Reading Teacher, 43,* (pp. 282–295).

Protheroe, D. (1979). Gi-Go: The content of content area reading. In R. T. Vacca & J. A. Meagher (Eds.), *Reading through content.* Storrs, CT: University Publications and the University of Connecticut Reading-Language Arts Center.

Raphael, T. E. (1982). Question-answering strategies for children. *The Reading Teacher, 36,* 186–191.

Raphael, T. E. (1986). Teaching question-answer relationships, revisited. *The Reading Teacher, 39,* 516–622.

Rasinski, T. V. (1989). Fluency for everyone: Incorporating fluency instruction in the classroom. *The Reading Teacher, 43*(9), 690–693.

Rasinski, T. V., & Fredericks, A. D. (1991). The Akron Paired reading project. *The Reading Teacher, 44*(7), (pp. 514–515).

Ravitch, D. (1993). Launching A Revolution in Standards & Assessments. *Phi Delta Kappan, 74*(10), pp. 767–772.

Read, C. (1971). Preschool children's knowledge of English phonology. *Harvard Educational Review, 41,* 1–34.

Read, C. (1975). *Children's categorization of speech sounds in English.* Urbana, IL: National Council of Teachers of English.

Reed, M. (1989). Teachers using picture books. In J. Hickman & B. Cullinan (Eds.), *Children's classroom: Weaving Charlotte's web* (pp. 89–98). Needham Heights, MA: Christopher-Gordon.

Reid, D., Hresko, W., & Hammill, D. (1981). *Test of early reading ability.* Chicago: Stoelting.

Reid, J. F. (1966). Learning to think about reading. *Educational Research, 9,* 56–62.

Reimer, K. M. (1992). Multiethnic literature: Holding fast to dreams. Technical Report No. 551. Champaign, IL: Reading Research and Educational Center, ERIC Document Reproduction Service, No. ED 343128.

Rentzel, D. R., & Cooter, R. B. (April, 1991). Organizing for effective instruction: The reading workshop. *The Reading Teacher, 44*(8), (pp. 548–554).

Reutzel, D. R. (1989). Point/counterpoint: The value of basal readers. *Reading Today, 7*(1), pp. 1, 18.

Reutzel, D. R., & Cooter, R. B. (1992). Teaching children to read: From basals to books. NY: Macmillan.

Reutzel, D. R., & Hollingsworth, P. M. (1991). Reading time in school: Effect on fourth graders' performance on a criterion-referenced comprehension test. *Journal of Educational Research, 84*(3), pp. 170–176.

Reyhner, J. (1986). Native Americans in basal reading textbooks: Are there enough? *Journal of American Indian Education, 26*(1), pp. 14–22.

Rhodes, L. K. (1981). I can read! Predictable books as resources for reading and writing instruction. *The Reading Teacher, 34,* 314–318.

Rhodes, L. and Shanklin, N. (1993). *Windows into literacy: Assessing learners K-8.* Portsmouth, NH: Heinemann.

Rigg, P. (1989). Language experience approach: Reading naturally. In P. Rigg, & V. Allen (Eds.), *When they don't all speak English: Integrating the ESL student into the regular classroom.* Urbana, IL: NCTE.

Roberts, P. (1985). Speech communities. In V. Clark, P. Escholz, & A. Rosa (Eds.), *Language* (4th ed.). NY: St. Martin's Press.

Rogers, W. C. (1986). *Congruency of theoretical orientation and practice and its relationship to spheres of influence on reading instruction.* Ph.D. diss. Kent State University.

Romance, N. R. & Vitale, M. R. (1992). A curriculum strategy that expands time for in-depth elementary science instruction by using science-based reading strategies: Effects of a year-long study in grade 4. *Journal of Reading in Science Teaching, 29*(6), pp. 545–554.

Rosaen, C. L. with Hazelwood, C. (1993). Creating a writing community: Revising collaborative goals, roles, and actions. Elementary Subjects Center Series No. 85. East Lansing, MI: Institute for Research on Teaching. ERIC Document Reproduction Service ED 355 521.

Rose, K. (1982). *Teaching language arts to children.* New York: Harcourt Brace Jovanovich.

Rosenblatt, L. (1982). The literary transaction: Evocation and response. *Theory into Practice, 21,* 268–277.

Rosenfield, P., Lambert, N. M., & Black, A. (1985). Desk arrangement effects on pupil classroom behavior. *Journal of Educational Psychology, 77,* 101–108.

Rosenshine, B., & Stevens, R. (1984). Classroom instruction in reading. In P. D. Pearson, R. Barr, M. L. Kamie, & P. Mosenthal (Eds.), *Handbook of reading research* (pp. 745–799). New York: Longman.

Roser, N., Hoffman, J. V., & Farest, C. (1990). Language, literacy, and at-risk children. *The Reading Teacher, 43,* 8, 554–559.

Roskos, K. (1986). *The nature of literate behavior in the pretend play episodes of four and five year old children.* Ph.D. diss. Kent State University.

Roskos, K. (1988). Literacy at work in play. *The Reading Teacher, 41,* 562–566.

Rosow, L. (1992). The story of Irma. *The Reading Teacher, 45,* 7, 525.

Routman, R. (1988). *Transitions: From literature to literacy.* Portsmouth, NH: Heinemann.

Routman, R. (1991). *Invitations.* Portsmouth, NH: Heinemann.

Rudman, M. K. (1976). *Children's literature: An issues approach.* Lexington, MA: Heath.

Rumelhart, D. E. (1982). Schemata: The building blocks of cognition. In J. Guthrie (Ed.), *Comprehension and teaching: Research reviews.* Newark, DE: International Reading Association.

Rupley, W. H., Garcia, J., & Longnion, B. (1981). Sex role portrayal in reading materials: Implications for the 1980s. *The Reading Teacher, 34,* 786–791.

Samuels, S. J. (1972). The effect of letter-name knowledge on learning to read. *American Educational Research Journal, 1,* 65–74.

Samuels, S. J. (1976). Hierarchical subskills in the reading acquisition process. In J. T. Guthrie (Ed.), *Aspects of reading acquisition.* Baltimore, MD: Johns Hopkins University Press.

Samuels, S. J. (1979). Method of repeated readings. *The Reading Teacher, 32,* 403–408.

Samuels, S. J. (1981). Characteristics of exemplary reading programs. In J. Guthrie (Ed.), *Comprehension and teaching: Research reviews.* Newark, DE: International Reading Association.

Samuels, S. J. (1986). Word Recognition. In H. Singer & R. Ruddell (Eds.), *Theoretical models and processes of reading* (3rd ed.). Newark, DE: International Reading Association.

Samuels, S. J. (1988). Decoding and automaticity. *The Reading Teacher, 41,* 756–760.

Santa, C. M., Dailey, S. C., & Nelson, M. (1985). Free response and opinion proof: A reading and writing strategy for middle grade and secondary teachers. *Journal of Reading, 28,* 346–352.

Schickendanz, J. A. (1986). *More than the ABC's.* Washington, DC: National Association for the Education of Young Children.

Schmidt, (1993).

Schramm, W., Lyle, J., & Parker, E. (1961). *Television in the lives of our children.* Stanford, CA: Stanford University Press.

Schreiber, P. (1980). On the acquisition of reading fluency. *Journal of Reading Behavior, 12,* 177–186.

Schwartz, R. M. (1988). Learning to learn: Vocabulary in content area textbooks. *Journal of Reading, 32,* 108–117.

Schwartz, R. M., & Raphael, T. E. (1985). Concept of definition: A key to improving students' vocabulary. *The Reading Teacher, 39,* 198–204.

Searcy, B. (1988). Getting children into the literacy club—and keeping them there. *Childhood Education, 65,* 74–77.

Sewell, G. T. (1987). *American history textbooks: An assessment of quality.* New York: Educational Excellence Network, Teachers College, Columbia University.

Shake, M. (1985). *The congruence between instructional philosophies and practices: A study of teacher thinking.* Paper presented at the International Reading Association Annual Convention, New Orleans, LA.

Shake, M. (1988). Teacher questioning: Is there an answer? *Reading Research and Instruction, 27*(2), 29–39.

Shanahan, T. (1988). The reading-writing relationship: Seven instructional principles. *The Reading Teacher, 41,* 636–647.

Shanahan, T. (1990). *Reading and writing together. New perspectives for the classroom.* Norwood, MA: Christopher-Gordon Publishers.

Shanahan, T., Robinson, B., and Schneider, M. (1993). Integration of curriculum or interaction of people? *The Reading Teacher, 47*(2), pp. 158–160.

Shannon, P. (1985). Reading instruction and social class. *Language Arts, 62,* 604–613.

Sharpley, A. M., and Sharpley, C. F. (1981). Peer tutoring: A review of the literature. In *Collected Original Resources in Education 5,* 3, 7–11.

Shatz, E. K., & Baldwin, R. S. (1986). Context clues are unreliable predictors of word meanings. *Reading Research Quarterly, 21,* 429–453.

Shields, C., & Vondrak, L. (1980). Good news about newspapers. *Journal of Reading, 24,* 259–260.

Shanklin, N. L., & Rhodes, L. K. (March, 1989). Comprehensive instruction as sharing and extending. *The Reading Teacher, 42*(7), (pp. 496–501).

Short, K. G., & Klassen, C. (1993). Literature Circles: Hearing children's voices. In Cullinan, B. E. (Ed.) *Children's Voices: Talk in the Classroom.* Newark, DE: IRA.

Shuman, R. B. (1982). Reading with a purpose: Strategies to interest reluctant readers. *Journal of Reading, 25,* 725–730.

Shuy, R. W. (1969). Some language and cultural differences in a theory of reading. In K. S. Goodman & J. T. Fleming (Eds.), *Psycholinguistics and the teaching of reading.* Newark, DE: International Reading Association.

Simons, H., & Elster, C. (1990). Picture dependence in first grade basal texts. *Journal of Educational Research, 84*(2), pp. 86–92.

Simpson, M. (1987). Alternative formats for evaluating content area vocabulary understanding. *Journal of Reading, 31,* 20–27.

Sinatra, R. (1981). Using visuals to help the second-language learner. *The Reading Teacher, 34,* 539–546.

Singer, D., Singer, J., & Zuckerman, D. (1981). *Getting the most out of TV.* Santa Monica, CA: Goodyear.

Singer, H. (1978). Active comprehension: From answering to asking questions. *The Reading Teacher, 31,* 901–908.

Singer, H., & Ruddell, R. (Eds.). (1985). *Theoretical models and processes of reading* (3rd ed.). Newark, DE: International Reading Association.

Sirota, B. S. (1971). The effect of a planned literature program of daily oral reading by the teacher on the voluntary reading of fifth-grade children. Ph.D. diss., New York University.

Slapin, B. (1992). How to tell the difference: A checklist for evaluating children's books for anti-Indian bias. Philadelphia, PA: New Society.

Slaughter, H. B. (1988). Indirect and direct teaching in a whole language program. *The Reading Teacher, 42,* 30–34.

Smith, F. (1976). Learning to read by reading. *Language Arts, 53,* 297–299, 322.

Smith, F. (1977). The uses of language. *Language Arts,* 54, 6, 638–644.

Smith, F. (1979). *Reading without nonsense.* New York: Teachers College Press.

Smith, F. (1985). *Reading without nonsense.* New York: Teachers College Press.

Smith, F. (1988). *Joining the literacy club: Further essays into education.* Portsmouth, NH: Heinemann.

Smith, F. (1989). Demonstrations, engagement, and sensitivity. The choice between people and programs. In Manning, G. & Manning, M. (Eds.) *Whole language: Beliefs and practices, K-8.* Washington, DC: National Education Association.

Smith, L. B. (1982). Sixth graders write about reading literature. *Language Arts,* 59, 357–366.

Smith, N. B. (1965). *American reading instruction.* Newark, DE: International Reading Association.

Smith, R. J., & Johnson, D. D. (1980). *Teaching children to read.* Reading, MA: Addison-Wesley.

Smith, S. (1979). *No easy answers: Teaching the learning disabled child.* Cambridge, MA: Winthrop.

Smitten, B. (1989). Point/counterpoint: The value of basal readers. *Reading Today, 7*(1), pp. 1, 18.

Snyder, G. V. (1979). Do basal characters read in their daily lives? *The Reading Teacher, 33,* 303–306.

Snyder, G. V. (1981). Learner verification of reading games. *The Reading Teacher, 34,* 686–691.

Soto, G. (1992). *Pacific Crossing.* San Diego, CA: Harcourt Brace Jovanovich.

Sowers, S. (1982). Six questions teachers ask about invented spelling. In T. Newkirk & N. Atwell (Eds.), *Understanding writing: Ways of observing, learning and teaching.* Chelmsford, MA: Northeast Regional Exchange.

Spearitt, D. (1972). Identification of subskills in reading comprehension by maximum likelihood factor analysis. *Reading Research Quarterly, 8,* 92–111.

Spiegel, D. L. (1981a). *Reading for pleasure: Guidelines.* Newark, DE: International Reading Association.

Spiegel, D. L. (1981b). Six alternatives to the directed reading activity. *The Reading Teacher, 34,* 914–922.

Spiegel, D. L. (1992). Blending whole language and systematic direct instruction. *The Reading Teacher, 46*(1), pp. 38–44.

Squire, J. R. (1984). Composing and comprehending: Two sides of the same basic process. In J. M. Jensen (Ed.), *Composing and Comprehending.* Urbana, IL: National Conference on Research in English.

Stahl, D. K., & Anzalone, D. (1970). *Individualized teaching in elementary schools.* West Nyack, NY: Parker.

Stahl, S. A. (1983). *Vocabulary instruction and the nature of word meanings.* Paper presented at a meeting of the College Reading Association, Atlanta, GA.

Stahl, S. A. (1986). Three principles of effective vocabulary instruction. *Journal of Reading, 29,* 662–668.

Stahl, S. A. (April, 1992). Saying the "p" word: Nine guidelines for exemplary phonic instruction. *The Reading Teacher, 45*(8), (pp. 618–625).

Stahl, S. A., & Fairbanks, M. (1986). The effects of vocabulary instruction: A model-based meta-analysis. *Review of Educational Research, 56,* 72–110.

Stahl, S. A., & Miller, P. D. (1989). Whole language and language experience approaches for beginning reading: A quantitative research synthesis. *Review of Educational Research, 59,* 87–116.

Stahl, S. A., & Vancil, S. (1985). *The importance of discussion in effective vocabulary instruction.* Macomb, IL: Western Illinois University.

Stanovich, K. E. (1986). Matthew effects in reading: Some consequences of individual differences in the acquisition of literacy. *Reading Research Quarterly, 21,* 360–407.

Stanovich, K. (1993). Romance and reality. *The Reading Teacher, 47,* 280–291.

Stauffer, R. G. (1970). *The language experience approach to the teaching of reading.* New York: Harper & Row.

Stauffer, R. G. (1975). *Directing in reading-thinking process.* New York: Harper & Row.

Stein, N., & Glenn, C. (1979). An analysis of story comprehension in elementary school children. In R. Freedle (Ed.), *New directions in discourse processing.* Norwood, NJ: Ablex.

Stennett, R. G., Smythe, P. C., & Hardy, M. (1975). Hierarchical organization of reading subskills: Statistical approaches. *Journal of Reading Behavior, 7,* 223–228.

Stewart, O., & Tei, E. (1983). Some implications of metacognition for reading instruction. *Journal of Reading, 27*, 36–43.

Stewig, J. W. (1980). *Read to write* (2nd ed.). New York: Holt, Rinehart & Winston.

Stone, J. M., & Kagan, S. (1989). *Cooperative learning and language arts: A multi-instructional approach.* San Juan Capistrano, CA: Resources for Teachers.

Stoodt, B. (1981). *Reading instruction.* Boston: Houghton Mifflin.

Stotdky, S. L. (1977). Teaching prefixes: Facts and fallacies. *Language Arts, 54*(8), (pp. 887–890).

Stotsky, S. (1983). Research on reading/writing relationships: A synthesis and suggested directions. *Language Arts, 60,* 627–643.

Strickland, R. (1962). *The language of elementary school children: Its relationship to the language of reading textbooks and the quality of reading of selected children.* Bloomington: Indiana University School of Education.

Strickland, D., & Ascher, C. (1992). Low-income African-American children and public schooling. *Handbook of Research on Curriculum,* pp. 609–625.

Sutherland, Z. (Ed.) (1980). *The best in children's books: The University of Chicago guide to children's literature* (1973–78). Chicago: University of Chicago Press.

Sutherland, Z. (1984). *The Scott, Foresman anthology of children's literature.* Glenview, IL: Scott, Foresman.

Swaby, B. (1983). *Teaching and learning reading.* Boston: Little, Brown.

Taba, H. (1975). *Teacher's handbook for elementary social studies.* Reading, MA: Addison-Wesley.

Talmage, H. (1985). Selecting instructional materials: A four-part series. Part 1. The antecedents of selection. *Curriculum Review, 24*(6), 17–39.

Talmage, H., & Walberg, H. (1978). Naturalistic, decision-oriented evaluation of a district reading program. *Journal of Reading Behavior, 10,* 185–195.

Tanner, N. (1983). Phonics. In J. E. Alexander (Ed.), *Teaching reading* (2nd ed.). Boston: Little, Brown.

Taylor, D. (1983). *Family literacy: Young children learning to read and write.* Portsmouth, NH: Heinemann.

Taylor, B., Short, R., Frye, B., & Shearer, B. (1992). Classroom teachers prevent reading failure in low-achieving first-grade students. *The Reading Teacher, 45,* (pp. 592–597).

Taylor, N. E., & Vawter, J. (1978). Helping children discover the functions of written language. *Language Arts, 55,* 941–945.

Teachers as readers book groups (1993). Newark, DE: International Reading Association.

Teale, W. H. (1978). Positive environments for learning to read: What studies of early readers tell us. *Language Arts, 55,* 922–932.

Teale, W., & Sulzby, E. (1986). *Emergent literacy: Writing and reading.* Norwood, NJ: Ablex.

The pot of gold: An Irish folk tale. (1974). Glenview, IL: Scott Foresman.

Thelen, J. (1984). *Improving reading in science.* Newark, DE: International Reading Association.

Thelen, J. (1986). Vocabulary instruction and meaningful learning. *Journal of Reading, 29,* 603–609.

Thomas, J. (1975). *Learning centers: Opening up the classroom.* Needham, MA: Allyn and Bacon.

Thorndyke, P. (1977). Cognitive structures in comprehension and memory of narrative discourse. *Cognitive Psychology, 9,* 77–110.

Thurstone, L. L. (1946). A note on a reanalysis of Davis' reading tests. *Psychometrika, 11,* 185–188.

Tierney, R., & LaZansky, J. (1980). The rights and responsibilities of readers and writers: A contractual agreement. *Language Arts, 57,* 606–613.

Tierney, R. J., & Shanahan, T. (1991). *Research on reading-writing relationships: Interactions, transactions, and outcomes.* In Pearson, P. D., Barr, R., Kamil, M., & Mosenthal, P. (Eds.). *Handbook of reading research* (2nd ed.) (pp. 246–280). New York: Longman.

Toch, T. (1984, February 8). The emerging politics of language. *Education Week, 3,* 20.

Tolstoy, A. (1971). *The Great Big Enormous Turnip.* Glenview, IL: Scott, Foresman.

Tom, C. L. (1969). What teachers read to pupils in the middle grades. Ph.D. diss., Ohio State University.

Topping, K. (1989). Peer tutoring and paired reading: Combining two powerful techniques. *The Reading Teacher, 42,* 488–494.

Torrey, J. W. (1969). Learning to read with a teacher: A case study. *Elementary English, 46,* 550–556, 658.

Trachtenburg, P. (May, 1990). Using children's literature to enhance phonic instruction. *The Reading Teacher,* 648–654.

Trelease, J. (1989). *The new read-aloud handbook.* New York: Penguin.

Tunnell, M., Calder, J., Justen, J., & Waldrop, P. (1988). An affective approach to reading: Effectively teaching reading to mainstreamed handicapped children. *The Pointer,* 32, 38–40.

Tuttle, F. (1991). Responding to individual differences: Teaching the gifted. In J. Flood, J. Jensen, D. Lapp, & J. Squire (Eds.), *Handbook of research on teaching the English language arts.* NY: Macmillan.

Tway, E. (1984). The resource center: Children's literature. *Language Arts, 61,* 312–315.

Vacca, J. L. (1977). Including attitude assessment in the classroom reading program. *Illinois Reading Council Journal,* 5, 8–10.

Vacca, J. L., and Vacca, R. T. (1976). Learning stations: How to in the middle grades. *Journal of Reading, 19,* 563–567.

Vacca, R. T. (1990). *Case study of a whole language teacher.* Unpublished paper, Kent State University, Kent, OH.

Vacca, R. T., & Newton, E. (1995). Responding to literary texts. In Hedley, C. N., Antonacci, P., & Rabinowitz, M. *Thinking and literacy: Mind at work in the classroom.* Hillsdale, NJ: Erlbaum.

Vacca, R. T., & Padak, N. D. (1990). Who's at-risk in reading? *Journal of Reading, 33,* 486–489.

Vacca, R. T., & Rasinski, T. V. (1992). *Case studies in whole language.* Fort Worth, TX: Harcourt Brace & Jovanovich.

Vacca, R. T., & Rasinski, T. V. (March, 1992). *Case studies in whole language.* New York: Harcourt Brace Jovanovich.

Vacca, R. T., & Vacca, J. L. (1983). Two less than fortunate consequences of reading research in the 1970s. *Reading Research Quarterly, 18,* 382–383.

Vacca, R. T., & Vacca, J. L. (1989). *Content Area Reading* (3rd ed.). Glenview, IL: Scott, Foresman.

Vacca, R. T., & Vacca, J. L. (1993). *Content area reading* (4th ed.). New York: HarperCollins.

Valencia, S., & Pearson, D. (1987). Reading assessment: Time for a change. *The Reading Teacher, 40,* 726–732.

Valeri-Gold, M. (1993). Unscramble me. In Olsen, M. & Homan, S. (Eds.), *Teacher to teacher: Strategies for the elementary classroom.* Newark, DE: IRA.

Veatch, J., & Acinapuro, P. (1966). *Reading in the elementary school.* New York: Owen.

Veatch, J., Sawicki, F., Elliot, G., Flake, E., & Blakey, J. (1979). *Key words to reading* (2nd ed.). Columbus, OH: Merrill.

Venezky, R. L. (1978). Reading acquisition: The occult and the obscure. In F. B. Murray & J. J. Pikulski (Eds.), *The acquisition of reading.* Baltimore: University Park Press.

Verble, M. (1980). *Dealing in discipline: Study guide.* Lincoln, NE: University of Mid-America Press.

Viechnicki, K. J., Barbour, N., Shaklee, B., Rhorer, J., and Ambrose, R. (1993). The impact of portfolio assessment on teacher classroom activities. *Journal of Teacher Education, 44*(5), 371–377.

Viorst, J. (1972). *Alexander's terrible, horrible, no good, very bad day.* New York: Atheneum.

Voss, M. M. (1992). Portfolios in first grade: A teacher's discoveries. In D. H. Graves & B. S. Sunstein (Eds.) *Portfolio portraits* (pp. 17–33). Portsmouth, NH: Heinemann.

Vygotsky, L. S. (1962). *Thought and language.* Cambridge: MIT Press.

Vygotsky, L. S. (1978). *Mind in society.* Cambridge: Harvard University Press.

Walberg, H. J. (1988). Synthesis of research on time and learning. *Educational Leadership, 45*(6), 76–85.

Walley, C. (March, 1993). An invitation to reading fluency. *The Reading Teacher, 46*(6), (pp. 526–527).

Watson, D. (1978). Reader selected miscues: Getting more from sustained silent reading. *English Education, 10,* 75–85.

Watson, D. (1985). Watching and listening to children read. In A. Jaggar & M. T. Smith-Burke (Eds.), *Observing the language learner.* Newark, DE: International Reading Association.

Watson, D. (1989). Defining and describing whole language. *The Elementary School Journal, 90,* 129–141.

Weaver, C. (1980). *Psycholinguistics and reading: From process to practice.* Boston: Little, Brown.

Wechsler, D. (1958). *The measurement and appraisal of adult intelligence.* Baltimore: Williams & Wilkins.

Wells, G. (1986). *The meaning-makers: Children learning language and using language.* Portsmouth, NH: Heinemann.

Wells, M. C. (1993). At the juncture of reading and writing: How dialogue journals contribute to students' reading development. *Journal of Reading, 36*(4), 294–303.

Wepner, S. B., (1989). Roles and responsibilities of reading personnel. In S. B. Wepner, J. T. Feeley, & D. S. Strickland (Eds.), *The administration and supervision of reading programs* (pp. 22–44). New York: Teachers College Press.

Wepner, S. B., & Feeley, J. T. (1993). *Moving toward with literature: Basals, books, and beyond.* New York: Macmillan.

Whaley, J. F. (1981). Story grammar and reading instruction. *The Reading Teacher, 34,* 762–771.

What works: Research about teaching and learning. (1986). Washington, DC: U.S. Department of Education.

Wheat, T. E., Galen, N. D., & Norwood, M. (1974). Initial reading experiences for linguistically diverse learners. *The Reading Teacher, 33,* 28–31.

Wiggins, G. (1989). A true test: Toward more authentic and equitable assessment. *Phi Delta Kappan, 70*(9), pp. 703–714.

Wiggins, G. (1993). News report in *The Council Chronicle, 2,* Urbana, IL: National Council of Teachers of English.

White, T. G., Sowelle, J., Yanagihara, A. (January, 1989). Teaching elementary students to use word-part clues. *The Reading Teacher,* (pp. 302–308).

Williams, S. (1989). Authors review authors. In N. Hall (Ed.), *Writing with reason: The emergence of authorship in young children* (pp. 109–118). Portsmouth, NH: Heinemann.

Witty, P. A. (1971). *Reading for the gifted and creative student.* Newark, DE. International Reading Association.

Witty, P. A. (1985). Rationale for fostering creative reading in the gifted and the creative. In M. Labuda (Ed.), *Creative learning for gifted learners* (2nd ed.). Newark, DE: International Reading Association.

Wixson, K., Bosky, A., Yochum, M. N., & Alvermann, D. (1984). An interview for assessing students' perceptions of classroom reading tasks. *The Reading Teacher, 37,* 346–352.

Wolf, J. (1985). Teaching young writers to revise. *The Ohio Reading Teacher, 19,* 28–30.

Wolf, J., & Vacca, R. T. (1985). *Teaching the writing process: A resource guide for elementary classroom teachers.* Kent, OH: Writing Process Demonstration Project, Kent State University.

Wylie, R. E., & Durrell, D. D. (1970). Teaching vowels through phonograms. *Elementary English, 47,* 787–791.

Yanok, J. (1988). Individualized instruction: A good approach. *Academic Therapy, 24,* 163–167.

Yakota, J. (1993). Issues in selecting multicultural literature for children and adolescents. *Language Arts, 70,* (pp. 156–167).

Yopp, H. K. (1992). Developing phonemic awareness in young children. *The Reading Teacher, 45, 9, 696–703.*

Yopp, R. H., & Yopp, H. K. (1993). *Literature-based reading activities.* Boston: Allyn and Bacon.

Zarrillo, J. (1989). Teachers' interpretations of literature-based reading. *The Reading Teacher, 43,* 22–28.

Zucker, C. (1993). Using whole language with students who have learning disabilities. *The Reading Teacher, 46,* (pp. 660–670).

Credits

Photos:

Page: 7: David Grossman; p. 19: Jeff Dunn/Stock Boston; p. 47: Michael Siluk/The Image Works; p. 54: Elizabeth Crews/Stock Boston; p. 73: Rhoda Sidney/Stock Boston; p. 100: Elizabeth Hamlin/Stock Boston; p. 114: © The Wright Group from Mrs. Wishy-Washy by Joy Crowley, reprinted by permission. Illustrations by Elizabeth Fuller; p. 125: Jean-Claude LeJeune/Stock Boston; p. 149: David Grossman; p. 165: David Grossman; p. 194: David Grossman; p. 215: David Grossman; p. 227: David Grossman; p. 230: Suzanne Arms/The Image Works; p. 272: Jean-Claude LeJeune/Stock Boston; p. 289: Frank Siteman/Stock Boston; p. 322: Elizabeth Crews/ The Image Works; p. 325: Spencer Grant/Stock Boston; p. 343: Jean-Claude LeJeune/ Stock Boston; p. 365: Nita Winter/The Image Works; p. 381: Courtesy Patricia Edwards; p. 382: Courtesy Jeanne Paratore; p. 383: Courtesy Lyndon Searfoss; p. 394: James L. Shaffer/ Photo Edit; p. 423: Jeffrey W. Myers/Stock Boston; p. 442: Elizabeth Crews/The Image Works; p. 451: James L. Shaffer/Photo Edit; p. 471: Elizabeth Crews/The Image Works; p. 498: Elizabeth Crews/Stock Boston; p. 501: Gale Zucker/Stock Boston; p. 522: Bob Daemmrich/ Stock Boston; and p. 527: David Grossman.

Color insert illustrations:

From *The People Could Fly* by Virginia Hamilton, illustrated by Leon and Diane Dillon. Illustrations copyright © 1985 by Leo and Diane Dillon. Reprinted by permission of Alfred A. Knopf, Inc.

From *Mrs. Katz and Tush* by Patricia Polacco. Copyright © 1992 by Patricia Polacco. Used by permission of Bantam Books, a division of Bantam Doubleday Dell Publishing Group, Inc.

Illustration by Jean and Mou-Sien Tseng from *The Boy Who Swallowed Snakes* by Lawrence Yep. Illustrations copyright © 1993 by Jean and Mou-Sien Tseng. Reprinted by permission of Scholastic Inc.

From *Kinda Blue* by Ann Grifalconi. Copyright © 1993 by Ann Grifalconi. By permission of Little, Brown and Company.

Reprinted with the permission of Bradbury Press, a Member of Paramount Publishing from *The Girl Who Loved Wild Horses* by Paul Goble. Copyright © 1978 by Paul Goble.

Illustration by Ed Young reprinted by permission of the G.P.Putnam's Sons from *Sadako* by Eleaner Coerr, illustrations copyright © 1993 by Ed Young.

From *Abuela* by Arthur Dorros, illustrated by Elisa Kleven. Copyright © 1991 by Elisa Kleven, illustrations. Used by permission of Dutton Children's Books, a division of Penguin Books USA Inc.

Illustration from *El Chino* by Allen Say. Copyright © 1990 by Allen Say. Reprinted by permission of Houghton Mifflin Co. All rights reserved.

Illustration from *Aunt Flossie's Hats (and Crab Cakes Later)* by Elizabeth Fitzgerald Howard. Illustrations copyright © 1991 by James Ransome. Reprinted by permission of Clarion Books/Houghton Mifflin Co. All rights reserved.

Text:

Chapter 1

Figure 1.1 Standards for Reading Professionals, 1992. Reprinted by permission of the International Reading Association.

Box 1.2 From a brochure entitled "Teachers as Readers Book Groups: Explore Your Own Literacy. Form a Book Group!" Reprinted by permission of the International Reading Association.

Chapter 2

Page 52 Xerox is a registered trademark of the Xerox Corporation.

Chapter 3

Box 3.2 *Recommendations from the Joint Committee on Reading in Pre-First Grade.* From "Reading and Pre-First Grade: A Joint Statement of Concerns About Present Practices in Pre-First Grade Reading Instruction," *The Reading Teacher,* April 1977. Reprinted by permission of the International Reading Association.

Table 3.1 *Types of props found in literary play centers.* From "Play, Print, and Purpose: Enriching Play Environments for Literacy Development" by Susan B. Neuman and Kathy Roskos, *The Reading Teacher,* November 1990, p. 217. Reprinted by permission of Susan B. Neuman and the International Reading Association.

Figure 3.2 *Writing Samples from Three Four-Year-Olds.* From "Children's Language and World: Initial Encounters with Print" by Jerome Harste, C. L. Burke, and V. A. Woodward from *Reader Meets Author/Bridging the Gap: A Psycholinguistic and Sociolinguistic Perspective,* J. A. Langer and M. T. Smith-Burke, eds. Reprinted by permission of Jerome C. Harste and the International Reading Association.

Chapter 4

Box 4.2 From "Joy of Big Books" by Joy Cowley, *Instructor,* October 1991, p. 19. Reprinted by permission of Scholastic, Inc.

Figure 4.2 From *Language, Literacy, and the Child* by L. Galda, B. Cullinan, and D. Strickland, pp. 102–103. Copyright © 1993 by Harcourt Brace and Company. Reprinted by permission.

Table 4.2 *Spellings by three kindergartners.* From "Three Steps to Teaching Beginning Readers to Spell" by J. R. Gentry and E. H. Henderson, *Developmental and Cognitive Aspects of Learning to Spell: A Reflection of Word Knowledge,* E. H. Henderson and J. W. Beers, eds., 1980, p. 115. Reprinted with permission of J. Richard Gentry and the International Reading Association.

Pages 139–141 From Gloria McDonnell and E. Bess Osburn, "New Thoughts on Reading Readiness," *Language Arts* 55:1, January 1978, pp. 27–29.

Box 4.3 From "Do-It-Yourself Big Books" by Ethel Huttar, *Instructor,* October 1991, p. 21. Reprinted by permission of Scholastic, Inc.

Chapter 5

Table 5.1 From *Read-On: A Conference Approach to Reading* by David Hornsby, Deborah Sukarna, and Jo-Ann Parry, p. 117. Copyright © 1986 by Heinemann Educational Books, Inc. Reprinted by permission.

Figure 5.3 *Krista and Michele's Buddy Journal Entries.* From "Buddy Journal Entries" by Karen Bromley, *The Reading Teacher,* November 1989, p. 12. Reprinted by permission of Karen Bromley and the International Reading Association.

Figure 5.4 and 5.5 *Jessica's First Draft on Pollution* and *Jessica's Second Draft on Pollution.* From "Teaching Young Writers to Revise" by Judi Wolf in *Ohio Reading Teacher,* Vol. 19, No. 4, July 1985, pp. 28–30. Reprinted with permission of Ohio Reading Teacher.

Chapter 6

Box 6.1 Adapted from *People of the Third Planet* by Dale Crail. Copyright © 1968 by Scholastic, Inc. Reprinted by permission of Scholastic, Inc.

Figure 6.7 *Potential Stopping Points in a DR-TA.* From "Developing Comprehension Skills in Primary Students Through the Use of Story Frames" by Gerald Fowler, *The Reading Teacher,* November 1982, p. 178. Reprinted by permission of Gerald L. Fowler and The International Reading Association.

Chapter 7

Figure 7.1 *Dale's Cone of Experience.* From *Audiovisual Methods in Teaching,* Third Edition, by Edgar Dale. Copyright © 1969 by Holt, Rinehart and Winston. Reprinted with permission of the publisher.

Page 240 Polaroid is a registered trademark of the Polaroid Corporation.

Box 7.2 *Think Sheet for Extended Definition of Self-Reliance.* Adapted from "Semantic Analysis to Writing: Connecting Words, Books, and Writing" by Janet M. Beyersdorfer and David K. Schaur, *Journal of Reading,* March 1989, pp. 643–649. Reprinted by permission of the International Reading Association.

Figure 7.8 *An Example of a Predict 'o Gram.* From Camille L. Z. Blachowicz, "Making Connections: Alternatives to the Vocabulary Notebook," *Journal of Reading,* April 1986, pp. 643–649.

Chapter 10

Figure 10.1 *People Hunt.* Adapted from J. M. Stone and S. Kagan, *Cooperative Learning and Language Arts: A Multi-Instructional Approach.* San Juan Capistrano, CA: Resources for Teachers, 1989.

Figure 10.2 From *Case Studies in Whole Language* by R. T. Vacca and T. R. Rasinski, p. 227. Copyright © 1992 by Harcourt Brace and C ompany. Reprinted by permission.

Table 10.2 Based on research by Marjorie R. Hancock, "Exploring and Extending Personal Response Through Literature Journals," *The Reading Teacher,* 46:6, 1993, 466–474. Reprinted by permission of Marjorie R. Hancock and the International Reading Association.

Chapter 11

Figure 11.1 *Sample Pages from the Appleton Reader.* From Appleton, *The Second Reader.* New York: American Book Company, 1878, pp. 28–29.

Figure 11.2 *Program Scope and Sequence Chart.* From *HBJ Treasury of Literature.*

Chapter 12

Figure 12.1 *Graphic Organizer.* Developed and used by permission of Janice Mark.

Box 12.3 From "Using Informational Books Extend the Curriculum" by M. Jean Greenlaw. *The Reading Teacher* (1988), p. 18. Reprinted by permission of The International Reading Association.

Box 12.9 *Model of a Reciprocal Teaching Lesson.* From "Two Approaches for Helping Poor Readers Become More Strategic" by Beth Ann Herrmann, *The Reading Teacher,* October 1988, p. 27. Reprinted by permission of Beth Ann Herrmann and The International Reading Association.

Chapter 13

Figure 13.4 and 13.5 *Louisa's Growth in Reading* and *Susan's Growth in Voluntary Reading.* From "Reporting Reading Progress: A Comparison Portfolio for Parents" by James Flood and Diane Lapp, *The Reading Teacher,* March 1989, pp. 511 and 513. Reprinted by permission of the International Reading Association and James Flood.

Chapter 14

Table 14.1 *Skills of Classroom Teacher of Reading.* Reprinted by permission of the publisher, from Wepner, Shelly, Feeley, John T., and Strickland, Dorothy S., *The Administration and Supervision of Reading Programs.* (New York: Teachers College Press, 1989, pp. 37–38). Copyright © 1989 by Teachers College, Columbia University. All rights reserved.

Figure 14.7 From "Assessing Student Action Beyond Reflection and Response" by J. Flood, D. Lapp, and G. Nagel. *Journal of Reading* 36:5, February 1993, 422. Reprinted by permission of the authors and the International Reading Association.

Figure 14.8 *Self-Evaluation Form.* From *Journal of Reading,* April 1976. Reprinted by permission of Jo Anne Vacca and The International Reading Association.

Appendix B

The DeFord Theoretical Orientation to Reading Profile (TORP). "Validating the Construct of Theoretical Orientation in Reading Instruction," by Diane E. DeFord, *Reading Research Quarterly* 20:3, Spring 1985. Reprinted by permission of The International Reading Association.

Name Index

Subject Index